GLEIM® | Aviation

2022 EDITION

COMMERCIAL PILOT

FAA Knowledge Test Prep

for the FAA Computer-Based Pilot Knowledge Test

Commercial Pilot - Airplane   *Military Competence - Non-Category*

by
Irvin N. Gleim, Ph.D., CFII, and Garrett W. Gleim, CFII

Gleim Publications, Inc.
PO Box 12848
Gainesville, Florida 32604

(352) 375-0772
(800) 87-GLEIM or (800) 874-5346
www.GleimAviation.com
aviationteam@gleim.com

For updates to the first printing of the 2022 edition of
Commercial Pilot FAA Knowledge Test Prep

Go To: www.GleimAviation.com/updates

Or: Email update@gleim.com with **CPKT 2022-1**
in the subject line. You will receive our current
update as a reply.

Updates are available until the next edition is published.

ISSN 1553-6904
ISBN 978-1-61854-449-0

Let Us Know!

This 2022 edition is designed specifically for pilots who aspire to the Commercial Certificate. Please send any corrections and suggestions for subsequent editions to us via the feedback links within the online components or using the form at www.GleimAviation.com/questions.

A companion volume, *Commercial Pilot Flight Maneuvers and Practical Test Prep*, focuses on the FAA practical test, just as this book focuses on the FAA knowledge test. Save time, money, and frustration--order online at www.GleimAviation.com today! Please bring these books to the attention of flight instructors, fixed-base operators, and others with a potential interest in acquiring their pilot ratings and certificates. Wide distribution of these books and increased interest in flying depend on your assistance and good word. Thank you.

Environmental Statement -- This book is printed on recycled paper sourced from suppliers certified using sustainable forestry management processes and is produced either TCF (Totally Chlorine-Free) or ECF (Elementally Chlorine-Free).

Our answers have been carefully researched and reviewed. Inevitably, there will be differences with competitors' books and even the FAA. If necessary, we will develop an UPDATE for *Commercial Pilot FAA Knowledge Test Prep*. Visit our website or email update@gleim.com for the latest updates. Updates for this 2022 edition will be available until the next edition is published. To continue providing our customers with first-rate service, we request that technical questions about our materials be sent to us via the feedback links within the online components. We will give each question thorough consideration and a prompt response. Questions concerning orders, prices, shipments, or payments will be handled via telephone by our competent and courteous customer service staff.

ABOUT THE AUTHORS

Irvin N. Gleim earned his private pilot certificate in 1965 from the Institute of Aviation at the University of Illinois, where he subsequently received his Ph.D. He is a commercial pilot and flight instructor (instrument) with multi-engine and seaplane ratings and is a member of the Aircraft Owners and Pilots Association, American Bonanza Society, Civil Air Patrol, Experimental Aircraft Association, National Association of Flight Instructors, and Seaplane Pilots Association. He is the author of flight maneuvers and practical test prep books for the sport, private, instrument, commercial, and flight instructor certificates/ratings and the author of study guides for the remote, sport, private/recreational, instrument, commercial, flight/ground instructor, fundamentals of instructing, airline transport pilot, and flight engineer FAA knowledge tests. Three additional pilot training books are *Pilot Handbook*, *Aviation Weather and Weather Services*, and *FAR/AIM*.

Dr. Gleim has also written articles for professional accounting and business law journals and is the author of widely used review manuals for the CIA (Certified Internal Auditor) exam, the CMA (Certified Management Accountant) exam, the CPA (Certified Public Accountant) Exam, and the EA (IRS Enrolled Agent) exam. He is Professor Emeritus, Fisher School of Accounting, University of Florida, and is a CFM, CIA, CMA, and CPA.

Garrett W. Gleim earned his private pilot certificate in 1997 in a Piper Super Cub. He is a commercial pilot (single- and multi-engine), ground instructor (advanced and instrument), and flight instructor (instrument and multi-engine), and he is a member of the Aircraft Owners and Pilots Association, the National Association of Flight Instructors, and the Society of Aviation and Flight Educators. He is the author of study guides for the remote, sport, private/recreational, instrument, commercial, flight/ground instructor, fundamentals of instructing, and airline transport pilot FAA knowledge tests. He received a Bachelor of Science in Economics from The Wharton School, University of Pennsylvania. Mr. Gleim is also a CPA.

REVIEWERS AND CONTRIBUTORS

Paul Duty, CFII, MEI, AGI, Remote Pilot, is a graduate of Embry-Riddle Aeronautical University with a Master of Business Administration-Aviation degree. He is our aviation product manager and the Gleim Part 141 Chief Ground Instructor. Mr. Duty is an active flight instructor, commercial pilot, and remote pilot. He researched questions, wrote and edited answer explanations, and incorporated revisions into the text.

Clayton Gamber, ATP, A&P, IA, is a graduate of Virginia Tech with over 40 years of experience in operations and maintenance for commercial aviation. He researched questions, wrote and edited answer explanations, and incorporated revisions into the text.

Ryan Jeff, CFI, AGI, Remote Pilot, graduated summa cum laude from Embry-Riddle Aeronautical University with a degree in Aeronautics and a minor in Applied Meteorology. He researched questions, wrote and edited answer explanations, and incorporated revisions into the text.

Karl Winters, CFII, AGI, IGI, Remote Pilot, is a graduate of Purdue University and is a 141 check airman and a flight instructor in the School of Aeronautics at Liberty University. Mr. Winters is also the Gleim Part 141 Assistant Chief Ground Instructor and one of our aviation editors. He researched questions, wrote and edited answer explanations, and incorporated revisions into the text.

The CFIs who have worked with us throughout the years to develop and improve our pilot training materials.

The many FAA employees who helped, in person or by telephone, primarily in Gainesville; Orlando; Oklahoma City; and Washington, DC.

The many pilots who have provided comments and suggestions about *Commercial Pilot FAA Knowledge Test Prep* during the past several decades.

A PERSONAL THANKS

This manual would not have been possible without the extraordinary effort and dedication of Jacob Bennett, Julie Cutlip, Ethan Good, Doug Green, Fernanda Martinez, Bree Rodriguez, Veronica Rodriguez, Teresa Soard, Joanne Strong, Elmer Tucker, Candace Van Doren, and Ryan Van Tress, who typed the entire manuscript and all revisions and drafted and laid out the diagrams, illustrations, and cover for this book.

The authors also appreciate the production and editorial assistance of Brianna Barnett, Brianna Bostick, Sirene Dagher, Michaela Giampaolo, Jessica Hatker, Katie Larson, Bryce Owen, Shane Rapp, David Sox, Michael Tamayo, and Alyssa Thomas.

The authors also appreciate the video production expertise of Gary Brook, Philip Brubaker, and Matthew Church, who helped produce and edit all Gleim Aviation videos.

Finally, we appreciate the encouragement, support, and tolerance of our families throughout this project.

TABLE OF CONTENTS

NOTE: The FAA does not release the complete database of test questions to the public. Instead, sample questions are released on the Airman Testing page of the FAA website. These questions are similar to the actual test questions, but they are not exact matches.

Gleim utilizes customer feedback and FAA publications to create additional sample questions that closely represent the topical coverage of each FAA knowledge test. In order to do well on the knowledge test, you must study the Gleim outlines in this book, answer all the questions under exam conditions (i.e., without looking at the answers first), and develop an understanding of the topics addressed. You should not simply memorize questions and answers. This will not prepare you for your FAA knowledge test, and it will not help you develop the knowledge you need to safely operate an aircraft.

Always refer to the Gleim update service (www.GleimAviation.com/updates) to ensure you have the latest information that is available. If you see topics covered on your FAA knowledge test that are not contained in this book, please contact us at www.GleimAviation.com/questions to report your experience and help us fine-tune our test preparation materials.

Thank you!

PREFACE

The primary purpose of this book is to provide you with the easiest, fastest, and least expensive means of passing the commercial pilot (airplane) knowledge test. Questions previously released by the FAA were not grouped together by topic. We have organized them for you. We have

1. Reproduced all previously released knowledge test questions published by the FAA. We have also included additional similar test questions, which we believe may appear in some form on your knowledge test.
2. Reordered the questions into logical topics.
3. Organized these topics into 11 study units.
4. Explained the answer immediately to the right of each question.
5. Provided an easy-to-study outline of exactly what you need to know (and no more) at the beginning of each study unit.

Accordingly, you can thoroughly prepare for the FAA pilot knowledge test by

1. Studying the brief outlines at the beginning of each study unit.
2. Answering the question on the left side of each page while covering up the answer explanations on the right side of each page.
3. Reading the answer explanation for each question that you answer incorrectly or have difficulty answering.
4. Facilitating this Gleim process with our **FAA Test Prep Online**. Our software emulates the FAA test given at PSI Exams Online (PSI). By practicing answering questions on a computer, you will become at ease with the computer testing process and have the confidence to **pass**. Refer to pages 17 and 18.
5. Using our **Online Ground School**, which provides you with our outlines, practice problems, and sample tests. We give you a money-back guarantee with our **Online Ground School**. If you are unsuccessful, you get your money back!

The secondary purpose of this book is to introduce *Commercial Pilot Flight Maneuvers and Practical Test Prep* and *Pilot Handbook*.

Commercial Pilot Flight Maneuvers and Practical Test Prep is designed to help prepare pilots for their flight training and the FAA commercial pilot practical test. Each task, objective, concept, and requirement is explained, analyzed, illustrated, and interpreted so pilots will be totally conversant with all aspects of the commercial pilot practical test.

Pilot Handbook is a textbook of aeronautical knowledge presented in easy-to-use outline format, with many charts, diagrams, figures, etc., included. While this book contains only the material needed to pass the FAA knowledge test, *Pilot Handbook* contains the textbook knowledge required to be a safe and proficient pilot.

Many books create additional work for the user. In contrast, this book and its companion, *Commercial Pilot Flight Maneuvers and Practical Test Prep*, facilitate your effort. They are easy to use. The outline/illustration format, type styles, and spacing are designed to improve readability. Concepts are often presented as phrases rather than as complete sentences–similar to notes that you would take in a class lecture.

Also, note that this study manual is concerned with **airplane** flight training, not balloon, glider, or helicopter training. We are confident this book, **FAA Test Prep Online**, and/or **Online Ground School** will facilitate speedy completion of your knowledge test. We wish you the very best as you complete your commercial pilot certificate, in subsequent flying, and in obtaining additional ratings and certificates.

Enjoy Flying Safely!

Irvin N. Gleim
Garrett W. Gleim

June 2021

INTRODUCTION: THE FAA PILOT KNOWLEDGE TEST

The beginning of this introduction explains how to obtain a commercial pilot certificate, and it explains the content and procedures of the Federal Aviation Administration (FAA) knowledge test, including how to take the test at a computer testing center. The remainder of this introduction discusses and illustrates the Gleim **Online Ground School** and **FAA Test Prep Online**. Achieving a commercial pilot certificate is fun. Begin today!

Commercial Pilot FAA Knowledge Test Prep is one of four books contained in the Gleim **Commercial Pilot Kit**. The other three books are

1. *Commercial Pilot Flight Maneuvers and Practical Test Prep*
2. *Commercial Pilot Syllabus*
3. *Commercial Pilot ACS and Oral Exam Guide*

Commercial Pilot Flight Maneuvers and Practical Test Prep presents each flight maneuver in outline/illustration format so you will know what to expect and what to do before each flight lesson. This book will thoroughly prepare you to complete your FAA practical (flight) test confidently and successfully.

Commercial Pilot Syllabus is a step-by-step syllabus of ground and flight training lesson plans for your commercial pilot training.

Commercial Pilot ACS and Oral Exam Guide contains the FAA Airman Certification Standards and hundreds of possible questions that applicants may face during the practical test.

While the following books are not included in the Commercial Pilot Kit, you may want to purchase them if you do not already have them:

Pilot Handbook is a complete pilot reference that combines over 100 FAA documents, including *AIM*, Federal Aviation Regulations, and ACs. Among the topics explained are aerodynamics, airplane systems, airspace, and navigation. This book, more than any other, will help make you a better pilot.

FAR/AIM is an essential part of every pilot's library. The Gleim *FAR/AIM* is an easy-to-read reference book containing all of the Federal Aviation Regulations applicable to general aviation flying, plus the full text of the FAA's *Aeronautical Information Manual (AIM)*.

The Gleim *Aviation Weather and Weather Services* book combines all of the information from the FAA's *Aviation Weather* (AC 00-6), *Aviation Weather Services* (AC 00-45), and numerous FAA publications into one easy-to-understand book.

WHAT IS A COMMERCIAL PILOT CERTIFICATE?

A commercial pilot certificate is identical to your private pilot certificate except it allows you to fly an airplane and carry passengers and/or property for compensation or hire. The certificate is sent to you by the FAA upon satisfactory completion of your training program, the pilot knowledge test, and a practical test. A sample commercial pilot certificate is reproduced below.

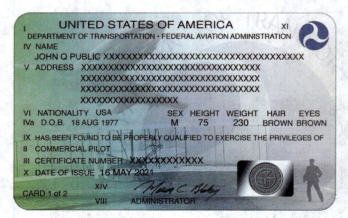 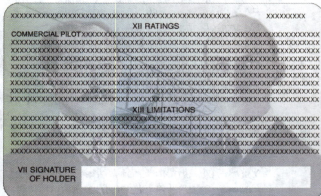

REQUIREMENTS TO OBTAIN A COMMERCIAL PILOT CERTIFICATE

1. Be at least 18 years of age and hold at least a private pilot certificate.

2. Be able to read, speak, write, and understand the English language. (Certificates with operating limitations may be available for medically related deficiencies.)

3. Hold at least a current third-class FAA medical certificate or meet the requirements of BasicMed. Later, if your flying requires a commercial pilot certificate, you must hold a second-class medical certificate.

    a. You must undergo a routine medical examination, which may only be administered by FAA-designated doctors called aviation medical examiners (AMEs).

        1) For operations requiring a commercial pilot certificate, a second-class medical certificate expires at the end of the last day of the month, 1 year after the date of examination shown on the certificate.

        2) For operations requiring a private or recreational pilot certificate, any class of medical certificate expires at the end of the last day of the month either

            a) 5 years after the date of examination shown on the certificate, if you have not reached your 40th birthday on or before the date of examination, or

            b) 2 years after the date of examination shown on the certificate, if you have reached your 40th birthday on or before the date of examination.

    b. Even if you have a physical disability, medical certificates can be issued in many cases. Operating limitations may be imposed depending upon the nature of the disability.

    c. Your certificated flight instructor (CFI) or fixed-base operator (FBO) will be able to recommend an AME.

        1) Also, the FAA maintains an online directory that lists all authorized AMEs by name and address. Copies of this directory are kept at all FAA offices, ATC facilities, and Flight Service Stations (FSSs).

4. Receive and log ground training from an authorized instructor or complete a home-study course (such as studying this book, **Commercial Pilot Flight Maneuvers and Practical Test Prep**, and **Pilot Handbook** or using the Gleim **Online Ground School**) to learn

    a. Applicable Federal Aviation Regulations that relate to commercial pilot privileges, limitations, and flight operations

    b. Accident reporting requirements of the National Transportation Safety Board

    c. Basic aerodynamics and the principles of flight

    d. Meteorology to include recognition of critical weather situations, wind shear recognition and avoidance, and the use of aeronautical weather reports and forecasts

    e. Safe and efficient operation of aircraft

    f. Weight and balance computations

    g. Use of performance charts

    h. Significance and effects of exceeding aircraft performance limitations

    i. Use of aeronautical charts and a magnetic compass for pilotage and dead reckoning

    j. Use of air navigation facilities

    k. Aeronautical decision making and judgment

    l. Principles and functions of aircraft systems

    m. Maneuvers, procedures, and emergency operations appropriate to the aircraft

    n. Night and high-altitude operations

    o. Procedures for operating within the National Airspace System

5. Pass a knowledge test with a score of 70% or better.

    a. All FAA knowledge tests are administered at FAA-designated computer testing centers.

    b. The commercial pilot test consists of 100 multiple-choice questions selected from the airplane-related questions in the FAA's commercial pilot test bank.

    c. Questions similar to those you will see on your knowledge test are provided in this book with complete answer explanations.

6. Accumulate flight experience (14 CFR 61.129). You must log at least 250 hr. of flight time as a pilot that consists of at least

    a. 100 hr. in powered aircraft, of which 50 hr. must be in airplanes

    b. 100 hr. as pilot in command flight time, which includes at least

        1) 50 hr. in airplanes
        2) 50 hr. in cross-country flight of which at least 10 hr. must be in airplanes

    c. 20 hr. of training in the areas of operation required for a single-engine or multi-engine rating that includes at least

        1) 10 hr. of instrument training of which at least 5 hr. must be in a single-engine or multi-engine airplane, as appropriate

        2) 10 hr. of training in a complex airplane, technologically advanced aircraft (TAA), or turbine-powered airplane

            a) For a multi-engine rating, the airplane must be a multi-engine airplane and meet the other requirements.

        3)   One cross-country flight of at least 2 hr. in a single-engine or multi-engine airplane (as appropriate) in daytime conditions, consisting of a total straight-line distance of more than 100 NM from the original point of departure

        4)   One cross-country flight of at least 2 hr. in a single-engine or multi-engine airplane (as appropriate) in nighttime conditions, consisting of a straight-line distance of more than 100 NM from the original point of departure

        5)   3 hr. in a single-engine or multi-engine airplane (as appropriate) with an authorized instructor in preparation for the practical test within the preceding 2 calendar months from the month of the test

    d.   10 hr. of solo flight (sole occupant of the aircraft) or 10 hr. of flight time performing the duties of pilot in command in a single- or multi-engine airplane (as appropriate) with an authorized instructor, training in the areas of operations required for a single- or multi-engine rating (as appropriate), which includes at least

        1)   One cross-country flight of not less than 300 NM total distance, with landings at a minimum of three points, one of which is a straight-line distance of at least 250 NM from the original departure point

            a)   In Hawaii, the longest segment need have only a straight-line distance of at least 150 NM.

        2)   5 hr. in night-VFR conditions with 10 takeoffs and 10 landings (with each landing involving a flight in the traffic pattern) at an airport with an operating control tower

    e.   The 250 hr. of flight time as a pilot may include 50 hr. in an approved flight simulator or training device that is representative of a single-engine or multi-engine airplane (as appropriate) and provided the aeronautical experience was obtained from an authorized instructor in a flight simulator or flight training device that represents that class of airplane appropriate to the rating sought.

7.   Hold an instrument rating. As a commercial pilot you are presumed to have an instrument rating. If not, your commercial certificate will be endorsed with a prohibition against carrying passengers for hire on flights beyond 50 NM, or at night.

8.   Demonstrate flight proficiency (14 CFR 61.127). You must receive and log ground and flight training from an authorized instructor in the following areas of operations for an airplane category rating with a single-engine or multi-engine class rating.

    a.   Preflight preparation

    b.   Preflight procedures

    c.   Airport and seaplane base operations

    d.   Takeoffs, landings, and go-arounds

    e.   Performance maneuvers

    f.   Ground reference maneuvers (single-engine only)

        1)   Multi-engine operations (multi-engine only)

    g.   Navigation

    h.   Slow flight and stalls

    i.   Emergency operations

    j.   High-altitude operations

    k.   Postflight procedures

9.   Alternatively, enroll in an FAA-certificated pilot school or training center that has an approved commercial pilot certification or test course (airplane).

   a.   These are known as Part 141 schools or Part 142 training centers because they are authorized by Part 141 or Part 142 of the Federal Aviation Regulations.

      1)   All other regulations concerning the certification of pilots are found in Part 61 of the Federal Aviation Regulations.

10. Successfully complete a practical (flight) test, which will be given as a final exam by an FAA inspector or designated pilot examiner. The flight test will be conducted as specified in the FAA Commercial Pilot Airman Certification Standards (FAA-S-ACS-7).

   a.   FAA inspectors are FAA employees and do not charge for their services.

   b.   FAA-designated pilot examiners are proficient, experienced flight instructors and pilots who are authorized by the FAA to conduct practical tests. They do charge a fee.

 The FAA's Commercial Pilot Airman Certification Standards are outlined and reprinted in the Gleim *Commercial Pilot Flight Maneuvers and Practical Test Prep* book.

FAA PILOT KNOWLEDGE TEST AND TESTING SUPPLEMENT

1.   This book is designed to help you prepare for and pass the following FAA knowledge tests:

   a.   Commercial Pilot - Airplane (CAX), which consists of 100 questions and has a 3-hour time limit. The testing candidate must be at least 16 years of age.

   b.   Military Competence - Non-Category (MCN), which consists of 50 questions covering airspace (see Study Unit 3), Federal Aviation Regulations (see Study Unit 4), and navigation (see Study Unit 9, Subunits 1-4). The testing candidate must be at least 18 years of age.

      1)   The MCN knowledge test time allowed is 2 hours.

2.   The FAA legends and figures are contained in a book titled *Airman Knowledge Testing Supplement for Commercial Pilot*, which you will be given to use at the time of your test.

   a.   For the purpose of test preparation, all of the airplane-related legends and figures are reproduced in color in this book.

3.   In an effort to develop better questions, the FAA frequently **pretests** questions on knowledge tests by adding up to five "pretest" questions. The pretest questions will not be graded.

   a.   You will **not** know which questions are real and which are pretest, so you must attempt to answer all questions correctly.

   b.   When you notice a question **not** covered by Gleim, it might be a pretest question.

      1)   We want to know about each pretest question you see.

      2)   Please contact us at www.GleimAviation.com/questions or call 800-874-5346 with your recollection of any possible pretest questions so we may improve our efforts to prepare future commercial pilots.

FAA'S KNOWLEDGE TESTS: CHEATING OR UNAUTHORIZED CONDUCT POLICY

The following is taken verbatim from an FAA knowledge test. It is reproduced here to remind all test takers about the FAA's policy against cheating and unauthorized conduct, a policy that Gleim consistently supports and upholds. Test takers must click "Yes" to proceed from this page into the actual knowledge test.

14 CFR part 61, section 61.37 Knowledge tests: Cheating or other unauthorized conduct

(a) An applicant for a knowledge test may not:
(1) Copy or intentionally remove any knowledge test;
(2) Give to another applicant or receive from another applicant any part or copy of a knowledge test;
(3) Give assistance on, or receive assistance on, a knowledge test during the period that test is being given;
(4) Take any part of a knowledge test on behalf of another person;
(5) Be represented by, or represent, another person for a knowledge test;
(6) Use any material or aid during the period that the test is being given, unless specifically authorized to do so by the Administrator; and
(7) Intentionally cause, assist, or participate in any act prohibited by this paragraph.

(b) An applicant who the Administrator finds has committed an act prohibited by paragraph (a) of this section is prohibited, for 1 year after the date of committing that act, from:
(1) Applying for any certificate, rating, or authorization issued under this chapter; and
(2) Applying for and taking any test under this chapter.

(c) Any certificate or rating held by an applicant may be suspended or revoked if the Administrator finds that person has committed an act prohibited by paragraph (a) of this section.

FAA PILOT KNOWLEDGE TEST QUESTION BANK

In an effort to keep applicants from simply memorizing test questions, the FAA does not disclose all the questions you might see on your FAA knowledge test. We encourage you to take the time to fully learn and understand the concepts explained in the knowledge transfer outlines contained in this book. Memorization greatly reduces the amount of information you will actually learn during your study.

Using this book or other Gleim test preparation material to merely memorize the questions and answers is unwise and unproductive, and it will not ensure your success on your FAA knowledge test.

The questions and answers provided in this book include all previously released FAA questions in addition to questions developed from current FAA reference materials that closely approximate the types of questions you should see on your knowledge test. We are confident that by studying our knowledge transfer outlines, answering our questions under exam conditions, and not relying on rote memorization, you will be able to successfully pass your FAA knowledge test and begin learning to become a safer and more competent pilot.

FAA QUESTIONS WITH TYPOGRAPHICAL ERRORS

Occasionally, FAA test questions contain typographical errors such that there is no correct answer. The FAA test development process involves many steps and people and, as you would expect, glitches occur in the system that are beyond the control of any one person. We indicate "best" rather than correct answers for some questions. Use these best answers for the indicated questions.

Note that the FAA corrects (rewrites) defective questions as they are discovered; these changes are explained in our updates (discussed on page ii). However, problems due to faulty or out-of-date figures printed in the FAA Airman Knowledge Testing Supplements are expensive to correct. Thus, it is important to carefully study questions that are noted to have a best answer in this book. Even though the best answer may not be completely correct, you should select it when taking your test.

REORGANIZATION OF FAA QUESTIONS

1. Questions previously released by the FAA were **not** grouped together by topic; i.e., they appeared to be presented randomly.

   a. We have reorganized and renumbered the questions into study units and subunits.
   b. Questions relating to helicopters, gliders, balloons, etc., are excluded.

2. Page 417 describes an online list of all of the questions in ACS code order, with cross-references to the study units and question numbers in this book.

HOW TO PREPARE FOR THE FAA PILOT KNOWLEDGE TEST

1. Begin by carefully reading the rest of this introduction. You need to have a complete understanding of the examination process prior to initiating your study. This knowledge will make your studying more efficient.

2. After you have spent an hour analyzing this introduction, set up a study schedule, including a target date for taking your knowledge test.

   a. Do not let the study process drag on and become discouraging; i.e., the quicker, the better.
   b. Consider enrolling in an organized ground school course, like the Gleim **Online Ground School**, or one held at your local FBO, community college, etc.
   c. Determine where and when you are going to take your knowledge test.

3. Work through Study Units 1 through 11.

   a. All previously released questions in the FAA's commercial pilot knowledge test question bank that are applicable to airplanes have been grouped into the following 11 categories, which are the titles of Study Units 1 through 11:

      Study Unit 1 -- Airplanes and Aerodynamics
      Study Unit 2 -- Airplane Instruments, Engines, and Systems
      Study Unit 3 -- Airports, Air Traffic Control, and Airspace
      Study Unit 4 -- Federal Aviation Regulations
      Study Unit 5 -- Airplane Performance and Weight and Balance
      Study Unit 6 -- Aeromedical Factors and Aeronautical Decision Making (ADM)
      Study Unit 7 -- Aviation Weather
      Study Unit 8 -- Aviation Weather Services
      Study Unit 9 -- Navigation: Charts, Publications, Flight Computers
      Study Unit 10 -- Navigation Systems
      Study Unit 11 -- Flight Operations

b.   Within each of the study units listed, questions relating to the same subtopic (e.g., thunderstorms, airplane stability, sectional charts, etc.) are grouped together to facilitate your study program. Each subtopic is called a subunit.

c.   To the right of each question, we present

1)   The correct answer.

2)   The appropriate source document for the answer explanation. These publications can be obtained from the FAA (www.faa.gov) and aviation bookstores.

14 CFR	Federal Aviation Regulations
AC	Advisory Circular
AC 00-6B	*Aviation Weather*
AC 00-45H	*Aviation Weather Services*
ACUG	Aeronautical Chart Users' Guide
AIM	*Aeronautical Information Manual*
E6B	Flight computer
FAA-H-8083-1B	*Weight and Balance Handbook*
FAA-H-8083-3B	*Airplane Flying Handbook*
FAA-H-8083-6	*Advanced Avionics Handbook*
FAA-H-8083-15B	*Instrument Flying Handbook*
FAA-H-8083-16B	*Instrument Procedures Handbook*
FAA-H-8083-25B	*Pilot's Handbook of Aeronautical Knowledge*
FAA-H-8083-32A	*Aviation Maintenance Technician Handbook–Powerplant*
FAA-P-8740-24	*Winter Flying Tips*
NTSB	National Transportation Safety Board regulations
P/C Glossary	Pilot/Controller Glossary *(AIM)*

a)   The codes may refer to an entire document, such as an advisory circular, or to a particular chapter or subsection of a larger document.

b)   A complete list of abbreviations and acronyms used in this book is on page 421.

3)   A comprehensive answer explanation, including

a)   A discussion of the correct answer or concept

b)   An explanation of why the other two answer choices are incorrect

4.   Each study unit begins with a list of its subunit titles. The number after each title is the number of questions that cover the information in that subunit. The two numbers following the number of questions are the page numbers on which the outline and the questions for that particular subunit begin, respectively.

5.   Begin by studying the outlines slowly and carefully. The outlines in this part of the book are very brief and have only one purpose: to help you pass the FAA knowledge test.

a.   **CAUTION:** The **sole purpose** of this book is to expedite your passing the FAA knowledge test for the commercial pilot certificate. Accordingly, all extraneous material (i.e., topics or regulations not directly tested on the FAA knowledge test) is omitted, even though much more knowledge is necessary to fly safely. This additional material is presented in four related Gleim books: *Commercial Pilot Flight Maneuvers and Practical Test Prep*, *FAR/AIM*, *Aviation Weather and Weather Services*, and *Pilot Handbook*.

6.   Next, answer the questions under exam conditions. Cover the answer explanations on the right side of each page with a piece of paper while you answer the questions.

 Remember, it is very important to the learning (and understanding) process that you honestly commit to an answer. If you are wrong, your memory will be reinforced by having discovered your error. Therefore, it is crucial to make an honest attempt to answer the question before reading the answer.

   a.   Study the answer explanation for each question that you answer incorrectly, do not understand, or have difficulty with.

   b.   Use our **Online Ground School** or **FAA Test Prep Online** to ensure that you do not refer to answers before committing to one AND to simulate actual computer testing center exam conditions.

7.   Note that this test book contains questions grouped by topic. Thus, some questions may appear repetitive, while others may be duplicates or near-duplicates. Accordingly, do not work question after question (i.e., waste time and effort) if you are already conversant with a topic and the type of questions asked.

8.   As you move through study units, you may need further explanation or clarification of certain topics. You may wish to obtain and use the following Gleim books described on page 1:
   a.   *Commercial Pilot Flight Maneuvers and Practical Test Prep*
   b.   *Pilot Handbook*
   c.   *FAR/AIM*
   d.   *Aviation Weather and Weather Services*

9.   Keep track of your work. As you complete a subunit, grade yourself with an A, B, C, or ? (use a ? if you need help on the subject) next to the subunit title at the front of the respective study unit.

   a.   The A, B, C, or ? is your self-evaluation of your comprehension of the material in that subunit and your ability to answer the questions.

      A   means a good understanding.
      B   means a fair understanding.
      C   means a shaky understanding.
      ?   means to ask your CFI or others about the material and/or questions, and read the pertinent sections in *Commercial Pilot Flight Maneuvers and Practical Test Prep* and/or *Pilot Handbook*.

   b.   This procedure will provide you with the ability to quickly see (by looking at the first page of each study unit) how much studying you have done (and how much remains) and how well you have done.

   c.   This procedure will also facilitate review. You can spend more time on the subunits that were more difficult for you.

   d.   **FAA Test Prep Online** provides you with your historical performance data.

     Follow the suggestions given throughout this introduction and you will have no trouble passing the FAA knowledge test the first time you take it.

     With this overview of exam requirements, you are ready to begin the easy-to-study outlines and rearranged questions with answers to build your knowledge and confidence and **pass the FAA's commercial pilot knowledge test**.

     The feedback we receive from users indicates that our materials reduce anxiety, improve FAA test scores, and build knowledge. Studying for each test becomes a useful step toward advanced certificates and ratings.

MULTIPLE-CHOICE QUESTION-ANSWERING TECHNIQUE

Because the commercial pilot knowledge test has a set number of questions (100) and a set time limit (3 hours), you can plan your test-taking session to ensure that you leave yourself enough time to answer each question with relative certainty. The following steps will help you move through the knowledge test efficiently and produce better test results.

1. **Budget your time.** We make this point with emphasis. Just as you would fill up your gas tank prior to reaching empty, so too should you finish your exam before time expires.

   a.   If you utilize the entire time limit for the test, you will have about 1.8 minutes per question.

   b.   If you are adequately prepared for the test, you should finish it well within the time limit.

      1)   Use any extra time you have to review questions that you are not sure about, cross-country planning questions with multiple steps and calculations, and similar questions in your exam that may help you answer other questions.

   c.   Time yourself when completing study sessions in this book and/or review your time investment reports from the Gleim **FAA Test Prep Online** to track your progress and adherence to the time limit and your own personal time allocation budget.

2. **Answer the questions in consecutive order.**

   a.   Do **not** agonize over any one item. Stay within your time budget.

      1)   We suggest that you skip cross-country planning questions and other similarly involved computational questions on your first pass through the exam. Come back to them after you have been through the entire test once.

   b.   Mark any questions you are unsure of and return to them later as time allows.

      1)   Once you initiate test grading, you will no longer be able to review/change any answers.

   c.   Never leave a multiple-choice question unanswered. Make your best educated guess in the time allowed. Remember, your score is based on the number of correct responses. You will not be penalized for guessing incorrectly.

3. **For each multiple-choice question,**

   a.   **Try to ignore the answer choices.** Do not allow the answer choices to affect your reading of the question.

      1)   If three answer choices are presented, two of them are incorrect. These choices are called **distractors** for good reason. Often, distractors are written to appear correct at first glance until further analysis.

      2)   In computational items, the distractors are carefully calculated such that they are the result of making common mistakes. Be careful, and double-check your computations if time permits.

   b.   **Read the question carefully** to determine the precise requirement.

      1)   Focusing on what is required enables you to ignore extraneous information, to focus on the relevant facts, and to proceed directly to determining the correct answer.

         a)   Be especially careful to note when the requirement is an **exception**; e.g., "Which of the following is **not** a type of hypoxia?"

   c.   **Determine the correct answer** before looking at the answer choices.

    d.   **Read the answer choices carefully.**

        1)   Even if the first answer appears to be the correct choice, do **not** skip the remaining answer choices. Questions often require the "best" answer of the choices provided. Thus, each choice requires your consideration.

        2)   Treat each answer choice as a true/false question as you analyze it.

    e.   **Click on the best answer.**

        1)   You have a 33% chance of answering the question correctly by blindly guessing; improve your odds with educated guessing.

        2)   For many multiple-choice questions, at least one answer choice can be eliminated with minimal effort, thereby increasing your educated guess to a 50-50 proposition.

4.   After you have been through all the questions in the test, consult the question status list to determine which questions are unanswered and which are marked for review.

    a.   Go back to the marked questions and finalize your answer choices.

    b.   Verify that all questions have been answered.

EDUCATED GUESSING

The FAA knowledge test sometimes includes questions that are poorly worded or confusing. Expect the unexpected and move forward. Do not let confusing questions affect your concentration or take up too much time; make your best guess and move on.

1.   If you don't know the answer, make an educated guess as follows:

    a.   Rule out answers that you think are incorrect.

    b.   Speculate on what the FAA is looking for and/or the rationale behind the question.

    c.   Select the best answer or guess between equally appealing answers. Your first guess is usually the most intuitive. If you cannot make an educated guess, re-read the stem and each answer choice and pick the most intuitive answer. It's just a guess!

2.   Avoid lingering on any question for too long. Remember your time budget and the overall test time limit.

SIMULATED FAA PRACTICE TEST

    Appendix A, "Commercial Pilot Practice Test," beginning on page 405, allows you to practice taking the FAA knowledge test without the answers next to the questions. This test has 100 questions randomly selected from the airplane-related questions in our commercial pilot knowledge test bank. Topical coverage in the practice test is similar to that of the FAA knowledge test.

    It is very important that you answer all 100 questions in one sitting. You should not consult the answers, especially when being referred to figures (charts, tables, etc.) throughout this book where the questions are answered and explained. Analyze your performance based on the answer key that follows the practice test.

    It is even better to practice with Test Sessions in the Gleim **FAA Test Prep Online**. These simulate actual computer testing conditions, including the screen layouts, instructions, etc., for PSI.

    More information on the Gleim **FAA Test Prep Online** is available on pages 17 and 18.

AUTHORIZATION TO TAKE THE FAA PILOT KNOWLEDGE TEST

Before taking the commercial pilot knowledge test, you must receive an endorsement from an authorized instructor who conducted the ground training or reviewed your home-study in the areas listed in item 4. on page 3, certifying that you are prepared to pass the knowledge test.

For your convenience, a standard authorization form for the commercial pilot knowledge test is reproduced on page 419, which can be easily completed, signed by a flight or ground instructor, torn out, and taken to the test site.

Note that if you use the Gleim **FAA Test Prep Online** or **Online Ground School**, the program will generate an authorization signed in facsimile by Dr. Gleim that is accepted at all PSI locations.

NOTE: An instructor endorsement is not required for the Military Competence - Non-Category (MCN) test.

WHEN TO TAKE THE FAA PILOT KNOWLEDGE TEST

1.   You must be at least 16 years of age to take the commercial pilot knowledge test.

2.   You must prepare for the test by successfully completing a ground instruction course or by using this book as your self-developed home study course.

    a.   See "Authorization to Take the FAA Pilot Knowledge Test" above.

3.   Take the FAA knowledge test within 30 days of beginning your study.

    a.   Complete the knowledge test early in your training so you can focus your effort toward building your skills through aeronautical experience.

4.   Your practical test must follow within 24 months.

    a.   Otherwise, you will have to retake your knowledge test.

WHAT TO TAKE TO THE FAA PILOT KNOWLEDGE TEST

1.   An approved flight computer (ideally the one that you use to solve the test questions in this book, i.e., one you are familiar with and have used before)

2.   Navigational plotter

3.   A pocket calculator you are familiar with and have used before (no instructional material for the calculator is allowed)

4.   Authorization to take the knowledge test (see above)

5.   Proper identification that contains your

    a.   Photograph
    b.   Signature
    c.   Date of birth
    d.   Actual residential address, if different from your mailing address

NOTE: Paper and pencils are supplied at the examination site.

 It is essential for each learner to own an approved E6B flight computer (manual or electronic) and a navigation plotter. These tools are necessary to answer some questions on the knowledge test and to use during your check ride. Go to www.GleimAviation.com/E6B to access complete instructions on the use of the Gleim E6B flight computer.

COMPUTER TESTING CENTERS

The FAA has contracted with a computer testing service (PSI) to administer FAA knowledge tests. PSI has testing centers throughout the country. To register for the knowledge test, call (844) 704-1487 or visit PSI's website at https://faa.psiexams.com/FAA/login. More information can be found at www.GleimAviation.com/testingcenters.

COMPUTER TESTING PROCEDURES

When you arrive at the testing center, you will be required to provide positive proof of identification and documentary evidence of your age. The identification must include your photograph, signature, and actual residential address if different from the mailing address. This information may be presented in more than one form of identification.

Next, you will sign in on the testing center's daily log. Your signature on the logsheet certifies that, if this is a retest, you meet the applicable requirements (discussed in "Failure on the FAA Pilot Knowledge Test" on page 15) and that you have not passed this test in the past 2 years.

Finally, you will present your logbook endorsement or authorization form from your instructor, which authorizes you to take the test. A standard authorization form is provided on page 419 for your use. Both **FAA Test Prep Online** and **Online Ground School** generate an authorization signed in facsimile by Dr. Gleim that is accepted at all PSI locations.

You will be taken into the testing room and seated at a computer terminal. A person from the testing center will assist you in logging onto the system, and you will be asked to confirm your personal data (e.g., name, Social Security number, etc.).

Then you will be given an online introduction to the computer testing system, and you will take a sample test. If you have used our **FAA Test Prep Online**, you will be conversant with the computer testing methodology and environment and will breeze through the sample test.

When you have completed your test, an Airman Knowledge Test Report will be printed out, validated, and given to you by a person from the testing center. Before you leave, you will be required to sign out on the testing center's daily log.

U.S. DEPARTMENT OF TRANSPORTATION
Federal Aviation Administration
Airman Knowledge Test Report

NAME:

FAA TRACKING NUMBER (FTN):   **EXAM ID:**

EXAM: Commercial Pilot Airplane (CAX)

EXAM DATE: 10/08/2021   **EXAM SITE:**

SCORE: 96   **GRADE:** Pass   **TAKE:** 1

The Airman Certification Standards (ACS) codes listed below represent incorrectly answered questions. These ACS codes and their associated Areas of Operation/Tasks/Elements may be found in the appropriate ACS document at http://www.faa.gov/training_testing/testing/acs.

A single code may represent more than one incorrect response.

CA.I.A.K2   CA.I.D.K3a

EXPIRATION DATE: 10/31/2023

DO NOT LOSE THIS REPORT

AUTHORIZED INSTRUCTOR'S STATEMENT: (if applicable)

On _____ (date) I gave the above named applicant _____ hours of additional instruction, covering each subject area shown to be deficient, and consider the applicant competent to pass the knowledge test.

Name _____

Cert. No. _____ *(print clearly)*

Type of instructor certificate _____

Signature _____

FRAUDULENT ALTERATION OF THIS FORM BY ANY PERSON IS A BASIS FOR SUSPENSION OR REVOCATION OF ANY CERTIFICATES OR RATINGS HELD BY THAT PERSON.
ISSUED BY: PSI Services LLC
FEDERAL AVIATION ADMINISTRATION

THIS INFORMATION IS PROTECTED BY THE PRIVACY ACT. FOR OFFICIAL USE ONLY.

YOUR FAA AIRMAN KNOWLEDGE TEST REPORT

1. You will receive your FAA Airman Knowledge Test Report upon completion of the test. An example test report is reproduced on the previous page.

   a. Note that you will receive only one grade as illustrated.

   b. The expiration date is the date by which you must take your FAA practical test.

   c. The report lists the ACS codes of the questions you missed so you can review the topics you missed prior to your practical test.

2. Refer to the Commercial Pilot Airplane ACS to determine which topics you had difficulty with.

   a. Look them over and review them with your CFI so (s)he can certify that (s)he reviewed the deficient areas and found you competent in them when you take your practical test. Have your CFI sign off your deficiencies on the FAA Airman Knowledge Test Report.

3. Keep your FAA Airman Knowledge Test Report in a safe place because you must submit it to the FAA evaluator when you take your practical test.

FAILURE ON THE FAA PILOT KNOWLEDGE TEST

1. If you fail (score less than 70%) the knowledge test (which is virtually impossible if you follow the Gleim system), you may retake it after your instructor endorses the bottom of your FAA Airman Knowledge Test Report certifying that you have received the necessary ground training to retake the test.

2. Upon retaking the test, you will find that the procedure is the same except that you must also submit your FAA Airman Knowledge Test Report indicating the previous failure to the computer testing center.

3. Note that the pass rate on the commercial pilot knowledge test is about 97%; i.e., fewer than 1 out of 10 fails the test initially. Reasons for failure include

   a. Failure to study the material tested and mere memorization of correct answers. (Relevant study material is contained in the outlines at the beginning of Study Units 1 through 11 of this book.)

   b. Failure to practice working through the questions under test conditions. (All of the previously released FAA questions appear in Study Units 1 through 11 of this book.)

   c. Poor examination technique, such as misreading questions and not understanding the requirements.

This Gleim Knowledge Test book will prepare you to pass the FAA knowledge test on your first attempt! In addition, the Gleim *Commercial Pilot Flight Maneuvers and Practical Test Prep* book will save you time and frustration as you prepare for the FAA practical test.

Just as this book organizes and explains the knowledge needed to pass your FAA knowledge test, *Commercial Pilot Flight Maneuvers and Practical Test Prep* will assist you in developing the competence and confidence to pass your FAA practical test.

Also, flight maneuvers are quickly perfected when you understand exactly what to expect before you get into an airplane to practice the flight maneuvers. You must be ahead of (not behind) your CFI and your airplane. Our flight maneuvers books explain and illustrate all flight maneuvers so the maneuvers and their execution are intuitively appealing to you. Visit www.GleimAviation.com or call (800) 874-5346 and order today!

GLEIM ONLINE GROUND SCHOOL

1. Gleim **Online Ground School (OGS)** course content is based on the Gleim Knowledge Test Prep books, **FAA Test Prep Online**, FAA publications, and Gleim reference books.

    a. Online Ground School courses are available for

        1) Sport Pilot
        2) Private Pilot
        3) Instrument Pilot
        4) Commercial Pilot
        5) Flight/Ground Instructor
        6) Fundamentals of Instructing
        7) Airline Transport Pilot
        8) Flight Engineer
        9) Canadian Certificate Conversion

    b. OGS courses are airplane-only and have lessons that correspond to the study units in the Gleim FAA Knowledge Test Prep books.

    c. Each course contains study outlines that automatically reference current FAA publications, the appropriate knowledge test questions, FAA figures, and Gleim answer explanations.

    d. OGS is always up to date.

    e. Users achieve very high knowledge test scores and a near-100% pass rate.

    f. **Gleim Online Ground School is the most flexible course available!** Access your OGS personal classroom from any computer with Internet access 24 hours a day, 7 days a week. Your virtual classroom is never closed!

    g. **Save time and study only the material you need to know!** Gleim **Online Ground School** Certificate Selection will provide you with a customized study plan. You save time because unnecessary questions will be automatically eliminated.

    h. **We are truly interactive. We help you focus on any weaker areas.** Answer explanations for wrong choices help you learn from your mistakes.

Register for Gleim Online Ground School today:
www.GleimAviation.com/OGS

or

Demo Study Unit 1 for FREE at
www.GleimAviation.com/Demos

GLEIM FAA TEST PREP ONLINE

Computer testing is consistent with aviation's use of computers (e.g., flight simulators, computerized flight decks, etc.). All FAA knowledge tests are administered by computer.

Computer testing is natural after computer study, and computer-assisted instruction is a very efficient and effective method of study. The Gleim **FAA Test Prep Online** is designed to prepare you for computer testing because our software simulates PSI. We make you comfortable with computer testing!

FAA Test Prep Online contains all of the questions in this book, context-sensitive outline material, and on-screen charts and figures. It allows you to choose either Study Mode or Test Mode.

In Study Mode, the software provides you with an explanation of each answer you choose (correct or incorrect). You design each Study Session:

- Topic(s) and/or FAA codes you wish to cover
- Number of questions
- Order of questions -- FAA, Gleim, or random
- Order of answers to each question -- Gleim or random
- Questions marked and/or missed from last session -- test, study, or both
- Questions marked and/or missed from all sessions -- test, study, or both
- Questions never seen, answered, or answered correctly

In Test Mode, the software emulates the operation of the FAA-approved PSI computer testing centers. When you finish your test, you can and should study the questions missed and access answer explanations. Thus, you have a complete understanding of how to take an FAA knowledge test and know exactly what to expect before you go to a computer testing center.

The Gleim **FAA Test Prep Online** is an all-in-one program designed to help anyone with a computer, Internet access, and an interest in flying pass the FAA knowledge tests.

Study Sessions and Test Sessions

Study Sessions give you immediate feedback on why your answer selection for a particular question is correct or incorrect and allow you to access the context-sensitive outline material that helps to explain concepts related to the question.

Choose from several different question sources: all questions available for that library; questions from a certain topic (Gleim study units and subunits); questions that you missed or marked in the last sessions you created; questions that you have never seen, answered, or answered correctly; questions from certain FAA codes; etc. You can mix up the questions by selecting to randomize the question and/or answer order so that you do not memorize answer letters.

You may then grade your study sessions and track your study progress using the performance analysis charts and graphs. The Performance Analysis information helps you to focus on areas where you need the most improvement, saving you time in the overall study process. You may then want to go back and study questions that you missed in a previous session, or you may want to create a Study Session of questions that you marked in the previous session. All of these options are made easy with **FAA Test Prep Online**'s Study Sessions.

After studying the outlines and questions in a Study Session, you can further test your skills with a Test Session. These sessions allow you to answer questions under actual testing conditions. In a Test Session, you will not know which questions you have answered correctly until the session is graded.

Recommended Study Program

1. Start with Study Unit 1 and proceed through study units in chronological order. Follow the three-step process below.

    a. First, carefully study the Gleim Outline.

    b. Second, create a Study Session of all questions in the study unit. Answer and study all questions in the Study Session.

    c. Third, create a Test Session of all questions in the study unit. Answer all questions in the Test Session.

2. After each Study Session and Test Session, create a new Study Session from questions answered incorrectly. This is of critical importance to allow you to learn from your mistakes.

Practice Test

Take an exam in the actual testing environment of the PSI testing centers. **FAA Test Prep Online** simulates the testing formats of these testing centers, making it easy for you to study questions under actual exam conditions. After studying with **FAA Test Prep Online**, you will know exactly what to expect when you go in to take your pilot knowledge test.

On-Screen Charts and Figures

One of the most convenient features of **FAA Test Prep Online** is the easily accessible on-screen charts and figures. Several of the questions refer to drawings, maps, charts, and other pictures that provide information to help answer the question. In **FAA Test Prep Online**, you can pull up any of these figures with the click of a button. You can increase or decrease the size of the images, and you may also use our drawing feature to calculate the true course between two given points (required only on the private pilot knowledge test).

Instructor Sign-Off Sheets

FAA Test Prep Online can generate an instructor sign-off for FAA knowledge tests that require one. This sign-off has been approved by the FAA and can be presented at the computer testing center as authorization to take your test--you do **not** need an additional endorsement from your instructor.

In order to obtain the instructor sign-off sheet for your test, you must first answer all relevant questions in **FAA Test Prep Online** correctly. Then, select "Sign-Off Forms" under the "Tools" area on the Main page. If you have answered all of the required questions, the instructor sign-off sheet will appear for you to print. If you have not yet answered all required questions, a list of the unanswered questions, along with their location, will appear.

Order FAA Test Prep Online today
(800) 874-5346 or www.GleimAviation.com
or
Demo Study Unit 1 for FREE at
www.GleimAviation.com/Demos

FREE UPDATES AND TECHNICAL SUPPORT

Gleim offers FREE technical support to all users of the current versions. Fill out the technical support request form online (www.GleimAviation.com/contact), send an email to support@gleim.com, or call (800) 874-5346. Additionally, Gleim **FAA Test Prep Online** is always up to date. The program is automatically updated when any changes are made, so you can be confident that Gleim will prepare you for your knowledge test. More information on our update service for books is on page ii.

STUDY UNIT ONE

AIRPLANES AND AERODYNAMICS

(11 pages of outline)

This study unit contains outlines of major concepts tested, sample test questions and answers regarding airplanes and aerodynamics, and an explanation of each answer. The table of contents above lists each subunit within this study unit, the number of questions pertaining to that particular subunit, and the pages on which the outlines and questions begin, respectively.

Recall that the **sole purpose** of this book is to expedite your passing of the FAA pilot knowledge test for the commercial pilot certificate. Accordingly, all extraneous material (i.e., topics or regulations not directly tested on the FAA pilot knowledge test) is omitted, even though much more knowledge is necessary to become a proficient commercial pilot. This additional material is presented in *Pilot Handbook* and *Commercial Pilot Flight Maneuvers and Practical Test Prep*, available from Gleim Publications, Inc. Order online at www.GleimAviation.com.

1.1 FLAPS

1. One of the main functions of flaps during the approach and landing is to increase angle of attack, which causes the wing to produce the same amount of lift at a slower airspeed.

2. The raising of flaps increases the stall speed.

1.2 AIRPLANE WINGS

1. Spoilers are fitted to many modern turbojets and other high performance aircraft.

    a. These aircraft are very clean aerodynamically and land at very high speeds.

    b. Spoilers fitted to the top of the wing can be deployed automatically or at the command of the PIC to disrupt airflow and destroy lift.

        1) When deployed just after landing, spoilers allow the brakes to be more effective.
        2) Ground spoilers used just after landing are more effective at high speed.

2. Rectangular wings generally are designed so that the wing root stalls first, with the stall progression toward the wingtip.

3. A change in the angle of attack of the wing changes the lift, drag, and airspeed.

4. The angle of attack of a wing directly controls the distribution of positive and negative pressure acting on the wing.

5. Frost on the upper surface of airplane wings disrupts the smooth flow of air over the top of the wing (which increases drag) and causes the airplane to stall at higher airspeeds and lower angles of attack than normal.

1.3 STALLS

1. The angle of attack at which a wing stalls (critical angle of attack) remains constant regardless of

    a. Weight

    b. Dynamic pressure (a component of the Bernoulli equation, which explains lift in terms of pressure differentials)

    c. Bank angle

    d. Pitch attitude

2. Stall speed is affected by the airplane's

    a. Weight
    b. Load factor
    c. Power setting

3. The stalling speed is most affected by variations in airplane loading, i.e., weight and CG.

    a. Design maneuvering speed, V_A, is listed in the POH/AFM on all recently designed aircraft. V_A defines the maximum speed at which an airplane can be safely stalled.

4. Turbulence can increase stall speed due to increased load factors.

    a. Slowing to V_A protects the airplane from excessive load stresses while providing a safe margin above stall speed.

5. Stall recovery becomes progressively more difficult when the CG moves aft.

6. Stall speed tables for various configurations at different angles of bank are provided for some airplanes, such as illustrated in Figure 2 below.

GROSS WEIGHT 2,750 LB			ANGLE OF BANK			
			LEVEL	30°	45°	60°
POWER			GEAR AND FLAPS UP			
ON	MPH		62	67	74	88
	KTS		54	58	64	76
OFF	MPH		75	81	89	106
	KTS		65	70	77	92
			GEAR AND FLAPS DOWN			
ON	MPH		54	58	64	76
	KTS		47	50	56	66
OFF	MPH		66	71	78	93
	KTS		57	62	68	81

Figure 2. Stall Speeds.

a. Note that the table portrays situations for a given weight at four angles of bank in two configurations (gear and flaps up or down) and with power on or off.

b. Note that stall speeds are generally lower with gear and flaps down.

c. Also, stall speeds are higher as bank increases.

1.4 SPINS

1. Recovery from spins as well as stalls may become difficult when the CG is too far rearward.

    a. The rotation of a spin is always around the CG.

2. Over-the-top spin.

    a. The aircraft can stall, then begin a spin. This begins as a cross-control stall.

        1) It usually occurs in the traffic pattern when turning base to final.

            a) The pilot compensates for overshooting the runway centerline with rudder alone.

            b) The proper action would be to increase the rate of turn while maintaining a coordinated turn.

        2) Improperly trained pilots are apt to hold the bank constant and try to increase the rate of turn by adding more rudder in an effort to get aligned with the runway centerline.

        3) While in this skidding turn, the aileron on the inside of the turn increases drag on the wing, slowing it down and decreasing its lift, which requires more aileron application.

        4) The airplane will then begin an uncommanded roll toward the inside wing. This roll may occur so quickly that it is possible the bank will be vertical or past vertical before it can be stopped.

        5) The airplane may continue to roll to an inverted position, which is usually the beginning of an over-the-top spin.

1.5 LIFT AND DRAG

1. An airplane wing produces lift resulting from relatively higher air pressure below the wing surface and lower air pressure above the wing surface.

    a. Lift is defined as the force acting perpendicular to the relative wind.
    b. An increase in the angle of attack will increase drag.

        1) Drag acts parallel to the flight path.

2. In all steady-state flight, including descent, the sum of all forward forces equals the sum of all rearward forces, and the sum of all upward forces equals the sum of all downward forces.

    a. During the transition from straight-and-level flight to a climb, the angle of attack must be increased and lift is momentarily increased.

3. Any given angle of attack has a corresponding airspeed to provide sufficient lift to maintain a given altitude.

    a. As airspeed decreases, the airfoils generate less lift. Accordingly, to maintain altitude, the angle of attack must be increased to compensate for the decrease in lift.

    b. To generate the same amount of lift as altitude increases, the airplane must be flown at a higher true airspeed for any given angle of attack.

4. As the angle of bank increases, the vertical component of lift decreases and the horizontal component of lift increases.

5. As airspeed increases, lift and parasite drag increase as the square of the increase in airspeed; e.g., doubling airspeed quadruples lift and parasite drag.

    a. Induced drag is a byproduct of lift and is also greatly affected by changes in airspeed.

6. Graphs including curves of the component of lift, the component of drag, and the lift/drag (L/D) ratio are frequently prepared to demonstrate the effect of the angle of attack on drag, lift, and the lift/drag ratio. Figure 3 on the next page is an example.

    a. For any given angle of attack, the L/D ratio can be converted into altitude loss (in feet) per forward distance traveled.

    b. The L/D ratio can be the same for two different angles of attack.

        1) EXAMPLE: At 3° angle of attack and at slightly over 12° angle of attack, the L/D ratio is approximately 10.

    c. This chart can be used to calculate an airplane's glide properties.

        1) EXAMPLE: If an airplane glides at an angle of attack of 10°, how much altitude will it lose in 1 SM?

            a) To determine the L/D ratio for a given angle of attack, you must use Figure 3.

                i) Locate 10° angle of attack at the bottom of the chart.
                ii) Draw a straight line along the 10° line to the L/D$_{MAX}$ line.
                iii) From that point, draw a straight line across to the right until you reach the L/D scale. The result is slightly over 11.
                iv) At a distance of 5,280 ft. (1 SM), the airplane will lose 480 ft. (5,280 ÷ 11) of altitude.

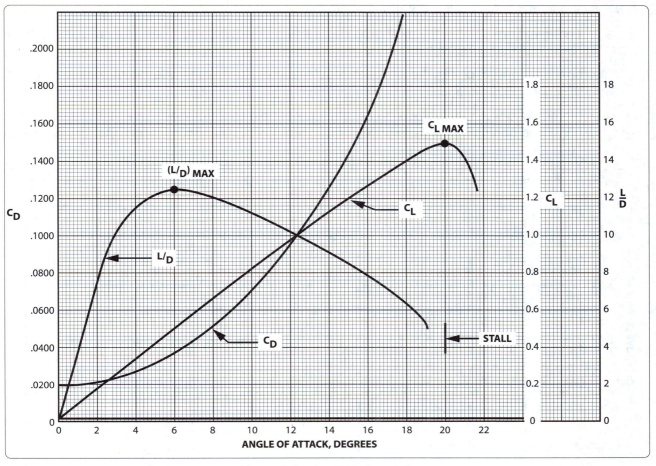

Figure 3. Angle of Attack vs. Lift.

7.   In the left diagram below, as airspeed increases above the maximum lift/drag (L/D$_{MAX}$) speed, total drag on the airplane increases due to the increased parasite drag. Figure 1 below is similar.

   a.   As airspeed decreases below the L/D$_{MAX}$ speed, total drag increases due to increased induced drag.

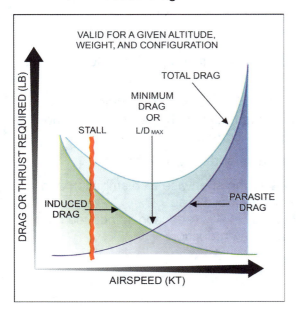

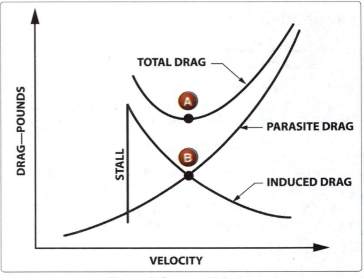

Figure 1. Drag vs. Velocity.

8.   By definition, the L/D$_{MAX}$ ratio is at the minimum (lowest) point of the total drag curve.

    a.   The minimum point in the total drag curve is the point where the parasite drag and induced drag curves intersect.

9.   In a propeller-driven airplane, the airspeed resulting in L/D$_{MAX}$ will provide the maximum range and maximum glide distance.

    a.   Many manufacturers provide glide data for a certain configuration. The best glide speed (V$_G$) and configuration were developed to provide the maximum glide distance. Figure 3A is an example.

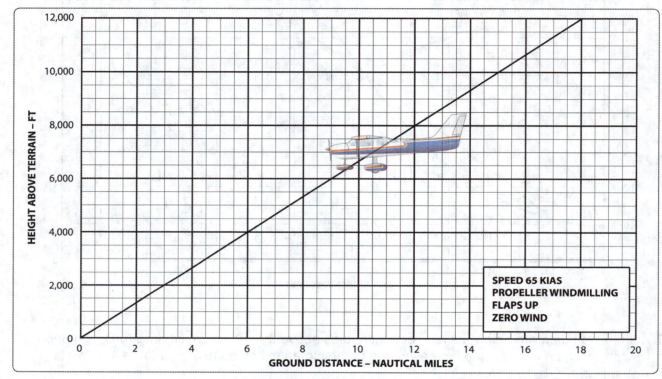

Figure 3A. Maximum Glide Distance.

10.   When flaps are extended, lift and drag increase.

1.6 GROUND EFFECT

1.   Ground effect is due to the interference of the ground (or water) surface with the airflow patterns about the airplane in flight.

    a.   When an airplane is within a distance of its wingspan to the surface, a change occurs in the three-dimensional flow pattern around the airplane because the vertical component of the airflow around the wing is restricted by the Earth's surface.

        1)   This change alters the wing's upwash, downwash, and wingtip vortices.

            a)   The reduction of the wingtip vortices alters the spanwise lift distribution and reduces the induced angle of attack and induced drag.

        2)   Within one wingspan above the surface, there is a 1.4% reduction in induced drag, while at one-tenth of a wingspan, there is a 47.6% reduction.

2.   An airplane leaving ground effect experiences an increase in induced drag and requires more thrust.

3.   While in ground effect, an airplane needs a lower angle of attack to produce the same lift as when out of ground effect.

    a.   If the same angle of attack is maintained in ground effect as when out of ground effect, lift will increase and induced drag will decrease.

1.7 AIRPLANE STABILITY

1.   Stability is the inherent ability of an object (e.g., airplane), after its equilibrium is disturbed, to return to its original position. In other words, a stable airplane will tend to return to the original condition of flight if disturbed by a force such as turbulent air.

2.   Static stability is the initial tendency that the airplane displays after its equilibrium is disturbed.

    a.   Positive static stability can be illustrated by a ball inside a round bowl. If the ball is displaced from its normal resting place, it will eventually return to its original position at the bottom of the bowl.

    b.   Neutral static stability can be illustrated by a ball on a flat plane. If the ball is displaced, it will come to rest at some new, neutral position and show no tendency to return to its original position.

    c.   Negative static stability is really instability. It can be illustrated by a ball on top of an inverted round bowl. Even the slightest displacement of the ball will activate greater forces, which will cause the ball to continue to move in the direction of the applied force (e.g., gravity).

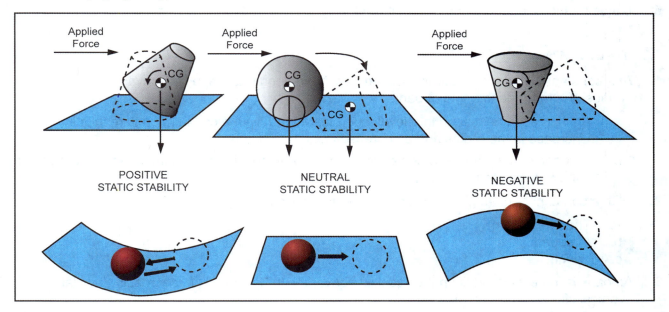

3. Dynamic stability is the overall tendency that the airplane displays after its equilibrium is disturbed.

    a. Positive dynamic stability is a property that dampens the oscillations set up by a statically stable airplane, enabling the oscillations to become smaller and smaller in magnitude until the airplane eventually settles down to its original condition of flight.

    b. Neutral dynamic stability means the oscillations remain unchanged.

    c. Negative dynamic stability is actually dynamic instability. It means the oscillations tend to increase.

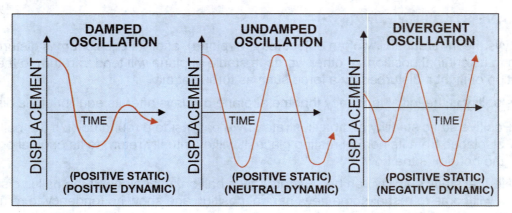

4. An airplane is said to have

    a. Longitudinal stability about the lateral axis

    b. Lateral stability about the longitudinal axis

    c. Directional stability about the vertical axis

5. If an airplane is loaded to the rear of its CG range, it will tend to be unstable about its lateral axis.

1.8 TURNS

1. At a constant altitude in a coordinated turn, each airspeed has a specific, unvarying rate and radius of turn for each angle of bank.

    a. An increase in airspeed in a level, coordinated turn with a constant bank results in an increase in the radius and a decrease in the rate of turn.

    b. Steepening the bank and decreasing the airspeed results in an increase in the rate of turn and a decrease in the radius.

2. With a constant bank angle, the load factor will be constant regardless of

    a. The rate of turn

    b. Airspeed

    c. Weight

3. As bank is increased, additional vertical lift converts into horizontal lift, decreasing available vertical lift.

    a. Thus, an increased angle of attack (back elevator pressure) is required in order to maintain a constant altitude during the turn.

4. When airspeed is increased during a level turn, the angle of attack must be decreased or the angle of bank increased to maintain level altitude.

5. A standard rate turn is, by definition, 2 min. for 360°, or 3°/second.

    a. To maintain a standard rate turn as the airspeed increases, the bank angle of the aircraft will need to increase.

1.9 LOAD FACTOR

1. Load factor is the ratio between the total airload imposed on the wing in flight and the gross weight of the airplane.

    a. The amount of excess load that can be imposed on an airplane's wings varies directly with the airplane's speed and the excess lift available.

        1) At low speeds, little excess lift is available, so little excess load can be imposed.

        2) At high speeds, the wings' lifting capacity is so great that the load factor can quickly exceed safety limits.

    b. An increased load factor will cause an airplane to stall at a higher airspeed.

    c. As bank angle increases, the load factor increases. The wings not only must carry the airplane's weight but also must bear the load imposed by the centrifugal force.

        1) The determinant of load factor in level, coordinated turns is the amount of bank.

        2) A change of airspeed does not affect load factor given a constant angle of bank, although it does directly affect the rate and radius of turn.

2. Load factor (or G units) is a multiple of the regular weight or, alternatively, a multiple of the force of gravity.

    a. Unaccelerated straight flight has a load factor of 1.0 (by definition).

    b. A 60° level bank has a load factor of 2.0. Thus, a 3,000-lb. airplane in a 60° bank would require the wings to provide lift for 6,000 pounds.

    c. The best indication of positive (+) or negative (–) Gs is the change in how heavy (positive) or light (negative) you feel in your seat.

3. Maximum safe load factors (limit load factors):

    a. The limit load factor is the ratio of maximum sustainable load imposed on the aircraft to the gross weight of the aircraft.

        1) Normal category airplanes are limited to +3.8 and –1.52 Gs.
        2) Utility aircraft are limited to +4.4 and –1.76 Gs.
        3) Aerobatic aircraft are limited to +6.0 and –3.0 Gs.

4. When baggage or other areas of the plane are placarded for weight, they are placarded for gross weight. The airplane is designed to accommodate the specified Gs (+3.8, +4.4, +6.0) given the weight placarded.

5.   A "stall speed vs. load factor" graph relates these variables to the degree of bank angle for a particular airplane, as illustrated in Figure 4 below.

 a.   Determine the load factor (or G units) for any bank angle by finding the bank angle on the horizontal axis, moving vertically up to the intersection with the load factor curve, and then proceeding horizontally to the right of the graph to find the number of G units on the vertical load factor scale.

 b.   To determine the increase in stall speed for any load factor, begin with the load factor on the far right vertical scale and move horizontally to intersect the load factor curve. From that point of intersection, move up vertically to the intersection with the stall speed increase curve. From that point, move horizontally to the left to the vertical axis to determine the percentage increase in stall speed.

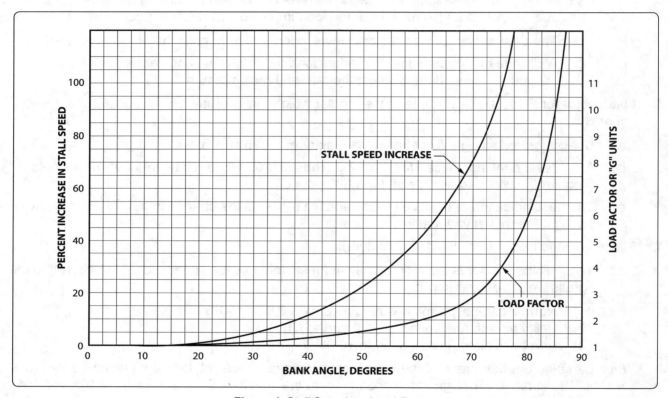

Figure 4. Stall Speed vs. Load Factor.

1.10 TRANSONIC AND SUPERSONIC FLIGHT

1.   Transonic and supersonic flight speeds are expressed by the ratio of the true airspeed in knots to the speed of sound in knots. This ratio is called the **Mach number**.

    a.   This ratio is not fixed because the speed of sound varies with altitude and temperature.

2.   At low flight speeds, the study of aerodynamics is greatly simplified by the fact that air may experience relatively small changes in pressure with only negligible changes in density.

    a.   This airflow is termed incompressible since the air may undergo changes in pressure without apparent changes in density.

    b.   The study of airflow at high speeds must account for these changes in air density and must consider that the air is compressible and there will be compressibility effects.

    c.   Local airflow velocities around an aerodynamic shape can be greater than flight speed.

        1)   Thus, an aircraft can experience compressibility effects at flight speeds well below the speed of sound.

3.   Because an aircraft can have both subsonic and supersonic airflows simultaneously, certain regimes have been defined.

    a.   Subsonic: Mach numbers below 0.75
    b.   Transonic: Mach numbers from 0.75 to 1.20
    c.   Supersonic: Mach numbers from 1.20 to 5.00
    d.   Hypersonic: Mach numbers above 5.00

4.   The **critical Mach number** is the highest flight speed possible without supersonic flow.

    a.   Accelerating past critical Mach is associated with trim and stability changes, an increase in drag, and a decrease in control surface effectiveness.

QUESTIONS AND ANSWER EXPLANATIONS: All of the commercial pilot knowledge test questions chosen by the FAA for release as well as additional questions selected by Gleim relating to the material in the previous outlines are provided on the following pages. These questions have been organized into the same subunits as the outlines. To the immediate right of each question are the correct answer and answer explanations. You should cover these answers and answer explanations while responding to the questions. Refer to the general discussion in the Introduction on how to take the FAA knowledge test.

Remember that the questions from the FAA knowledge test bank have been reordered by topic and organized into a meaningful sequence. Also, the first line of the answer explanation gives the citation of the authoritative source for the answer.

QUESTIONS

1.1 Flaps

1. One of the main functions of flaps during the approach and landing is to

    A. decrease the angle of descent without increasing the airspeed.

    B. provide the same amount of lift at a slower airspeed.

    C. decrease lift, thus enabling a steeper-than-normal approach to be made.

Answer (B) is correct. (FAA-H-8083-25B Chap 6 & 11)
    DISCUSSION: Extending the flaps increases the wing camber, the wing area (some types), and the angle of attack of the wing. This allows the wing to provide the same amount of lift at a slower airspeed.
    Answer (A) is incorrect. Flaps increase, not decrease, the angle of descent without increasing the airspeed. **Answer (C) is incorrect.** Flaps increase, not decrease, lift. They also increase induced drag.

2. Which is true regarding the use of flaps during level turns?

    A. The lowering of flaps increases the stall speed.

    B. The raising of flaps increases the stall speed.

    C. Raising flaps will require added forward pressure on the yoke or stick.

Answer (B) is correct. (FAA-H-8083-25B Chap 6)
    DISCUSSION: Raising the flaps decreases the wing camber and the angle of attack of the wing. This decreases wing lift and results in a higher stall speed.
    Answer (A) is incorrect. Flaps decrease, not increase, the stall speed. **Answer (C) is incorrect.** Raising the flaps will decrease the lift provided by the wings. Thus, back, not forward, pressure on the yoke or stick is required to maintain altitude.

1.2 Airplane Wings

3. The angle of attack of a wing directly controls the

    A. angle of incidence of the wing.

    B. amount of airflow above and below the wing.

    C. distribution of pressures acting on the wing.

Answer (C) is correct. (FAA-H-8083-25B Chap 4)
    DISCUSSION: The angle of attack of an airfoil directly controls the distribution of pressure below and above it. When a wing is at a low but positive angle of attack, most of the lift is due to the wing's negative pressure (upper surface) and downwash. NOTE: Negative pressure is any pressure less than atmospheric, and positive pressure is pressure greater than atmospheric.
    Answer (A) is incorrect. The angle of incidence is a fixed relationship between the wing chord line and the longitudinal axis of the airplane and is thus unrelated to the angle of attack. **Answer (B) is incorrect.** The same amount of air must flow above and below (over and under) the wing.

4. Some aircraft are fitted with wing spoilers to decrease

    A. drag.

    B. takeoff speed.

    C. lift.

Answer (C) is correct. (FAA-H-8083-25B Chap 5)
    DISCUSSION: Some aircraft require the use of spoilers. Many modern high-speed aircraft are very clean aerodynamically. Upon landing, spoilers are deployed on the top of the wing to reduce lift and improve braking performance.
    Answer (A) is incorrect. Spoilers increase drag while subsequently reducing lift. **Answer (B) is incorrect.** Spoilers are not used on takeoff. Spoilers reduce lift, the opposite of what is required for optimal takeoff performance.

5. A rectangular wing, as compared to other wing planforms, has a tendency to stall first at the

    A. wingtip, with the stall progression toward the wing root.

    B. wing root, with the stall progression toward the wingtip.

    C. center trailing edge, with the stall progression outward toward the wing root and tip.

Answer (B) is correct. (FAA-H-8083-25B Chap 5)
    DISCUSSION: A rectangular wing, as compared to other wing planforms, has a tendency to stall first at the wing root, with the stall progression toward the wingtip. Because the wingtips and the ailerons stall later, the pilot can use aileron control in avoiding and recovering from the stall.
    Answer (A) is incorrect. The wing root, not wingtip, will stall first. **Answer (C) is incorrect.** The wing root, not the center trailing edge, will stall first.

6. An aircraft airfoil is designed to produce lift resulting from a difference in the

A. negative air pressure below and a vacuum above the airfoil's surface.

B. vacuum below the airfoil's surface and greater air pressure above the airfoil's surface.

C. higher air pressure below the airfoil's surface and lower air pressure above the airfoil's surface.

Answer (C) is correct. (FAA-H-8083-25B Chap 4)
   DISCUSSION: As air molecules flow over the top portion of the wing, which is cambered, they travel a greater distance than the molecules that flow over the relatively flat underside of the wing. The airflow over the top of the wing is forced to accelerate. It is this increase in velocity that causes a pressure differential, creating an area of low pressure above the wing.
   Answer (A) is incorrect. Wings create areas of low pressure, not a vacuum. A vacuum by definition is an area of zero pressure. An area of negative pressure does not exist below the wing; rather, the underside of the wing is an area of high pressure. An area of low pressure, not a vacuum, exists above the top portion of the wing. **Answer (B) is incorrect.** Wings create areas of low pressure, not a vacuum. A vacuum by definition is an area of zero pressure. The area of greatest pressure is located on the underside of the wing with an area of low pressure forming above the wing.

7. Frost covering the upper surface of an airplane wing usually will cause

A. the airplane to stall at an angle of attack that is higher than normal.

B. the airplane to stall at an angle of attack that is lower than normal.

C. drag factors so large that sufficient speed cannot be obtained for takeoff.

Answer (B) is correct. (FAA-H-8083-25B Chap 5)
   DISCUSSION: Frost on the surface of a wing interferes with the smooth flow of air over the wing surface; i.e., parasite drag is increased. The air flowing over the wing is thus disrupted and stalls at a lower angle of attack (a higher speed) when there is frost on the wing surface.
   Answer (A) is incorrect. Frost on the wing surface will usually cause the airplane to stall at a lower, not higher, angle of attack. **Answer (C) is incorrect.** The drag created by frost usually will not be so disruptive as to prevent the aircraft from obtaining takeoff speed.

8. By changing the angle of attack of a wing, the pilot can control the airplane's

A. lift, airspeed, and drag.

B. lift, airspeed, and CG.

C. lift and airspeed, but not drag.

Answer (A) is correct. (FAA-H-8083-25B Chap 5)
   DISCUSSION: The pilot can control the airplane's lift, airspeed, and drag by changing the angle of attack of the wing. As the angle of attack is increased, the lift increases to the critical angle of attack, airspeed decreases, and induced drag increases with the increase in lift.
   Answer (B) is incorrect. The angle of attack has no effect on the CG of an airplane. **Answer (C) is incorrect.** Drag, as well as lift and airspeed, is determined by the angle of attack.

9. When a pilot increases the angle of attack on a symmetrical airfoil, the center of pressure will

A. move forward.

B. move aft.

C. be unchanged.

Answer (C) is correct. (FAA-H-8083-25B Chap 5)
   DISCUSSION: An increase in the angle of attack has no effect on the center of pressure on a symmetrical wing.
   Answer (A) is incorrect. The center of pressure on a symmetrical wing does not move forward with an increase in angle of attack; it is unaffected. **Answer (B) is incorrect.** The center of pressure on a symmetrical wing does not move aft with an increase in angle of attack; it is unaffected.

10. Ground spoilers used after landing are

A. more effective at low speed.

B. equally effective at any speed.

C. more effective at high speed.

Answer (C) is correct. (FAA-H-8080-3B Chap 15)
   DISCUSSION: Aerodynamic drag is initially the principal source of deceleration at high speed. As the speed lowers to 60-70% of landing speed, aerodynamic drag produced by ground spoilers is of little consequence.
   Answer (A) is incorrect. As the speed lowers to 60-70% of landing speed, aerodynamic drag produced by ground spoilers is of little consequence. **Answer (B) is incorrect.** Ground spoiler effectiveness is directly proportional to speed.

1.3 Stalls

11. The critical angle of attack is exceeded when

    A. airflow separates from the wing's trailing edge.

    B. a stall occurs.

    C. indicated airspeed equals $V_{SO} \times 1.3$.

Answer (B) is correct. (FAA-H-8083-25B Chap 5)
    DISCUSSION: Exceeding the critical angle of attack will result in a stall.
    Answer (A) is incorrect. When an airfoil exceeds its critical angle of attack, the airflow separates from the airfoil, causing a stall. This separation affects the entire wing, not just the trailing edge. **Answer (C) is incorrect.** $V_{SO} \times 1.3$ is a typical approach to landing speed; it is not the result of the critical angle of attack being exceeded.

12. The angle of attack at which a wing stalls remains constant regardless of

    A. weight, dynamic pressure, bank angle, or pitch attitude.

    B. dynamic pressure, but varies with weight, bank angle, and pitch attitude.

    C. weight and pitch attitude, but varies with dynamic pressure and bank angle.

Answer (A) is correct. (FAA-H-8083-3B Chap 4)
    DISCUSSION: The angle of attack at which a wing stalls is constant regardless of weight, bank, pitch, etc.
    Answer (B) is incorrect. The stall speed, not angle of attack, varies with weight and bank angle. **Answer (C) is incorrect.** The stall speed, not angle of attack, varies with bank angle.

13. The design maneuvering speed is

    A. the maximum speed an airplane can be safely stalled.

    B. 1.3 times the normal stalling speed.

    C. maximum takeoff weight divided by V_{SO}.

Answer (A) is correct. (FAA-H-8083-25B Chap 5)
    DISCUSSION: The maximum speed at which an airplane may be stalled safely is called the "design maneuvering speed" (V_A). V_A is the speed below which you can move a single flight control, one time, to its full deflection, for one axis of airplane rotation only (pitch, roll, or yaw), in smooth air, without risk of damage to the airplane.
    Answer (B) is incorrect. For older general aviation aircraft (aircraft not recently designed), the design maneuvering speed is approximately 1.7 times the normal stalling speed, not 1.3 times the normal stalling speed. **Answer (C) is incorrect.** Dividing the takeoff weight by V_{SO} does not calculate design maneuvering speed.

14. The need to slow an aircraft below V_A is brought about by the following weather phenomenon:

    A. High density altitude which increases the indicated stall speed.

    B. Turbulence which causes an increase in stall speed.

    C. Turbulence which causes a decrease in stall speed.

Answer (B) is correct. (FAA-H-8083-25B Chap 5)
    DISCUSSION: Turbulence, in the form of vertical air currents, can cause severe load stress on a wing. It is wise, in extremely rough air, to reduce the speed to V_A (design maneuvering speed). Speeds up to, but not exceeding, the design maneuvering speed allow an aircraft to stall prior to experiencing an increase in load factor that would exceed the limit load of the aircraft.
    Answer (A) is incorrect. Changes in density altitude do not affect indicated stall speed. **Answer (C) is incorrect.** Turbulence increases the load factors imposed on the aircraft, which increases, not decreases, stall speed.

15. Stall speed is affected by

    A. weight, load factor, and power.

    B. load factor, angle of attack, and power.

    C. angle of attack, weight, and air density.

Answer (A) is correct. (FAA-H-8083-25B Chap 5)
    DISCUSSION: Stall speed may vary under different circumstances. Factors such as weight, load factor, power, center of gravity, altitude, temperature, and the presence of snow, ice, or frost on the wings will affect an aircraft's stall speed.
    Answer (B) is incorrect. Stall speed is not affected by the angle of attack. **Answer (C) is incorrect.** Stall speed is not affected by the angle of attack.

16. A stall will occur

   A. when airspeed is no longer sufficient to generate the required lift.

   B. when the wing reaches the critical angle of attack.

   C. when the critical angle of attack is exceeded.

Answer (C) is correct. (FAA-H-8083-3B Chap 4)
    DISCUSSION: An airfoil stalls when the air can no longer flow smoothly over the top cambered surface of the wing. This phenomenon, known as early airflow separation, occurs when the wing exceeds the critical angle of attack.
    Answer (A) is incorrect. A stall can occur at any airspeed, and airspeed is not a determining factor in the cause of a stall. **Answer (B) is incorrect.** A wing stalls when exceeding, not reaching, the critical angle of attack.

17. An airplane will stall at the same

   A. angle of attack regardless of the attitude with relation to the horizon.

   B. airspeed regardless of the attitude with relation to the horizon.

   C. angle of attack and attitude with relation to the horizon.

Answer (A) is correct. (FAA-H-8083-3B Chap 4)
    DISCUSSION: An airplane will always stall at the same angle of attack. The airplane's attitude with relation to the horizon has no significance to the stall.
    Answer (B) is incorrect. The stall speed will vary with changing load factors, weight, and power. **Answer (C) is incorrect.** An airplane can stall in any attitude with relation to the horizon.

18. (Refer to Figure 2 below.) Select the correct statement regarding stall speeds.

   A. Power-off stalls occur at higher airspeeds with the gear and flaps down.

   B. In a 60° bank the airplane stalls at a lower airspeed with the gear up.

   C. Power-on stalls occur at lower airspeeds in shallower banks.

Answer (C) is correct. (FAA-H-8083-25B Chap 11)
    DISCUSSION: Using Fig. 2, work through each of the answers to determine which is true. Power-on stalls occur at lower airspeeds in shallower banks.
    Answer (A) is incorrect. With power off, stall speed is lower, not higher, with gear and flaps down. **Answer (B) is incorrect.** In a 60° bank, the gear position alone will not affect stall speed.

19. (Refer to Figure 2 below.) Select the correct statement regarding stall speeds. The airplane will stall

   A. 10 knots higher in a power-on, 60° bank, with gear and flaps up, than with gear and flaps down.

   B. 25 knots lower in a power-off, flaps-up, 60° bank, than in a power-off, flaps-down, wings-level configuration.

   C. 10 knots higher in a 45° bank, power-on stall, than in a wings-level stall with flaps up.

Answer (A) is correct. (FAA-H-8083-25B Chap 11)
    DISCUSSION: The airplane stalls at 76 knots with power on, gear and flaps up at 60° bank but stalls at 66 knots with gear and flaps down (i.e., a difference of 10 knots).
    Answer (B) is incorrect. The airplane stalls 35 knots higher, not 25 knots lower, with power off, flaps up, and a 60° bank than with power off, flaps down, and wings level. **Answer (C) is incorrect.** The gear position and power setting are not specified, so there is not enough information to make a proper determination.

GROSS WEIGHT 2,750 LB			ANGLE OF BANK			
			LEVEL	30°	45°	60°
POWER			**GEAR AND FLAPS UP**			
ON		MPH	62	67	74	88
		KTS	54	58	64	76
OFF		MPH	75	81	89	106
		KTS	65	70	77	92
			GEAR AND FLAPS DOWN			
ON		MPH	54	58	64	76
		KTS	47	50	56	66
OFF		MPH	66	71	78	93
		KTS	57	62	68	81

Figure 2. Stall Speeds.

20. In a rapid recovery from a dive, the effects of load factor would cause the stall speed to

    A. increase.

    B. decrease.

    C. not vary.

Answer (A) is correct. *(FAA-H-8083-3B Chap 4)*
    DISCUSSION: In a rapid recovery from a dive, the load factor would be increased because of the rapid change in the angle of attack, because gravity and centrifugal force would prevent the airplane from immediately altering its flight path. Because the relative wind is opposite the flight path, the critical angle of attack will be reached at a higher airspeed.
    Answer (B) is incorrect. As load factor increases, so does stall speed. **Answer (C) is incorrect.** As load factor increases, so does stall speed.

21. (Refer to Figure 3 below.) Use the diagram to determine the critical angle of attack.

    A. 15°

    B. 16°

    C. 20°

Answer (C) is correct. *(FAA-H-8083-3B Chap 4)*
    DISCUSSION: The peak point in the C_L curve is the maximum lift production point for a given airfoil, $C_{L\ MAX}$. This is also known as the critical angle of attack. Increasing the angle of attack beyond this point will cause the airfoil to stall.
    Answer (A) is incorrect. The critical angle of attack is 20°, not 15°, as indicated by the peak point of the C_L curve, $C_{L\ MAX}$. **Answer (B) is incorrect.** The critical angle of attack is 20°, not 16°, as indicated by the peak point of the C_L curve, $C_{L\ MAX}$.

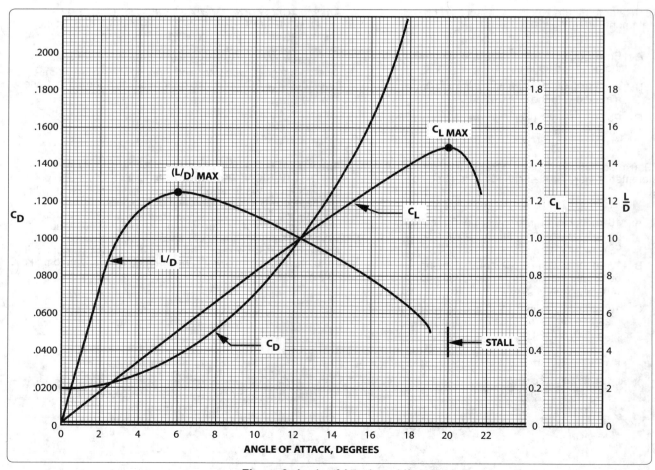

Figure 3. Angle of Attack vs. Lift.

22. The stalling speed of an airplane is most affected by

    A. changes in air density.

    B. variations in flight altitude.

    C. variations in airplane loading.

Answer (C) is correct. (FAA-H-8083-3B Chap 4)
    DISCUSSION: Indicated stall speed is most affected by the gross weight and how it is distributed within the airplane.
    Answer (A) is incorrect. Air density does not affect indicated stall speed. **Answer (B) is incorrect.** Flight altitude does not affect indicated stall speed.

23. Recovery from a stall in any airplane becomes more difficult when its

    A. center of gravity moves aft.

    B. center of gravity moves forward.

    C. elevator trim is adjusted nose down.

Answer (A) is correct. (FAA-H-8083-3B Chap 3)
    DISCUSSION: The recovery from a stall in any airplane becomes progressively more difficult as the airplane's center of gravity moves aft. This difficulty is due to the decreasing stability in pitch, which results in the decrease of elevator effectiveness in lowering the nose.
    Answer (B) is incorrect. Recovery from a stall becomes easier, not more difficult, as the center of gravity moves forward. **Answer (C) is incorrect.** The center of gravity, not the elevator trim adjustment, has an effect on the stall recovery characteristics of an airplane.

1.4 Spins

24. In small airplanes, normal recovery from spins may become difficult if the

    A. CG is too far rearward, and rotation is around the longitudinal axis.

    B. CG is too far rearward, and rotation is around the CG.

    C. spin is entered before the stall is fully developed.

Answer (B) is correct. (FAA-H-8083-25B Chap 5)
    DISCUSSION: Because rotation is around the CG in a spin, with a rearward CG, the control arm at the rudder is sufficiently shortened that it may make spin recovery difficult, if not impossible. Intuitively, if there is too much weight near the tail, it is also hard to get the nose down to produce an angle of attack below the critical angle.
    Answer (A) is incorrect. Rotation is around the CG, not the longitudinal axis, in a spin. **Answer (C) is incorrect.** In order for an airplane to spin, it must first stall.

25. A left side slip is used to counteract a crosswind drift during the final approach for landing. An over-the-top spin would most likely occur if the controls were used in which of the following ways? Holding the stick

    A. in the neutral position and applying full right rudder.

    B. too far to the left and applying full left rudder.

    C. too far back and applying full right rudder.

Answer (C) is correct. (FAA-H-8083-3B Chap 8)
    DISCUSSION: The down aileron on the inside of the turn increases drag on the wing, slowing it down and decreasing its lift, which requires more aileron application. This causes the airplane to roll. This roll may occur so quickly that it is possible for the bank to be vertical or past vertical before it can be stopped. With these control inputs, the inside wing may suddenly drop and the airplane may continue to roll to an inverted position. This is usually the beginning of a spin.
    Answer (A) is incorrect. If the stick were kept in the neutral position, the airplane would descend, increasing airspeed while yawing to the right. **Answer (B) is incorrect.** This would lead to a slipping turn.

1.5 Lift and Drag

26. Which statement is true relative to changing angle of attack?

    A. A decrease in angle of attack will increase pressure below the wing, and decrease drag.

    B. An increase in angle of attack will increase drag.

    C. An increase in angle of attack will decrease pressure below the wing, and increase drag.

Answer (B) is correct. (FAA-H-8083-25B Chap 5)
    DISCUSSION: As the angle of attack is increased, up to the critical angle of attack, the greater the amount of lift is developed and the greater the induced drag.
    Answer (A) is incorrect. A decrease in the angle of attack will decrease, not increase, the pressure below the wing. **Answer (C) is incorrect.** An increase in angle of attack will increase, not decrease, the pressure below the wing.

27. To generate the same amount of lift as altitude is increased, an airplane must be flown at

    A. the same true airspeed regardless of angle of attack.

    B. a lower true airspeed and a greater angle of attack.

    C. a higher true airspeed for any given angle of attack.

Answer (C) is correct. (FAA-H-8083-25B Chap 5)
    DISCUSSION: At an altitude of 18,000 feet MSL, the air has one-half the density of air at sea level. Thus, in order to maintain the same amount of lift as altitude increases, an airplane must be flown at a higher true airspeed for any given angle of attack.
    Answer (A) is incorrect. True airspeed must be increased, not remain the same, as altitude increases to generate the same amount of lift. **Answer (B) is incorrect.** True airspeed must be increased, not decreased, as altitude increases to generate the same amount of lift.

28. A pilot who intends to maintain level flight must coordinate the angle of attack and

    A. thrust.

    B. drag.

    C. lift.

Answer (A) is correct. (FAA-H-8083-25B Chap 5)
    DISCUSSION: To maintain level flight, a pilot must coordinate thrust and the angle of attack. If the angle of attack is increased, more lift will be generated so a reduction in thrust is required. If the angle of attack is reduced, lift will be reduced and more thrust will be required.
    Answer (B) is incorrect. Drag is a byproduct of lift production and the basic shape of the aircraft. A change in angle of attack will change the total drag generated, but the pilot has very little control on the amount of drag produced by the aircraft in flight, especially in a clean, cruise configuration. **Answer (C) is incorrect.** A pilot changes the angle of attack to control the lift generated. When the total amount of lift generated is changed, a change in thrust is required to maintain straight-and-level flight.

29. As the angle of bank is increased, the vertical component of lift

    A. decreases and the horizontal component of lift increases.

    B. increases and the horizontal component of lift decreases.

    C. decreases and the horizontal component of lift remains constant.

Answer (A) is correct. (FAA-H-8083-25B Chap 5)
    DISCUSSION: In level flight, all lift is vertical (upwards). As bank is increased, however, a portion of the airplane's lift is transferred from a vertical component to a horizontal component. Thus, the vertical component of lift decreases and the horizontal component of lift increases as the angle of bank is increased.
    Answer (B) is incorrect. The vertical component of lift decreases and the horizontal component of lift increases. **Answer (C) is incorrect.** The horizontal component of lift increases.

30. Which is true regarding the forces acting on an aircraft in a steady-state descent? The sum of all

    A. upward forces is less than the sum of all downward forces.

    B. rearward forces is greater than the sum of all forward forces.

    C. forward forces is equal to the sum of all rearward forces.

Answer (C) is correct. (FAA-H-8083-25B Chap 5)
    DISCUSSION: In any steady-state flight, whether level flight, climbs, or descents, the sum of all forward forces is equal to the sum of all rearward forces, and the upward forces equal the downward forces.
    Answer (A) is incorrect. Upward forces are equal to, not less than, downward forces in steady-state flight. **Answer (B) is incorrect.** Rearward forces are equal to, not greater than, forward forces in steady-state flight.

31. During the transition from straight-and-level flight to a climb, the angle of attack is increased and lift

    A. is momentarily decreased.

    B. remains the same.

    C. is momentarily increased.

Answer (C) is correct. (FAA-H-8083-25B Chap 5)
    DISCUSSION: During the transition from straight-and-level flight to a climb, a change in lift occurs as back elevator pressure is first applied, causing an increase in the angle of attack. Lift at this moment is now greater than weight and starts the airplane's climb.
    Answer (A) is incorrect. During the transition from straight-and-level flight to a climb, lift is momentarily increased, not decreased, as the angle of attack is increased. **Answer (B) is incorrect.** During the transition from straight-and-level flight to a climb, lift is momentarily increased, rather than remaining the same, as the angle of attack is increased.

32. What changes in airplane longitudinal control must be made to maintain altitude while the airspeed is being decreased?

    A. Increase the angle of attack to produce more lift than drag.

    B. Increase the angle of attack to compensate for the decreasing lift.

    C. Decrease the angle of attack to compensate for the increasing drag.

Answer (B) is correct. (FAA-H-8083-25B Chap 5)
    DISCUSSION: As airspeed decreases, the airfoils generate less lift. Accordingly, to maintain altitude, the angle of attack must be adjusted to compensate for the decrease in lift.
    Answer (A) is incorrect. If the angle of attack is increased to produce more lift than weight, not drag, the airplane will begin to climb. **Answer (C) is incorrect.** The angle of attack must be increased, not decreased, and the objective is to compensate for the decreased lift, not increased drag.

33. In theory, if the airspeed of an airplane is doubled while in level flight, parasite drag will become

    A. twice as great.

    B. half as great.

    C. four times greater.

Answer (C) is correct. (FAA-H-8083-25B Chap 5)
    DISCUSSION: Tests show that lift and drag vary as the square of the velocity. The velocity of the air passing over the wing in flight is determined by the airspeed of the airplane. Thus, if an airplane doubles its airspeed, lift and drag will be four times greater (assuming that the angle of attack remains the same).
    Answer (A) is incorrect. The relationship between parasite drag and airspeed is not linear. **Answer (B) is incorrect.** Parasite drag will increase, not decrease, with an increase in airspeed.

34. In theory, if the angle of attack and other factors remain constant and the airspeed is doubled, the lift produced at the higher speed will be

    A. the same as at the lower speed.

    B. two times greater than at the lower speed.

    C. four times greater than at the lower speed.

Answer (C) is correct. (FAA-H-8083-25B Chap 5)
    DISCUSSION: If the angle of attack and other factors remain constant, lift is proportional to the square of the airplane's velocity. For example, an airplane traveling at 200 knots has four times the lift as the same airplane traveling at 100 knots.
    Answer (A) is incorrect. As airspeed is doubled, lift produced is four times greater than, not the same as, at the lower speed. **Answer (B) is incorrect.** As airspeed is doubled, lift produced is four, not two, times greater than at the lower speed.

35. As airspeed decreases in level flight below that speed for maximum lift/drag ratio, total drag of an airplane

    A. decreases because of lower parasite drag.

    B. increases because of increased induced drag.

    C. increases because of increased parasite drag.

Answer (B) is correct. (FAA-H-8083-25B Chap 5)
    DISCUSSION: Total drag is at a minimum for the maximum lift/drag (L/D_{MAX}) ratio at one specific angle of attack and lift coefficient. As airspeed decreases, the induced drag will increase because a greater angle of attack is required to maintain level flight. The amount of induced drag varies inversely as the square of the airspeed.
    Answer (A) is incorrect. Total drag increases, not decreases, with decreases in airspeed below L/D_{MAX} because of increased induced drag. **Answer (C) is incorrect.** Parasite drag changes directly, not inversely, with airspeed. Thus, below L/D_{MAX}, parasite drag decreases, not increases.

36. If airspeed remains constant, but the air density increases, what will be the effect on both lift and drag?

    A. Lift will decrease and drag will decrease.

    B. Drag will decrease and lift will increase.

    C. Lift will increase and drag will increase.

Answer (C) is correct. (FAA-H-8083-25B Chap 5)
    DISCUSSION: Air density is a determining factor in lift production. The greater the density of the air, the greater the lift produced by an airfoil. Induced drag is a byproduct of lift production. As lift increases, induced drag increases as well.
    Answer (A) is incorrect. An increase in air density results in an increase, not a decrease, in both lift and drag. **Answer (B) is incorrect.** An increase in air density results in an increase in both lift and drag. An increase in lift always results in an increase of drag because induced drag increases as lift production increases.

37. What performance is characteristic of flight at maximum lift/drag ratio in a propeller-driven airplane? Maximum

    A. gain in altitude over a given distance.

    B. range and maximum distance glide.

    C. coefficient of lift and minimum coefficient of drag.

Answer (B) is correct. (FAA-H-8083-25B Chap 5)
    DISCUSSION: If the airplane is operated in steady flight at L/D_{MAX}, the total drag is at a minimum. Many important items of airplane performance are obtained in flight at L/D_{MAX}. For a propeller-driven airplane, these items include maximum range and maximum power-off glide range.
    Answer (A) is incorrect. The best angle of climb (e.g., to clear an obstacle) is at a high angle of attack with both high lift and high drag coefficients, which would not result in an L/D_{MAX} ratio. **Answer (C) is incorrect.** L/D_{MAX} is neither at the maximum coefficient of lift nor at the minimum coefficient of drag, but at a point somewhere in between.

38. Both lift and drag would be increased when which of these devices are extended?

    A. Flaps.

    B. Spoilers.

    C. Slats.

Answer (A) is correct. (FAA-H-8083-3B Chap 5)
    DISCUSSION: Flaps increase both lift and (induced) drag for any given angle of attack.
    Answer (B) is incorrect. Spoilers decrease lift and increase drag. **Answer (C) is incorrect.** Slats increase the wing area, thereby increasing lift without increasing drag.

39. (Refer to Figure 1 below.) At the airspeed represented by point A, in steady flight, the airplane will

    A. have its maximum L/D ratio.

    B. have its minimum L/D ratio.

    C. be developing its maximum coefficient of lift.

Answer (A) is correct. (FAA-H-8083-25B Chap 5)
    DISCUSSION: Point A (Fig. 1) is at the minimum point on the total drag curve. By definition, this is the point of maximum L/D ratio. Note that airspeed is on the horizontal axis and drag is on the vertical axis.
    Answer (B) is incorrect. The minimum, not maximum, L/D ratio occurs at high airspeeds at which parasite drag is very high. **Answer (C) is incorrect.** The maximum coefficient of lift is produced at lower airspeeds, which have high induced drag and resulting lower L/D ratio.

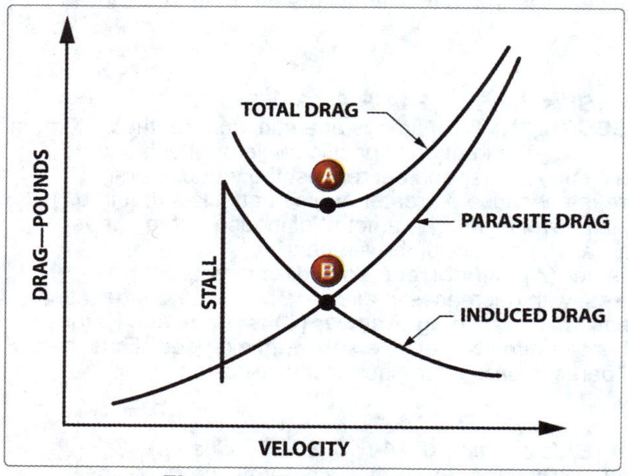

Figure 1. Drag vs. Velocity.

40. (Refer to Figure 1 above.) At an airspeed represented by point B, in steady flight, the pilot can expect to obtain the airplane's maximum

    A. endurance.

    B. glide range.

    C. coefficient of lift.

Answer (B) is correct. (FAA-H-8083-25B Chap 5)
    DISCUSSION: Point B (Fig. 1) is the intersection of the parasite and induced drag curves, which is the point where the total drag is at its minimum (also known as the point of maximum L/D ratio). L/D_{MAX} is the airspeed at which the pilot of either a jet or a propeller-driven airplane can expect to obtain that airplane's maximum glide range.
    Answer (A) is incorrect. Only a jet-powered aircraft will obtain its maximum endurance at L/D_{MAX}. **Answer (C) is incorrect.** The maximum coefficient of lift is at the critical angle of attack, where total drag is also high because of an increase in induced drag.

41. Which is true regarding the force of lift in steady, unaccelerated flight?

    A. At lower airspeeds the angle of attack must be less to generate sufficient lift to maintain altitude.

    B. There is a corresponding indicated airspeed required for every angle of attack to generate sufficient lift to maintain altitude.

    C. An airfoil will always stall at the same indicated airspeed; therefore, an increase in weight will require an increase in speed to generate sufficient lift to maintain altitude.

Answer (B) is correct. (FAA-H-8083-25B Chap 5)
    DISCUSSION: Different angles of attack provide different lift coefficients (amounts of lift). Accordingly, any given angle of attack has a corresponding airspeed to provide sufficient lift to maintain altitude.
    Answer (A) is incorrect. As airspeed is reduced, the angle of attack must be increased, not decreased, to provide sufficient lift. **Answer (C) is incorrect.** An airfoil will always stall at the same angle of attack, not the same indicated airspeed.

42. An aircraft wing is designed to produce lift resulting from a difference in the

    A. negative air pressure below and a vacuum above the wing's surface.

    B. vacuum below the wing's surface and greater air pressure above the wing's surface.

    C. higher air pressure below the wing's surface and lower air pressure above the wing's surface.

Answer (C) is correct. (FAA-H-8083-25B Chap 5)
    DISCUSSION: An airplane's lift is produced by a pressure differential resulting from relatively lower (i.e., less than atmospheric) pressure above the wing and higher (i.e., greater than atmospheric) pressure below the wing's surface.
    Answer (A) is incorrect. The air pressure below the wing is relatively higher, not negative, and the pressure above the wing is lower, not a vacuum. **Answer (B) is incorrect.** The air pressure below the wing is relatively higher, not a vacuum, and the pressure above the wing is lower, not higher.

43. Lift on a wing is most properly defined as the

    A. force acting perpendicular to the relative wind.

    B. differential pressure acting perpendicular to the chord of the wing.

    C. reduced pressure resulting from a laminar flow over the upper camber of an airfoil, which acts perpendicular to the mean camber.

Answer (A) is correct. (FAA-H-8083-25B Chap 5)
    DISCUSSION: Lift opposes the downward force of weight, is produced by the dynamic effect of the air acting on the wing, and acts perpendicular to the relative wind through the wing's center of lift.
    Answer (B) is incorrect. Lift acts perpendicular to the relative wind, not the chord line. **Answer (C) is incorrect.** Lift is produced by pressure resulting from flow under as well as over the wing, and it acts perpendicular to relative wind, not the mean camber of the wing.

44. To hold an airplane in level flight at airspeeds from very slow to very fast, a pilot must coordinate thrust and

    A. angle of incidence.

    B. gross weight.

    C. angle of attack.

Answer (C) is correct. (FAA-H-8083-25B Chap 5)
    DISCUSSION: If a reduction in thrust and airspeed occurs, the force of gravity (weight) will overpower lift. A pilot must increase the angle of attack to generate more lift, thus compensating for the loss of thrust. If thrust and airspeed increase, lift will overpower gravity (weight), the aircraft will climb, and the pilot must decrease the angle of attack to maintain straight-and-level flight.
    Answer (A) is incorrect. The angle of incidence defines the wing's chord line and its relationship to the longitudinal axis of the airplane. A pilot cannot change the angle of incidence. **Answer (B) is incorrect.** A pilot cannot alter the gross weight of an aircraft in flight.

45. In theory, if the airspeed of an aircraft is cut in half while in level flight, parasite drag will become

    A. one-third as much.

    B. one-half as much.

    C. one-fourth as much.

Answer (C) is correct. (FAA-H-8083-25B Chap 3)
    DISCUSSION: If an aircraft in a steady flight condition at 100 knots is accelerated to 200 knots, the parasite drag becomes four times as great; therefore, if you reduce the airspeed by half, the parasite drag will be one-fourth as much.
    Answer (A) is incorrect. Induced drag increases as speed goes down. **Answer (B) is incorrect.** Parasite drag would be one-fourth as much, not one-half as much.

46. (Refer to Figure 3 below.) If an airplane glides at an angle of attack of 10°, how much altitude will it lose in 1 mile?

A. 240 feet.

B. 480 feet.

C. 960 feet.

Answer (B) is correct. (FAA-H-8083-3B Chap 4)
DISCUSSION: Use Fig. 3 to determine the L/D ratio for a given angle of attack. At the bottom of the chart, locate 10 (i.e., 10° angle of attack) and move vertically up to the L/D curve (the third curve as you move up). Then move right to the margin to determine the L/D ratio of 11:1 (i.e., 1-ft. loss of altitude for every 11 ft. of horizontal distance traveled). Thus, at a distance of 5,280 ft. (1 SM), the airplane will lose 480 ft. (5,280 ÷ 11) of altitude.
Answer (A) is incorrect. The airplane would lose 240 ft. in 1/2, not 1, SM at an angle of attack of 10°. **Answer (C) is incorrect.** The airplane would lose 960 ft. of altitude in 1 SM at an angle of attack of 1.5° or 19°, not 10°.

47. (Refer to Figure 3 below.) The L/D ratio at a 2° angle of attack is approximately the same as the L/D ratio for a

A. 9.75° angle of attack.

B. 10.5° angle of attack.

C. 16.5° angle of attack.

Answer (C) is correct. (FAA-H-8083-3B Chap 4)
DISCUSSION: Enter the bottom of the chart in Fig. 3 at 2° angle of attack and move vertically up to the L/D curve. From this point, move right horizontally to the point where the L/D curve intersects. Then move vertically down to the bottom of the chart to determine a 16.5° angle of attack. Thus, the L/D ratio is approximately the same at both a 2° and 16.5° angle of attack.
Answer (A) is incorrect. An angle of attack of 9.75° would have the same L/D ratio as a 3.75°, not 2.0°, angle of attack. **Answer (B) is incorrect.** An angle of attack of 10.5° would have the same L/D ratio as a 3.5°, not 2.0°, angle of attack.

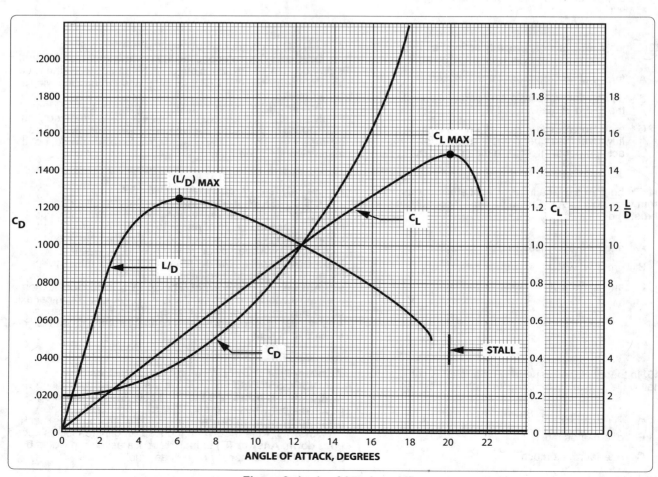

Figure 3. Angle of Attack vs. Lift.

48. (Refer to Figure 3 on page 40.) How much altitude will this airplane lose in 3 statute miles of gliding at an angle of attack of 8°?

    A. 440 feet.

    B. 880 feet.

    C. 1,320 feet.

Answer (C) is correct. (FAA-H-8083-3B Chap 4)
    DISCUSSION: Use Fig. 3 to determine the L/D ratio for a given angle of attack. At the bottom of the chart, locate 8 (i.e., 8° angle of attack) and move vertically up to the L/D curve (the third curve as you move up). Then move right to the margin to determine the L/D ratio of 12:1 (i.e., 1-ft. loss of altitude for every 12 ft. of horizontal distance traveled). Thus, at a distance of 15,840 ft. (5,280 ft./SM × 3 SM), the airplane will lose 1,320 ft. (15,840 ÷ 12) of altitude.
    Answer (A) is incorrect. The airplane would lose 440 ft. in 1 mile. **Answer (B) is incorrect.** The airplane would lose 880 ft. in 2 miles.

49. On a wing, the force of lift acts perpendicular to and the force of drag acts parallel to the

    A. chord line.

    B. flightpath.

    C. longitudinal axis.

Answer (B) is correct. (FAA-H-8083-3B Chap 5)
    DISCUSSION: Lift acts perpendicular to the relative wind, which is opposite the flight path. Drag acts parallel to the flight path.
    Answer (A) is incorrect. There is no fixed relationship between lift and drag with respect to the chord line. **Answer (C) is incorrect.** There is no fixed relationship between lift and drag and the longitudinal axis.

50. Which statement is true regarding the opposing forces acting on an airplane in steady-state level flight?

    A. These forces are equal.

    B. Thrust is greater than drag and weight and lift are equal.

    C. Thrust is greater than drag and lift is greater than weight.

Answer (A) is correct. (FAA-H-8083-3B Chap 5)
    DISCUSSION: In steady-state level flight, the sum of the opposing forces is equal to zero.
    Answer (B) is incorrect. Thrust is equal to, not greater than, drag in steady-state level flight. If thrust is greater than drag, airspeed will increase. **Answer (C) is incorrect.** Thrust is equal to, not greater than, drag and lift is equal to, not greater than, weight in steady-state level flight. If lift is greater than weight, the airplane will enter a climb.

51. When transitioning from straight-and-level flight to a constant airspeed climb, the angle of attack and lift

    A. are increased and remain at a higher lift-to-weight ratio to maintain the climb.

    B. remain the same and maintain a steady state lift-to-weight ratio during the climb.

    C. are momentarily increased and lift returns to a steady state during the climb.

Answer (C) is correct. (FAA-H-8083-25B Chap 5)
    DISCUSSION: During the transition from straight-and-level flight to a climb, a change in lift occurs when back elevator pressure is first applied. Raising the aircraft's nose increases the angle of attack and momentarily increases the lift. Lift at this moment is now greater than weight and starts the aircraft climbing. After the flight path is stabilized on the upward incline, the angle of attack and lift again revert to about the level flight values.
    Answer (A) is incorrect. Angle of attack and lift initially increase, but after the flight path is stabilized on the upward incline, the angle of attack and lift again revert to about the level flight values. **Answer (B) is incorrect.** Angle of attack and lift initially increase. It is not until after the flight path is stabilized on the upward incline that the angle of attack and lift again revert to about the level flight values.

52. (Refer to Figure 3A below.) As you are flying with a headwind from the coastline inland toward your destination airport, your aircraft has engine failure. You would expect your glide path to be

- A. greater than the ground distance estimate provided.
- B. shorter than the ground distance estimate provided.
- C. very close to the ground distance estimate provided.

Answer (B) is correct. *(FAA-H-8083-3B Chap 3)*
 DISCUSSION: Fig. 3A assumes a speed of 65 KIAS, propeller windmilling, flaps up, and zero wind. It is also important to note that the vertical (y) axis is in height above terrain. You should think of this as AGL instead of MSL and consider whether the area underneath you is a forest or open grasslands. Because you have a headwind, the distance you will travel is shorter. Moreover, if you are using your altimeter, which indicates MSL, not AGL, altitude, you need to consider how high the elevation (and terrain obstructions) are below you.
 Answer (A) is incorrect. If you had a tailwind instead of a headwind, you would expect a longer ground distance covered. **Answer (C) is incorrect.** Fig. 3A assumes a speed of 65 KIAS, propeller windmilling, flaps up, and zero wind. It is also important to note that the vertical (y) axis is height above terrain. Because there is a headwind, you cannot assume that the numbers on this chart will be accurate. You should expect less ground distance covered.

53. (Refer to Figure 3A below.) At an altitude of 2,000 feet AGL, how far would you expect to glide?

- A. 1,400 feet.
- B. 3 feet.
- C. 18,228 feet.

Answer (C) is correct. *(FAA-H-8083-3B Chap 3)*
 DISCUSSION: Note the axis labeled Height Above Terrain - FT (y-axis) and the axis labeled Ground Distance - Nautical Miles (x-axis). Locate 2,000 feet on the vertical (y) axis and then move to the right until you come to the diagonal line. Once you are at the diagonal line, move directly down to find your ground distance in nautical miles. A distance of 3 NM equals 18,228 feet (6,076 feet per mile × 3 miles).
 Answer (A) is incorrect. The altitude of 1,400 feet is achieved if you first referenced the 2 on the x-axis, not the y-axis. **Answer (B) is incorrect.** The answer is 3 nautical miles or 18,228 feet, not 3 feet. Always pay close attention to the units of measure.

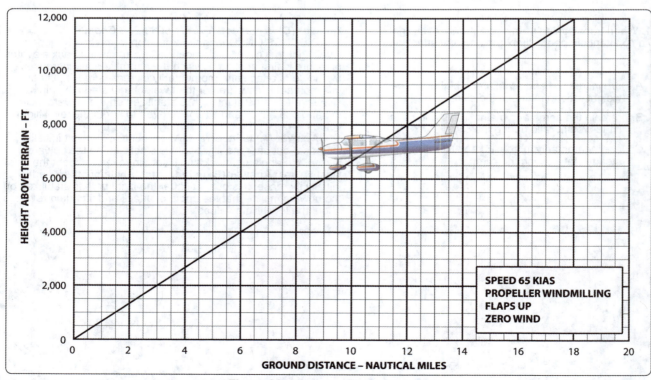

Figure 3A. Maximum Glide Distance.

1.6 Ground Effect

54. An airplane leaving ground effect will

A. experience a reduction in ground friction and require a slight power reduction.

B. experience an increase in induced drag and require more thrust.

C. require a lower angle of attack to maintain the same lift coefficient.

Answer (B) is correct. (FAA-H-8083-3B Chap 5)
   DISCUSSION: An airplane leaving ground effect (a height greater than the wingspan) will

1. Require an increase in angle of attack to maintain the same lift coefficient,
2. Experience an increase in induced drag and thrust required,
3. Experience a decrease in stability and a nose-up change in moment, and
4. Produce a reduction in static source pressure and increase in indicated airspeed.

   Answer (A) is incorrect. Ground friction is reduced when breaking ground, not leaving ground effect, and an increase, not decrease, in power may be required. **Answer (C) is incorrect.** A higher, not lower, angle of attack is required to maintain the same lift coefficient when leaving ground effect.

55. To produce the same lift while in ground effect as when out of ground effect, the airplane requires

A. a lower angle of attack.

B. the same angle of attack.

C. a greater angle of attack.

Answer (A) is correct. (FAA-H-8083-3B Chap 5)
   DISCUSSION: In ground effect, induced drag decreases due to a reduction in wingtip vortices (caused by a reduction in the wing's downwash), which alters the spanwise lift distribution and reduces the induced angle of attack. Thus, the wing will require a lower angle of attack in ground effect to produce the same lift as when out of ground effect.
   Answer (B) is incorrect. A lower, not the same, angle of attack is required to maintain the same lift while in ground effect as when out of ground effect. **Answer (C) is incorrect.** A lower, not greater, angle of attack is required to maintain the same lift while in ground effect as when out of ground effect.

56. If the same angle of attack is maintained in ground effect as when out of ground effect, lift will

A. increase, and induced drag will decrease.

B. decrease, and parasite drag will increase.

C. increase, and induced drag will increase.

Answer (A) is correct. (FAA-H-8083-3B Chap 5)
   DISCUSSION: In ground effect, induced drag decreases due to a reduction in wingtip vortices (caused by a reduction in the wing's downwash), which alters the spanwise lift distribution and reduces the induced angle of attack. Thus, if an airplane is brought into ground effect with a constant angle of attack, an increase in lift will result.
   Answer (B) is incorrect. At the same angle of attack in ground effect as when out of ground effect, lift will increase, not decrease, and parasite drag does not significantly change in ground effect. **Answer (C) is incorrect.** Induced drag decreases, not increases, in ground effect.

1.7 Airplane Stability

57. Longitudinal stability involves the motion of the airplane controlled by its

    A. rudder.

    B. elevator.

    C. ailerons.

Answer (B) is correct. (FAA-H-8083-25B Chap 5)
    DISCUSSION: Longitudinal stability is the quality that makes an airplane stable about its lateral (i.e., pitch) axis. This motion is controlled by the elevators.
    Answer (A) is incorrect. The rudder affects the directional, not longitudinal, stability of the airplane. **Answer (C) is incorrect.** The ailerons affect the lateral, not longitudinal, stability of the airplane.

58. Longitudinal dynamic instability in an airplane can be identified by

    A. bank oscillations becoming progressively steeper.

    B. pitch oscillations becoming progressively steeper.

    C. trilatitudinal roll oscillations becoming progressively steeper.

Answer (B) is correct. (FAA-H-8083-25B Chap 5)
    DISCUSSION: Dynamic stability is the overall tendency that the airplane displays after its equilibrium is disturbed. Negative dynamic stability (dynamic instability) is a property that causes oscillations set up by a statically stable airplane to become progressively greater. Longitudinal instability refers to pitch oscillations.
    Answer (A) is incorrect. Roll (bank) oscillations refer to lateral, not longitudinal, stability. **Answer (C) is incorrect.** Roll (bank) oscillations refer to lateral, not longitudinal, stability.

59. If the airplane attitude remains in a new position after the elevator control is pressed forward and released, the airplane displays

    A. neutral longitudinal static stability.

    B. positive longitudinal static stability.

    C. neutral longitudinal dynamic stability.

Answer (A) is correct. (FAA-H-8083-25B Chap 5)
    DISCUSSION: When an airplane's attitude is momentarily displaced and it remains at its new attitude, it is said to have neutral longitudinal static stability. Longitudinal stability is the quality that makes an airplane stable about its lateral axis (pitch).
    Answer (B) is incorrect. Positive longitudinal static stability is the initial tendency of the airplane to return to its original attitude after the elevator control is pressed forward and released. **Answer (C) is incorrect.** The longitudinal dynamic stability is the overall, not initial, tendency that the airplane displays after the elevator control is pressed forward and released. Neutral dynamic stability is indicated if the airplane attempts to return to its original state of equilibrium, but the pitch oscillations neither increase nor decrease in magnitude in time.

60. If the airplane attitude initially tends to return to its original position after the elevator control is pressed forward and released, the airplane displays

    A. positive dynamic stability.

    B. positive static stability.

    C. neutral dynamic stability.

Answer (B) is correct. (FAA-H-8083-25B Chap 5)
    DISCUSSION: When an airplane's elevator control is pressed forward and released and its attitude initially tends to return to its original position, the airplane displays positive static stability.
    Answer (A) is incorrect. Dynamic stability is the overall, not initial, tendency the airplane displays after its equilibrium is disturbed. Positive dynamic stability means the airplane will return to its original position directly, or through a series of decreasing pitch oscillations in time. **Answer (C) is incorrect.** Dynamic stability is the overall, not initial, tendency the airplane displays after its equilibrium is disturbed. Neutral dynamic stability means the airplane attempts to return to its original position, but the pitch oscillations neither increase nor decrease in magnitude in time.

61. If an airplane is loaded to the rear of its CG range, it will tend to be unstable about its

    A. vertical axis.

    B. lateral axis.

    C. longitudinal axis.

Answer (B) is correct. (FAA-H-8083-25B Chap 5)
    DISCUSSION: As the CG is moved rearward, it may move behind the center of lift, in which case the airplane is said to have negative stability about its lateral axis. Recall that the CG should be forward of the center of lift and that the tail surface is designed to have negative lift.
    Answer (A) is incorrect. The CG position has relatively little to do with the stability about the vertical axis. **Answer (C) is incorrect.** Stability about the longitudinal axis is not greatly affected by CG location. Remember that the airplane rolls about the longitudinal axis.

1.8 Turns

62. If airspeed is increased during a level turn, what action would be necessary to maintain altitude? The angle of attack

   A. and angle of bank must be decreased.

   B. must be increased or angle of bank decreased.

   C. must be decreased or angle of bank increased.

Answer (C) is correct. (FAA-H-8083-25B Chap 5)
   DISCUSSION: To compensate for the added lift that would result if the airspeed were increased during a turn, the angle of attack must be decreased, or the angle of bank increased, to maintain a constant altitude.
   Answer (A) is incorrect. Either the angle of attack can be decreased or the angle of bank increased, not decreased, to maintain altitude as airspeed is increased in a turn. **Answer (B) is incorrect.** To maintain a constant altitude in a turn as the airspeed is decreased, not increased, the angle of attack must be increased or angle of bank decreased.

63. If a standard rate turn is maintained, how long would it take to turn 360°?

   A. 1 minute.

   B. 2 minutes.

   C. 3 minutes.

Answer (B) is correct. (FAA-H-8083-25B Chap 8)
   DISCUSSION: A standard rate turn is one during which the heading changes at a rate of 3°/sec. Thus, a 360° turn would take 2 min. (360° ÷ 3°/sec. = 120 sec., or 2 min.).
   Answer (A) is incorrect. At standard rate, a 180°, not 360°, turn would take 1 minute. **Answer (C) is incorrect.** At standard rate, a 540°, not 360°, turn would take 3 minutes.

64. While holding the angle of bank constant in a level turn, if the rate of turn is varied the load factor would

   A. remain constant regardless of air density and the resultant lift vector.

   B. vary depending upon speed and air density provided the resultant lift vector varies proportionately.

   C. vary depending upon the resultant lift vector.

Answer (A) is correct. (FAA-H-8083-25B Chap 5)
   DISCUSSION: For any given angle of bank, the rate of turn varies with the airspeed. For example, if the angle of bank is held constant and the airspeed is increased, the rate of turn will decrease and vice versa. Because of this, there is no change in centrifugal force while holding a constant angle of bank; thus, the load factor remains constant.
   Answer (B) is incorrect. The rate of turn, not load factor, will vary depending on airspeed while holding a constant angle of bank. **Answer (C) is incorrect.** Load factor will vary depending on the resultant load, not lift, vector.

65. Which is correct with respect to rate and radius of turn for an airplane flown in a coordinated turn at a constant altitude?

   A. For a specific angle of bank and airspeed, the rate and radius of turn will not vary.

   B. To maintain a steady rate of turn, the angle of bank must be increased as the airspeed is decreased.

   C. The faster the true airspeed, the faster the rate and larger the radius of turn regardless of the angle of bank.

Answer (A) is correct. (FAA-H-8083-25B Chap 5)
   DISCUSSION: At a constant altitude in a coordinated turn, each airspeed has a specific, unvarying rate and radius of turn for each angle of bank.
   Answer (B) is incorrect. You must decrease, not increase, the angle of bank when the airspeed is decreased if you are to maintain a steady rate of turn. **Answer (C) is incorrect.** The faster the airspeed, the slower, not faster, the rate of turn at a constant angle of bank.

66. To increase the rate of turn and at the same time decrease the radius, a pilot should

   A. maintain the bank and decrease airspeed.

   B. increase the bank and increase airspeed.

   C. increase the bank and decrease airspeed.

Answer (C) is correct. (FAA-H-8083-25B Chap 5)
   DISCUSSION: At slower airspeeds, an airplane can make a turn in less distance (smaller radius) and at a faster rate. Thus, to decrease the radius and increase the rate, a pilot should steepen the bank and decrease airspeed.
   Answer (A) is incorrect. At a given angle of bank, a decrease in airspeed will increase the rate of turn and decrease the radius, but the effect will be less than that of steepening the bank and decreasing airspeed. **Answer (B) is incorrect.** You decrease, not increase, airspeed to decrease the turn radius.

67. While maintaining a constant angle of bank and altitude in a coordinated turn, an increase in airspeed will

   A. decrease the rate of turn resulting in a decreased load factor.

   B. decrease the rate of turn resulting in no change in load factor.

   C. increase the rate of turn resulting in no change in load factor.

Answer (B) is correct. (FAA-H-8083-25B Chap 5)
   DISCUSSION: When in a constant bank in a coordinated turn, an increase in airspeed will decrease the rate of turn. Because the bank is held constant, there will be no change in load factor.
   Answer (A) is incorrect. There is no change in load factor in a coordinated turn if the angle of bank is held constant. **Answer (C) is incorrect.** The rate of turn decreases, not increases, with an increase in airspeed, and since the angle of bank is held constant, the load factor remains constant, not decreases.

68. Why is it necessary to increase back elevator pressure to maintain altitude during a turn? To compensate for the

   A. loss of the vertical component of lift.

   B. loss of the horizontal component of lift and the increase in centrifugal force.

   C. rudder deflection and slight opposite aileron throughout the turn.

Answer (A) is correct. (FAA-H-8083-25B Chap 5)
   DISCUSSION: As you enter a turn, lift is divided into horizontal and vertical components. This division reduces the amount of vertical lift, which is opposing weight, and thus the airplane loses altitude unless additional lift is created by increasing back elevator pressure to increase the angle of attack and the vertical component of lift.
   Answer (B) is incorrect. When the horizontal component of lift is less than centrifugal force, the airplane is in a skidding turn, which is corrected by increasing bank or decreasing the rate of turn (or a combination of both). **Answer (C) is incorrect.** Slight opposite aileron pressure may be needed in a steep bank to overcome the airplane's overbanking tendency.

69. To maintain altitude during a turn, the angle of attack must be increased to compensate for the decrease in the

   A. forces opposing the resultant component of drag.

   B. vertical component of lift.

   C. horizontal component of lift.

Answer (B) is correct. (FAA-H-8083-25B Chap 5)
   DISCUSSION: As you enter a turn, lift is divided into horizontal and vertical components. This division reduces the amount of vertical lift, which is opposing weight, and thus the airplane loses altitude unless additional lift is created by increasing back elevator pressure to increase the angle of attack and the vertical component of lift.
   Answer (A) is incorrect. The resultant component of drag is a nonsense term. **Answer (C) is incorrect.** As the horizontal component of lift decreases, the vertical component increases; thus, the angle of attack will need to be decreased, not increased.

70. To maintain a standard rate turn as the airspeed increases, the bank angle of the aircraft will need to

   A. remain constant.

   B. increase.

   C. decrease.

Answer (B) is correct. (FAA-H-8083-15B)
   DISCUSSION: A standard rate turn, although always 3° per sec., requires higher angles of bank as airspeed increases.
   Answer (A) is incorrect. A standard rate turn, although always 3° per sec., requires higher angles of bank as airspeed increases. **Answer (C) is incorrect.** To maintain a standard rate turn as the airspeed increases, the bank angle of the aircraft will need to increase, not decrease.

71. To maintain a standard rate turn as the airspeed decreases, the bank angle of the airplane will need to

   A. decrease.

   B. increase.

   C. remain constant.

Answer (A) is correct. (FAA-H-8083-15B)
   DISCUSSION: A standard rate turn, although always 3° per sec., requires lower angles of bank as airspeed decreases.
   Answer (B) is incorrect. A standard rate turn, although always 3° per sec., requires lower angles of bank, not higher, as airspeed decreases. **Answer (C) is incorrect.** To maintain a standard rate turn as the airspeed decreases, the bank angle of the aircraft will need to decrease.

1.9 Load Factor

72. The ratio between the total airload imposed on the wing and the gross weight of an aircraft in flight is known as

    A. load factor and directly affects stall speed.

    B. aspect load and directly affects stall speed.

    C. load factor and has no relation with stall speed.

Answer (A) is correct. (FAA-H-8083-25B Chap 5)
    DISCUSSION: A load factor is the ratio of the total airload acting on the airplane to the gross weight of the airplane. For example, if the airload imposed on the wing is twice the actual weight of the airplane, the load factor is said to be 2 Gs, and the stall speed increases.
    Answer (B) is incorrect. The ratio between the total airload imposed on the wing and the gross weight of an airplane is known as a load factor, not aspect load. **Answer (C) is incorrect.** The airplane's stalling speed increases in proportion to the square root of the load factor.

73. Load factor is the lift generated by the wings of an aircraft at any given time,

    A. divided by the total weight of the aircraft.

    B. multiplied by the total weight of the aircraft.

    C. divided by the basic empty weight of the aircraft.

Answer (A) is correct. (FAA-H-8083-25B Chap 5)
    DISCUSSION: Since the load factor is the ratio between the total airload imposed on the wing and the gross weight of the airplane, the load factor is the lift generated by the wings divided by the total weight of the airplane. For example, 4,000 lb. of lift ÷ 2,000 lb. aircraft = 2 Gs load factor.
    Answer (B) is incorrect. Load factor times airplane weight equals required lift. **Answer (C) is incorrect.** The total weight of the airplane, not the basic empty weight, is relevant.

74. For a given angle of bank, in any airplane, the load factor imposed in a coordinated constant-altitude turn

    A. is constant and the stall speed increases.

    B. varies with the rate of turn.

    C. is constant and the stall speed decreases.

Answer (A) is correct. (FAA-H-8083-25B Chap 5)
    DISCUSSION: In any airplane at any airspeed, if a constant altitude is maintained during the turn, the load factor for a given degree of bank is the same, which is the resultant of weight and centrifugal force. Because of the increased load factor in a turn, the stall speed is also increased in proportion to the square root of the load factor.
    Answer (B) is incorrect. The load factor is not affected by changes in the rate of turn (which is determined by airspeed when at a constant bank). **Answer (C) is incorrect.** When the load factor is increased as a turn is entered, the stall speed is also increased in proportion to the square root of the load factor.

75. Airplane wing loading during a level coordinated turn in smooth air depends upon the

    A. rate of turn.

    B. angle of bank.

    C. true airspeed.

Answer (B) is correct. (FAA-H-8083-25B Chap 5)
    DISCUSSION: The load factor for a given airplane during a level coordinated turn is determined solely by the angle of bank.
    Answer (A) is incorrect. In a coordinated turn, rate of turn has no impact on load factor. **Answer (C) is incorrect.** In a coordinated turn, true airspeed has no impact on wing loading.

76. The load factor for an airplane in a 60° banked turn is

    A. 1.7 Gs.

    B. 2 Gs.

    C. 3 Gs.

Answer (B) is correct. (FAA-H-8083-25B Chap 5)
    DISCUSSION: Any airplane in a 60° banked turn has a load factor of 2 Gs.
    Answer (A) is incorrect. An airplane in a 60° banked turn has a load factor of 2 Gs, not 1.7 Gs. **Answer (C) is incorrect.** An airplane in a 60° banked turn has a load factor of 2 Gs, not 3 Gs.

77. A load factor of 1.2 means the total load on an aircraft's structure is 1.2 times its

    A. gross weight.

    B. load limit.

    C. gust factor.

Answer (A) is correct. (FAA-H-8083-25B Chap 5)
    DISCUSSION: Load factor is the ratio of an airplane's gross weight to the maximum load the airframe can support measured in Gs. Any time the aircraft's flight path is disrupted or altered, a load factor is placed on the airframe.
    Answer (B) is incorrect. Load limit is the maximum load factor the airframe can withstand. Exceeding the load limit will result in severe airframe damage and structural failure. **Answer (C) is incorrect.** A gust factor is applied to the airplane's approach speed when landing in windy conditions.

78. If an aircraft with a gross weight of 2,000 pounds was subjected to a 60° constant-altitude bank, the total load would be

A. 3,000 pounds.

B. 4,000 pounds.

C. 12,000 pounds.

Answer (B) is correct. (FAA-H-8083-25B Chap 5)
    DISCUSSION: In a constant-altitude, 60° bank turn, the wings are loaded at 2 Gs. Therefore, the total load of a 2,000-lb. airplane is 4,000 lb. (2,000 × 2).
    Answer (A) is incorrect. This would be the total load of a 1,500-lb. airplane in a 60° bank. **Answer (C) is incorrect.** This would be the total load of a 6,000-lb. airplane in a 60° bank.

79. If the airspeed is increased from 90 knots to 135 knots during a level 60° banked turn, the load factor will

A. increase as well as the stall speed.

B. decrease and the stall speed will increase.

C. remain the same but the radius of turn will increase.

Answer (C) is correct. (FAA-H-8083-25B Chap 5)
    DISCUSSION: Because the only determinant of load factor in level, coordinated turns is the amount of bank, a change in airspeed does not change the load factor. When airspeed is increased, however, the rate of turn decreases and the radius of turn increases.
    Answer (A) is incorrect. The load factor and stall speed will remain the same for a constant-altitude, constant-banked turn. **Answer (B) is incorrect.** The load factor and stall speed will remain the same for a constant-altitude, constant-banked turn.

80. If the airspeed is decreased from 98 knots to 85 knots during a coordinated level 45° banked turn, the load factor will

A. remain the same, but the radius of turn will decrease.

B. decrease, and the rate of turn will decrease.

C. remain the same, but the radius of turn will increase.

Answer (A) is correct. (FAA-H-8083-25B Chap 5)
    DISCUSSION: Because the only determinant of load factor in level, coordinated turns is the amount of bank, a change in airspeed does not change the load factor. When airspeed is decreased, however, the rate of turn increases and the radius of turn decreases.
    Answer (B) is incorrect. The load factor will remain the same for a constant-altitude, constant-banked turn, and the rate of turn will actually increase, not decrease. The radius of turn, however, will decrease. **Answer (C) is incorrect.** While the load factor will remain the same for a constant-altitude, constant-banked turn, the radius of turn will actually decrease, not increase.

81. Baggage weighing 90 pounds is placed in a normal category airplane's baggage compartment which is placarded at 100 pounds. If this airplane is subjected to a positive load factor of 3.5 Gs, the total load of the baggage would be

A. 315 pounds and would be excessive.

B. 315 pounds and would not be excessive.

C. 350 pounds and would not be excessive.

Answer (B) is correct. (FAA-H-8083-25B Chap 5)
    DISCUSSION: Because 90 lb. is less than the amount of placarded weight (100 lb.), there is no problem with the weight. The positive load factor of 3.5 Gs is within the normal operational limit of 3.8 Gs of normal category airplanes. When 100 lb. was set as a baggage limit in this particular case, it was understood that it may be subjected to 3.8 Gs, i.e., 380 pounds. The baggage weight of 90 lb. is multiplied by 3.5 Gs to get a load of 315 pounds.
    Answer (A) is incorrect. The baggage weight is not excessive. Load factor does not need to be figured in to determine maximum weight for any compartment. **Answer (C) is incorrect.** This would be the total load of 100 lb. of baggage at 3.5 Gs.

82. While executing a 60° level turn, your aircraft is at a load factor of 2.0. What does this mean?

A. The total load on the aircraft's structure is two times its weight.

B. The load factor is over the load limit.

C. The gust factor is two times the total load limit.

Answer (A) is correct. (FAA-H-8083-25B)
    DISCUSSION: A load factor of 2.0 means the total load on an aircraft's structure is two times its weight. Since load factors are expressed in terms of Gs, a load factor of 2.0 may be spoken of as 2 Gs, or a load factor of 4 as 4 Gs.
    Answer (B) is incorrect. A load factor of 2.0 would be within all category load factor limits. The maximum safe load factors (limit load factors) are as follows: normal category airplanes are limited to 3.8 and –1.52 Gs, utility aircraft are limited to 4.4 and –1.76 Gs, and aerobatic aircraft are limited to 6.0 and –3.0 Gs. **Answer (C) is incorrect.** The gust factor is an increasing function of speed. A load factor of 2.0 is not referencing a gust factor but rather the total load on an aircraft's structure, which would be two times its weight.

83. Which factor below is the best indication of positive or negative Gs in an aircraft?

 A. Change in the amount of pressure by the pilot needed on the controls.

 B. Change in how heavy or light you feel in your seat.

 C. Change in control-surface effectiveness.

Answer (B) is correct. *(FAA-H-8083-25B Chap 5)*
 DISCUSSION: Positive or negative load factor is most easily observed by considering how heavy or light you feel in the seat. This effect is one of the primary considerations in the design of the structure for all airplanes.
 Answer (A) is incorrect. Pilot pressure on the flight controls can be affected by speed and/or load factor.
 Answer (C) is incorrect. Control surface effectiveness can be affected by speed and/or load factor.

84. If the airspeed is increased from 89 knots to 98 knots during a coordinated level 45° banked turn, the load factor will

 A. remain the same, but the radius of turn will increase.

 B. decrease, and the rate of turn will decrease.

 C. increase, but the rate of turn will decrease.

Answer (A) is correct. *(FAA-H-8083-25B Chap 5)*
 DISCUSSION: Because the only determinant of load factor in level, coordinated turns is the amount of bank, a change in airspeed does not change the load factor. When airspeed is increased, however, the rate of turn decreases and the radius of turn increases.
 Answer (B) is incorrect. The load factor will remain the same for a constant-altitude, constant-banked turn, and the rate of turn will decrease. The radius of turn, however, will increase.
 Answer (C) is incorrect. The load factor will remain the same for a constant-altitude, constant-banked turn, and the rate of turn decreases. However, the radius of turn will increase.

85. Which of the following would best indicate to the pilot that the load factor placed on the airframe has been increased?

 A. An increase in the sensation of being pushed into the seat.

 B. An increase in airspeed.

 C. More effort is required to operate the controls.

Answer (A) is correct. *(FAA-H-8083-25B Chap 5)*
 DISCUSSION: Load factor can be judged by noting the seat pressure. Increases in load factor ("pulling Gs") result in increased pressure pushing you into the seat.
 Answer (B) is incorrect. An increase in airspeed is not an indication of an increased load factor. In fact, airspeed often decreases with increases in load factor in balanced flight.
 Answer (C) is incorrect. The feedback provided by the flight control system will vary by aircraft type and the design of the flight control system. Some flight control systems are fly-by-wire, hydraulic, or conventional cables and pulleys. Because of these factors, the pressure applied to the controls by the pilot is not an accurate method for judging load factor.

86. Limit load factor is the ratio of

 A. angle of attack to stall speed.

 B. angle of attack to power-on configuration-specific stall speed.

 C. maximum sustainable load to the gross weight of the airplane.

Answer (C) is correct. *(FAA-H-8083-25B Chap 5)*
 DISCUSSION: Limit load factors are the highest load factors that can be expected in normal operation under various operational situations. The limit load factor is the ratio of maximum positive or negative load imposed on the aircraft to the gross weight of the aircraft.
 Answer (A) is incorrect. The relationship between angle of attack and stall speed is the critical angle of attack, not the load factor. **Answer (B) is incorrect.** The relationship between angle of attack and stall speed is the critical angle of attack, not the load factor.

87. (Refer to Figure 4 on page 51.) What increase in load factor would take place if the angle of bank were increased from 60° to 80°?

    A. 3 G's.

    B. 3.5 G's.

    C. 4 G's.

Answer (C) is correct. (FAA-H-8083-25B Chap 5)
    DISCUSSION: In Fig. 4, the relationship between bank angle degrees on the horizontal axis is related to both load factor or "G" units on the vertical scale and percent increase in stall speed on the vertical axis. There are two curves on the graph. Each curve relates to the vertical scale or the vertical axis. At a 60° bank, find 60° on the horizontal axis, go up to the load factor curve, and then horizontally right to the far right vertical scale to determine approximately 2 Gs. At 80° there are approximately 6 Gs. Thus, the increase in load factor is 4 Gs (6 − 2) when the angle of bank is increased from 60° to 80°.
    Answer (A) is incorrect. An additional 3 Gs results from increasing bank from 60° to 77°. **Answer (B) is incorrect.** An additional 3.5 Gs results from increasing bank from 60° to 78°.

88. (Refer to Figure 4 on page 51.) What is the stall speed of an airplane under a load factor of 2.5 Gs if the unaccelerated stall speed is 60 knots?

    A. 62 knots.

    B. 84 knots.

    C. 96 knots.

Answer (C) is correct. (FAA-H-8083-25B Chap 5)
    DISCUSSION: In Fig. 4, find 2.5 Gs on the far right axis labeled Load Factor or "G" Units. Draw a horizontal line to intersect the Load Factor curve. At this intersection, draw a vertical line to intersect the Stall Speed Increase curve. From here, draw a horizontal line to intersect the far left axis labeled Percent Increase in Stall Speed to find an increase of about 60%. Apply this increase to the unaccelerated stall speed of 60 kt. to get the stall speed of 96 kt. (60 kt. × 1.6 = 96 kt.).
    Answer (A) is incorrect. Sixty-two knots is a 1% increase, not a 60% increase, in stall speed. **Answer (B) is incorrect.** Eighty-four knots is a 40% increase, not a 60% increase, in stall speed.

89. (Refer to Figure 4 on page 51.) What is the stall speed of an airplane under a load factor of 2 Gs if the unaccelerated stall speed is 60 knots?

    A. 66 knots.

    B. 74 knots.

    C. 84 knots.

Answer (C) is correct. (FAA-H-8083-25B Chap 5)
    DISCUSSION: Use Fig. 4 to determine the percentage increase in stall speed under a load factor of 2 Gs. First, find 2 Gs on the far right vertical scale and move horizontally to the left to the load factor curve, which intersects at about a 60° bank. Then move vertically up from that point to the intersection of the stall speed increase curve. Next move left horizontally to the vertical axis to determine a 40% increase in stall speed. If the unaccelerated stall speed is 60 kt., the accelerated stall speed is 84 kt. (60 kt. × 140%).
    Answer (A) is incorrect. This is a 10%, not 40%, increase in stall speed. **Answer (B) is incorrect.** This is a 23%, not 40%, increase in stall speed.

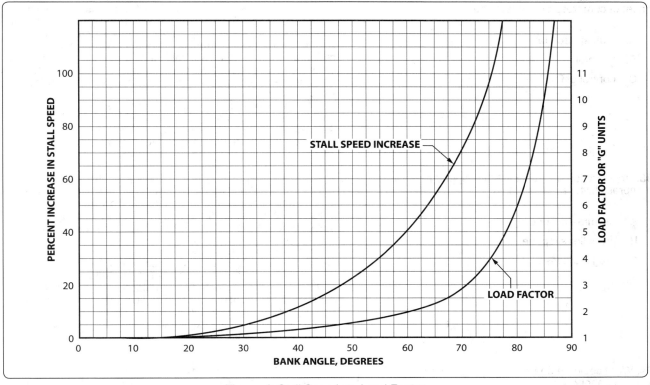

Figure 4. Stall Speed vs. Load Factor.

1.10 Transonic and Supersonic Flight

90. Transonic airflow typically occurs in airplane speed regimes between Mach

    A. 0.75 and 0.95.

    B. 0.95 and 1.01.

    C. 0.75 and 1.20.

Answer (C) is correct. *(FAA-H-8083-25B Chap 5)*
    DISCUSSION: Because there is the possibility of having both subsonic and supersonic flows existing on the aircraft, it is convenient to define certain regimes of flight. Transonic airflow is defined between Mach 0.75 and 1.20.
    Answer (A) is incorrect. Transonic airflow is defined between Mach 0.75 and 1.20. **Answer (B) is incorrect.** Transonic airflow is defined between Mach 0.75 and 1.20.

91. The ratio of an airplane's true airspeed to the speed of sound in the same atmospheric conditions is

    A. equivalent airspeed.

    B. transonic airflow.

    C. mach number.

Answer (C) is correct. *(FAA-H-8083-25B Chap 5)*
    DISCUSSION: Mach number is the ratio of an airplane's true airspeed to the speed of sound in the same atmospheric conditions. The speed of sound varies with a change of altitude and temperature. At sea level with a standard temperature of 15°C, the speed of sound is 661 knots. At 40,000 with a temperature of –55°C, the speed of sound is 574 knots.
    Answer (A) is incorrect. Equivalent airspeed is the indicated airspeed corrected for position error, installation error, and adiabatic compressibility for a particular altitude. **Answer (B) is incorrect.** Airplanes operating between .75 and 1.20 Mach experience transonic airflow over the wings and airframe. The shock wave created by transonic airflow over the wings often alters the center of pressure, resulting in a change to the airplane's pitch attitude.

92. Accelerating past critical Mach may result in the onset of compressibility effects such as

    A. high speed stalls.

    B. P factor.

    C. control difficulties.

Answer (C) is correct. (FAA-H-8083-25B Chap 5)
    DISCUSSION: The critical Mach number is the highest flight speed possible without supersonic flow. As critical Mach is exceeded, an area of supersonic airflow is created and a normal shockwave forms as the boundary between the supersonic flow and the subsonic flow on the aft portion of the airfoil surface. Accelerating past critical Mach is associated with trim and stability changes and a decrease in control surface effectiveness.
    Answer (A) is incorrect. High-speed stalls do not necessarily result from accelerating past critical Mach.
    Answer (B) is incorrect. P-factor affects propeller-driven airplanes, which are not designed for Mach speeds.

93. Acceleration past critical Mach speed may cause compressibility issues such as

    A. asymmetric loading.

    B. propeller slippage.

    C. drag increases.

Answer (C) is correct. (FAA-H-8083-25B Chap 5)
    DISCUSSION: The critical Mach number is the highest flight speed possible without supersonic flow. Accelerating past critical Mach is associated with a large increase in drag due to the initial formation of a weak shockwave on the wing, creating a barrier to the oncoming airflow.
    Answer (A) is incorrect. Asymmetrical loading is not associated with flight near the critical Mach speed. Rather, it is most commonly referred to as P-factor (the unbalanced production of thrust created by the blades of a propeller).
    Answer (B) is incorrect. Propeller slippage is not associated with flight near the critical Mach speed. Rather, it has to do with the loss in efficiency inherent in the operation of any propeller-driven aircraft, particularly with fixed-pitch propellers.

94. What could be one result of exceeding critical Mach number?

    A. Propeller stall.

    B. Reduction in drag.

    C. Aircraft control difficulties.

Answer (C) is correct. (FAA-H-8083-25B)
    DISCUSSION: The critical Mach number is the boundary between subsonic and transonic flight and is largely dependent on the wing and airfoil design. The critical Mach number is an important point in transonic flight. When shock waves form on the aircraft, airflow separation followed by buffet and aircraft control difficulties can occur.
    Answer (A) is incorrect. Propeller slippage is not associated with flight near the critical Mach speed. Rather, it has to do with the loss in efficiency inherent in the operation of any propeller-driven aircraft, particularly with fixed-pitch propellers. **Answer (B) is incorrect.** The critical Mach number is the highest flight speed possible without supersonic flow. Accelerating past critical Mach is associated with a large increase in drag, not a reduction in drag. This is due to the initial formation of a weak shockwave on the wing, creating a barrier to the oncoming airflow.

STUDY UNIT TWO

AIRPLANE INSTRUMENTS, ENGINES, AND SYSTEMS

(6 pages of outline)

This study unit contains outlines of major concepts tested; sample test questions and answers regarding airplane instruments, engines, and systems; and an explanation of each answer. The table of contents above lists each subunit within this study unit, the number of questions pertaining to that particular subunit, and the pages on which the outlines and questions begin, respectively.

Recall that the **sole purpose** of this book is to expedite your passing of the FAA pilot knowledge test for the commercial pilot certificate. Accordingly, all extraneous material (i.e., topics or regulations not directly tested on the FAA pilot knowledge test) is omitted, even though much more knowledge is necessary to become a proficient commercial pilot. This additional material is presented in *Pilot Handbook* and *Commercial Pilot Flight Maneuvers and Practical Test Prep*, available from Gleim Publications, Inc. Order online at www.GleimAviation.com.

2.1 MAGNETIC COMPASS

1. The difference between direction indicated by a magnetic compass not installed in an airplane and one installed in an airplane is called compass deviation.

    a. Magnetic fields produced by metals and electrical accessories in an airplane disturb the compass needle.

    b. The compass deviation usually varies for different headings of the same aircraft.

2.2 AIRSPEED INDICATOR

1. Airspeed indicators have several color-coded markings.

    a. The white arc is the flap operating range.

        1) The lower limit is the power-off stalling speed or the minimum steady flight speed with wing flaps and landing gear in the landing position (V_{S0}).

        2) The upper limit is the maximum flap extended speed (V_{FE}).

    b. The green arc is the normal operating range.

        1) The lower limit is the power-off stalling speed with the wing flaps up and landing gear retracted (V_{S1}).

        2) The upper limit is the maximum structural cruising speed for normal operation (V_{NO}).

    c. The yellow arc is the range of airspeed that is safe in smooth air only.

        1) It is known as the caution range.

    d. The red line is the speed that should never be exceeded (V_{NE}).

        1) Design limit load factors could be exceeded with airspeeds in excess of V_{NE} from a variety of phenomena.

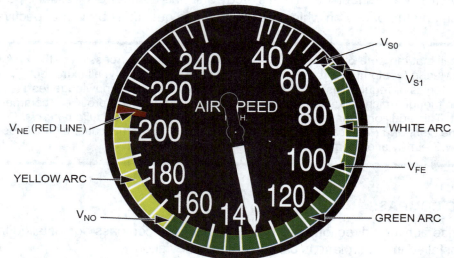

2. The most important speed limitation that is **not** color-coded is the design maneuvering speed (V_A).

    a. The design maneuvering speed is the speed below which you can move a single flight control one time to its full deflection for one axis of airplane rotation only (pitch, roll, or yaw), in smooth air, without risk of damage to the airplane.

    b. It is the maximum speed for flight in turbulent air.

    c. It is the maximum speed at which an airplane may be stalled safely.

3. The maximum landing gear extended speed (V_{LE}) is not color-coded.

    a. It is usually placarded and is included in the airplane's flight manual.

4. Types of Airspeed

    a. Indicated airspeed (IAS) is read directly off the airspeed indicator.

    b. Calibrated airspeed (CAS) is IAS corrected for installation and instrument error.

    c. True airspeed (TAS) is CAS corrected for pressure altitude and nonstandard temperature.

    d. Equivalent airspeed (EAS) is CAS corrected for the adiabatic compressible flow of air for a particular altitude. EAS is equal to CAS when at sea level in a standard atmosphere.

5. The V-G diagram (velocity vs. "G" loads) shows the flight operating strength of an airplane.

    a. In the diagram below, load factor is on the vertical axis with airspeed on the horizontal axis.

    b. The dashed lines, the first important items on the diagram, show maximum lift capability.

        1) The subject airplane in the diagram below is capable of developing no more than one positive "G" at 64 MPH, which is the wings-level stall speed of the airplane.

        2) The maximum load factor increases dramatically with airspeed. The airplane's maximum positive lift capability is 2 "G" at 96 MPH, 3 "G" at 116 MPH, 3.8 "G" at 126 MPH, etc. These are the "coordinates" of points on the curved line up to point C.

        3) Any load factor above this dashed line is unavailable aerodynamically. That is, the subject airplane cannot fly above the line of maximum lift capability (it will stall).

    c. Point C is the intersection of the positive limit load factor (line CDE) and the line of maximum positive lift capability (dashed line up to point C).

        1) The airspeed at this point [usually called the design maneuvering speed (V_A)] is the minimum airspeed at which the limit load can be developed aerodynamically.

        2) Any airspeed greater than point C provides a positive lift capability sufficient to damage the airplane. Any airspeed less than point C does **not** provide positive lift capability sufficient to cause damage from excessive flight loads.

    d. The limit airspeed V_{NE} is a design reference point for the airplane. The subject airplane is limited to 196 MPH (line EF). If flight is attempted beyond the limit airspeed, structural damage or structural failure may result from a variety of phenomena.

    e. Thus, the airplane in flight is limited to a regime of airspeeds and Gs that do not exceed

        1) The limit (or red-line) speed (line EF)
        2) Normal stall speed (line AJ)
        3) The positive and negative limit load factors (lines CDE and IHG)
        4) The maximum lift capability (dashed lines up to C, down to I)

    f. A caution range is indicated between points D, E, F, and G. Within this range, certain factors must be considered to maintain flight in the envelope. Line DG represents the maximum structural cruising speed (V_{NO}).

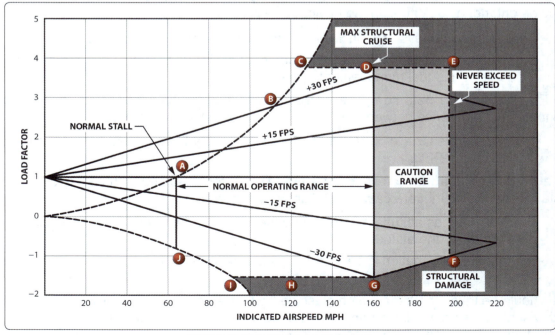

Figure 5. Velocity vs. Load Factor.

2.3   TURN COORDINATOR/TURN-AND-SLIP INDICATOR

1.   The turn coordinator and the turn-and-slip indicator are usually electric-driven instruments. Each instrument has an inclinometer (i.e., ball).

    a.   The turn coordinator indicates roll rate, rate of turn, and coordination.

    b.   The turn-and-slip indicator indicates rate of turn and coordination.

2.   The advantage of having an electric turn coordinator (or turn-and-slip indicator) is to provide bank information in case the vacuum-driven attitude indicator and heading indicator fail.

2.4   GLASS COCKPITS

1.   Glass cockpits, or systems of advanced avionics, are replacing the older round-dial gauges common in many training aircraft.

    a.   These systems vary widely but generally provide flight information such as flight progress, engine monitoring, navigation, terrain, traffic, and weather.

    b.   These systems are designed to decrease pilot workload, enhance situational awareness, and increase the safety margin.

    c.   These systems are displayed in an electronic flight display (EFD).

2.   A **primary flight display (PFD)** integrates all flight instruments critical to safe flight on one screen. It is a type of EFD.

    a.   Some PFDs incorporate or overlay navigation instruments on top of primary flight instruments.

        1)   EXAMPLE: An ILS or VOR may be integrated with the heading indicator.

3.   A **multi-function display (MFD)** not only shows primary instrumentation but can combine information from multiple systems on one page or screen. It is another type of EFD.

    a.   Moving maps provide a pictorial view of the aircraft's location, route, airspace, and geographical features.

    NOTE: A moving map should not be used as the primary navigation instrument; it should be a supplement, not a substitute, in the navigational process.

    b.   Onboard weather systems, including radar, may provide real-time weather.

    c.   Other information that could be included on MFDs include terrain and traffic avoidance, checklists, and fuel management systems.

4.   An EFD utilizes an **air data computer (ADC)**, which receives the pitot and static inputs and computes the difference between the total pressure and the static pressure.

    a.   It then generates the information necessary to display the airspeed, altitude, and vertical speed on the PFD.

5.   The **attitude and heading reference system (AHRS)** replaces free-spinning gyros with solid-state laser systems that are capable of flight at any attitude without tumbling.

    a.   The AHRS sends attitude information to the PFD in order to generate the pitch and bank information of the attitude indicator.

    b.   The heading information is derived from a magnetometer that senses the Earth's lines of magnetic flux.

6.   Care should be taken that reliance on glass cockpits does not negate safety. A regular scan, both visually outside and inside on backup gauges, should be combined with other means of navigation and checklists to ensure safe flight.

2.5 FUEL/AIR MIXTURE

1. As altitude increases, the density (weight) of air entering the carburetor decreases.

    a. If no adjustment is made, the amount of fuel remains constant and the fuel/air ratio (mixture) becomes excessively rich.

    b. Thus, the pilot adjusts the fuel flow with the mixture control to maintain the proper fuel/air ratio at all altitudes.

2. The fuel/air ratio, by definition, is the ratio between the weight of fuel and the weight of air entering the cylinder.

    a. The best power mixture refers to the fuel/air ratio that will provide the most power at any given power setting.

3. Spark plug fouling results from operating at high altitudes with an excessively rich mixture due to the below-normal temperatures in the combustion chambers.

4. In gas turbine (as well as reciprocating) engines, as temperature increases and air density decreases, thrust decreases.

2.6 CARBURETOR HEAT

1. Carburetor heat enriches the fuel/air mixture because warm air is less dense than cold air.

2. Applying carburetor heat decreases engine output and increases operating temperature due to the warmer, less dense air entering the carburetor.

    a. Leaving the carburetor heat on during takeoff will increase the ground roll.

2.7 DETONATION AND PREIGNITION

1. Detonation occurs in a reciprocating aircraft engine when the unburned fuel/air charge in the cylinders is subjected to instantaneous combustion.

2. Detonation is usually caused by using a lower-than-specified grade of aviation fuel and too lean a mixture or by excessive engine temperature caused by high-power settings.

3. Preignition is the uncontrolled firing of the fuel/air charge in advance of the normal spark ignition.

2.8 AIRPLANE IGNITION SYSTEMS

1. Dual ignition systems provide improved combustion of the fuel/air mixture.

2. Aircraft magnetos generate their own electricity by self-contained magnets.

3. An engine that continues to run after the ignition switch has been turned off probably has a broken or disconnected ground wire between the magneto and the ignition switch.

    a. Thus, a potentially dangerous situation exists because the engine could accidentally start if the propeller is moved with fuel in the cylinder.

4. A good practice before shutdown is to idle the engine and momentarily turn the ignition off.

5. Rapid opening and closing of the throttle may cause detuning of engine crankshaft counterweights (throwing the crankshaft out of balance).

2.9   ENGINE COOLING

1.   Aircraft engines are largely cooled by the flow of oil through the lubrication system.

2.   An excessively low oil level will prevent the oil from cooling adequately and result in an abnormally high engine oil temperature.

3.   Exhaust manifold type heating systems are used as a heat source for the cabin and carburetor. The risks of operating an aircraft with a defective exhaust heating system include carbon monoxide poisoning, a decrease in engine performance, and an increased potential for fire. Because of these risks, the exhaust manifold should be periodically inspected.

2.10   AIRPLANE PROPELLERS

1.   Propeller efficiency is the ratio of thrust horsepower to brake horsepower.

2.   A fixed-pitch propeller can be most efficient only at a specified combination of airspeed and RPM.

   a.   A cruise propeller has a higher pitch and therefore more drag. More drag results in lower RPM and less horsepower capability, which decreases performance during takeoffs and climbs but increases efficiency during cruising flight.

3.   The propeller's geometric pitch varies along the propeller blade because the propeller tip goes through the air faster than the section of propeller near the hub.

   a.   This pitch variation (i.e., twist) permits a relatively constant angle of attack and the same amount of lift to be created along the blade's length when in cruising flight.

4.   Pitch setting is the propeller blade setting determined by the blade angle measured in a manner, and at a radius, specified in the propeller's instruction manual.

5.   A constant-speed (controllable-pitch) propeller adjusts the pitch angle of the propeller blade so that the engine is maintained at a selected RPM.

6.   For takeoff, to develop maximum power and thrust, you should use a small angle of attack and high RPM on a controllable-pitch (constant-speed) propeller.

7.   To establish climb power after takeoff in an airplane equipped with a constant-speed propeller, you should first decrease manifold pressure and then decrease RPM. When the propeller control is moved to reduce the RPM, the propeller blade angle increases.

   a.   When increasing power, increase RPM first; then increase manifold pressure to avoid placing undue stress on the engine.

8.   Spiraling slipstream describes the propeller blade forcing air rearward in a spiraling clockwise direction around the fuselage when the propeller rotates through the air in a clockwise direction as viewed from the rear.

   a.   As a result, the airplane yaws left around the vertical axis.

QUESTIONS AND ANSWER EXPLANATIONS: All of the commercial pilot knowledge test questions chosen by the FAA for release as well as additional questions selected by Gleim relating to the material in the previous outlines are provided on the following pages. These questions have been organized into the same subunits as the outlines. To the immediate right of each question are the correct answer and answer explanations. You should cover these answers and answer explanations while responding to the questions. Refer to the general discussion in the Introduction on how to take the FAA knowledge test.

Remember that the questions from the FAA knowledge test bank have been reordered by topic and organized into a meaningful sequence. Also, the first line of the answer explanation gives the citation of the authoritative source for the answer.

QUESTIONS

2.1 Magnetic Compass

1. Which statement is true about magnetic deviation of a compass? Deviation

A. varies over time as the agonic line shifts.

B. varies for different headings of the same aircraft.

C. is the same for all aircraft in the same locality.

Answer (B) is correct. (FAA-H-8083-25B Chap 8)
   DISCUSSION: The difference between the direction indicated by a compass not installed in an airplane and one installed in an airplane is called compass deviation. Magnetic fields produced by the metal and electrical accessories in the airplane disturb the compass needle and produce errors. The amount of deviation varies with different headings.
   Answer (A) is incorrect. The position of the agonic line determines magnetic variation, not compass deviation. **Answer (C) is incorrect.** Compass deviation varies from aircraft to aircraft.

2.2 Airspeed Indicator

2. Maximum structural cruising speed is the maximum speed at which an airplane can be operated during

A. abrupt maneuvers.

B. normal operations.

C. flight in smooth air.

Answer (B) is correct. (FAA-H-8083-25B Chap 8)
   DISCUSSION: The maximum structural cruising speed (V_{NO}) is the upper limit of the green arc on the airspeed indicator. It is the maximum speed for normal operations.
   Answer (A) is incorrect. V_A is the design maneuvering speed, which is the rough air penetration speed and maximum speed for abrupt maneuvers. **Answer (C) is incorrect.** The yellow arc (V_{NO} to V_{NE}) is the caution range where flight is allowed only in smooth air.

3. Why should flight speeds above V_{NE} be avoided?

A. Excessive induced drag will result in structural failure.

B. Design limit load factors may be exceeded, if gusts are encountered.

C. Control effectiveness is so impaired that the aircraft becomes uncontrollable.

Answer (B) is correct. (FAA-H-8083-25B Chap 8)
   DISCUSSION: At speeds above V_{NE}, the design limit load factors for the airplane may be exceeded if gusts are encountered. Thus, this airspeed should never be exceeded, even in smooth air.
   Answer (A) is incorrect. Induced drag decreases, not increases, as airspeed increases. **Answer (C) is incorrect.** Control effectiveness increases, not decreases, as airspeed increases.

4. Which airspeed would a pilot be unable to identify by the color coding of an airspeed indicator?

A. The never-exceed speed.

B. The power-off stall speed.

C. The maneuvering speed.

Answer (C) is correct. (FAA-H-8083-25B Chap 8)
   DISCUSSION: The maneuvering speed (V_A) is not color coded on an airspeed indicator. It is usually placarded and included in the airplane's flight manual.
   Answer (A) is incorrect. The never-exceed speed is identified by the red radial line at the top of the yellow arc. **Answer (B) is incorrect.** Two power-off stall speeds are represented on the airspeed indicator; the stall speeds in the landing and clean configurations are represented by the lower limits of the white and green arcs, respectively.

5. Calibrated airspeed is best described as indicated airspeed corrected for

A. installation and instrument error.

B. instrument error.

C. non-standard temperature.

Answer (A) is correct. (FAA-H-8083-25B Chap 8)
   DISCUSSION: Calibrated airspeed (CAS) is indicated airspeed corrected for installation and instrument error. An airspeed calibration chart is provided in the airplane's Pilot's Operating Handbook (POH).
   Answer (B) is incorrect. Calibrated airspeed is indicated airspeed corrected for both installation and instrument error, not only for instrument error. **Answer (C) is incorrect.** Calibrated airspeed is indicated airspeed corrected for installation and instrument error, not for nonstandard temperature.

6. True airspeed is best described as calibrated airspeed corrected for

    A. installation or instrument error.

    B. non-standard temperature.

    C. altitude and nonstandard temperature.

Answer (C) is correct. (FAA-H-8083-25B Chap 8)
DISCUSSION: True airspeed (TAS) is calibrated airspeed corrected for pressure altitude and nonstandard temperature. Thus, TAS is calibrated airspeed corrected for density altitude.
Answer (A) is incorrect. Calibrated airspeed, not true airspeed, is indicated airspeed corrected for installation and, not or, instrument error. **Answer (B) is incorrect.** True airspeed is calibrated airspeed corrected for both nonstandard temperature and pressure altitude, not only nonstandard temperature.

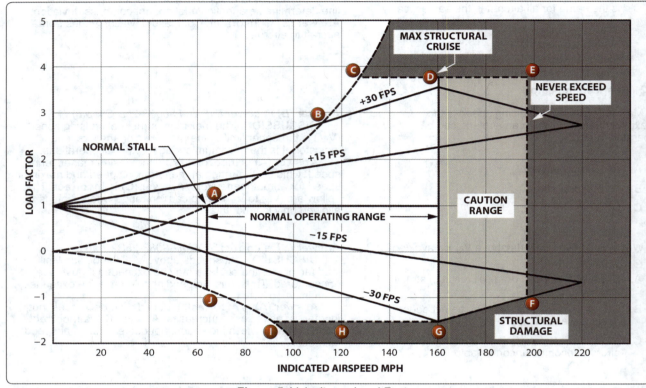

Figure 5. Velocity vs. Load Factor.

7. (Refer to Figure 5 above.) Point C references

    A. V_{NE}.

    B. V_{NO}.

    C. V_A.

Answer (C) is correct. (FAA-H-8083-25B Chap 5)
DISCUSSION: Point C on the V-G diagram references V_A (design maneuvering speed), which is not displayed on the airspeed indicator.
Answer (A) is incorrect. V_{NE} (never-exceed speed) is represented by points E and F on the V-G diagram and by a red line on the airspeed indicator. **Answer (B) is incorrect.** V_{NO} (normal operating speed) is represented by point G on the V-G diagram and by the upper limit of the green arc on the airspeed indicator.

8. (Refer to Figure 5 above.) The horizontal dashed line from point C to point E represents the

    A. ultimate load factor.

    B. positive limit load factor.

    C. airspeed range for normal operations.

Answer (B) is correct. (FAA-H-8083-25B Chap 5)
DISCUSSION: In Fig. 5, the line from point C to point E represents the positive limit load factor, i.e., the greatest positive load that may be placed on the aircraft without risk of structural damage.
Answer (A) is incorrect. Ultimate load factor is the limit load factor multiplied by 1.5 as a safety measure. While structural damage may occur at the limit load factor, structural failure may occur at the ultimate load factor. **Answer (C) is incorrect.** The airspeed range for normal operations, the green arc on the airspeed indicator, is the horizontal distance from the vertical line from point A to point J to the vertical line from point D to point G.

9. (Refer to Figure 5 on page 60.) The vertical line from point E to point F is represented on the airspeed indicator by the

A. upper limit of the yellow arc.

B. upper limit of the green arc.

C. blue radial line.

Answer (A) is correct. (FAA-H-8083-25B Chap 5)
　　DISCUSSION: In Fig. 5, the line from point E to point F is labeled as the never-exceed speed (V_{NE}). This speed is represented on the airspeed indicator by the upper limit of the yellow arc (the red radial line).
　　Answer (B) is incorrect. The upper limit of the green arc represents the maximum structural cruising speed (V_{NO}), which is the line from point D to point G, not E to F. **Answer (C) is incorrect.** The blue radial line represents the single-engine best rate-of-climb speed (V_{YSE}) in a multi-engine airplane. V_{YSE} is not shown on the V-G diagram.

10. (Refer to Figure 5 on page 60.) The vertical line from point D to point G is represented on the airspeed indicator by the maximum speed limit of the

A. green arc.

B. yellow arc.

C. white arc.

Answer (A) is correct. (FAA-H-8083-25B Chap 5)
　　DISCUSSION: In Fig. 5, the line from point D to point G is labeled as the maximum structural cruising speed (V_{NO}). This speed is represented on the airspeed indicator by the upper limit of the green arc.
　　Answer (B) is incorrect. The upper limit of the yellow arc represents the never-exceed speed (V_{NE}), which is the line from point E to point F, not D to G. **Answer (C) is incorrect.** The upper limit of the white arc is the maximum flap extended speed (V_{FE}), which is not shown on the V-G diagram.

11. Structural damage or failure is more likely to occur in smooth air at speeds above

A. V_{NO}.

B. V_A.

C. V_{NE}.

Answer (C) is correct. (FAA-H-8083-25B)
　　DISCUSSION: Never exceed speed (V_{NE}) is a design limit speed where load factors could be exceeded with airspeeds in excess of V_{NE} from a variety of phenomena. Operating above this speed is prohibited because it may result in damage or structural failure.
　　Answer (A) is incorrect. V_{NO} is the maximum structural cruising speed. Do not exceed this speed except in smooth air. **Answer (B) is incorrect.** V_A is the design maneuvering speed. It is the speed below which you can move a single flight control one time to its full deflection for one axis of airplane rotation only (pitch, roll, or yaw), in smooth air, without risk of damage to the airplane.

2.3 Turn Coordinator/Turn-and-Slip Indicator

12. What is an advantage of an electric turn coordinator if the airplane has a vacuum system for other gyroscopic instruments?

A. It is a backup in case of vacuum system failure.

B. It is more reliable than the vacuum-driven indicators.

C. It will not tumble as will vacuum-driven turn indicators.

Answer (A) is correct. (FAA-H-8083-25B Chap 8)
　　DISCUSSION: The principal uses of the turn coordinator are to indicate rate of turn and to serve as an emergency source of bank information in case the vacuum-driven attitude indicator fails.
　　Answer (B) is incorrect. The vacuum-driven and electric-driven indicators are equally reliable. **Answer (C) is incorrect.** Both the vacuum-driven and the electric-driven turn indicator can tumble.

13. What is an operational difference between the turn coordinator and the turn-and-slip indicator? The turn coordinator

A. is always electric; the turn-and-slip indicator is always vacuum-driven.

B. indicates bank angle only; the turn-and-slip indicator indicates rate of turn and coordination.

C. indicates roll rate, rate of turn, and coordination; the turn-and-slip indicator indicates rate of turn and coordination.

Answer (C) is correct. (FAA-H-8083-25B Chap 8)
　　DISCUSSION: The turn-and-slip indicator indicates the rate and direction of the turn. The turn coordinator displays the movement of the aircraft along the longitudinal axis in an amount proportional to the roll rate. When the roll rate is reduced to zero (i.e., a constant bank), the instrument provides an indication of rate of turn. Both the turn coordinator and the turn indicator possess a ball that indicates rudder/aileron coordination.
　　Answer (A) is incorrect. The turn coordinator and the turn-and-slip indicator are usually electric-driven instruments. **Answer (B) is incorrect.** The turn coordinator indicates roll rate and coordination, not angle of bank.

2.4 Glass Cockpits

14. You are flying an aircraft equipped with an electronic flight display and the air data computer fails. What instrument is affected?

    A. ADS-B in capability.

    B. Airspeed indicator.

    C. Attitude indicator.

Answer (B) is correct. (FAA-H-8083-25B Chap 8)
    DISCUSSION: An electronic flight display (EFD) utilizes an air data computer (ADC), which receives the pitot and static inputs and computes the difference between the total pressure and the static pressure. It then generates the information necessary to display the airspeed, altitude, and vertical speed on the PFD.
    Answer (A) is incorrect. ADS-B in capability is not affected by the air data computer (ADC). **Answer (C) is incorrect.** The attitude indicator receives its information from the attitude and heading reference system (AHRS).

15. What steps must be taken when flying with glass cockpits to ensure safe flight?

    A. Use the moving map for primary means of navigation, use the MFD to check engine systems and weather, back up with supplementary forms of information.

    B. Regularly scan each item on the PFD, confirm on the MFD.

    C. Regularly scan both inside and outside, use all appropriate checklists, and cross-check with other forms of information.

Answer (C) is correct. (FAA-H-8083-6 Chap 5)
    DISCUSSION: A regular scan, both visually outside and inside on backup gauges, should be combined with other means of navigation and checklists to ensure safe flight.
    Answer (A) is incorrect. The moving map should not be the sole means of navigation. Moving maps should be used as a supplement, not as a replacement. **Answer (B) is incorrect.** While you should scan both the PFD and MFD, more is needed to ensure a safe flight, such as visually scanning outside and confirming indications from other sources.

16. What is a benefit of flying with a glass cockpit?

    A. There is no longer a need to carry paper charts in flight.

    B. Situational awareness is increased.

    C. Terrain avoidance is guaranteed.

Answer (B) is correct. (FAA-H-8083-25B Chap 2)
    DISCUSSION: Glass cockpits are designed to decrease pilot workload, enhance situational awareness, and increase the safety margin.
    Answer (A) is incorrect. Pilots should still have current information and backup electronic navigation to enhance safety. **Answer (C) is incorrect.** Terrain avoidance is not guaranteed solely by means of relying on advanced avionics.

17. An aircraft which is equipped with an Electronic Flight Display (EFD) can

    A. compensate for an airman's lack of skill or knowledge.

    B. offer new capabilities and simplify the basic flying task.

    C. improve flight awareness by allowing the pilot to simply watch for alerts.

Answer (B) is correct. (FAA-H-8083-25B Chap 2)
    DISCUSSION: EFDs offer new capabilities, such as enhanced situational awareness, and simplify basic flying tasks, such as traditional cross-country flight planning and fuel management.
    Answer (A) is incorrect. It is important to remember that EFDs do not replace basic flight knowledge and skills. An EFD is a tool for improving flight safety. Risk increases when the pilot believes gadgets will compensate for lack of skill and knowledge. It is especially important to recognize there are limits to what the electronic systems in any light GA aircraft can do. Being PIC requires sound ADM, which sometimes means saying "no" to a flight. **Answer (C) is incorrect.** An advanced avionics aircraft offers increased safety with enhanced situational awareness. Tools like the moving map, topography, terrain awareness, traffic, and weather datalink displays give the pilot unprecedented information for enhanced situational awareness, but, without a well-planned information management strategy, these tools also make it easy for an unwary pilot to slide into the complacent role of passenger in command.

SU 2: Airplane Instruments, Engines, and Systems

2.5 Fuel/Air Mixture

18. At high altitudes, an excessively rich mixture will cause the

    A. engine to overheat.

    B. fouling of spark plugs.

    C. engine to operate smoother even though fuel consumption is increased.

Answer (B) is correct. (FAA-H-8083-25B Chap 7)
    DISCUSSION: As an aircraft gains altitude, the mixture must be leaned to compensate for the decrease in air density. If the mixture is not adjusted, it becomes too rich, i.e., contains too much fuel in terms of the weight of the air. Because of excessive fuel, a cooling effect takes place, which causes below-normal temperatures in the combustion chambers, resulting in spark plug fouling.
    Answer (A) is incorrect. A lean, not rich, mixture will cause the engine to overheat. **Answer (C) is incorrect.** An engine runs smoothest when the mixture is appropriate, not excessively rich.

19. What will occur if no leaning is made with the mixture control as the flight altitude increases?

    A. The volume of air entering the carburetor decreases and the amount of fuel decreases.

    B. The density of air entering the carburetor decreases and the amount of fuel increases.

    C. The density of air entering the carburetor decreases and the amount of fuel remains constant.

Answer (C) is correct. (FAA-H-8083-25B Chap 7)
    DISCUSSION: As altitude increases, the density of air entering the carburetor decreases. If no leaning is done with the mixture control, the amount of fuel will remain constant, resulting in an excessively rich mixture.
    Answer (A) is incorrect. The density, not volume, of air decreases, and the amount of fuel remains the same, not decreases. **Answer (B) is incorrect.** The amount of fuel remains the same, not decreases.

20. The basic purpose of adjusting the fuel/air mixture control at altitude is to

    A. decrease the fuel flow to compensate for decreased air density.

    B. decrease the amount of fuel in the mixture to compensate for increased air density.

    C. increase the amount of fuel in the mixture to compensate for the decrease in pressure and density of the air.

Answer (A) is correct. (FAA-H-8083-25B Chap 7)
    DISCUSSION: The purpose of adjusting the fuel/air mixture control at altitude is to decrease the fuel flow to compensate for the decreased air density.
    Answer (B) is incorrect. Air density decreases, not increases, at altitude. **Answer (C) is incorrect.** At altitude the amount of fuel is decreased, not increased, to compensate for decreased air density.

21. Fuel/air ratio is the ratio between the

    A. volume of fuel and volume of air entering the cylinder.

    B. weight of fuel and weight of air entering the cylinder.

    C. weight of fuel and weight of air entering the carburetor.

Answer (B) is correct. (FAA-H-8083-25B Chap 7)
    DISCUSSION: The fuel/air ratio, i.e., mixture, is the ratio between the weight of fuel and the weight of air entering the cylinder.
    Answer (A) is incorrect. As altitude increases, the amount of air in a fixed volume (i.e., air density) decreases. Thus, the ratio is between weights, not volume. **Answer (C) is incorrect.** The carburetor is where the fuel/air ratio is established prior to entering the cylinders.

22. The pilot controls the air/fuel ratio with the

    A. throttle.

    B. manifold pressure.

    C. mixture control.

Answer (C) is correct. (FAA-H-8083-25B Chap 7)
    DISCUSSION: The mixture control is used to adjust the ratio of fuel-to-air mixture entering the combustion chamber.
    Answer (A) is incorrect. The throttle regulates the total volume of fuel and air, not the fuel-to-air ratio, entering the combustion chamber. **Answer (B) is incorrect.** The manifold pressure indicates an engine's power output as controlled by the throttle; it is not directly related to the air/fuel mixture.

23. What effect, if any, would a change in ambient temperature or air density have on gas turbine engine performance?

    A. As air density decreases, thrust increases.

    B. As temperature increases, thrust increases.

    C. As temperature increases, thrust decreases.

Answer (C) is correct. (FAA-H-8083-32A Chap 1)
    DISCUSSION: A high ambient air temperature at a given pressure altitude relates to a high density altitude, or a decrease in air density. Thrust is reduced because of low air density and low mass flow. Also, thrust and fuel flow are reduced further because of high compressor inlet temperature.
    Answer (A) is incorrect. As air density decreases, thrust decreases, not increases. **Answer (B) is incorrect.** Thrust decreases, not increases, with an increase in temperature.

24. Fouling of spark plugs is more apt to occur if the aircraft

    A. gains altitude with no mixture adjustment.

    B. descends from altitude with no mixture adjustment.

    C. throttle is advanced very abruptly.

Answer (A) is correct. (FAA-H-8083-25B Chap 7)
    DISCUSSION: As an aircraft gains altitude, the mixture must be leaned to compensate for the decrease in air density. If the mixture is not adjusted, it becomes too rich, i.e., contains too much fuel in terms of the weight of the air. Because of excessive fuel, a cooling effect takes place, which causes below-normal temperatures in the combustion chambers, resulting in spark plug fouling.
    Answer (B) is incorrect. Descending with no mixture adjustment, i.e., operating with an excessively lean mixture, results in overheating, rough engine operation, a loss of power, and detonation, not spark plug fouling. **Answer (C) is incorrect.** Advancing the throttle abruptly may cause the engine to sputter or stop, not foul the spark plugs.

25. The mixture control can be adjusted, which

    A. prevents the fuel/air combination from becoming too rich at higher altitudes.

    B. regulates the amount of airflow through the carburetor's venturi.

    C. prevents the fuel/air combination from becoming lean as the airplane climbs.

Answer (A) is correct. (FAA-H-8083-25B Chap 7)
    DISCUSSION: As an aircraft gains altitude, the mixture must be leaned to compensate for the decrease in air density. If the mixture is not adjusted, it becomes too rich, i.e., contains too much fuel in terms of the weight of the air.
    Answer (B) is incorrect. The throttle, not the mixture control, regulates the airflow through the carburetor's venturi. **Answer (C) is incorrect.** The fuel/air ratio becomes richer, not leaner, as the airplane climbs.

26. Unless adjusted, the fuel/air mixture becomes richer with an increase in altitude because the amount of fuel

    A. decreases while the volume of air decreases.

    B. remains constant while the volume of air decreases.

    C. remains constant while the density of air decreases.

Answer (C) is correct. (FAA-H-8083-25B Chap 7)
    DISCUSSION: As altitude increases, the density of air entering the carburetor decreases. If no leaning is done with the mixture control, the amount of fuel will remain constant, resulting in an excessively rich mixture.
    Answer (A) is incorrect. The amount of fuel remains the same, not decreases, and the density, not volume, of air decreases. **Answer (B) is incorrect.** The density, not the volume, of air decreases.

27. The best power mixture is that fuel/air ratio at which

    A. cylinder head temperatures are the coolest.

    B. the most power can be obtained for any given throttle setting.

    C. a given power can be obtained with the highest manifold pressure or throttle setting.

Answer (B) is correct. (FAA-H-8083-25B Chap 7)
    DISCUSSION: Engines are more efficient when they are supplied the proper mixture of fuel and air. The best power mixture refers to the fuel/air ratio that provides the most power at any given throttle setting.
    Answer (A) is incorrect. The engine's cylinder heads will be coolest when the mixture is richest, not when it is at its best power setting. **Answer (C) is incorrect.** It describes the highest power setting, not the best power mixture.

2.6 Carburetor Heat

28. Which statement is true concerning the effect of the application of carburetor heat?

    A. It enriches the fuel/air mixture.

    B. It leans the fuel/air mixture.

    C. It has no effect on the fuel/air mixture.

Answer (A) is correct. (FAA-H-8083-25B Chap 7)
    DISCUSSION: The application of carburetor heat reduces the density of air entering the carburetor because the air is warmer. As a result, it enriches the fuel/air mixture because there is no change in the weight of fuel being combusted.
    Answer (B) is incorrect. Warmer air is less dense, so the mixture is enriched, not leaned. **Answer (C) is incorrect.** Warmer air is less dense, so the mixture is enriched, not unaffected.

29. Applying carburetor heat will

    A. not affect the mixture.

    B. lean the fuel/air mixture.

    C. enrich the fuel/air mixture.

Answer (C) is correct. (FAA-H-8083-25B Chap 7)
    DISCUSSION: The application of carburetor heat reduces the density of air entering the carburetor because the air is warmer. As a result, it enriches the fuel/air mixture because there is no change in the weight of fuel being combusted.
    Answer (A) is incorrect. Warmer air is less dense, so the mixture is enriched, not unaffected. **Answer (B) is incorrect.** Warmer air is less dense, so the mixture is enriched, not leaned.

30. Leaving the carburetor heat on during takeoff

A. leans the mixture for more power on takeoff.

B. will decrease the takeoff distance.

C. will increase the ground roll.

Answer (C) is correct. (FAA-H-8083-25B Chap 7)
DISCUSSION: Use of carburetor heat tends to reduce the output of the engine due to the warmer, less dense air entering the carburetor. Thus, the use of carburetor heat reduces performance during critical phases of flight, e.g., takeoff and climb. During the takeoff, it will increase the ground roll.
Answer (A) is incorrect. Carburetor heat enriches, not leans, the mixture for less, not more, power. **Answer (B) is incorrect.** The use of carburetor heat will increase, not decrease, takeoff performance.

2.7 Detonation and Preignition

31. Detonation occurs in a reciprocating aircraft engine when

A. there is an explosive increase of fuel caused by too rich a fuel/air mixture.

B. the spark plugs receive an electrical jolt caused by a short in the wiring.

C. the unburned fuel/air charge in the cylinders is subjected to instantaneous combustion.

Answer (C) is correct. (FAA-H-8083-25B Chap 7)
DISCUSSION: Detonation (or knock) is a sudden explosion, or instantaneous combustion, of the fuel/air mixture in the cylinders, producing extreme heat and severe structural stresses on the engine. It is caused by low-grade fuel, too lean a mixture, or excessively high engine temperatures.
Answer (A) is incorrect. Detonation is caused by too lean, not too rich, a mixture. **Answer (B) is incorrect.** Detonation is caused by excessively high engine temperatures, not a short in spark plug wiring.

32. Detonation may occur at high-power settings when

A. the fuel mixture ignites instantaneously instead of burning progressively and evenly.

B. an excessively rich fuel mixture causes an explosive gain in power.

C. the fuel mixture is ignited too early by hot carbon deposits in the cylinder.

Answer (A) is correct. (FAA-H-8083-25B Chap 7)
DISCUSSION: Detonation (or knock) is a sudden explosion, or instantaneous combustion, of the fuel/air mixture in the cylinders, producing extreme heat and severe structural stresses on the engine. It is caused by low-grade fuel, too lean a mixture, or excessively high engine temperatures.
Answer (B) is incorrect. Detonation may occur with an excessively lean, not rich, fuel mixture that causes a loss, not gain, in power. **Answer (C) is incorrect.** The fuel mixture being ignited too early describes preignition, not detonation.

33. The uncontrolled firing of the fuel/air charge in advance of normal spark ignition is known as

A. instantaneous combustion.

B. detonation.

C. preignition.

Answer (C) is correct. (FAA-H-8083-25B Chap 7)
DISCUSSION: Preignition is the ignition of the fuel prior to normal ignition or ignition before the electrical arcing occurs at the spark plug. Preignition may be caused by excessively hot exhaust valves, carbon particles, or spark plugs and electrodes heated to an incandescent, or glowing, state. These hot spots are usually caused by high temperatures encountered during detonation. A significant difference between preignition and detonation is that, if the conditions for detonation exist in one cylinder, they may exist in all cylinders, but preignition could take place in only one or two cylinders.
Answer (A) is incorrect. Instantaneous combustion is detonation, which will cause extremely high engine temperatures and can result in preignition. **Answer (B) is incorrect.** Detonation is the instantaneous combustion of the fuel/air mixture, which can be caused by using too lean a mixture, by using too low a grade of fuel, or by operating in temperatures that are too high.

34. Detonation can be caused by

A. a "rich" mixture.

B. low engine temperatures.

C. using a lower grade of fuel than recommended.

Answer (C) is correct. (FAA-H-8083-25B Chap 7)
DISCUSSION: Detonation (or knock) is a sudden explosion, or instantaneous combustion, of the fuel/air mixture in the cylinders, producing extreme heat and severe structural stresses on the engine. It is caused by low-grade fuel, too lean a mixture, or excessively high engine temperatures.
Answer (A) is incorrect. Detonation is caused by the mixture being too lean, not rich. **Answer (B) is incorrect.** Detonation is caused by excessively high, not low, engine temperatures.

2.8 Airplane Ignition Systems

35. Before shutdown, while at idle, the ignition key is momentarily turned OFF. The engine continues to run with no interruption; this

    A. is normal because the engine is usually stopped by moving the mixture to idle cutoff.

    B. should not normally happen. Indicates a magneto not grounding in OFF position.

    C. is an undesirable practice, but indicates that nothing is wrong.

Answer (B) is correct. (FAA-H-8083-25B Chap 7)
    DISCUSSION: An engine that continues to run after the ignition switch has been turned off probably has a broken magneto ground wire. The ignition switch is not able to ground the magneto to stop the generation of electrical impulses that provide electricity to the spark plug. Thus, momentarily turning off the ignition prior to shutdown is a recommended procedure to check for a faulty ground wire.
    Answer (A) is incorrect. Turning the ignition key to OFF should stop the engine. **Answer (C) is incorrect.** Turning off the ignition key is a recommended procedure prior to shutdown to check for a faulty ground wire.

36. A way to detect a broken magneto primary grounding lead is to

    A. idle the engine and momentarily turn the ignition off.

    B. add full power, while holding the brakes, and momentarily turn off the ignition.

    C. run on one magneto, lean the mixture, and look for a rise in manifold pressure.

Answer (A) is correct. (FAA-H-8083-25B Chap 7)
    DISCUSSION: An engine that continues to run after the ignition switch has been turned off probably has a broken magneto ground wire. The ignition switch is not able to ground the magneto to stop the generation of electrical impulses that provide electricity to the spark plug. Thus, momentarily turning off the ignition prior to shutdown is a recommended procedure to check for a faulty ground wire.
    Answer (B) is incorrect. It is not necessary to add full power when performing this check. **Answer (C) is incorrect.** This is a nonsense procedure.

37. A detuning of engine crankshaft counterweights is a source of overstress that may be caused by

    A. rapid opening and closing of the throttle.

    B. carburetor ice forming on the throttle valve.

    C. operating with an excessively rich fuel/air mixture.

Answer (A) is correct. (AC 20-103)
    DISCUSSION: A detuning of counterweights on balance weight-equipped crankshafts is a source of overstress for the crankshaft. The counterweights are designed to position themselves by the inertia forces generated during crankshaft rotation and to absorb and dampen crankshaft vibration effectively. If the counterweights are detuned (allowed to slam on mounts), the vibrations are not properly dampened and crankshaft failure can occur. Counterweight detuning can occur from rapid opening and closing of the throttle, excessive speed or power, and operating at high RPMs and low manifold pressure.
    Answer (B) is incorrect. Carburetor ice causes the engine to stop running when the carburetor is sufficiently clogged but does not affect the engine crankshaft counterweights. **Answer (C) is incorrect.** Operating with an excessively rich fuel/air mixture fouls the spark plugs but does not affect the crankshaft.

38. If the ground wire between the magneto and the ignition switch becomes disconnected, the engine

    A. will not operate on one magneto.

    B. cannot be started with the switch in the BOTH position.

    C. could accidentally start if the propeller is moved with fuel in the cylinder.

Answer (C) is correct. (FAA-H-8083-25B Chap 7)
    DISCUSSION: If the magneto switch ground wire is disconnected, the magneto is ON even though the ignition switch is in the OFF position. Thus, the engine could fire if the propeller is moved from outside the airplane.
    Answer (A) is incorrect. Disconnecting the ground wire causes both magnetos to remain on; i.e., they will operate even when the ignition switch is in the OFF position. The dual ignition system is designed so that, in case one magneto fails, the other magneto can operate alone. **Answer (B) is incorrect.** The engine can still be started; the magnetos cannot be turned OFF.

39. The reason a 4-cylinder reciprocating engine continues to run after the ignition switch is positioned to OFF may be a

    A. fouled spark plug.

    B. wire between the magneto and spark plug in contact with the engine casing.

    C. broken magneto ground wire.

Answer (C) is correct. (FAA-H-8083-25B Chap 7)
    DISCUSSION: A broken magneto ground wire will cut off grounding for the magneto, allowing it to continue sending electricity to the spark plugs for the engine to run.
    Answer (A) is incorrect. A fouled spark plug will cause the engine to run rough. However, the engine can still be shut off when the ignition switch is turned to the OFF position. **Answer (B) is incorrect.** A wire between the magneto and the spark plug in contact with the engine casing will cause the engine to run rough, but the engine can still be shut off when the ignition switch is turned to the OFF position.

40. The most probable reason an engine continues to run after the ignition switch has been turned off is

A. carbon deposits glowing on the spark plugs.

B. a magneto ground wire is in contact with the engine casing.

C. a broken magneto ground wire.

Answer (C) is correct. *(FAA-H-8083-25B Chap 7)*
DISCUSSION: An engine that continues to run after the ignition switch has been turned off probably has a broken magneto ground wire. The ignition switch is not able to ground the magneto to stop the generation of electrical impulses that provide electricity to the spark plug. Thus, momentarily turning off the ignition prior to shutdown is a recommended procedure to check for a faulty ground wire.
Answer (A) is incorrect. Glowing carbon deposits result in preignition, not in the continued running of the engine.
Answer (B) is incorrect. The magneto ground wire should be in contact with the engine casing to provide effective grounding.

2.9 Engine Cooling

41. An abnormally high engine oil temperature indication may be caused by

A. a defective bearing.

B. the oil level being too low.

C. operating with an excessively rich mixture.

Answer (B) is correct. *(FAA-H-8083-25B Chap 7)*
DISCUSSION: Operating with an excessively low oil level prevents the oil from cooling adequately; i.e., an inadequate supply of oil cannot to transfer engine heat to the engine's oil cooler (similar to a car engine's water radiator). Insufficient oil may also damage an engine from excessive friction within the cylinders and on other metal-to-metal contact parts.
Answer (A) is incorrect. A defective bearing results in local heat and wear, which will probably increase metal particles in the oil, but it should not affect oil temperature significantly.
Answer (C) is incorrect. A rich fuel/air mixture results in lower engine operating temperatures and thus does not increase engine oil temperature.

42. Your aircraft has an exhaust manifold type heating system. The exhaust manifold is periodically inspected to avoid

A. carbon monoxide poisoning.

B. overheating on the flight deck.

C. extremely cold temperatures in the cabin.

Answer (A) is correct. *(FAA-H-8083-25B Chap 7)*
DISCUSSION: An exhaust manifold type heating system is used as a heat source for the cabin and carburetor. Risks of operating with a defective exhaust heating system include carbon monoxide poisoning, a decrease in engine performance, and an increased potential for fire. Because of these risks, the exhaust manifold should be periodically inspected.
Answer (B) is incorrect. The risks of operating an aircraft with a defective exhaust heating system include carbon monoxide poisoning, a decrease in engine performance, and an increased potential for fire, not overheating on the flight deck. Because of these risks, the exhaust manifold should be periodically inspected. **Answer (C) is incorrect.** The risks of operating an aircraft with a defective exhaust heating system include carbon monoxide poisoning, a decrease in engine performance, and an increased potential for fire, not extremely cold temperatures in the cabin. Because of these risks, the exhaust manifold should be periodically inspected.

43. For internal cooling, reciprocating aircraft engines are especially dependent on

A. a properly functioning cowl flap augmenter.

B. the circulation of lubricating oil.

C. the proper freon/compressor output ratio.

Answer (B) is correct. *(FAA-H-8083-25B Chap 7)*
DISCUSSION: An engine accomplishes much of its cooling by the flow of oil through the lubrication system. The lubrication system aids in cooling by reducing friction as well as by absorbing heat from internal engine parts. Many airplane engines also use an oil cooler, a small radiator device that cools the oil before it is recirculated through the engine.
Answer (A) is incorrect. The cowl flaps aid in controlling engine temperatures but are not the primary cooling source.
Answer (C) is incorrect. The freon/compressor output ratio determines the effectiveness of cabin, not engine, cooling.

2.10 Airplane Propellers

44. Propeller efficiency is the

    A. ratio of thrust horsepower to brake horsepower.

    B. actual distance a propeller advances in one revolution.

    C. ratio of geometric pitch to effective pitch.

Answer (A) is correct. (FAA-H-8083-25B Chap 5)
    DISCUSSION: The efficiency of any machine is the ratio of useful power output to actual power output. Thus, propeller efficiency is the ratio of thrust horsepower (amount of thrust the propeller produces) to brake horsepower (amount of torque the engine imparts on the propeller). Propeller efficiency generally varies between 50% and 85%, depending upon propeller slippage.
    Answer (B) is incorrect. The distance a propeller travels in one revolution is effective pitch, not propeller efficiency. **Answer (C) is incorrect.** The ratio of geometric pitch to effective pitch is propeller slippage, which is related to, but is not, propeller efficiency.

45. A fixed-pitch propeller is designed for best efficiency only at a given combination of

    A. altitude and RPM.

    B. airspeed and RPM.

    C. airspeed and altitude.

Answer (B) is correct. (FAA-H-8083-25B Chap 5)
    DISCUSSION: A fixed-pitch propeller is most efficient only at a specified combination of airspeed and RPM. When designing a fixed-pitch propeller, the manufacturer usually selects a pitch that will operate most efficiently at the expected cruising speed of the airplane.
    Answer (A) is incorrect. Altitude does not necessarily affect the efficiency of a fixed-pitch propeller. **Answer (C) is incorrect.** Altitude does not necessarily affect the efficiency of a fixed-pitch propeller.

46. The reason for variations in geometric pitch (twisting) along a propeller blade is that it

    A. permits a relatively constant angle of incidence along its length when in cruising flight.

    B. prevents the portion of the blade near the hub from stalling during cruising flight.

    C. permits a relatively constant angle of attack along its length when in cruising flight.

Answer (C) is correct. (FAA-H-8083-25B Chap 5)
    DISCUSSION: Variations in the geometric pitch of the blades permit the propeller to operate with a relatively constant angle of attack along its length when in cruising flight. Propeller blades have variations to change the blade in proportion to the differences in speed of rotation along the length of the propeller and thereby keep thrust more nearly equalized along this length.
    Answer (A) is incorrect. Variations in geometric pitch permit a constant angle of attack, not incidence, along its length. **Answer (B) is incorrect.** If there were no variation in geometric pitch, the propeller tips, not the root, would be stalled during cruising flight.

47. Which statement best describes the operating principle of a constant-speed propeller?

    A. As throttle setting is changed by the pilot, the prop governor causes pitch angle of the propeller blades to remain unchanged.

    B. A high blade angle, or increased pitch, reduces the propeller drag and allows more engine power for takeoffs.

    C. The propeller control regulates the engine RPM and in turn the propeller RPM.

Answer (C) is correct. (FAA-H-8083-25B Chap 5)
    DISCUSSION: A constant-speed propeller, as the name implies, adjusts the pitch angle of the propeller blades so that the engine is maintained at a selected RPM. This variation permits use of a blade angle that will result in the most efficient performance for each particular flight condition.
    Answer (A) is incorrect. The prop governor causes pitch angle of the propeller blades to change, not remain unchanged, to maintain a specified RPM. **Answer (B) is incorrect.** A high blade angle increases, not reduces, propeller drag, and allows less, not more, engine power.

48. When referring to a constant speed propeller, the pitch setting is

    A. varied in flight by a governor maintaining constant RPM despite varying air loads.

    B. set to a specific blade angle by the pilot.

    C. unchanged; the manifold pressure changes, not the propeller pitch.

Answer (A) is correct. (FAA-H-8083-25B Chap 5)
    DISCUSSION: A constant-speed propeller uses a governor to regulate and maintain a constant RPM. The governor changes the propeller blade pitch angles to adjust for air loads and airspeed changes.
    Answer (B) is incorrect. A pilot selects a specific RPM, not a blade angle. The blade angle is constantly varied by the governor to maintain the specified RPM. **Answer (C) is incorrect.** Propeller pitch is always changing on aircraft fitted with a constant-speed propeller to maintain the RPM set by the pilot. The manifold pressure may be adjusted by the pilot with the throttle or may be affected by altitude change.

49. To develop maximum power and thrust, a constant-speed propeller should be set to a blade angle that will produce a

A. large angle of attack and low RPM.

B. small angle of attack and high RPM.

C. large angle of attack and high RPM.

Answer (B) is correct. (FAA-H-8083-25B Chap 5)
DISCUSSION: When using a constant-speed propeller, the maximum engine power for maximum thrust can be obtained by using a small angle of attack, which results in a high RPM.
Answer (A) is incorrect. A large angle of attack and low RPM result in less, not maximum, power and thrust. **Answer (C) is incorrect.** Maximum power is obtained by using a small, not large, propeller angle of attack.

50. In aircraft equipped with constant-speed propellers and normally-aspirated engines, which procedure should be used to avoid placing undue stress on the engine components? When power is being

A. decreased, reduce the RPM before reducing the manifold pressure.

B. increased, increase the RPM before increasing the manifold pressure.

C. increased or decreased, the RPM should be adjusted before the manifold pressure.

Answer (B) is correct. (FAA-H-8083-25B Chap 5)
DISCUSSION: To avoid placing undue stress on an engine equipped with a constant-speed propeller, you should avoid high manifold pressure settings with low RPM. Thus, when power is being increased, you should increase the RPM before increasing the manifold pressure.
Answer (A) is incorrect. When power is being decreased, you should reduce the manifold pressure before reducing the RPM, not vice versa. **Answer (C) is incorrect.** When power is being decreased, you should reduce the manifold pressure before reducing the RPM, not vice versa.

51. For takeoff, the blade angle of a controllable-pitch propeller should be set at a

A. small angle of attack and high RPM.

B. large angle of attack and low RPM.

C. large angle of attack and high RPM.

Answer (A) is correct. (FAA-H-8083-25B Chap 5)
DISCUSSION: For takeoff with a controllable-pitch (i.e., constant-speed) propeller, the blade angle should be set for maximum power, which is a small angle of attack and high RPM.
Answer (B) is incorrect. A large angle of attack and low RPM result in low, not maximum, power. **Answer (C) is incorrect.** Maximum takeoff power requires a small, not large, propeller angle of attack.

52. To establish a climb after takeoff in an aircraft equipped with a constant-speed propeller, the output of the engine is reduced to climb power by decreasing manifold pressure and

A. increasing RPM by decreasing propeller blade angle.

B. decreasing RPM by decreasing propeller blade angle.

C. decreasing RPM by increasing propeller blade angle.

Answer (C) is correct. (FAA-H-8083-3B Chap 3)
DISCUSSION: To establish climb power after takeoff using a constant-speed propeller, you should first decrease manifold pressure and then decrease RPM. When the propeller control is moved to reduce the RPM, the propeller blade angle increases.
Answer (A) is incorrect. To reduce power, you should decrease, not increase, RPM by increasing, not decreasing, propeller blade angle. **Answer (B) is incorrect.** To reduce power, you should decrease RPM by increasing, not decreasing, propeller blade angle.

53. A propeller rotating clockwise as seen from the rear, creates a spiraling slipstream. The spiraling slipstream, along with torque effect, tends to rotate the airplane to the

A. right around the vertical axis, and to the left around the longitudinal axis.

B. left around the vertical axis, and to the right around the longitudinal axis.

C. left around the vertical axis, and to the left around the longitudinal axis.

Answer (B) is correct. (FAA-H-8083-25B Chap 5)
DISCUSSION: As the airplane propeller rotates through the air in a clockwise direction as viewed from the rear, the propeller blade forces the air rearward in a spiraling, clockwise direction of flow around the fuselage. This clockwise flow also attempts to roll the airplane to the right about the longitudinal axis. A portion of this spiraling slipstream strikes the left side of the vertical stabilizer, forcing the airplane's tail to the right, causing the airplane to rotate to the left around the vertical axis. Note that the rolling moment caused by the corkscrew flow of the slipstream is to the right, while the rolling moment caused by torque reaction is to the left about the longitudinal axis. NOTE: This answer corresponds with FAA guidance.
Answer (A) is incorrect. The rotation is to the left, not right, around the vertical axis and to the right, not left, around the longitudinal axis. **Answer (C) is incorrect.** The rolling moment caused by torque reaction, not by the corkscrew flow of the slipstream, is to the left about the longitudinal axis. The corkscrew flow of the slipstream causes a rotation to the right.

54. What is pitch setting?

A. The propeller blade setting determined by the blade angle measured in a manner, and at a radius, specified in the propeller's instruction manual.

B. The propeller setting as manipulated by the pilot with the propeller control.

C. A specific blade angle set by the pilot.

Answer (A) is correct. (14 CFR 1.1)
   DISCUSSION: According to 14 CFR 1.1, pitch setting is the propeller blade setting as determined by the blade angle measured in a manner, and at a radius, specified by the instruction manual for the propeller.
   Answer (B) is incorrect. The propeller control sets the RPM, not the pitch. **Answer (C) is incorrect.** The pitch setting cannot be directly manipulated by the pilot. Moreover, the pitch changes automatically to maintain the RPM selected by the pilot with the propeller control.

55. A propeller's angle of incidence is the greatest

A. Near the center of the blade, so the same amount of lift is created along the blade's length.

B. At the tip, so the same amount of lift is created along the blade's length.

C. At the hub, which permits the same amount of lift to be created along the blade's length.

Answer (C) is correct. (FAA-H-8083-25B Chap 7)
   DISCUSSION: The propeller's geometric pitch varies along the propeller blade because the propeller tip goes through the air faster than the section of propeller near the hub. This pitch variation (i.e., twist) permits the same amount of lift to be created along the blade's length when in cruising flight.
   Answer (A) is incorrect. The angle of incidence is greater near the hub of a propeller, not at the center. **Answer (B) is incorrect.** The angle of incidence is at its minimum value near the tip. This is because the tip travels faster and can produce the same lift at a lower angle of attack.

56. The angle of attack of a cruise propeller is

A. Lower than that of a climb propeller and creates more drag.

B. Higher than that of a climb propeller and creates more drag.

C. Lower than that of a climb propeller and creates less drag.

Answer (B) is correct. (FAA-H-8083-25B Chap 7)
   DISCUSSION: The cruise propeller has a higher pitch and therefore more drag. More drag results in lower RPM and less horsepower capability, which decreases performance during takeoffs and climbs but increases efficiency during cruising flight.
   Answer (A) is incorrect. A cruise propeller has a higher, not lower, angle of attack than a climb propeller. Moreover, a lower angle of attack would create less, not more, drag. **Answer (C) is incorrect.** A cruise propeller has a higher, not lower, angle of attack than a climb propeller. Furthermore, the higher angle of attack results in more, not less, drag.

STUDY UNIT THREE

AIRPORTS, AIR TRAFFIC CONTROL, AND AIRSPACE

(16 pages of outline)

This study unit contains outlines of major concepts tested; sample test questions and answers regarding airports, air traffic control, and airspace; and an explanation of each answer. The table of contents above lists each subunit within this study unit, the number of questions pertaining to that particular subunit, and the pages on which the outlines and questions begin, respectively.

Recall that the **sole purpose** of this book is to expedite your passing of the FAA pilot knowledge test for the commercial pilot certificate. Accordingly, all extraneous material (i.e., topics or regulations not directly tested on the FAA pilot knowledge test) is omitted, even though much more knowledge is necessary to become a proficient commercial pilot. This additional material is presented in *Pilot Handbook* and *Commercial Pilot Flight Maneuvers and Practical Test Prep*, available from Gleim Publications, Inc. Order online at www.GleimAviation.com.

3.1 AIRSPACE

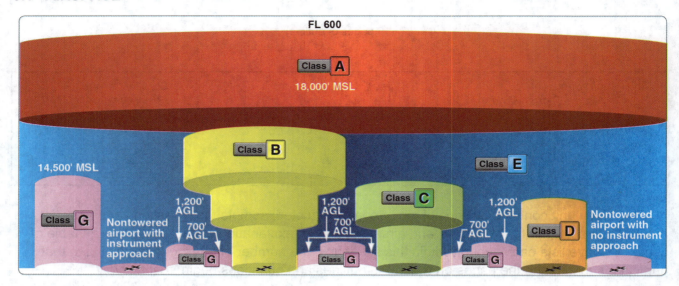

1. **Class A Airspace**

   a.   Class A airspace is generally the airspace from 18,000 ft. MSL up to and including FL 600, including the airspace overlying the waters within 12 NM of the coast of the 48 contiguous states and Alaska.

   b.   Operating Rules and Equipment Requirements

      1)   An IFR clearance to enter and operate within Class A airspace is mandatory. Pilots must be instrument rated to act as PIC of an airplane in Class A airspace.

      2)   Two-way radio communication, appropriate navigational capability, a Mode C transponder with altitude reporting capability, and ADS-B Out equipment that operates on the frequency of 1090 MHz are required.

   c.   Basic VFR Weather Minimums

      1)   There are no applicable VFR weather minimums for aircraft operating in Class A airspace. All aircraft in Class A airspace must be on an IFR flight plan.

2. **Class B Airspace**

   a.   Class B airspace is generally the airspace from the surface to 10,000 ft. MSL surrounding the nation's busiest airports.

      1)   The configuration of each Class B airspace area is individually tailored and consists of a surface area and two or more layers.

   b.   Operating Rules and Equipment Requirements

      1)   An ATC clearance is required prior to operating within Class B airspace.

      2)   Two-way radio communication capability is required.

      3)   An operating ATC (4096 code or Mode S) transponder and automatic altitude reporting equipment (Mode C) are required within and above the lateral limits of Class B airspace and within 30 NM of the primary airport.

      4)   ADS-B Out equipment that either operates on the frequency of 1090 MHz or operates using a universal access transceiver (UAT) on the frequency of 978 MHz is required.

      5)   The PIC must be at least a private pilot.

         a)   A student or recreational pilot may fly solo in Class B airspace only if (s)he has met the requirements listed in 14 CFR 61.95.

6) For IFR operations, an operable VOR is required in addition to a two-way radio and a Mode C transponder.

7) The maximum indicated speed authorized when operating an airplane in the airspace underlying Class B airspace is 200 kt.

a) If the minimum safe airspeed for any particular operation is greater than the maximum airspeed prescribed in 14 CFR Part 91, the airplane may be operated at that speed.

b) In such cases, pilots are expected to advise ATC of the airspeed that will be used.

c. Mode C Veil

1) The Mode C veil is the airspace within 30 NM of a Class B primary airport from the surface up to 10,000 ft. MSL.

2) Unless otherwise authorized by ATC, aircraft (with some exceptions) operating within this airspace must be equipped with a Mode C transponder and ADS-B Out equipment that either operates on the frequency of 1090 MHz or operates using a UAT on the frequency of 978 MHz if the airport is listed in Appendix D, Section 1, of 14 CFR Part 91.

3. **Class C Airspace**

a. Class C airspace surrounds airports that have an operational control tower, are serviced by a radar approach control, and have a certain number of IFR operations or passenger enplanements.

1) Class C airspace normally consists of

a) A surface area with a 5-NM radius that extends from the surface to 4,000 ft. AGL
b) A shelf area with a 10-NM radius that extends from 1,200 ft. to 4,000 ft. AGL

b. The general structure of Class C airspace is shown in the airspace diagram on the previous page.

1) The outer area, which is the airspace between 10 NM and 20 NM from the primary Class C airport, is not considered Class C airspace.

a) Radar services in this area are available but not mandatory.

c. Operating Rules and Equipment Requirements

1) Two-way radio communications must be established and maintained with ATC before entering and while operating in Class C airspace.

2) The minimum equipment needed to operate within and above Class C airspace includes

a) A 4096 code transponder with Mode C (altitude encoding) capability,
b) Two-way communication capability, and
c) ADS-B Out equipment that either operates on the frequency of 1090 MHz or operates using a UAT on the frequency of 978 MHz.

3) When departing from a satellite airport without an operating control tower, pilots must contact ATC as soon as practicable after takeoff.

4) Unless otherwise authorized or required by ATC, the maximum indicated airspeed permitted when at or below 2,500 ft. AGL within 4 NM of a Class C or Class D primary airport is 200 kt.

4. **Class D Airspace**

    a.   Class D airspace surrounds airports that have both an operating control tower and weather services available not associated with Class B or C airspace.

        1)   Airspace at an airport with a part-time control tower is classified as Class D airspace only when the control tower is operating.

            a)   When a part-time control tower at the primary airport in Class D airspace is not in operation, the airspace at the surface becomes either Class E or Class G with an overlying Class E area beginning at 700 ft. AGL.

        2)   Class D airspace normally extends from the surface up to and including 2,500 ft. AGL (charted on the sectional chart as ft. MSL).

            a)   The lateral dimensions of Class D airspace are based on local needs.

    b.   Operating Rules and Equipment Requirements

        1)   Two-way communications must be established and maintained with ATC prior to entering and while operating in Class D airspace.

            a)   When departing from a non-towered satellite airport within Class D airspace, pilots must establish and maintain two-way radio communication with the primary airport's control tower.

                i)   The primary airport is the airport for which the Class D is designated.
                ii)   A satellite airport is any other airport within the Class D airspace area.

        2)   Special VFR

            a)   The flight requirements to operate under special VFR in Class D airspace are the following:

                i)   Remain clear of clouds, and
                ii)   Have flight visibility of at least 1 SM if ground visibility is not reported.

            b)   Flight under special VFR clearance at night is permitted only if the pilot is instrument rated and the airplane is equipped for instrument flight.

            c)   To take off or land under special VFR requires ground visibility of at least 1 SM.

                i)   If ground visibility is not reported, flight visibility during takeoff or landing must be at least 1 SM.

5. **Class E Airspace**

   a. Class E airspace is any controlled airspace that is not Class A, B, C, or D airspace.

      1) Except for 18,000 ft. MSL (the floor of Class A airspace), Class E airspace has no defined vertical limit but extends upward from either the surface or a designated altitude to the overlying or adjacent controlled airspace.

      2) In most areas, the Class E airspace base is 1,200 ft. AGL. In many other areas, the Class E airspace base is either the surface or 700 ft. AGL.

         a) Some Class E airspace begins at an MSL altitude depicted on the charts instead of an AGL altitude.

   b. The Federal airways are Class E airspace areas. Unless otherwise specified, they extend upward from 1,200 ft. AGL to, but not including, 18,000 ft. MSL.

   c. There are no minimum pilot certification requirements to operate under VFR in Class E airspace.

      1) ADS-B Out equipment that either operates on the frequency of 1090 MHz or operates using a UAT on the frequency of 978 MHz is required in Class E airspace

         a) Above 10,000 ft. MSL over the 48 states and D.C., excluding airspace at and below 2,500 ft. AGL, and

         b) Over the Gulf of Mexico at and above 3,000 ft. MSL within 12 NM of the coastline of the United States.

6. **Class G Airspace**

   a. Class G airspace is airspace that has not been designated as Class A, B, C, D, or E airspace (i.e., it is uncontrolled airspace).

      1) Class G airspace exists beneath the floor of controlled airspace in areas where the controlled airspace does not extend down to the surface.

   b. No minimum pilot certification or airplane equipment is required in Class G airspace.

      1) While no specific equipment is generally required to operate under VFR in Class G airspace (beyond the general requirements established in 14 CFR 91.205), there are some airports with operational control towers within the surface area of Class G airspace.

         a) In these circumstances, the pilot must establish and maintain two-way radio communication with the control tower if planning to operate to, from, or through an area within 4 NM from the airport, from the surface up to and including 2,500 ft. AGL.

   c. When approaching to land at an airport without an operating control tower in Class G airspace, pilots should make all turns to the left, unless otherwise indicated.

7.   The basic VFR weather minimums are listed in the chart below.

Cloud Clearance and Visibility Required for VFR

Basic VFR Weather Minimums				
Airspace			**Flight Visibility**	**Distance from Clouds**
Class A			Not applicable	Not applicable
Class B			3 statute miles	Clear of clouds
Class C			3 statute miles	1,000 feet above 500 feet below 2,000 feet horizontal
Class D			3 statute miles	1,000 feet above 500 feet below 2,000 feet horizontal
Class E	At or above 10,000 feet MSL		5 statute miles	1,000 feet above 1,000 feet below 1 statute mile horizontal
	Less than 10,000 feet MSL		3 statute miles	1,000 feet above 500 feet below 2,000 feet horizontal
Class G	1,200 feet or less above the surface (regardless of MSL altitude).	Day, except as provided in section 91.155(b)	1 statute mile	Clear of clouds
		Night, except as provided in section 91.155(b)	3 statute miles	1,000 feet above 500 feet below 2,000 feet horizontal
	More than 1,200 feet above the surface but less than 10,000 feet MSL.	Day	1 statute mile	1,000 feet above 500 feet below 2,000 feet horizontal
		Night	3 statute miles	1,000 feet above 500 feet below 2,000 feet horizontal
	More than 1,200 feet above the surface and at or above 10,000 feet MSL.		5 statute miles	1,000 feet above 1,000 feet below 1 statute mile horizontal

3.2 AIRPORT SIGNS/MARKINGS

1. Airport signs are used to provide information to pilots.

2. Destination signs have black characters on a yellow background with an arrow showing the direction of the taxiing route to the destination listed. Outbound destinations commonly show directions to the takeoff runways.

    a. Examples of destination signs are shown in Figure 51 below.

        1) They are signs I, J, and K.
        2) Sign K designates the direction of taxiway Bravo.

3. Taxiway location signs identify the taxiway on which an aircraft is currently located.

    a. Location signs feature a black background with yellow lettering and do not have directional arrows.

4. Taxiway directional signs indicate the designation and direction of a taxiway.

    a. When turning from one taxiway to another, a taxiway directional sign indicates the designation and direction of a taxiway leading out of the intersection.

    b. Taxiway directional signs feature a yellow background with black lettering and directional arrows.

5. When approaching taxiway holding lines from the side with continuous lines, the pilot should not cross the lines without an ATC clearance.

    a. Taxiway holding lines are painted across the width of the taxiway and are yellow.

6. A runway holding position sign is a mandatory instruction sign with white characters on a red background. It is located at the holding position on taxiways that intersect a runway or on runways that intersect other runways.

7. Each of the letters below corresponds to the type of sign or marking in Figure 51.

    a. Runway Holding Position Sign

    b. Holding Position Sign for a Runway Approach Area

    c. Holding Position Sign for ILS Critical Area

    d. No Entry Sign

    e. Taxiway Location Sign

    f. Runway Location Sign

    g. Runway Boundary Sign

    h. ILS Critical Area Boundary Sign

    i. Direction Sign for Terminal

    j. Direction Sign for Common Taxiing Route to Runway

    k. Direction Sign for Runway Exit

    l. Runway Distance Remaining Sign

    m. Hold Short Position Sign

    n. Taxiway Ending Sign

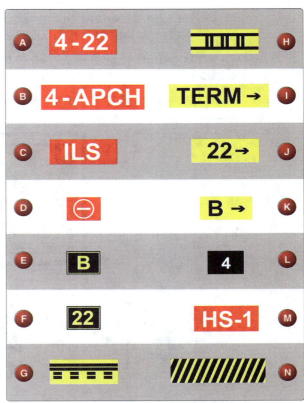

Figure 51. Airport Signs.

8. A no entry sign (to the right) is a type of mandatory instruction sign that has a red background with a white inscription.

    a. A no entry sign prohibits an aircraft from entering an area.

    b. Typically, this sign is located on a taxiway intended to be used in only one direction or at the intersection of vehicle roadways with runways, taxiways, or aprons where the roadway may be mistaken as a taxiway or other aircraft movement surface.

9. A runway boundary sign (below) is a type of location sign that has a yellow background with a black inscription and graphic depicting the pavement holding position marking.

    a. This sign, which faces the runway and is visible to you when you are exiting the runway, is located adjacent to the holding position marking on the pavement.

        1) The sign provides another visual cue for deciding when you are clear of the runway.

    b. You are clear of the runway when your airplane is on the solid-line side of the holding position marking.

10. An ILS critical area boundary sign (to the right) is a location sign that has a yellow background with a black inscription and graphic depicting the ILS pavement holding position marking.

    a. This sign is located adjacent to the ILS holding position marking on the pavement. You can see it when you are leaving or approaching the critical area.

        1) The sign provides another visual cue for deciding when you are clear of, or about to enter, the ILS critical area.

11. A taxiway ending marker sign is a type of information sign that consists of alternating yellow and black diagonal stripes [Figure 60 (Sign 1) below].

    a. This sign indicates that the taxiway does not continue beyond the sign.

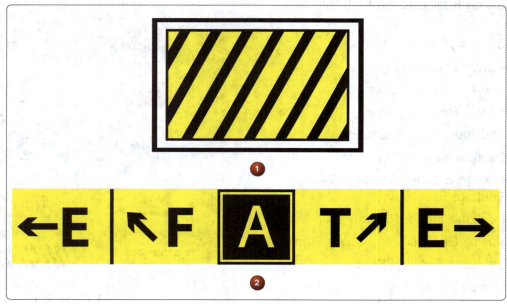

Figure 60. Two Signs.

12. Figure 59 below consists of a taxiway diagram and a direction sign array.

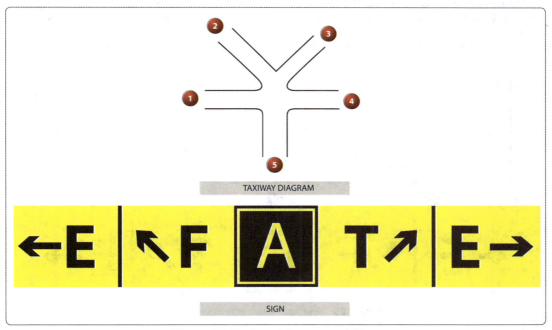

Figure 59. Taxiway Diagram and Sign.

a. The taxiway designations and their associated arrows on the sign are arranged clockwise starting from the first taxiway on the pilot's left.

b. Therefore, at number 5, you are on taxiway Alpha, and if you turn to taxi toward number 3, it would be taxiway Tango. Number 4 is Echo, 2 is Foxtrot, and 1 is also Echo.

13. Direction signs consist of black lettering on a yellow background.

a. These signs indicate the designation (name) and direction (orientation) of taxiways leading out of an intersection.

b. Figures 61 and 62 below are similar to the direction sign array in Figure 59 above. You may encounter pretest questions with these figures.

1) The difference between Figures 61 and 62 is that Figure 61 includes a location sign, which is the letter A. This signifies that you are on taxiway Alpha.

Figure 61. Sign.

Figure 62. Sign.

c.   Figure 63 below is very similar to Figure 59. You may encounter a question that asks which taxiway diagram is associated with the taxiway directional sign. In Figure 63, the taxiway diagram labeled 2 is the correct taxiway diagram for the taxiway direction sign.

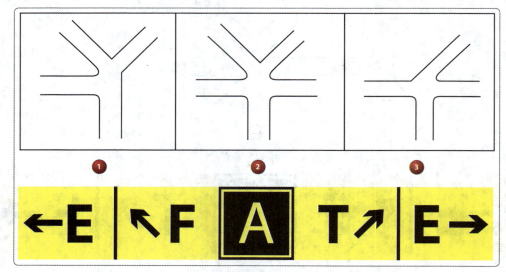

Figure 63. Sign and Intersection Diagram.

d.   Figure 57 below is similar to the previous taxiway diagram and directional signs. However, the center of the destination sign indicates a common route, straight ahead, for Runways 10 and 21. Also, if you were to use the taxiway to the left, you would encounter Runway 4. If you were to use the taxiway to the right, you would encounter Runway 22.

Figure 57. Sign.

e.   Figure 60 below has two signs: (1) a taxiway ending marker and (2) a taxiway directional sign. You may encounter a pretest question referencing this figure.

Figure 60. Two Signs.

14. Vehicle Roadway Markings (Figure 99 below).

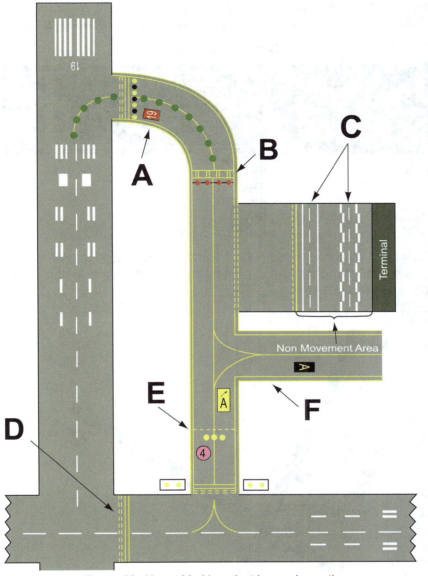

Figure 99. Airport Markings (not in supplement).

a. Vehicle roadway markings define pathways for vehicles to cross areas of the airport used by aircraft.

  1) Vehicle roadway markings exist in two forms, as indicated in Letter C above.

    a) The edge of vehicle roadway markings may be defined by a solid white line or white zipper markings.

  2) A dashed white line separates opposite-direction vehicle traffic inside the roadway.

15. Yellow Demarcation Bar.

a.   The yellow demarcation bar is a 3-foot-wide, painted yellow bar that separates a displaced threshold from a blast pad, stopway, or taxiway that precedes the runway.

Yellow Demarcation Bar

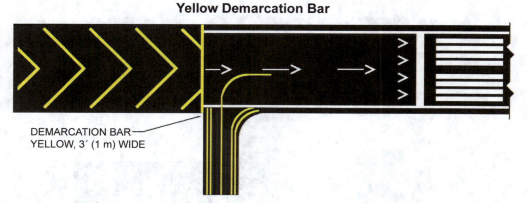

16. Figure 58 below is an airport diagram with a runway airport sign for Runway 16-34. You will be asked where the runway hold position sign might appear on the airport diagram. The answer would be at points 10 and 11.

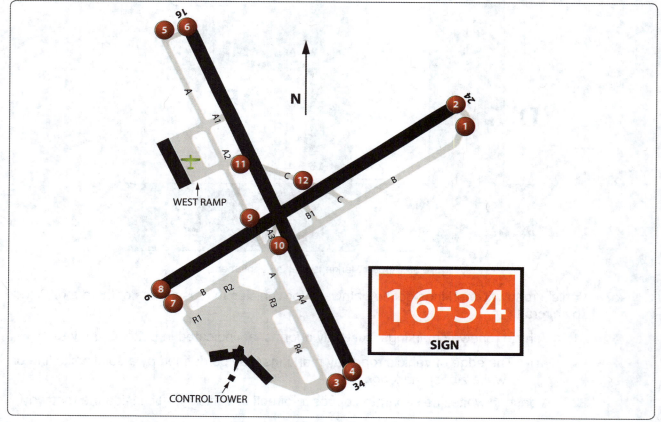

Figure 58. Airport Diagram and Sign.

17. Figures 56 and 64 below contain more runway indicator signs. In Figure 56, Sign 1 shows that you are approaching Runway 22, and Sign 2 indicates that you are holding short of Runway 4. Figure 64 indicates that you are at an intersection of Runway 26-8.

Figure 56. Two Signs.   **Figure 64.** Sign.

a. If you were holding short at an intersection and saw the sign pictured in Figure 64, it would tell you that taking off on Runway 8 would require a left turn onto the runway and a takeoff on Runway 26 would require a right turn onto the runway.

1) If you were holding short at an intersection, saw the sign pictured in Figure 64, and wanted to back taxi for a full length takeoff on Runway 8, you would turn to the right. Once you reach the threshold, you would turn 180 degrees to take off on Runway 8.

18. The runway exit sign defines the direction and designation of the exit taxiway from the runway.

a. The sign features a yellow background with a black letter and arrow that directs pilots to the appropriate exit point.

3.3 COLLISION AVOIDANCE

1. Navigation lights consist of a steady red light on the left wing, a steady green light on the right wing, and a steady white light on the tail. In night flight, when an airplane is heading away from you, you will observe a steady white light and a rotating red light.

2. Any aircraft that has no apparent relative motion is likely to be on a collision course.

3. In the vicinity of VORs, you should look carefully for other aircraft converging on the VOR from all directions.

4. ADS-B (Automatic Dependent Surveillance-Broadcast) is technology that allows air traffic controllers (and ADS-B equipped aircraft) to see traffic with more precision. Instead of relying on old radar technology, ADS-B uses highly accurate GPS signals. Because of this, ADS-B works where radar often will not.

a. This system

1) Works in remote areas such as mountainous terrain

2) Functions at low altitudes and even on the ground

3) Can be used to monitor traffic on the taxiways and runways

4) Allows air traffic controllers as well as aircraft with certain equipment to receive ADS-B traffic

5) Provides subscription-free weather information to all aircraft flying over the U.S.

b. ADS-B has been required since January 1, 2020. This system helps make our skies safer. For more information, visit www.garmin.com/us/intheair/ads-b.

3.4 WAKE TURBULENCE

1.   Wingtip vortices (wake turbulence) are created when airplanes develop lift.

2.   The greatest wingtip vortex strength occurs behind heavy, clean (flaps and gear up), and slow aircraft.

3.   When landing behind a large aircraft on the same runway, stay at or above the other aircraft's final approach flight path and land beyond that airplane's touchdown point.

   a.   When taking off after a large aircraft has just landed, become airborne past the large airplane's touchdown point.

4.   When taking off behind a jet, take off before the rotation point of the jet, and then climb above and stay upwind of the jet's flight path until you are able to turn clear of the wake.

5.   Wingtip vortex turbulence tends to sink into the flight path of airplanes operating below the airplane generating the turbulence.

   a.   Thus, you should fly above the flight path of a large jet rather than below.

6.   The primary hazard of wake turbulence is loss of control because of induced roll.

7.   In forward flight, helicopters produce a pair of high velocity trailing vortices similar to wing tip vortices of large fixed wing aircraft.

3.5 LAND AND HOLD SHORT OPERATIONS (LAHSO)

1.   Land and hold short operations (LAHSO) take place at some airports with an operating control tower in order to increase airport capacity and improve the flow of traffic.

   a.   LAHSO requires that you land and hold short of an intersecting runway, an intersecting taxiway, or some other designated point on a runway.

2.   Before accepting a clearance to land and hold short, you must determine that you can safely land and stop in the available landing distance (ALD).

   a.   Pilots should have readily available the published ALD and runway slope information for all LAHSO runway combinations at each airport of intended landing.

   b.   ATC will provide ALD data upon request.

3.   The pilot in command has the final authority to accept or decline any LAHSO clearance.

   a.   You are expected to decline a LAHSO clearance if you determine it will compromise safety.

   b.   Once a LAHSO is accepted, it must be adhered to unless an amended clearance is obtained or an emergency occurs. A LAHSO clearance does not preclude a rejected landing.

4.   You should receive a LAHSO clearance only when there is a minimum ceiling of 1,000 ft. and 3 SM visibility.

   a.   The intent of having "basic" VFR weather conditions is to allow pilots to maintain visual contact with other aircraft and ground vehicle operations.

3.6 SEGMENTED CIRCLES

1. The segmented circle system provides traffic pattern information at airports without operating control towers. It consists of the

    a. Segmented circle–located in a position affording maximum visibility to pilots in the air and on the ground. It provides a centralized point for the other elements of the system.

    b. Landing strip indicators–L-shaped symbols that look like legs sticking out of the segmented circle. They are always in pairs, with each pair representing one runway. For each pair, the Ls are directly opposite each other.

       1) For each opposing pair of Ls, the long leg of the L represents the runway direction.

    c. Traffic pattern indicators–indicators at right angles to the landing strip indicator.

       1) For each opposing pair of Ls, the short leg of the L shows the direction of turn from base to final and upwind to crosswind.

       2) In Figure 101 below, Runways 36 and 09 use left traffic, while Runways 18 and 27 use right.

    d. Wind direction indicator–a wind cone, wind sock, or wind tee installed near the runways to indicate wind direction.

       1) The large end of the wind cone/wind sock points into the wind, as does the large end (cross bar) of the wind tee.

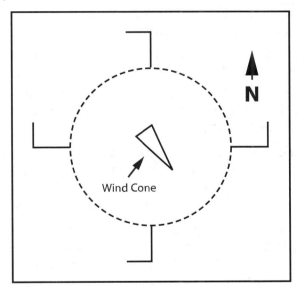

Figure 101. Wind Sock Airport
Landing Indicator (not in supplement).

3.7 TRANSPONDERS AND TRANSPONDER CODES

1.   There are three kinds of civilian transponders used in U.S. airspace:

   a.   Mode A

      1)   A Mode A transponder, when requested by the air traffic control radar beacon system (ATCRBS), transmits a four-digit squawk code to ATC.

   b.   Mode C (Automatic Altitude Reporting)

      1)   This type of transponder converts your airplane's altitude in 100-ft. increments to coded digital information, which is transmitted in the reply to the interrogating radar facility. A Mode C transponder provides this information in addition to transmitting the four-digit squawk code.

      2)   If your airplane is Mode C-equipped, you must set your transponder to reply Mode C (i.e., set function switch to ALT) unless ATC requests otherwise.

      3)   Mode C is required when flying

         a)   At or above 10,000 ft. MSL, except in that airspace below 2,500 ft. AGL
         b)   Within 30 NM of a Class B airspace primary airport
         c)   Within and above a Class C airspace area
         d)   Into, within, or across the U.S. ADIZ (Air Defense Identification Zone)

   c.   Mode S (Selective)

      1)   Mode S (Selective) transponders are designed to help air traffic control in busy areas and allow automatic collision avoidance.

         a)   Mode S transponders allow TCAS (Traffic Alert and Collision Avoidance System) and TIS (Traffic Information System) to function.

      2)   Mode S transponders broadcast information about the equipped aircraft to the Secondary Surveillance Radar (SSR) system, TCAS receivers on board aircraft, and to the ADS-B system.

         a)   This information includes the call sign of the aircraft and/or the transponder's permanent unit code (i.e., not the four-digit user-entered squawk code).

         b)   These transponders also receive ground-based radar information through a datalink and can display that information to pilots to aid in collision avoidance.

2.   The military has multiple kinds of transponders, and the military type that corresponds to civilian Mode A and civilian Mode C is referred to as military Mode 3. You may see FAA questions that refer to Mode A/3 or Mode C/3. The "3" is referring to military transponders, so just think "Mode A" or "Mode C."

3.   Code 1200 is the standard VFR transponder code.

4.   The ident feature should not be engaged unless instructed by ATC.

5.   Certain special codes should never be engaged (except in an emergency), as they may cause problems at ATC centers. These include the following:

   a.   Code 7500 – hijacking
   b.   Code 7600 – lost radio communication
   c.   Code 7700 – general emergency
   d.   Code 7777 – military interceptor

QUESTIONS AND ANSWER EXPLANATIONS: All of the commercial pilot knowledge test questions chosen by the FAA for release as well as additional questions selected by Gleim relating to the material in the previous outlines are provided on the following pages. These questions have been organized into the same subunits as the outlines. To the immediate right of each question are the correct answer and answer explanations. You should cover these answers and answer explanations while responding to the questions. Refer to the general discussion in the Introduction on how to take the FAA knowledge test.

Remember that the questions from the FAA knowledge test bank have been reordered by topic and organized into a meaningful sequence. Also, the first line of the answer explanation gives the citation of the authoritative source for the answer.

QUESTIONS

3.1 Airspace

1. Which is true regarding flight operations in Class A airspace?

A. Aircraft must be equipped with approved distance measuring equipment (DME).

B. Must conduct operations under instrument flight rules.

C. Aircraft must be equipped with an approved ATC transponder.

Answer (B) is correct. (14 CFR 91.135)
DISCUSSION: Each person operating an airplane in Class A airspace must conduct that operation under instrument flight rules (IFR).
Answer (A) is incorrect. If VOR navigational equipment is required, the airplane must be equipped with DME for operations at or above FL 240. Since Class A airspace begins at FL 180, DME is not required for all operations. **Answer (C) is incorrect.** In Class A airspace, all airplanes must be equipped with an operable transponder and altitude reporting equipment, not only an approved ATC transponder.

2. Which is true regarding pilot certification requirements for operations in Class B airspace?

A. The pilot in command must hold at least a private pilot certificate with an instrument rating.

B. The pilot in command must hold at least a private pilot certificate.

C. Solo student pilot operations are not authorized.

Answer (B) is correct. (14 CFR 91.131)
DISCUSSION: No person may take off or land at an airport within Class B airspace or operate an airplane within Class B airspace unless the pilot in command holds at least a private pilot certificate. However, a student pilot or a recreational pilot seeking private pilot certification may fly solo in Class B airspace if (s)he has met the requirements listed in 14 CFR 61.95.
Answer (A) is incorrect. There is no requirement for the pilot in command to be instrument rated if (s)he is operating under VFR in Class B airspace. **Answer (C) is incorrect.** Solo student pilot operations are authorized in Class B airspace, as long as the requirements of 14 CFR 61.95 have been met.

3. Which is true regarding flight operations in Class A airspace?

A. Aircraft must be equipped with approved distance measuring equipment (DME).

B. Aircraft must be equipped with an ATC transponder and altitude reporting equipment.

C. May conduct operations under visual flight rules.

Answer (B) is correct. (14 CFR 91.135)
DISCUSSION: All aircraft operating in Class A airspace must be equipped with an ATC transponder and altitude reporting capability, unless otherwise authorized by ATC.
Answer (A) is incorrect. If VOR navigational equipment is required, the airplane must be equipped with DME for operations at or above FL 240. Since Class A airspace begins at FL 180, DME is not required for all operations in Class A airspace. **Answer (C) is incorrect.** Flight operations in Class A airspace are conducted under IFR, not VFR.

4. Which is true regarding flight operations in Class B airspace?

A. Flight under VFR is not authorized unless the pilot in command is instrument rated.

B. The pilot must receive an ATC clearance before operating an aircraft in that area.

C. Solo student pilot operations are not authorized.

Answer (B) is correct. (14 CFR 91.131)
DISCUSSION: The pilot must receive an ATC clearance before operating an airplane in Class B airspace.
Answer (A) is incorrect. Flight under special VFR at night, not VFR operations in Class B airspace, requires the pilot in command to be instrument rated. **Answer (C) is incorrect.** Solo student pilot operations are authorized in Class B airspace, as long as the requirements of 14 CFR 61.95 have been met.

5. Which is true regarding flight operations in Class B airspace?

A. The aircraft must be equipped with an ATC transponder and altitude reporting equipment.

B. The pilot in command must hold at least a private pilot certificate with an instrument rating.

C. The pilot in command must hold at least a student pilot certificate.

Answer (A) is correct. (14 CFR 91.131)
DISCUSSION: To operate in Class B airspace, the airplane must be equipped with an operating ATC transponder and automatic altitude reporting equipment.
Answer (B) is incorrect. The pilot in command is not required to be instrument rated to operate in Class B airspace under VFR. **Answer (C) is incorrect.** To operate solo in Class B airspace, a student pilot must also have met the requirements of 14 CFR 61.95.

6. What is the maximum indicated airspeed authorized in the airspace underlying Class B airspace?

A. 156 knots.

B. 200 knots.

C. 230 knots.

Answer (B) is correct. (14 CFR 91.117)
DISCUSSION: No person may operate an aircraft in the airspace underlying a Class B airspace area designated for an airport at an indicated airspeed of more than 200 knots (230 MPH).
Answer (A) is incorrect. The figure 156 knots is not a maximum speed associated with any type of airspace. **Answer (C) is incorrect.** The figure 230 MPH, not 230 knots, is the maximum indicated airspeed allowed in the airspace underlying Class B airspace.

7. What transponder equipment is required for airplane operations within Class B airspace? A transponder

A. with 4096 code or Mode S, and Mode C capability.

B. with 4096 code capability is required except when operating at or below 1,000 feet AGL under the terms of a letter of agreement.

C. is required for airplane operations when visibility is less than 3 miles.

Answer (A) is correct. (14 CFR 91.215)
DISCUSSION: Unless otherwise authorized or directed by ATC, no person may operate an airplane within Class B airspace unless it is equipped with an operable transponder having either 4096 code capability or Mode S capability. Additionally, the airplane must be equipped with automatic pressure altitude reporting equipment having Mode C capability.
Answer (B) is incorrect. In Class B airspace, the transponder must have both 4096 code capability and Mode C capability, not only 4096 code capability. Additionally, any letter of agreement with the controlling ATC facility would be geographically specific; it would not make an exception simply for any operation below 1,000 ft. AGL. **Answer (C) is incorrect.** An operable transponder with 4096 code, or Mode S, capability and Mode C capability is required at all times within Class B airspace, not only at times when the visibility is less than 3 statute miles.

8. Unless otherwise authorized, which situation requires Automatic Dependent Surveillance-Broadcast (ADS-B)?

A. Landing at an airport with an operating control tower.

B. Overflying Class C airspace below 10,000 feet MSL.

C. Flying under the shelf of Class C airspace.

Answer (B) is correct. (FAA-H-8083-3B Chap 3)
DISCUSSION: ADS-B equipment meeting the requirements of 14 CFR 91.227 is required above the ceiling and within the lateral boundaries of a Class C airspace area designated for an airport upward to 10,000 ft. MSL.
Answer (A) is incorrect. ADS-B equipment is not a requirement for operations in Class D airspace, regardless of whether the control tower is operating. **Answer (C) is incorrect.** Flight under a Class C shelf does not directly require the aircraft to be equipped with ADS-B. However, if the Class C airport is located within a Mode C veil surrounding a Class B airport, then ADS-B equipment is required.

9. Unless otherwise authorized by ATC, which airspace requires the appropriate Automatic Dependent Surveillance-Broadcast (ADS-B) Out equipment installed?

A. Within Class E airspace below the upper shelf of Class C Airspace.

B. Above the ceiling and within the lateral boundaries of Class D airspace up to 10,000 feet MSL.

C. Within Class G airspace 25 nautical miles from a Class B airport.

Answer (C) is correct. (FAA-H-8083-3B Chap 3)
DISCUSSION: Though ADS-B Out equipment is not a requirement for operation within Class G airspace, it is required by all aircraft operating in any airspace within the 30-NM Mode C veil that shrouds each Class B airport from the surface up to 10,000 ft. MSL.
Answer (A) is incorrect. ADS-B Out equipment is not a requirement for operations beneath the upper shelf of Class C airspace, though it is required while operating above the upper shelf of Class C airspace up to 10,000 ft. MSL. **Answer (B) is incorrect.** ADS-B Out equipment is not a requirement for operation within Class D airspace or above the Class D ceiling.

10. Unless otherwise authorized or required by ATC, the maximum indicated airspeed permitted when at or below 2,500 feet AGL within 4 NM of the primary airport within Class C or D airspace is

A. 180 knots.

B. 200 knots.

C. 230 knots.

Answer (B) is correct. (14 CFR 91.117)
DISCUSSION: Unless otherwise authorized or required by ATC, the maximum airspeed permitted when at or below 2,500 feet AGL within 4 NM of the primary airport of a Class C or Class D airspace is 200 knots (230 MPH).
Answer (A) is incorrect. The figure 180 knots is not a maximum indicated airspeed associated with any air space classification and/or altitude. **Answer (C) is incorrect.** The figure 230 MPH, not 230 knots, is the maximum indicated airspeed permitted when at or below 2,500 feet AGL within 4 NM of the primary airport in Class C or Class D airspace.

11. The radius of the uncharted Outer Area of Class C airspace is normally

A. 20 NM.

B. 30 NM.

C. 40 NM.

Answer (A) is correct. (AIM Para 3-2-4)
DISCUSSION: Class C airspace areas have a procedural outer area that normally consists of a 20-NM radius from the primary airport in the Class C airspace. This area is not charted and generally does not require action from the pilot.
Answer (B) is incorrect. A 30-NM uncharted space does not exist around Class C airspace; however, a 30-NM Mode C veil surrounds Class B airspace. **Answer (C) is incorrect.** A 40-NM outer area does not exist for any form of airspace.

12. If the minimum safe speed for any particular operation is greater than the maximum speed prescribed in 14 CFR Part 91, the

A. operator must have a Memorandum of Agreement (MOA) with the controlling agency.

B. aircraft may be operated at that speed.

C. operator must have a Letter of Agreement with ATC.

Answer (B) is correct. (14 CFR 91.117)
DISCUSSION: If the minimum safe airspeed for any particular operation is greater than the maximum airspeed prescribed in Part 91, the aircraft may be operated at that minimum airspeed. In such cases, the pilot is expected to advise ATC of the airspeed that will be used.
Answer (A) is incorrect. If the minimum safe airspeed for any particular operation is greater than the maximum airspeed prescribed in Part 91, the aircraft may be operated at that airspeed. The pilot is expected to advise ATC of the airspeed to be used. A memorandum of agreement is not required. **Answer (C) is incorrect.** If the minimum safe airspeed for any particular operation is greater than the maximum airspeed prescribed in Part 91, the aircraft may be operated at that minimum airspeed. The pilot is expected to advise ATC of the airspeed to be used. A letter of agreement is not required.

13. At some airports located in Class D airspace where ground visibility is not reported, takeoffs and landings under special VFR are

A. not authorized.

B. authorized by ATC if the flight visibility is at least 1 SM.

C. authorized only if the ground visibility is observed to be at least 3 SM.

Answer (B) is correct. (14 CFR 91.157)
DISCUSSION: No person may take off or land an aircraft (other than a helicopter) at any airport in Class D airspace under special VFR unless ground visibility at that airport is at least 1 SM or, if ground visibility is not reported at that airport, unless flight visibility during landing or takeoff is at least 1 SM.
Answer (A) is incorrect. Special VFR is still authorized if flight visibility is at least 1 SM. **Answer (C) is incorrect.** The visibility requirement for special VFR is 1 SM, not 3 SM.

14. Which is true regarding flight operations to or from a satellite airport, without an operating control tower, within the Class C airspace area?

A. Prior to entering that airspace, a pilot must establish and maintain communication with the ATC serving facility.

B. Aircraft must be equipped with an ATC transponder.

C. Prior to takeoff, a pilot must establish communication with the ATC controlling facility.

Answer (A) is correct. (14 CFR 91.130)
DISCUSSION: Prior to entering Class C airspace, a pilot must establish and maintain two-way radio communications with the ATC facility providing air traffic services.
Answer (B) is incorrect. To operate in Class C airspace, an aircraft must be equipped with an ATC transponder and altitude reporting equipment (Mode C transponder), not just a transponder. **Answer (C) is incorrect.** When departing from a satellite airport without an operating control tower, you must establish communication with the ATC controlling facility as soon as practicable after, not prior to, takeoff.

15. Which is true regarding flight operations to or from a satellite airport, without an operating control tower, within the Class C airspace area?

   A. Prior to takeoff, a pilot must establish communication with the ATC controlling facility.

   B. Aircraft must be equipped with an ATC transponder and altitude reporting equipment.

   C. Prior to landing, a pilot must establish and maintain communication with an ATC facility.

Answer (B) is correct. (14 CFR 91.130)
   DISCUSSION: No person may operate an airplane within Class C airspace unless the airplane is equipped with an ATC transponder and altitude reporting equipment (Mode C transponder).
   Answer (A) is incorrect. When departing a satellite airport without an operating control tower, you must establish communication with the ATC controlling facility as soon as practicable after, not prior to, takeoff. **Answer (C) is incorrect.** Prior to entering Class C airspace, not prior to landing at a satellite airport without an operating control tower, you must establish communication with the controlling ATC facility.

16. When operating an airplane for the purpose of takeoff or landing within Class D airspace under special VFR, what minimum distance from clouds and what visibility are required?

   A. Remain clear of clouds, and the ground visibility must be at least 1 SM.

   B. 500 feet beneath clouds, and the ground visibility must be at least 1 SM.

   C. Remain clear of clouds, and the flight visibility must be at least 1 NM.

Answer (A) is correct. (14 CFR 91.157)
   DISCUSSION: Under special VFR weather minimums, you may take off or land an airplane within Class D airspace if you remain clear of clouds and if the ground visibility is at least 1 SM.
   Answer (B) is incorrect. You must only remain clear of clouds, not 500 feet below the clouds, when operating an airplane under special VFR in Class D airspace. **Answer (C) is incorrect.** If ground visibility is not reported, the flight visibility must be at least 1 SM, not 1 NM.

17. When approaching to land at an airport with an ATC facility, in Class D airspace, the pilot must establish communications prior to

   A. 10 NM, up to and including 3,000 feet AGL.

   B. 30 SM, and be transponder equipped.

   C. 4 NM, up to and including 2,500 feet AGL.

Answer (C) is correct. (14 CFR 91.129)
   DISCUSSION: A pilot must establish communications with ATC prior to entering Class D airspace. Class D airspace extends from the surface to 2,500 feet AGL, and the lateral dimensions are set by local needs. NOTE: When approaching to land at an airport with an ATC facility in Class E or Class G airspace, the pilot must establish communications prior to 4 NM, up to and including 2,500 feet AGL.
   Answer (A) is incorrect. A pilot must establish communications with ATC prior to entering Class D airspace, not prior to 10 NM, up to and including 3,000 feet AGL. **Answer (B) is incorrect.** A pilot must establish communications with ATC prior to entering Class D airspace, not prior to 30 SM, and the airplane must be transponder equipped.

18. To operate an airplane under SPECIAL VFR (SVFR) within Class D airspace at night, which is required?

   A. The pilot must hold an instrument rating, but the airplane need not be equipped for instrument flight, as long as the weather will remain at or above SVFR minimums.

   B. The Class D airspace must be specifically designated as a night SVFR area.

   C. The pilot must hold an instrument rating, and the airplane must be equipped for instrument flight.

Answer (C) is correct. (14 CFR 91.157)
   DISCUSSION: No person may operate an airplane in Class D airspace under special VFR at night unless that person is instrument rated and the airplane is equipped for instrument flight.
   Answer (A) is incorrect. The airplane must also be equipped for instrument flight to operate under SVFR at night in Class D airspace. **Answer (B) is incorrect.** There is no such designation as a "night special VFR area."

19. The upper limits of Class D airspace are depicted

   A. on the sectional chart as feet MSL.

   B. in the Chart Supplements U.S. in feet MSL and feet AGL.

   C. on the sectional chart as feet AGL.

Answer (A) is correct. (AIM Para 3-2-5)
   DISCUSSION: The upper limits of Class D airspace are depicted as feet MSL on the sectional chart.
   Answer (B) is incorrect. The upper limits of Class D airspace are not listed in the Chart Supplement. **Answer (C) is incorrect.** The upper limits of Class D airspace are depicted as feet MSL, not AGL, on the sectional chart.

20. Excluding Hawaii, the vertical limits of the Federal Low Altitude airways extend from

A. 700 feet AGL up to, but not including, 14,500 feet MSL.

B. 1,200 feet AGL up to, but not including, 18,000 feet MSL.

C. 1,200 feet AGL up to, but not including, 14,500 feet MSL.

Answer (B) is correct. (AIM Para 3-2-6)
 DISCUSSION: Federal airways are Class E airspace, which extends upward from 1,200 feet AGL to, but not including, 18,000 feet MSL.
 Answer (A) is incorrect. The amount of 700 feet AGL is the floor of Class E airspace when designated in conjunction with an airport that has an IAP, not in conjunction with a Federal airway. Also, Class E airspace extends up to, but does not include, 18,000 feet MSL, not 14,500 feet MSL. **Answer (C) is incorrect.** Class E airspace that is designated as a Federal airway extends from 1,200 feet AGL up to, but not including, 18,000 feet MSL, not 14,500 feet MSL.

21. When operating an aircraft in the vicinity of an airport with an operating control tower, in Class E airspace, a pilot must establish communications prior to

A. 8 NM, and up to and including 3,000 feet AGL.

B. 5 NM, and up to and including 3,000 feet AGL.

C. 4 NM, and up to and including 2,500 feet AGL.

Answer (C) is correct. (14 CFR 91.127)
 DISCUSSION: When operating an airplane to, from, through, or on an airport with an operating control tower in Class E airspace, a pilot must establish communications prior to 4 NM from the airport, up to and including 2,500 feet AGL.
 Answer (A) is incorrect. When operating an airplane in the vicinity of an airport with an operating control tower in Class E airspace, a pilot must establish communications prior to 4 NM, not 8 NM, from the airport, and up to and including 2,500 feet AGL, not 3,000 feet AGL. **Answer (B) is incorrect.** When operating an airplane in the vicinity of an airport with an operating control tower in Class E airspace, a pilot must establish communications prior to 4 NM, not 5 NM, from the airport, and up to and including 2,500 feet AGL, not 3,000 feet AGL.

22. What designated airspace associated with an airport becomes inactive when the control tower at that airport is not in operation?

A. Class D, which then becomes Class C.

B. Class D, which then becomes Class E.

C. Class B.

Answer (B) is correct. (AIM Para 3-2-5)
 DISCUSSION: Class D airspace is located at airports that have an operating control tower which is not associated with Class B or Class C airspace. Airspace at an airport with a part-time control tower is classified as Class D airspace when the control tower is in operation and as Class E airspace when the control tower is not in operation.
 During the hours the tower is not in operation, the Class E surface area rules or a combination of Class E rules to 700 feet AGL and Class G rules to the surface will become applicable. Check the Chart Supplement for specific information about a given airspace area.
 Answer (A) is incorrect. When a part-time control tower is not in operation, the Class D airspace becomes Class E, not Class C, airspace. **Answer (C) is incorrect.** The primary airport of Class B airspace will have a control tower that operates full-time, not part-time.

23. When approaching to land at an airport without an operating control tower, in Class G airspace, the pilot should

A. make all turns to the left, unless otherwise indicated.

B. fly a left-hand traffic pattern at 800 feet AGL.

C. enter and fly a traffic pattern at 800 feet AGL.

Answer (A) is correct. (14 CFR 91.126)
 DISCUSSION: When approaching to land at an airport without an operating control tower in Class G airspace, the pilot of an airplane must make all turns to the left, unless otherwise indicated.
 Answer (B) is incorrect. When approaching to land at an airport without an operating control tower in Class G airspace, the pilot should fly a left-hand traffic pattern, unless otherwise indicated by traffic pattern indicators around the segment circle. Additionally, the recommended pattern altitude is 1,000 feet AGL, unless otherwise published. **Answer (C) is incorrect.** When approaching to land at an airport without an operating control tower in Class G airspace, the pilot should make all turns to the left (unless otherwise indicated), not fly any traffic pattern direction. Additionally, the recommended pattern altitude is 1,000 feet AGL, unless otherwise published.

24. You would like to enter Class B airspace and contact the approach controller. The controller responds to your initial radio call with "N125HF standby." May you enter the Class B airspace?

    A. You must remain outside Class B airspace until controller gives you a specific clearance.

    B. You may continue into the Class B airspace and wait for further instructions.

    C. You may continue into the Class B airspace without a specific clearance, if the aircraft is ADS-B equipped.

Answer (A) is correct. (14 CFR 91.131, AIM Para 3-2-3)
    DISCUSSION: In order to operate an aircraft within Class B airspace, a pilot must receive an ATC clearance from the ATC facility having jurisdiction for that area before entering the Class B airspace.
    Answer (B) is incorrect. An ATC clearance is required prior to entering Class B airspace. **Answer (C) is incorrect.** An ATC clearance is required prior to entering Class B airspace.

25. What is the minimum flight visibility and proximity to cloud requirements for VFR flight, at 6,500 feet MSL, in Class C, D, and E airspace?

    A. 1 mile visibility; clear of clouds.

    B. 3 miles visibility; 1,000 feet above and 500 feet below.

    C. 5 miles visibility; 1,000 feet above and 1,000 feet below.

Answer (B) is correct. (14 CFR 91.155)
    DISCUSSION: At 6,500 ft. MSL in Class C, D, or E airspace, the basic VFR flight visibility requirement is 3 SM. The distance from clouds requirement is 500 ft. below, 1,000 ft. above, and 2,000 ft. horizontal.
    Answer (A) is incorrect. One SM visibility and clear of clouds is the basic VFR weather minimums when at or below 1,200 ft. AGL (regardless of MSL altitude) in Class G airspace during the day. **Answer (C) is incorrect.** Five SM visibility and a distance from clouds of 1,000 ft. above or below is the basic VFR weather minimums in Class E airspace at or above, not below, 10,000 ft. MSL.

26. The minimum flight visibility for VFR flight increases to 5 statute miles beginning at an altitude of

    A. 14,500 feet MSL.

    B. 10,000 feet MSL if above 1,200 feet AGL.

    C. 10,000 feet MSL regardless of height above ground.

Answer (B) is correct. (14 CFR 91.155)
    DISCUSSION: The minimum flight visibility for VFR flight increases to 5 SM beginning at an altitude of 10,000 ft. MSL if above 1,200 ft. AGL in Class G airspace. In Class E airspace, the minimum flight visibility for VFR flight increases to 5 SM beginning at an altitude of 10,000 ft. MSL regardless of height above ground. This is the best answer because it includes both Class E and Class G airspace.
    Answer (A) is incorrect. This is not an altitude associated with basic VFR minimums. **Answer (C) is incorrect.** While the minimum flight visibility for VFR flight increases to 5 SM at an altitude of 10,000 ft. MSL regardless of the height above ground for Class E airspace, it does not include that in Class G airspace. The minimum flight visibility increases to 5 SM when at 10,000 ft. MSL and above 1,200 ft. AGL.

27. Your VFR flight will be conducted above 10,000 ft. MSL in Class E airspace. What is the minimum flight visibility?

    A. 3 SM.

    B. 5 SM.

    C. 1 SM.

Answer (B) is correct. (14 CFR 91.155)
    DISCUSSION: At or above 10,000 ft. MSL in Class E airspace requires at least 5 mi. of flight visibility.
    Answer (A) is incorrect. The visibility requirement when operating at less than 10,000 ft. MSL in Class E airspace is 3 SM. Operating above 10,000 ft. MSL in Class E airspace requires at least 5 mi. of flight visibility. **Answer (C) is incorrect.** The lowest allowable flight visibility in Class E airspace is 3 mi.; however, above 10,000 ft. MSL, the minimum visibility requirement is increased to 5 SM.

28. You have received a VFR clearance to enter the San Francisco Class B airspace at 8,500 ft. What are the VFR cloud clearance and visibility requirements in the Class B airspace?

    A. 3 SM visibility and clear of clouds.

    B. 3 SM visibility; 500 ft. below, 1,000 ft. above, and 2,000 ft. horizontally from clouds.

    C. 5 SM visibility; 1,000 ft. below, 1,000 ft. above, and 1,000 ft. horizontally from clouds.

Answer (A) is correct. (14 CFR 91.155)
    DISCUSSION: In Class B airspace, the minimum in-flight visibility and cloud clearance requirements for VFR flight are 3 SM visibility and clear of clouds.
    Answer (B) is incorrect. In Class C, Class D, or Class E airspace (below 10,000 ft. MSL), not Class B airspace, the cloud clearance requirements are 500 ft. below, 1,000 ft. above, and 2,000 ft. horizontal. **Answer (C) is incorrect.** The VFR weather minimums in Class E airspace at or above 10,000 ft. MSL, not Class B airspace, are 5 SM visibility; 1,000 ft. below, 1,000 ft. above, and 1,000 ft. horizontally from clouds.

3.2 Airport Signs/Markings

29. The runway holding position sign is located on

A. runways that intersect other runways.

B. taxiways protected from an aircraft approaching a runway.

C. runways that intersect other taxiways.

***Answer (A) is correct.** (AIM Para 2-3-5)*
   DISCUSSION: The runway holding position sign is used to delineate the holding point on a taxiway that intersects a runway or on a runway that intersects another runway.
   Answer (B) is incorrect. Runway holding position signs do not protect taxiways from aircraft approaching the runway.
Answer (C) is incorrect. Runway holding position signs are placed on a runway to delineate intersecting runways, not taxiways.

30. (Refer to Figure 99 below.) Which marking indicates a vehicle lane?

A. A.

B. C.

C. E.

***Answer (B) is correct.** (AIM Para 2-3-6)*
   DISCUSSION: Vehicle roadway markings define pathways for vehicles to cross areas of the airport used by aircraft and exist in two forms. Vehicle roadway markings may be defined by either a solid while line or white zipper markings. A dashed white line separates opposite direction vehicle traffic inside the roadway.
   Answer (A) is incorrect. The marking on the pavement defines a holding position sign at the beginning of the takeoff runway. **Answer (C) is incorrect.** The pavement marking delineates the movement and nonmovement surface areas.

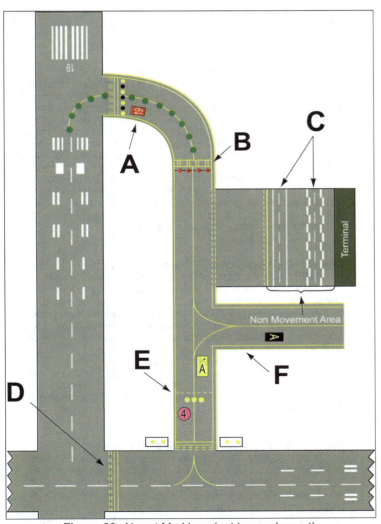

Figure 99. Airport Markings (not in supplement).

31. (Refer to Figure 51 on page 95.) The ILS Critical Area Boundary Sign indicates

A. you are about to enter, or you are clear of, the ILS critical area.

B. an area you are prohibited from entering.

C. an area in which aircraft over 30 feet tall may conflict with aircraft on the ILS approach.

Answer (A) is correct. (AIM Para 2-3-8)
DISCUSSION: This sign (symbol H) is located adjacent to the ILS holding position marking on the pavement. The sign is intended to provide you with a visual reference when entering the critical area while taxiing to a runway and when exiting the area while taxiing away from a runway.
Answer (B) is incorrect. You are not prohibited from entering the ILS critical area. However, you must hold short of the critical area when the ILS approach is in use or when so instructed by ATC. **Answer (C) is incorrect.** Aircraft on the ground, in the ILS critical area, pose no collision risk to aircraft on the ILS approach.

32. (Refer to Figure 51 on page 95.) The pilot generally calls ground control after landing when the aircraft is completely clear of the runway. This is when the aircraft

A. passes symbol D.

B. is on the dashed-line side of symbol G.

C. is past the solid-line side of symbol G.

Answer (C) is correct. (AIM Para 2-3-9)
DISCUSSION: Symbol G is a runway boundary sign that has a yellow background with a black inscription and graphic depicting the pavement holding position marking. This sign, which faces the runway and is visible to the pilot exiting the runway, is located adjacent to the holding position marking on the pavement. The sign is intended to provide you with another visual cue to use as a guide to determine when you are clear of the runway. Thus, you are clear of the runway when your entire airplane is on the solid-line side of the holding marking.
Answer (A) is incorrect. If you pass symbol D, you will enter an area prohibited to aircraft; it does not mean that you are clear of the runway. **Answer (B) is incorrect.** You are considered still on, not clear of, the runway if you are on the dashed-line side of symbol G.

33. (Refer to Figure 51 on page 95.) While clearing an active runway you are most likely clear of the ILS critical area when you pass which symbol?

A. D.

B. G.

C. H.

Answer (C) is correct. (AIM Para 2-3-9)
DISCUSSION: Symbol H is an ILS critical area boundary sign, which has a yellow background with a black inscription and graphic depicting the ILS pavement holding position marking. The sign is located adjacent to the ILS holding position marking on the pavement and can be seen by pilots leaving the critical area. The sign is intended to provide you with another visual cue to use as a guide in deciding when you are clear of the ILS critical area.
Answer (A) is incorrect. Symbol D is a sign prohibiting aircraft entry into an area, not a sign that you have cleared the ILS critical area. **Answer (B) is incorrect.** While clearing the active runway, you are most likely clear of the runway, not the ILS critical area, when you pass symbol G.

34. (Refer to Figure 51 on page 95.) Symbol D would most likely be found

A. upon exiting all runways prior to calling ground control.

B. at an intersection where a roadway may be mistaken as a taxiway.

C. near the approach end of ILS runways.

Answer (B) is correct. (AIM Para 2-3-8)
DISCUSSION: Symbol D (red background with white inscription) is a mandatory instruction sign that prohibits an aircraft from entering an area. Typically, this sign is located on a taxiway intended to be used in only one direction or at an intersection of vehicle roadways with runways, taxiways, or aprons where the roadway may be mistaken as a taxiway or other aircraft movement surface.
Answer (A) is incorrect. Symbol G, not Symbol D, would most likely be found upon exiting all runways prior to calling ground control. **Answer (C) is incorrect.** Symbol H, not symbol D, would most likely be found near the approach end of ILS runways.

35. (Refer to Figure 51 on page 95.) (Refer to E.) This sign is a visual clue that

A. confirms the aircraft's location to be on taxiway "B."

B. warns the pilot of approaching taxiway "B."

C. indicates "B" holding area is ahead.

Answer (A) is correct. (AIM Para 2-3-9)
DISCUSSION: The taxiway location sign consists of a yellow letter on a black background with a yellow border. This sign confirms the pilot is on taxiway "B."
Answer (B) is incorrect. A direction sign with a yellow background, a black letter, and an arrow pointing to taxiway "B" would be required to warn a pilot that (s)he is approaching taxiway "B." **Answer (C) is incorrect.** A taxiway location sign defines a position on a taxiway, not a holding area.

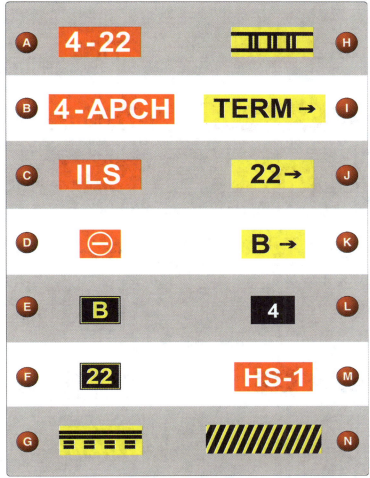

Figure 51. Airport Signs.

36. (Refer to Figure 51 above.) (Refer to F.) This sign confirms your position on

A. runway 22.

B. routing to runway 22.

C. taxiway 22.

Answer (A) is correct. (AIM Para 2-3-9)
  DISCUSSION: A runway location sign has a black background with a yellow inscription and a yellow border. The inscription on the sign informs the pilot (s)he is located on Runway 22.
  Answer (B) is incorrect. A direction sign with a yellow background and black inscription would be required to inform a pilot (s)he is routing to Runway 22. **Answer (C) is incorrect.** Only runways are numbered. Taxiways are always identified by a letter.

37. (Refer to Figure 51 above.) From the flight deck, symbol G confirms the aircraft to be

A. on a taxiway, about to enter the runway zone.

B. on a runway, about to clear.

C. near an instrument approach clearance zone.

Answer (B) is correct. (AIM Chap 4)
  DISCUSSION: When the runway holding position line is viewed from the runway side, the pilot is presented with two dashed bars. The PIC must ensure the entire aircraft has cleared the runway holding position line prior to coming to a stop.
  Answer (A) is incorrect. A pilot entering a runway from a taxiway is presented with the two solid bars, not dashed lines, on the runway holding position marking. **Answer (C) is incorrect.** The marking depicted is a runway holding position marking and is not related to any form of clearance zone.

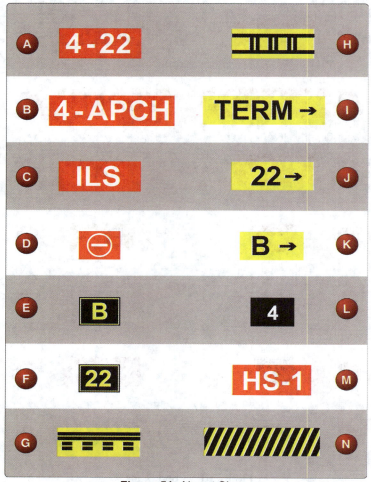

Figure 51. Airport Signs.

38. (Refer to Figure 51 above.) When taxiing up to an active runway, you are likely to be clear of the ILS critical area when short of which symbol?

A. H.

B. D.

C. G.

Answer (A) is correct. (AIM Para 2-3-9)
   DISCUSSION: Symbol H is an ILS critical area boundary sign, which has a yellow background with a black inscription depicting the ILS pavement holding position marking. The sign is located adjacent to the ILS holding position marking on the pavement and can be seen by pilots approaching the ILS critical area. Thus, you will be clear of the ILS critical area, when taxiing to an active runway, when short of the ILS critical area boundary sign.
   Answer (B) is incorrect. Symbol D prohibits an aircraft from entering an area and is not used to mark the ILS critical area. **Answer (C) is incorrect.** Symbol G is a runway boundary sign that faces toward the runway to help pilots to decide when they are clear of the runway, not the ILS critical area.

39. (Refer to Figure 51 above.) Which of the signs in the figure is a mandatory instruction sign?

A. D.

B. G.

C. H.

Answer (A) is correct. (AIM Para 2-3-8)
   DISCUSSION: Mandatory signs have a red background with a white inscription and are used to denote an entrance to a runway or critical area and areas where an aircraft is prohibited from entering. Symbol D is a "No Entry" sign.
   Answer (B) is incorrect. Symbol G is a runway boundary sign. It is located on taxiways on the back side of certain runway/taxiway holding position signs or runway approach area signs. **Answer (C) is incorrect.** The ILS critical area sign (symbol H) has a yellow background and black lines drawn that look like a sideways ladder. This sign identifies the ILS critical area exit boundary. If an aircraft is on this line and instrument approaches are in progress, the ILS signal may be blocked. Do not cross or block this during IMC unless clearance is given.

40. (Refer to Figure 51 on page 96.) Which sign is a designation and direction of an exit taxiway from a runway?

A. J.

B. F.

C. K.

Answer (C) is correct. (AIM Para 2-3-11)
DISCUSSION: Sign K designates the direction of taxiway B; while both J and K are destination signs, only K designates the route to a taxiway.
Answer (A) is incorrect. Though a destination sign, sign J designates the direction of Runway 22, not the direction of a taxiway. Answer (B) is incorrect. Sign F is a location sign indicating that the aircraft is located on Runway 22.

41. (Refer to Figure 51 on page 96.) Which sign identifies where aircraft are prohibited from entering?

A. D.

B. G.

C. B.

Answer (A) is correct. (AIM Para 2-3-8)
DISCUSSION: Mandatory instruction signs have a red background with a white inscription and are used to denote an entrance to a runway or critical area and areas where an aircraft is prohibited from entering.
Answer (B) is incorrect. Sign "G" is a runway boundary sign. Answer (C) is incorrect. Sign "B" is a holding position sign for a runway approach area.

42. (Refer to Figure 51 on page 96.) Which symbol does not directly address runway incursion with other aircraft?

A. D.

B. G.

C. H.

Answer (A) is correct. (AIM Para 2-3-8)
DISCUSSION: Symbol D (red background with white inscription) is a mandatory instruction sign that prohibits an aircraft from entering an area. Typically, this sign would be located on a taxiway intended to be used in only one direction or at an intersection of vehicle roadways with runways, taxiways, or aprons where the roadway may be mistaken as a taxiway or other aircraft movement surface. Thus, it does not directly address runway incursion with other aircraft.
Answer (B) is incorrect. Symbol G is used to help indicate when you are clear of the runway. If you are not clear of the active runway, you will interfere with runway operations. Answer (C) is incorrect. Symbol H is used to help indicate when you are clear of the ILS critical area. An aircraft that is not clear of the ILS critical area may cause ILS course distortion, which will interfere with ILS approaches being conducted.

43. When turning onto a taxiway from another taxiway, the "taxiway directional sign" indicates

A. direction to the take-off runway.

B. designation and direction of taxiway leading out of an intersection.

C. designation and direction of exit taxiway from runway.

Answer (B) is correct. (AIM Para 2-3-10)
DISCUSSION: Direction signs consist of black lettering on a yellow background. These signs identify the designations of taxiways leading out of an intersection. An arrow next to each taxiway designation indicates the direction that an aircraft must turn in order to taxi onto that taxiway.
Answer (A) is incorrect. Outbound destination signs, not direction signs, indicate the direction that must be taken out of an intersection in order to follow the preferred taxi route to a runway. Answer (C) is incorrect. The question specifies that you are turning onto a taxiway from another taxiway, not from a runway.

44. (Refer to Figure 57 below.) You are directed to taxi to runway 10. You see this sign at a taxiway intersection while taxiing. Which way should you proceed?

A. Left.

B. Right.

C. Straight ahead.

Answer (C) is correct. (AIM Para 2-3-10)
DISCUSSION: A direction sign has a yellow background with black numbers or letters and an arrow indicating the direction to travel. In this case, the direction sign indicates that runway 10 is straight ahead. The sign also indicates that runway 21 is straight ahead.
Answer (A) is incorrect. A turn to the left would take you to runway 4, not runway 10. Answer (B) is incorrect. A turn to the right would take you to runway 22, not runway 10.

Figure 57. Sign.

45. Which of the following best describes a destination sign?

    A. Indicates a runway on which the aircraft is presently located.

    B. Indicates the direction to the takeoff runway.

    C. Indicates the entrance to a taxiway from a runway.

Answer (B) is correct. (AIM Para 2-3-11)
    DISCUSSION: A destination sign has a yellow background with a black inscription. The destination sign indicates the direction of taxi required to reach a particular destination.
    Answer (A) is incorrect. A destination sign indicates the direction of travel to a particular destination; it does not provide information on your present location. This answer choice best describes a runway position sign. **Answer (C) is incorrect.** Runway exit signs, not destination signs, indicate the entrance to a taxiway from a runway.

46. (Refer to Figure 59 below.) Use the sign and taxiway diagram. You are approaching the intersection on taxiway 5 and see the sign at the left of the intersection. Taxiway number 2 is identified as

    A. A.

    B. F.

    C. T.

Answer (B) is correct. (AIM Para 2-3-10)
    DISCUSSION: The taxiway diagram shows that taxiway 2 is forward and to the left (which is not to be confused with directly to the left). The sign shows that the taxiway to the forward left is taxiway Foxtrot (F).
    Answer (A) is incorrect. The airplane is currently positioned on Taxiway Alpha (A), shown on the taxiway diagram as taxiway 5. **Answer (C) is incorrect.** Taxiway Tango (T) is shown as being forward and right, that is, as taxiway 3 on the taxiway diagram.

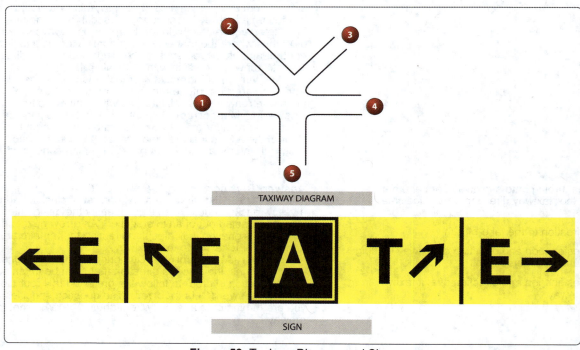

Figure 59. Taxiway Diagram and Sign.

47. (Refer to Figure 60 on page 99.) As you taxi you see sign 2 on the right side of the aircraft and sign 1 directly in front of you on the opposite side of the intersection. Does the taxiway continue on the opposite side of the intersection?

    A. Yes, taxiway A is on the opposite side of the intersection.

    B. Yes, taxiway T is on the opposite side of the intersection.

    C. No, the taxiway does not continue.

Answer (C) is correct. (AIM Para 2-3-5)
    DISCUSSION: The taxiway array sign (sign 2) shows that the pilot is currently on taxiway A. The taxiway ending sign (sign 1) indicates that taxiway A does not continue.
    Answer (A) is incorrect. The pilot is on taxiway A, which ends as denoted by the taxiway ending sign. **Answer (B) is incorrect.** Taxiway T is to the right. The taxiway array sign shows that the pilot is currently on taxiway A. The taxiway ending sign indicates that taxiway A ends ahead of the intersection.

48. (Refer to Figure 60 below.) Sign 1 is an indication

    A. of an area where aircraft are prohibited.

    B. that the taxiway does not continue.

    C. of the general taxiing direction to a taxiway.

Answer (B) is correct. (AIM Para 2-3-12)
    DISCUSSION: A taxiway ending marker sign consists of alternating yellow and black diagonal stripes. Taxiway ending marker signs indicate that the taxiway does not continue beyond the sign.
    Answer (A) is incorrect. No entry signs, not taxiway ending marker signs, identify an area where aircraft are prohibited from entering. No entry signs consist of a white horizontal line surrounded by a white circle on a red background. **Answer (C) is incorrect.** A direction sign, not a taxiway ending marker sign, indicates the general taxiing direction to a taxiway. Direction signs consist of black lettering on a yellow background with an arrow indicating the direction of turn.

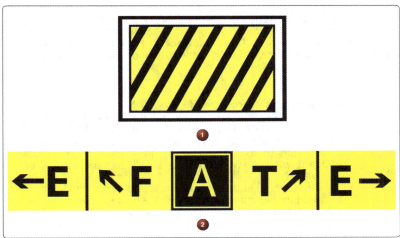

Figure 60. Two Signs.

49. (Refer to Figure 61 below.) This sign is a visual clue that

    A. confirms the aircraft's location to be on taxiway "A."

    B. warns the pilot of approaching taxiway "A."

    C. indicates "A" holding area is ahead.

Answer (A) is correct. (AIM Para 2-3-10)
    DISCUSSION: The taxiway location sign consists of a yellow letter on a black background with a yellow border. This sign confirms the pilot is on taxiway "A."
    Answer (B) is incorrect. A direction sign with a yellow background, a black letter, and an arrow pointing to taxiway "A" would be required to warn a pilot that (s)he is approaching taxiway "A." **Answer (C) is incorrect.** A taxiway location sign defines a position on a taxiway, not a holding area.

50. (Refer to Figure 61 below.) Ground control has instructed you to taxi Alpha to Foxtrot to the active runway. According to the sign in the figure, which direction would you turn at this intersection to comply with ATC?

    A. No turn is required.

    B. The turn will be made to the right.

    C. The turn will be made to the left.

Answer (C) is correct. (FAA-H-8083-25B Chap 14)
    DISCUSSION: The black location sign signifies that you are on taxiway Alpha. Taxiway Foxtrot angles to the left, so a left turn must be made onto Foxtrot to comply with ATC.
    Answer (A) is incorrect. A left turn must be made onto taxiway Foxtrot to comply with ATC. **Answer (B) is incorrect.** A left turn, not a right turn, must be made onto taxiway Foxtrot to comply with ATC.

Figure 61. Sign.

51. What is the purpose of the runway exit sign?

A. Defines direction and designation of runway when exiting a taxiway.

B. Defines direction and designation of exit taxiway from runway.

C. Defines a mandatory exit point from the runway during Land and Hold Short Operations (LAHSO).

Answer (B) is correct. (AIM Para 2-3-10)
   DISCUSSION: A runway exit sign defines the direction and designation of an exit taxiway from the runway.
   Answer (A) is incorrect. A runway exit sign is positioned on the runway, not on a taxiway. This answer choice describes a runway destination sign. **Answer (C) is incorrect.** Runway exit signs are not mandatory exit points during LAHSO. This answer choice partially describes runway holding position markings.

52. The 'yellow demarcation bar' marking indicates

A. runway with a displaced threshold that precedes the runway.

B. a hold line from a taxiway to a runway.

C. the beginning of available runway for landing on the approach side.

Answer (A) is correct. (AIM Para 2-3-4)
   DISCUSSION: A demarcation bar is a 3-foot-wide yellow stripe that separates a runway with a displaced threshold from a blast pad, stopway, or taxiway that precedes the runway.
   Answer (B) is incorrect. A set of solid yellow and dashed yellow lines represents the hold lines between a taxiway and runway. **Answer (C) is incorrect.** The yellow demarcation bar delineates the beginning of the displaced threshold, which is not a landing surface.

53. (Refer to Figure 64 on page 101.) You are viewing this sign from the flight deck as you hold short of the runway. The air traffic controller clears you to back taxi on the runway for a full length departure on Runway 8. Which way would you turn to begin the back taxi?

A. Right.

B. Left.

C. Not enough information provided.

Answer (A) is correct. (AIM Para 2-3-8)
   DISCUSSION: The runway hold position sign depicts the runway thresholds. The "8" is on the right side of the sign, indicating the threshold for Runway 8 is to the right. To back taxi for a full length takeoff, you would turn to the right. At the end of the runway, you would perform a 180° turn and take off on Runway 8.
   Answer (B) is incorrect. You would turn to the left if you intended to take off on Runway 8 for an intersection departure without a back taxi for a full length takeoff or if you intended to back taxi for a Runway 26 takeoff. **Answer (C) is incorrect.** There is sufficient information provided to determine the appropriate direction of turn.

54. (Refer to Figure 64 on page 101.) You are viewing this sign from the flight deck as you hold short of the runway. The air traffic controller clears you to back taxi on the runway for a full length departure on Runway 26. Which way would you turn to begin the back taxi?

A. Right.

B. Left.

C. Not enough information provided.

Answer (B) is correct. (AIM Para 2-3-8)
   DISCUSSION: The runway hold position sign depicts the runway thresholds. The "26" is on the left side of the sign, indicating the threshold for Runway 26 is to the left. A turn to the right would place you on Runway 26. To back taxi for a full length takeoff, you would turn to the left. At the end of the runway, you would perform a 180° turn and take off on Runway 26.
   Answer (A) is incorrect. You would turn to the right if you intended to take off on Runway 26 for an intersection departure without a back taxi for a full length takeoff or if you intended to back taxi for a Runway 8 take off. **Answer (C) is incorrect.** Sufficient information is provided to determine the appropriate direction of turn.

55. (Refer to Figure 64 on page 101.) You are holding short for an intersection departure on Runway 8 with the sign in front of you. Which way should you turn when taxiing onto the runway to depart Runway 8?

A. Turn right.

B. Turn left.

C. Insufficient information is given.

Answer (B) is correct. (AIM Para 2-3-8)
   DISCUSSION: You would turn to the left because the runway holding position sign shown in Fig. 64 shows the actual runway layout. Therefore, you would turn away from the position of the runway designation on the sign just like you would if you were taxiing onto the end of the runway for takeoff.
   Answer (A) is incorrect. Turning right would result in a takeoff from Runway 26. **Answer (C) is incorrect.** The runway holding position sign provides sufficient information to answer this question.

56. (Refer to Figure 64 below.) You are holding short for an intersection departure on Runway 26 with the sign in front of you. Which way should you turn when taxiing onto the runway for departure?

A. Turn right.

B. Turn left.

C. Insufficient information is given.

Answer (A) is correct. (AIM Para 2-3-8)
    DISCUSSION: You would turn to the right because the runway holding position sign shown in Fig. 64 shows the actual runway layout and will be located at an intersection. Therefore, you would turn away from the position of the runway designation on the sign just like you would if you were taxiing onto the end of the runway for takeoff; in this instance turn right to 260.
    Answer (B) is incorrect. Turning left would result in a takeoff from Runway 8. **Answer (C) is incorrect.** The runway holding position sign provides sufficient information to answer this question.

Figure 64. Sign.

57. (Refer to Figure 64 above.) If cleared for an intersection takeoff on runway 8, you see this sign at the intersection hold short position. Which way should you turn when taxiing onto the runway?

A. Left.

B. Right.

C. Need more information.

Answer (A) is correct. (AIM Para 2-3-8)
    DISCUSSION: The numbers on the runway holding position sign correspond to the runway threshold; in this case, the threshold for Runway 8 is on the right. Therefore, for an intersection takeoff on Runway 8, you would turn left when taxiing onto the runway.
    Answer (B) is incorrect. A turn to the right at the intersection would be for a full-length runway departure. **Answer (C) is incorrect.** All of the information you need to make a decision is provided by the runway holding position sign.

58. (Refer to Figure 64 above.) You see this sign when holding short of the runway. You receive clearance to back taxi on the runway for a full-length runway 8 departure. Which way should you turn when taxiing onto the runway?

A. Left.

B. Right.

C. Need more information.

Answer (B) is correct. (AIM Para 2-3-8)
    DISCUSSION: The numbers on the runway holding position sign correspond to the runway threshold; in this case, the threshold for Runway 8 is on the right. Therefore, for a full-length departure on Runway 8, you would turn right to back taxi. Upon reaching the threshold, you would turn 180° for a takeoff on Runway 8.
    Answer (A) is incorrect. A turn to the left at the intersection would not be a full-length runway departure. **Answer (C) is incorrect.** All of the information you need to make a decision is provided by the runway holding position sign.

59. (Refer to Figure 64 above.) This taxiway sign would be expected

A. at the intersection of runway 08/26 departure end and the taxiway.

B. near the intersection of runways 08 and 26.

C. at a taxiway intersecting runway 08/26.

Answer (C) is correct. (AIM Para 2-3-8)
    DISCUSSION: The runway holding position sign consists of white numbers on a red background. In this example, the pilot would be on a taxiway intersection of Runways 8 and 26.
    Answer (A) is incorrect. The pilot would see the holding position sign if (s)he were at the departure end of the runway. The holding position sign consists of white numbers on a red background. Since the holding position sign is on the departure end of the runway, only one runway, as opposed to both, is listed. **Answer (B) is incorrect.** The sign indicates that the pilot is at a specific location, not nearing a location.

60. (Refer to Figure 65 below.) The "taxiway ending" marker

A. indicates taxiway does not continue.

B. identifies area where aircraft are prohibited.

C. provides general taxiing direction to named taxiway.

Answer (A) is correct. (AIM Para 2-3-12)
DISCUSSION: A taxiway ending marker sign consists of alternating yellow and black diagonal stripes. Taxiway ending marker signs indicate that the taxiway does not continue beyond the sign. **Answer (B) is incorrect.** No entry signs, not taxiway ending marker signs, identify an area where aircraft are prohibited from entering. No entry signs consist of a white horizontal line surrounded by a white circle on a red background. **Answer (C) is incorrect.** A direction sign, not a taxiway ending marker sign, indicates the general direction to take out of an intersection in order to taxi onto the named taxiway. Direction signs consist of black lettering on a yellow background with an arrow indicating the direction of turn.

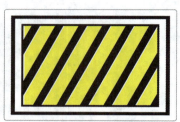

Figure 65. Sign.

61. (Refer to Figure 56 below.) If you were on a taxiway approaching or leading to Runway 22, which sign would you see?

A. 1

B. 2

C. Neither 1 or 2.

Answer (A) is correct. (AIM Para 2-3-11)
DISCUSSION: Image 1 is a destination sign pointing you in the direction of Runway 22. **Answer (B) is incorrect.** Image 2 is a hold position sign indicating that you are at the takeoff end of Runway 4. **Answer (C) is incorrect.** Image 1 is a destination sign pointing you in the direction of Runway 22.

Figure 56. Two Signs.

62. (Refer to Figure 56 above.) Sign 1 confirms your position on

A. runway 22.

B. routing to runway 22.

C. taxiway 22.

Answer (B) is correct. (AIM Para 2-3-11)
DISCUSSION: A direction sign has a yellow background with black numbers or letters and an arrow indicating the direction to travel. In this case, the direction sign indicates that Runway 22 is straight ahead. **Answer (A) is incorrect.** The sign indicates that you are routing to Runway 22, not already at Runway 22. If a pilot were already at Runway 22, (s)he would see the runway holding position sign, a red sign with white letters. **Answer (C) is incorrect.** Only runways are numbered. Taxiways are always identified by a letter.

63. 'Runway Holding Position Markings' on taxiways

A. identify where aircraft are prohibited to taxi when not cleared to proceed by ground control.

B. identify where aircraft are supposed to stop when not cleared to proceed onto the runway.

C. allow an aircraft permission onto the runway.

Answer (B) is correct. (AIM Para 2-3-4)
DISCUSSION: Runway holding position markings identify where aircraft are supposed to stop when not cleared onto the runway. When told to hold short of a runway, a pilot must come to a stop prior to the runway holding position markings and ensure no portion of his or her aircraft extends beyond them. At an uncontrolled airport, a pilot must ensure the runway is clear and confirm the area is clear of arriving or departing traffic on the runway prior to crossing the runway holding position markings.
Answer (A) is incorrect. Runway holding position markings are used at both controlled and uncontrolled airports. A clearance to cross runway holding position markings will not be available from ground control at a non-towered facility. It is, however, the PIC's responsibility to ensure the area is clear of traffic prior to crossing the runway holding position markings. **Answer (C) is incorrect.** Access and/or a clearance onto an active runway can be granted only by ATC or the PIC at an uncontrolled airport after carefully ensuring the area is clear and (s)he is safe to cross the runway holding position markings.

64. (Refer to Figure 58 below.) At what point on the airport diagram could a pilot expect to see this sign?

A. 3 and 5.

B. 10 and 11.

C. 3, 5, 10, and 11.

Answer (B) is correct. (AIM Para 2-3-8)
DISCUSSION: The runway holding position sign will be located at the intersection of a taxiway and runway or the intersection of two runways. In this figure, you could expect to see this sign at points 10 and 11.
Answer (A) is incorrect. The runway holding position sign at the beginning of the takeoff runway may only display the designation of the takeoff runway. All other signs will have the designation of both runway directions. **Answer (C) is incorrect.** The runway holding position sign at the beginning of the takeoff runway may only display the designation of the takeoff runway. All other signs will have the designation of both runway directions.

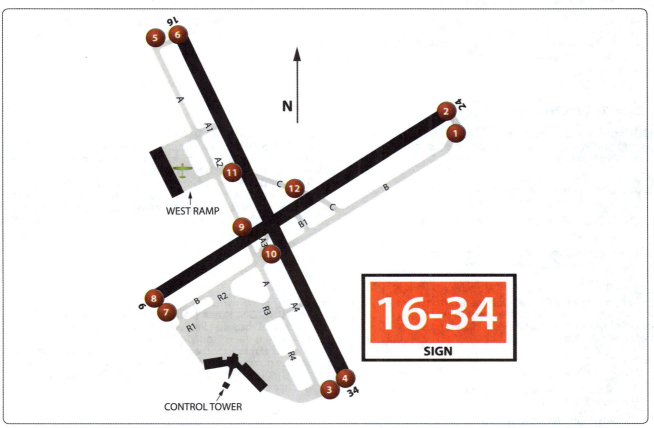

Figure 58. Airport Diagram and Sign.

3.3   Collision Avoidance

65. How can you determine if another aircraft is on a collision course with your aircraft?

    A. The nose of each aircraft is pointed at the same point in space.

    B. The other aircraft will always appear to get larger and closer at a rapid rate.

    C. There will be no apparent relative motion between your aircraft and the other aircraft.

Answer (C) is correct. *(AIM Para 8-1-8)*
    DISCUSSION: Any aircraft that appears to have no relative motion and stays in one scan quadrant is likely to be on a collision course. Also, if a target shows no lateral or vertical movements but increases in size, take evasive action.
    Answer (A) is incorrect. Even if you could determine the direction of the other airplane, you may not be able to accurately project the flight paths and speeds of the two airplanes to determine if they indeed point to the same point in space and will arrive there at the same time (i.e., collide). **Answer (B) is incorrect.** Aircraft on collision courses may not always appear to grow larger or to close at a rapid rate. Frequently, the degree of proximity cannot be detected.

66. What is the general direction of movement of the other aircraft if during a night flight you observe a steady white light and a rotating red light ahead and at your altitude? The other aircraft is

    A. headed away from you.

    B. crossing to your left.

    C. approaching you head-on.

Answer (A) is correct. *(FAA-H-8083-3B Chap 10)*
    DISCUSSION: A steady white light is the tail light. The other airplane is heading away from you. The rotating red light is the beacon light. The red and green wingtip position lights cannot be seen from the rear.
    Answer (B) is incorrect. You would observe a steady red light if the other airplane was crossing to your left. **Answer (C) is incorrect.** You would see the red and green wingtip (not white) position lights if the other aircraft was approaching you head-on.

67. When in the vicinity of a VOR which is being used for navigation on VFR flight, it is important to

    A. make 90° left and right turns to scan for other traffic.

    B. exercise sustained vigilance to avoid aircraft that may be converging on the VOR from other directions.

    C. pass the VOR on the right side of the radial to allow room for aircraft flying in the opposite direction on the same radial.

Answer (B) is correct. *(AIM Para 4-4-15)*
    DISCUSSION: When operating VFR in highly congested areas, such as in the vicinity of a VOR that is being used for VFR navigation, you should exercise constant vigilance to avoid aircraft that may be converging on the VOR from other directions.
    Answer (A) is incorrect. Ninety-degree turns (i.e., clearing turns) are appropriate prior to practicing stalls, etc., but not while en route. **Answer (C) is incorrect.** There is no convention to pass on the right side of VORs or stay on the right side of airways. Federal Aviation Regulations require you to be on the centerline of the airway.

3.4   Wake Turbulence

68. During a takeoff made behind a departing large jet airplane, the pilot can minimize the hazard of wingtip vortices by

    A. being airborne prior to reaching the jet's flightpath until able to turn clear of its wake.

    B. maintaining extra speed on takeoff and climbout.

    C. extending the takeoff roll and not rotating until well beyond the jet's rotation point.

Answer (A) is correct. *(AIM Para 7-4-6)*
    DISCUSSION: When departing behind a larger aircraft, you should rotate prior to the larger aircraft's rotation point and climb above its climb path until turning clear of its wake.
    Answer (B) is incorrect. Even at maximum speed, you will probably not have enough control effectiveness to counteract the induced roll of the vortices. **Answer (C) is incorrect.** The vortices sink below the jet's flight path, so you want to be above them, not below them.

69. To avoid possible wake turbulence from a large jet aircraft that has just landed prior to your takeoff, at which point on the runway should you plan to become airborne?

    A. Past the point where the jet touched down.

    B. At the point where the jet touched down, or just prior to this point.

    C. Approximately 500 feet prior to the point where the jet touched down.

Answer (A) is correct. *(AIM Para 7-4-6)*
    DISCUSSION: When taking off on a runway on which a large jet aircraft has just landed, plan to become airborne past the point where the jet touched down.
    Answer (B) is incorrect. You should rotate past, not at or prior to, the point where the jet touched down. **Answer (C) is incorrect.** You should rotate past, not 500 feet prior to, where the jet touched down.

70. Which procedure should you follow to avoid wake turbulence if a large jet crosses your course from left to right approximately 1 mile ahead and at your altitude?

    A. Make sure you are slightly above the path of the jet.

    B. Slow your airspeed to V_A and maintain altitude and course.

    C. Make sure you are slightly below the path of the jet and perpendicular to the course.

Answer (A) is correct. (AIM Para 7-4-6)
    DISCUSSION: To avoid the wake turbulence of a large jet at your altitude, you should increase your altitude slightly to get above the flight path of the jet.
    Answer (B) is incorrect. The greatest danger is induced roll, not turbulence. **Answer (C) is incorrect.** Flight below and behind a larger aircraft's path should be avoided.

71. Choose the correct statement regarding wake turbulence.

    A. Vortex generation begins with the initiation of the takeoff roll.

    B. The primary hazard is loss of control because of induced roll.

    C. The greatest vortex strength is produced when the generating airplane is heavy, clean, and fast.

Answer (B) is correct. (AIM Para 7-4-3)
    DISCUSSION: The usual hazard associated with wake turbulence is the induced rolling movements, which can exceed the rolling capability of the encountering aircraft.
    Answer (A) is incorrect. Vortex generation begins at the rotation point when the airplane takes off, not the initiation of the takeoff roll. **Answer (C) is incorrect.** The greatest vortex strength is when the generating aircraft is slow, not fast.

72. When landing behind a large aircraft, which procedure should be followed for vortex avoidance?

    A. Stay above its final approach flightpath all the way to touchdown.

    B. Stay below and to one side of its final approach flightpath.

    C. Stay well below its final approach flightpath and land at least 2,000 feet behind.

Answer (A) is correct. (AIM Para 7-4-6)
    DISCUSSION: When landing behind a large aircraft, stay above its final approach flight path all the way to touchdown; i.e., touch down beyond the touchdown point of the large aircraft.
    Answer (B) is incorrect. You should stay at or above, not below, its flight path. **Answer (C) is incorrect.** You should stay at or above, not below, its flight path, and land beyond, not behind, its touchdown point.

73. Which is true with respect to vortex circulation in the wake turbulence generated by an aircraft?

    A. Helicopters generate downwash turbulence only, not vortex circulation.

    B. The vortex strength is greatest when the generating aircraft is heavy, clean, and slow.

    C. When vortex circulation sinks into ground effect, it tends to dissipate rapidly and offer little danger.

Answer (B) is correct. (FAA-H-8083-25B Chap 14)
    DISCUSSION: Airplanes produce wingtip vortices in all phases of flight. The vortex circulation and wake turbulence is at its greatest when the airplane is heavy, clean, and slow. To compensate for a heavy, clean, and slow configuration, a pilot must operate the aircraft at a higher angle of attack to produce the required lift, resulting in greater wake turbulence. This is commonplace in and around the airport environment as aircraft are operating at a high angle of attack to generate the required lift for takeoff and landing.
    Answer (A) is incorrect. A helicopter in forward flight creates strong vortices that trail the helicopter in a similar fashion to the vortices generated by a large, fixed-wing airplane. **Answer (C) is incorrect.** A vortex cannot sink into ground effect since ground effect is formed by the relationship of an airplane's wings to the earth's surface. It could be stated that wake turbulence generated by an airplane in ground effect is reduced.

74. With respect to vortex circulation, which is true?

    A. Helicopters generate downwash turbulence, not vortex circulation.

    B. The vortex strength is greatest when the generating aircraft is flying fast.

    C. Vortex circulation generated by helicopters in forward flight trail behind in a manner similar to wingtip vortices generated by airplanes.

Answer (C) is correct. (AIM Para 7-4-7)
    DISCUSSION: In forward flight, helicopters produce a pair of high velocity trailing vortices similar to wing tip vortices of large fixed wing aircraft.
    Answer (A) is incorrect. Helicopters create both downwash turbulence and wingtip vortices. **Answer (B) is incorrect.** The vortex strength is greatest when flying slow, not fast.

75. Which is true with respect to vortex circulation?

A. Helicopters generate downwash turbulence only, not vortex circulation.

B. The vortex strength is greatest when the generating aircraft is heavy, clean, and slow.

C. When vortex circulation sinks into ground effect, it tends to dissipate rapidly and offer little danger.

Answer (B) is correct. (AIM Para 7-4-3)
DISCUSSION: The greatest vortex strength occurs when the generating aircraft is heavy, clean, and slow.
Answer (A) is incorrect. Helicopters generate both downwash turbulence and wingtip vortices. **Answer (C) is incorrect.** Vortices remain active in ground effect for a period of time.

76. Your flight takes you in the path of a large aircraft. In order to avoid the vortices you should fly

A. at the same altitude as the large aircraft.

B. below the altitude of the large aircraft.

C. above the flight path of the large aircraft.

Answer (C) is correct. (AIM Para 7-4-6, FAA-H-8083-25B)
DISCUSSION: When flying behind a large aircraft, stay at or above the other aircraft's flight path. Wingtip vortex turbulence tends to sink into the flight path of airplanes operating below the airplane generating the turbulence.
Answer (A) is incorrect. In order to avoid the vortices, avoid flying through another aircraft's flight path. **Answer (B) is incorrect.** Wingtip vortex turbulence tends to sink into the flight path of airplanes operating below the airplane generating the turbulence.

3.5   Land and Hold Short Operations (LAHSO)

77. What should you expect when you are told that LAHSO operations are in effect at your destination airport?

A. All aircraft must operate on an IFR clearance due to high traffic volume.

B. That ATC will give you a clearance to land and hold short of a specified point on the runway.

C. Delays due to low IFR conditions and high traffic volume.

Answer (B) is correct. (FAA-H-8083-25B Chap 14)
DISCUSSION: Land and hold short operations (LAHSO) is an ATC procedure for when simultaneous operations (takeoffs and landings) are being conducted on intersecting runways. Pilots may be asked to land and hold short of an intersecting runway, an intersecting taxiway, or some other designated point on a runway.
Answer (A) is incorrect. LAHSO is an ATC procedure for when simultaneous operations (takeoffs and landings) are being conducted on intersecting runways. An IFR clearance is not required to participate in LAHSO. **Answer (C) is incorrect.** LAHSO clearances are only given when VFR conditions exist (there is a minimum ceiling of 1,000 ft. and 3 SM of visibility).

78. Who has the final authority to accept or decline any "land and hold short" (LAHSO) clearance?

A. ATC tower controller.

B. ATC approach controller.

C. Pilot-in-command.

Answer (C) is correct. (AIM Para 4-3-11)
DISCUSSION: The pilot in command has the final authority to accept or decline any LAHSO clearance. The safety and operation of the airplane remain the responsibility of the pilot. Pilots are expected to decline a LAHSO clearance if they determine it will compromise safety.
Answer (A) is incorrect. Although an ATC tower controller will issue a LAHSO clearance, the pilot in command has the final authority to accept or decline the LAHSO clearance. **Answer (B) is incorrect.** ATC approach controllers do not issue landing or LAHSO clearances.

79. The commercial pilot operating as the pilot in command of an aircraft may accept or decline a land and hold short clearance (LAHSO)

A. when operating for hire.

B. any time.

C. at night.

Answer (B) is correct. (AIM Para 4-3-11)
DISCUSSION: The pilot in command has the final authority to accept or decline any LAHSO clearance. The safety and operation of the airplane remain the responsibility of the pilot, and pilots are expected to decline a LAHSO clearance if they determine it will compromise safety.
Answer (A) is incorrect. A pilot in command may accept or decline a LAHSO clearance regardless of the mission profile. **Answer (C) is incorrect.** A pilot in command may accept or decline a LAHSO clearance during both day and night operations.

80. Once a pilot-in-command accepts a "land and hold short" (LAHSO) clearance, the clearance must be adhered to, just as any other ATC clearance, unless

    A. an amended clearance is obtained or an emergency occurs.

    B. the wind changes or Available Landing Distance decreases.

    C. Available Landing Distance decreases or density altitude increases.

Answer (A) is correct. (AIM Para 4-3-11)
    DISCUSSION: If, for any reason, the pilot elects to request to land on the full length of the runway, to land on another runway, or to decline LAHSO, a pilot is expected to promptly inform air traffic, ideally even before the clearance is issued. A LAHSO clearance, once accepted, must be adhered to, just as any other ATC clearance, unless an amended clearance is obtained or an emergency occurs. A LAHSO clearance does not preclude a rejected landing.
    Answer (B) is incorrect. A wind shift does not cancel a LAHSO clearance and Available Landing Distance is a fixed value that cannot spontaneously change. **Answer (C) is incorrect.** Available Landing Distance is a fixed value that cannot spontaneously change and a density altitude increase does not cancel a LAHSO clearance.

81. When should pilots decline a "land and hold short" (LAHSO) clearance?

    A. When it will compromise safety.

    B. If runway surface is contaminated.

    C. Only when the tower controller concurs.

Answer (A) is correct. (AIM Para 4-3-11)
    DISCUSSION: The pilot in command has the final authority to accept or decline a LAHSO clearance. The safety and operation of the airplane remain the responsibility of the pilot. Pilots are expected to decline a LAHSO clearance if they determine it will compromise safety.
    Answer (B) is incorrect. ATC should not issue a LAHSO clearance if the runway is contaminated (e.g., snow, ice, etc.), which would affect the braking action of an airplane. **Answer (C) is incorrect.** The pilot in command has the final authority to accept a LAHSO clearance whether or not the tower controller concurs.

82. What is the minimum visibility and ceiling required for a pilot to receive a "land and hold short" clearance?

    A. 3 statute miles and 1,000 feet.

    B. 3 nautical miles and 1,000 feet.

    C. 3 statute miles and 1,500 feet.

Answer (A) is correct. (AIM Para 4-3-11)
    DISCUSSION: You should only receive a LAHSO clearance when there is a minimum ceiling of 1,000 ft. and 3 SM visibility. The intent of having "basic" VFR weather conditions is to allow pilots to maintain visual contact with other aircraft and ground vehicle operations.
    Answer (B) is incorrect. The minimum visibility and ceiling required for you to receive a LAHSO clearance is 3 SM, not 3 NM, and 1,000 ft. **Answer (C) is incorrect.** The minimum visibility and ceiling required for you to receive a LAHSO clearance is 3 SM and 1,000 ft., not 1,500 ft.

83. What information should a pilot have available when encountering LAHSO?

    A. FAA Advisory Circular on airport markings, signs, and LAHSO.

    B. Published available landing distance data for the expected destination.

    C. Aeronautical Information Manual content relating to LAHSO.

Answer (B) is correct. (AIM Para 4-3-11)
    DISCUSSION: To conduct LAHSO, pilots should become familiar with all available information concerning LAHSO at their destination airport. Pilots should have readily available the published Available Landing Distance (ALD) and runway slope information for all LAHSO runway combinations at each airport of intended landing.
    Answer (A) is incorrect. There is no FAA Advisory Circular that deals with airport markings, signs, and LAHSO. **Answer (C) is incorrect.** Although the AIM is a useful tool for learning about LAHSO, it does not contain LAHSO information for specific airports.

84. To conduct LAHSO a pilot should have readily available

   A. runway slope information.

   B. published LAHSO procedure.

   C. current ATC guide for airport runway markings, lights, signs, LAHSO, and runway safety.

Answer (A) is correct. (AIM Para 4-3-11)
   DISCUSSION: To conduct LAHSO, pilots should become familiar with all available information concerning LAHSO at their destination airport. Pilots should have readily available the published Available Landing Distance (ALD) and runway slope information for all LAHSO runway combinations at each airport of intended landing.
   Answer (B) is incorrect. There are no published LAHSO procedures for airports, only Available Landing Distance (ALD) information provided in the Chart Supplement. **Answer (C) is incorrect.** An ATC guide on airport runway markings, lights, signs, LAHSO, and runway safety will contain information about general airport operations, not operations specific to a given airport. The PIC must use information relevant to the destination airport to determine if LAHSO is in effect and if (s)he can comply with the landing requirements.

85. (Refer to Figure 58 below.) While on final approach for Runway 24, you have been asked to Land and Hold Short on Runway 34-16. Based on the controller's report of the available landing distance, you are concerned you may not be able to land and stop prior to crossing Runway 34-16. You must

   A. use maximum braking as soon as you touch down.

   B. decline the Land and Hold Short clearance.

   C. divert to your alternate airport.

Answer (B) is correct. (AIM Para 4-3-11)
   DISCUSSION: If you are unsure that you will be able to land and hold short of the runway, you should decline the controller's request, since it could compromise safety.
   Answer (A) is incorrect. Since you are concerned that you may not be able to land and stop prior to crossing Runway 34-16, the LAHSO request should be declined. **Answer (C) is incorrect.** A diversion to an alternate airport is not necessary if you are unable to comply with a LAHSO request. The controller should still be able to accommodate you, although you may have to wait or land on another runway.

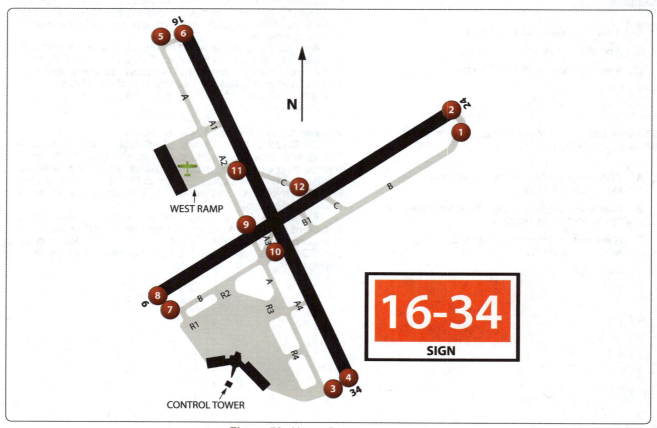

Figure 58. Airport Diagram and Sign.

86. Prior to accepting a "land and hold short" clearance (LAHSO) a pilot must confirm the aircraft can stop

   A. in the Available Landing Distance.
   B. prior to the intersecting taxiway.
   C. prior to the intersecting runway.

Answer (A) is correct. (AIM Para 4-3-11)
   DISCUSSION: To conduct LAHSO, pilots should become familiar with all available information concerning runway availability, length, and any specific LAHSO procedures at their destination airport. Pilots should have readily available the published Available Landing Distance (ALD) and runway slope information for all LAHSO runway combinations at each airport of intended landing.
   Answer (B) is incorrect. Pilots must confirm the aircraft can come to a stop in the Available Landing Distance (ALD), not prior to an intersecting taxiway. While stopping prior to an intersecting taxiway might be part of your LAHSO clearance, the most accurate answer to this question is to ensure that you can stop within the ALD. **Answer (C) is incorrect.** Pilots must confirm the aircraft can come to a stop in the Available Landing Distance (ALD), not prior to an intersecting runway. While stopping prior to an intersecting runway might be part of your LAHSO clearance, the most accurate answer to this question is to ensure that you can stop within the ALD.

87. A 'land and hold short' (LAHSO) clearance

   A. precludes a "Go Around" by ATC.
   B. does not preclude a rejected landing.
   C. requires a runway exit at the first taxiway.

Answer (B) is correct. (AIM Para 4-3-11)
   DISCUSSION: Once a LAHSO is accepted, it must be adhered to unless an amended clearance is obtained or when an emergency occurs. A LAHSO does not preclude a rejected landing.
   Answer (A) is incorrect. A LAHSO clearance does not preclude a rejected landing. **Answer (C) is incorrect.** A LAHSO requires the aircraft to stop at the hold line or exit at any taxiway instructed to by ATC. This taxiway exit would be before the LAHSO hold line.

88. If given a landing clearance on runway 16 and told to hold short of runway 6, how can a pilot determine the available landing distance?

   A. The full runway length is available.
   B. Use rule of thumb to determine the distance.
   C. Ask the controller.

Answer (C) is correct. (AIM Para 4-3-11)
   DISCUSSION: To conduct land and hold short operations (LAHSO), pilots should have readily available the published Available Landing Distance (ALD) and runway slope information for all LAHSO runway combinations at each airport of intended landing. If the controller gives a LAHSO clearance and the pilot is unsure of the landing distance available, (s)he can always ask the controller. The controller will provide the exact distance available in feet.
   Answer (A) is incorrect. When a land and hold short clearance is given, the pilot is expected to hold short of a specified point on the runway. The full runway length is not available. **Answer (B) is incorrect.** A pilot should not use a rule of thumb to determine the available landing distance. The pilot should have readily available the published Available Landing Distance (ALD) for all LAHSO runway combinations at each airport of intended landing.

3.6 Segmented Circles

89. (Refer to Figure 101 below.) The segmented circle indicates that the airport traffic is

   A. left-hand for Runway 36 and right-hand for Runway 18.

   B. left-hand for Runway 18 and right-hand for Runway 36.

   C. right-hand for Runway 9 and left-hand for Runway 27.

Answer (A) is correct. (AIM Para 4-3-4)
    DISCUSSION: A segmented circle (as shown in Fig. 101) is installed at uncontrolled airports to provide traffic pattern information. The landing runway indicators are shown coming out of the segmented circle to show the alignment of landing runways. In the figure provided (given the answer choices), the available runways are 18-36 and 9-27. The traffic pattern indicators show left-hand traffic for Runway 36 and right-hand traffic for Runway 18.
    Answer (B) is incorrect. Runway 18 is right, not left, traffic, and Runway 36 is left, not right, traffic. **Answer (C) is incorrect.** Runway 9 is left, not right, traffic, and Runway 27 is right, not left, traffic.

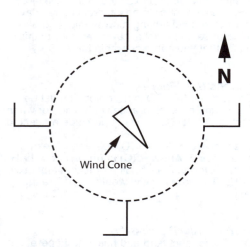

Figure 101. Wind Sock Airport Landing Indicator (not in supplement).

90. You are on approach to land on Runway 19 of a non-towered airport. You observe ripples on the southeast side of a small lake 3/4 mi. east of the airport. What is the most appropriate course of action?

   A. Proceed with your approach to Runway 19.

   B. Maneuver for an approach to Runway 01.

   C. Check the wind sock to determine the appropriate runway.

Answer (C) is correct. (AIM Para 4-3-4)
    DISCUSSION: Checking the wind sock would enable you to verify the wind direction over the field and determine the best runway for landing.
    Answer (A) is incorrect. Landing on Runway 19 would put you in a tailwind condition. **Answer (B) is incorrect.** Although landing on Runway 01 would allow you to land in a headwind, it is advisable to check the wind sock to ensure that the winds on the field agree with the wind direction over the lake.

3.7 Transponders and Transponder Codes

91. When making routine transponder code changes, pilots should avoid inadvertent selection of which codes?

- A. 7200
- B. 7000
- C. 7500

Answer (C) is correct. (AIM Para 4-1-20)
DISCUSSION: Some special codes set aside for emergencies should be avoided during routine VFR flights. They are 7500 for hijacking, 7600 for lost radio communications, and 7700 for a general emergency. Additionally, you should know that code 7777 is reserved for military interceptors.
Answer (A) is incorrect. Code 7200 may be assigned by ATC. **Answer (B) is incorrect.** Code 7000 may be assigned by ATC.

92. When making routine transponder code changes, pilots should avoid inadvertent selection of which code?

- A. 1200
- B. 7600
- C. 4096

Answer (B) is correct. (AIM Para 4-1-20)
DISCUSSION: Some special codes set aside for emergencies should be avoided during routine VFR flights. They are 7500 for hijacking, 7600 for lost radio communications, and 7700 for a general emergency. Additionally, you should know that code 7777 is reserved for military interceptors.
Answer (A) is incorrect. Code 1200 is the standard VFR code. **Answer (C) is incorrect.** The number 4096 is the number of possible codes, not an actual code itself. Additionally, the transponder digits only go up to 7, so a 9 is not possible.

93. At an altitude below 18,000 feet MSL, which transponder code should be selected?

- A. Mode A/3, Code 1200.
- B. Mode F, Code 1200.
- C. Mode C, Code 4096.

Answer (A) is correct. (AIM Para 4-1-20)
DISCUSSION: The standard VFR transponder code is 1200. Because all flight operations above 18,000 feet MSL are to be IFR, code 1200 is not used above that height.
Answer (B) is incorrect. The standard VFR transponder code is 1200, but Mode F is not a valid transponder type. **Answer (C) is incorrect.** Mode C is a valid transponder type, but 4096 is the number of possible codes, not an actual code itself. Additionally, the transponder digits only go up to 7, so a 9 is not possible.

94. Unless otherwise authorized, if flying a transponder equipped aircraft, a pilot should squawk which VFR code?

- A. 1200
- B. 7600
- C. 7700

Answer (A) is correct. (AIM Para 4-1-20)
DISCUSSION: A pilot flying a transponder-equipped aircraft should set that transponder on code (squawk) 1200, which is the VFR code.
Answer (B) is incorrect. Code 7600 is the lost communication code. **Answer (C) is incorrect.** Code 7700 is the general emergency code.

95. What is the appropriate transponder code in response to lost communications?

- A. 7400
- B. 7500
- C. 7600

Answer (C) is correct. (14 CFR 91.185, AIM Para 4-1-20)
DISCUSSION: Code 7600 is used in the event of a radio failure or lost communications. Other emergency codes are 7500 for hijacking and 7700 for a general emergency. Additionally, code 7777 is reserved for military interceptors.
Answer (A) is incorrect. Code 7400 is reserved for an unmanned aircraft experiencing a lost link. **Answer (B) is incorrect.** Code 7500 is used in the event of unlawful interference or hijacking.

96. In the event of unlawful interference or hijacking, which transponder code should you input immediately?

- A. 7500
- B. 7600
- C. 7777

Answer (A) is correct. (14 CFR 91.185, AIM Para 4-1-20)
DISCUSSION: The nondiscrete transponder code 7500 is used in the event of unlawful interference or hijacking. Once input, this code triggers a special emergency indicator in all radar ATC facilities.
Answer (B) is incorrect. Code 7600 is used in the event of a radio failure or lost communications. **Answer (C) is incorrect.** Code 7777 is the highest value code that may be entered on a 4096 transponder and a discrete code reserved for military interceptor operations.

97. A pilot mistakenly entered transponder code 7500 in response to an emergency. The correct code would have been

A. 7777

B. 7700

C. 7600

Answer (B) is correct. (14 CFR 91.185, AIM Para 4-1-20)
DISCUSSION: Nondiscrete code 7700 is used to communicate an emergency, whereas 7500 should only be used in response to unlawful interference or hijacking.
Answer (A) is incorrect. Code 7777 is reserved for military interceptor operations, 7500 is for unlawful interference or hijacking, and the correct code for an emergency is 7700.
Answer (C) is incorrect. Code 7600 is reserved for radio failure or lost communications, 7500 is used for unlawful interference or hijacking, and the correct code for an emergency is 7700.

98. What is the hijack code?

A. 7200

B. 7500

C. 7777

Answer (B) is correct. (14 CFR 91.185, AIM Para 4-1-20)
DISCUSSION: Transponder code 7500 means: "I am being hijacked/forced to a new destination." Code 7500 will never be assigned by ATC without prior notification from the pilot that his or her airplane is being subjected to unlawful interference. Code 7500 will trigger special emergency indicators in all radar ATC facilities.
Answer (A) is incorrect. Code 7200 is used for normal operating procedures. **Answer (C) is incorrect.** Under no circumstances should a pilot of a civil airplane operate the transponder on Code 7777. This code is reserved for military interceptor operations.

STUDY UNIT FOUR

FEDERAL AVIATION REGULATIONS

(18 pages of outline)

This study unit contains outlines of major concepts tested, sample test questions and answers regarding Federal Aviation Regulations, and an explanation of each answer. The table of contents above and on the previous page lists each subunit within this study unit, the number of questions pertaining to that particular subunit, and the pages on which the outlines and questions begin, respectively.

Recall that the **sole purpose** of this book is to expedite your passing of the FAA pilot knowledge test for the commercial pilot certificate. Accordingly, all extraneous material (i.e., topics or regulations not directly tested on the FAA pilot knowledge test) is omitted, even though much more knowledge is necessary to become a proficient commercial pilot. This additional material is presented in *Pilot Handbook* and *Commercial Pilot Flight Maneuvers and Practical Test Prep*, available from Gleim Publications, Inc. Order online at www.GleimAviation.com.

NOTE: The FAA refers to the Federal Aviation Regulations as "14 CFR" rather than "FAR." CFR stands for Code of Federal Regulations, and the Federal Aviation Regulations are in Title 14. For example, FAR Part 1 and FAR 61.109 are now referred to as 14 CFR Part 1 and 14 CFR 61.109, respectively.

4.1 14 CFR PART 1

1.1 General Definitions

1. Airports are areas of land or water that are used or intended to be used for the landing and takeoff of aircraft, and includes its buildings and facilities, if any.

2. Commercial operators engage in carriage by aircraft in air commerce of persons or property for compensation or hire, other than as an air carrier.

3. An operator is a person who causes the aircraft to be used or authorizes its use.

4. Operational control of a flight means exercising authority over initiating, conducting, or terminating a flight.

1.2 Abbreviations and Symbols

1. V_{EF} means the speed at which the critical engine is assumed to fail during takeoff.

2. V_F means the design flap speed.

3. V_{LE} means the maximum landing gear extended speed.

4. V_{MC} means the minimum control speed with the critical engine inoperative.

5. V_{MO}/M_{MO} means the maximum operating limit speed.

6. V_{NE} means the never-exceed speed.

7. V_{NO} means the maximum structural cruising speed.

8. V_S means the stalling speed or minimum steady flight speed at which the airplane is controllable.

9. V_{S1} means the stalling speed or minimum steady flight speed in a specified configuration.

10. V_X means the speed for the best angle of climb.

11. V_Y means the best rate of climb speed.

12. V_1 means the maximum speed in the takeoff at which the pilot must take the first action (e.g., apply brakes, reduce thrust, deploy speed brakes) to stop the airplane within the accelerate-stop distance. V_1 also means the minimum speed in the takeoff, following a failure of the critical engine at V_{EF}, at which the pilot can continue the takeoff and achieve the required height above the takeoff surface within the takeoff distance.

13. V_2 means the takeoff safety speed.

4.2 14 CFR PART 21

21.181 Duration of Airworthiness Certificates

1.   Airworthiness certificates remain in force as long as maintenance, preventive maintenance, and alterations of the aircraft are performed according to the Federal Aviation Regulations.

4.3 14 CFR PART 23

23.2005 Certification of Normal Category Airplanes

NOTE: The FAA proposes to eliminate commuter, utility, and acrobatic airplane categories from 14 CFR Part 23. All newly certificated airplanes under Part 23 are certified in the normal category. Airplanes already certified in the commuter, utility, acrobatic, or normal categories will continue to be in those categories.

1.   Certification in the normal category applies to airplanes with a passenger seating configuration of 19 or fewer and a maximum certificated takeoff weight of 19,000 lb. or less.

    a.   Airplane certification levels are as follows:

        1)   Level 1: Maximum seating configuration of 0 to 1 passengers
        2)   Level 2: Maximum seating configuration of 2 to 6 passengers
        3)   Level 3: Maximum seating configuration of 7 to 9 passengers
        4)   Level 4: Maximum seating configuration of 10 to 19 passengers

    b.   Airplane performance levels are as follows:

        1)   Low speed: For airplanes with a V_{NO} and $V_{MO} \leq 250$ knots calibrated airspeed (KCAS) and a $M_{MO} \leq 0.6$

        2)   High speed: For airplanes with a V_{NO} or $V_{MO} > 250$ KCAS or a $M_{MO} > 0.6$

    c.   Airplanes not certified for aerobatics may be used to perform any maneuver incident to normal flying, including stalls, lazy eights, chandelles, and steep turns, in which the angle of bank is not more than 60°.

        1)   Airplanes certified for aerobatics may be used to perform maneuvers without limitations.

2.   The preceding utility operational category of an airplane permits limited aerobatics, including spins (if approved for that particular type of airplane), lazy eights, chandelles, and steep turns between 60° and 90°.

4.4 14 CFR PART 39

39.3 Definition of Airworthiness Directives

1.   Airworthiness Directives (ADs) are mandatory rules that apply to aircraft, aircraft engines, propellers, and appliances.

4.5 14 CFR PART 43

43.9 Maintenance Records

1.   After preventive maintenance has been performed, the signature, certificate number, and kind of certificate held by the person approving the work; the date; and a description of the work must be entered in the aircraft maintenance records.

4.6   14 CFR PART 61

61.3   Requirements for Certificates, Ratings, and Authorizations

1. A current and appropriate pilot and medical certificate is required to be in a pilot's personal possession or readily accessible in the aircraft whenever the pilot is acting as pilot in command or as a required flight crewmember.

2. Each person who holds a pilot certificate or a medical certificate shall present it for inspection upon the request of the Administrator of the FAA; an authorized representative of the National Transportation Safety Board; or any federal, state, or local law enforcement officer.

61.5   Certificates and Ratings Issued under This Part

1. Aircraft class ratings (with respect to airmen) are single-engine land, multi-engine land, single-engine sea, and multi-engine sea.

61.15   Offenses Involving Alcohol or Drugs

1. A pilot convicted of operating a motor vehicle while intoxicated by, impaired by, or under the influence of alcohol or a drug is required to provide a written report to the FAA Security and Hazardous Materials Safety Office (AXE-700) no later than 60 days after the conviction.

2. A pilot convicted for the violation of any federal or state statute relating to the process, manufacture, transportation, distribution, or sale of narcotic drugs is grounds for suspension or revocation of any certificate, rating, or authorization issued under Part 61.

3. A pilot convicted of operating an aircraft as a crewmember under the influence of alcohol or using drugs that affect the person's faculties (acts which are prohibited by Sec. 91.17), is grounds for denial of an application for a certificate, rating, or authorization issued under Part 61 for a period of one year after the date of that act.

61.19   Duration of Pilot and Instructor Certificates

1. Commercial pilot certificates are issued without a specific expiration date.

61.23   Medical Certificates: Requirement and Duration

1. A person must hold

    a. A first-class medical certificate when exercising the privileges of an ATP certificate

    b. At least a second-class medical certificate when exercising the privileges of a commercial pilot certificate

    c. At least a third-class medical certificate

        1) When exercising the privileges of a private, recreational, or student pilot certificate

        2) When exercising the privileges of a flight instructor certificate if the CFI is acting as PIC

        3) Prior to taking a practical test for a recreational, private, commercial, or ATP certificate or rating

2.   Duration of a Medical Certificate

    a.   A first-class medical certificate expires at the end of the last day of

        1)   The 12th month after the date of examination for operations requiring an ATP certificate if the person is under age 40

        2)   The 6th month after the date of examination for operations requiring an ATP certificate if the person is age 40 or older

        3)   The 12th month after the date of examination for operations requiring only a commercial pilot certificate

        4)   The period specified in item c. below for operations requiring only a private, recreational, flight instructor (when acting as PIC), or student pilot certificate

    b.   A second-class medical certificate expires at the end of the last day of

        1)   The 12th month after the date of examination for operations requiring a commercial pilot certificate

        2)   The period specified in item c. below for operations requiring only a private, recreational, flight instructor (when acting as PIC), or student pilot certificate

    c.   A third-class medical certificate for operations requiring a private, recreational, flight instructor (when acting as PIC), or student pilot certificate expires at the end of the last day of

        1)   The 60th month after the date of examination if the person has not reached his or her 40th birthday on or before the date of the examination

        2)   The 24th month after the date of examination if the person has reached his or her 40th birthday on or before the date of examination

3.   A U.S. Armed Forces medical examination may be used in place of an FAA medical certificate for flights that do not require higher than a third-class medical certificate. It may not be used for commercial pilot certificate privileges because a second-class medical certificate is required.

4.   BasicMed allows a pilot to conduct certain operations using a U.S. driver's license instead of a medical certificate as long as the pilot meets the following conditions:

    a.   Has held an FAA medical certificate at any time after July 14, 2006, the most recent of which

        1)   May have been a special issuance medical certificate

             a)   A one-time special issuance medical certificate must be obtained for certain cardiovascular, neurological, and mental health conditions.

        2)   May be expired

        3)   Cannot have been suspended, revoked, withdrawn, or denied

    b.   Completes an approved medical education course in the preceding 24 calendar months in accordance with 14 CFR Part 68

    c.   Receives a comprehensive medical examination from a state-licensed physician in the previous 48 months in accordance with 14 CFR Part 68

        1)   The exam is not required to be conducted by an aviation medical examiner (AME).

61.31 Type Rating Requirements, Additional Training, and Authorization Requirements

1. For flights carrying passengers, the pilot must hold a category and class rating appropriate to the aircraft being flown.

2. A type rating is required when operating any turbojet-powered airplane or an airplane having a gross weight of more than 12,500 lb.

3. To act as pilot in command of a complex airplane (an airplane that has retractable landing gear, flaps, and a controllable pitch propeller), the pilot must receive and log ground and flight training in such an airplane and obtain a logbook endorsement of competence.

4. To act as pilot in command of a high-performance airplane (an airplane with an engine of more than 200 horsepower), the pilot must receive and log ground and flight training from an authorized instructor in such an airplane.

   a. In addition, that pilot must receive a one-time endorsement in his or her logbook from an authorized instructor who certifies (s)he is proficient to operate a high-performance airplane.

5. To act as a pilot in command of a tailwheel airplane, without prior experience, a pilot must receive and log flight training from an authorized instructor in a tailwheel airplane and receive a one-time logbook endorsement.

61.51 Pilot Logbooks

1. Pilots may log as second-in-command time all flight time when qualified and occupying a crewmember station in an aircraft that requires more than one pilot.

2. The aeronautical training and experience used to meet the requirements for a certificate, rating, or flight review and recent flight experience must be documented and recorded in a manner acceptable to the FAA, e.g., a logbook.

61.55 Second-in-Command Qualifications

1. To serve as second in command of an airplane type certificated for more than one pilot crewmember and operated under Part 91, (in part) a person, within the last 12 months, must have

   a. Become familiar with the required information (systems operations, performance, limitations, etc.) and

   b. Logged pilot time in the type of airplane for which privileges are requested.

61.56 Flight Review

1. To act as pilot in command of an aircraft, a commercial pilot must have satisfactorily completed a flight review or proficiency check within the preceding 24 months.

61.57 Recent Flight Experience: Pilot in Command

1. If a pilot does not meet the recent night experience requirements, (s)he may not carry passengers during the period from 1 hr. after sunset to 1 hr. before sunrise.

2. Prior to carrying passengers, the pilot in command must accomplish required takeoffs and landings in the same category, class, and type of aircraft (if a type rating is required).

3. To act as pilot in command under IFR or in weather conditions that are less than the minimums prescribed for VFR, a pilot must have, within the preceding 6 months, performed and logged (under actual or simulated instrument conditions) at least six instrument approaches, holding procedures, and intercepting and tracking courses through the use of navigation systems.

    a. Alternatively, the pilot may have passed an instrument proficiency check in the appropriate category of aircraft within the preceding 6 months.

61.58 Pilot-in-Command Proficiency Check: Operation of Aircraft Requiring More than One Pilot Flight Crewmember

1. To serve as pilot in command of an airplane that is certificated for more than one pilot crewmember and operated under Part 91, a person must have completed a pilot-in-command proficiency check within the preceding 12 calendar months in an airplane that is type certificated for more than one pilot.

61.60 Change of Address

1. To exercise privileges, one must report a change of permanent mailing address to the FAA Airmen Certification Branch within 30 days of moving.

61.69 Glider and Unpowered Ultralight Vehicle Towing: Experience and Training Requirements

1. To act as pilot in command of an airplane towing a glider, the tow pilot

    a. Is required to hold at least a current private pilot certificate with a category rating for powered aircraft, have a logbook endorsement from an authorized glider instructor certifying receipt of ground and flight training in gliders, and be proficient with techniques and procedures for the safe towing of gliders.

    b. Must have accomplished, within the preceding 24 months, at least three actual or simulated glider tows while accompanied by a qualified tow pilot.

61.113 Private Pilot Privileges and Limitations: Pilot in Command

1. A commercial pilot who chooses to operate under BasicMed is restricted to private pilot privileges and may not conduct flights for compensation or hire.

2. A pilot in command of an aircraft operating under BasicMed must adhere to the following limitations:

    a. The aircraft may not

        1) Be certificated to carry more than six occupants
        2) Have a maximum certificated takeoff weight of more than 6,000 lb.

    b. No portion of the flight may be

        1) Carried out above 18,000 ft. MSL

        2) Conducted outside of the United States unless authorized by the country in which the flight is conducted

        3) Carried out at an indicated airspeed greater than 250 kt.

    c. The pilot must have available in his or her logbook (in paper or electronic format) the

        1) Completed medical examination checklist
        2) Medical education course completion certificate

61.133 Commercial Pilot Privileges and Limitations

1. Commercial pilots without an instrument rating cannot carry passengers for hire on cross-country flights during the day beyond a radius of 50 NM.

    a. Carrying passengers for hire at night is prohibited without an instrument rating.

2. A person who holds a commercial pilot certificate may act as pilot in command of an airplane that

    a. Carries persons or property for compensation or hire, provided the person is qualified in accordance with Part 61 and any other 14 CFR Parts that apply to the operation

    b. Operates for compensation or hire, provided the person is qualified in accordance with Part 61 and any other 14 CFR Parts that apply to the operation

4.7   14 CFR PART 91

91.3 Responsibility and Authority of the Pilot in Command

1. If you, as pilot in command, deviate from any rule in 14 CFR Part 91 (due to an in-flight emergency requiring immediate action), you must submit a written report to the FAA, if requested.

2. The pilot in command is directly responsible for, and is the final authority as to, the operation of the airplane.

91.7 Civil Aircraft Airworthiness

1. You, as pilot in command, are responsible for determining whether your aircraft is in condition for safe flight.

91.9 Civil Aircraft Flight Manual, Marking, and Placard Requirements

1. You may not operate a U.S.-registered civil aircraft without complying with the operating limitations found in the current FAA-approved flight manual, approved manual material, markings, and placards, or any combination thereof.

2. You may not operate a U.S.-registered civil aircraft unless there is a current, approved Airplane Flight Manual available in the aircraft.

91.15 Dropping Objects

1. As pilot in command of a civil aircraft, you may not allow any object to be dropped from that aircraft in flight if it creates a hazard to persons or property. The dropping of an object is not prohibited if reasonable precautions are taken to avoid injury or damage to persons or property.

91.21 Portable Electronic Devices

1. Portable electronic devices that may cause interference with the navigation or communication system may not be operated on any of the following U.S.-registered civil aircraft operations:

    a. Air carrier
    b. Any other aircraft under IFR

2. The determination on potential device usage is to be made by the operator. In the case of aircraft, it may be made by the PIC.

91.23 Truth-in-Leasing Clause Requirement in Leases and Conditional Sales Contracts

1. In order to operate a large civil aircraft of U.S. registry that is subject to a lease, the lessee must have mailed a copy of the lease to the FAA in Oklahoma City within 24 hr. of its execution.

91.103 Preflight Action

1. Pilots are required to familiarize themselves with all available information concerning the flight prior to every flight, and specifically to determine

    a. For any flight, runway lengths at airports of intended use and the airplane's takeoff and landing requirements

    b. For IFR flights **or** flights not in the vicinity of an airport,

        1) Weather reports and forecasts
        2) Fuel requirements
        3) Alternatives available if the planned flight cannot be completed
        4) Any known traffic delays

91.105 Flight Crewmembers at Stations

1. Required flight crewmembers' seat belts must be fastened while the crewmembers are at their stations.

2. Each required flight crewmember is required to keep his or her shoulder harness fastened during takeoff and landing unless

    a. The crewmember would be unable to perform required duties with the shoulder harness fastened.

    b. The seat at the crewmember's station is not equipped with a shoulder harness.

91.107 Use of Safety Belts, Shoulder Harnesses, and Child Restraint Systems

1. All occupants of airplanes must wear a safety belt and shoulder harness (if installed) during taxiing, takeoffs, and landings. The pilot in command must ensure that all passengers are briefed on how to fasten and unfasten all safety belts and harnesses.

91.109 Flight Instruction; Simulated Instrument Flight and Certain Flight Tests

1. No person may operate an airplane in simulated instrument flight conditions unless the other control seat is occupied by a safety pilot who possesses at least a private pilot certificate with category and class ratings appropriate to the airplane being flown.

91.111 Operating near Other Aircraft

1. No person may operate an aircraft so close to another aircraft as to create a collision hazard.

2. Formation flights are not authorized, except by arrangement with the pilot in command of each aircraft.

3. Formation flights are not authorized when carrying passengers for hire.

91.113 Right-of-Way Rules: Except Water Operations

1. When an airplane is overtaking another, the airplane being passed has the right-of-way.

    a. The passing (overtaking) airplane shall alter course to the right to pass well clear.

2. When aircraft of the same category are converging at approximately the same altitude (except head on, or nearly so), the aircraft to the other's right has the right-of-way.

    a. EXAMPLE: On a night flight, if the pilot of aircraft #1 sees only the green navigation light of aircraft #2, and the aircraft are converging, aircraft #1 has the right-of-way because it is to the right of aircraft #2.

    b. Airplanes and helicopters are equally maneuverable and have equal rights-of-way.

3. When two or more aircraft are approaching an airport for the purpose of landing, the aircraft at the lower altitude has the right-of-way.

    a. This rule shall not be abused by cutting in front of or overtaking another aircraft.

4. An aircraft towing or refueling another aircraft has the right-of-way over all other engine-driven aircraft.

91.117 Aircraft Speed

1.   The speed limit is 250 kt. (288 MPH) when flying below 10,000 ft. MSL.

2.   The speed limit within Class B airspace is 250 kt. (288 MPH).

   a.   When flying under Class B airspace or in VFR corridors through Class B airspace, the speed limit is 200 kt. (230 MPH).

3.   When at or below 2,500 ft. AGL and within 4 NM of the primary airport of Class C or Class D airspace, the speed limit is 200 kt. (230 MPH).

91.119 Minimum Safe Altitudes: General

1.   Over congested areas (cities, towns, settlements, or open-air assemblies), a pilot must maintain an altitude of 1,000 ft. above the highest obstacle within a horizontal radius of 2,000 ft. of the airplane.

2.   The minimum altitude over uncongested areas is 500 ft. AGL.

   a.   Over open water or sparsely populated areas, an airplane may not be operated closer than 500 ft. to any person, vessel, vehicle, or structure.

3.   Altitude in all areas must be sufficient to permit an emergency landing without undue hazard to persons or property on the surface in case a power unit fails.

91.121 Altimeter Settings

1.   When a pilot is operating an airplane at or above 18,000 ft. MSL, the altimeter should be set to 29.92 in. Hg.

91.123 Compliance with ATC Clearances and Instructions

1.   After obtaining an ATC clearance, a pilot may not deviate from that clearance unless an amended clearance is obtained, an emergency exists, or the deviation is in response to a traffic alert and collision avoidance system (TCAS) resolution advisory.

91.144 Temporary Restriction on Flight Operations during Abnormally High Barometric Pressure Conditions

1.   When any information indicates that barometric pressure on the route of flight currently exceeds or will exceed 31.00 in. of mercury, no person may operate an aircraft or initiate a flight contrary to the requirements established by the FAA and published in NOTAMs.

91.147 Passenger-Carrying Flights for Compensation or Hire

1.   Each operator conducting nonstop passenger-carrying flights (that begin and end at the same airport and are conducted within a 25-SM radius of that airport) in an airplane for compensation or hire must apply for and receive a Letter of Authorization from the Flight Standards office for that operation.

91.159 VFR Cruising Altitude or Flight Level

1. Specified altitudes are required for VFR cruising flight at more than 3,000 ft. AGL and below 18,000 ft. MSL.

    a. On a magnetic course of 0° through 179°, altitudes flown must be odd thousands plus 500 ft.

        1) EXAMPLE: 3,500, 5,500, 7,500, etc.

    b. On a magnetic course of 180° through 359°, altitudes flown must be even thousands plus 500 ft.

        1) EXAMPLE: 4,500, 6,500, 8,500, etc.

91.167 Fuel Requirements for Flight in IFR Conditions

1. When an alternate airport is required on an IFR flight plan, you must have sufficient fuel to complete the flight to the first airport of intended landing, fly to the alternate, and thereafter fly for 45 min. at normal cruising speed.

91.169 IFR Flight Plan: Information Required

1. For an airport with an approved instrument approach procedure to be listed as an alternate airport on an IFR flight plan, the forecast weather conditions at the time of arrival must be at or above the following alternate airport weather minimums:

    a. Nonprecision approach -- ceiling 800 ft. and visibility 2 SM
    b. Precision approach -- ceiling 600 ft. and visibility 2 SM

2. For an airport with no instrument approach procedure to be listed as an alternate airport, the forecast weather conditions at the time of arrival must have a ceiling and visibility that allow descent from the MEA, approach, and landing under basic VFR.

91.171 VOR Equipment Check for IFR Operations

1. To operate an airplane under IFR using the VOR, you must ensure that the VOR equipment has been operationally checked within the preceding 30 days and found to be within prescribed limits.

2. The maximum bearing error allowed for an operational VOR equipment check when using an FAA-approved ground test signal (such as a VOT) is ±4°.

    a. When performing an operational check using an airborne checkpoint, the maximum tolerance is ±6°.

3. Each person making the VOR operational check must enter the date, place, and bearing error and sign the aircraft log or other record.

91.175 Takeoff and Landing under IFR

1. One requirement for a pilot on an instrument approach to operate below the MDA or DH, or to continue the approach, is that the airplane continuously be in a position from which a descent to landing on the intended runway can be made at a normal rate using normal maneuvers.

2. A pilot is not authorized to land an airplane from an instrument approach unless the flight visibility is at, or exceeds, the visibility prescribed in the approach procedure being used.

3. In the case of a radar vector to a final approach course or fix, a timed approach from a holding fix, or an approach for which the procedure specifies "No PT," a pilot may not make a procedure turn unless cleared to do so by ATC.

91.177 Minimum Altitudes for IFR Operations

1.   Except during takeoff or landing, the minimum altitude for IFR flight, within a horizontal distance of 4 NM from the course to be flown, is 2,000 ft. above the highest obstacle over designated mountainous terrain or 1,000 ft. above the highest obstacle over terrain elsewhere.

91.183 IFR Communications

1.   The pilot in command of an airplane operated under IFR in controlled airspace, and not in radar contact, shall report by radio as soon as possible the time and altitude of passing each designated reporting point.

91.187 Operation under IFR in Controlled Airspace: Malfunction Reports

1.   The pilot in command of an airplane operated under IFR in controlled airspace shall report to ATC, as soon as practicable, any malfunctions of navigational, approach, or communication equipment occurring in flight.

91.203 Civil Aircraft: Certifications Required

1.   No person may operate a civil aircraft unless the aircraft has a U.S. airworthiness certificate displayed in a manner that makes it legible to passengers and crew.

2.   To operate a civil aircraft, a valid U.S. registration issued to the owner of the aircraft must be on board.

91.205 Powered Civil Aircraft with Standard Category U.S. Airworthiness Certificates: Instrument and Equipment Requirements

1.   For a flight for hire over water beyond power-off gliding distance from shore, approved flotation gear must be readily available to each occupant.

2.   An anticollision light system is required for powered aircraft during VFR night flights.

3.   An electric landing light is required for VFR night flights when operated for hire.

91.207 Emergency Locator Transmitters

1.   Emergency locator transmitter (ELT) batteries must be replaced (or recharged, if rechargeable batteries) after 1 cumulative hour of use or after 50% of their useful life expires.

2.   An ELT is required to be inspected every 12 months for proper installation, battery corrosion, operation of the controls and crash sensor, and the presence of a sufficient signal radiated from its antenna.

91.209 Aircraft Lights

1.   Airplanes operating between sunset and sunrise must display lighted position (navigation) lights.

2.   If an airplane is not equipped with an anticollision light system, no one may operate that airplane after sunset.

91.211 Supplemental Oxygen

1. At cabin pressure altitudes above 15,000 ft. MSL, each passenger of the aircraft **must be provided** with supplemental oxygen.

   a. At cabin pressure altitudes above 14,000 ft. MSL, each required crewmember **must be provided and must use** supplemental oxygen.

2. If a flight is conducted at cabin pressure altitudes above 12,500 ft. MSL up to and including 14,000 ft. MSL, oxygen must be used by required crewmembers for the time in excess of 30 min. at that altitude.

91.213 Inoperative Instruments and Equipment

1. The primary purpose of a minimum equipment list (MEL) is to list the equipment that can be inoperative and still not affect the airworthiness of an aircraft. An MEL allows aircraft to be operated with inoperative equipment determined to be nonessential for safe flight.

2. Authority for approval of an MEL must be obtained from the responsible FAA Flight Standards office.

3. If an aircraft operating under 14 CFR Part 91, for which a master MEL has not been developed, is determined to have an inoperative instrument or piece of equipment that does not constitute a hazard to the aircraft,

   a. The item should be removed or deactivated.
   b. The item should be placarded as "Inoperative."
   c. Repairs can be deferred indefinitely.

      1) Consideration should be given to the effect that an inoperative component may have on aircraft operation, particularly if other items are inoperative.

91.215 ATC Transponder and Altitude Reporting Equipment and Use

1. A transponder with altitude encoding (Mode C) equipment is required

   a. In all airspace above 10,000 ft. MSL, excluding airspace at or below 2,500 ft. AGL.

   b. In Class A, Class B, and Class C airspace.

   c. Within 30 NM of Class B airports listed in Appendix A, Section 1, of 14 CFR 91.25, from the surface up to 10,000 feet MSL.

2. In order to enter Class B airspace, you must submit a request for a deviation from the controlling ATC facility at least 1 hr. before the proposed flight.

91.225 ADS-B Out Equipment and Use

1. No person may operate an aircraft in the following airspace unless the aircraft has the appropriate ADS-B Out equipment installed:

   a. Within Class A airspace
   b. Within and above Class B airspace
   c. Within 30 NM of the Class B airspace primary airport
   d. Within and above Class C airspace
   e. At and above 10,000 ft. MSL except at and below 2,500 ft. AGL
   f. At and above 3,000 ft. MSL over the Gulf of Mexico from the U.S. coastline out to 12 NM

2.   These requirements do not apply to any aircraft not originally certificated with an electrical system or that has not subsequently been certified with such a system installed.

3.   Requests for ATC-authorized deviations from these requirements must be made to the appropriate ATC facility

   a.   At any time for an aircraft with an inoperative ADS-B Out

   b.   At least 1 hr. before the proposed operation of an aircraft that is not equipped with ADS-B Out

4.   Aircraft operating with ADS-B Out must operate this equipment in the transmit mode at all times unless

   a.   Authorized by the Administrator in the interest of national defense, security, intelligence, or law enforcement purposes or

   b.   Directed by ATC for safe air traffic control functions.

91.227 ADS-B Out Equipment Performance Requirements

1.   ADS-B Out is a function of an aircraft's onboard avionics that periodically broadcasts the aircraft's state vector (3-dimensional position and 3-dimensional velocity).

2.   Aircraft operating in Class A airspace are required to have ADS-B Out equipment installed that operates on the frequency of 1090 MHz.

3.   Aircraft operating in airspace designated for ADS-B Out, but outside of Class A airspace, must have ADS-B Out equipment installed that either

   a.   Operates on the frequency of 1090 MHz or
   b.   Operates using a universal access transceiver (UAT) on the frequency of 978 MHz.

91.311 Towing: Other than under Sec. 91.309

1.   In order to operate an aircraft towing an advertising banner, the pilot must obtain a certificate of waiver from the administrator of the FAA.

91.313 Restricted Category Civil Aircraft: Operating Limitations

1.   Persons or property cannot be transported for compensation or hire in a restricted category airplane.

91.315 Limited Category Civil Aircraft: Operating Limitations

1.   Persons or property cannot be transported for compensation or hire in a limited category aircraft.

91.319 Aircraft Having Experimental Certificates: Operating Limitations

1.   Persons or property cannot be transported for compensation or hire in an airplane that has an experimental certificate.

91.325 Primary Category Aircraft: Operating Limitations

1.   Persons or property cannot be transported for compensation or hire in a primary category aircraft.

91.403 General

1. The owner or operator of an aircraft is primarily responsible for

    a. Maintaining that aircraft in an airworthy condition
    b. Assuring compliance with all Airworthiness Directives

2. An operator is a person who uses, causes to use, or authorizes to use an aircraft for the purpose of air navigation, including the piloting of an aircraft, with or without the right of legal control (i.e., owner, lessee, or otherwise).

    a. Thus, the pilot in command is also responsible for maintaining the aircraft in an airworthy condition and for complying with all Airworthiness Directives.

91.405 Maintenance Required

1. After an annual inspection has been completed and the aircraft has been returned to service, an appropriate notation must be made in the aircraft maintenance records.

2. A standard airworthiness certificate remains in effect as long as the airplane receives required maintenance and inspections.

91.407 Operation after Maintenance, Preventive Maintenance, Rebuilding, or Alteration

1. When aircraft alterations or repairs substantially change the flight characteristics, the aircraft documents must show that it was test flown and approved for return to service prior to carrying passengers.

    a. The pilot test flying the aircraft must be at least a private pilot and rated for the type of aircraft being tested.

91.409 Inspections

1. For commercial operations, an inspection is required every 100 hr.

    a. The 100 hr. may be exceeded by no more than 10 hr. if necessary to reach a place at which an inspection can be performed.
    b. An annual inspection may be substituted for a 100-hr. inspection but not vice versa.

91.413 ATC Transponder Tests and Inspections

1. An ATC transponder may not be used unless, within the preceding 24 calendar months, that transponder has been tested, inspected, and found to comply with appropriate regulations.

91.417 Maintenance Records

1. Each owner or operator must keep maintenance records for each airplane. The records must include

    a. Current status of life-limited parts of the airframe and each engine, propeller, rotor, and appliance
    b. Current status of each Airworthiness Directive (AD)
    c. Preventive maintenance accomplished by a pilot

91.421 Rebuilt Engine Maintenance Records

1. A new maintenance record may be used for a rebuilt (zero-time) engine, but the new records must include the status of previous Airworthiness Directives.

4.8   14 CFR PART 119

119.1 Applicability

1.   A commercial pilot may act as pilot in command of the following operations, which are not regulated by 14 CFR Part 119:

    a.   Nonstop flights within a 25 SM radius of an airport for the purpose of carrying persons for intentional parachute jumps

    b.   Aerial application (e.g., crop dusting, spraying), aerial photography, and bird surveying.

4.9 NTSB PART 830

830.2 Definitions

1.   For an injury to be defined as a "serious injury" on the basis of hospitalization, the injury must require hospitalization for more than 48 hours, commencing within 7 days from the date the injury was received.

830.5 Immediate Notification

1.   Even when no injuries occur to occupants, an airplane accident resulting in substantial damage must be reported to the nearest National Transportation Safety Board (NTSB) field office immediately.

    a.   Damage to the landing gear, wheels, and tires is not considered "substantial damage," and thus no notification or report is required.

2.   The following incidents must also be reported immediately to the NTSB:

    a.   Inability of any required crewmember to perform normal flight duties because of in-flight injury or illness

    b.   In-flight fire (but not a ground fire)

    c.   Flight control system malfunction or failure

830.15 Reports and Statements to Be Filed

1.   A written accident report is required to be filed with the nearest NTSB field office within 10 days of an accident.

2.   A written incident report is required only upon request.

4.10 NEAR MIDAIR COLLISION REPORTING

1. The primary purpose of the Near Midair Collision (NMAC) Reporting Program is to provide information for use in enhancing the safety and efficiency of the National Airspace System.

   a. Data obtained from NMAC reports are used by the FAA to improve the quality of FAA services to users and to develop programs, policies, and procedures aimed at the reduction of NMAC occurrences.

2. A near midair collision is defined as an incident associated with the operation of an aircraft in which a possibility of collision occurs as a result of proximity of less than 500 feet to another aircraft, or a report is received from a pilot or a flight crew member stating that a collision hazard existed between two or more aircraft.

3. It is the responsibility of the pilot and/or flight crew to determine whether a near midair collision did actually occur and, if so, to initiate an NMAC report.

   a. Be specific, as ATC will not interpret a casual remark to mean that an NMAC is being reported. The pilot should state, "I wish to report a near midair collision."

4. Pilots and/or flight crew members involved in NMAC occurrences are urged to report each incident immediately

   a. By radio or telephone to the nearest FAA ATC facility or FSS.
   b. In writing, in lieu of the above, to the responsible Flight Standards office.

5. The Flight Standards office in whose area the incident occurred is responsible for the investigation and reporting of NMACs.

QUESTIONS AND ANSWER EXPLANATIONS: All of the commercial pilot knowledge test questions chosen by the FAA for release as well as additional questions selected by Gleim relating to the material in the previous outlines are provided on the following pages. These questions have been organized into the same subunits as the outlines. To the immediate right of each question are the correct answer and answer explanations. You should cover these answers and answer explanations while responding to the questions. Refer to the general discussion in the Introduction on how to take the FAA knowledge test.

Remember that the questions from the FAA knowledge test bank have been reordered by topic and organized into a meaningful sequence. Also, the first line of the answer explanation gives the citation of the authoritative source for the answer.

QUESTI

4.1 14   t 1

1.1   Definitions

1. Which of the following terms describes an airport?

A. An area of land or water that is used or intended to be used for the landing and takeoff of aircraft, and includes its buildings and facilities, if any.

B. An area of land that is used for the takeoff and landing of aircraft, but does not include buildings since not all airports have buildings.

C. All runway, taxiway, and ramp areas created for use by aircraft.

Answer (A) is correct. (14 CFR 1.1)
DISCUSSION: Section 1.1 of the Federal Aviation Regulations defines an airport as "an area of land or water that is used or intended to be used for the landing and takeoff of aircraft, and includes its buildings and facilities, if any."
Answer (B) is incorrect. Section 1.1 of the Federal Aviation Regulations includes areas of water and any buildings and facilities in the definition of an airport. **Answer (C) is incorrect.** Section 1.1 of the Federal Aviation Regulations includes areas of land and water and any buildings and facilities in the definition of an airport.

2. Regulations which refer to "operate" relate to that person who

A. acts as pilot in command of the aircraft.

B. is the sole manipulator of the aircraft controls.

C. causes the aircraft to be used or authorizes its use.

Answer (C) is correct. (14 CFR 1.1)
DISCUSSION: To operate an aircraft means to use, cause to use, or authorize to use aircraft for the purpose of air navigation, including the piloting of aircraft, with or without the right of legal control (as owner, lessee, or otherwise).
Answer (A) is incorrect. The pilot in command may not necessarily be the operator of the aircraft. **Answer (B) is incorrect.** The sole manipulator may not necessarily be the operator of the aircraft.

3. Regulations which refer to "commercial operators" relate to that person who

A. is the owner of a small scheduled airline.

B. for compensation or hire, engages in the carriage by aircraft in air commerce of persons or property, as an air carrier.

C. for compensation or hire, engages in the carriage by aircraft in air commerce of persons or property, other than as an air carrier.

Answer (C) is correct. (14 CFR 1.1)
DISCUSSION: A commercial operator is a person who, for compensation or hire, engages in the carriage by aircraft in air commerce of persons or property, other than as an air carrier or foreign air carrier or under the authority of Part 375.
Answer (A) is incorrect. Commercial operations do not apply to airlines. **Answer (B) is incorrect.** Commercial operations do not apply to airlines.

4. Regulations which refer to the "operational control" of a flight are in relation to

A. the specific duties of any required crewmember.

B. acting as the sole manipulator of the aircraft controls.

C. exercising authority over initiating, conducting, or terminating a flight.

Answer (C) is correct. (14 CFR 1.1)
DISCUSSION: Operational control of a flight means the exercise of authority over initiating, conducting, or terminating a flight.
Answer (A) is incorrect. Assigning specific duties to a crewmember is only a small portion of exercising operational control. **Answer (B) is incorrect.** Acting as sole manipulator of an aircraft is a flight crew, not an operator, responsibility.

1.2 Abbreviations and Symbols

5. Which is the correct symbol for the stalling speed or the minimum steady flight speed in a specified configuration?

A. V_S.

B. V_{S1}.

C. V_{S0}.

Answer (B) is correct. (14 CFR 1.2)
DISCUSSION: V_{S1} means the stalling speed or the minimum steady flight speed obtained in a specified configuration. This configuration is generally specified as gear and flaps retracted.
Answer (A) is incorrect. V_S means the stalling speed or the minimum steady flight speed at which the airplane is controllable with no particular configuration specified. **Answer (C) is incorrect.** V_{S0} means the stalling speed or the minimum steady flight speed in the landing configuration.

6. Which is the correct symbol for the stalling speed or the minimum steady flight speed at which the airplane is controllable?

    A. V_S.

    B. V_{S1}.

    C. V_{S0}.

Answer (A) is correct. (14 CFR 1.2)
    DISCUSSION: V_S means the stalling speed or the minimum steady flight speed at which the airplane is controllable. No configuration is specified.
    Answer (B) is incorrect. V_{S1} means the stalling speed or the minimum steady flight speed obtained in a specified configuration. **Answer (C) is incorrect.** V_{S0} means the stalling speed or the minimum steady flight speed in the landing configuration.

7. 14 CFR Part 1 defines V_F as

    A. design flap speed.

    B. flap operating speed.

    C. maximum flap extended speed.

Answer (A) is correct. (14 CFR 1.2)
    DISCUSSION: V_F means design flap speed.
    Answer (B) is incorrect. The flap operating range, not speed, is indicated by the white arc on the airspeed indicator. **Answer (C) is incorrect.** V_{FE} means maximum flap extended speed.

8. 14 CFR Part 1 defines V_{NO} as

    A. maximum structural cruising speed.

    B. normal operating speed.

    C. maximum operating speed.

Answer (A) is correct. (14 CFR 1.2)
    DISCUSSION: V_{NO} means maximum structural cruising speed.
    Answer (B) is incorrect. The normal operating range, not speed, is indicated by the green arc on the airspeed indicator. **Answer (C) is incorrect.** V_{MO}, not V_{NO}, means maximum operating limit speed.

9. 14 CFR Part 1 defines V_{LE} as

    A. maximum landing gear extended speed.

    B. maximum landing gear operating speed.

    C. maximum leading edge flaps extended speed.

Answer (A) is correct. (14 CFR 1.2)
    DISCUSSION: V_{LE} means maximum landing gear extended speed.
    Answer (B) is incorrect. V_{LO} means maximum landing gear operating speed. **Answer (C) is incorrect.** Maximum leading edge flaps extended speed is not defined in 14 CFR Part 1.

10. 14 CFR Part 1 defines V_{NE} as

    A. maximum nose wheel extend speed.

    B. never-exceed speed.

    C. maximum landing gear extended speed.

Answer (B) is correct. (14 CFR 1.2)
    DISCUSSION: V_{NE} is defined as the never-exceed speed.
    Answer (A) is incorrect. V_{NE} means the never-exceed speed, not the maximum nosewheel extend speed. **Answer (C) is incorrect.** V_{LE}, not V_{NE}, means the maximum landing gear extended speed.

11. 14 CFR Part 1 defines V_Y as

    A. speed for best rate of descent.

    B. speed for best angle of climb.

    C. speed for best rate of climb.

Answer (C) is correct. (14 CFR 1.2)
    DISCUSSION: V_Y means the speed for the best rate of climb.
    Answer (A) is incorrect. V_Y means the speed for the best rate of climb, not descent. **Answer (B) is incorrect.** V_X, not V_Y, means the speed for the best angle of climb.

12. 14 CFR Part 1 defines V_{NO} as

    A. maximum structural cruising speed.

    B. maximum operating limit speed.

    C. never-exceed speed.

Answer (A) is correct. (14 CFR 1.2)
    DISCUSSION: V_{NO} means maximum structural cruising speed.
    Answer (B) is incorrect. V_{MO}, not V_{NO}, means maximum operating limit speed. **Answer (C) is incorrect.** V_{NE}, not V_{NO}, means never-exceed speed.

61.5 Certificates and Ratings Issued under This Part

21. Which of the following are considered aircraft class ratings?

    A. Transport, normal, utility, and acrobatic.

    B. Airplane, rotorcraft, glider, and lighter-than-air.

    C. Single-engine land, multiengine land, single-engine sea, and multiengine sea.

Answer (C) is correct. (14 CFR 61.5)
    DISCUSSION: Aircraft class ratings (with respect to airmen) are single-engine land, multiengine land, single-engine sea, and multiengine sea.
    Answer (A) is incorrect. Transport, normal, utility, and acrobatic are aircraft categories with respect to the certification of aircraft, not airmen. **Answer (B) is incorrect.** Airplane, rotorcraft, glider, and lighter-than-air are categories, not classes, of aircraft with respect to airmen.

61.15 Offenses Involving Alcohol or Drugs

22. A pilot convicted of operating a motor vehicle while either intoxicated by, impaired by, or under the influence of alcohol or a drug is required to provide a

    A. written report to the FAA Civil Aerospace Medical Institute (CAMI) within 60 days after the motor vehicle action.

    B. written report to the FAA Security and Hazardous Materials Safety Office (AXE-700) not later than 60 days after the conviction.

    C. the notification of the conviction to an FAA Aviation Medical Examiner (AME) not later than 60 days after the motor vehicle action.

Answer (B) is correct. (14 CFR 61.15)
    DISCUSSION: A pilot convicted of operating a motor vehicle while either intoxicated by, impaired by, or under the influence of alcohol or a drug is required to provide a written report to the FAA Security and Hazardous Materials Safety Office (AXE-700) not later than 60 days after the conviction.
    Answer (A) is incorrect. A pilot convicted of operating a motor vehicle while either intoxicated by, impaired by, or under the influence of alcohol or a drug is required to provide a written report to the FAA Security and Hazardous Materials Safety Office, not the FAA CAMI, within 60 days after the motor vehicle action. **Answer (C) is incorrect.** A pilot convicted of operating a motor vehicle while either intoxicated by, impaired by, or under the influence of alcohol or a drug is required to provide a written report to the FAA Security and Hazardous Materials Safety Office, not notify an AME, not later than 60 days after the motor vehicle action.

23. A pilot convicted of a motor vehicle offense involving alcohol or drugs is required to provide a written report to the

    A. FAA Flight Standards office within 60 days after such action.

    B. FAA Civil Aerospace Medical Institute (CAMI) within 60 days after the conviction.

    C. FAA Security and Hazardous Materials Safety Office (AXE-700) within 60 days after such action.

Answer (C) is correct. (14 CFR 61.15)
    DISCUSSION: A pilot convicted of a motor vehicle offense involving alcohol or drugs is required to provide a written report to the FAA Security and Hazardous Materials Safety Office (AXE-700) within 60 days after such action.
    Answer (A) is incorrect. A pilot convicted of a motor vehicle offense involving alcohol or drugs is required to provide a written report to the FAA Security and Hazardous Materials Safety Office, not a Flight Standards office, within 60 days after such action. **Answer (B) is incorrect.** A pilot convicted of a motor vehicle offense involving alcohol or drugs is required to provide a written report to the FAA Security and Hazardous Materials Safety Office, not the FAA CAMI, within 60 days after the conviction.

24. A pilot convicted for the violation of any Federal or State statute relating to the process, manufacture, transportation, distribution, or sale of narcotic drugs is grounds for

    A. a written report to be filed with the FAA Security and Hazardous Materials Safety Office (AXE-700) not later than 60 days after the conviction.

    B. notification of this conviction to the FAA Civil Aerospace Medical Institute (CAMI) within 60 days after the conviction.

    C. suspension or revocation of any certificate, rating, or authorization issued under 14 CFR Part 61.

Answer (C) is correct. (14 CFR 61.15)
    DISCUSSION: A pilot convicted for the violation of any Federal or State statute relating to the process, manufacture, transportation, distribution, or sale of narcotic drugs is grounds for suspension or revocation of any certificate, rating, or authorization issued under 14 CFR Part 61.
    Answer (A) is incorrect. A written report must be filed with the FAA Security and Hazardous Materials Safety Office not later than 60 days after a pilot is convicted of a motor vehicle offense involving alcohol or drugs, not for a conviction for the violation of any Federal or State statute relating to the process, manufacture, transportation, or sale of narcotic drugs. **Answer (B) is incorrect.** A pilot convicted for the violation of any Federal or State statute relating to the process, manufacture, transportation, distribution, or sale of narcotic drugs is grounds for suspension or revocation of any certificate, rating, or authorization issued under 14 CFR Part 61. The pilot is not required to notify CAMI of the conviction.

25. A pilot convicted of operating an aircraft as a crewmember under the influence of alcohol, or using drugs that affect the person's faculties, is grounds for a

   A. written report to be filed with the FAA Security and Hazardous Materials Safety Office (AXE-700) not later than 60 days after the conviction.

   B. written notification to the FAA Civil Aerospace Medical Institute (CAMI) within 60 days after the conviction.

   C. denial of an application for an FAA certificate, rating, or authorization issued under 14 CFR Part 61.

Answer (C) is correct. (14 CFR 61.15)
   DISCUSSION: A pilot convicted of operating an aircraft as a crewmember under the influence of alcohol, or using drugs that affect the person's faculties (acts prohibited by Sec. 91.17), is grounds for denial of an application for a certificate or rating, or authorization issued under 14 CFR Part 61 for a period of one year after the date of that act.
   Answer (A) is incorrect. A written report must be filed with the FAA Security and Hazardous Materials Safety Office not later than 60 days after a pilot is convicted of a motor vehicle offense involving alcohol or drugs, not for being convicted of operating an aircraft as a crewmember under the influence of alcohol, or using drugs that affect the person's faculties.
Answer (B) is incorrect. A pilot convicted of operating an aircraft as a crewmember under the influence of alcohol, or using drugs that affect a person's faculties, is grounds for denial of an application for an FAA certificate or rating. The pilot is not required to notify CAMI of the conviction.

61.19 Duration of Pilot and Instructor Certificates

26. Does a commercial pilot certificate have a specific expiration date?

   A. No, it is issued without an expiration date.

   B. Yes, it expires at the end of the 24th month after the month in which it was issued.

   C. No, but commercial privileges expire if a flight review is not satisfactorily completed each 12 months.

Answer (A) is correct. (14 CFR 61.19)
   DISCUSSION: Any pilot certificate (other than a student pilot or flight instructor certificate) issued under Part 61 is issued without a specific expiration date.
   Answer (B) is incorrect. A flight instructor certificate, not a commercial pilot certificate, expires at the end of the 24th month after the month in which it was issued. **Answer (C) is incorrect.** A flight review is required at the end of the 24th month, not the 12th month.

61.23 Medical Certificates: Requirement and Duration

27. A second-class medical certificate issued to a commercial pilot on April 10, this year, permits the pilot to exercise which of the following privileges?

   A. Commercial pilot privileges through April 30, next year.

   B. Commercial pilot privileges through April 10, 2 years later.

   C. Private pilot privileges through, but not after, March 31, next year.

Answer (A) is correct. (14 CFR 61.23)
   DISCUSSION: A second-class medical certificate expires at the end of the last day of the 12th month after the examination for operations requiring a commercial pilot certificate (e.g., April 30, next year).
   Answer (B) is incorrect. A second-class medical is valid for commercial operations for 12 months, not 24 months, and expires on the last day of the month. **Answer (C) is incorrect.** A second-class medical is valid for private or recreational pilot operations, not commercial pilot operations, for 24 months (if over age 40 at the time of examination) or 60 months (if under age 40 at the time of examination).

28. May a pilot in the U.S. Military use a current U.S. Armed Forces medical examination to exercise the privileges of an FAA Commercial Pilot Certificate?

   A. Yes, the military examination may be used for any civilian flight operations.

   B. No, the medical examination may not be used to exercise the privileges of an FAA Commercial Pilot Certificate.

   C. No, a military medical examination may not be used for any civilian flight operations.

Answer (B) is correct. (14 CFR 61.23)
   DISCUSSION: A U.S. Armed Forces medical examination may be used in place of an FAA medical certificate only for flights that do not require higher than a third-class medical certificate. A military medical examination may not be used for commercial pilot certificate privileges since a second-class medical certificate is required.
   Answer (A) is incorrect. A U.S. Armed Forces medical examination may only be used for flights that do not require higher than a third-class medical certificate. **Answer (C) is incorrect.** A U.S. Armed Forces medical examination may be used for flights that do not require higher than a third-class medical certificate if the flight conducted is a domestic flight operation within U.S. airspace.

29. To exercise the privileges of a Commercial Pilot Certificate, a person must

    A. hold at least a Second-Class Medical Certificate.

    B. have a BasicMed checklist signed by a certifying physician.

    C. have received an endorsement from an authorized instructor.

Answer (A) is correct. (14 CFR 61.23)

    DISCUSSION: At least a second-class medical certificate is required when exercising the privileges of a commercial pilot certificate.

    Answer (B) is incorrect. BasicMed allows a person to exercise private pilot privileges with some additional restrictions, not commercial pilot privileges. **Answer (C) is incorrect.** An endorsement from an instructor does not authorize a person to exercise commercial pilot privileges. A commercial pilot certificate and second-class medical certificate are required.

30. In order to qualify for BasicMed, you must have received a comprehensive examination from:

    A. An FAA-designated Aviation Medical Examiner within the previous 60 months.

    B. A state-licensed physician within the previous 24 months.

    C. A state-licensed physician within the previous 48 months.

Answer (C) is correct. (14 CFR 61.23)

    DISCUSSION: In order to qualify for BasicMed, you must have received a comprehensive examination from a state-licensed physician within the previous 48 months.

    Answer (A) is incorrect. You are required to have received the examination from a state-licensed physician, not an FAA-designated Aviation Medical Examiner, and you must have received the examination within the previous 48 months, not the previous 60 months. **Answer (B) is incorrect.** You must have received the examination from a state-licensed physician within the previous 48 months, not the previous 24 months.

61.31 Type Rating Requirements, Additional Training, and Authorization Requirements

31. To act as pilot in command of an airplane that is equipped with retractable landing gear, flaps, and controllable pitch propeller, a person is required to

    A. hold a multiengine airplane class rating.

    B. make at least six takeoffs and landings in such an airplane within the preceding 6 months.

    C. receive and log ground and flight training in such an airplane, and obtain a logbook endorsement certifying proficiency.

Answer (C) is correct. (14 CFR 61.31)

    DISCUSSION: No person may act as pilot in command of a complex airplane (an airplane that has retractable landing gear, flaps, and a controllable pitch propeller), unless the person has received and logged ground and flight training from an authorized instructor in a complex airplane and obtained a logbook endorsement certifying proficiency.

    Answer (A) is incorrect. It is not necessary to hold a multiengine rating to pilot a single-engine complex airplane. **Answer (B) is incorrect.** To act as pilot in command of a complex airplane, a person is required to receive and log ground and flight training in a complex airplane and obtain a logbook endorsement certifying proficiency, not just make at least six takeoffs and landings in a complex airplane within the preceding 6 months.

32. To act as pilot-in-command of an airplane with more than 200 horsepower, a person is required to

    A. receive and log ground and flight training from a qualified pilot in such an airplane.

    B. obtain an endorsement from a qualified pilot stating that the person is proficient to operate such an airplane.

    C. receive and log ground and flight training from an authorized instructor in such an airplane.

Answer (C) is correct. (14 CFR 61.31)

    DISCUSSION: To act as pilot in command of an airplane with an engine of more than 200 hp. (high-performance), a person is required to receive and log ground and flight training from an authorized instructor in a high-performance airplane, simulator, or flight training device and receive a one-time logbook endorsement from an authorized instructor who certifies the person is proficient to operate a high-performance airplane.

    Answer (A) is incorrect. The ground and flight training must be given by an authorized instructor, not a qualified pilot. Additionally, a one-time logbook endorsement stating that the person is proficient to operate a high-performance airplane is required. **Answer (B) is incorrect.** The endorsement must be given by an authorized instructor, not any qualified pilot, and the endorsement will certify, not state, that the person is proficient to operate such an airplane.

33. When is the pilot in command required to hold a category and class rating appropriate to the aircraft being flown?

    A. On flights when carrying another person.

    B. All solo flights.

    C. On practical tests given by an examiner or FAA inspector.

Answer (A) is correct. (14 CFR 61.31)

    DISCUSSION: To serve as pilot in command of an aircraft carrying passengers, a person must hold the appropriate category, class, and type rating (if a class rating and a type rating are required) for the aircraft to be flown.

    Answer (B) is incorrect. The pilot in command must hold a category and class rating on flights when carrying passengers. **Answer (C) is incorrect.** The pilot in command is not required to hold a category and class rating to the aircraft being flown on a practical test.

34. To act as pilot in command of a tailwheel airplane, without prior experience, a pilot must

A. log ground and flight training from an authorized instructor.

B. pass a competency check and receive an endorsement from an authorized instructor.

C. receive and log flight training from an authorized instructor.

Answer (C) is correct. (14 CFR 61.31)
   DISCUSSION: To act as pilot in command of a tailwheel airplane without prior experience, you must receive and log flight training from an authorized instructor in a tailwheel airplane and have your instructor endorse your logbook stating that you are proficient in the operation of a tailwheel airplane. This is the best answer of the choices given.
   Answer (A) is incorrect. To act as pilot in command of a tailwheel airplane without prior experience, you must receive and log flight training from an authorized instructor. There is no requirement to log ground training. **Answer (B) is incorrect.** To act as pilot in command of a tailwheel airplane without prior experience, you must receive and log flight training and receive a logbook endorsement from an authorized instructor. There is no requirement to pass a competency check.

35. To act as PIC of a high-performance airplane, which training or experience would meet the additional requirements?

A. Logged at least five hours as SIC in a high-performance or turbine-powered airplane in the last 12 calendar months.

B. Received and logged ground and flight training in an airplane with retractable landing gear, flaps, and controllable-pitch propeller.

C. Received and logged ground and flight training in a high-performance airplane and received a logbook endorsement.

Answer (C) is correct. (14 CFR 61.31)
   DISCUSSION: To act as PIC of a high-performance aircraft, the pilot must receive and log ground and flight training from an authorized instructor in a high-performance airplane (an aircraft with more than 200 horsepower) or in a flight simulator or training device that is representative of a high-performance airplane. In addition, that pilot must receive a one-time endorsement in the pilot's logbook from an authorized instructor who certifies that the pilot is proficient to operate a high-performance airplane.
   Answer (A) is incorrect. No specific hourly flight time or recency requirements are necessary to act as PIC of a high-performance airplane. However, the pilot is required to receive and log ground and flight training and to receive a logbook endorsement to act as PIC of a high-performance airplane. **Answer (B) is incorrect.** This answer choice defines a complex airplane rather than a high-performance airplane; a high-performance airplane is one with an engine of more than 200 horsepower. To act as PIC of a high-performance airplane, the pilot must have received and logged ground and flight training in a high-performance airplane and received a one-time logbook endorsement of proficiency.

36. To act as pilot in command of a tailwheel airplane, without prior experience, a pilot must

A. log ground and flight training from an authorized instructor.

B. receive and log flight training from an authorized instructor as well as receive a logbook endorsement from an authorized instructor who finds the person proficient in a tailwheel airplane.

C. pass a competency check and receive an endorsement from an authorized instructor.

Answer (B) is correct. (14 CFR 61.31)
   DISCUSSION: To act as a pilot in command of a tailwheel airplane without prior experience, you must receive and log flight training from an authorized instructor in a tailwheel airplane and have your instructor endorse your logbook stating that you are proficient in the operation of a tailwheel airplane.
   Answer (A) is incorrect. To act as a pilot in command of a tailwheel airplane without prior experience, you must receive and log flight training from an authorized instructor as well as receive a logbook endorsement from an authorized instructor. There is no requirement to log ground training. **Answer (C) is incorrect.** To act as pilot in command of a tailwheel airplane without prior experience, you must receive and log flight training and receive a logbook endorsement from an authorized instructor. There is no requirement to pass a competency check.

37. Unless otherwise authorized, the pilot in command is required to hold a type rating when operating any

A. aircraft that is certificated for more than one pilot.

B. aircraft of more than 12,500 pounds maximum certificated takeoff weight.

C. multiengine airplane having a gross weight of more than 12,000 pounds.

Answer (B) is correct. (14 CFR 61.31)
   DISCUSSION: A person may not act as pilot in command of any aircraft of more than 12,500 lb. maximum takeoff weight unless (s)he holds a type rating for that aircraft.
   Answer (A) is incorrect. An aircraft that is certificated for more than one pilot does not necessarily require a type rating. **Answer (C) is incorrect.** A type rating is required for any, not only multiengine, aircraft having a maximum gross weight of more than 12,500 lb., not 12,000 lb.

61.51 Pilot Logbooks

38. What flight time may a pilot log as second in command?

A. All flight time while acting as second in command in aircraft configured for more than one pilot.

B. Only that flight time during which the second in command is the sole manipulator of the controls.

C. All flight time when qualified and occupying a crewmember station in an aircraft that requires more than one pilot.

Answer (C) is correct. (14 CFR 61.51)
DISCUSSION: A person may log second-in-command flight time only for that flight time during which that person is qualified in accordance with 14 CFR 61.55 and occupies a crewmember station in an aircraft that requires more than one pilot by the aircraft's type certificate.
Answer (A) is incorrect. A pilot may log second-in-command flight time only if (s)he is qualified and the aircraft or regulations required more than one pilot, not if the aircraft is configured for more than one pilot. **Answer (B) is incorrect.** A pilot may log all second-in-command flight time if (s)he is qualified and the aircraft requires more than one pilot, not just when the pilot is the sole manipulator of the controls. If the pilot is rated in that aircraft, (s)he can log PIC when (s)he is the sole manipulator of the controls.

39. What flight time must be documented and recorded by a pilot exercising the privileges of a commercial certificate?

A. All flight time flown for compensation or hire.

B. Only flight time for compensation or hire with passengers aboard which is necessary to meet the recent flight experience requirements.

C. Flight time showing training and aeronautical experience to meet requirements for a certificate, rating, or flight review.

Answer (C) is correct. (14 CFR 61.51)
DISCUSSION: Flight time showing training and aeronautical experience used to meet the requirements for a certificate, rating, or flight review must be documented and recorded in a reliable record (logbook). Additionally, the aeronautical experience required for meeting the recent flight experience requirements must be recorded in your logbook.
Answer (A) is incorrect. You must log the training and aeronautical experience used to meet the requirements for a certificate, rating, or flight review and the recent flight experience requirements, not all flight time for compensation or hire. **Answer (B) is incorrect.** While you are required to log the experience required for meeting the recent flight experience requirements, it can be done at any time, not only when a flight is for compensation or hire with passengers on board.

61.55 Second-in-Command Qualifications

40. To serve as second in command of an airplane that is certificated for more than one pilot crewmember, and operated under Part 91, a person must

A. receive and log flight training from an authorized flight instructor in the type of airplane privileges are requested.

B. hold at least a commercial pilot certificate with an airplane category rating.

C. within the last 12 months become familiar with the required information, and perform and log pilot time in the type of airplane for which privileges are requested.

Answer (C) is correct. (14 CFR 61.55)
DISCUSSION: To serve as second in command of an airplane type certificated for more than one required pilot flight crewmember and operated under Part 91, a person, within the previous 12 calendar months, must become familiar with the required information (system operations, performance and limitations, normal and emergency operations, and the flight manual and placards) and have logged pilot time in the type of airplane for which privileges are requested.
Answer (A) is incorrect. To serve as second in command of an airplane that is certificated for more than one pilot flight crewmember, a person, within the previous 12 calendar months, must become familiar with the required information and must have performed and logged pilot time, not just received and logged flight training, in the type of airplane for which privileges are requested. **Answer (B) is incorrect.** To serve as second in command of an airplane that is certificated for more than one pilot flight crewmember under Part 91, a person must hold at least a private pilot certificate, not a commercial pilot certificate, with an airplane and appropriate class rating.

61.56 Flight Review

41. To act as pilot in command of an aircraft under 14 CFR Part 91, a commercial pilot must have satisfactorily accomplished a flight review or completed a proficiency check within the preceding

A. 24 calendar months.

B. 12 calendar months.

C. 6 calendar months.

Answer (A) is correct. (14 CFR 61.56)
DISCUSSION: No person may act as pilot in command of an aircraft unless, within the preceding 24 calendar months, (s)he has accomplished a flight review; a pilot proficiency check for a certificate, rating, or operating privilege; or one or more phases of the FAA Wings program.
Answer (B) is incorrect. A flight review or a proficiency check must have been accomplished within the preceding 24 months, not 12 months. **Answer (C) is incorrect.** A flight review or a proficiency check must have been accomplished within the preceding 24 months, not 6 months.

61.57 Recent Flight Experience: Pilot in Command

42. If a pilot does not meet the recency of experience requirements for night flight and official sunset is 1900 CST, the latest time passengers should be carried is

A. 1900 CST.

B. 1800 CST.

C. 1959 CST.

Answer (C) is correct. (14 CFR 61.57)
DISCUSSION: If a pilot does not meet the recent night experience requirements, (s)he may not carry passengers during the period from 1 hr. after sunset to 1 hr. before sunrise. If sunset is 1900 CST, the latest that passengers may be carried is 1959 CST.
Answer (A) is incorrect. Without recent night experience, a pilot may not carry passengers beginning 1 hr. after sunset, not at sunset. At sunset, the airplane must have lighted position lights. **Answer (B) is incorrect.** Without recent night experience, a pilot may not carry passengers beginning 1 hr. after, not before, sunset.

43. Prior to carrying passengers at night, the pilot in command must have accomplished the required takeoffs and landings in

A. any category aircraft.

B. the same category and class of aircraft to be used.

C. the same category, class, and type of aircraft (if a type rating is required).

Answer (C) is correct. (14 CFR 61.57)
DISCUSSION: No person may act as pilot in command of an aircraft carrying passengers at night unless that person has made at least three takeoffs and landings to a full stop within the preceding 90 days; that person was the sole manipulator of the controls; and the takeoffs and landings were performed in the same category, class, and type (if a type rating is required) of aircraft.
Answer (A) is incorrect. The takeoffs and landings must be in the same category, class, and type (if a type rating is required) of aircraft, not just the same category. **Answer (B) is incorrect.** If a type rating is required in a particular aircraft, then the takeoffs and landings must also be done in the same type of aircraft, not only the same category and class.

44. To act as pilot in command of an aircraft under IFR, what is the minimum instrument flight experience you must have logged during the preceding six months, in the same category of aircraft?

A. Holding procedures, intercepting and tracking courses through the use of navigation systems, and six instrument approaches.

B. Six hours of instrument time in any aircraft, and six instrument approaches.

C. Six instrument approaches, three of which must be in the same category and class of aircraft to be flown, and 6 hours of instrument time in any aircraft.

Answer (A) is correct. (14 CFR 61.57)
DISCUSSION: Acting as PIC of an aircraft under IFR requires a minimum of six approaches logged in the 6 calendar months preceding the month of the flight, holding procedures, and intercepting and tracking courses through the use of navigation systems. This can be recalled with 66-HIT: 6 approaches, 6 months, holding, intercepting, and tracking.
Answer (B) is incorrect. There are no minimum hourly requirements for maintaining instrument experience. **Answer (C) is incorrect.** All six of the minimum required six instrument approaches must be conducted in an airplane, powered-lift, helicopter, or airship, as appropriate, for the instrument rating privileges to be maintained in actual weather conditions or under simulated conditions using a view-limiting device.

45. No pilot may act as pilot in command of an aircraft under IFR or in weather conditions less than the minimums prescribed for VFR unless that pilot has, within the past 6 months, performed and logged under actual or simulated instrument conditions, at least

A. six instrument approaches, holding procedures, intercepting and tracking courses, or passed an instrument proficiency check in an aircraft that is appropriate to the aircraft category.

B. six instrument flights and six approaches.

C. three instrument approaches and logged 3 hours of instruments.

Answer (A) is correct. (14 CFR 61.57)
DISCUSSION: No pilot may act as pilot in command when operating under IFR or in weather conditions less than the minimums prescribed for VFR unless (s)he has, within the 6 calendar months preceding the month of the flight, logged instrument time under actual or simulated IFR conditions in the category of aircraft involved or in an appropriate flight simulator or flight training device and has performed at least six instrument approaches, holding procedures, and intercepting and tracking courses through the use of navigation systems. An alternative way to remain current is to pass an instrument proficiency check in the category of aircraft involved.
Answer (B) is incorrect. Only six approaches, not six instrument flights, are required, and holding procedures and intercepting and tracking courses must also be performed. **Answer (C) is incorrect.** Six, not three, instrument approaches are required, and there is no instrument time requirement.

46. You have accomplished 25 takeoffs and landings in multi-engine land airplanes in the previous 45 days. For a flight you plan to conduct today, this meets the PIC recency of experience requirements to carry passengers in which airplanes?

A. Multi- or single-engine land.
B. Single-engine land airplane.
C. Multi-engine land airplane.

Answer (C) is correct. (14 CFR 61.57)
DISCUSSION: No person may act as a pilot in command of an aircraft carrying passengers unless that person has made at least three takeoffs and three landings within the preceding 90 days and the required takeoffs and landings were performed in an aircraft of the same category (airplane, rotorcraft, glider, etc.), class (single-engine, multi-engine, land, water, gyroplane, etc.), and type (if a type rating is required). Therefore, this meets PIC recency of experience requirements to carry passengers in multi-engine land airplanes.
Answer (A) is incorrect. The required takeoffs and landings must be performed in an aircraft of the same category (airplane, rotorcraft, glider, etc.), class (single-engine, multi-engine, land, water, gyroplane, etc.), and type (if a type rating is required). Therefore, this meets PIC recency of experience requirements to carry passengers in multi-engine land airplanes, not multi- or single-engine land. **Answer (B) is incorrect.** The required takeoffs and landings must be performed in an aircraft of the same category (airplane, rotorcraft, glider, etc.), class (single-engine, multi-engine, land, water, gyroplane; etc.), and type (if a type rating is required). Therefore, this meets PIC recency of experience requirements to carry passengers in multi-engine land airplanes, not single-engine land airplanes.

61.58 Pilot-in-Command Proficiency Check: Operation of Aircraft Requiring More than One Pilot Flight Crewmember

47. To serve as pilot in command of an airplane that is certified for more than one pilot crewmember, and operated under Part 91, a person must

A. complete a flight review within the preceding 24 calendar months.
B. receive and log ground and flight training from an authorized flight instructor.
C. complete a pilot-in-command proficiency check within the preceding 12 calendar months in an airplane that is type certified for more than one pilot.

Answer (C) is correct. (14 CFR 61.58)
DISCUSSION: To serve as pilot in command of an aircraft that is type certified for more than one required pilot flight crewmember and operated under Part 91, a person must have completed a pilot-in-command proficiency check within the preceding 12 calendar months in an airplane that is type certified for more than one required pilot flight crewmember. Additionally, that person must also have completed a pilot-in-command proficiency check within the preceding 24 calendar months in the particular type of aircraft in which that person will serve as pilot in command.
Answer (A) is incorrect. To serve as pilot in command of an airplane that is certified for more than one pilot crewmember, a person must complete a pilot-in-command proficiency check in an appropriate airplane every 12 calendar months, which meets the flight review requirement. **Answer (B) is incorrect.** To serve as pilot in command of an airplane that is certified for more than one pilot crewmember, a person must have completed a pilot proficiency check within the preceding 12 calendar months in an airplane that is type certified for more than one pilot, not just receive and log ground and flight training from an authorized flight instructor.

61.60 Change of Address

48. Pilots who change their permanent mailing address and fail to notify the FAA Airmen Certification Branch of this change, are entitled to exercise the privileges of their pilot certificate for a period of

A. 30 days.
B. 60 days.
C. 90 days.

Answer (A) is correct. (14 CFR 61.60)
DISCUSSION: The holder of a pilot or flight instructor certificate who has made a change in his or her permanent mailing address may not, after 30 days from the date (s)he moved, exercise the privileges of the certificate unless (s)he has notified the FAA in writing. NOTE: While you must notify the FAA if your address changes, you are not required to carry a certificate that shows your current address. The FAA will not issue a new certificate upon receipt of your new address unless you also send a written request and a $2 fee.
Answer (B) is incorrect. The FAA must be notified within 30, not 60, days of moving. **Answer (C) is incorrect.** The FAA must be notified within 30, not 90, days of moving.

61.69 Glider and Unpowered Ultralight Vehicle Towing: Experience and Training Requirements

49. To act as pilot in command of an airplane towing a glider, the tow pilot is required to have

A. at least a private pilot certificate with a category rating for powered aircraft, and made and logged at least three flights as pilot or observer in a glider being towed by an airplane.

B. a logbook endorsement from an authorized glider instructor certifying receipt of ground and flight training in gliders, and be proficient with techniques and procedures for safe towing of gliders.

C. a logbook record of having made at least three flights as sole manipulator of the controls of a glider being towed by an airplane.

Answer (B) is correct. (14 CFR 61.69)
DISCUSSION: No person may act as a pilot in command of an aircraft towing a glider unless (s)he has a logbook endorsement in his or her pilot logbook from an authorized glider instructor certifying that (s)he has received ground and flight training in gliders and is proficient in the techniques and procedures essential for safe towing of gliders.
Answer (A) is incorrect. To act as pilot in command of an airplane towing a glider, the pilot must have logged at least three flights as the sole manipulator of the controls of an airplane towing a glider, not as a pilot or an observer in a glider being towed by an airplane. **Answer (C) is incorrect.** To act as pilot in command of an airplane towing a glider, the tow pilot must have made at least three flights as pilot in command of a glider towed by an aircraft within the preceding 12 months, not just have logged three flights as sole manipulator of the controls of a glider towed by an airplane.

50. To act as pilot in command of an airplane towing a glider, a pilot must have accomplished, within the preceding 24 months, at least

A. three actual glider tows under the supervision of a qualified tow pilot.

B. three actual or simulated glider tows while accompanied by a qualified tow pilot.

C. ten flights as pilot in command of an aircraft while towing a glider.

Answer (B) is correct. (14 CFR 61.69)
DISCUSSION: To act as pilot in command of an airplane towing a glider, a pilot must have accomplished, within the preceding 24 months, at least three actual or simulated glider tows while accompanied by a qualified tow pilot or must have made at least three flights as pilot in command of a glider towed by an aircraft.
Answer (A) is incorrect. The glider tows may be actual or simulated and the pilot must be accompanied by, not just under the supervision of, a qualified tow pilot. **Answer (C) is incorrect.** Ten flights as pilot in command of an aircraft while towing a glider is a requirement for a person to be authorized to endorse the logbook of a pilot seeking glider-towing privileges. This does not meet the 24-month requirement of three actual or simulated glider tows while accompanied by another qualified tow pilot.

61.113 Private Pilot Privileges and Limitations: Pilot in Command

51. A pilot recently passed the commercial pilot checkride while operating under BasicMed and has been offered a job as a jump pilot at a skydiving operation. Is the pilot qualified for this role?

A. Yes, because the pilot holds a commercial pilot certificate, he is fully qualified.

B. No, the pilot must first receive a jump pilot endorsement to fly skydivers.

C. No, the pilot is not medically qualified.

Answer (C) is correct. (14 CFR 61.113)
DISCUSSION: Pilots may not fly for compensation or hire while operating under BasicMed. A second-class medical certificate is required to exercise the privileges of a commercial pilot certificate.
Answer (A) is incorrect. Although a commercial pilot certificate allows a pilot to fly for compensation or hire, the pilot must also hold a second-class medical certificate to exercise commercial pilot privileges. Pilots may not fly for compensation or hire while operating under BasicMed. **Answer (B) is incorrect.** A jump pilot endorsement is not required to fly skydivers.

52. If you are operating under BasicMed, you may fly an aircraft with

A. an actual takeoff weight of no more than 6,000 lb.

B. a maximum certificated takeoff weight of no more than 6,000 lb.

C. any weight, as long as you do not exceed the aircraft's maximum certificated takeoff weight.

Answer (B) is correct. (14 CFR 61.113)
DISCUSSION: If you are operating under BasicMed, you may fly an aircraft with a maximum certificated takeoff weight of no more than 6,000 lb.
Answer (A) is incorrect. To operate under BasicMed, you must fly aircraft with a maximum certificated takeoff weight, not an actual takeoff weight, of no more than 6,000 lb. **Answer (C) is incorrect.** To operate under BasicMed, you must fly aircraft with a maximum certificated takeoff weight of no more than 6,000 lb.

53. If you are operating under BasicMed, what is the maximum speed at which you may fly?

A.   250 KIAS.

B.   250 KIAS below 10,000 feet, and 230 KIAS above 10,000 feet.

C.   200 KIAS below 10,000 feet, and 230 KIAS above 10,000 feet.

Answer (A) is correct. (14 CFR 61.113)
   DISCUSSION: If you are operating under BasicMed, you may fly an aircraft at a maximum speed of 250 KIAS.
   Answer (B) is incorrect. If you are operating under BasicMed, you may fly an aircraft at a maximum speed of 250 KIAS, whether you are above or below 10,000 ft.
   Answer (C) is incorrect. If you are operating under BasicMed, you may fly an aircraft at a maximum speed of 250 KIAS, whether you are above or below 10,000 ft.

54. You own an aircraft which is certificated to carry 8 occupants and has a total of 8 seats installed, including the pilot's seat. You have recently elected to fly under BasicMed. May you continue to fly the aircraft?

A.   Yes, if you remove two of the seats.

B.   Yes, as long as you carry no more than 5 passengers.

C.   No.

Answer (C) is correct. (14 CFR 61.113)
   DISCUSSION: If you are operating under BasicMed, you may only fly aircraft that are certificated to carry no more than 6 occupants.
   Answer (A) is incorrect. If you are operating under BasicMed, you are limited to flying aircraft that are certificated to carry no more than 6 occupants. Removing 2 of the seats will not change the fact that the aircraft is certificated to carry more than 6 occupants. **Answer (B) is incorrect.** If you are operating under BasicMed, you are limited to carrying no more than 5 passengers and to flying aircraft that are certificated to carry no more than 6 occupants. However, carrying 5 passengers will not change the fact that the aircraft is certificated to carry more than 6 occupants.

61.133 Commercial Pilot Privileges and Limitations

55. What limitation is imposed on a newly certificated commercial pilot-airplane, if that person does not hold an instrument rating? The carriage of passengers

A.   or property for hire on cross-country flights at night is limited to a radius of 50 NM.

B.   for hire on cross-country flights is limited to 50 NM for night flights, but not limited for day flights.

C.   for hire on cross-country flights in excess of 50 NM, or for hire at night is prohibited.

Answer (C) is correct. (14 CFR 61.133)
   DISCUSSION: If a commercial airplane pilot does not hold an instrument rating, his or her certificate will carry a limitation prohibiting the carriage of passengers for hire in airplanes on cross-country flights of more than 50 NM or at night.
   Answer (A) is incorrect. The carriage of property is not restricted. **Answer (B) is incorrect.** The carriage of passengers is prohibited at night and is limited to 50 NM during the day.

56. A person with a Commercial Pilot certificate may act as pilot in command of an aircraft for compensation or hire, if that person

A.   is qualified in accordance with 14 CFR Part 61 and with the applicable parts that apply to the operation.

B.   is qualified in accordance with 14 CFR Part 61 and has passed a pilot competency check given by an authorized check pilot.

C.   holds appropriate category, class ratings, and meets the recent flight experience requirements of 14 CFR Part 61.

Answer (A) is correct. (14 CFR 61.133)
   DISCUSSION: A person who holds a commercial pilot certificate may act as pilot in command of an airplane for compensation or hire, provided that person is qualified in accordance with 14 CFR Part 61 and any other 14 CFR parts that apply to the operation.
   Answer (B) is incorrect. A commercial pilot may act as pilot in command of an airplane operating for compensation or hire, if that person is qualified in accordance with Part 61 and any other 14 CFR parts that apply to the operation, not if that person passes a competency check given by an authorized check pilot. **Answer (C) is incorrect.** A commercial pilot may act as pilot in command of an airplane operating for compensation or hire, if that person is qualified in accordance with Part 61 and any other 14 CFR parts that apply to the operation, not only if that person holds the appropriate category and class ratings and meets the recent flight experience requirements.

4.7 14 CFR Part 91

91.3 Responsibility and Authority of the Pilot in Command

57. What action must be taken when a pilot in command deviates from any rule in 14 CFR Part 91?

A. Upon landing, report the deviation to the responsible FAA Flight Standards office.

B. Advise ATC of the pilot in command's intentions.

C. Upon the request of the Administrator, send a written report of that deviation to the Administrator.

Answer (C) is correct. (14 CFR 91.3)
DISCUSSION: If a pilot in command deviates from any rule in 14 CFR Part 91 (due to an in-flight emergency requiring immediate action), (s)he must submit a written report to the Administrator (FAA), if requested.
Answer (A) is incorrect. The pilot in command must submit a written report of any rule deviation only when requested by the FAA, not upon landing. **Answer (B) is incorrect.** The pilot in command must inform ATC of any deviation of an ATC clearance or instruction and should advise ATC of his or her intentions, even if no rule in 14 CFR Part 91 was violated.

58. What person is directly responsible for the final authority as to the operation of the airplane?

A. Certificate holder.

B. Pilot in command.

C. Airplane owner/operator.

Answer (B) is correct. (14 CFR 91.3)
DISCUSSION: The pilot in command of an airplane is directly responsible for, and is the final authority as to, the operation of that airplane.
Answer (A) is incorrect. The pilot in command, not the certificate holder, is directly responsible for, and is the final authority as to, the operation of that airplane. **Answer (C) is incorrect.** The pilot in command, not the airplane owner or operator, is directly responsible for, and the final authority as to, the operation of that airplane.

91.7 Civil Aircraft Airworthiness

59. An aircraft is on a stop 460 NM from base. It develops a mechanical problem. You get a technician to fix the problem. Who is responsible for the airworthiness of the aircraft?

A. Owner or operator.

B. Pilot in command.

C. Technician.

Answer (B) is the best answer. (14 CFR 91.7)
DISCUSSION: The pilot in command is directly responsible for determining whether the airplane is in condition for safe flight.
Answer (A) is incorrect. The pilot in command (who is considered the operator when piloting an airplane), not the owner, is directly responsible for determining whether an airplane is in condition for safe flight. **Answer (C) is incorrect.** While the technician is responsible for ensuring his or her work meets regulatory standards, it is the responsibility of the pilot in command to determine whether the aircraft is airworthy before operating it.

60. Who is responsible for determining if an aircraft is in condition for safe flight?

A. A certificated aircraft mechanic.

B. The pilot in command.

C. The owner or operator.

Answer (B) is correct. (14 CFR 91.7)
DISCUSSION: The pilot in command is directly responsible for determining whether the airplane is in condition for safe flight.
Answer (A) is incorrect. The pilot in command, not a certificated aircraft mechanic, is responsible for determining if an airplane is in condition for safe flight. **Answer (C) is incorrect.** The pilot in command (who is considered the operator when piloting an airplane), not the owner, is directly responsible for determining if an airplane is in condition for safe flight.

61. You are PIC of a flight. During your preflight, you notice a mechanical discrepancy that you think makes the aircraft unairworthy. Who is responsible for this determination?

A. A certificated aircraft mechanic.

B. The pilot-in-command.

C. The owner or operator.

Answer (B) is correct. (14 CFR 91.7)
DISCUSSION: The pilot in command is responsible for ensuring the aircraft is in an airworthy condition before each flight.
Answer (A) is incorrect. A certificated mechanic should perform maintenance or repairs on an aircraft but is not responsible for ensuring the aircraft is in an airworthy condition before each flight. **Answer (C) is incorrect.** The owner or operator of an aircraft is primarily responsible for maintaining that aircraft in an airworthy condition, but the pilot in command is responsible for determining the aircraft remains airworthy before each flight.

91.9 Civil Aircraft Flight Manual, Marking, and Placard Requirements

62. When operating a U.S.-registered civil aircraft, which document is required by regulation to be available in the aircraft?

    A. A manufacturer's Operations Manual.

    B. A current, approved Airplane Flight Manual.

    C. An Owner's Manual.

Answer (B) is correct. (14 CFR 91.9)
    DISCUSSION: No person may operate a U.S.-registered civil aircraft unless there is available in the aircraft a current, approved Airplane Flight Manual.
    Answer (A) is incorrect. Anyone operating a U.S.-registered civil aircraft is required by regulation to have available in the aircraft a current, approved Airplane Flight Manual, not a manufacturer's Operations Manual. **Answer (C) is incorrect.** Anyone operating a U.S.-registered civil aircraft is required by regulation to have available in the aircraft a current, approved Airplane Flight Manual, not an Owner's Manual.

63. Where may an aircraft's operating limitations be found?

    A. On the Standard Airworthiness Certificate issued by the FAA for the aircraft type certificated.

    B. In the current, FAA-approved flight manual, approved manual material, markings, and placards, or any combination thereof.

    C. In the airframe and engine maintenance handbooks.

Answer (B) is correct. (14 CFR 91.9)
    DISCUSSION: An aircraft's operating limitations may be found in the current FAA-approved flight manual, approved manual material, markings, and placards, or any combination thereof.
    Answer (A) is incorrect. The airworthiness certificate only indicates the airplane was in an airworthy condition when delivered from the factory, not its operating limitations. **Answer (C) is incorrect.** The airframe and engine maintenance handbooks are reference books used by aviation maintenance technicians preparing for mechanic certification and by current technicians as a reference guide. They do not contain the operating limitations for a specific aircraft.

91.15 Dropping Objects

64. A pilot in command (PIC) of a civil aircraft may not allow any object to be dropped from that aircraft in flight

    A. if it creates a hazard to persons and property.

    B. unless the PIC has permission to drop any object over private property.

    C. unless reasonable precautions are taken to avoid damage to property.

Answer (A) is correct. (14 CFR 91.15)
    DISCUSSION: A pilot in command of a civil aircraft may not allow any object to be dropped from that aircraft in flight if it creates a hazard to persons or property. However, an object may be dropped from an aircraft if reasonable precautions are taken to avoid injury or damage to persons or property.
    Answer (B) is incorrect. An object may be dropped from an aircraft if reasonable precautions are taken to avoid injury or damage to persons or property. Permission from a property owner is not required. **Answer (C) is incorrect.** An object may be dropped from an aircraft if reasonable precautions are taken to avoid injury or damage to persons or property, not only damage to property.

91.21 Portable Electronic Devices

65. Portable electronic devices which may cause interference with the navigation or communication system may not be operated on a U.S.-registered civil aircraft being flown

    A. along Federal airways.

    B. within the U.S.

    C. in air carrier operations.

Answer (C) is correct. (14 CFR 91.21)
    DISCUSSION: Portable electronic devices that may cause interference with the navigation or communication system may not be operated on a U.S.-registered civil aircraft being flown in air carrier operations or other operations requiring an operating certificate, or on any aircraft while it is operated under IFR.
    Answer (A) is incorrect. Portable electronic devices that may cause interference with the navigation or communication system may be operated on an aircraft being flown along Federal airways, as long as the aircraft is not an air carrier or an aircraft operating under IFR. **Answer (B) is incorrect.** Portable electronic devices that may cause interference with the navigation or communication system may be operated within the U.S., as long as the aircraft is not an air carrier or an aircraft operating under IFR.

66. Portable electronic devices which may cause interference with the navigation or communication system may not be operated on U.S.-registered civil aircraft being operated

    A. under IFR.

    B. in passenger carrying operations.

    C. along Federal airways.

Answer (A) is correct. (14 CFR 91.21)
    DISCUSSION: Portable electronic devices that may cause interference with the navigation or communication system may not be operated on a U.S.-registered civil aircraft being operated under IFR or an aircraft being operated under an air carrier operating certificate or other operating certificate.
    Answer (B) is incorrect. Portable electronic devices that may cause interference with the navigation or communication system may be operated on an aircraft in passenger-carrying operations, as long as the aircraft is not operated under an air carrier or other operating certificate or under IFR. **Answer (C) is incorrect.** Portable electronic devices that may cause interference with the navigation or communication system may be operated on an aircraft operating along Federal airways, as long as the airplane is not operated under IFR.

91.23 Truth-in-Leasing Clause Requirement in Leases and Conditional Sales Contracts

67. No person may operate a large civil aircraft of U.S.-registry which is subject to a lease, unless the lessee has mailed a copy of the lease to the FAA Aircraft Registration Branch, Oklahoma City, OK, within how many hours of its execution?

    A. 24

    B. 48

    C. 72

Answer (A) is correct. (14 CFR 91.23)
    DISCUSSION: A copy of the lease or contract to a large civil aircraft must be mailed to the FAA within 24 hr. of its execution.
    Answer (B) is incorrect. The lease must be mailed within 24 hr., not 48 hr. **Answer (C) is incorrect.** The lease must be mailed within 24 hr., not 72 hr.

91.103 Preflight Action

68. When is preflight action required, relative to alternatives available, if the planned flight cannot be completed?

    A. IFR flights only.

    B. Any flight not in the vicinity of an airport.

    C. Any flight conducted for hire or compensation.

Answer (B) is correct. (14 CFR 91.103)
    DISCUSSION: Each pilot in command shall, before beginning a flight, familiarize himself or herself with all available information concerning that flight. This information must include, for a flight under IFR or a flight not in the vicinity of an airport, weather reports and forecasts, fuel requirements, alternatives available if the planned flight cannot be completed, and any known traffic delays of which (s)he has been advised by ATC. For any flight, runway lengths at airports of intended use and certain takeoff and landing distance information should be obtained.
    Answer (A) is incorrect. Preflight action relative to alternate airports is required for all flights not in the vicinity of an airport, not just IFR flights. **Answer (C) is incorrect.** Preflight action relative to alternate airports is required for all flights not in the vicinity of an airport, not just commercial flights.

69. The required preflight action relative to weather reports and fuel requirements is applicable to

    A. any flight conducted for compensation or hire.

    B. any flight not in the vicinity of an airport.

    C. IFR flights only.

Answer (B) is correct. (14 CFR 91.103)
    DISCUSSION: A required preflight action by the pilot in command of a flight not in the vicinity of an airport or a flight under IFR is to become familiar with all available information concerning that flight, including weather reports and forecasts and fuel requirements. Additional preflight information for the flight includes alternatives available, runway length at airports of intended use, and takeoff and landing distance information.
    Answer (A) is incorrect. Preflight action relative to weather reports and fuel requirements is applicable to a flight under IFR or a flight not in the vicinity of an airport, not just any flight conducted for compensation or hire. **Answer (C) is incorrect.** Preflight action relative to weather reports and fuel requirements is applicable to a flight under IFR or a flight not in the vicinity of an airport, not IFR flights only.

70. A pilot in command is required to be aware of all of the information pertinent to the flight. This should include what information about the destination airport?

A. Customs availability at an airport of entry.

B. Land and hold short operations (LAHSO).

C. Available airport services.

Answer (B) is correct. *(14 CFR 91.103)*
   DISCUSSION: Prior to a flight, the PIC of the aircraft must be aware of all of the information available for the flight, including takeoff and landing distances, which may be affected by land and hold short operations (LAHSO).
   Answer (A) is incorrect. Customs availability at an airport of entry would only be required for international flights arriving in the United States. **Answer (C) is incorrect.** While it is certainly good operating practice, pilots are not required to know the services available at an airport.

71. Before beginning any flight under IFR, the pilot in command must become familiar with all available information concerning that flight. In addition, the pilot must

A. be familiar with all instrument approaches at the destination airport.

B. list an alternate airport on the flight plan, and confirm adequate takeoff and landing performance at the destination airport.

C. be familiar with the runway lengths at airports of intended use, and the alternatives available, if the flight cannot be completed.

Answer (C) is correct. *(14 CFR 91.103)*
   DISCUSSION: Each pilot in command shall, before beginning a flight, familiarize himself or herself with all available information concerning that flight. For a flight under IFR or a flight not in the vicinity of an airport, this information should include weather reports and forecasts, fuel requirements, alternatives available if the planned flight cannot be completed, and any known traffic delays of which (s)he has been advised by ATC. For any flight, the preflight information should include runway lengths at airports of intended use and takeoff and landing distance information.
   Answer (A) is incorrect. IFR pilots should carry instrument approach charts for their destination airports and possible alternates. **Answer (B) is incorrect.** An alternate is not always required.

72. Before beginning any flight under IFR, the pilot in command must become familiar with all available information concerning that flight. In addition, the pilot must

A. list an alternate airport on the flight plan, and confirm adequate takeoff and landing performance at the destination airport.

B. be familiar with all instrument approaches at the destination airport.

C. be familiar with the runway lengths at airports of intended use, weather reports, fuel requirements, and alternatives available, if the planned flight cannot be completed.

Answer (C) is correct. *(14 CFR 91.103)*
   DISCUSSION: Before beginning any flight under IFR, the pilot in command must become familiar with all available information concerning the flight. This information must include the runway lengths at airports of intended use, weather reports and forecasts, alternatives available if the planned flight cannot be completed, and any known traffic delays that have been advised by ATC.
   Answer (A) is incorrect. An alternate airport may not be required for the flight, based on the weather reports and forecast at the destination. **Answer (B) is incorrect.** While the pilot in command should be familiar with the instrument approaches at the destination airport (especially if (s)he should expect to conduct an instrument approach), it is not a required preflight action for any flight under IFR.

73. You are pilot-in-command of a VFR flight that you think will be within the fuel range of your aircraft. As part of your preflight planning you must

A. be familiar with all instrument approaches at the destination airport.

B. list an alternate airport on the flight plan, and confirm adequate takeoff and landing performance at the destination airport.

C. obtain weather reports, forecasts, and fuel requirements for the flight.

Answer (C) is correct. *(14 CFR 91.103, 91.153)*
   DISCUSSION: A required preflight action by the pilot in command of a flight not in the vicinity of an airport or a flight under IFR is to become familiar with all available information concerning that flight, including weather reports and forecasts and fuel requirements. Additional preflight information for the flight includes alternative airport availability, runway length at airports of intended use, and takeoff and landing distance information.
   Answer (A) is incorrect. Under VFR, it is not necessary to be familiar with instrument approaches at the destination airport. **Answer (B) is incorrect.** It is important that information for alternate airports is analyzed; however, it is not a requirement to list an alternate on a VFR flight plan.

91.105 Flight Crewmembers at Stations

74. Required flight crewmembers' seatbelts must be fastened

    A. only during takeoff and landing.

    B. while the crewmembers are at their stations.

    C. only during takeoff and landing when passengers are aboard the aircraft.

Answer (B) is correct. (14 CFR 91.105)
    DISCUSSION: During takeoff and landing, and while en route, each required flight crewmember shall keep his or her seatbelt fastened while at his or her station.
    Answer (A) is incorrect. Crewmembers are required to keep their seatbelts fastened while at their stations, not only during takeoff and landing. **Answer (C) is incorrect.** Crewmembers are required to keep their seatbelts fastened while at their stations, not only during takeoff and landing when passengers are aboard.

75. Each required flight crewmember is required to keep his or her shoulder harness fastened

    A. during takeoff and landing only when passengers are aboard the aircraft.

    B. while the crewmembers are at their stations, unless he or she is unable to perform required duties.

    C. during takeoff and landing, unless he or she is unable to perform required duties.

Answer (C) is correct. (14 CFR 91.105)
    DISCUSSION: Each required flight crewmember is required to keep his or her shoulder harness fastened during takeoff or landing while at his or her assigned duty station, unless (s)he would be unable to perform required duties or the seat is not equipped with a shoulder harness.
    Answer (A) is incorrect. A required flight crewmember is required to keep his or her shoulder harness fastened during takeoff and landing, regardless of whether or not passengers are aboard the airplane. **Answer (B) is incorrect.** Each required flight crewmember is required to keep his or her shoulder harness fastened during takeoff and landing while at their stations, not all the time while at their stations.

91.107 Use of Safety Belts, Shoulder Harnesses, and Child Restraint Systems

76. Operating regulations for U.S.-registered civil airplanes require that during movement on the surface, takeoffs, and landings, a seat belt and shoulder harness (if installed) must be properly secured about each

    A. flight crewmember only.

    B. person on board.

    C. flight and cabin crewmembers.

Answer (B) is correct. (14 CFR 91.107)
    DISCUSSION: Each person on board a U.S.-registered civil airplane must occupy an approved seat or berth with a safety belt and, if installed, shoulder harness properly secured about him or her during movement on the surface, takeoffs, and landings.
    Answer (A) is incorrect. Each person on board, not only the flight crewmembers, must have a safety belt and, if installed, shoulder harness properly secured about him or her during movement on the surface, takeoffs, and landings. **Answer (C) is incorrect.** Each person on board, not only the flight and cabin crewmembers, must have a safety belt and, if installed, a shoulder harness properly secured about him or her during movement on the surface, takeoffs, and landings.

77. With U.S.-registered civil airplanes, the use of safety belts is required during movement on the surface, takeoffs, and landings for

    A. safe operating practice, but not required by regulations.

    B. each person over 2 years of age on board.

    C. commercial passenger operations only.

Answer (B) is correct. (14 CFR 91.107)
    DISCUSSION: Each person over 2 years of age on a U.S.-registered civil airplane must occupy an approved seat or berth with a safety belt and, if installed, shoulder harness properly secured about him or her during movement on the surface, takeoff, and landing.
    Answer (A) is incorrect. While the use of safety belts is a safe operating practice, it is also required by regulations during movement on the surface, takeoffs, and landings for each person over 2 years of age on board. **Answer (C) is incorrect.** The use of safety belts is required on all U.S.-registered civil airplanes, not only commercial passenger airplanes, during movement on the surface, takeoffs, and landings for each person over 2 years of age on board.

78. You are planning a trip and one of your passengers states that he prefers not to use his shoulder harness because it is uncomfortable. You should

    A. explain that it is a mandatory requirement and that he must use the shoulder harness during takeoff and landing.

    B. allow him to use his seat belt for the entire trip without the shoulder harness.

    C. allow him to use his seat belt for takeoff and landing and the shoulder harness while en route.

Answer (A) is correct. (14 CFR 91.107)
    DISCUSSION: Each person on board a U.S.-registered civil aircraft must occupy an approved seat with a safety belt and, if installed, a shoulder harness, properly secured during movement on the surface, takeoff, and landing.
    Answer (B) is incorrect. Use of the shoulder harness is not required en route, but it is required during taxi, takeoff, and landing. **Answer (C) is incorrect.** Passengers are required to wear both seat belts and shoulder harnesses during taxi, takeoff, and landing; neither is required while en route.

91.109 Flight Instruction; Simulated Instrument Flight and Certain Flight Tests

79. No person may operate an aircraft in simulated instrument flight conditions unless the

    A. other control seat is occupied by at least an appropriately rated commercial pilot.

    B. pilot has filed an IFR flight plan and received an IFR clearance.

    C. other control seat is occupied by a safety pilot, who holds at least a private pilot certificate and is appropriately rated.

Answer (C) is correct. (14 CFR 91.109)
    DISCUSSION: No person may operate an aircraft in simulated instrument flight conditions unless the other control seat is occupied by a safety pilot who possesses at least a private pilot certificate with category and class ratings appropriate to the aircraft being flown.
    Answer (A) is incorrect. The safety pilot must hold at least a private, not commercial, pilot certificate with the category and class ratings appropriate to the aircraft being flown. **Answer (B) is incorrect.** There is no requirement that a person file an IFR flight plan and receive an IFR clearance to operate in simulated flight conditions. Normally, a person will be operating under VFR while operating in simulated instrument flight conditions.

91.111 Operating near Other Aircraft

80. Which is true with respect to operating near other aircraft in flight? They are

    A. not authorized, when operated so close to another aircraft they can create a collision hazard.

    B. not authorized, unless the pilot in command of each aircraft is trained and found competent in formation.

    C. authorized when carrying passengers for hire, with prior arrangement with the pilot in command of each aircraft in the formation.

Answer (A) is correct. (14 CFR 91.111)
    DISCUSSION: No person may operate an aircraft so close to another aircraft as to create a collision hazard.
    Answer (B) is incorrect. Formation flights are authorized when an arrangement is made with the pilot in command of each aircraft in the formation. There is no regulatory requirement for any type of training in formation flying. **Answer (C) is incorrect.** Formation flight is not authorized when carrying passengers for hire.

81. Which is true with respect to formation flights? Formation flights are

    A. not authorized, except by arrangement with the pilot in command of each aircraft.

    B. not authorized, unless the pilot in command of each aircraft is trained and found competent in formation.

    C. authorized when carrying passengers for hire, with prior arrangement with the pilot in command of each aircraft in the formation.

Answer (A) is correct. (14 CFR 91.111)
    DISCUSSION: Formation flights are not authorized, except by arrangement with the pilot in command of each aircraft in the formation.
    Answer (B) is incorrect. Formation flights are not authorized, except by arrangement with the pilot in command of each aircraft in the formation. There is no regulatory requirement for any specific training in formation flying. **Answer (C) is incorrect.** Formation flights are not authorized when carrying passengers for hire.

82. Which is true with respect to formation flights? Formation flights are

A. authorized when carrying passengers for hire, with prior arrangement with the pilot in command of each aircraft in the formation.

B. not authorized when visibilities are less than 3 SM.

C. not authorized when carrying passengers for hire.

Answer (C) is correct. (14 CFR 91.111)
   DISCUSSION: No person may operate an aircraft carrying passengers for hire in formation flight.
   Answer (A) is incorrect. Formation flights are prohibited when carrying passengers for hire. **Answer (B) is incorrect.** Formation flights are authorized when visibility is less than 3 SM.

91.113 Right-of-Way Rules: Except Water Operations

83. Airplane A is overtaking airplane B. Which airplane has the right-of-way?

A. Airplane A; the pilot should alter course to the right to pass.

B. Airplane B; the pilot should expect to be passed on the right.

C. Airplane B; the pilot should expect to be passed on the left.

Answer (B) is correct. (14 CFR 91.113)
   DISCUSSION: Each aircraft that is being overtaken has the right-of-way, and each pilot of an overtaking aircraft shall alter course to the right to pass well clear.
   Answer (A) is incorrect. The airplane being overtaken has the right-of-way. **Answer (C) is incorrect.** When overtaking another aircraft, you pass to the right, not left.

84. A pilot flying a single-engine airplane observes a multiengine airplane approaching from the left. Which pilot should give way?

A. The pilot of the multiengine airplane should give way; the single-engine airplane is to its right.

B. The pilot of the single-engine airplane should give way; the other airplane is to the left.

C. Each pilot should alter course to the right.

Answer (A) is correct. (14 CFR 91.113)
   DISCUSSION: When aircraft of the same category are converging at the same altitude (except head-on, or nearly so), the aircraft to the other's right has the right-of-way. Since the single-engine airplane is to the right of the multiengine airplane, the pilot of the multiengine airplane should give way to the single-engine airplane.
   Answer (B) is incorrect. The airplane to the right, not left, has the right-of-way. Thus, the pilot of the multiengine airplane should give way to the single-engine airplane. **Answer (C) is incorrect.** Each pilot should alter course to the right if the airplanes are approaching each other head-on, not converging.

85. An airplane is overtaking a helicopter. Which aircraft has the right-of-way?

A. Helicopter; the pilot should expect to be passed on the right.

B. Airplane; the airplane pilot should alter course to the left to pass.

C. Helicopter; the pilot should expect to be passed on the left.

Answer (A) is correct. (14 CFR 91.113)
   DISCUSSION: Each aircraft that is being overtaken (the helicopter) has the right-of-way, and each pilot of an overtaking aircraft (the airplane) shall alter course to the right to pass well clear.
   Answer (B) is incorrect. The helicopter has the right-of-way because it is being overtaken and the airplane should alter course to the right, not left, to pass well clear. **Answer (C) is incorrect.** The airplane should alter course to the right, not left, to pass well clear.

86. Two aircraft of the same category are approaching an airport for the purpose of landing. The right-of-way belongs to the aircraft

A. at the higher altitude.

B. at the lower altitude, but the pilot shall not take advantage of this rule to cut in front of or to overtake the other aircraft.

C. that is more maneuverable, and that aircraft may, with caution, move in front of or overtake the other aircraft.

Answer (B) is correct. (14 CFR 91.113)
   DISCUSSION: When two or more aircraft are approaching an airport for the purpose of landing, the aircraft at the lower altitude has the right-of-way, but it shall not take advantage of this rule to cut in front of another that is on final approach to land, or to overtake that aircraft.
   Answer (A) is incorrect. The right-of-way belongs to the aircraft at the lower, not higher, altitude. **Answer (C) is incorrect.** The right-of-way belongs to the aircraft at the lower altitude, not to the more maneuverable aircraft.

87. During a night operation, the pilot of aircraft #1 sees only the green light of aircraft #2. If the aircraft are converging, which pilot has the right-of-way? The pilot of aircraft

A. #2; aircraft #2 is to the left of aircraft #1.

B. #2; aircraft #2 is to the right of aircraft #1.

C. #1; aircraft #1 is to the right of aircraft #2.

Answer (C) is correct. (14 CFR 91.113)
DISCUSSION: When aircraft of the same category are converging at approximately the same altitude (except head-on or nearly so), the aircraft to the other's right has the right-of-way. Since the green position light is on aircraft #2's right wing, aircraft #1 is to the right of aircraft #2 and thus has the right-of-way.
Answer (A) is incorrect. When two aircraft are converging, the aircraft to the right, not left, has the right-of-way. Since aircraft #2 is to the left of aircraft #1, aircraft #1 has the right-of-way. **Answer (B) is incorrect.** The green position light is on the right wing of aircraft #2. Since aircraft #1 can see only the green position light, aircraft #1 is to the right, not left, of aircraft #2, and aircraft #1 has the right-of-way.

88. An airplane is converging with a helicopter. Which aircraft has the right-of-way?

A. The aircraft on the left.

B. The aircraft on the right.

C. The faster of the two aircraft.

Answer (B) is correct. (14 CFR 91.113)
DISCUSSION: When aircraft of the same category are converging at approximately the same altitude (except head on, or nearly so), the aircraft to the other's right has the right-of-way. Airplanes and helicopters are equally maneuverable and have equal rights-of-way.
Answer (A) is incorrect. When aircraft of the same category are converging at approximately the same altitude (except head on, or nearly so), the aircraft to the other's right has the right-of-way, not the aircraft to the other's left. **Answer (C) is incorrect.** When aircraft of the same category are converging at approximately the same altitude (except head on, or nearly so), the aircraft to the other's right has the right-of-way, not the faster of the two aircraft.

89. While in flight a helicopter and an airplane are converging at a 90° angle, and the helicopter is located to the right of the airplane. Which aircraft has the right-of-way, and why?

A. The helicopter, because it is to the right of the airplane.

B. The helicopter, because helicopters have the right-of-way over airplanes.

C. The airplane, because airplanes have the right-of-way over helicopters.

Answer (A) is correct. (14 CFR 91.113)
DISCUSSION: When aircraft are converging at approximately the same altitude, the aircraft to the other's right has the right-of-way. Since the helicopter is to the airplane's right, it has the right-of-way. Since helicopters and airplanes are considered equally maneuverable, neither has the right-of-way over the other.
Answer (B) is incorrect. Helicopters do not have the right-of-way over airplanes. **Answer (C) is incorrect.** Airplanes do not have the right-of-way over helicopters.

91.117 Aircraft Speed

90. Unless otherwise authorized or required by air traffic control, what is the maximum indicated airspeed at which a person may operate an aircraft below 10,000 feet MSL?

A. 200 knots.

B. 250 MPH.

C. 250 knots.

Answer (C) is correct. (14 CFR 91.117)
DISCUSSION: Unless otherwise authorized, no person may operate an aircraft below 10,000 ft. MSL at an indicated airspeed of more than 250 kt. (288 MPH).
Answer (A) is incorrect. The speed limit of 200 kt. is for 2,500 ft. AGL or below within 4 NM of a Class C or Class D primary airport, as well as for beneath (or in a VFR corridor through) Class B airspace. **Answer (B) is incorrect.** The speed limit below 10,000 ft. MSL is 250 kt., not 250 MPH.

91. Unless otherwise authorized, what is the maximum indicated airspeed at which an aircraft may be flown in a satellite airport traffic pattern located within Class B airspace?

A. 200 MPH.

B. 200 knots.

C. 250 knots.

Answer (C) is correct. (14 CFR 91.117)
DISCUSSION: Unless otherwise authorized, no person may operate an aircraft within Class B airspace at an indicated airspeed of more than 250 kt. (288 MPH).
Answer (A) is incorrect. No person may operate an aircraft at or below 2,500 ft. AGL within 4 NM of the primary airport of a Class C or Class D airspace area at an indicated airspeed of more than 200 kt., not 200 MPH. **Answer (B) is incorrect.** No person may operate an aircraft at or below 2,500 ft. AGL within 4 NM of the primary airport of a Class C or Class D airspace area, not within Class B airspace, at an indicated airspeed of more than 200 kt.

92. When flying in a VFR corridor designated through Class B airspace, the maximum speed authorized is

A. 180 knots.

B. 200 knots.

C. 250 knots.

Answer (B) is correct. (14 CFR 91.117)
   DISCUSSION: No person may operate an airplane in a VFR corridor designated through Class B airspace at an indicated airspeed of more than 200 kt. (230 MPH).
   Answer (A) is incorrect. When flying in a VFR corridor designated through Class B airspace, the maximum speed authorized is 200 (not 180) kt. **Answer (C) is incorrect.** The maximum speed authorized below 10,000 ft. MSL, not when flying in a VFR corridor through Class B airspace, is 250 kt.

93. Unless otherwise authorized, the maximum indicated airspeed at which aircraft may be flown when at or below 2,500 feet AGL and within 4 nautical miles of the primary airport of Class C airspace is

A. 200 knots.

B. 230 knots.

C. 250 knots.

Answer (A) is correct. (14 CFR 91.117)
   DISCUSSION: Unless otherwise authorized, the maximum indicated airspeed at which an airplane may be flown when at or below 2,500 feet AGL and within 4 nautical miles of the primary airport of Class C airspace is 200 knots (230 MPH).
   Answer (B) is incorrect. The amount of 230 MPH, not 230 knots, is the maximum indicated airspeed at which an airplane may be flown when at or below 2,500 feet AGL and within 4 nautical miles of the primary airport of a Class C airspace area. **Answer (C) is incorrect.** The amount of 250 knots is the maximum indicated airspeed at which an airplane may be flown below 10,000 feet MSL or in Class B airspace, not when at or below 2,500 feet AGL and within 4 nautical miles of the primary airport of a Class C airspace area.

94. The maximum indicated airspeed permitted when operating an aircraft within 4 NM of the primary airport in Class D airspace is

A. 200 MPH.

B. 200 knots.

C. 250 knots.

Answer (B) is correct. (14 CFR 91.117)
   DISCUSSION: Unless otherwise authorized or required by ATC, no person may operate an aircraft at or below 2,500 ft. AGL within 4 NM of the primary airport of a Class C or Class D airspace area at an indicated airspeed of more than 200 kt. Note that Class D airspace generally extends upward from the surface to 2,500 ft. AGL.
   Answer (A) is incorrect. The speed limit within 4 NM of a primary Class D airport is 200 kt., not 200 MPH. **Answer (C) is incorrect.** The general speed limit below 10,000 ft. MSL or in Class B airspace is 250 kt., but not within 4 NM of a primary Class C or Class D airport.

95. When flying beneath the lateral limits of Class B airspace, the maximum indicated airspeed authorized is

A. 156 knots.

B. 200 knots.

C. 250 knots.

Answer (B) is correct. (14 CFR 91.117)
   DISCUSSION: No person may operate an aircraft in the airspace underlying a Class B airspace area designated for an airport, or in a VFR corridor designated through such a Class B airspace area, at an indicated airspeed of greater than 200 kt. (230 MPH).
   Answer (A) is incorrect. The old speed limit in airport traffic areas for reciprocating-engine aircraft is 156 kt.
   Answer (C) is incorrect. The speed limit of aircraft within, not beneath the lateral limits of, Class B airspace, is 250 kt.

91.119 Minimum Safe Altitudes: General

96. According to 14 CFR Part 91, at what minimum altitude may an airplane be operated unless necessary for takeoff and landing?

A. In congested areas, you must maintain 500 feet over obstacles, and no closer than 500 feet to any person, vessel, vehicle, or structure.

B. In uncongested areas, 1,000 feet over any obstacle within a horizontal radius of 2,000 feet.

C. An altitude allowing for an emergency landing without undue hazard, if a power unit fails.

Answer (C) is correct. (14 CFR 91.119)
   DISCUSSION: Except when necessary for takeoff or landing, an aircraft should always be operated at an altitude high enough to permit an emergency landing without endangering people or property on the ground.
   Answer (A) is incorrect. In a congested area, you must maintain an altitude of 1,000 ft. above the highest obstacle within a horizontal radius of 2,000 ft. of the aircraft. Over uncongested areas, you must maintain an altitude of 500 ft. above the surface, except over open water or sparsely populated areas. In those cases, the aircraft may not be operated closer than 500 ft. to any person, vessel, vehicle, or structure. **Answer (B) is incorrect.** An aircraft must be 1,000 ft. over any obstacle within a horizontal radius of 2,000 ft. over a congested area (city, town, settlement, or assembly of people). This does not apply to an uncongested area.

91.121 Altimeter Settings

97. What altimeter setting is required when operating an aircraft at 18,000 feet MSL?

A. Current reported altimeter setting of a station along the route.

B. 29.92" Hg.

C. Altimeter setting at the departure or destination airport.

Answer (B) is correct. (14 CFR 91.121)
DISCUSSION: When operating an airplane at or above 18,000 feet MSL, the altimeter should be set to 29.92" Hg.
Answer (A) is incorrect. The altimeter is set to the current reported altimeter setting of a station along the route when below 18,000 feet MSL, not at or above 18,000 feet MSL. **Answer (C) is incorrect.** The altimeter is set to 29.92" Hg when operating at or above 18,000 feet MSL, not to the altimeter setting at the departure or destination airport.

91.123 Compliance with ATC Clearances and Instructions

98. After an ATC clearance has been obtained, a pilot may not deviate from that clearance, unless the pilot

A. requests an amended clearance.

B. is operating VFR on top.

C. receives an amended clearance or has an emergency.

Answer (C) is correct. (14 CFR 91.123)
DISCUSSION: After an ATC clearance has been obtained, a pilot may not deviate from that clearance unless an amended clearance is obtained, an emergency exists, or the deviation is in response to a traffic alert and collision avoidance system (TCAS) resolution advisory.
Answer (A) is incorrect. A pilot may not deviate from an ATC clearance until an amended clearance has been received, not when the pilot requests an amended clearance. **Answer (B) is incorrect.** Operating VFR-on-top is an IFR clearance; thus, a pilot may not deviate from VFR-on-top unless an amended clearance is received or an emergency exists.

99. As pilot-in-command of an aircraft, you may deviate from an ATC clearance when

A. flying in the outer ring of Class C airspace.

B. operating under VFR in Class B airspace.

C. there is an in-flight emergency requiring immediate action.

Answer (C) is correct. (14 CFR 91.123)
DISCUSSION: A pilot may deviate from ATC clearance or instruction only in the case of an in-flight emergency requiring immediate action. In such a case, the pilot should notify ATC of the deviation as soon as possible.
Answer (A) is incorrect. You must follow ATC instructions within any part of Class C airspace unless there is an in-flight emergency requiring immediate action. **Answer (B) is incorrect.** Even while operating VFR within Class B airspace, you must comply with ATC clearances unless a deviation is necessary for the safety of the flight.

91.144 Temporary Restriction on Flight Operations during Abnormally High Barometric Pressure Conditions

100. When weather information indicates that abnormally high barometric pressure exists, or will be above ____ inches of mercury, flight operations will not be authorized contrary to the requirements published in NOTAMs.

A. 31.00

B. 32.00

C. 30.50

Answer (A) is correct. (14 CFR 91.144)
DISCUSSION: When weather information indicates that barometric pressure on the route of flight exceeds 31.00 in. of mercury, no person may operate an aircraft or initiate a flight contrary to the requirements published in NOTAMs.
Answer (B) is incorrect. Flight operations will not be authorized contrary to the requirements published in NOTAMs when barometric pressure exceeds, or will exceed, 31.00 in., not 32.00 in., of mercury. **Answer (C) is incorrect.** Flight operations will not be authorized contrary to the requirements published in NOTAMs when barometric pressure exceeds, or will exceed, 31.00 in., not 30.50 in., of mercury.

91.147 Passenger-Carrying Flights for Compensation or Hire

101. As a commercial pilot, you decide to start a small business flying non-stop tours to look at Christmas lights during the holiday season. What authorizations, if any, are required to conduct Christmas light tours?

    A. No authorizations or approvals are required if you hold the appropriate category and class rating for the aircraft that will be flown.

    B. You must apply for and receive a Letter of Authorization from a Flight Standards office.

    C. You must apply to the FAA to receive an exemption to carry passengers at night within a 50 mile radius of your departure airport.

Answer (B) is correct. (14 CFR 91.147)
    DISCUSSION: Each operator conducting passenger-carrying flights for compensation or hire must apply for and receive a Letter of Authorization from the responsible Flight Standards office for its principal place of business. Passenger-carrying flights of this nature are considered a commercial air tour operation, as defined by 14 CFR 91.147, and are subject to the requirements of 14 CFR 91.147, which include applying for and receiving a Letter of Authorization from a Flight Standards office for that operation.
    Answer (A) is incorrect. Passenger-carrying flights of this nature are considered a commercial air tour operation as defined by 14 CFR 91.147 and are subject to its requirements, which include applying for and receiving a Letter of Authorization from a Flight Standards office for that operation. **Answer (C) is incorrect.** Passenger-carrying flights of this nature are considered a commercial air tour operation, as defined by 14 CFR 91.147, and require a Letter of Authorization from a Flight Standards office for that operation, not an exemption to carry passengers at night within a 50-mile radius of the departure airport.

91.159 VFR Cruising Altitude or Flight Level

102. VFR cruising altitudes are required to be maintained when flying

    A. at 3,000 feet or more AGL; based on true course.

    B. more than 3,000 feet AGL; based on magnetic course.

    C. at 3,000 feet or more above MSL; based on magnetic heading.

Answer (B) is correct. (14 CFR 91.159)
    DISCUSSION: VFR cruising altitudes are prescribed for level flight above 3,000 feet AGL and are based on magnetic course.
    Answer (A) is incorrect. VFR cruising altitudes are based upon magnetic (not true) course. **Answer (C) is incorrect.** VFR cruising altitudes apply for flight above 3,000 feet AGL (not MSL) and are based on magnetic course (not heading).

103. According to 14 CFR Part 91, what is the appropriate VFR cruising altitude, when above 3,000 ft. AGL, for a flight on a magnetic course of 090°?

    A. 4,500 ft.

    B. 5,500 ft.

    C. 5,000 ft.

Answer (B) is correct. (14 CFR 91.159)
    DISCUSSION: When operating a VFR flight above 3,000 ft. AGL on a magnetic course of 0° through 179°, fly any odd thousand-foot MSL altitude plus 500 ft. Thus, on a magnetic course of 090°, an appropriate VFR cruising altitude is 5,500 ft.
    Answer (A) is incorrect. An acceptable VFR cruising altitude would be 4,500 ft. if you were on a magnetic course of 180° through 359°, not 090°. **Answer (C) is incorrect.** On a magnetic course of 090°, the acceptable VFR cruising altitude is an odd thousand plus 500 ft. (i.e., 5,500 ft., not 5,000 ft., in this case).

91.167 Fuel Requirements for Flight in IFR Conditions

104. If weather conditions are such that it is required to designate an alternate airport on your IFR flight plan, you should plan to carry enough fuel to arrive at the first airport of intended landing, fly from that airport to the alternate airport, and fly thereafter for

    A. 30 minutes at slow cruising speed.

    B. 45 minutes at normal cruising speed.

    C. 1 hour at normal cruising speed.

Answer (B) is correct. (14 CFR 91.167)
    DISCUSSION: No person may operate a civil aircraft in IFR conditions unless it carries enough fuel (considering weather reports, forecasts, and conditions) to complete the flight to the first airport of intended landing; fly from that airport to the alternate airport; and fly after that for 45 min. at normal cruising speed.
    Answer (A) is incorrect. Enough fuel must be carried to fly for 45 (not 30) min. at normal (not slow) cruising speed after reaching the alternate airport. **Answer (C) is incorrect.** Enough fuel must be carried to fly for 45 min. (not 1 hr.) at normal cruising speed after reaching the alternate airport.

91.169 IFR Flight Plan: Information Required

105. For an airport with an approved instrument approach procedure to be listed as an alternate airport on an IFR flight plan, the forecasted weather conditions at the time of arrival must be at or above the following weather minimums.

    A. Ceiling 600 feet and visibility 2 NM for precision.

    B. Ceiling 800 feet and visibility 2 SM for nonprecision.

    C. Ceiling 800 feet and visibility 2 NM for nonprecision.

Answer (B) is correct. *(14 CFR 91.169)*
    DISCUSSION: For an airport with an approved instrument approach procedure to be listed as an alternate airport on an IFR flight plan, the forecasted weather conditions at the time of arrival for a nonprecision approach must be at or above a ceiling of 800 feet and visibility of 2 SM.
    Answer (A) is incorrect. For a precision approach, the weather minimums are a ceiling of 600 feet and visibility of 2 SM, not 2 NM. **Answer (C) is incorrect.** For a nonprecision approach, the weather minimums are a ceiling of 800 feet and visibility of 2 SM, not 2 NM.

106. For an airport without an approved instrument approach procedure to be listed as an alternate airport on an IFR flight plan, the forecasted weather conditions at the time of arrival must have at least a

    A. ceiling of 2,000 feet and visibility 3 SM.

    B. ceiling and visibility that allows for a descent, approach, and landing under basic VFR.

    C. ceiling of 1,000 feet and visibility 3 NM.

Answer (B) is correct. *(14 CFR 91.169)*
    DISCUSSION: For an airport without an approved instrument approach procedure to be listed as an alternate airport on an IFR flight plan, the forecasted weather conditions at the time of arrival must have ceiling and visibility minimums that allow for descent from the MEA, approach, and landing under basic VFR.
    Answer (A) is incorrect. The weather minimums for an alternate airport without an approved instrument approach must allow for a descent from the MEA, approach, and landing under basic VFR, not a ceiling of 2,000 feet and visibility of 3 SM. **Answer (C) is incorrect.** The weather minimums for an alternate airport without an approved instrument approach must allow for a descent from the MEA, approach, and landing under basic VFR, not a ceiling of 1,000 feet and visibility of 3 SM.

91.171 VOR Equipment Check for IFR Operations

107. When must an operational check on the aircraft VOR equipment be accomplished to operate under IFR? Within the preceding

    A. 30 days or 30 hours of flight time.

    B. 10 days or 10 hours of flight time.

    C. 30 days.

Answer (C) is correct. *(14 CFR 91.171)*
    DISCUSSION: To use the aircraft VOR equipment under IFR, the VOR equipment must have been operationally checked within the preceding 30 days.
    Answer (A) is incorrect. Prior to operating under IFR, an operational check of the VOR must have been accomplished within the preceding 30 days, regardless of the flight time. **Answer (B) is incorrect.** Prior to operating under IFR, an operational check of the VOR must have been accomplished within the preceding 30 days, not 10 days, regardless of the flight time.

108. What is the maximum bearing error (+ or –) allowed for an operational VOR equipment check when using an FAA-approved ground test signal?

    A. 4 degrees.

    B. 6 degrees.

    C. 8 degrees.

Answer (A) is correct. *(14 CFR 91.171)*
    DISCUSSION: When using an FAA-approved ground test signal (such as a VOT) for an operational VOR equipment check, the maximum allowable bearing error is ±4°.
    Answer (B) is incorrect. The permissible bearing error when using an airborne checkpoint, not a ground test signal, is ±6°. **Answer (C) is incorrect.** This is not a permissible bearing error on VOR checks.

109. Which data must be recorded in the aircraft logbook or other record by a pilot making a VOR operational check for IFR operations?

A. VOR name or identification, place of operational check, amount of bearing error, and date of check.

B. Date of check, place of operational check, bearing error, and signature.

C. VOR name or identification, amount of bearing error, date of check, and signature.

Answer (B) is correct. (14 CFR 91.171)
DISCUSSION: When you make a VOR operational check, you must enter the date of check, place of operational check, and bearing error, and sign the airplane logbook or other record. **Answer (A) is incorrect.** When you make a VOR operational check, you must enter in the airplane logbook or other record the date, place, and bearing error. The VOR name or identification is not required, but you must sign the airplane logbook or other record. **Answer (C) is incorrect.** When you make a VOR operational check, you must enter in the airplane logbook or other record the date, bearing error, and your signature. Additionally, the place of the operational check, not the VOR name or identification, must be entered.

91.175 Takeoff and Landing under IFR

110. On an instrument approach where a DH or MDA is applicable, the pilot may not operate below, or continue the approach unless the

A. aircraft is continuously in a position from which a descent to a normal landing, on the intended runway, can be made.

B. approach and runway lights are distinctly visible to the pilot.

C. flight visibility and ceiling are at, or above, the published minimums for that approach.

Answer (A) is correct. (14 CFR 91.175)
DISCUSSION: On an instrument approach when a DH or MDA is applicable, the pilot may not operate below the DH or MDA, or continue the approach, unless (among other items) the airplane is continuously in a position from which a descent to a landing on the intended runway can be made at a normal rate of descent using normal maneuvers. **Answer (B) is incorrect.** To operate below the DH or MDA, or to continue the approach, a pilot needs only to (among other requirements) maintain visual reference to either the approach lights or the runway lights, not both. **Answer (C) is incorrect.** A pilot may not operate below the DH or MDA, or continue the approach, unless the flight visibility, not the ceiling, is at or above the published minimums for that approach.

111. Pilots are not authorized to land an aircraft from an instrument approach unless the

A. flight visibility is at, or exceeds, the visibility prescribed in the approach procedure being used.

B. flight visibility and ceiling are at, or exceed, the minimums prescribed in the approach being used.

C. visual approach slope indicator and runway references are distinctly visible to the pilot.

Answer (A) is correct. (14 CFR 91.175)
DISCUSSION: Pilots are not authorized to land an airplane from an instrument approach unless the flight visibility is at, or exceeds, the visibility prescribed in the instrument approach procedure being used. **Answer (B) is incorrect.** A pilot may not land an airplane from an instrument approach unless the flight visibility, not the ceiling, is at, or exceeds, the visibility prescribed for that instrument approach. **Answer (C) is incorrect.** A pilot may not descend below the DH or MDA unless runway references or the VASI is available. To land, the flight visibility must be at, or must exceed, the visibility minimum prescribed in the instrument approach procedure being used.

112. A pilot performing a published instrument approach is not authorized to perform a procedure turn when

A. receiving a radar vector to a final approach course or fix.

B. maneuvering at minimum safe altitudes.

C. maneuvering at radar vectoring altitudes.

Answer (A) is correct. (14 CFR 91.175)
DISCUSSION: In the case of a radar vector to a final approach or fix or an approach for which the procedure specifies "No PT," a pilot may not make a procedure turn unless cleared to do so by ATC. **Answer (B) is incorrect.** A pilot performing a published instrument approach is not authorized to perform a procedure turn when receiving a radar vector to a final approach course or fix, rather than when maneuvering at minimum safe altitudes. **Answer (C) is incorrect.** A pilot performing a published instrument approach is not authorized to perform a procedure turn when receiving a radar vector to a final approach course or fix, rather than when maneuvering at minimum radar vector altitudes.

91.177 Minimum Altitudes for IFR Operations

113. Except when necessary for takeoff or landing or unless otherwise authorized by the Administrator, the minimum altitude for IFR flight is

    A. 2,000 feet over all terrain.

    B. 3,000 feet over designated mountainous terrain; 2,000 feet over terrain elsewhere.

    C. 2,000 feet above the highest obstacle over designated mountainous terrain; 1,000 feet above the highest obstacle over terrain elsewhere.

Answer (C) is correct. (14 CFR 91.177)
DISCUSSION: No one may operate an aircraft under IFR below the published minimum altitudes or, if none are prescribed, below an altitude of 2,000 ft. above the highest obstacle in a mountainous area or an altitude of 1,000 ft. above the highest obstacle over terrain elsewhere.
    Answer (A) is incorrect. This is the minimum altitude for IFR operations over mountainous terrain; elsewhere the minimum altitude is 1,000 ft. **Answer (B) is incorrect.** The minimum altitude is 2,000 ft., not 3,000 ft., over mountainous terrain and 1,000 ft., not 2,000 ft., over terrain elsewhere.

91.183 IFR Communications

114. The pilot in command of an aircraft operated under IFR, in controlled airspace, not in radar contact, shall report by radio as soon as possible when

    A. passing FL 180.

    B. passing each designated reporting point, to include time and altitude.

    C. changing control facilities.

Answer (B) is correct. (14 CFR 91.183)
DISCUSSION: The pilot in command of an airplane operated under IFR in controlled airspace and not in radar contact shall report by radio as soon as possible the time and altitude of passing each designated reporting point.
    Answer (A) is incorrect. When operating under IFR in controlled airspace and not in radar contact, the pilot must report passing each designated reporting point, not passing FL 180. **Answer (C) is incorrect.** When operating under IFR in controlled airspace and not in radar contact, the pilot must report passing each designated reporting point, not changing control facilities. When changing control facilities, the pilot will check in with the new facility whether operating in radar contact or not.

91.187 Operation under IFR in Controlled Airspace: Malfunction Reports

115. The pilot in command of an aircraft operated under IFR, in controlled airspace, shall report as soon as practical to ATC when

    A. climbing or descending to assigned altitudes.

    B. experiencing any malfunctions of navigational, approach, or communications equipment, occurring in flight.

    C. requested to contact a new controlling facility.

Answer (B) is correct. (14 CFR 91.187)
DISCUSSION: The pilot in command of an airplane operated under IFR in controlled airspace shall report as soon as practicable to ATC any malfunctions of navigational, approach, or communication equipment occurring in flight.
    Answer (A) is incorrect. A pilot should inform ATC that (s)he is climbing or descending to an assigned altitude only on initial contact with an ATC facility, not at all times. The reports that the pilot shall (must) make while operating under IFR are found in 14 CFR Part 91, while the reports the pilot should make (established general procedures) are found in the *AIM*. **Answer (C) is incorrect.** As a general procedure, the pilot should acknowledge and select the new frequency as soon as possible and make the initial call as soon as practical. The reports that the pilot shall (must) make while operating under IFR are found in 14 CFR Part 91; established general IFR procedures are found in the *AIM* and include acknowledging ATC directives, clearances, etc.

91.203 Civil Aircraft: Certifications Required

116. Which list accurately reflects some of the documents required to be current and carried in a U.S. registered civil airplane flying in the United States under day Visual Flight Rules (VFR)?

A. Proof of insurance certificate, VFR flight plan or flight itinerary, and the aircraft logbook.

B. VFR sectional(s) chart(s) for the area in which the flight occurs, aircraft logbook, and engine logbook.

C. Airworthiness certificate, approved airplane flight manual, and aircraft registration certificate.

Answer (C) is correct. (14 CFR 91.9/91.203)
   DISCUSSION: No person may operate a civil aircraft unless it has within it an appropriate and current airworthiness certificate and an effective U.S. registration certificate. No person may operate a U.S. registered civil aircraft unless there is available in the aircraft a current and approved Airplane Flight Manual.
   Answer (A) is incorrect. A proof of insurance certificate, VFR flight plan or flight itinerary, and aircraft logbook are not required for flight in day VFR conditions. **Answer (B) is incorrect.** Sectional charts, aircraft logbook, and engine logbook are not requirements for flight in day VFR conditions.

117. Which of the following preflight actions is the pilot in command required to take in order to comply with the United States Code of Federal Regulations regarding day Visual Flight Rules (VFR)?

A. File a VFR flight plan with a Flight Service Station.

B. Verify the airworthiness certificate is legible to passengers.

C. Verify approved position lights are not burned out.

Answer (B) is correct. (14 CFR 91.203)
   DISCUSSION: No person may operate a civil aircraft unless the airworthiness certificate or a special flight authorization is displayed at the cabin or flight deck entrance so that it is legible to passengers and crew.
   Answer (A) is incorrect. A VFR flight plan is not required to conduct VFR flight operations. **Answer (C) is incorrect.** A pilot is only required to have approved position lights for night VFR operations.

118. A commercial pilot is preparing for a VFR flight that will involve carrying passengers 150 NM at night. Prior to the flight what action must the PIC perform?

A. Confirm the Airworthiness Certificate is on board and visible to passengers.

B. File a flight plan.

C. Confirm the proof of insurance is on board.

Answer (A) is correct. (14 CFR 91.203)
   DISCUSSION: No person may operate a civil aircraft unless an airworthiness certificate or special flight authorization is displayed at the cabin or flight deck entrance so it is visible to passengers and crew.
   Answer (B) is incorrect. A flight plan is not required for VFR night cross-country flying. **Answer (C) is incorrect.** Proof of insurance is not required to be on board U.S.-registered civil aircraft while operating within the National Airspace System.

119. You are taking a 123 nautical mile VFR flight from one airport to another. Which of the following actions must the pilot in command take?

A. Ensure each passenger has a legible photo identification.

B. Verify the airworthiness certificate is legible to passengers.

C. File a VFR flight plan with a Flight Service Station.

Answer (B) is correct. (14 CFR 91.203)
   DISCUSSION: No person may operate a civil aircraft unless the airworthiness certificate or a special flight authorization is displayed at the cabin or flight deck entrance so that it is legible to passengers and crew.
   Answer (A) is incorrect. It is not required for the pilot in command to ensure that each passenger has photo identification. **Answer (C) is incorrect.** A VFR flight plan is not required to conduct VFR flight operations.

120. You are taking a 196 nautical mile VFR cross country flight in mountainous terrain. Which of the following actions must the pilot in command take?

A. Verify the airworthiness certificate is legible to passengers.

B. File a VFR flight plan with a Flight Service Station.

C. Ensure all items in the baggage area are strapped down.

Answer (A) is correct. (14 CFR 91.203)
   DISCUSSION: No person may operate a civil aircraft unless the airworthiness certificate or a special flight authorization is displayed at the cabin or flight deck entrance so that it is legible to passengers and crew.
   Answer (B) is incorrect. A VFR flight plan is not required to conduct VFR flight operations. **Answer (C) is incorrect.** This is not the best answer because most baggage areas use cargo nets to keep baggage in place and not necessarily strapped down.

121. Prior to departing on a VFR cross country flight over mountainous terrain, what action must the pilot in command perform?

A. Confirm the Airworthiness certificate is visible to passengers and crew.

B. Perform a VOR check.

C. Take a mountain flying awareness course (MFAC).

Answer (A) is correct. (14 CFR 91.203)
DISCUSSION: No person may operate a civil aircraft unless an airworthiness certificate or special flight authorization is displayed at the cabin or flight deck entrance so it is visible to passengers and crew.
Answer (B) is incorrect. A VOR check is required every 30 days for flight under instrument flight rules. A VFR cross-country flight does not require the use of a VOR. **Answer (C) is incorrect.** A mountain flying awareness course (MFAC) is not required to operate over mountainous terrain.

91.205 Powered Civil Aircraft with Standard Category U.S. Airworthiness Certificates: Instrument and Equipment Requirements

122. Approved flotation gear, readily available to each occupant, is required on each airplane if it is being flown for hire over water,

A. in amphibious aircraft beyond 50 NM from shore.

B. beyond power-off gliding distance from shore.

C. more than 50 statute miles from shore.

Answer (B) is correct. (14 CFR 91.205)
DISCUSSION: If an airplane is operated for hire over water and beyond power-off gliding distance from shore, approved flotation gear, readily available to each occupant, and at least one pyrotechnic signaling device are required.
Answer (A) is incorrect. The flotation gear requirement applies to all aircraft operated for hire when flying beyond power-off gliding distance, not 50 NM, from shore. **Answer (C) is incorrect.** Flotation gear is required for each occupant if the airplane is flown beyond the power-off gliding distance from shore, not more than 50 statute miles from shore.

123. Which is required equipment for powered aircraft during VFR night flights?

A. Flashlight with red lens, if the flight is for hire.

B. An electric landing light, if the flight is for hire.

C. Sensitive altimeter adjustable for barometric pressure.

Answer (B) is correct. (14 CFR 91.205)
DISCUSSION: For VFR flights at night, the required equipment includes one electric landing light if the aircraft is operated for hire.
Answer (A) is incorrect. No specific requirement concerns flashlights and the color of the lens. **Answer (C) is incorrect.** Sensitive altimeters are required only for IFR flight.

124. Which is required equipment for powered aircraft during VFR night flights?

A. Anticollision light system.

B. Gyroscopic direction indicator.

C. Gyroscopic bank-and-pitch indicator.

Answer (A) is correct. (14 CFR 91.205)
DISCUSSION: For VFR flight at night, the required instruments and equipment include an approved aviation red or aviation white anticollision light system on all U.S.-registered civil aircraft.
Answer (B) is incorrect. A gyroscopic direction indicator is required for IFR, not VFR night, flight. **Answer (C) is incorrect.** A gyroscopic bank-and-pitch indicator is required for IFR, not VFR night, flight.

91.207 Emergency Locator Transmitters

125. The maximum cumulative time that an emergency locator transmitter may be operated before the rechargeable battery must be recharged is

A. 30 minutes.

B. 45 minutes.

C. 60 minutes.

Answer (C) is correct. (14 CFR 91.207)
DISCUSSION: An ELT battery must be replaced or recharged when the transmitter has been in use for more than 1 cumulative hr. or when 50% of its useful life (or useful life of charge) has expired.
Answer (A) is incorrect. An ELT battery must be replaced or recharged after 1 hr. (not 30 min.) of cumulative use. **Answer (B) is incorrect.** An ELT battery must be replaced or recharged after 1 hr. (not 45 min.) of cumulative use.

126. You are conducting your preflight of an aircraft and notice that the last inspection of the emergency locator transmitter was 11 calendar months ago. You may

A. depart if you get a special flight permit.

B. depart because the ELT is within the inspection requirements.

C. not depart until a new inspection is conducted.

Answer (B) is correct. (14 CFR 91.207)
DISCUSSION: Each required ELT must be inspected within 12 calendar months after the last inspection for proper installation, battery corrosion, operation of the controls and crash sensor, and the presence of a sufficient signal radiating from its antenna. In this scenario, you may depart because the last inspection was conducted 11 months ago.
Answer (A) is incorrect. ELTs must be inspected within 12 calendar months; therefore, the inspection is current and a special flight permit is not necessary. **Answer (C) is incorrect.** The ELT was inspected 11 months ago; therefore, the next inspection is not due for another month and you may depart.

91.209 Aircraft Lights

127. If not equipped with required position lights, an aircraft must terminate flight

A. at sunset.

B. 30 minutes after sunset.

C. 1 hour after sunset.

Answer (A) is correct. (14 CFR 91.209)
DISCUSSION: No person may, during the period from sunset to sunrise, operate an aircraft unless it has lighted position lights.
Answer (B) is incorrect. Position lights are required at, not 30 min. after, sunset. **Answer (C) is incorrect.** Position lights are required at, not 1 hr. after, sunset.

128. If an aircraft is not equipped with an electrical or anticollision light system, no person may operate that aircraft

A. after dark.

B. 1 hour after sunset.

C. after sunset to sunrise.

Answer (C) is correct. (14 CFR 91.209)
DISCUSSION: If an aircraft is not equipped with an electrical or anticollision light system, you may not operate that aircraft during the period from sunset to sunrise.
Answer (A) is incorrect. You may not operate an aircraft that is not equipped with an electrical or anticollision light system after sunset, not after dark. **Answer (B) is incorrect.** You may not operate an aircraft that is not equipped with an electrical or anticollision light system after sunset, not 1 hr. after sunset. The logging of night flight time, to meet recent experience requirements for carrying passengers at night, begins 1 hr. after sunset.

91.211 Supplemental Oxygen

129. What are the oxygen requirements when operating at cabin pressure altitudes above 15,000 feet MSL?

A. Oxygen must be available for the flightcrew.

B. Oxygen is not required at any altitude in a balloon.

C. The flightcrew and passengers must be provided with supplemental oxygen.

Answer (C) is correct. (14 CFR 91.211)
DISCUSSION: No person may operate a civil aircraft of U.S. registry at cabin pressure altitudes above 15,000 ft. MSL unless each occupant of the aircraft is provided with supplemental oxygen.
Answer (A) is incorrect. The flightcrew must use oxygen (not just have it available) above 14,000 ft. MSL. **Answer (B) is incorrect.** Each occupant, not only the flightcrew, must be provided with supplemental oxygen at cabin pressure altitudes above 15,000 ft. MSL.

130. In accordance with 14 CFR Part 91, supplemental oxygen must be used by the required minimum flightcrew for that time exceeding 30 minutes while at cabin pressure altitudes of

A. 10,500 feet MSL up to and including 12,500 feet MSL.

B. 12,000 feet MSL up to and including 18,000 feet MSL.

C. 12,500 feet MSL up to and including 14,000 feet MSL.

Answer (C) is correct. (14 CFR 91.211)
DISCUSSION: No one may operate a U.S. civil aircraft at cabin pressure altitudes above 12,500 feet MSL up to and including 14,000 feet MSL, unless the required minimum flight crew is provided with and uses supplemental oxygen for that part of the flight at those altitudes that is of more than 30 min. duration.
Answer (A) is incorrect. Supplemental oxygen is not required below 12,500 feet MSL. **Answer (B) is incorrect.** Supplemental oxygen is not required below 12,500 feet MSL and is required at all times above 14,000 feet MSL.

91.213 Inoperative Instruments and Equipment

131. The primary purpose of a minimum equipment list (MEL) is to

A. provide a list of equipment that must be operational at all times on the aircraft.

B. list the equipment that can be inoperative and still not affect the airworthiness of an aircraft.

C. list the minimum equipment that must be installed in all aircraft as required by airworthiness directives.

Answer (B) is correct. (14 CFR 91.213)
   DISCUSSION: No person may take off in an aircraft with inoperative instruments or equipment installed unless the following conditions are met:

1. An approved minimum equipment list exists for that aircraft.
2. The aircraft has within it a letter of authorization, issued by the FAA Flight Standards office having jurisdiction over the area in which the operator is located, authorizing operation of the aircraft under the minimum equipment list.
3. The approved minimum equipment list must provide for the operation of the aircraft with the instruments and equipment in an inoperable condition.

   Answer (A) is incorrect. This information is covered by regulations for each condition of flight and the aircraft flight manual. **Answer (C) is incorrect.** This information is covered by the governing airworthiness directive.

132. Authority for approval of a minimum equipment list (MEL) must be obtained from the

A. Administrator.

B. FAA district office.

C. aircraft manufacturer.

Answer (B) is correct. (14 CFR 91.213)
   DISCUSSION: No person may take off in an aircraft with inoperative instruments or equipment installed unless the following conditions are met:

1. An approved minimum equipment list exists for that aircraft.
2. The aircraft has within it a letter of authorization, issued by the FAA Flight Standards office having jurisdiction over the area in which the operator is located, authorizing operation of the aircraft under the minimum equipment list.
3. The approved minimum equipment list must provide for the operation of the aircraft with the instruments and equipment in an inoperable condition.

   Answer (A) is incorrect. Authority for approval of an MEL comes from the responsible Flight Standards office, not the FAA Administrator. **Answer (C) is incorrect.** Authority for approval of an MEL comes from the responsible Flight Standards office, not the aircraft manufacturer.

133. Which action is appropriate if an aircraft, operating under 14 CFR Part 91 and for which a master minimum equipment list has not been developed, is determined to have an inoperative instrument or piece of equipment that does not constitute a hazard to the aircraft? The item should be

A. removed and repaired prior to the next flight.

B. placarded "inoperative" and repaired during the next inspection.

C. deactivated and placarded "inoperative" but repairs can be deferred indefinitely.

Answer (C) is correct. (14 CFR 91.213)
   DISCUSSION: A person may take off in an aircraft for which a master minimum equipment list has not been developed under Part 91 with inoperative instruments and equipment provided

1. The item is not required by the aircraft's equipment list or kinds of operations list.
2. The item is not required by the VFR-day type certification requirements prescribed in the airworthiness certification regulations.
3. The item is not required by an airworthiness directive, 14 CFR 91.205, 14 CFR 91.207, or any other 14 CFR.
4. The item is either removed or deactivated and placarded "Inoperative."
5. A determination is made that the inoperative instrument or equipment does not constitute a hazard to the anticipated operation.

While the operator should have all inoperative items repaired at the next inspection, the operator may elect to defer the repairs indefinitely.
   Answer (A) is incorrect. The item does not need to be removed and/or repaired until the next inspection, not the next flight. **Answer (B) is incorrect.** In addition to being placarded, the item must also be either removed or deactivated. While it is recommended that repairs be done at the next inspection, it is not required.

91.215 ATC Transponder and Altitude Reporting Equipment and Use

134. A coded transponder equipped with altitude reporting equipment is required for

A. Class A, Class B, and Class C airspace areas.

B. all airspace of the 48 contiguous U.S. and the District of Columbia at and above 10,000 feet MSL (including airspace at and below 2,500 feet above the surface).

C. both of the other answers.

Answer (A) is correct. (14 CFR 91.215)
   DISCUSSION: An operable coded transponder with altitude reporting capability (i.e., Mode C) is required in Class A, Class B, and Class C airspace areas.
   Answer (B) is incorrect. An operable coded transponder equipped with altitude reporting capability is required in all airspace of the 48 contiguous U.S. and the District of Columbia at and above 10,000 feet MSL excluding, not including, airspace at and below 2,500 feet AGL. **Answer (C) is incorrect.** An operable coded transponder equipped with altitude reporting capability is required in all airspace of the 48 contiguous U.S. and the District of Columbia at and above 10,000 feet MSL excluding, not including, airspace at and below 2,500 feet AGL.

135. In the contiguous U.S., excluding the airspace at and below 2,500 feet AGL, an operable coded transponder equipped with Mode C capability is required in all airspace above

A. 10,000 feet MSL.

B. 12,500 feet MSL.

C. 14,500 feet MSL.

Answer (A) is correct. (14 CFR 91.215)
   DISCUSSION: An operable transponder with altitude reporting capability (i.e., Mode C) is required for all operations above 10,000 feet MSL, excluding the airspace at and below 2,500 feet AGL.
   Answer (B) is incorrect. The altitude above which crewmembers are required to use oxygen after 30 min. in an unpressurized aircraft is 12,500 feet MSL. **Answer (C) is incorrect.** The base of Class E airspace is 14,500 feet MSL.

136. Your transponder is inoperative. In order to enter Class B airspace, you must submit a request for a deviation from the

A. ATC facility no less than 24 hr. before the proposed operation.

B. nearest FSDO 24 hr. before the proposed operation.

C. controlling ATC facility at least 1 hr. before the proposed flight.

Answer (C) is correct. (14 CFR 91.215)
   DISCUSSION: ATC may authorize deviations on a continuing basis, or for individual flights, for operations of aircraft without an operative transponder. The request for a deviation must be submitted to the ATC facility having jurisdiction over the airspace concerned at least 1 hr. before the proposed operation.
   Answer (A) is incorrect. A request for a deviation to operate in Class B airspace in an airplane not equipped with an operative transponder must be submitted to the controlling ATC facility at least 1 hr. before the proposed flight, not 24 hr. before the operation. **Answer (B) is incorrect.** FSDOs are not responsible for controlling air traffic. Instead, a request should be submitted to the controlling ATC facility.

91.225 ADS-B Out Equipment and Use

137. Automatic Dependent Surveillance-Broadcast (ADS-B) Out is mandated for aircraft operations in

A. Class A, B, and C airspace.

B. Class A, B, and C airspace above 2,500 ft. AGL.

C. all airspace within the 48 contiguous states above 2,000 ft. AGL.

Answer (A) is correct. (14 CFR 91.225)
   DISCUSSION: ADS-B Out equipment must be installed for all operations (1) in Class A, B, and C airspace; (2) above the ceiling and within the lateral boundaries of Class B and C airspace; and (3) in Class E airspace within the 48 contiguous states and the District of Columbia at and above 10,000 ft. MSL, excluding the airspace at and below 2,500 ft. above the surface.
   Answer (B) is incorrect. ADS-B Out equipment is required in all Class A, B, and C airspace, not only the airspace above 2,500 ft. AGL. **Answer (C) is incorrect.** ADS-B Out equipment is required only in certain airspace areas as specified in 14 CFR 91.225.

138. Each person operating an aircraft equipped with ADS-B Out must operate it in the transmit mode

A. at all times unless otherwise authorized by the FAA or directed by ATC.

B. when operating in Class B and C airspace, excluding operations conducted under day VFR.

C. all classes of airspace when the flight is operated for compensation or hire but not otherwise.

Answer (A) is correct. (14 CFR 91.225)
   DISCUSSION: As per 14 CFR 91.225, each person operating an aircraft equipped with ADS-B Out must operate this equipment in the transmit mode at all times unless otherwise authorized by the FAA or directed by ATC.
   Answer (B) is incorrect. ADS-B Out equipment is required to be operated in transmit mode at all times unless otherwise authorized by the FAA or directed by ATC. **Answer (C) is incorrect.** ADS-B Out equipment is not a requirement for operation within Class D airspace or above the Class D ceiling.

139. Aircraft that operate in Class A airspace must be equipped with

    A. ADS-B.

    B. ADS-B with TIS-B.

    C. ADS-B with FIS-B.

Answer (B) is correct. (14 CFR 91.225)
    DISCUSSION: Operations in Class A airspace require aircraft to be equipped with extended squitter Automatic Dependent Surveillance-Broadcast (ADS-B) and Traffic Information Service-Broadcast (TIS-B) equipment operating on the frequency of 1090 MHz.
    Answer (A) is incorrect. Operations in Class A airspace require Traffic Information Service-Broadcast (TIS-B) equipment in addition to Automatic Dependent Surveillance-Broadcast (ADS-B) equipment operating on 1090-ES. **Answer (C) is incorrect.** The aircraft equipment requirements for operating in Class A airspace include Automatic Dependent Surveillance-Broadcast (ADS-B) and Traffic Information Service-Broadcast (TIS-B) equipment operating on the frequency of 1090 MHz, not Flight Information Services-Broadcast (FIS-B).

140. An aircraft fitted with ADS-B Out equipment does not need to be operated in the transmit mode when

    A. the aircraft was not originally certificated with an electrical system under 14 CFR 91.225.

    B. the aircraft is in uncontrolled airspace where ADS-B Out is not a requirement.

    C. operating under a mission of law enforcement or intelligence purposes.

Answer (C) is correct. (14 CFR 91.225)
    DISCUSSION: An ADS-B Out-equipped aircraft may operate without this equipment in transmit mode when performing a sensitive government mission for national defense, homeland security, intelligence, or law enforcement purposes wherein transmitting would compromise the operations security of the mission or pose a safety risk to the aircraft, crew, or people and property in the air or on the ground.
    Answer (A) is incorrect. Any aircraft that is equipped with ADS-B Out is required to have this equipment operating in transmit mode at all times as per 14 CFR 91.225. **Answer (B) is incorrect.** Irrespective of airspace requirements, if the aircraft is equipped with ADS-B Out, this equipment must be operated in the transmit mode at all times as per 14 CFR 91.225.

141. Which of the following flights may be made without ADS-B Out equipment installed?

    A. A VFR flight that departs a Class E airport and cruises at 12,500 ft. MSL to a Class G destination airport.

    B. A VFR flight that overflies, but does not enter, a Class C airspace while en route at 6,500 ft. MSL.

    C. A VFR flight that departs a Class D airport, cruises in Class E airspace at 7,500 ft. MSL, and arrives at another Class D airport.

Answer (C) is correct. (14 CFR 91.225)
    DISCUSSION: A VFR flight that departs a Class D airport, cruises in Class E airspace at 7,500 ft. MSL, and arrives at another Class D airport may be made without ADS-B Out equipment installed because ADS-B Out is not required in Class D airspace or Class E airspace below 10,000 ft. MSL. ADS-B Out equipment must be installed for all operations (1) in Class A, B, and C airspace; (2) above the ceiling and within the lateral boundaries of Class B and Class C airspace; and (3) in Class E airspace within the 48 contiguous states and the District of Columbia at and above 10,000 ft. MSL, excluding the airspace at and below 2,500 ft. above the surface.
    Answer (A) is incorrect. ADS-B Out equipment is required for flights at and above 10,000 ft. MSL. **Answer (B) is incorrect.** ADS-B Out equipment is required for flights within and above Class C airspace.

142. When is Automatic Dependent Surveillance-Broadcast (ADS-B) Out equipment required?

    A. Under the shelf of Class C airspace.

    B. In Class E airspace above 10,000 ft. MSL, except at and below 2,500 ft. AGL.

    C. In all controlled airspace.

Answer (B) is correct. (14 CFR 91.225)
    DISCUSSION: ADS-B Out equipment must be installed for all operations (1) in Class A airspace; (2) above the ceiling and within the lateral boundaries of Class B and C airspace (within the Mode C veil where applicable); and (3) in Class E airspace within the 48 contiguous states and the District of Columbia at and above 10,000 ft. MSL, excluding the airspace at and below 2,500 ft. above the surface. It is also required over the Gulf of Mexico at and above 3,000 ft. MSL within 12 NM of the United States coastline.
    Answer (A) is incorrect. ADS-B Out is required within and above Class C airspace, not underneath Class C airspace. **Answer (C) is incorrect.** ADS-B Out equipment is not required in all controlled airspace, only the airspace designated by 14 CFR 91.225. It is not required in Class D airspace and some Class E airspace.

91.227 ADS-B Out Equipment Performance Requirements

143. What type of ADS-B equipment is required in Class A airspace?

A. ADS-B Out that operates on the frequency 1090 MHz.

B. ADS-B Out that operates with UAT on the frequency 978 MHz.

C. Any type of certified ADS-B In.

Answer (A) is correct. (14 CFR 91.227)
DISCUSSION: Aircraft operating in Class A airspace are required to have ADS-B Out equipment installed that operates on the frequency of 1090 MHz.
Answer (B) is incorrect. ADS-B Out that operates with a universal access transceiver (UAT) on the frequency 978 MHz may be used in airspace below 18,000 ft., but not in Class A airspace. **Answer (C) is incorrect.** ADS-B Out, not ADS-B In, is required in Class A airspace.

144. Aircraft operating in class A airspace are required to use which type of ADS-B equipment?

A. Universal access transceiver (978 UAT).

B. 1090-ES.

C. 1090-ES or universal access transceiver (978 UAT).

Answer (B) is correct. (14 CFR 91.227)
DISCUSSION: As per 14 CFR 91.227, each aircraft operating in Class A airspace must meet the installed equipment requirements as defined in TSO-C166b, Extended Squitter Automatic Dependent Surveillance-Broadcast (ADS-B) and Traffic Information Service-Broadcast (TIS-B) Equipment Operating on the Radio Frequency of 1090 Megahertz (MHz) or 1090-ES.
Answer (A) is incorrect. Aircraft operating in Class A airspace require 1090-ES ADS-B Out equipment, whereas aircraft operating solely under 18,000 ft. MSL may use 1090-ES or UAT equipment. **Answer (C) is incorrect.** Aircraft that operate in Class A airspace must use 1090-ES ADS-B Out equipment.

91.311 Towing: Other than under Sec. 91.309

145. Which is required to operate an aircraft towing an advertising banner?

A. Approval from ATC to operate in Class E airspace.

B. A certificate of waiver issued by the Administrator.

C. A safety link at each end of the towline which has a breaking strength not less than 80 percent of the aircraft's gross weight.

Answer (B) is correct. (14 CFR 91.311)
DISCUSSION: No pilot of a civil aircraft may tow anything with that aircraft (other than a glider) except in accordance with the terms of a certificate of waiver issued by the Administrator of the FAA.
Answer (A) is incorrect. ATC approval for flight in Class E airspace is required only during IFR conditions. **Answer (C) is incorrect.** The breaking strength of the safety link applies to towing gliders, not banners.

91.313 Restricted Category Civil Aircraft: Operating Limitations

146. Which is true with respect to operating limitations of a "restricted" category airplane?

A. A pilot of a "restricted" category airplane is required to hold a commercial pilot certificate.

B. A "restricted" category airplane is limited to an operating radius of 25 miles from its home base.

C. No person may operate a "restricted" category airplane carrying passengers or property for compensation or hire.

Answer (C) is correct. (14 CFR 91.313)
DISCUSSION: Persons or property cannot be transported for compensation or hire in a restricted category airplane.
Answer (A) is incorrect. With respect to operating limitations of a restricted category airplane, there is no minimum pilot certification level. If the pilot is receiving compensation, then, due to that type of operation, a commercial pilot certificate may be required. **Answer (B) is incorrect.** With respect to operating limitations of a restricted category airplane, there is no limitation as to how far from the airplane's home base it may be operated.

91.315 Limited Category Civil Aircraft: Operating Limitations

147. The carriage of passengers for hire by a commercial pilot is

A. not authorized in limited category aircraft.

B. not authorized in utility category airplane.

C. authorized in restricted category aircraft.

Answer (A) is correct. (14 CFR 91.315)
DISCUSSION: Persons or property cannot be transported for compensation or hire in a limited category civil aircraft.
Answer (B) is incorrect. Carriage of passengers for hire is permitted in utility category aircraft. **Answer (C) is incorrect.** Carriage of passengers for hire is not permitted in restricted category aircraft.

91.319 Aircraft Having Experimental Certificates: Operating Limitations

148. No person may operate an aircraft that has an experimental airworthiness certificate

    A.   under instrument flight rules (IFR).

    B.   when carrying property for hire.

    C.   when carrying persons or property for hire.

Answer (C) is correct. (14 CFR 91.319)
    DISCUSSION: No person may operate an aircraft that has an experimental airworthiness certificate when carrying persons or property for hire.
    Answer (A) is incorrect. While an experimental aircraft is to be flown only in VFR-day weather conditions, the FAA may specifically authorize IFR operations. **Answer (B) is incorrect.** No person may operate an aircraft that has an experimental certificate when carrying persons or property for hire, not only property.

91.325 Primary Category Aircraft: Operating Limitations

149. Which is true with respect to operating limitations of a "primary" category airplane?

    A.   A "primary" category airplane is limited to a specified operating radius from its home base.

    B.   No person may operate a "primary" category airplane carrying passengers or property for compensation or hire.

    C.   A pilot of a "primary" category airplane must hold a commercial pilot certificate when carrying passengers for compensation or hire.

Answer (B) is correct. (14 CFR 91.325)
    DISCUSSION: With respect to operating limitations of a primary category airplane, no person may operate a primary category airplane carrying persons or property for compensation or hire.
    Answer (A) is incorrect. With respect to operating limitations of a primary category airplane, there is no limitation as to how far from the airplane's home base it may be operated. **Answer (C) is incorrect.** With respect to operating limitations of a primary category airplane, there is no minimum level of pilot certification required.

91.403 General

150. Assuring compliance with an Airworthiness Directive is the responsibility of the

    A.   pilot in command and the FAA certificated mechanic assigned to that aircraft.

    B.   pilot in command of that aircraft.

    C.   owner or operator of that aircraft.

Answer (C) is correct. (14 CFR 91.403)
    DISCUSSION: The owner or operator of an aircraft is primarily responsible for maintaining that aircraft in an airworthy condition, including compliance with all Airworthiness Directives. The term "operator" includes the pilot in command.
    Answer (A) is incorrect. Although a mechanic will perform the maintenance required to comply with an Airworthiness Directive, assuring compliance is the responsibility of the owner or operator. **Answer (B) is incorrect.** The owner or operator, not only the pilot in command, is responsible for assuring compliance with all Airworthiness Directives.

151. Who is primarily responsible for maintaining an aircraft in an airworthy condition?

    A.   The lead mechanic responsible for that aircraft.

    B.   Pilot in command or operator.

    C.   Owner or operator of the aircraft.

Answer (C) is correct. (14 CFR 91.403)
    DISCUSSION: The owner or operator of an aircraft is primarily responsible for maintaining that aircraft in an airworthy condition. The term "operator" includes the pilot in command.
    Answer (A) is incorrect. Mechanics work at the direction of the owner or operator. **Answer (B) is incorrect.** The owner or operator, not only the operator, of an aircraft is primarily responsible for an aircraft's airworthiness. The term "operator" includes the pilot in command.

152. You are PIC of a flight and determine that the aircraft you planned to fly has an overdue Airworthiness Directive (AD). Which of the following is an appropriate decision?

    A.   No maintenance is available so you wait until after the trip to comply with the AD.

    B.   You make the flight because you can overfly an AD by 10 hours.

    C.   You cancel the flight and have the aircraft scheduled for maintenance.

Answer (C) is correct. (14 CFR 91.403)
    DISCUSSION: The pilot in command is responsible for ensuring the aircraft is maintained in an airworthy condition and for complying with all ADs. ADs are regulatory and must be complied with unless a specific exemption is granted.
    Answer (A) is incorrect. If an AD is overdue, then the aircraft is not airworthy and should not be flown. **Answer (B) is incorrect.** An aircraft with an overdue AD cannot be flown without a ferry permit.

91.405 Maintenance Required

153. After an annual inspection has been completed and the aircraft has been returned to service, an appropriate notation should be made

    A. on the airworthiness certificate.

    B. in the aircraft maintenance records.

    C. in the FAA-approved flight manual.

Answer (B) is correct. (14 CFR 91.405)
    DISCUSSION: Each owner or operator shall ensure that maintenance personnel make appropriate entries in the aircraft maintenance records indicating that an annual inspection has been completed and that the aircraft has been approved for return to service.
    Answer (A) is incorrect. Annual inspections are recorded in maintenance records, not on the Airworthiness Certificate.
    Answer (C) is incorrect. Annual inspections are recorded in maintenance records, not in the flight manual.

154. A standard airworthiness certificate remains in effect as long as the aircraft receives

    A. required maintenance and inspections.

    B. an annual inspection.

    C. an annual inspection and a 100-hour inspection prior to their expiration dates.

Answer (A) is correct. (14 CFR 91.405)
    DISCUSSION: A standard airworthiness certificate remains in effect as long as the aircraft receives the required maintenance and inspections. This includes compliance with Airworthiness Directives, annual inspections, 100-hr. inspections, repairs between inspections, etc.
    Answer (B) is incorrect. A standard airworthiness certificate remains in effect as long as the aircraft receives the required maintenance and inspections. An annual inspection is just one part of the inspections and maintenance requirements, and some aircraft have an inspection program, which means an annual inspection is not required. **Answer (C) is incorrect.** A standard airworthiness certificate remains in effect as long as the aircraft receives the required maintenance and inspections. Not all aircraft require an annual and a 100-hr. inspection.

91.407 Operation after Maintenance, Preventive Maintenance, Rebuilding, or Alteration

155. If an aircraft's operation in flight was substantially affected by an alteration or repair, the aircraft documents must show that it was test flown and approved for return to service by an appropriately-rated pilot prior to being operated

    A. under VFR or IFR rules.

    B. with passengers aboard.

    C. for compensation or hire.

Answer (B) is correct. (14 CFR 91.407)
    DISCUSSION: No person may carry any person (other than crewmembers) in an altered aircraft that may have appreciably changed its flight characteristics or substantially affected its operation in flight until an appropriately rated pilot with at least a private pilot certificate flies the aircraft, makes an operational check of the maintenance performed or alteration made, and logs the flight in the aircraft records.
    Answer (A) is incorrect. An altered aircraft must be test flown before passengers are carried. A maintenance logbook entry by an appropriate maintenance person returns the aircraft to service, which allows the airplane to be flown under VFR or IFR. **Answer (C) is incorrect.** An altered aircraft must be test flown before passengers are carried regardless of whether the flight is for compensation or hire.

91.409 Inspections

156. Which is true concerning required maintenance inspections?

    A. A 100-hour inspection may be substituted for an annual inspection.

    B. An annual inspection may be substituted for a 100-hour inspection.

    C. An annual inspection is required even if a progressive inspection system has been approved.

Answer (B) is correct. (14 CFR 91.409)
    DISCUSSION: No person may operate an aircraft within the preceding 12 calendar months unless it has had an annual inspection. If the aircraft is required to have a 100-hr. inspection, an annual inspection may be substituted for a 100-hr. inspection.
    Answer (A) is incorrect. An annual inspection may be substituted for a 100-hr. inspection (not vice versa).
    Answer (C) is incorrect. An annual inspection is not required if a progressive inspection system has been approved.

157. An aircraft carrying passengers for hire has been on a schedule of inspection every 100 hours of time in service. Under which condition, if any, may that aircraft be operated beyond 100 hours without a new inspection?

    A. The aircraft may be flown for any flight as long as the time in service has not exceeded 110 hours.

    B. The aircraft may be dispatched for a flight of any duration as long as 100 hours has not been exceeded at the time it departs.

    C. The 100-hour limitation may be exceeded by not more than 10 hours if necessary to reach a place at which the inspection can be done.

Answer (C) is correct. (14 CFR 91.409)
    DISCUSSION: The 100-hr. limitation may be exceeded by not more than 10 hr. if necessary to reach a place at which the inspection can be done. The excess time, however, is included in computing the next 100 hr. of time in service.
    Answer (A) is incorrect. The 10-hr. leeway is applicable only if necessary to reach a place to perform the 100-hr. inspection. **Answer (B) is incorrect.** There is a 10-hr. leeway in excess of the 100-hr. limitation, and the 10-hr. leeway is applicable only if necessary to reach a place to perform the 100-hr. inspection.

91.413 ATC Transponder Tests and Inspections

158. If an ATC transponder installed in an aircraft has not been tested, inspected, and found to comply with regulations within a specified period, what is the limitation on its use?

    A. Its use is not permitted.

    B. It may be used when in Class G airspace.

    C. It may be used for VFR flight only.

Answer (A) is correct. (14 CFR 91.413)
    DISCUSSION: No person may use an ATC transponder unless, within the preceding 24 calendar months, that ATC transponder has been tested and inspected and found to comply with the appropriate regulations.
    Answer (B) is incorrect. There are no exceptions. The installed ATC transponder must meet the inspection requirements as outlined in 14 CFR 91.413. **Answer (C) is incorrect.** There are no exceptions. According to 14 CFR 91.413, no person may use an ATC transponder unless it has been inspected within the preceding 24 calendar months and found to comply with regulations.

159. An ATC transponder is not to be used unless it has been tested, inspected, and found to comply with regulations within the preceding

    A. 30 days.

    B. 12 calendar months.

    C. 24 calendar months.

Answer (C) is correct. (14 CFR 91.413)
    DISCUSSION: No person may use an ATC transponder unless, within the preceding 24 calendar months, that ATC transponder has been tested and inspected and found to comply with the appropriate regulations.
    Answer (A) is incorrect. A VOR (not a transponder) must be checked every 30 days. **Answer (B) is incorrect.** A transponder must be inspected every 24 (not 12) calendar months.

91.417 Maintenance Records

160. Which is true relating to Airworthiness Directives (AD's)?

    A. AD's are advisory in nature and are, generally, not addressed immediately.

    B. Noncompliance with AD's renders an aircraft unairworthy.

    C. Compliance with AD's is the responsibility of maintenance personnel.

Answer (B) is correct. (14 CFR 91.417)
    DISCUSSION: 14 CFR 91.405 requires annual inspections with appropriate entries in the airplane maintenance records. 14 CFR 91.417 requires that the current status of applicable ADs and the method of compliance be specified. Noncompliance means the airplane is unairworthy and may not be flown.
    Answer (A) is incorrect. ADs are regulatory in nature, i.e., mandatory. **Answer (C) is incorrect.** Compliance with ADs as well as maintenance is the responsibility of the operator/owner, not maintenance personnel.

161. Aircraft maintenance records must include the current status of the

    A. applicable airworthiness certificate.

    B. life-limited parts of only the engine and airframe.

    C. life-limited parts of each airframe, engine, propeller, rotor, and appliance.

Answer (C) is correct. (14 CFR 91.417)
    DISCUSSION: Each owner or operator must keep certain records for each airplane:

1. Records of maintenance, preventive maintenance, and alteration, and of the 100-hr., annual, progressive, and other required of approved inspections for each aircraft
2. Records containing total time in service of the airframe, each engine, and each propeller; current status of life-limited parts of each airframe, engine, propeller, rotor, and appliance; all items which are required to be overhauled on a specified time basis; the current inspection of the aircraft; airworthiness directives; and copies of forms prescribed for major alterations

    Answer (A) is incorrect. Airworthiness certificates are issued only at the time of manufacture. **Answer (B) is incorrect.** The current status of the life-limited parts of the propeller, rotor, and appliance is required as well.

162. Which is correct concerning preventive maintenance, when accomplished by a pilot?

    A. A record of preventive maintenance is not required.

    B. A record of preventive maintenance must be entered in the maintenance records.

    C. Records of preventive maintenance must be entered in the FAA-approved flight manual.

Answer (B) is correct. (14 CFR 91.417)
    DISCUSSION: Each owner or operator must keep certain records for each airplane:

1. Records of maintenance, preventive maintenance, and alteration, and of the 100-hr., annual, progressive, and other required of approved inspections for each aircraft
2. Records containing total time in service of the airframe, each engine, and each propeller; current status of life-limited parts of each airframe, engine, propeller, rotor, and appliance; all items which are required to be overhauled on a specified time basis; the current inspection of the aircraft; airworthiness directives; and copies of forms prescribed for major alterations

    Answer (A) is incorrect. Preventive maintenance records are required. **Answer (C) is incorrect.** Maintenance must be recorded in the maintenance records, not the flight manual.

91.421 Rebuilt Engine Maintenance Records

163. A new maintenance record being used for an aircraft engine rebuilt by the manufacturer must include previous

    A. operating hours of the engine.

    B. annual inspections performed on the engine.

    C. changes as required by Airworthiness Directives.

Answer (C) is correct. (14 CFR 91.421)
    DISCUSSION: Each manufacturer or agency that grants zero time to an engine rebuilt by it shall enter, in the new record, a signed statement of the date the engine was rebuilt; each change made as required by AD; and each change made in compliance with manufacturer's service bulletins, if the entry is specifically requested in that bulletin.
    Answer (A) is incorrect. A rebuilt engine is considered to have zero operating hours. **Answer (B) is incorrect.** A record of previous inspections is not required on a rebuilt engine.

164. Under what condition could an aircraft's engine logbook show no previous operating history?

    A. If the aircraft had been imported from a foreign country.

    B. This would indicate an error by maintenance personnel.

    C. When the aircraft's engine has been rebuilt by the manufacturer.

Answer (C) is correct. (14 CFR 91.421)
    DISCUSSION: A new maintenance record, without previous operating history, may be used for an aircraft engine rebuilt by the manufacturer or by an agency approved by the manufacturer.
    Answer (A) is incorrect. An aircraft that has been imported from a foreign country should have the previous operating history available in the logbook. **Answer (B) is incorrect.** An aircraft engine logbook having no previous operating history is not necessarily an error by maintenance personnel. A new maintenance record may be used for an aircraft engine rebuilt by the manufacturer.

4.8 14 CFR Part 119

119.1 Applicability

165. In what type of operation, not regulated by 14 CFR Part 119, may a commercial pilot act as pilot in command and receive compensation for services?

   A. Part-time contract pilot.

   B. Nonstop flights within a 25 SM radius of an airport to carry persons for intentional parachute jumps.

   C. Nonstop flights within a 25 SM radius of an airport to carry cargo only.

Answer (B) is correct. (14 CFR 119.1)
   DISCUSSION: Certification of air carriers and commercial operators is regulated by Part 119. Section 119.1 lists several types of operations to which Part 119 does not apply, including nonstop flights within a 25 SM radius of an airport to carry persons for intentional parachute jumps.
   Answer (A) is incorrect. Part 119 regulates the types of operations which need an operating certificate, not how a pilot is employed. A commercial pilot may act as PIC (and receive compensation for services) as a part-time contract pilot for any of the operations regulated or not regulated under Part 119, provided the pilot complies with all applicable regulations for those operations. **Answer (C) is incorrect.** Operators conducting nonstop cargo-only flights within a 25 SM radius of an airport are regulated by Part 119.

166. In what type of operation, not regulated by 14 CFR Part 119, may a commercial pilot act as pilot in command and receive compensation for services?

   A. Aerial application and bird chasing.

   B. On-demand, nine or less passenger, charter flights.

   C. On-demand cargo flights.

Answer (A) is correct. (14 CFR 119.1)
   DISCUSSION: Part 119 regulates the certification of air carriers and commercial operators. Section 119.1 lists several types of operations to which Part 119 does not apply, including crop dusting, seeding, spraying, and bird chasing.
   Answer (B) is incorrect. Operators of on-demand charter flights are regulated by Part 119. **Answer (C) is incorrect.** Operators of on-demand cargo flights are regulated by Part 119.

167. You are acting as a commercial pilot, but are not operating under the regulations of 14 CFR Part 119. Which of these operations are you authorized to conduct?

   A. On-demand, passenger-carrying flights of nine persons or less.

   B. Aerial application and aerial photography.

   C. On-demand cargo flights.

Answer (B) is correct. (14 CFR 119.1)
   DISCUSSION: 14 CFR Part 119, Certification of Air Carriers and Commercial Operators, specifically excludes aerial application and aerial photography; therefore, a pilot conducting these commercial operations is not subject to this part.
   Answer (A) is incorrect. An on-demand operation is an example of a commercial operation that is governed by 14 CFR Part 135. Commercial operators and air carriers are certificated in accordance with 14 CFR Part 119. **Answer (C) is incorrect.** An on-demand operation is an example of a commercial operation that is governed by 14 CFR Part 135. Commercial operators and air carriers are certificated in accordance with 14 CFR Part 119.

4.9 NTSB Part 830

830.2 Definitions

168. What period of time must a person be hospitalized before an injury may be defined by the NTSB as a "serious injury"?

    A. 10 days, with no other extenuating circumstances.

    B. 48 hours; commencing within 7 days after date of the injury.

    C. 72 hours; commencing within 10 days after date of the injury.

Answer (B) is correct. (NTSB 830.2)
    DISCUSSION: A serious injury is defined as an injury that requires hospitalization for more than 48 hours, commencing within 7 days from the date of the injury; results in the fracture of any bone other than simple fractures of the fingers, toes, or nose; causes severe hemorrhages, nerve, muscle, or tendon damage; involves any internal organ; or involves second- or third-degree burns or any burns affecting more than 5% of the body surface.
    Answer (A) is incorrect. For an injury to be considered a serious injury on the basis of hospitalization, the injury must require hospitalization for more than 48 hours, not 10 days, commencing within 7 days from the date of the injury, not without other extenuating circumstances or requirements. **Answer (C) is incorrect.** For an injury to be considered a serious injury on the basis of hospitalization, the injury must require hospitalization for more than 48 hours, not 72 hours, commencing within 7 days, not 10 days, from the date of the injury.

830.5 Immediate Notification

169. NTSB Part 830 requires an immediate notification as a result of which incident?

    A. Engine failure for any reason during flight.

    B. Damage to the landing gear as a result of a hard landing.

    C. Any required flight crewmember being unable to perform flight duties because of illness.

Answer (C) is correct. (NTSB 830.5)
    DISCUSSION: Immediate notification is required when an aircraft accident or any of the following listed incidents occurs: flight control system malfunction or failure; inability of any required flight crewmember to perform normal flight duties as a result of injury or illness; failure of structural components of a turbine engine excluding compressor and turbine blades and vanes; in-flight fire; or aircraft collision in flight. Immediate notice is also required when an aircraft is overdue and is believed to have been involved in an accident.
    Answer (A) is incorrect. Engine failure, in itself, is not considered "substantial damage" requiring immediate notification. **Answer (B) is incorrect.** Damage to landing gear is not considered "substantial damage" requiring immediate notification.

170. Notification to the NTSB is required when there has been substantial damage

    A. which requires repairs to landing gear.

    B. to an engine caused by engine failure in flight.

    C. which adversely affects structural strength or flight characteristics.

Answer (C) is correct. (NTSB 830.5)
    DISCUSSION: An accident is an occurrence associated with the operation of an aircraft that takes place between the time any person boards the aircraft with the intention of flight and all such persons have disembarked, and in which any person suffers death or serious injury, or in which the aircraft receives substantial damage. Substantial damage means damage or failure that adversely affects the structural strength, performance, or flight characteristics of the aircraft and that would normally require major repair or replacement of the affected component. An accident causing substantial damage requires immediate notification to the NTSB.
    Answer (A) is incorrect. Damage to landing gear is not considered "substantial damage" requiring immediate notification. **Answer (B) is incorrect.** Damage to an engine caused by engine failure is not considered "substantial damage" requiring immediate notification.

171. The NTSB must be notified immediately when there is

    A. an in-flight fire.

    B. a ground fire.

    C. a hangar fire.

Answer (A) is correct. (NTSB 830.5)
    DISCUSSION: An in-flight fire is included in the list of serious incidents in NTSB 830.5 and must be reported to the NTSB immediately.
    Answer (B) is incorrect. A ground fire is not considered serious enough to require immediate NTSB notification. **Answer (C) is incorrect.** A hangar fire does not require notification of the NTSB.

172. Which airborne incident would require that the nearest NTSB field office be notified immediately?

A. Cargo compartment door malfunction or failure.

B. Cabin door opened in-flight.

C. Flight control systems malfunction or failure.

Answer (C) is correct. (NTSB 830.5)
   DISCUSSION: Immediate notification is required when an aircraft accident or any of the following listed incidents occurs: flight control system malfunction or failure; inability of any required flight crewmember to perform normal flight duties as a result of an injury or illness; failure of structural components of a turbine engine excluding compressor and turbine blades and vanes; in-flight fire; or aircraft collision in flight. Immediate notification is also required when an aircraft is overdue and believed to have been involved in an accident.
   Answer (A) is incorrect. A flight control system, not a cargo compartment door, malfunction or failure requires immediate notification. **Answer (B) is incorrect.** A cabin door that comes open in flight is not considered an incident that requires immediate notification.

173. While taxiing on the parking ramp, the landing gear, wheel, and tire are damaged by striking ground equipment. What action would be required to comply with NTSB Part 830?

A. An immediate notification must be filed by the operator of the aircraft with the nearest NTSB field office.

B. A report must be filed with the nearest FAA field office within 7 days.

C. No notification or report is required.

Answer (C) is correct. (NTSB 830.5)
   DISCUSSION: No report or notification is required unless an accident or a specified incident has occurred or unless an aircraft is overdue and believed to have been in an accident. The described incident is not one specified that requires notification or a report, and it is not considered an accident under NTSB Part 830. One requirement of an accident is substantial damage. Under NTSB Sec. 830.2, damage to landing gear, wheels, and tires is not considered "substantial damage."
   Answer (A) is incorrect. Immediate notification is required only for accidents or certain incidents. Damage to the landing gear, wheel, and tire is not considered an accident or an incident that requires immediate notification under NTSB Part 830. **Answer (B) is incorrect.** No report is required to be filed under NTSB Part 830. Additionally, NTSB Part 830 deals with notification and reports to the NTSB only, not the FAA.

174. Which incident would require that the nearest NTSB field office be notified immediately?

A. In-flight fire.

B. Ground fire resulting in fire equipment dispatch.

C. Fire of the primary aircraft while in a hangar which results in damage to other property of more than $25,000.

Answer (A) is correct. (NTSB 830.5)
   DISCUSSION: Immediate notification is required when an aircraft accident or any of the following listed incidents occurs: flight control system malfunction or failure; inability of any required flight crewmember to perform normal flight duties as a result of injury or illness; failure of structural components of a turbine engine excluding compressor and turbine blades and vanes; in-flight fire; or aircraft collision in flight. Immediate notice is also required when an aircraft is overdue and is believed to have been involved in an accident.
   Answer (B) is incorrect. Only in-flight incidents require immediate notification. **Answer (C) is incorrect.** Only in-flight incidents require immediate notification.

175. When should notification of an aircraft accident be made to the NTSB if there was substantial damage and no injuries?

A. Immediately.

B. Within 10 days.

C. Within 30 days.

Answer (A) is correct. (NTSB 830.5)
   DISCUSSION: An accident is an occurrence associated with the operation of an aircraft that takes place between the time any person boards the aircraft with the intention of flight and all such persons have disembarked, and in which any person suffers death or serious injury, or in which the aircraft receives substantial damage. The operator of an aircraft must immediately notify the nearest NTSB field office when an accident occurs.
   Answer (B) is incorrect. Ten days is the time specified to file a detailed aircraft accident report with the NTSB. **Answer (C) is incorrect.** Thirty days is not a deadline specified in NTSB Part 830.

176. While taxiing for takeoff, a small fire burned the insulation from a transceiver wire. What action would be required to comply with NTSB Part 830?

A. No notification or report is required.

B. A report must be filed with the avionics inspector at the nearest FAA field office within 48 hours.

C. An immediate notification must be filed by the operator of the aircraft with the nearest NTSB field office.

Answer (A) is correct. (NTSB 830.5)
DISCUSSION: An in-flight fire is an incident that requires immediate notification. The minor fire described did not occur in flight, however. Moreover, it did not cause substantial damage and was thus not classifiable as an accident. No report or notification is required unless an accident or a specified incident has occurred or unless an aircraft is overdue and believed to have been in an accident.
Answer (B) is incorrect. An immediate report is required only if certain items occur such as an in-flight fire. Also, the reports are to go to the NTSB, not the FAA offices. **Answer (C) is incorrect.** An immediate report is required only if certain items occur such as an in-flight fire.

177. During flight a fire, which was extinguished, burned the insulation from a transceiver wire. What action is required by regulations?

A. No notification or report is required.

B. A report must be filed with the avionics inspector at the responsible FAA Flight Standards office within 48 hours.

C. An immediate notification by the operator of the aircraft to the nearest NTSB field office.

Answer (C) is correct. (NTSB 830.5)
DISCUSSION: Immediate notification is required when an aircraft accident or any of the following listed incidents occurs: flight control system malfunction or failure, inability of any required flight crewmember to perform normal flight duties as a result of injury or illness, failure of structural components of a turbine engine excluding compressor and turbine blades and vanes, in-flight fire, or aircraft collision in flight. Immediate notice is also required when an aircraft is overdue and is believed to have been involved in an accident.
Answer (A) is incorrect. An in-flight fire (in contrast to an on-ground fire) does require immediate notification. **Answer (B) is incorrect.** No report to the avionics inspector is required.

178. On a post flight inspection of your aircraft after an aborted takeoff due to an elevator malfunction, you find that the elevator control cable has broken. According to NTSB 830, you

A. must immediately notify the nearest NTSB office.

B. should notify the NTSB within 10 days.

C. must file a NASA report immediately.

Answer (A) is correct. (NTSB 830.5)
DISCUSSION: According to NTSB 830.5, immediate notification to the nearest NTSB office is required for certain serious incidents, such as when a flight control system malfunctions or fails.
Answer (B) is incorrect. A written report for an accident must be filed within 10 days, while immediate notification to the nearest NTSB office is required for certain serious incidents, such as when a flight control system malfunctions or fails. **Answer (C) is incorrect.** Although it is advisable to file a NASA ASRS report, it is not required. Immediate notification to the nearest NTSB office is required for certain serious incidents, such as when a flight control system malfunctions or fails.

830.15 Reports and Statements to Be Filed

179. How many days after an accident is a report required to be filed with the nearest NTSB field office?

A. 2

B. 7

C. 10

Answer (C) is correct. (NTSB 830.15)
DISCUSSION: The operator of an aircraft must file a report within 10 days after an accident, or after 7 days if an overdue aircraft is still missing. A report on an incident for which notification is required should be filed only as requested by an authorized representative of the NTSB.
Answer (A) is incorrect. Two days is not a reporting requirement in NTSB Part 830. **Answer (B) is incorrect.** Seven days is the limitation with respect to an overdue aircraft that is missing.

180. The operator of an aircraft that has been involved in an incident is required to submit a report to the nearest field office of the NTSB

A. within 7 days.

B. within 10 days.

C. only if requested to do so.

Answer (C) is correct. (NTSB 830.15)
DISCUSSION: The operator of an aircraft must file a report within 10 days after an accident, or after 7 days if an overdue aircraft is still missing. A report on an incident for which notification is required shall be filed only as requested by an authorized representative of the Board.
Answer (A) is incorrect. Seven days is the time limitation for reporting overdue (missing) aircraft. **Answer (B) is incorrect.** Ten days is the limitation on filing a report for accidents.

4.10   Near Midair Collision Reporting

181. Who is responsible for filing a Near Midair Collision (NMAC) Report?

    A. A passenger on board the involved aircraft.

    B. Local law enforcement.

    C. Pilot and/or flight crew of aircraft involved in the incident.

Answer (C) is correct. (AIM Chap 7)
    DISCUSSION: The primary purpose of the Near Midair Collision (NMAC) Reporting Program is to provide information for use in enhancing the safety and efficiency of the National Airspace System. Data obtained from NMAC reports are used by the FAA to improve the quality of FAA services to users and to develop programs, policies, and procedures aimed at the reduction of NMAC occurrences. A near midair collision is defined as an incident associated with the operation of an aircraft in which a possibility of collision occurs as a result of proximity of less than 500 feet to another aircraft, or a report is received from a pilot or a flight crewmember stating that a collision hazard existed between two or more aircraft. It is the responsibility of the pilot and/or flight crew to determine whether a near midair collision did actually occur and, if so, to initiate an NMAC report. Be specific, as ATC will not interpret a casual remark to mean that an NMAC is being reported. The pilot should state, "I wish to report a near midair collision."
    Answer (A) is incorrect. A passenger is not responsible because it is the responsibility of the pilot and/or flight crew to determine whether a near midair collision did actually occur and, if so, to initiate an NMAC report. **Answer (B) is incorrect.** The pilot and/or flight crew is responsible for initiating an NMAC report. The Flight Standards Office in whose area the incident occurred in is responsible for investigating and reporting the NMAC.

182. Pilots and/or Flight Crew members involved in NMAC occurrences are urged to report each incident immediately:

    A. By radio or phone to the nearest FAA ATC Facility or FSS.

    B. To local law enforcement.

    C. By phone to the responsible Flight Standards office as this is an emergency.

Answer (A) is correct. (AIM Chap 7)
    DISCUSSION: Pilots and/or flight crew members involved in NMAC occurrences are urged to report each incident immediately by radio or phone to the responsible FAA ATC facility or FSS.
    Answer (B) is incorrect. The *AIM* states to report each incident immediately by radio or phone to the responsible FAA ATC facility or FSS. **Answer (C) is incorrect.** Contacting the responsible Flight Standards office is in lieu of contacting the nearest FAA ATC facility or FSS, and an NMAC is not deemed an emergency.

STUDY UNIT FIVE

AIRPLANE PERFORMANCE AND WEIGHT AND BALANCE

(20 pages of outline)

This study unit contains outlines of major concepts tested, sample test questions and answers regarding airplane performance and weight and balance, and an explanation of each answer. The table of contents above lists each subunit within this study unit, the number of questions pertaining to that particular subunit, and the pages on which the outlines and questions begin, respectively.

Recall that the **sole purpose** of this book is to expedite your passing of the FAA pilot knowledge test for the commercial pilot certificate. Accordingly, all extraneous material (i.e., topics or regulations not directly tested on the FAA pilot knowledge test) is omitted, even though much more knowledge is necessary to become a proficient commercial pilot. This additional material is presented in *Pilot Handbook* and *Commercial Pilot Flight Maneuvers and Practical Test Prep*, available from Gleim Publications, Inc. Order online at www.GleimAviation.com.

5.1 DENSITY ALTITUDE

1. Density altitude is a measurement of the density of the air in terms of altitude on a standard day.

    a. Air density varies inversely with altitude, temperature, and humidity and varies directly with barometric pressure.

        1) As altitude, air temperature, or humidity increases, density altitude increases.
        2) As barometric pressure increases, density altitude decreases.

    b. The scale of air density to altitude was made using a constant (standard) temperature and barometric pressure.

        1) Standard temperature at sea level is 15°C.
        2) Standard pressure at sea level is 29.92" Hg.

    c. Pressure altitude is the height above the standard pressure plane.

        1) To determine pressure altitude, the altimeter is set to 29.92 and the altimeter indication is noted.

    d. Density altitude is pressure altitude corrected for nonstandard temperature.

2. The performance tables of an aircraft are based on pressure/density altitude.

    a. High density altitude reduces an airplane's performance.

        1) Climb performance is lower.
        2) Takeoff distance is longer.
        3) Propellers also have less efficiency because there is less air for the propeller to grip.

    b. However, the same indicated airspeed is used for takeoffs and landings, regardless of altitude or air density, because the airspeed indicator is also directly affected by air density.

5.2 DENSITY ALTITUDE COMPUTATIONS

1. Density altitude is determined by finding the pressure altitude (the indicated altitude when your altimeter is set to 29.92) and adjusting for the temperature.

    a. This adjustment is made using your flight computer or a density altitude chart. This part of the FAA knowledge test requires you to use your flight computer.

    b. On your flight computer, set the air temperature (°C) over the pressure altitude in the center right.

        1) In the adjacent density altitude window, read the density altitude.

    c. Note that humidity affects air density and aircraft performance slightly but is not taken into account on performance charts.

2. To convert °F to °C, you may use a conversion chart (on most flight computers) or calculate by using the following formula:

$$°C = \frac{5}{9} \times (°F - 32)$$

3. EXAMPLE: Pressure altitude   12,000 ft.
                       True air temperature   +50°F

    From the conditions given, the approximate density altitude is 14,130 feet. This is determined as follows:

    a. Convert +50°F to °C by using the formula above.

$$\frac{5}{9} \times (50 - 32) = +10°C$$

    b. Under the "True Airspeed and Density Altitude" window on your flight computer, put the pressure altitude of 12,000 ft. under the true air temperature of +10°C.

    c. In the window above ("Density Altitude"), read the density altitude above the index mark to be approximately 14,130 feet.

5.3 TAKEOFF DISTANCE

1. Takeoff distance is displayed in the airplane operating manual in graph form or on a chart. The variables are

   a. Pressure altitude and temperature
   b. Airplane weight
   c. Headwind component

2. In either case, it is usually presented in terms of pressure altitude and temperature. Thus, one must first adjust the airport elevation for barometric pressure. Associated conditions are often listed in legends, e.g., paved runway, sloping runway, etc.

   a. An upslope runway increases takeoff distance.

3. In the graph used on this exam (Figure 32 on the next page), the first section on the left uses outside air temperature and pressure altitude to obtain density altitude.

   a. The line labeled "ISA" is standard atmosphere, which you use when the question calls for standard temperature.

   b. The second section of the graph, to the right of the first reference line, takes the weight in pounds into account.

   c. The third section of the graph, to the right of the second reference line, takes the headwind into account.

4. EXAMPLE: Given an outside air temperature of 75°F, an airport pressure altitude of 4,000 ft., a takeoff weight of 3,100 lb., and a headwind component of 20 kt., find the ground roll.

   a. The solution to the example problem is marked with arrows on the graph in Figure 32.

      1) Move straight up from 75°F to the pressure altitude of 4,000 ft. and then horizontally to the right.

      2) From the first reference line (2,400 lb.), you must proceed up and to the right, parallel to the guide lines, to 3,100 pounds.

      3) From that point, continue horizontally to the right to the second reference line.

      4) The headwind component of 20 kt. requires you to move down and to the right parallel to the guide lines to the 20-kt. point.

      5) Finally, moving horizontally to the right gives the total takeoff distance over a 50-ft. obstacle of 1,350 feet.

   b. A note above the graph states that the ground roll is approximately 73% of the total takeoff distance over a 50-ft. obstacle. Thus, the ground roll is 986 ft. (1,350 ft. × .73).

   c. You may be asked the maximum weight that may be carried under specified conditions to meet a certain takeoff distance requirement.

      1) To solve this, simply work backward on the chart to find the maximum weight.

ASSOCIATED CONDITIONS:

POWER	TAKEOFF POWER
	SET BEFORE
	BRAKE RELEASE
FLAPS	20°
RUNWAY	PAVED, LEVEL, DRY SURFACE
TAKEOFF SPEED	IAS AS TABULATED

NOTE: GROUND ROLL IS APPROX 73% OF TOTAL TAKEOFF DISTANCE OVER A 50 FT OBSTACLE

EXAMPLE:

OAT	75 °F
PRESSURE ALTITUDE	4,000 FT
TAKEOFF WEIGHT	3,100 LB
HEADWIND	20 KNOTS

TOTAL TAKEOFF DISTANCE	
OVER A 50 FT OBSTACLE	1,350 FT
GROUND ROLL (73% OF 1,350)	986 FT
IAS TAKEOFF SPEED	
LIFT-OFF	74 MPH
AT 50 FT	74 MPH

WEIGHT (LB)	IAS TAKEOFF SPEED (ASSUMES ZERO INSTR ERROR)			
	LIFT-OFF		50 FEET	
	MPH	KNOTS	MPH	KNOTS
3,400	77	67	77	67
3,200	75	65	75	65
3,000	72	63	72	63
2,800	69	60	69	60
2,600	66	57	66	57
2,400	63	55	63	55

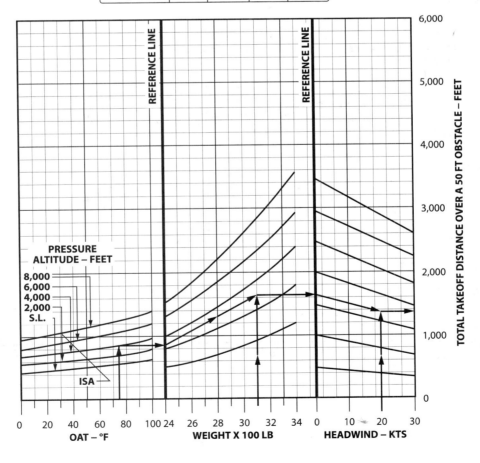

Figure 32. Obstacle Take-off Chart.

5.4 TIME, FUEL, AND DISTANCE TO CLIMB

1. Performance data concerning time, fuel, and distance to climb are often presented in operating handbooks for both normal conditions (Figure 14 below) and maximum rate of climb (Figure 13 on the next page). The variables involved are

   a. Airplane weight
   b. Pressure altitude and temperature
   c. Climb speed (indicated airspeed)
   d. Rate of climb in feet per minute (fpm)
   e. Data from sea level

      1) Time in minutes
      2) Pounds of fuel used
      3) Distance in nautical miles

NORMAL CLIMB – 110 KIAS

CONDITIONS:
FLAPS UP
GEAR UP
2,500 RPM
30 INCHES HG
120 PPH FUEL FLOW
COWL FLAPS OPEN
STANDARD TEMPERATURE

NOTES:
1. ADD 16 POUNDS OF FUEL FOR ENGINE START, TAXI, AND TAKEOFF ALLOWANCE.
2. INCREASE TIME, FUEL, AND DISTANCE BY 10% FOR EACH 7 °C ABOVE STANDARD TEMPERATURE.
3. DISTANCES SHOWN ARE BASED ON ZERO WIND.

WEIGHT (LB)	PRESS ALT (FT)	RATE OF CLIMB (FPM)	FROM SEA LEVEL		
			TIME (MIN)	FUEL USED (LB)	DISTANCE (NM)
4,000	S.L.	605	0	0	0
	4,000	570	7	14	13
	8,000	530	14	28	27
	12,000	485	22	44	43
	16,000	430	31	62	63
	20,000	365	41	82	87
3,700	S.L.	700	0	0	0
	4,000	665	6	12	11
	8,000	625	12	24	23
	12,000	580	19	37	37
	16,000	525	26	52	53
	20,000	460	34	68	72
3,400	S.L.	810	0	0	0
	4,000	775	5	10	9
	8,000	735	10	21	20
	12,000	690	16	32	31
	16,000	635	22	44	45
	20,000	565	29	57	61

Figure 14. Fuel, Time, and Distance to Climb.

2. EXAMPLE (Figure 13 below): At 4,000 lb., to climb from sea level to a pressure altitude of 8,000 ft., the indicated climb speed is 100 kt., and the average rate of climb is 845 fpm, requiring 9 min. using 24 lb. of fuel and covering a distance of 16 nautical miles.

   a. Often, you start at a pressure altitude other than sea level, so you must do the computation twice. The difference between the two calculations is the time, fuel, and distance to climb.

      1) For example, if you depart with a pressure altitude of 4,000 ft. and are going to cruise at a pressure altitude of 8,000 ft., you must compute the values for both and then subtract the values at 4,000 ft. from those at 8,000 ft. to determine the time, fuel, and distance for climbing from a pressure altitude of 4,000 ft. to 8,000 ft.

   b. Adjust for differences from standard temperature, if necessary.

      1) Recall that the formula for computing standard temperature at altitude is 15°C − (N × 2°C), where N is the altitude divided by 1,000.

      2) EXAMPLE: At 8,000 ft. MSL, standard temperature is −1°C [15°C − (8 × 2°C)]

   c. Note 1 states that you must add 16 lb. of fuel for engine start, taxi, and takeoff allowance.

   d. You can interpolate to find the values for an altitude not specifically shown in the table.

MAXIMUM RATE OF CLIMB

CONDITIONS:
FLAPS UP
GEAR UP
2,600 RPM
COWL FLAPS OPEN
STANDARD TEMPERATURE

MIXTURE SETTING		
PRESS ALT	MP	PPH
S.L. TO 17,000	35	162
18,000	34	156
20,000	32	144
22,000	30	132
24,000	28	120

NOTES:
1. ADD 16 POUNDS OF FUEL FOR ENGINE START, TAXI, AND TAKEOFF ALLOWANCE.
2. INCREASE TIME, FUEL, AND DISTANCE BY 10% FOR EACH 10 °C ABOVE STANDARD TEMPERATURE.
3. DISTANCES SHOWN ARE BASED ON ZERO WIND.

WEIGHT (LB)	PRESS ALT (FT)	CLIMB SPEED (KIAS)	RATE OF CLIMB (FPM)	FROM SEA LEVEL		
				TIME (MIN)	FUEL USED (LB)	DISTANCE (NM)
4,000	S.L.	100	930	0	0	0
	4,000	100	890	4	12	7
	8,000	100	845	9	24	16
	12,000	100	790	14	38	25
	16,000	100	720	19	52	36
	20,000	99	515	26	69	50
	24,000	97	270	37	92	74
3,700	S.L.	99	1,060	0	0	0
	4,000	99	1,020	4	10	6
	8,000	99	975	8	21	13
	12,000	99	915	12	33	21
	16,000	99	845	17	45	30
	20,000	97	630	22	59	42
	24,000	95	370	30	77	60
3,400	S.L.	97	1,205	0	0	0
	4,000	97	1,165	3	9	5
	8,000	97	1,120	7	19	12
	12,000	97	1,060	11	29	18
	16,000	97	985	15	39	26
	20,000	96	760	19	51	36
	24,000	94	485	26	65	50

Figure 13. Fuel, Time, and Distance to Climb.

3. As an alternative to a table, the fuel, time, and distance to climb may be presented in graph form, as in Figure 15 below. The same variables are involved.

   a. Note the example in Figure 15 for computing fuel, time, and distance for departing an airport with a pressure altitude of 1,400 ft. with an OAT of 15°C to a cruise pressure altitude of 12,000 ft. that has an OAT of 0°C.

      1) Here again, note that the solution is the difference between calculations at the airport elevation and at the desired cruise altitude.

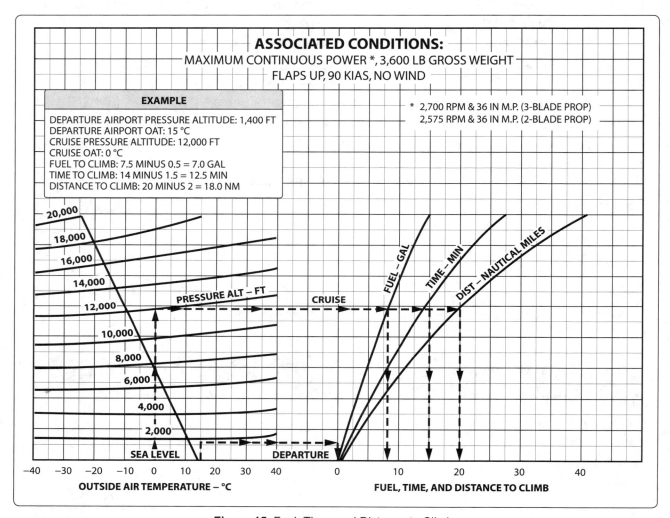

Figure 15. Fuel, Time, and Distance to Climb.

5.5 MAXIMUM RATE OF CLIMB

1. The rate of climb for maximum climb is dependent upon

    a. Pressure altitude and temperature
    b. Airplane weight
    c. Use of the best rate of climb speed

2. The maximum rate of climb can be presented in a table such as Figure 33 below.

    a. EXAMPLE: At 3,700 lb., the rate of climb at an 8,000-ft. pressure altitude at +20°C is 815 fpm.

    b. You may need to interpolate to find the value for an altitude that is not specifically shown in the table.

CONDITIONS:
FLAPS UP
GEAR UP
2,600 RPM
COWL FLAPS OPEN

PRESS ALT	MP	PPH
S.L. TO 17,000	35	162
18,000	34	156
20,000	32	144
22,000	30	132
24,000	28	120

WEIGHT (LB)	PRESS ALT (FT)	CLIMB SPEED (KIAS)	RATE OF CLIMB (FPM)			
			−20 °C	0 °C	20 °C	40 °C
4,000	S.L.	100	1,170	1,035	895	755
	4,000	100	1,080	940	800	655
	8,000	100	980	840	695	555
	12,000	100	870	730	590	---
	16,000	100	740	605	470	---
	20,000	99	485	355	---	---
	24,000	97	190	70	---	---
3,700	S.L.	99	1,310	1,165	1,020	875
	4,000	99	1,215	1,070	925	775
	8,000	99	1,115	965	815	670
	12,000	99	1,000	855	710	---
	16,000	99	865	730	590	---
	20,000	97	600	470	---	---
	24,000	95	295	170	---	---
3,400	S.L.	97	1,465	1,320	1,165	1,015
	4,000	97	1,370	1,220	1,065	910
	8,000	97	1,265	1,110	955	795
	12,000	97	1,150	995	845	---
	16,000	97	1,010	865	725	---
	20,000	96	730	595	---	---
	24,000	94	405	275	---	---

Figure 33. Maximum Rate of Climb Chart.

5.6   CRUISE AND RANGE PERFORMANCE

1.   Cruise performance is based upon the pressure altitude and temperature, the manifold pressure, and the engine RPM setting.

2.   Given these variables, charts provide the following information:

   a.   The percentage of brake horsepower (%BHP)
   b.   True airspeed (TAS)
   c.   Pounds of fuel per hour (PPH) or gallons of fuel per hour (GPH)

3.   Also used is a cruise and range performance chart, as in Figure 11 below.

GROSS WEIGHT – 2,300 LB
STANDARD CONDITIONS
ZERO WIND LEAN MIXTURE

NOTE: MAXIMUM CRUISE IS NORMALLY LIMITED TO 75% POWER.

ALT.	RPM	% BHP	TAS MPH	GAL/ HOUR	38 GAL (NO RESERVE)		48 GAL (NO RESERVE)	
					ENDR (HOURS)	RANGE (MILES)	ENDR (HOURS)	RANGE (MILES)
2,500	2,700	86	134	9.7	3.9	525	4.9	660
	2,600	79	129	8.6	4.4	570	5.6	720
	2,500	72	123	7.8	4.9	600	6.2	760
	2,400	65	117	7.2	5.3	620	6.7	780
	2,300	58	111	6.7	5.7	630	7.2	795
	2,200	52	103	6.3	6.1	625	7.7	790
5,000	2,700	82	134	9.0	4.2	565	5.3	710
	2,600	75	128	8.1	4.7	600	5.9	760
	2,500	68	122	7.4	5.1	625	6.4	790
	2,400	61	116	6.9	5.5	635	6.9	805
	2,300	55	108	6.5	5.9	635	7.4	805
	2,200	49	100	6.0	6.3	630	7.9	795
7,500	2,700	78	133	8.4	4.5	600	5.7	755
	2,600	71	127	7.7	4.9	625	6.2	790
	2,500	64	121	7.1	5.3	645	6.7	810
	2,400	58	113	6.7	5.7	645	7.2	820
	2,300	52	105	6.2	6.1	640	7.7	810
10,000	2,650	70	129	7.6	5.0	640	6.3	810
	2,600	67	125	7.3	5.2	650	6.5	820
	2,500	61	118	6.9	5.5	655	7.0	830
	2,400	55	110	6.4	5.9	650	7.5	825
	2,300	49	100	6.0	6.3	635	8.0	800

Figure 11. Cruise and Range Performance.

   a.   Note that the range assumes a zero wind component.

   b.   Note each of the nine columns in the chart (Figure 11).

   c.   Given altitude and RPM in the first two columns, the last seven columns are the results.

   d.   EXAMPLE: At a gross weight of 2,300 lb., 5,000-ft. pressure altitude, and 2300 RPM, you are operating at 55% power and will achieve a true airspeed of 108 mph, burn 6.5 GPH, and have a range of 635 statute miles with a 38-gal. tank of 5.9 hr.

4. See the cruise performance chart, Figure 12 below.

PRESSURE ALTITUDE – 18,000 FEET

CONDITIONS:
4,000 POUNDS
RECOMMENDED LEAN MIXTURE
COWL FLAPS CLOSED

NOTES:
FOR BEST FUEL ECONOMY AT 70% POWER OR LESS, OPERATE AT 6 PPH LEANER THAN SHOWN IN THIS CHART OR AT PEAK EGT.

RPM	MP	20 °C BELOW STANDARD TEMPERATURE −41 °C			STANDARD TEMPERATURE −21 °C			20 °C ABOVE STANDARD TEMP −1 °C		
		% BHP	KTAS	PPH	% BHP	KTAS	PPH	% BHP	KTAS	PPH
2,500	30	---	---	---	81	188	106	76	185	100
	28	80	184	105	76	182	99	71	178	93
	26	75	178	99	71	176	93	67	172	88
	24	70	171	91	66	168	86	62	164	81
	22	63	162	84	60	159	79	56	155	75
2,400	30	81	185	107	77	183	101	72	180	94
	28	76	179	100	72	177	94	67	173	88
	26	71	172	93	67	170	88	63	166	83
	24	66	165	87	62	163	82	58	159	77
	22	61	158	80	57	155	76	54	150	72
2,300	30	79	182	103	74	180	97	70	176	91
	28	74	176	97	70	174	91	65	170	86
	26	69	170	91	65	167	86	61	163	81
	24	64	162	84	60	159	79	56	155	75
	22	58	154	77	55	150	73	51	145	65
2,200	26	66	166	87	62	163	82	58	159	77
	24	61	158	80	57	154	76	54	150	72
	22	55	148	73	51	144	69	48	138	66
	20	49	136	66	46	131	63	43	124	59

Figure 12. Cruise Performance.

a. Note each of the columns in the chart.

b. Given the pressure altitude of 18,000 ft. and the manifold pressure (MP) and RPM, the last nine columns are the results.

c. EXAMPLE: At 2500 RPM, 28" MP, −41°C, you are using 80% power, will achieve a true airspeed of 184 kt., and will burn 105 PPH.

    1) If you have 315 lb. of usable fuel on board, you have a total available flight time of 3 hr. (315 ÷ 105).

    2) Allowing for day-VFR reserve, your maximum endurance is 2 hr. 30 min. (3 hr. − 30 minutes).

5. Finally, a fuel consumption versus brake horsepower graph is sometimes available. It relates the fuel flow in GPH (vertical scale) to brake horsepower (horizontal scale), based upon various power settings at various altitudes, as illustrated in Figure 8 below.

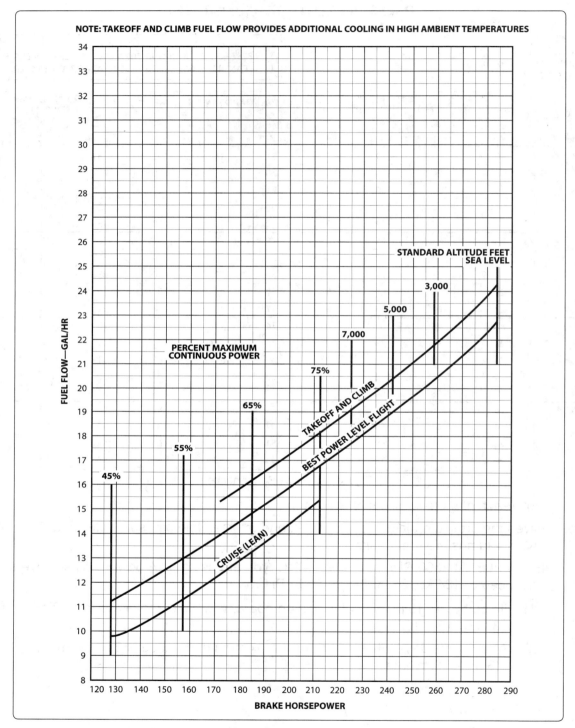

Figure 8. Fuel Consumption vs. Brake Horsepower.

    a. EXAMPLE: To determine the amount of fuel consumed when climbing at 75% power for 10 min., find the intersection of the takeoff and climb curve with the 75% brake horsepower line. From there, move horizontally to the left to the margin to read a fuel flow of 18.3 GPH.

        1) Since 10 min. is 1/6 hr., divide 18.3 by 6 to determine the amount consumed in 10 min.

6. As gross weight decreases, maximum range airspeed decreases.

5.7 CROSSWIND/HEADWIND COMPONENT

1. Many airplanes have an upper limit as to the amount of direct crosswind in which they can land. Crosswinds of less than 90° (i.e., direct) can be converted into a 90° component by using charts.

   a. Variables on the crosswind component charts are (a) angle between wind and runway and (b) knots of total wind velocity.

2. The variables are plotted on the graph; tracing the coordinates to the vertical and horizontal axes indicates the headwind and crosswind components of a quartering headwind.

3. In the crosswind component chart below, the example is of a 40-kt. wind at a 30° angle.

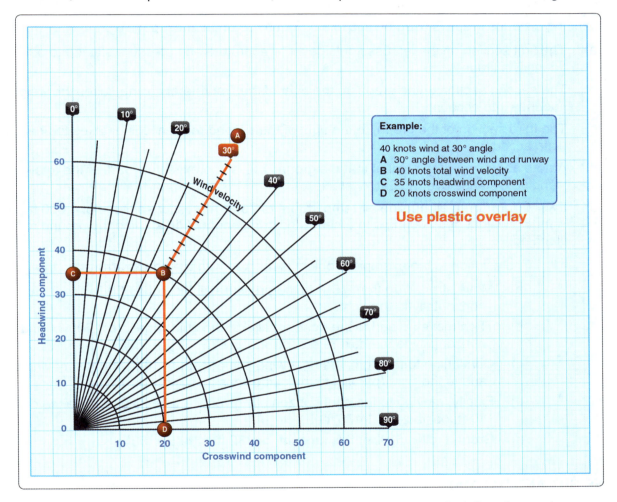

   a. Find the 30° wind angle line. This is the angle between the wind direction and runway direction, e.g., runway 16 and wind from 190°.

   b. Find the 40-kt. wind velocity arc. Note the intersection of the wind arc and the 30° angle line (point B).

   c. Drop straight down from point B to determine the crosswind component of 20 kt.; i.e., landing in this situation is like having a direct crosswind of 20 knots.

   d. Move horizontally to the left from point B to determine the headwind component of 35 kt.; i.e., landing in this situation is like having a headwind component of 35 knots.

   e. Note whether you are being asked for the headwind or the crosswind component.

4. An airplane's crosswind capability may be expressed in terms of a fraction of its V_{S0}.

   a. EXAMPLE: Given a .2-V_{S0} crosswind capability and V_{S0} of 65 kt., the crosswind capability is 13 kt. (65 × .2).

5.8 LANDING DISTANCE

1. Required landing distances differ at various altitudes and temperatures due to changes in air density.

    a.   However, indicated airspeed for landing is the same at all altitudes.

2. Landing distance information is given in airplane operating manuals in chart or graph form to adjust for headwind, temperature, and dry grass runways.

3. You must distinguish between the distance for clearing a 50-ft. obstacle and the distance without a 50-ft. obstacle at the beginning of the runway (the latter is described as the ground roll).

4. A landing distance graph is used on this exam (Figure 35 on the next page).

    a.   The first section on the left uses outside air temperature and pressure altitude to obtain density altitude.

    b.   The second section of the graph, to the right of the first reference line, takes the weight in pounds into account.

    c.   The third section of the graph, to the right of the second reference line, takes the headwind into account.

    d.   A note above the graph states that the ground roll is approximately 53% of the total landing distance over a 50-ft. obstacle.

    e.   EXAMPLE: Given an outside air temperature of 75°F, a pressure altitude of 4,000 ft., a landing weight of 3,200 lb., and a headwind component of 10 kt., find the ground roll for landing.

        1)   The solution to the example problem is marked with the dotted arrows on the graph.

            a)   Move straight up from 75°F to the pressure altitude of 4,000 ft. and then horizontally to the right.

            b)   Then move up and to the right, parallel to the guide lines, to 3,200 lb. and then horizontally to the next reference line.

            c)   Continuing to the right, the headwind component of 10 kt. means moving down and to the right (parallel to the guide lines to 10 knots).

            d)   Finally, moving to the right horizontally gives the total landing distance over a 50-ft. obstacle of 1,475 feet.

            e)   Ground roll is 53% of this amount, or 782 ft. (1,475 × .53).

5.9 WEIGHT AND BALANCE

1. Empty weight consists of the airframe, the engine, and all installed optional equipment, including fixed ballast, unusable fuel, full operating fluids, and full oil.

2. The center of gravity (CG) by definition is total moments divided by total weight.

    a.   Total moment is the position of weight (measured in index units) from some fixed point (called the datum) times that weight.

3. If all index units (arms) are positive when computing weight and balance, the location of the datum is at the nose or out in front of the airplane.

ASSOCIATED CONDITIONS:

POWER	AS REQUIRED TO MAINTAIN 800 FT/MIN DESCENT ON APPROACH
FLAPS	DOWN
RUNWAY	PAVED, LEVEL, DRY SURFACE
APPROACH SPEED	IAS AS TABULATED

NOTE: GROUND ROLL IS APPROX 53% OF TOTAL LANDING DISTANCE OVER A 50 FT OBSTACLE.

EXAMPLE:

OAT	75 °F
PRESSURE ALTITUDE	4,000 FT
LANDING WEIGHT	3,200 LB
HEADWIND	10 KNOTS

TOTAL LANDING DISTANCE OVER A 50 FT OBSTACLE	1,475 FT
GROUND ROLL (53% OF 1,475)	782 FT
IAS TAKEOFF SPEED	87 MPH IAS

WEIGHT (LB)	IAS APPROACH SPEED (ASSUMES ZERO INSTR ERROR)	
	MPH	KNOTS
3,400	90	78
3,200	87	76
3,000	84	73
2,800	81	70
2,600	78	68
2,400	75	65

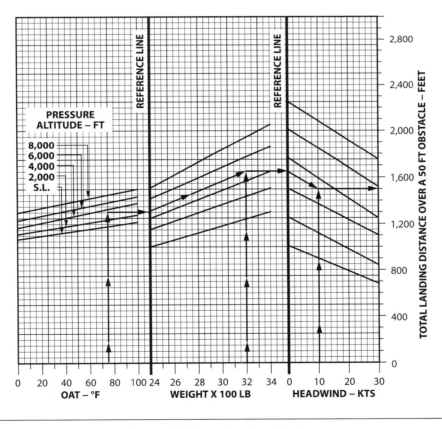

Figure 35. Normal Landing Chart.

5.10 WEIGHT AND MOMENT COMPUTATIONS

1.   Airplanes must be loaded in a manner such that the CG is in front of the center of lift. This placement provides airplane stability about the lateral axis (for pitch).

2.   The CG is a point of balance in an airplane determined in relation to the weight of objects put into the airplane times their distance from a specified point in the airplane (either positive or negative). This distance is called the arm. The CG determination can be made by calculation or by chart.

3.   The basic formula for weight and balance is

Weight × Arm = Moment

a.   Arm is the distance from the datum (a fixed position on the longitudinal axis of the airplane).

b.   The weight/arm/moment calculation computes the location of the CG.

1)   Multiply the weight of each item loaded into the airplane by its arm (distance from datum) to determine "moment."

2)   Add moments.

3)   Divide total weight into total moments to obtain CG (expressed in distance from the datum).

c.   EXAMPLE: You have placed items A, B, and C into the airplane. Note that the airplane's empty weight is given as 1,500 lb. with a 20-in. arm.

	Weight		Arm		Moment
Empty airplane	1,500	×	20	=	30,000
A (pilot and passenger)	300	×	25	=	7,500
B (25 gal. of fuel)	150	×	30	=	4,500
C (baggage)	100	×	40	=	4,000
	2,050				46,000

The total loaded weight of the airplane is 2,050 pounds. Divide the total moments of 46,000 in.-lb. by the total weight of 2,050 lb. to obtain the CG of 22.44 inches. Then check to see whether the weight and the CG are within allowable limits.

4.   Some manufacturers provide a loading graph (Figure 38 on the next page) that is used to plot weight vs. moment of various items. The graph can save you the steps of multiplying and dividing to obtain moments and CG.

a.   The load weight in pounds is listed on the left side. Using Figure 38, move horizontally to the right across the chart from the amount of weight to intersect the line indicating where the weight is located; e.g., different diagonal lines usually exist for fuel, baggage, pilot and front seat passengers, and center seat and back seat passengers.

b.   From the point of intersection of the weight with the appropriate diagonal line, drop straight down to the bottom of the chart where the moments are located.

1)   Note that you may have to estimate some moments when it is not clear exactly where the diagonal line intersects. For instance, the pilot and copilot diagonal at 300 lb. on Figure 38 intersects somewhere between 27.0 and 28.0 in.-lb. of moment. Do not let this worry you, as using 27.0 in.-lb. will be close enough.

c.   Total the weights and moments.

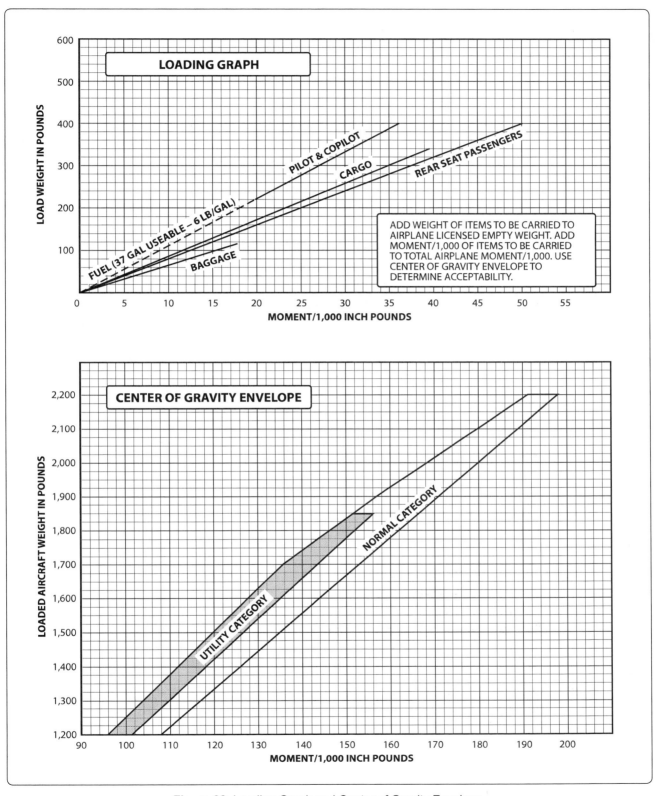

Figure 38. Loading Graph and Center of Gravity Envelope.

d.   EXAMPLE: Determine the center of gravity moment/1,000 in.-lb. given the following situation. The "/1,000" reduces the number to manageable proportions by eliminating a lot of zeros. First, set up a schedule of what you are given and what you must find (below).

	Weight (lb.)	Moment/1000 in.-lb.
Empty weight	1,271	102.04
Pilot and copilot	340	?
Rear-seat passengers	140	?
Cargo	60	?
Fuel (25 gal. × 6 lb./gal.)	150	?

1)   Compute the moment of the pilot and copilot by referring to the loading graph (Figure 38 on the next page). Locate 340 lb. on the weight scale. Move horizontally across the graph to intersect the diagonal line representing the pilot and front passenger. Then move vertically to the bottom scale, which indicates a moment of approximately 31.0 inch-pounds.

2)   Locate 140 lb. on the weight scale for the rear-seat passengers. Move horizontally across the graph to intersect the diagonal line that represents rear-seat passengers. Then move down vertically to the bottom scale, which indicates a moment of approximately 18.0 inch-pounds.

3)   Use the graph in the same manner to locate moments for cargo and fuel.

4)   Now add the weights and the moments.

	Weight (lb.)	Moment/1000 in.-lb.
Empty weight	1,271	102.04
Pilot and copilot	340	31.0
Rear-seat passengers	140	18.0
Cargo	60	7.0
Fuel (25 gal. × 6 lb./gal.)	150	13.5
	1,961	171.54

5)   Use the center-of-gravity envelope graph to see whether the total weight and the CG are within acceptable limits.

6)   Find the total weight of 1,961 lb. on the weight scale (left margin) and draw a horizontal line from it across the graph.

7)   Find the total moment of 171.54 in.-lb. on the moment scale (bottom of graph) and draw a vertical line from it up the graph.

8)   Because the lines intersect inside the normal-category envelope, the airplane is loaded within acceptable limits for normal-category operations.

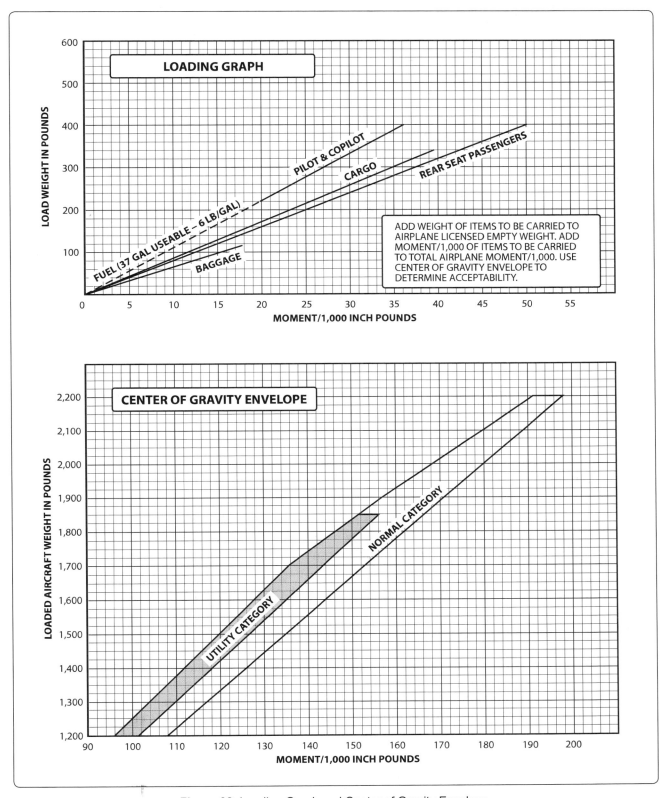

Figure 38. Loading Graph and Center of Gravity Envelope.

5.11 WEIGHT CHANGE AND WEIGHT SHIFT COMPUTATIONS

1.   Authors' note: The following is an effective, intuitively appealing handout used by
     Dr. Melville R. Byington at Embry-Riddle Aeronautical University (used with permission).

   a.   **Background** -- Center of gravity shift problems can be intimidating when an organized
        approach is not followed. If one goes to the usual texts for assistance, the result is often

       1)   "Just plug this/these formulas" (without adequate rationale), or
       2)   Follow a set of (up to six) formulas to solve the problems, or
       3)   Follow a tabular approach, which is often lengthy and tedious.

   b.   **Basic theory** -- The foregoing "methods" obscure what can and should be a logical,
        straightforward approach. The standard question is, **"If the CG started out there, and
        certain changes occurred, where is it now?"** It can be answered directly using a
        SINGLE, UNIVERSAL, UNCOMPLICATED FORMULA.

       1)   At **any** time, the CG is simply the sum of all moments (ΣM) divided by the sum of all
            weights (ΣW).

$$CG = \frac{\Sigma M}{\Sigma W}$$

       2)   Because CG was known at some previous (#1) loading condition (with moment = M_1
            and weight = W_1), it is logical that this become the point of departure. Due to weight
            addition, removal, or shift, the moment has changed by some amount, ΔM. The
            total weight has also changed **if**, and only if, weight has been added or removed.
            Therefore, the current CG is merely the current total moment divided by the current
            total weight. In equation format,

$$CG = \text{Current Moment/Current Weight becomes } CG = \frac{M_1 \pm \Delta M}{W_1 \pm \Delta W}$$

   c.   **Application** -- This universal formula will accommodate any CG shift problem! Before
        proceeding, certain conventions deserve review:

       1)   Any weight added causes a + moment change (Weight removed is –).
       2)   Weight **shifted** rearward causes a + moment change (Forward is –).
       3)   A weight **shift** changes only the moment ($\Delta W = 0$).

   d.   **Example 1** -- An airplane takes off at 3,000 lb. with CG at station 60. Since takeoff, 25 gal.
        (150 lb.) of fuel has been consumed. Fuel cell CG is station 65. Find the new CG.

$$CG = \frac{M_1 \pm \Delta M}{W_1 \pm \Delta W} = \frac{(3{,}000 \times 60) - (150 \times 65)}{3{,}000 - 150} = 59.74 \text{ in.}$$

   e.   **Example 2** -- An airplane has a gross weight of 10,000 pounds. Five hundred lb. of cargo
        is shifted 50 inches. How far does the CG shift? (Note that the original CG and direction
        of shift are unspecified. Since datum is undefined, why not define it, temporarily, as
        the initial CG location, even though it is unknown? This causes M_1 to become zero!
        Incidentally, the **direction** of CG shift corresponds precisely to the **direction** of the
        weight shift.)

$$CG = \frac{M_1 \pm \Delta M}{W_1 \pm \Delta W} = \frac{500 \times 50}{10{,}000} = 2.5 \text{ in.}$$

QUESTIONS AND ANSWER EXPLANATIONS: All of the commercial pilot knowledge test questions chosen by the FAA for release as well as additional questions selected by Gleim relating to the material in the previous outlines are provided on the following pages. These questions have been organized into the same subunits as the outlines. To the immediate right of each question are the correct answer and answer explanations. You should cover these answers and answer explanations while responding to the questions. Refer to the general discussion in the Introduction on how to take the FAA knowledge test.

Remember that the questions from the FAA knowledge test bank have been reordered by topic and organized into a meaningful sequence. Also, the first line of the answer explanation gives the citation of the authoritative source for the answer.

QUESTIONS

5.1 Density Altitude

1. The performance tables of an aircraft for takeoff and climb are based on

A. pressure/density altitude.

B. cabin altitude.

C. true altitude.

Answer (A) is correct. (FAA-H-8083-25B Chap 4)
DISCUSSION: Performance tables of an aircraft for takeoff, climb, cruise, and landing are based on pressure and/or density altitude. They are an index to the efficiency of airplane performance at various air densities. Pressure altitude is the indicated altitude when the altimeter is set to 29.92 (the standard datum plane). Density altitude is pressure altitude adjusted for nonstandard temperature.
Answer (B) is incorrect. Cabin altitude is the altitude that corresponds to the pressure within the cabin of a pressurized airplane. **Answer (C) is incorrect.** True altitude is the height above sea level. Airport, terrain, and obstacle elevations found on aeronautical charts are true altitudes.

2. Density altitude is the vertical distance above mean sea level in the standard atmosphere at which

A. pressure altitude is corrected for standard temperature.

B. a given atmospheric density is to be found.

C. temperature, pressure, altitude, and humidity are considered.

Answer (B) is correct. (FAA-H-8083-25B Chap 4)
DISCUSSION: Density altitude is defined as the vertical distance above mean sea level at which a given atmospheric density is to be found.
Answer (A) is incorrect. Density altitude is pressure altitude corrected for nonstandard temperature, not standard temperature. **Answer (C) is incorrect.** Temperature, pressure, altitude, and humidity all can affect density altitude, but they do not define density altitude.

3. To determine pressure altitude prior to takeoff, the altimeter should be set to

A. the current altimeter setting.

B. 29.92" Hg and the altimeter indication noted.

C. the field elevation and the pressure reading in the altimeter setting window noted.

Answer (B) is correct. (FAA-H-8083-25B Chap 4)
DISCUSSION: Pressure altitude can be determined by either of two methods: (1) Set the barometric scale of the altimeter to 29.92 and read the indicated altitude, or (2) apply a correction factor to the airport elevation according to the reported altimeter setting.
Answer (A) is incorrect. With the current altimeter setting in the altimeter, the altimeter should indicate the airport elevation (i.e., true altitude), not pressure altitude. **Answer (C) is incorrect.** The pressure reading in the altimeter setting window should be the current altimeter setting, which should indicate the airport elevation (i.e., true, not pressure, altitude).

4. At higher elevation airports the pilot should know that indicated airspeed

    A. will be unchanged, but groundspeed will be faster.

    B. will be higher, but groundspeed will be unchanged.

    C. should be increased to compensate for the thinner air.

Answer (A) is correct. (FAA-H-8083-25B Chap 11)
    DISCUSSION: If an airplane of given weight and configuration is operated at greater heights above standard sea level, the airplane will still require the same dynamic pressure to become airborne at the takeoff lift coefficient. Thus, the airplane at altitude will take off at the same indicated airspeed as at sea level, but because of the reduced air density, the true airspeed (and groundspeed) will be greater.
    Answer (B) is incorrect. The indicated airspeed will remain the same, not higher, and the groundspeed will be higher, not unchanged. **Answer (C) is incorrect.** The true, not indicated, airspeed will increase at higher elevation airports due to the thinner (i.e., reduced air density) air.

5. As air temperature increases, density altitude will

    A. decrease.

    B. increase.

    C. remain the same.

Answer (B) is correct. (FAA-H-8083-25B Chap 4)
    DISCUSSION: Increasing the temperature of a substance decreases its density, and a decrease in air density means a higher density altitude. Thus, with an increase in temperature, the air density decreases, providing a higher density altitude.
    Answer (A) is incorrect. As temperature increases, the density altitude will increase, not decrease. **Answer (C) is incorrect.** Density varies inversely with temperature. Increasing the temperature of a substance decreases its density, and a decrease in air density means a higher density altitude.

5.2 Density Altitude Computations

6. GIVEN:

Pressure altitude	12,000 ft
True air temperature	+50°F

From the conditions given, the approximate density altitude is

    A. 11,900 feet.

    B. 14,130 feet.

    C. 18,150 feet.

Answer (B) is correct. (E6B Instructions)
    DISCUSSION: To convert from °F to °C, use the formula

$$°C = \frac{5}{9} \times (°F - 32)$$

Thus, convert +50°F to °C as follows:

$$\frac{5}{9} \times (50 - 32) = +10°C$$

    On the center of the computer side of your flight computer, put the pressure altitude of 12,000 feet under the true air temperature of +10°C. The density altitude is indicated in the window as 14,130 feet.
    Answer (A) is incorrect. This is the density altitude for −10°C, not +10°C. **Answer (C) is incorrect.** This is the density for +50°C, not +50°F.

7. GIVEN:

Pressure altitude	5,000 ft
True air temperature	+30°C

From the conditions given, the approximate density altitude is

    A. 7,800 feet.

    B. 7,200 feet.

    C. 9,000 feet.

Answer (A) is correct. (E6B Instructions)
    DISCUSSION: On the center of the computer side of your flight computer, put the pressure altitude of 5,000 feet under the true air temperature of +30°C. The density altitude is indicated in the window as 7,800 feet.
    Answer (B) is incorrect. This is the approximate density altitude at a temperature of 25°C, not 30°C. **Answer (C) is incorrect.** This is the approximate density altitude at a temperature of 42°C, not 30°C.

8. GIVEN:

Pressure altitude   6,000 ft
True air temperature   +30°F

From the conditions given, the approximate density altitude is

    A. 9,000 feet.

    B. 5,500 feet.

    C. 5,000 feet.

Answer (B) is correct. (E6B Instructions)
    DISCUSSION: To convert from °F to °C, use the formula

$$°C = \frac{5}{9} \times (°F - 32)$$

Thus, convert +30°F to °C as follows:

$$\frac{5}{9} \times (30 - 32) = -1°C$$

    On the center of the computer side of your flight computer, put the pressure altitude of 6,000 feet under the true air temperature of −1°C. The density altitude is indicated in the window as 5,500 feet.
    Answer (A) is incorrect. This is the density altitude for +30°C, not +30°F. **Answer (C) is incorrect.** This is the density altitude for −5°C, not −1°C.

9. GIVEN:

Pressure altitude   12,000 feet
True air temperature   +15°F

From the conditions given, the approximate density altitude is

    A. 11,900 feet.

    B. 14,130 feet.

    C. 18,150 feet.

Answer (A) is correct. (E6B Instructions)
    DISCUSSION: To convert from °F to °C, use the bottom of the computer side of the E6B flight computer, where the temperature conversion scale is located. The bottom of the conversion scale is °F and the top of the scale is °C. Find +15 on the °F side of the scale and you will see it is lined up about halfway between the first tick mark to the right of −10 of the °C scale. This is about −9.5°C. Therefore, +15°F = −9.5°C.
    On the center of the computer side of your flight computer, in the window to the right, put the pressure altitude of 12,000 feet under the air temperature of −9.5°C. The density altitude is indicated in the window as about 12,000 feet. The best and closest answer is 11,900 feet.
    Answer (B) is incorrect. This is the density altitude for +50°F, not −9.5°C. **Answer (C) is incorrect.** This is the density altitude for +50°C, not +15°F.

10. GIVEN:

Pressure altitude   7,000 ft
True air temperature   +15°C

From the conditions given, the approximate density altitude is

    A. 5,000 feet.

    B. 8,500 feet.

    C. 9,500 feet.

Answer (B) is correct. (E6B Instructions)
    DISCUSSION: On the center of the computer side of your flight computer, put the pressure altitude of 7,000 feet under the true air temperature of +15°C. The density altitude is indicated in the window as 8,500 feet.
    Answer (A) is incorrect. This is the density altitude for −15°C, not +15°C. **Answer (C) is incorrect.** This is the density altitude for +23°C, not +15°C.

5.3 Takeoff Distance

11. What effect does an uphill runway slope have on takeoff performance?

A.   Increases takeoff speed.

B.   Increases takeoff distance.

C.   Decreases takeoff distance.

Answer (B) is correct. (FAA-H-8083-25B Chap 11)
DISCUSSION: The upslope or downslope of the runway (runway gradient) is quite important when runway length and takeoff distance are critical. Upslope provides a retarding force that impedes acceleration because the engine has to overcome gravity as well as surface friction and drag, resulting in a longer ground run or takeoff.
Answer (A) is incorrect. The indicated takeoff speed is the same on a level, downhill, or uphill runway at a given density altitude. **Answer (C) is incorrect.** A downhill, not an uphill, runway slope will decrease the takeoff distance.

12. (Refer to Figure 32 on page 199.)

GIVEN:

Temperature	30°F
Pressure altitude	6,000 ft
Weight	3,300 lb
Headwind	20 kts

What is the total takeoff distance over a 50-foot obstacle?

A.   1,100 feet.

B.   1,300 feet.

C.   1,500 feet.

Answer (C) is correct. (FAA-H-8083-25B Chap 11)
DISCUSSION: Fig. 32 presents the takeoff distance graph. Find the total takeoff distance over a 50-ft. obstacle as follows:

1.   Move up vertically from 30°F to the 6,000-ft. pressure altitude line.
2.   Move to the right horizontally to the first reference line.
3.   Move up and to the right, parallel to the guideline, to the weight of 3,300 pounds.
4.   Move to the right horizontally to the second reference line.
5.   Move down and to the right, parallel to the guideline, to the headwind of 20 knots.
6.   Move to the right horizontally to the right margin of the graph and read the distance, which is 1,500 feet.

Answer (A) is incorrect. The figure of 1,100 feet (73% of 1,500 feet) is the approximate ground roll, not total takeoff, distance. **Answer (B) is incorrect.** The figure of 1,300 feet is required for an aircraft weighing 3,000 lb., not 3,300 pounds.

13. (Refer to Figure 32 on page 199.)

GIVEN:

Temperature	100°F
Pressure altitude	4,000 ft
Weight	3,200 lb
Wind	Calm

What is the ground roll required for takeoff over a 50-foot obstacle?

A.   1,180 feet.

B.   1,350 feet.

C.   1,850 feet.

Answer (B) is correct. (FAA-H-8083-25B Chap 11)
DISCUSSION: Fig. 32 presents the takeoff distance graph. Find the ground roll required for takeoff over a 50-ft. obstacle as follows:

1.   Move up vertically from 100°F to the 4,000-ft. pressure altitude line.
2.   Move to the right horizontally to the first reference line.
3.   Move up and to the right, parallel to the guideline, to the weight of 3,200 pounds.
4.   Since the wind is calm, move right horizontally to the right margin to determine the total takeoff distance of 1,850 feet.
5.   Ground roll is approximately 73% of the total takeoff distance (as stated in the note below the Associated Conditions). Thus, the ground roll is approximately 1,350 feet (1,850 × .73).

Answer (A) is incorrect. This is the required ground roll for a 2,950-lb., not 3,200-lb., aircraft. **Answer (C) is incorrect.** This is the total takeoff, not ground roll, distance to clear a 50-ft. obstacle.

14. (Refer to Figure 32 on page 199.)

GIVEN:

Temperature	50°F
Pressure altitude	2,000 ft
Weight	2,700 lb
Wind	Calm

What is the total takeoff distance over a 50-foot obstacle?

A.   800 feet.

B.   650 feet.

C.   1,050 feet.

Answer (A) is correct. (FAA-H-8083-25B Chap 11)
DISCUSSION: Fig. 32 presents the takeoff distance graph. Find the total takeoff distance over a 50-ft. obstacle as follows:

1.   Move up vertically from 50°F to the 2,000 feet pressure altitude line.
2.   Move to the right horizontally to the first reference line.
3.   Move up and to the right, parallel to the guideline, to the weight of 2,700 pounds.
4.   Since the wind is calm, move right horizontally to the right margin of the graph to determine the total takeoff distance, which is 800 feet.

Answer (B) is incorrect. This is required for a pressure altitude of sea level, not 2,000 feet. **Answer (C) is incorrect.** This is required for an aircraft weighing 2,900 lb., not 2,700 pounds.

ASSOCIATED CONDITIONS:

POWER   TAKEOFF POWER
               SET BEFORE
               BRAKE RELEASE
FLAPS   20°
RUNWAY   PAVED, LEVEL, DRY SURFACE
TAKEOFF SPEED IAS AS TABULATED

NOTE: GROUND ROLL IS APPROX 73% OF TOTAL TAKEOFF
      DISTANCE OVER A 50 FT OBSTACLE

EXAMPLE:

OAT	75 °F
PRESSURE ALTITUDE	4,000 FT
TAKEOFF WEIGHT	3,100 LB
HEADWIND	20 KNOTS

TOTAL TAKEOFF DISTANCE	
OVER A 50 FT OBSTACLE	1,350 FT
GROUND ROLL (73% OF 1,350)	986 FT
IAS TAKEOFF SPEED	
LIFT-OFF	74 MPH
AT 50 FT	74 MPH

WEIGHT (LB)	IAS TAKEOFF SPEED (ASSUMES ZERO INSTR ERROR)			
	LIFT-OFF		50 FEET	
	MPH	KNOTS	MPH	KNOTS
3,400	77	67	77	67
3,200	75	65	75	65
3,000	72	63	72	63
2,800	69	60	69	60
2,600	66	57	66	57
2,400	63	55	63	55

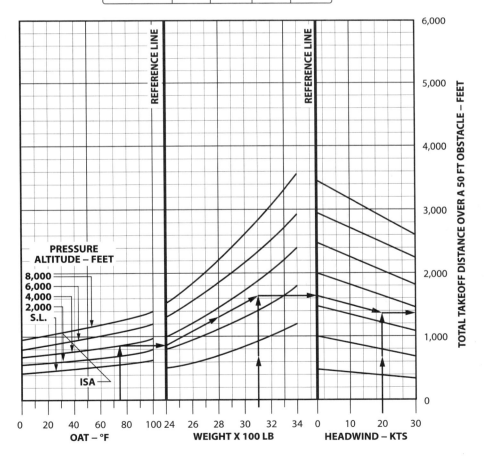

Figure 32. Obstacle Take-off Chart.

15. (Refer to Figure 32 on page 201.)

GIVEN:

Temperature	75°F
Pressure altitude	6,000 ft
Weight	2,900 lb
Headwind	20 kts

To safely take off over a 50-foot obstacle in 1,000 feet, what weight reduction is necessary?

   A. 50 pounds.

   B. 100 pounds.

   C. 300 pounds.

Answer (C) is correct. (FAA-H-8083-25B Chap 11)
    DISCUSSION: Fig. 32 presents the takeoff distance graph. Find the weight reduction necessary to safely take off over a 50-ft. obstacle in 1,000 feet as follows:

1. Move up vertically from 75°F to the 6,000-ft. pressure altitude line.
2. Move to the right horizontally to the first reference line.
3. Move up and to the right, parallel to the guideline, to the weight of 2,900 pounds.
4. Move to the right horizontally to the second reference line.
5. Move down and to the right, parallel to the guideline, to the headwind of 20 knots.
6. Move to the right horizontally to the margin of the graph to indicate a total takeoff distance of 1,400 ft. This exceeds the 1,000-ft. limit by 400 ft., or 2 grid squares on the graph.
7. Return to the weight segment of the graph.
8. From the original point of 2,900 lb., move down and to the left, parallel to the guideline, to a point that is 3 grid squares less than 2,900 lb. This would be 2,600 pounds.
9. The total weight reduction required is 300 lb. (2,900 − 2,600).

    Answer (A) is incorrect. A 50-lb. reduction requires a takeoff distance of 1,350 feet, not 1,000 feet. **Answer (B) is incorrect.** A 100-lb. reduction requires a takeoff distance of 1,300 feet, not 1,000 feet.

16. (Refer to Figure 32 on page 201.)

GIVEN:

Temperature	40°F
Pressure altitude	4,000 ft.
Weight	3,200 lb.
Headwind	15 kts.

Determine the approximate runway length necessary for takeoff.

   A. 1,300 feet.

   B. 850 feet.

   C. 950 feet.

Answer (C) is correct. (FAA-H-8083-25B Chap 11)
    DISCUSSION: Start by finding 40°F on the bottom left of the chart. Draw a vertical line up to the pressure altitude, 4,000 ft.; then draw a horizontal line to the first reference line. Follow the curved lines until you reach the weight, 3,200 lb. From there, draw a horizontal line to the second reference line. Follow the angled lines down until you reach 15 kt. of headwind; then draw a horizontal line to determine the total takeoff distance over a 50-ft. obstacle, 1,300 ft. Finally, to find runway length necessary for takeoff, see the note at the top of the chart. Ground roll is approximately 73% of total takeoff distance over a 50-ft. obstacle, so the approximate runway length necessary for takeoff is 950 ft. (1,300 × .73).
    Answer (A) is incorrect. This is the total takeoff distance over a 50-ft. obstacle. **Answer (B) is incorrect.** This is the approximate runway length necessary for takeoff with a 20-kt. headwind.

17. (Refer to Figure 32 on page 201.) What is the total takeoff distance required to clear a 50-foot obstacle with the following conditions?

Temperature	50°F
Pressure altitude	4,000 ft.
Weight	3,200 lb.
Headwind	15 kts.

   A. 1,200 feet.

   B. 880 feet.

   C. 700 feet.

Answer (A) is correct. (FAA-H-8083-25B Chap 11)
    DISCUSSION: Fig. 32 presents the takeoff distance graph. Find the total takeoff distance over a 50-ft. obstacle as follows:

1. Move up vertically from 50°F to the 4,000-ft. pressure altitude line.
2. Move to the right horizontally to the first reference line.
3. Move up and to the right, parallel to the guideline, to the weight of 3,200 lb.
4. Move to the right horizontally to the second reference line.
5. Move down and to the right, parallel to the guideline, to the headwind of 15 kt.
6. Move to the right horizontally to the right margin of the graph and read the distance, which is approximately 1,200 ft.

    Answer (B) is incorrect. The ground roll, not the total takeoff distance required to clear a 50-ft. obstacle, is 880 ft. **Answer (C) is incorrect.** If the weight of the aircraft was 2,600 lb., not 3,200 lb., the total takeoff distance required to clear a 50-ft. obstacle would be 700 ft.

ASSOCIATED CONDITIONS:

POWER	TAKEOFF POWER SET BEFORE BRAKE RELEASE
FLAPS	20°
RUNWAY	PAVED, LEVEL, DRY SURFACE
TAKEOFF SPEED	IAS AS TABULATED

NOTE: GROUND ROLL IS APPROX 73% OF TOTAL TAKEOFF DISTANCE OVER A 50 FT OBSTACLE

EXAMPLE:

OAT	75 °F
PRESSURE ALTITUDE	4,000 FT
TAKEOFF WEIGHT	3,100 LB
HEADWIND	20 KNOTS

TOTAL TAKEOFF DISTANCE OVER A 50 FT OBSTACLE	1,350 FT
GROUND ROLL (73% OF 1,350)	986 FT
IAS TAKEOFF SPEED	
LIFT-OFF	74 MPH
AT 50 FT	74 MPH

WEIGHT (LB)	IAS TAKEOFF SPEED (ASSUMES ZERO INSTR ERROR)			
	LIFT-OFF		50 FEET	
	MPH	KNOTS	MPH	KNOTS
3,400	77	67	77	67
3,200	75	65	75	65
3,000	72	63	72	63
2,800	69	60	69	60
2,600	66	57	66	57
2,400	63	55	63	55

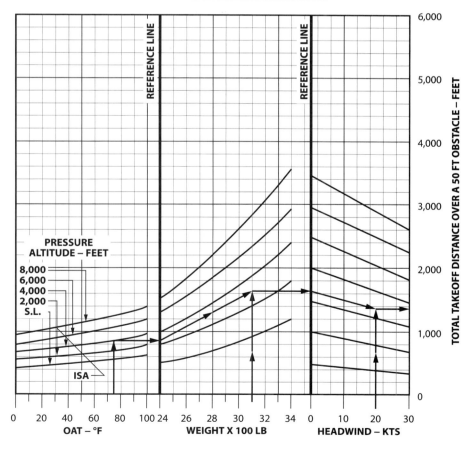

Figure 32. Obstacle Take-off Chart.

5.4 Time, Fuel, and Distance to Climb

18. (Refer to Figure 13 on page 203.)

GIVEN:

Aircraft weight	4,000 lb
Airport pressure altitude	2,000 ft
Temperature at 2,000 ft	32°C

Using a maximum rate of climb under the given conditions, how much time would be required to climb to a pressure altitude of 8,000 feet?

A. 7 minutes.

B. 8.4 minutes.

C. 11.2 minutes.

Answer (B) is correct. (FAA-H-8083-25B Chap 11)
  DISCUSSION: The time to climb from 2,000 feet to 8,000 feet at an aircraft weight of 4,000 lb. is computed using Fig. 13 as follows: The time required to climb from sea level to 8,000 feet (9 minutes) minus the time required to climb from sea level to 2,000 feet (2 minutes, interpolated) equals 7 minutes. Standard temperature is 11°C [15°C − (2°C × 2)], so the temperature is 21°C above standard. Thus, the total time required to climb from 2,000 feet to 8,000 feet is 8.4 minutes (7 × 1.21).
  Answer (A) is incorrect. Seven minutes is the time required for the climb at standard temperature. **Answer (C) is incorrect.** The time required to climb from sea level, not 2,000 feet, to 8,000 feet is 11.2 minutes.

19. (Refer to Figure 13 on page 203.)

GIVEN:

Aircraft weight	3,400 lb
Airport pressure altitude	6,000 ft
Temperature at 6,000 ft	10°C

Using a maximum rate of climb under the given conditions, how much fuel would be used from engine start to a pressure altitude of 16,000 feet?

A. 43 pounds.

B. 45 pounds.

C. 49 pounds.

Answer (A) is correct. (FAA-H-8083-25B Chap 11)
  DISCUSSION: The procedure is to note the difference on Fig. 13 between fuel usage on a climb to 16,000 feet and on a climb to 6,000 feet. Also note that the temperature is not standard. Standard temperature at sea level is 15°C, and there is a lapse rate of 2°C per 1,000 feet, so the standard temperature at 6,000 feet would be 3°C [15°C − (6 × 2°C)]. On a climb from sea level to 16,000 feet with an aircraft weight of 3,400 lb., the amount of fuel used is 39 pounds. For a climb from sea level to 6,000 feet, interpolate to find a fuel burn of 14 pounds. The difference between the two altitudes is 25 lb. (39 − 14), but this difference must be increased by 7%, which is 1.75 lb., to allow for the 7°C above standard. Do not forget the 16 lb. for engine start, taxi, and takeoff. Thus, the total fuel used is approximately 43 lb. (25 + 1.75 + 16).
  Answer (B) is incorrect. Forty-five lb. of fuel is required to climb from approximately 5,000 feet, not 6,000 feet, to 16,000 feet. **Answer (C) is incorrect.** Forty-nine lb. of fuel is required to climb from approximately 3,000 feet, not 6,000 feet, to 16,000 feet.

MAXIMUM RATE OF CLIMB

CONDITIONS:
FLAPS UP
GEAR UP
2,600 RPM
COWL FLAPS OPEN
STANDARD TEMPERATURE

MIXTURE SETTING		
PRESS ALT	MP	PPH
S.L. TO 17,000	35	162
18,000	34	156
20,000	32	144
22,000	30	132
24,000	28	120

NOTES:
1. ADD 16 POUNDS OF FUEL FOR ENGINE START, TAXI, AND TAKEOFF ALLOWANCE.
2. INCREASE TIME, FUEL, AND DISTANCE BY 10% FOR EACH 10 °C ABOVE STANDARD TEMPERATURE.
3. DISTANCES SHOWN ARE BASED ON ZERO WIND.

WEIGHT (LB)	PRESS ALT (FT)	CLIMB SPEED (KIAS)	RATE OF CLIMB (FPM)	FROM SEA LEVEL		
				TIME (MIN)	FUEL USED (LB)	DISTANCE (NM)
4,000	S.L.	100	930	0	0	0
	4,000	100	890	4	12	7
	8,000	100	845	9	24	16
	12,000	100	790	14	38	25
	16,000	100	720	19	52	36
	20,000	99	515	26	69	50
	24,000	97	270	37	92	74
3,700	S.L.	99	1,060	0	0	0
	4,000	99	1,020	4	10	6
	8,000	99	975	8	21	13
	12,000	99	915	12	33	21
	16,000	99	845	17	45	30
	20,000	97	630	22	59	42
	24,000	95	370	30	77	60
3,400	S.L.	97	1,205	0	0	0
	4,000	97	1,165	3	9	5
	8,000	97	1,120	7	19	12
	12,000	97	1,060	11	29	18
	16,000	97	985	15	39	26
	20,000	96	760	19	51	36
	24,000	94	485	26	65	50

Figure 13. Fuel, Time, and Distance to Climb.

20. (Refer to Figure 14 on page 205.)

GIVEN:

Aircraft weight	3,700 lb
Airport pressure altitude	4,000 ft
Temperature at 4,000 ft	21°C

Using a normal climb under the given conditions, how much fuel would be used from engine start to a pressure altitude of 12,000 feet?

    A. 30 pounds.

    B. 37 pounds.

    C. 46 pounds.

Answer (C) is correct. (FAA-H-8083-25B Chap 11)
    DISCUSSION: The amount of fuel needed to climb from 4,000 feet (airport pressure altitude) to 12,000 feet pressure altitude with a weight of 3,700 lb. is calculated as the amount needed to climb from sea level to 12,000 feet (37 lb.) minus the amount to climb to 4,000 feet (12 pounds). The difference is 25 pounds. However, you must adjust (add) 10% for every 7°C above standard. Here, standard temperature at the 4,000-ft. pressure altitude is 7°C [15°C – (2°C × 4)], so OAT of 21°C is 14°C above standard. If you increase time, fuel, and distance by 10% for each 7°C above standard, multiply standard conditions usage by 120% for 14°C over standard. Fuel needed to climb is thus 30 lb. (25 lb. × 1.20). Finally, you must add 16 lb. for engine start, taxi, and takeoff. Total fuel needed to climb from engine start is thus 46 lb. (30 + 16).
    Answer (A) is incorrect. Thirty lb. is the fuel required for the climb without taking into consideration the 16 lb. for engine start, taxi, and takeoff. **Answer (B) is incorrect.** Thirty-seven lb. is the fuel required for a climb from sea level to 12,000 feet at standard temperature.

21. (Refer to Figure 14 on page 205.)

GIVEN:

Weight	3,400 lb
Airport pressure altitude	4,000 ft
Temperature at 4,000 ft	14°C

Using a normal climb under the given conditions, how much time would be required to climb to a pressure altitude of 8,000 feet?

    A. 4.8 minutes.

    B. 5 minutes.

    C. 5.5 minutes.

Answer (C) is correct. (FAA-H-8083-25B Chap 11)
    DISCUSSION: The time to climb to 8,000 feet from 4,000 feet with a weight of 3,400 lb. is calculated as the time to climb from sea level to 8,000 feet (10 minutes) minus the time to climb to 4,000 feet (5 minutes). The difference is 5 minutes. However, you must adjust (add) 10% for every 7°C above standard. Here, standard temperature at the 4,000-ft. pressure altitude is 7°C [15°C – (2°C × 4)], so OAT of 14°C at 4,000 feet is 7°C above standard. Time to climb is thus 5.5 minutes (5 min. × 1.10).
    Answer (A) is incorrect. This figure was not arrived at by subtracting the climb from sea level to 4,000 feet from the climb from sea level to 8,000 feet and factoring in nonstandard temperature. **Answer (B) is incorrect.** Five minutes would be the time required for the climb before the correction for nonstandard temperature is made.

NORMAL CLIMB – 110 KIAS

CONDITIONS:
FLAPS UP
GEAR UP
2,500 RPM
30 INCHES HG
120 PPH FUEL FLOW
COWL FLAPS OPEN
STANDARD TEMPERATURE

NOTES:
1. ADD 16 POUNDS OF FUEL FOR ENGINE START, TAXI, AND TAKEOFF ALLOWANCE.
2. INCREASE TIME, FUEL, AND DISTANCE BY 10% FOR EACH 7 °C ABOVE STANDARD TEMPERATURE.
3. DISTANCES SHOWN ARE BASED ON ZERO WIND.

WEIGHT (LB)	PRESS ALT (FT)	RATE OF CLIMB (FPM)	FROM SEA LEVEL		
			TIME (MIN)	FUEL USED (LB)	DISTANCE (NM)
4,000	S.L.	605	0	0	0
	4,000	570	7	14	13
	8,000	530	14	28	27
	12,000	485	22	44	43
	16,000	430	31	62	63
	20,000	365	41	82	87
3,700	S.L.	700	0	0	0
	4,000	665	6	12	11
	8,000	625	12	24	23
	12,000	580	19	37	37
	16,000	525	26	52	53
	20,000	460	34	68	72
3,400	S.L.	810	0	0	0
	4,000	775	5	10	9
	8,000	735	10	21	20
	12,000	690	16	32	31
	16,000	635	22	44	45
	20,000	565	29	57	61

Figure 14. Fuel, Time, and Distance to Climb.

22. (Refer to Figure 15 on page 207.)

GIVEN:

Airport pressure altitude	4,000 ft
Airport temperature	12°C
Cruise pressure altitude	9,000 ft
Cruise temperature	–4°C

What will be the distance required to climb to cruise altitude under the given conditions?

   A. 6 miles.

   B. 8.5 miles.

   C. 11 miles.

Answer (B) is correct. (FAA-H-8083-25B Chap 11)
   DISCUSSION: Start at the lower left corner of Fig. 15. Go up from –4°C cruise temperature to the 9,000-ft. cruise pressure altitude. From there, proceed horizontally to the right to the intersection of the third curve (distance). Then proceed down to the bottom of the chart, which is at approximately 13.5 nautical miles. Note that this is the distance from sea level to 9,000 feet.
   Because the airport pressure altitude is 4,000 ft., go back to the left lower corner and go up from the airport temperature of 12°C to the pressure altitude line of 4,000 feet. Then proceed horizontally to the third curve (distance) and move downward to determine the distance of 5.5 NM to climb to 4,000 ft. from sea level. Thus, the distance to climb from 4,000 ft. to 9,000 ft. is 8 NM (13.5 – 5.5). Therefore, the best answer is 8.5 miles.
   Answer (A) is incorrect. The distance required to climb from 4,000 ft. to 9,000 ft. is 8 NM, not 6 NM. **Answer (C) is incorrect.** The distance required to climb from 4,000 ft. to 9,000 ft. is 8 NM, not 11 NM.

23. (Refer to Figure 15 on page 207.)

GIVEN:

Airport pressure altitude	2,000 ft
Airport temperature	20°C
Cruise pressure altitude	10,000 ft
Cruise temperature	0°C

What will be the fuel, time, and distance required to climb to cruise altitude under the given conditions?

   A. 5 gallons, 9 minutes, 13 NM.

   B. 6 gallons, 11 minutes, 16 NM.

   C. 7 gallons, 12 minutes, 18 NM.

Answer (A) is correct. (FAA-H-8083-25B Chap 11)
   DISCUSSION: Start at the lower left corner of Fig. 15. Go up from 0°C cruise temperature to the 10,000-ft. cruise pressure altitude. From there, proceed horizontally to the right to the intersection of each of the curves (fuel, time, and distance). From there, proceed down to 6 gallons, 11 minutes, and 16 NM. Note that these are the fuel, time, and distance from sea level to 10,000 feet.
   Because the airport pressure altitude is 2,000 ft., go back to the left lower corner and go up from the airport temperature of 20°C to the pressure altitude line of 2,000 feet. Then proceed horizontally to each of the curves and move downward to determine the fuel of 1 gallon, time of 2 minutes, and distance of 3 NM to climb to 2,000 ft. from sea level.
   Thus, to climb from 2,000 ft. to 10,000 ft. requires 5 gallons (6 – 1), 9 min. (11 – 2), and 13 NM (16 – 3).
   Answer (B) is incorrect. Six gallons, 11 minutes, and 16 NM are required for a climb from sea level, not 2,000 ft., to 10,000 ft. **Answer (C) is incorrect.** To climb from 2,000 ft. to 10,000 ft. requires 5 gallons, not 7 gallons; 9 minutes, not 12 minutes; and 13 NM, not 18 NM.

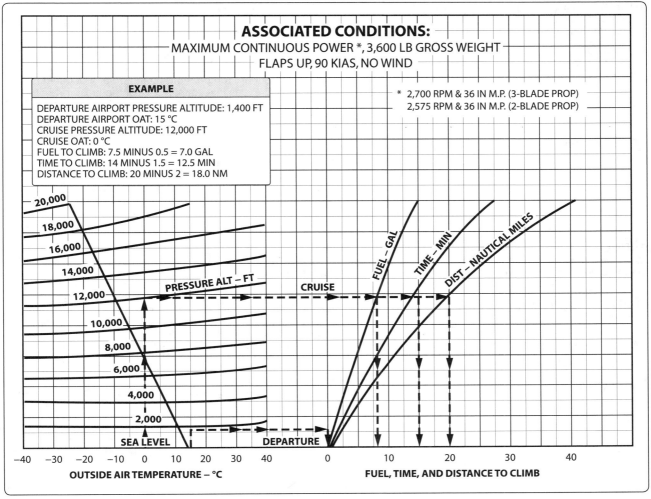

Figure 15. Fuel, Time, and Distance to Climb.

24. (Refer to Figure 9 on page 209.) Using a normal climb, how much fuel would be used from engine start to 12,000 feet pressure altitude?

Aircraft weight	3,800 lb
Airport pressure altitude	4,000 ft
Temperature	26°C

    A. 46 pounds.

    B. 51 pounds.

    C. 58 pounds.

Answer (C) is correct. (FAA-H-8083-25B Chap 11)
    DISCUSSION: At 3,800 lb., 51 lb. of fuel is required to climb from sea level to 12,000 feet, according to Fig. 9. From sea level to 4,000 feet, only 12 lb. is required. The net difference is 39 lb. to climb from 4,000 feet pressure altitude to 12,000 feet pressure altitude. The air temperature of 26°C, however, is 19°C over standard temperature (standard at 4,000 feet is 7°C, which is 15°C at sea level minus 8°C for the lapse rate). Note that there is an increase of 10% for each 10°C above standard. Accordingly, you must increase the 39 lb. by 19% (39 × 1.19) to get 46.41 lb. Then add 12 lb. for taxi, takeoff, etc., which is approximately 58 lb.
    Answer (A) is incorrect. This is the fuel required to make the climb without factoring in the 12 lb. required for engine start, taxi, and takeoff. **Answer (B) is incorrect.** This amount of fuel is required for the climb from sea level to 12,000 feet before adjustments are made for nonstandard temperature; the 4,000-feet airport altitude; and engine start, taxi, and takeoff.

25. (Refer to Figure 9 on page 209.) Using a normal climb, how much fuel would be used from engine start to 10,000 feet pressure altitude?

Aircraft weight	3,500 lb
Airport pressure altitude	4,000 ft
Temperature	21°C

    A. 23 pounds.

    B. 31 pounds.

    C. 35 pounds.

Answer (C) is correct. (FAA-H-8083-25B Chap 11)
    DISCUSSION: At 3,500 lb., 31 lb. of fuel is required to climb from sea level to 10,000 feet, per Fig. 9. From sea level to 4,000 feet, only 11 lb. is required. The net difference is 20 lb. to climb from 4,000 feet pressure altitude to 10,000 feet pressure altitude. The air temperature of 21°C, however, is 14°C over standard temperature (standard at 4,000 feet is 7°C, which is 15°C at sea level minus 8°C for the lapse rate). Note that there is an increase of 10% for each 10°C above standard. Accordingly, you must increase the 20 lb. by 14% (20 × 1.14) to get 22.8 lb. Then add 12 lb. for taxi, takeoff, etc., which is approximately 35 lb.
    Answer (A) is incorrect. This amount of fuel is required for the climb itself. The fuel required for engine start, taxi, and takeoff must be factored in. **Answer (B) is incorrect.** This amount of fuel is required to climb from sea level to 10,000 feet. Adjustments must be made for nonstandard temperature; a 4,000-ft. airport altitude; and the engine start, taxi, and takeoff.

NORMAL CLIMB—100 KIAS

CONDITIONS:
FLAPS UP
GEAR UP
2,550 RPM
25 INCHES MP OR FULL THROTTLE
COWL FLAPS OPEN
STANDARD TEMPERATURE

MIXTURE SETTING	
PRESS ALT	PPH
S.L. to 4,000	108
8,000	96
12,000	84

NOTES:
1. INCREASE TIME, FUEL, AND DISTANCE BY 10% FOR EACH 10 °C ABOVE STANDARD TEMPERATURE.
2. ADD 12 POUNDS OF FUEL FOR ENGINE START, TAXI, AND TAKEOFF ALLOWANCE.
3. DISTANCES SHOWN ARE BASED ON ZERO WIND.

WEIGHT (LB)	PRESS ALT (FT)	RATE OF CLIMB (FPM)	FROM SEA LEVEL		
			TIME (MIN)	FUEL USED (LB)	DISTANCE (NM)
3,800	S.L.	580	0	0	0
	2,000	580	3	6	6
	4,000	570	7	12	12
	6,000	470	11	19	19
	8,000	365	16	27	28
	10,000	265	22	37	40
	12,000	165	32	51	59
3,500	S.L.	685	0	0	0
	2,000	685	3	5	5
	4,000	675	6	11	10
	6,000	565	9	16	16
	8,000	455	13	23	23
	10,000	350	18	31	33
	12,000	240	25	41	46
3,200	S.L.	800	0	0	0
	2,000	800	2	4	4
	4,000	795	5	9	8
	6,000	675	8	14	13
	8,000	560	11	19	19
	10,000	445	15	25	27
	12,000	325	20	33	37

Figure 9. Fuel, Time, and Distance to Climb.

26. (Refer to Figure 10 on page 211.) Using a maximum rate of climb, how much fuel would be used from engine start to 6,000 feet pressure altitude?

Aircraft weight	3,200 lb
Airport pressure altitude	2,000 ft
Temperature	27°C

    A. 10 pounds.

    B. 14 pounds.

    C. 24 pounds.

Answer (C) is the best answer. (FAA-H-8083-25B Chap 11)
    DISCUSSION: At 3,200 lb., 14 lb. of fuel is required to climb from sea level to 6,000 feet per Fig. 10. From sea level to 2,000 feet, only 4 lb. is required. The net difference is 10 lb. to climb from 2,000 feet pressure altitude to 6,000 feet pressure altitude. The air temperature of 27°C, however, is 16°C over standard temperature (standard at 2,000 feet is 11°C, which is 15°C at sea level minus 4°C for the lapse rate). Note that there is an increase of 10% for each 10°C above standard. Accordingly, you must increase the 10 lb. by 16% (10 × 1.16) to get 11.6 lb. Then add 12 lb. for taxi, takeoff, etc., which is approximately 24 lb. NOTE: As the #2 note in the figure states, a 10% increase equals 11 lb., and then adding 12 lb. for taxi, takeoff, etc., yields an answer of 23 lb. Therefore, 24 pounds is the most correct answer.
    Answer (A) is incorrect. This is required for the climb from 2,000 feet to 6,000 feet without factoring in nonstandard temperature or the fuel required for the engine start, taxi, and takeoff adjustment. **Answer (B) is incorrect.** This is required for a climb from sea level, not 2,000 feet, to 6,000 feet.

27. (Refer to Figure 10 on page 211.) Using a maximum rate of climb, how much fuel would be used from engine start to 10,000 feet pressure altitude?

Aircraft weight	3,800 lb
Airport pressure altitude	4,000 ft
Temperature	30°C

    A. 28 pounds.

    B. 35 pounds.

    C. 40 pounds.

Answer (C) is correct. (FAA-H-8083-25B Chap 11)
    DISCUSSION: At 3,800 lb., 35 lb. of fuel is required to climb from sea level to 10,000 feet, per Fig. 10. From sea level to 4,000 feet, only 12 lb. is required. The net difference is 23 lb. to climb from 4,000 feet pressure altitude to 10,000 feet pressure altitude. The air temperature of 30°C, however, is 23°C over standard temperature (standard at 4,000 feet is 7°C, which is 15°C at sea level minus 8°C for the lapse rate). Note that there is an increase of 10% for each 10°C above standard. Accordingly, you must increase the 23 lb. by 23% (23 × 1.23) to get 28.29 lb. Then add 12 lb. for taxi, takeoff, etc., which is approximately 40 lb.
    Answer (A) is incorrect. This amount of fuel is required to climb from 4,000 feet to 10,000 feet, but the 12 lb. of fuel required for engine start, taxi, and takeoff has not been added to the total. **Answer (B) is incorrect.** This amount of fuel is required to climb from sea level, not 4,000 feet, to 10,000 feet.

MAXIMUM RATE OF CLIMB

CONDITIONS:
FLAPS UP
GEAR UP
2,700 RPM
FULL THROTTLE
MIXTURE SET AT PLACARD FUEL FLOW
COWL FLAPS OPEN
STANDARD TEMPERATURE

MIXTURE SETTING	
PRESS ALT	PPH
S.L.	138
4,000	126
8,000	114
12,000	102

NOTES:
1. ADD 12 POUNDS OF FUEL FOR ENGINE START, TAXI, AND TAKEOFF ALLOWANCE.
2. INCREASE TIME, FUEL, AND DISTANCE BY 10% FOR EACH 10 °C ABOVE STANDARD TEMPERATURE.
3. DISTANCES SHOWN ARE BASED ON ZERO WIND.

WEIGHT (LB)	PRESS ALT (FT)	CLIMB SPEED (KIAS)	RATE OF CLIMB (FPM)	FROM SEA LEVEL		
				TIME (MIN)	FUEL USED (LB)	DISTANCE (NM)
3,800	S.L.	97	860	0	0	0
	2,000	95	760	2	6	4
	4,000	94	660	5	12	9
	6,000	93	565	9	18	14
	8,000	91	465	13	26	21
	10,000	90	365	18	35	29
	12,000	89	265	24	47	41
3,500	S.L.	95	990	0	0	0
	2,000	94	885	2	5	3
	4,000	93	780	5	10	7
	6,000	91	675	7	16	12
	8,000	90	570	11	22	17
	10,000	89	465	15	29	24
	12,000	87	360	20	38	32
3,200	S.L.	94	1,135	0	0	0
	2,000	92	1,020	2	4	3
	4,000	91	910	4	9	6
	6,000	90	800	6	14	10
	8,000	88	685	9	19	14
	10,000	87	575	12	25	20
	12,000	86	465	16	32	26

Figure 10. Fuel, Time, and Distance to Climb.

5.5 Maximum Rate of Climb

28. (Refer to Figure 33 on page 213.)

GIVEN:

Weight	3,700 lb
Pressure altitude	22,000 ft
Temperature	−10°C

What is the maximum rate of climb under the given conditions?

   A. 305 ft/min.

   B. 320 ft/min.

   C. 384 ft/min.

Answer (C) is correct. (FAA-H-8083-25B Chap 11)
DISCUSSION: The maximum rate of climb at a pressure altitude of 22,000 ft., temperature of −10°C, and 3,700 lb. is found by using the 3,700 lb. weight section of Fig. 33. Note that you must interpolate for both 22,000 ft. and −10°C.
First, interpolate for 22,000 ft. At 0°C, the difference between 20,000 ft. and 24,000 ft. is 300 fpm (470 − 170). One-half of 300 added to 170 is 320 (170 + 150).
At −20°C, the difference is 305 (600 − 295). Adding one-half of 305 to 295 is 447.5 (295 + 152.5).
The next step is to interpolate the 22,000 ft. values for −10°C: 320 at 0° and 447.5 at −20°. The difference is 127.5 (447.5 − 320). Adding one-half of 127.5 to 320 to split the difference between 0° and −20° gives 384 fpm (320 + 64).
Answer (A) is incorrect. The difference in rate of climb between 20,000 feet and 24,000 ft. at −20°C is 305 fpm. **Answer (B) is incorrect.** The maximum rate of climb at 22,000 ft. and a temperature of 0°C, not −10°C, is 320 fpm.

29. (Refer to Figure 33 on page 213.)

GIVEN:

Weight	4,000 lb
Pressure altitude	5,000 ft
Temperature	30°C

What is the maximum rate of climb under the given conditions?

   A. 655 ft/min.

   B. 702 ft/min.

   C. 774 ft/min.

Answer (B) is correct. (FAA-H-8083-25B Chap 11)
DISCUSSION: The maximum rate of climb at a pressure altitude of 5,000 ft., temperature of 30°C, and 4,000 lb. is found by using the 4,000 lb. weight section of Fig. 33. Note that you must interpolate for both 5,000 ft. and 30°C.
First, interpolate for 5,000 ft. At 20°C, the difference between 4,000 ft. and 8,000 ft. is 105 fpm (800 − 695). Five thousand ft. is 1/4 of the way between 4,000 ft. and 8,000 feet; 105 × .25 = 26.25, and 800 − 26.25 = 773.75. At 40°C, the difference is 100 (655 − 555). Subtracting one-fourth of 100 from 655 gives 630 (655 − 25).
Using these values, interpolate for 30°C between 773.75 at 20° and 630 at 40°. The difference is 143.75 fpm (773.75 − 630). Subtracting one-half of 143.75 (about 72) from 773.75 to split the difference between 40° and 30° gives about 702 fpm.
Answer (A) is incorrect. This is the maximum rate of climb at 4,000 ft., not 5,000 ft., at 40°C, not 30°C. **Answer (C) is incorrect.** This is the maximum rate of climb at 5,000 ft. at 20°C, not 30°C.

CONDITIONS:
FLAPS UP
GEAR UP
2,600 RPM
COWL FLAPS OPEN

PRESS ALT	MP	PPH
S.L. TO 17,000	35	162
18,000	34	156
20,000	32	144
22,000	30	132
24,000	28	120

WEIGHT (LB)	PRESS ALT (FT)	CLIMB SPEED (KIAS)	RATE OF CLIMB (FPM)			
			−20 °C	0 °C	20 °C	40 °C
4,000	S.L.	100	1,170	1,035	895	755
	4,000	100	1,080	940	800	655
	8,000	100	980	840	695	555
	12,000	100	870	730	590	---
	16,000	100	740	605	470	---
	20,000	99	485	355	---	---
	24,000	97	190	70	---	---
3,700	S.L.	99	1,310	1,165	1,020	875
	4,000	99	1,215	1,070	925	775
	8,000	99	1,115	965	815	670
	12,000	99	1,000	855	710	---
	16,000	99	865	730	590	---
	20,000	97	600	470	---	---
	24,000	95	295	170	---	---
3,400	S.L.	97	1,465	1,320	1,165	1,015
	4,000	97	1,370	1,220	1,065	910
	8,000	97	1,265	1,110	955	795
	12,000	97	1,150	995	845	---
	16,000	97	1,010	865	725	---
	20,000	96	730	595	---	---
	24,000	94	405	275	---	---

Figure 33. Maximum Rate of Climb Chart.

5.6 Cruise and Range Performance

30. (Refer to Figure 11 on page 215.) If the cruise altitude is 7,500 feet, using 64 percent power at 2,500 RPM, what would be the range with 48 gallons of usable fuel?

    A. 635 miles.

    B. 645 miles.

    C. 810 miles.

Answer (C) is correct. (FAA-H-8083-25B Chap 11)
    DISCUSSION: On Fig. 11 at 7,500 feet and 2500 RPM, which is 64% power, go to the far right-hand column to determine range of 810 mi. with 48 gallons of usable fuel.
    Answer (A) is incorrect. The range at 7,500 feet and 2500 RPM is found in the far right column to be 810 mi., not 635 miles. **Answer (B) is incorrect.** This is the range at 7,500 feet and 2,500 RPM with 38 gallons, not 48 gallons, of usable fuel.

31. (Refer to Figure 11 on page 215.) What would be the endurance at an altitude of 7,500 feet, using 52 percent power?

NOTE: (With 48 gallons of fuel – no reserve.)

    A. 6.1 hours.

    B. 7.7 hours.

    C. 8.0 hours.

Answer (B) is correct. (FAA-H-8083-25B Chap 11)
    DISCUSSION: On Fig. 11 at 7,500 feet and 2300 RPM, which is 52% power, go to the endurance column at 48 gallons of usable fuel to determine 7.7 hours.
    Answer (A) is incorrect. The endurance for 38 gallons, not 48 gallons, of usable fuel is 6.1 hours. **Answer (C) is incorrect.** The endurance at 10,000 feet, not 7,500 feet, and 49%, not 52%, power is 8.0 hours.

32. (Refer to Figure 11 on page 215.) What would be the approximate true airspeed and fuel consumption per hour at an altitude of 7,500 feet, using 52 percent power?

    A. 103 MPH TAS, 6.3 GPH.

    B. 105 MPH TAS, 6.6 GPH.

    C. 105 MPH TAS, 6.2 GPH.

Answer (C) is correct. (FAA-H-8083-25B Chap 11)
    DISCUSSION: On Fig. 11 at 7,500 feet and 2300 RPM, which is 52% power, the TAS is 105 mph and the fuel consumption is 6.2 GPH.
    Answer (A) is incorrect. At 52% power, a TAS of 103 mph and a fuel consumption of 6.3 GPH are for an altitude of 2,500 feet, not 7,500 feet. **Answer (B) is incorrect.** The figure of 6.6 is not a performance value (i.e., fuel consumption or endurance) that appears on the chart.

| | | | | | GROSS WEIGHT – 2,300 LB
STANDARD CONDITIONS
ZERO WIND LEAN MIXTURE | | | |

NOTE: MAXIMUM CRUISE IS NORMALLY LIMITED TO 75% POWER.

ALT.	RPM	% BHP	TAS MPH	GAL/ HOUR	38 GAL (NO RESERVE)		48 GAL (NO RESERVE)	
					ENDR (HOURS)	RANGE (MILES)	ENDR (HOURS)	RANGE (MILES)
2,500	2,700	86	134	9.7	3.9	525	4.9	660
	2,600	79	129	8.6	4.4	570	5.6	720
	2,500	72	123	7.8	4.9	600	6.2	760
	2,400	65	117	7.2	5.3	620	6.7	780
	2,300	58	111	6.7	5.7	630	7.2	795
	2,200	52	103	6.3	6.1	625	7.7	790
5,000	2,700	82	134	9.0	4.2	565	5.3	710
	2,600	75	128	8.1	4.7	600	5.9	760
	2,500	68	122	7.4	5.1	625	6.4	790
	2,400	61	116	6.9	5.5	635	6.9	805
	2,300	55	108	6.5	5.9	635	7.4	805
	2,200	49	100	6.0	6.3	630	7.9	795
7,500	2,700	78	133	8.4	4.5	600	5.7	755
	2,600	71	127	7.7	4.9	625	6.2	790
	2,500	64	121	7.1	5.3	645	6.7	810
	2,400	58	113	6.7	5.7	645	7.2	820
	2,300	52	105	6.2	6.1	640	7.7	810
10,000	2,650	70	129	7.6	5.0	640	6.3	810
	2,600	67	125	7.3	5.2	650	6.5	820
	2,500	61	118	6.9	5.5	655	7.0	830
	2,400	55	110	6.4	5.9	650	7.5	825
	2,300	49	100	6.0	6.3	635	8.0	800

Figure 11. Cruise and Range Performance.

33. (Refer to Figure 12 on page 217.)

GIVEN:

Pressure altitude	18,000 ft
Temperature	–21°C
Power	2,400 RPM – 28" MP
Recommended lean mixture usable fuel	425 lb

What is the approximate flight time available under the given conditions? (Allow for VFR day fuel reserve.)

A. 3 hours 46 minutes.

B. 4 hours 1 minute.

C. 4 hours 31 minutes.

Answer (B) is correct. (FAA-H-8083-25B Chap 11)
DISCUSSION: Given 2400 RPM and manifold pressure of 28", use Fig. 12 to find 94 lb. of fuel per hour at –21°C. Because you have 425 lb. of usable fuel, you can cruise for 4 hours 31 minutes, less the 30-minutes VFR-day fuel reserve, or 4 hours 1 minute. The time, calculated as 425 lb. of fuel divided by 94 lb./hr., equals 4.52 hours. Sixty min./hr. times .52 hours equals 31 minutes.

Alternatively, you can use your flight computer. Put 94 over 60 minutes on the time index (dark triangle). Then look to 425 on the outer scale and find that it corresponds to 4 hours 31 minutes on the inner scale. Note that the question asks for the flight time, not flight time plus VFR-day reserve; i.e., compute 4 hours 31 minutes and subtract 30 minutes to get 4 hours 1 minute.

Answer (A) is incorrect. The flight time available with a VFR-night, not VFR-day, fuel reserve of 45 minutes is 3 hours 46 minutes. **Answer (C) is incorrect.** The flight time available with no reserve is 4 hours 31 minutes.

34. (Refer to Figure 12 on page 217.)

GIVEN:

Pressure altitude	18,000 ft
Temperature	–41°C
Power	2,500 RPM – 26" MP
Recommended lean mixture usable fuel	318 lb

What is the approximate flight time available under the given conditions? (Allow for VFR night fuel reserve.)

A. 2 hours 27 minutes.

B. 3 hours 12 minutes.

C. 3 hours 42 minutes.

Answer (A) is correct. (FAA-H-8083-25B Chap 11)
DISCUSSION: Given 2500 RPM and manifold pressure of 26", use Fig. 12 to find 99 lb. of fuel per hour at –41°C. Because you have 318 lb. of usable fuel, you can cruise for 3 hours 12 minutes, less the 45-minute VFR-night fuel reserve, or 2 hours 27 minutes.

Calculate the time as 318 lb. of fuel divided by 99 lb./hr., which equals 3.21 hours. Sixty min./hr. times .21 hr. equals about 12 minutes.

Answer (B) is incorrect. The flight time available with no fuel reserve is 3 hours 12 minutes. **Answer (C) is incorrect.** The flight time with no reserve at a fuel consumption of 86 PPH, not 99 PPH, is 3 hours 42 minutes.

35. (Refer to Figure 12 on page 217.)

GIVEN:

Pressure altitude	18,000 ft
Temperature	–1°C
Power	2,200 RPM – 20" MP
Best fuel economy usable fuel	344 lb

What is the approximate flight time available under the given conditions? (Allow for VFR day fuel reserve.)

A. 4 hours 50 minutes.

B. 5 hours 20 minutes.

C. 5 hours 59 minutes.

Answer (C) is correct. (FAA-H-8083-25B Chap 11)
DISCUSSION: Given 2200 RPM and manifold pressure of 20", use Fig. 12 to find 59 lb. of fuel per hour at –1°C. The "Note" indicates to use 6 lb./hr. less for "best fuel economy." Thus, use 53 lb./hr. (59 – 6). Because you have 344 lb. of usable fuel, you can cruise for 6 hours 29 minutes (344 lb. ÷ 53 lb. per hr.), less the 30-minute VFR-day fuel reserve, or 5 hours 59 minutes.

Answer (A) is incorrect. Using 53 PPH, the flight time available is 5 hours 59 minutes, not 4 hours 50 minutes. **Answer (B) is incorrect.** This is the endurance, with a VFR-day reserve, using the recommended lean mixture, not the best fuel economy, fuel flow.

PRESSURE ALTITUDE – 18,000 FEET

CONDITIONS:
4,000 POUNDS
RECOMMENDED LEAN MIXTURE
COWL FLAPS CLOSED

NOTES:
FOR BEST FUEL ECONOMY AT 70% POWER OR LESS, OPERATE AT 6 PPH LEANER THAN SHOWN IN THIS CHART OR AT PEAK EGT.

RPM	MP	20 °C BELOW STANDARD TEMPERATURE −41 °C			STANDARD TEMPERATURE −21 °C			20 °C ABOVE STANDARD TEMP −1 °C		
		% BHP	KTAS	PPH	% BHP	KTAS	PPH	% BHP	KTAS	PPH
2,500	30	---	---	---	81	188	106	76	185	100
	28	80	184	105	76	182	99	71	178	93
	26	75	178	99	71	176	93	67	172	88
	24	70	171	91	66	168	86	62	164	81
	22	63	162	84	60	159	79	56	155	75
2,400	30	81	185	107	77	183	101	72	180	94
	28	76	179	100	72	177	94	67	173	88
	26	71	172	93	67	170	88	63	166	83
	24	66	165	87	62	163	82	58	159	77
	22	61	158	80	57	155	76	54	150	72
2,300	30	79	182	103	74	180	97	70	176	91
	28	74	176	97	70	174	91	65	170	86
	26	69	170	91	65	167	86	61	163	81
	24	64	162	84	60	159	79	56	155	75
	22	58	154	77	55	150	73	51	145	65
2,200	26	66	166	87	62	163	82	58	159	77
	24	61	158	80	57	154	76	54	150	72
	22	55	148	73	51	144	69	48	138	66
	20	49	136	66	46	131	63	43	124	59

Figure 12. Cruise Performance.

36. (Refer to Figure 34 on page 219.)

GIVEN:

Pressure altitude	6,000 ft
Temperature	+3°C
Power	2,200 RPM – 22" MP
Usable fuel available	465 lb

What is the maximum available flight time under the conditions stated?

    A. 6 hours 27 minutes.

    B. 6 hours 39 minutes.

    C. 6 hours 56 minutes.

Answer (B) is correct. (FAA-H-8083-25B Chap 11)
    DISCUSSION: Using Fig. 34 at 2,200 RPM, find the 22" MP line. Then go across to the PPH column in the middle section for standard temperatures and find 70 PPH. Divide 465 lb. of usable fuel by 70 PPH to determine a time of 6.64 hours, which translates to about 6 hours 39 minutes.
    Alternatively, use your flight computer. Put 70 PPH on the outer scale over the time index on the inner scale. Then find 465 on the outer scale and read about 6 hours 40 minutes on the inner scale.
    Answer (A) is incorrect. The maximum available flight time at 2,200 RPM, 22" MP, and –17°C, not +3°C, is 6 hours 27 minutes. **Answer (C) is incorrect.** The maximum available flight time at 2,200 RPM, 22" MP, and +23°C, not +3°C, is 6 hours 56 minutes.

37. (Refer to Figure 34 on page 219.)

GIVEN:

Pressure altitude	6,000 ft
Temperature	–17 °C
Power	2,300 RPM – 23" MP
Usable fuel available	370 lb

What is the maximum available flight time under the conditions stated?

    A. 4 hours 20 minutes.

    B. 4 hours 30 minutes.

    C. 4 hours 50 minutes.

Answer (B) is correct. (FAA-H-8083-25B Chap 11)
    DISCUSSION: Using Fig. 34 at 2300 RPM, find the 23" MP line. Then go across to the PPH column in the section for 20° below standard temperature and find 82 PPH. Divide 370 lb. of usable fuel by 82 PPH to determine a time of 4.51 hours, which translates to about 4 hours 30 minutes.
    Alternatively, use your flight computer. Put 82 PPH on the outer scale over the time index on the inner scale. Then find 370 on the outer scale and find about 4 hours 30 minutes on the inner scale.
    Answer (A) is incorrect. The maximum available flight time of 4 hours 20 minutes is achieved by using an MP of 24 in., not 23 in. **Answer (C) is incorrect.** The maximum flight time of 4 hours 50 minutes is achieved by using an MP of 22 in., not 23 in.

38. (Refer to Figure 34 on page 219.)

GIVEN:

Pressure altitude	6,000 ft
Temperature	+13°C
Power	2,500 RPM – 23" MP
Usable fuel available	460 lb

What is the maximum available flight time under the conditions stated?

    A. 4 hours 58 minutes.

    B. 5 hours 7 minutes.

    C. 5 hours 12 minutes.

Answer (C) is correct. (FAA-H-8083-25B Chap 11)
    DISCUSSION: Using Fig. 34 at 2500 RPM, find the 23" MP line. Then, notice that 13°C, 10° above standard temperature (ST), is not given. You must interpolate between standard temperature and 20° above ST. At standard temperature, fuel flow equals 90 PPH; at 20° above ST, fuel flow equals 87 PPH, a difference of 3 PPH. Since the required 10° above ST is exactly halfway between ST and ST + 20°, half of 3 PPH, or 1.5, should be added to the value of 87 PPH, giving 88.5 PPH. Divide 460 lb. of usable fuel by 88.5 PPH to determine a time of 5.19 hours, which translates to about 5 hours 12 minutes.
    Answer (A) is incorrect. The maximum flight time of 4 hours 58 minutes is at a temperature of –17°C, not +13°C. **Answer (B) is incorrect.** The maximum flight time of 5 hours 7 minutes is at a temperature of +3°C, not +13°C.

39. Which maximum range factor decreases as weight decreases?

    A. Altitude.

    B. Airspeed.

    C. Angle of attack.

Answer (B) is correct. (FAA-H-8083-25B Chap 11)
    DISCUSSION: As weight decreases, the maximum range is achieved when the airplane is flown at the airspeed which maximizes the lift/drag ratio. As weight decreases, the L/D_{MAX} airspeed decreases.
    Answer (A) is incorrect. Maximum range altitude may increase, not decrease, with weight decrease. **Answer (C) is incorrect.** Angle of attack is not a maximum range factor (as are weight, altitude, and power setting).

PRESSURE ALTITUDE 6,000 FEET

CONDITIONS:
3,800 POUNDS
RECOMMENDED LEAN MIXTURE
COWL FLAPS CLOSED

RPM	MP	20 °C BELOW STANDARD TEMPERATURE −17 °C			STANDARD TEMPERATURE 3 °C			20 °C ABOVE STANDARD TEMPERATURE 23 °C		
		% BHP	KTAS	PPH	% BHP	KTAS	PPH	% BHP	KTAS	PPH
2,550	24	---	---	---	78	173	97	75	174	94
	23	76	167	96	74	169	92	71	171	89
	22	72	164	90	69	166	87	67	167	84
	21	68	160	85	65	162	82	63	163	80
2,500	24	78	169	98	75	171	95	73	172	91
	23	74	166	93	71	167	90	69	169	87
	22	70	162	88	67	164	85	65	165	82
	21	66	158	83	63	160	80	61	160	77
2,400	24	73	165	91	70	166	88	68	167	85
	23	69	161	87	67	163	84	64	164	81
	22	65	158	82	63	159	79	61	160	77
	21	61	154	77	59	155	75	57	155	73
2,300	24	68	161	86	66	162	83	64	163	80
	23	65	158	82	62	159	79	60	159	76
	22	61	154	77	59	155	75	57	155	72
	21	57	150	73	55	150	71	53	150	68
2,200	24	63	156	80	61	157	77	59	158	75
	23	60	152	76	58	153	73	56	154	71
	22	57	149	72	54	149	70	53	149	67
	21	53	144	68	51	144	66	49	143	64
	20	50	139	64	48	138	62	46	137	60
	19	46	133	60	44	132	58	43	131	57

Figure 34. Cruise Performance Chart.

40. (Refer to Figure 8 on page 221.)

GIVEN:

Fuel quantity	47 gal
Power-cruise (lean)	55 percent

Approximately how much flight time would be available with a night VFR fuel reserve remaining?

    A. 3 hours 8 minutes.

    B. 3 hours 22 minutes.

    C. 3 hours 43 minutes.

Answer (B) is correct. (FAA-H-8083-25B Chap 11)
    DISCUSSION: Given 47 gallons of fuel available at cruise power (55%), how much time is available, not counting a 45-min. fuel reserve? On Fig. 8, find the intersection of the cruise (lean) curve and 55% power. From the intersection, proceed horizontally to the left to determine 11.4 GPH. Divide 47 gallons usable fuel by 11.4 GPH to determine 4.122 hours, which translates to 4 hours 7 minutes. Subtract 45 minutes to determine 3 hours 22 minutes.
    Alternatively, use your flight computer. Put 11.4 over the true index. Then, on the outer scale, find 47, which gives you about 4 hours 7 minutes. Subtract 45 minutes to get 3 hours 22 minutes.
    Answer (A) is incorrect. This is the flight time at best power, not cruise, and with a VFR-day, not VFR-night (i.e., 45-min.), reserve. **Answer (C) is incorrect.** The flight time with a VFR-night reserve (45 minutes) at cruise (lean) power is 3 hours 22 minutes, not 3 hours 43 minutes.

41. (Refer to Figure 8 on page 221.)

GIVEN:

Fuel quantity	65 gal
Best power (level flight)	55 percent

Approximately how much flight time would be available with a day VFR fuel reserve remaining?

    A. 4 hours 17 minutes.

    B. 4 hours 30 minutes.

    C. 5 hours 4 minutes.

Answer (B) is correct. (FAA-H-8083-25B Chap 11)
    DISCUSSION: Given 65 gallons of fuel available at best power (55%), how much time is available, not counting a 30-minute fuel reserve? On Fig. 8, find the intersection of the level flight curve and 55% power. From the intersection, proceed horizontally to the left to determine 13 GPH. Divide 65 gallons usable fuel by 13 GPH to determine 5 hours. Subtract 30 minutes to determine 4 hours 30 minutes.
    Answer (A) is incorrect. This is the approximate flight time with a VFR-night, not VFR-day, fuel reserve. **Answer (C) is incorrect.** The approximate flight time with no fuel reserve is 5 hours 4 minutes.

42. (Refer to Figure 8 on page 221.) Approximately how much fuel would be consumed when climbing at 75 percent power for 7 minutes?

    A. 1.82 gallons.

    B. 1.97 gallons.

    C. 2.12 gallons.

Answer (C) is correct. (FAA-H-8083-25B Chap 11)
    DISCUSSION: To determine the amount of fuel to be burned in 7 minutes, on Fig. 8, find the intersection of the takeoff and climb curve with 75% power. From the intersection, proceed horizontally to the left to determine about 18.2 GPH. Multiply this by 7/60 to determine 2.12 gallons.
    Answer (A) is incorrect. The amount of 1.8 gallons is used with a fuel flow of 15.6 GPH, not 18.2 GPH. **Answer (B) is incorrect.** The amount of 1.97 gallons is used with a fuel flow of 16.8 GPH, not 18.2 GPH.

43. (Refer to Figure 8 on page 221.) Determine the amount of fuel consumed during takeoff and climb at 70 percent power for 10 minutes.

    A. 2.66 gallons.

    B. 2.88 gallons.

    C. 3.2 gallons.

Answer (B) is correct. (FAA-H-8083-25B Chap 11)
    DISCUSSION: To determine the amount of fuel to be burned in 10 minutes, on Fig. 8, find the intersection of the takeoff and climb curve with 70% power (the 70% power line is approximately one-half of the way between 65% and 75%), which is about 17.3 GPH. One-sixth of this is 2.88 gallons.
    Answer (A) is incorrect. The amount of 2.66 gallons is used with a fuel flow of 16 GPH, not 17.3 GPH. **Answer (C) is incorrect.** The amount of 3.2 gallons is used with a fuel flow of 19.2 GPH, not 17.3 GPH.

44. (Refer to Figure 8 on page 221.) With 38 gallons of fuel aboard at cruise power (55 percent), how much flight time is available with night VFR fuel reserve still remaining?

    A. 2 hours 34 minutes.

    B. 2 hours 49 minutes.

    C. 3 hours 18 minutes.

Answer (A) is correct. (FAA-H-8083-25B Chap 11)
    DISCUSSION: On Fig. 8, find the intersection of the cruise (lean) curve and 55% power. From the intersection, proceed horizontally to the left to determine 11.4 GPH. Divide 38 gallons usable fuel by 11.4 GPH to determine 3 hours 19 minutes. Subtract 45 minutes to determine 2 hours 34 minutes.
    Answer (B) is incorrect. This time requires a fuel flow of 10.7 GPH, not 11.4 GPH. **Answer (C) is incorrect.** This time is the approximate flight time without considering the 45-min. VFR-night fuel reserve.

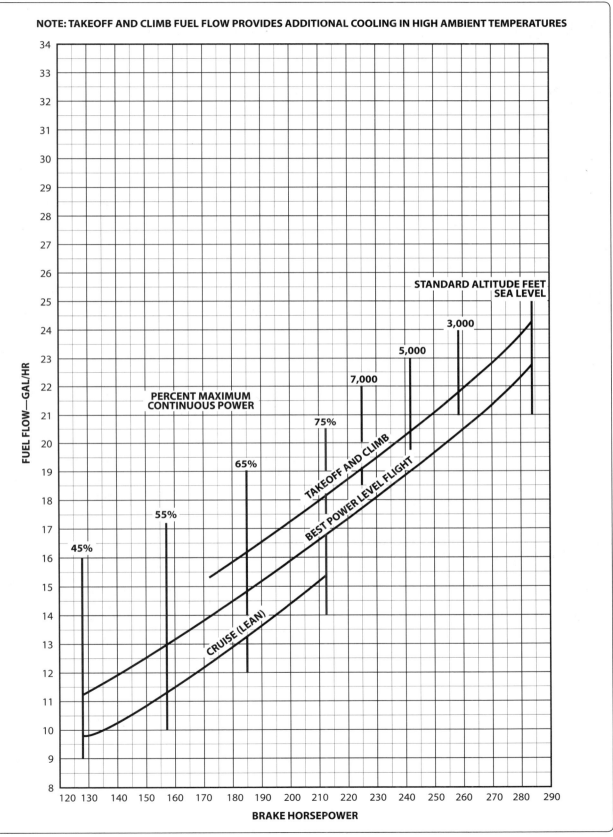

Figure 8. Fuel Consumption vs. Brake Horsepower.

5.7   Crosswind/Headwind Component

45. (Refer to Figure 31 on page 223.) Rwy 30 is being used for landing. Which surface wind would exceed the airplane's crosswind capability of 0.2 V_{s0}, if V_{s0} is 60 knots?

    A.   260° at 20 knots.

    B.   275° at 25 knots.

    C.   315° at 35 knots.

Answer (A) is correct. (FAA-H-8083-25B Chap 11)
    DISCUSSION: The crosswind capability of .2 V_{s0} with a V_{s0} of 60 knots means a crosswind capability of 12 knots (60 × .2). Thus, you must go through each of the situations to determine which crosswind component is in excess of 12 knots.
    With a wind of 260° and a landing on Rwy 30 (i.e., at 300°), the crosswind angle is 40° (300° − 260°). Go out to the 20-kt. arc and then down vertically to determine a 13-kt. crosswind component, which exceeds the 12-kt. capability.
    Answer (B) is incorrect. The crosswind angle is 25° (300° − 275°). Go out to the 25-kt. arc and then down vertically to determine a 10.5-kt. crosswind component, which is less than the airplane's 12-kt. crosswind capability. **Answer (C) is incorrect.** The crosswind angle is 15° (315° − 300°). Go out to the 35-kt. arc and then down vertically to determine a 9-kt. crosswind component, which is less than the airplane's 12-kt. crosswind capability.

46. (Refer to Figure 31 on page 223.) The surface wind is 180° at 25 knots. What is the crosswind component for a Rwy 13 landing?

    A.   19 knots.

    B.   21 knots.

    C.   23 knots.

Answer (A) is correct. (FAA-H-8083-25B Chap 11)
    DISCUSSION: When landing on Rwy 13 with a surface wind of 180°, the crosswind will be at 50° (180° − 130°). On Fig. 31, go out the 50° line to the 25-kt. wind arc. From that intersection, go vertically down to the horizontal scale at the bottom of the graph and find a 19-kt. crosswind component.
    Answer (B) is incorrect. A 21-knot crosswind component requires a surface wind of 180° at 28 knots, not 25 knots. **Answer (C) is incorrect.** A 23-knot crosswind component requires a surface wind of 180° at 30 knots, not 25 knots.

47. (Refer to Figure 31 on page 223.) What is the headwind component for a Rwy 13 takeoff if the surface wind is 190° at 15 knots?

    A.   7 knots.

    B.   13 knots.

    C.   15 knots.

Answer (A) is correct. (FAA-H-8083-25B Chap 11)
    DISCUSSION: When landing on Rwy 13 with a surface wind of 190°, the crosswind will be at 60° (190° − 130°). On Fig. 31, go out the 60° line to the 15-kt. wind arc. From that intersection, go horizontally across to the left to the vertical scale at the side of the graph and find a 7-kt. headwind component.
    Answer (B) is incorrect. This is the crosswind, not headwind, component. **Answer (C) is incorrect.** This is the surface wind, not headwind, component.

48. (Refer to Figure 31 on page 223.) If the tower-reported surface wind is 010° at 18 knots, what is the crosswind component for a Rwy 08 landing?

    A.   7 knots.

    B.   15 knots.

    C.   17 knots.

Answer (C) is correct. (FAA-H-8083-25B Chap 11)
    DISCUSSION: When landing on Rwy 08 with a surface wind of 10° the crosswind will be at 70° (80° − 10°). On Fig. 31, go out the 70° line to the 18-kt. wind arc. From that intersection, go vertically down to the horizontal scale at the bottom of the graph and find a 17-kt. crosswind component.
    Answer (A) is incorrect. A 7-kt. crosswind component requires a 7-kt., not an 18-kt., surface wind at 010°. **Answer (B) is incorrect.** A 15-kt. crosswind component requires a 16-kt., not an 18-kt., surface wind at 010°.

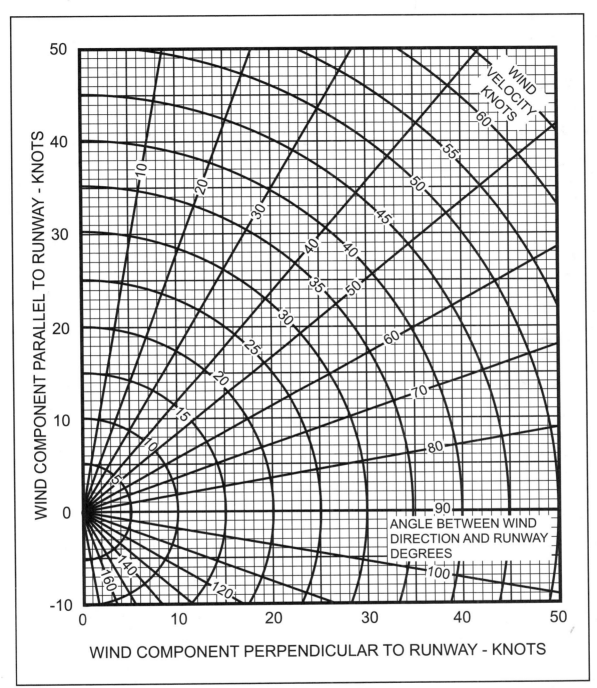

Figure 31. Wind Component Chart.

5.8 Landing Distance

49. (Refer to Figure 35 on page 225.)

GIVEN:

Temperature	50°F
Pressure altitude	Sea level
Weight	3,000 lb
Headwind	10 kts

Determine the approximate ground roll.

    A. 425 feet.

    B. 636 feet.

    C. 836 feet.

Answer (B) is correct. (FAA-H-8083-25B Chap 11)
    DISCUSSION: Determine the ground roll on Fig. 35 by computing 53% of the total landing distance over a 50-ft. obstacle, which is listed on the right-hand side of the figure. Begin with the temperature of 50°F at the lower left. Proceed upward to the sea-level line. From that intersection, proceed horizontally to the right to the first reference line. From that point, proceed up and to the right, parallel to the guidelines, to the 3,000-lb. point, as shown at the bottom of the graph. From that point, proceed horizontally to the second reference line. Then proceed to the right and down, parallel to the headwind guidelines, until you intersect the 10-kt. line. From that point, proceed horizontally to the right to determine about 1,200 feet to clear a 50-foot obstacle. Multiply this amount by .53 to get the ground roll of 636 feet.
    Answer (A) is incorrect. This is the ground roll for a total landing distance over a 50-ft. obstacle of 802 feet. **Answer (C) is incorrect.** This is the ground roll for a total landing distance over a 50-foot obstacle of 1,577 feet.

50. (Refer to Figure 35 on page 225.)

GIVEN:

Temperature	70°F
Pressure altitude	Sea level
Weight	3,400 lb
Headwind	16 kts

Determine the approximate ground roll.

    A. 689 feet.

    B. 716 feet.

    C. 1,275 feet.

Answer (A) is correct. (FAA-H-8083-25B Chap 11)
    DISCUSSION: Determine the ground roll on Fig. 35 by computing 53% of the total landing distance over a 50-ft. obstacle, which is listed on the right-hand side of the figure. Begin with the temperature of 70°F at the lower left. Proceed upward to the sea-level line. From that intersection, proceed horizontally to the right to the first reference line. From that point, proceed up and to the right, parallel to the guidelines, to the 3,400-lb. point, as shown at the bottom of the graph. From that point, proceed horizontally to the second reference line. Then proceed to the right and down, parallel to the headwind guidelines, until you intersect the 16-kt. line. From that point, proceed horizontally to the right to determine a total landing distance of 1,300 feet to clear a 50-foot obstacle. Multiply this amount by .53 to get the ground roll of 689 feet.
    Answer (B) is incorrect. A ground roll of 716 feet requires a headwind of 14 knots, not 16 knots. **Answer (C) is incorrect.** This is the total landing distance over a 50-ft. obstacle, not ground roll, with a 19-knot, not 16-knot, headwind.

51. (Refer to Figure 35 on page 225.)

GIVEN:

Temperature	85°F
Pressure altitude	6,000 ft
Weight	2,800 lb
Headwind	14 kts

Determine the approximate ground roll.

    A. 742 feet.

    B. 1,280 feet.

    C. 1,480 feet.

Answer (A) is correct. (FAA-H-8083-25B Chap 11)
    DISCUSSION: Determine the ground roll on Fig. 35 by computing 53% of the total landing distance over a 50-ft. obstacle, which is listed on the right-hand side of the figure. Begin with the temperature of 85°F at the lower left. Proceed upward to the 6,000-ft. line. From that intersection, proceed horizontally to the right to the first reference line. From that point, proceed up and to the right, parallel to the guidelines, to the 2,800-lb. point, as shown at the bottom of the graph. From that point, proceed horizontally to the second reference line. Then proceed to the right and down, parallel to the headwind guidelines, until you intersect the 14-kt. line. From that point, proceed horizontally to the right to determine about 1,400 feet to clear a 50-ft. obstacle. Multiply this amount by .53 to get the ground roll of 742 feet.
    Answer (B) is incorrect. A 1,280-ft. ground roll requires a 2,415-ft. total landing distance. **Answer (C) is incorrect.** This is the total landing distance, not the ground roll, with a 10-kt., not 14-kt., headwind.

52. (Refer to Figure 35 below.)

GIVEN:

Temperature	80°F
Pressure altitude	4,000 ft
Weight	2,800 lb
Headwind	24 kts

What is the total landing distance over a 50-foot obstacle?

   A. 1,125 feet.

   B. 1,250 feet.

   C. 1,325 feet.

Answer (B) is correct. *(FAA-H-8083-25B Chap 11)*
    DISCUSSION: Begin with the temperature of 80°F at the lower left on Fig. 35. Proceed upward to the 4,000-ft. line. From that intersection, proceed horizontally to the right to the first reference line. From that point, proceed up and to the right, parallel to the guidelines, to the 2,800-lb. point, as shown at the bottom of the graph. From that point, proceed horizontally to the second reference line. From that point on the second reference line, proceed to the right and down, parallel to the headwind guidelines, until you intersect the 24-kt. line. From that point, proceed horizontally to the right to determine about 1,250 feet to clear a 50-foot obstacle.
    Answer (A) is incorrect. This figure requires a headwind of 28 knots, not 24 knots. **Answer (C) is incorrect.** This figure requires a headwind of 10 knots, not 24 knots.

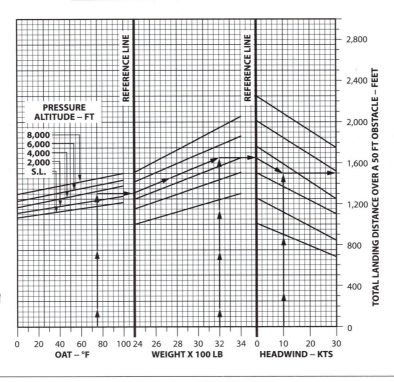

Figure 35. Normal Landing Chart.

5.9 Weight and Balance

53. When computing weight and balance, the basic empty weight includes the weight of the airframe, engine(s), and all installed optional equipment. Basic empty weight also includes

   A. the unusable fuel, full operating fluids, and full oil.

   B. all usable fuel, full oil, hydraulic fluid, but does not include the weight of pilot, passengers, or baggage.

   C. all usable fuel and oil, but does not include any radio equipment or instruments that were installed by someone other than the manufacturer.

Answer (A) is correct. (FAA-H-8083-25B Chap 10)
   DISCUSSION: Empty weight consists of the airframe, the engine, and all installed optional equipment, including fixed ballast, unusable fuel, full operating fluids, and full oil.
   Answer (B) is incorrect. Empty weight does not include usable fuel. **Answer (C) is incorrect.** Empty weight does not include usable fuel, but it does include all installed equipment.

54. The CG of an aircraft can be determined by which of the following methods?

   A. Dividing total arms by total moments.

   B. Multiplying total arms by total weight.

   C. Dividing total moments by total weight.

Answer (C) is correct. (FAA-H-8083-25B Chap 10)
   DISCUSSION: The center of gravity, by definition, is the total moment of the airplane divided by its total weight. Moment is the position of weight from some fixed point (called the datum) multiplied by that weight.
   Answer (A) is incorrect. Arms are the distances of weight from the datum; each arm is individually multiplied by its respective weight to determine an individual moment. **Answer (B) is incorrect.** Arms are the distances of weight from the datum; each arm is individually multiplied by its respective weight to determine an individual moment.

55. The CG of an aircraft may be determined by

   A. dividing total arms by total moments.

   B. dividing total moments by total weight.

   C. multiplying total weight by total moments.

Answer (B) is correct. (FAA-H-8083-25B Chap 10)
   DISCUSSION: The center of gravity, by definition, is the total moment of the airplane divided by its total weight. Moment is the position of weight from some fixed point (called the datum) multiplied by that weight.
   Answer (A) is incorrect. Arms are the distances of weight from the datum; each arm is individually multiplied by its respective weight to determine an individual moment. **Answer (C) is incorrect.** You must divide total moments by total weight (not vice versa).

56. If all index units are positive when computing weight and balance, the location of the datum would be at the

   A. centerline of the main wheels.

   B. nose, or out in front of the airplane.

   C. centerline of the nose or tailwheel, depending on the type of airplane.

Answer (B) is correct. (FAA-H-8083-1B Chap 2)
   DISCUSSION: Index units refer to arms. If all the arms are positive in computing weight and balance, the datum (or starting point) must be at the nose or out in front of the nose of the airplane. If it is somewhere between the nose and the tail, some items (those between the datum and the nose) would be negative.
   Answer (A) is incorrect. If the datum were at the centerline of the main wheels, the engine would have a negative arm (or index unit). **Answer (C) is incorrect.** If the datum were at the centerline of the nose or tailwheel, at least the propeller would have a negative arm (or index unit).

5.10 Weight and Moment Computations

57. GIVEN:

Weight A -- 155 pounds at 45 inches aft of datum
Weight B -- 165 pounds at 145 inches aft of datum
Weight C -- 95 pounds at 185 inches aft of datum

Based on this information, where would the CG be located aft of datum?

    A. 86.0 inches.

    B. 116.8 inches.

    C. 125.0 inches.

Answer (B) is correct. (FAA-H-8083-1B Chap 5)
    DISCUSSION: To determine the CG, use a three-step process:

1.   First, multiply the individual weights by their arms to get the individual moments.

		W	×	A	=	M
A	=	155	×	45	=	6,975
B	=	165	×	145	=	23,925
C	=	95	×	185	=	17,575
		415				48,475

2.   Compute total weight and total moments.
3.   Divide total moments by total weight to get the CG.

$$CG = \frac{48,475}{415} = 116.8 \text{ in.}$$

    Answer (A) is incorrect. The CG is 116.8 in., not 86.0 in.
    Answer (C) is incorrect. The CG is 116.8 in., not 125.0 in.

58. GIVEN:

Weight A -- 140 pounds at 17 inches aft of datum
Weight B -- 120 pounds at 110 inches aft of datum
Weight C -- 85 pounds at 210 inches aft of datum

Based on this information, the CG would be located how far aft of datum?

    A. 89.11 inches.

    B. 96.89 inches.

    C. 106.92 inches.

Answer (B) is correct. (FAA-H-8083-1B Chap 5)
    DISCUSSION: To determine the CG, use a three-step process:

1.   First, multiply the individual weights by their arms to get the individual moments.

		W	×	A	=	M
A	=	140	×	17	=	2,380
B	=	120	×	110	=	13,200
C	=	85	×	210	=	17,850
		345				33,430

2.   Compute total weight and total moments.
3.   Divide total moments by total weight to get the CG.

$$CG = \frac{33,430}{345} = 96.89 \text{ in.}$$

    Answer (A) is incorrect. The CG is 96.89 in., not 89.11 in.
    Answer (C) is incorrect. The CG is 96.89 in., not 106.92 in.

59. GIVEN:

	WEIGHT	ARM	MOMENT
Empty weight	957	29.07	?
Pilot (fwd seat)	140	−45.30	?
Passenger (aft seat)	170	+1.60	?
Ballast	15	−45.30	?
TOTALS	?	?	?

The CG is located at station

    A. −6.43.

    B. +16.43.

    C. +27.38.

Answer (B) is correct. (FAA-H-8083-1B Chap 5)
    DISCUSSION: To determine the CG, use a three-step process:

1.   Multiply the individual weights by individual arms to get individual moments.

		W	×	A	=	M
A	=	957	×	29.07	=	27,819.99
B	=	140	×	−45.30	=	−6,342.00
C	=	170	×	1.60	=	272.00
D	=	15	×	−45.30	=	−679.50
		1,282				21,070.49

2.   Compute total weight and total moments.
3.   Divide total moments by total weight to get the CG.

$$CG = \frac{21,070.49}{1,282} = +16.43$$

    Answer (A) is incorrect. The CG is +16.43, not −6.43.
    Answer (C) is incorrect. The CG is +16.43, not +27.38.

60. GIVEN:

Weight A -- 135 pounds at 15 inches aft of datum
Weight B -- 205 pounds at 117 inches aft of datum
Weight C -- 85 pounds at 195 inches aft of datum

Based on this information, the CG would be located how far aft of datum?

   A. 100.2 inches.

   B. 109.0 inches.

   C. 121.7 inches.

Answer (A) is correct. (FAA-H-8083-1B Chap 5)
   DISCUSSION: To determine the CG, use a three-step process:

1. Multiply the individual weights by their arms to get the individual moments.

		W	×	A	=	M
A	=	135	×	15	=	2,025
B	=	205	×	117	=	23,985
C	=	85	×	195	=	16,575
		425				42,585

2. Compute total weight and total moments.
3. Divide total moments by total weight to get the CG.

$$CG = \frac{42,585}{425} = 100.2 \text{ in.}$$

   Answer (B) is incorrect. The CG is 100.2 in., not 109.0 in.
Answer (C) is incorrect. The CG is 100.2 in., not 121.7 in.

61. GIVEN:

Weight A -- 175 pounds at 135 inches aft of datum
Weight B -- 135 pounds at 115 inches aft of datum
Weight C -- 75 pounds at 85 inches aft of datum

The CG for the combined weights would be located how far aft of datum?

   A. 91.76 inches.

   B. 111.67 inches.

   C. 118.24 inches.

Answer (C) is correct. (FAA-H-8083-1B Chap 5)
   DISCUSSION: To determine the CG, use a three-step process:

1. Multiply the individual weights by their arms to get the individual moments.

		W	×	A	=	M
A	=	175	×	135	=	23,625
B	=	135	×	115	=	15,525
C	=	75	×	85	=	6,375
		385				45,525

2. Compute total weight and total moments.
3. Divide total moments by total weight to get the CG.

$$CG = \frac{45,525}{385} = 118.24 \text{ in.}$$

   Answer (A) is incorrect. The CG is 118.24 in., not 91.76 in. **Answer (B) is incorrect.** The CG is 118.24 in., not 111.67 in.

62. (Refer to Figure 38 on page 229.)

GIVEN:

Empty weight (oil is included)	1,271 lb
Empty weight moment (in-lb/1,000)	102.04
Pilot and copilot	260 lb
Rear seat passenger	120 lb
Cargo	60 lb
Fuel	37 gal

Under these conditions, the CG is determined to be located

   A. within the CG envelope.

   B. on the forward limit of the CG envelope.

   C. within the shaded area of the CG envelope.

Answer (A) is correct. (FAA-H-8083-1B Chap 5)
   DISCUSSION: Use the loading graph at the top of Fig. 38 to determine the moment for each individual weight.

	Weight	Moment/ 1,000 in.-lb.
Empty weight	1,271	102.04
Pilot and copilot	260	23.5
Rear-seat passenger	120	15.0
Cargo	60	7.0
Fuel (37 gal. × 6 lb./gal.)	222	20.0
	1,933	167.54

The intersection of total weight of 1,933 lb. and total moment of 167.54 in.-lb. is within the CG moment envelope in Fig. 38.
   Answer (B) is incorrect. A total moment of approximately 160.5 in.-lb., not 167.54 in.-lb., would put the CG at the forward limit of the CG envelope at a weight of 1,933 lb. **Answer (C) is incorrect.** Both the weight and the moment are outside the shaded (utility category) area.

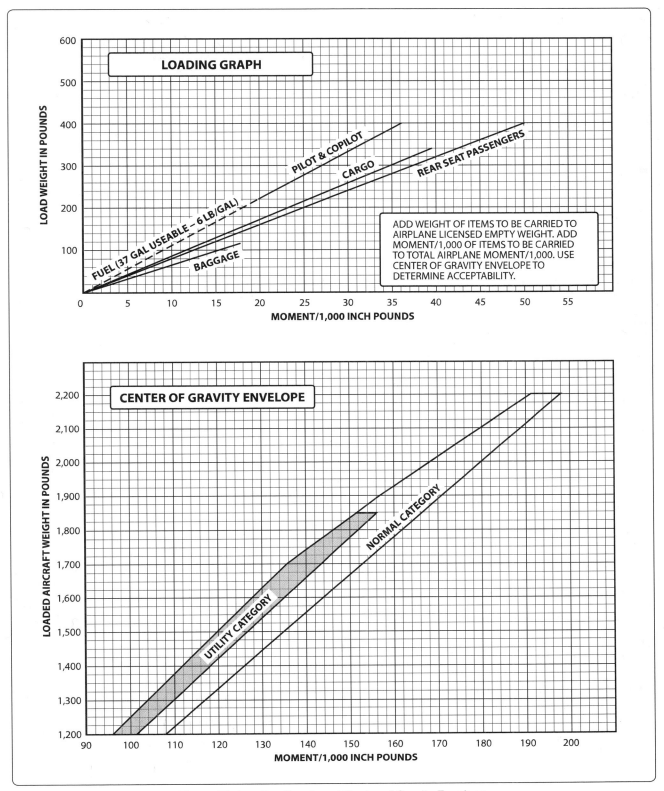

Figure 38. Loading Graph and Center of Gravity Envelope.

63. (Refer to Figure 38 on page 231.)

GIVEN:

Empty weight (oil is included)	1,271 lb
Empty weight moment (in-lb./1,000)	102.04
Pilot and copilot	360 lb
Cargo	340 lb
Fuel	37 gal

Will the CG remain within limits after 30 gallons of fuel has been used in flight?

A. Yes, the CG will remain within limits.

B. No, the CG will be located aft of the aft CG limit.

C. Yes, but the CG will be located in the shaded area of the CG envelope.

Answer (A) is correct. (FAA-H-8083-1B Chap 5)

DISCUSSION: Use the loading graph at the top of Fig. 38 to determine the moment for each individual weight. Fuel remaining is determined by 37 gallons to start – 30 gallons burned = 7 gallons left × 6 lb. per gallon.

	Weight	Moment/ 1,000 in.-lb.
Empty weight	1,271	102.04
Pilot and copilot	360	32.5
Cargo	340	39.5
Fuel (7 gal. × 6 lb./gal.)	42	4.0
	2,013	178.04

The intersection of total weight of 2,013 lb. and total moment of 178.04 in.-lb. is within the CG moment envelope in Fig. 38.

Answer (B) is incorrect. The amount of 178.04 in.-lb. is less than the aft CG limit at 2,013 lb. of 180 in.-lb. **Answer (C) is incorrect.** Both the weight and the moment are outside the shaded (utility category) area.

64. (Refer to Figure 38 on page 231.) Given the following information, does the weight of the aircraft and center of gravity fall within allowable limits?

Empty weight (oil is included)	1,275 lb.
Empty weight moment (in-lb./1,000)	102.05
Pilot and copilot	390 lb.
Rear-seat passenger	145 lb.
Cargo	95 lb.
Fuel	35 gal.

Is the airplane loaded within limits?

A. Yes, the weight and center of gravity is within allowable limits.

B. No, the weight exceeds the maximum allowable.

C. No, the weight is acceptable, but the center of gravity is aft of the allowable limits.

Answer (A) is correct. (FAA-H-8083-1B Chap 5)

DISCUSSION: Use the loading graph at the top of Fig. 38 to determine the moment for each individual weight.

	Weight	Moment/ 1,000 in.-lb.
Empty weight	1,275	102.05
Pilot and copilot	390	35.5
Rear-seat passenger	145	18.0
Cargo	95	11.0
Fuel (35 gal. × 6 lb./gal.)	210	19.0
	2,115	185.55

The intersection of total weight (2,115 lb.) and total moment (185.55 in.-lb.) is within the CG moment envelope in Fig. 38.

Answer (B) is incorrect. A weight of 2,115 lb. is less than the maximum allowable weight of 2,200 lb. **Answer (C) is incorrect.** The moment of 185.55 in.-lb. is less than the aft limit at 2,115 lb. of 190 in.-lb.

65. (Refer to Figure 38 on page 231.)

GIVEN:

Empty weight (oil is included)	1,271 lb
Empty weight moment (in-lb/1,000)	102.04
Pilot and copilot	400 lb
Rear seat passenger	140 lb
Cargo	100 lb
Fuel	37 gal

Is the airplane loaded within limits?

A. Yes, the weight and CG is within limits.

B. No, the weight exceeds the maximum allowable.

C. No, the weight is acceptable, but the CG is aft of the aft limit.

Answer (A) is correct. (FAA-H-8083-1B Chap 5)

DISCUSSION: Use the loading graph at the top of Fig. 38 to determine the moment for each individual weight.

	Weight	Moment/ 1,000 in.-lb.
Empty weight	1,271	102.04
Pilot and copilot	400	36.0
Rear-seat passenger	140	18.0
Cargo	100	11.5
Fuel (37 gal. × 6 lb./gal.)	222	20.0
	2,133	187.54

The intersection of total weight of 2,133 lb. and total moment of 187.54 in.-lb. is within the CG moment envelope in Fig. 38.

Answer (B) is incorrect. A weight of 2,133 lb. is less than the maximum allowable weight of 2,200 lb. **Answer (C) is incorrect.** The amount of 187.54 in.-lb. is less than the aft limit at 2,133 lb. of 193 in.-lb.

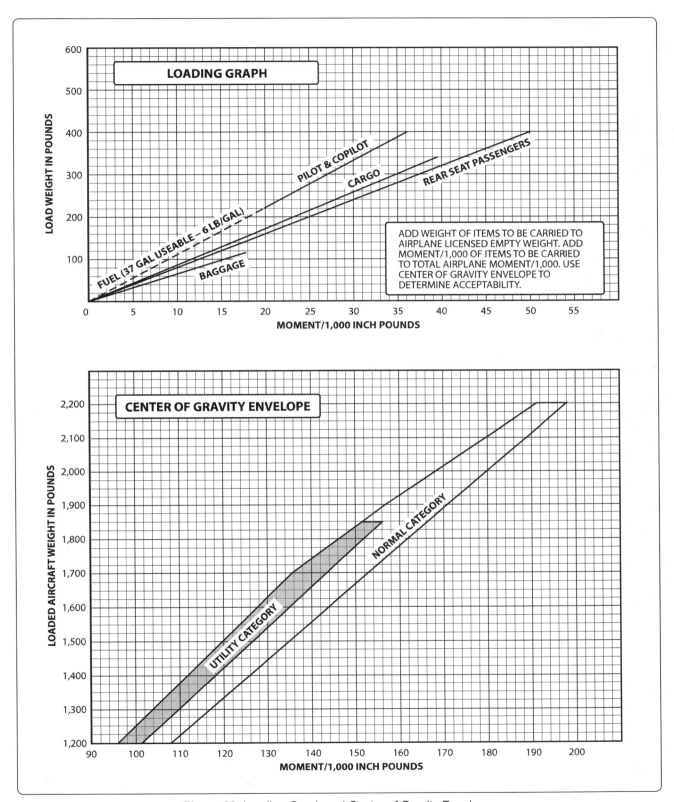

Figure 38. Loading Graph and Center of Gravity Envelope.

5.11 Weight Change and Weight Shift Computations

66. GIVEN:

Total weight	4,137 lb
CG location	Station 67.8
Fuel consumption	13.7 GPH
Fuel CG	Station 68.0

After 1 hour 30 minutes of flight time, the CG would be located at station

   A. 67.79

   B. 68.79

   C. 70.78

Answer (A) is correct. (FAA-H-8083-1B Chap 2)
   DISCUSSION: To determine the new CG, complete the following steps:

1. Weight change = Fuel consumption (GPH) × flight time × 6 lb./gal.

$$= 13.7 \times 1.5 \times 6$$
$$= 123.3 \text{ lb.}$$

2. Use the following formula to determine the new CG:

$$\text{New CG} = \frac{M_1 \pm \Delta M}{W_1 \pm \Delta W}$$

where M_1 = original moment and W_1 = original weight.

$$\text{New CG} = \frac{(4,137 \times 67.8) - (123.3 \times 68.0)}{4,137 - 123.3}$$

$$= \frac{280,488.6 - 8,384.4}{4,013.7}$$

$$= \frac{272,104.2}{4,013.7} = 67.79$$

   Answer (B) is incorrect. The new CG is 67.79, not 68.79.
Answer (C) is incorrect. The new CG is 67.79, not 70.78.

67. GIVEN:

Total weight	3,037 lb
CG location	Station 68.8
Fuel consumption	12.7 GPH
Fuel CG	Station 68.0

After 1 hour 45 minutes of flight time, the CG would be located at station

   A. 68.77

   B. 68.83

   C. 69.77

Answer (B) is correct. (FAA-H-8083-1B Chap 2)
   DISCUSSION: To determine the new CG, complete the following steps:

1. Weight change = Fuel consumption (GPH) × flight time × 6 lb./gal.

$$= 12.7 \times 1.75 \times 6$$
$$= 133.35 \text{ lb.}$$

2. Use the following formula to determine the new CG:

$$\text{New CG} = \frac{M_1 \pm \Delta M}{W_1 \pm \Delta W}$$

where M_1 = original moment and W_1 = original weight.

$$\text{New CG} = \frac{(3,037 \times 68.8) - (133.35 \times 68.0)}{3,037 - 133.35}$$

$$= \frac{208,945.6 - 9,067.8}{2,903.65}$$

$$= \frac{199,877.8}{2,903.65} = 68.83$$

   Answer (A) is incorrect. The new CG is 68.83, not 68.77.
Answer (C) is incorrect. The new CG is 68.83, not 69.77.

68. An airplane is loaded to a gross weight of 4,800 pounds, with three pieces of luggage in the rear baggage compartment. The CG is located 98 inches aft of datum, which is 1 inch aft of limits. If luggage which weighs 90 pounds is moved from the rear baggage compartment (145 inches aft of datum) to the front compartment (45 inches aft of datum), what is the new CG?

   A. 96.13 inches aft of datum.

   B. 95.50 inches aft of datum.

   C. 99.87 inches aft of datum.

Answer (A) is correct. (FAA-H-8083-1B Chap 2)
   DISCUSSION: To determine the new CG, use the following formula:

$$\text{New CG} = \frac{M_1 \pm \Delta M}{W_1 \pm \Delta W}$$

where M_1 = original moment and W_1 = original weight.

   Since there is no change in weight, $\Delta W = 0$ and weight shifted forward causes a "–" moment change.

$$\text{New CG} = \frac{(4,800 \times 98) - 90(145 - 45)}{4,800}$$

$$= \frac{470,400 - 9,000}{4,800}$$

$$= \frac{461,400}{4,800} = 96.13$$

   Answer (B) is incorrect. The new CG is 96.13, not 95.50.
Answer (C) is incorrect. The new CG is 96.13, not 99.87.

69. An aircraft is loaded with a ramp weight of 3,650 pounds and having a CG of 94.0, approximately how much baggage would have to be moved from the rear baggage area at station 180 to the forward baggage area at station 40 in order to move the CG to 92.0?

   A. 52.14 pounds.

   B. 62.24 pounds.

   C. 78.14 pounds.

Answer (A) is correct. (FAA-H-8083-1B Chap 2)
   DISCUSSION: To determine how much weight needs to be shifted forward (causing a "–" moment change), use the following formula:

M_1 = original moment
W_1 = original weight
$\Delta W = 0$ (because there is no change in weight)

$$\text{New CG} = \frac{M_1 \pm \Delta M}{W_1 \pm \Delta W}$$

$$92.0 \text{ lb./in.} = \frac{(3,650 \text{ lb.} \times 94.0 \text{ lb./in.}) - x(180 \text{ lb./in.} - 40 \text{ lb./in.})}{3,650 \text{ lb.}}$$

$$92.0 \text{ lb./in.} \times 3,650 \text{ lb.} = (3,650 \text{ lb.} \times 94.0 \text{ lb./in.}) - x(140 \text{ lb./in.})$$

$$335,800 \text{ lb.}^2/\text{in.} = 343,100 \text{ lb.}^2/\text{in.} - x(140 \text{ lb./in.})$$

$$-7,300 \text{ lb.}^2/\text{in.} = -x(140 \text{ lb./in.})$$

$$\frac{-7,300 \text{ lb.}^2/\text{in.}}{-140 \text{ lb./in.}} = x$$

$$52.14 \text{ lb.} = x$$

   Answer (B) is incorrect. Only 52.14 lb., not 62.24 lb., of baggage needs to be shifted. **Answer (C) is incorrect.** Only 52.14 lb., not 78.14 lb., of baggage needs to be shifted.

234

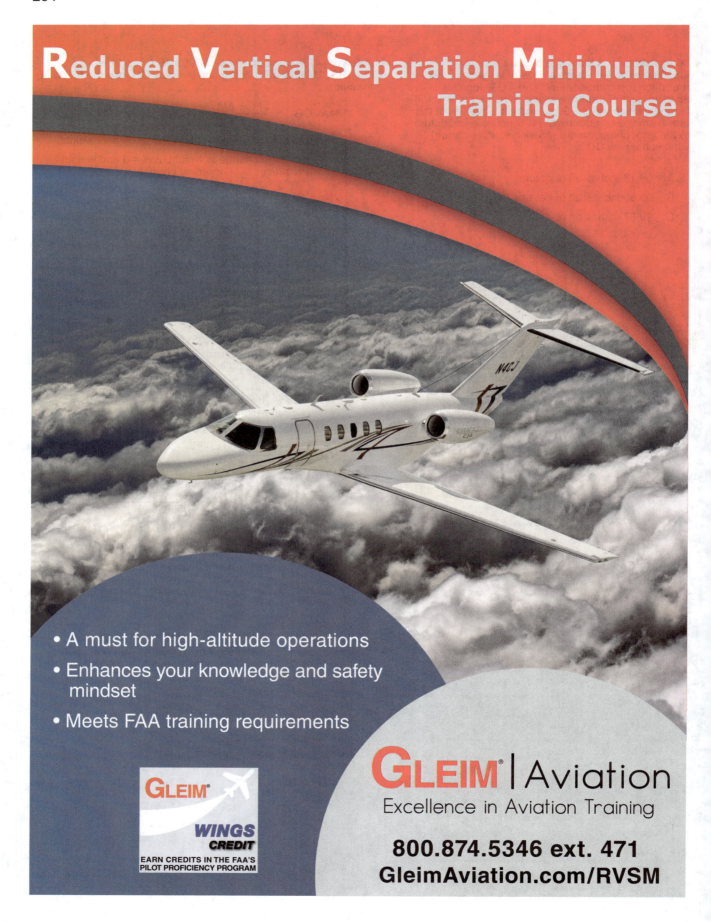

STUDY UNIT SIX

AEROMEDICAL FACTORS AND AERONAUTICAL DECISION MAKING (ADM)

(6 pages of outline)

This study unit contains outlines of major concepts tested, sample test questions and answers regarding aeromedical factors and aeronautical decision making (ADM), and an explanation of each answer. The table of contents above lists each subunit within this study unit, the number of questions pertaining to that particular subunit, and the pages on which the outlines and questions begin, respectively.

Recall that the **sole purpose** of this book is to expedite your passing of the FAA pilot knowledge test for the commercial pilot certificate. Accordingly, all extraneous material (i.e., topics or regulations not directly tested on the FAA pilot knowledge test) is omitted, even though much more knowledge is necessary to become a proficient commercial pilot. This additional material is presented in *Pilot Handbook* and *Commercial Pilot Flight Maneuvers and Practical Test Prep*, available from Gleim Publications, Inc. Order online at www.GleimAviation.com.

6.1 HYPOXIA AND ALCOHOL

1.   Hypoxia is a state of oxygen deficiency in the body sufficient to impair functions of the brain and other organs.

2.   The following are four types of hypoxia based on their causes:

    a.   **Hypoxic hypoxia** is a result of insufficient oxygen available to the body as a whole.

        1)   EXAMPLE: Reduction of partial pressure at higher altitudes

    b.   **Anemic (hypemic) hypoxia** occurs when blood is not able to take up and transport a sufficient amount of oxygen to the cells in the body. The result is a deficiency in the oxygen-carrying capacity of blood rather than a lack of inhaled oxygen.

        1)   EXAMPLE: Carbon monoxide poisoning or a reduced blood volume as a result of blood donation

    c.   **Stagnant hypoxia** results when oxygen-rich blood in the lungs is not moving.

        1)   EXAMPLE: Shock, reduced circulation due to extreme cold, or pulling excessive Gs in flight

    d.   **Histotoxic hypoxia** is the inability of cells to effectively use oxygen.

        1)   EXAMPLE: Impairment due to alcohol and drugs

3.   Symptoms of hypoxia include an initial feeling of euphoria but lead to more serious concerns such as headache, delayed reaction time, visual impairment, and eventual unconsciousness.

4.   The correct response to counteract feelings of hypoxia is to lower altitude or use supplemental oxygen.

5.   Alcohol is a central nervous system depressant that interferes with the brain's ability to use oxygen.

    a.   Even small amounts of alcohol in the body adversely affect judgment and decision-making abilities.

    b.   While experiencing a hangover, a pilot is still under the influence of alcohol and will have impaired motor and mental responses.

6.   Altitude multiplies the effects of alcohol on the brain; at higher altitudes, alcohol from two drinks may have the same effect as three or four drinks at lower altitudes.

7.   14 CFR 91.17 requires that blood alcohol level be less than 0.04% and that a minimum of 8 hr. passes between consuming alcohol and piloting an aircraft.

    a.   The body requires about 3 hr. to rid itself of all the alcohol contained in one mixed drink, one beer, or one glass of wine.

6.2 HYPERVENTILATION

1. Hyperventilation occurs when an excessive amount of air is breathed in and out of the lungs, e.g., when you become excited or undergo stress, tension, fear, or anxiety.

    a. This results in insufficient carbon dioxide in the body.

    b. Symptoms include lightheadedness, suffocation, drowsiness, tingling in the extremities, and coolness. Incapacitation and finally unconsciousness can occur.

    c. To overcome hyperventilation, a pilot should slow his or her breathing rate.

6.3 SPATIAL DISORIENTATION

1. Spatial disorientation, e.g., not knowing whether you are going up, going down, or turning, is a state of temporary confusion resulting from misleading information being sent to the brain by various sensory organs.

2. If you lose outside visual references and become disoriented, you are experiencing spatial disorientation. This occurs when you rely on the sensations of muscles and the inner ear to tell you what the airplane's attitude is.

    a. This might occur during a night flight, in clouds, or in dust.
    b. Examples of spatial disorientation in flight could include the following:

        1) **Graveyard spiral.** An observed loss of altitude during a coordinated constant-rate turn that has ceased stimulating the motion-sensing system can create the illusion of being in a descent with the wings level.

            a) The disoriented pilot will pull back on the controls, tightening the spiral and increasing the loss of altitude.

        2) **False horizon.** Sloping cloud formations, an obscured horizon, or certain geometric patterns of ground lights can create the illusion of not being correctly aligned with the true horizon.

            a) Without reference to instruments, a pilot may place the airplane in a dangerous attitude based on incorrect visual cues.

        3) **Somatogravic illusion.** A rapid acceleration, such as one experienced during takeoff, may create the illusion of being in a nose-up attitude, especially in conditions with poor visual references.

            a) The disoriented pilot may push the aircraft into a nose-low or dive attitude.

3. Ways to overcome the effects of spatial disorientation include relying on the airplane instruments, avoiding sudden head movements, and ensuring that outside visual references are fixed points on the surface.

6.4 PILOT VISION

1. Scanning for traffic is best accomplished by bringing small portions of the sky into the central field of vision slowly and in succession.

    a. Each movement should not exceed 10°, and each area should be observed for at least 1 second.

2. Haze can create the illusion of traffic or terrain being farther away than they actually are.

3. Visual illusions may affect a pilot's ability to properly judge a landing.

    a. Rain on a windscreen can create the illusion of greater height from the runway.

    b. Haze can create the illusion of greater distance from the runway.

    c. Landing errors from these illusions can be overcome by knowledge and anticipation of the illusions.

4. A narrower-than-usual runway may create the illusion that the airplane is higher than it actually is.

    a. This illusion results in a lower-than-normal approach.
    b. A wider-than-usual runway creates the opposite illusion and problem.

5. An upward-sloping runway may create the illusion that the airplane is at a higher-than-actual altitude.

    a. This illusion results in a lower-than-normal approach.
    b. A downward-sloping runway creates the opposite illusion and problem.

6.5 AERONAUTICAL DECISION MAKING (ADM)

1. **Aeronautical decision making (ADM)** is a systematic approach to the mental process used by pilots to consistently determine the best course of action in response to a given set of circumstances.

2. **Risk management** is the part of the ADM process that relies on situational awareness, problem recognition, and good judgment to reduce risks and manage external pressures associated with each flight.

3. The ADM process addresses all aspects of decision making on the flight deck and identifies the steps involved in good decision making.

    a. One of the steps for good decision making is to identify personal hazardous attitudes to safe flight.

        1) This is accomplished by taking a Self-Assessment Hazardous Attitude Inventory Test.

4. There are a number of classic behavioral traps to which pilots are susceptible.

    a. Experienced pilots, as a rule, always try to complete a flight as planned, please passengers, meet schedules, and generally demonstrate that they have the "right stuff."

    b. The basic drive to demonstrate the "right stuff" can have an adverse effect on safety and can impose an unrealistic assessment of piloting skills under stressful conditions.

        1) These tendencies ultimately may lead to practices that are dangerous and often illegal and that may result in a mishap.

5. Most pilots have fallen prey to dangerous tendencies or behavioral problems at some time. Some of these dangerous tendencies or behavioral patterns, which must be identified and eliminated, include

   a. Peer pressure
   b. Get-there-itis
   c. Loss of positional or situational awareness
   d. Operating without adequate fuel reserves

6. ADM addresses the following five hazardous attitudes:

   a. Antiauthority -- "Don't tell me!"

      1) EXAMPLE: The passengers for a charter flight have arrived almost an hour late for a flight that requires a reservation. An antiauthority attitude (reaction) by the pilot would be to think that those reservation rules do not apply to this flight.

   b. Impulsivity -- "Do something quickly without thinking!"

      1) EXAMPLE: The pilot and the passengers are anxious to get to their destination for a business presentation, but level 4 thunderstorms are reported to be in a line across their intended route of flight. An impulsivity attitude (reaction) would be for the pilot to "hurry and get going" before things get worse.

   c. Invulnerability -- "It won't happen to me."

      1) EXAMPLE: During an operational check of the cabin pressurization system, the pilot discovers that the rate control feature is inoperative. Since the pilot knows that (s)he can manually control the system, the pilot elects to disregard the discrepancy. An invulnerability attitude (reaction) would be to think, "What is the worst that could happen? (Problems happen to other people.)"

   d. Macho -- "I can do it!"

      1) EXAMPLE: While on an IFR flight, a pilot emerges from a cloud to find himself within 300 ft. of a helicopter. A macho attitude (reaction) by the pilot would be to fly a little closer to the helicopter, just to "show" the other pilot.

   e. Resignation -- "What's the use?"

      1) EXAMPLE: A pilot and friends are going to fly to an out-of-town football game. When the passengers arrive, the pilot determines that the loaded airplane will be over the maximum gross weight for takeoff with the existing fuel load. A resignation attitude (reaction) by the pilot would be to think, "Well, nobody told me about the extra weight."

7. Hazardous attitudes that contribute to poor pilot judgment can be effectively counteracted by redirecting those hazardous attitudes so that appropriate action can be taken.

8. Recognition of hazardous thoughts is the first step in neutralizing them in the ADM process.

9. When you recognize a hazardous thought, you should label it as hazardous and then correct it by stating the corresponding antidote.

10. The hazardous attitude antidotes shown below should be learned thoroughly and practiced.

Hazardous Attitude	Antidote
Antiauthority: *Don't tell me!*	Follow the rules. They are usually right.
Impulsivity: *Do something quickly!*	Not so fast. Think first.
Invulnerability: *It won't happen to me.*	It could happen to me.
Macho: *I can do it.*	Taking chances is foolish.
Resignation: *What's the use?*	I'm not helpless. I can make a difference.

11. Good flight deck stress management begins with good life stress management.

  a.   Since many of the stress coping techniques practiced for life stress management are not usually practiced in flight, you must condition yourself to relax and think rationally when stress occurs.

12. Fatigue can be treacherous because it may not be apparent until serious errors are made.

  a.   Acute fatigue is the everyday tiredness felt after long periods of physical or mental strain.

   1)   Consequently, coordination and alertness can be reduced.

   2)   Acute fatigue is prevented by adequate rest and sleep as well as regular exercise and proper nutrition.

  b.   Chronic fatigue occurs when there is not enough time for a full recovery between episodes of acute fatigue.

   1)   Performance continues to fall off, and judgment becomes impaired.

   2)   Recovery from chronic fatigue requires a prolonged period of rest.

13. The Decide Model is comprised of a six-step process to provide pilots with a logical way of approaching ADM. The six steps (in order) are

  a.   **D**etect. The decision maker detects the fact that change has occurred.

  b.   **E**stimate. The decision maker estimates the need to counter or react to the change.

  c.   **C**hoose. The decision maker chooses a desirable outcome (in terms of success) for the flight.

  d.   **I**dentify. The decision maker identifies actions that could successfully control the change.

  e.   **D**o. The decision maker takes the necessary action.

  f.   **E**valuate. The decision maker evaluates the effect(s) of his or her action countering the change.

14. Crew resource management (CRM) is the application of team management concepts in the flight deck environment. CRM refers to the effective use of all resources available, such as human resources (e.g., aircraft dispatchers, flight attendants, maintenance personnel, air traffic controllers, and flight crew), hardware (e.g., computers and flight directories), and information (e.g., Chart Supplements).

  a.   This definition includes all groups routinely working with the flight crew who are involved in decisions required to operate a flight safely. These groups include, but are not limited to, pilots, dispatchers, cabin crewmembers, maintenance personnel, and air traffic controllers.

  b.   The mission of CRM training has always been to prevent aviation accidents by improving crew performance through better crew coordination.

  c.   The goal of all flight crews is good ADM. Using CRM is one way to make good decisions that proactively recognize safety-related hazards and mitigate the associated risks.

QUESTIONS AND ANSWER EXPLANATIONS: All of the commercial pilot knowledge test questions chosen by the FAA for release as well as additional questions selected by Gleim relating to the material in the previous outlines are provided on the following pages. These questions have been organized into the same subunits as the outlines. To the immediate right of each question are the correct answer and answer explanations. You should cover these answers and answer explanations while responding to the questions. Refer to the general discussion in the Introduction on how to take the FAA knowledge test.

Remember that the questions from the FAA knowledge test bank have been reordered by topic and organized into a meaningful sequence. Also, the first line of the answer explanation gives the citation of the authoritative source for the answer.

QUESTIONS

6.1 Hypoxia and Alcohol

1. Which is not a type of hypoxia?

    A. Histotoxic.

    B. Hypoxic.

    C. Hypertoxic.

Answer (C) is correct. (FAA-H-8083-25B Chap 17)
    DISCUSSION: There is no such thing as hypertoxic hypoxia. The four types of hypoxia are histotoxic, hypoxic, anemic, and stagnant hypoxia.
    Answer (A) is incorrect. The four types of hypoxia are histotoxic, hypoxic, anemic, and stagnant hypoxia. **Answer (B) is incorrect.** The four types of hypoxia are histotoxic, hypoxic, anemic, and stagnant hypoxia.

2. Which of the following is a correct response to counteract the feelings of hypoxia in flight?

    A. Promptly descend to a lower altitude.

    B. Increase cabin air flow.

    C. Avoid sudden inhalations.

Answer (A) is correct. (FAA-H-8083-25B Chap 17)
    DISCUSSION: The correct response to counteract feelings of hypoxia is to descend to a lower altitude or use supplemental oxygen, if the aircraft is so equipped.
    Answer (B) is incorrect. Increasing the amount of air flowing inside an aircraft will not help counteract hypoxia. Because of the reduction of partial pressure at higher altitudes, there is less oxygen in the air to draw from. **Answer (C) is incorrect.** Breathing deeply or suddenly will not counteract feelings of hypoxia.

3. Hypoxia susceptibility due to inhalation of carbon monoxide increases as

    A. altitude increases.

    B. humidity decreases.

    C. oxygen demand increases.

Answer (A) is correct. (FAA-H-8083-25B Chap 17)
    DISCUSSION: The inhalation of carbon monoxide reduces body's ability to transport oxygen. The red blood cells will pick up carbon monoxide molecules instead of oxygen. This problem is compounded by increasing altitude, which also limits the body's ability to transport oxygen.
    Answer (B) is incorrect. A change in humidity does not change the body's susceptibility to hypoxia due to the inhalation of carbon monoxide. **Answer (C) is incorrect.** An increase in altitude, not an increase in oxygen demand, increases the susceptibility to hypoxia when carbon monoxide is inhaled.

4. Altitude-induced hypoxia is caused by what atmospheric condition?

    A. Significantly less oxygen molecules at high altitude.

    B. Insufficient partial pressure of the inhaled oxygen.

    C. Incorrect balance of oxygen and carbon dioxide.

Answer (B) is correct. (AIM Para 8-1-2)
    DISCUSSION: As altitude is increased, the partial pressure of oxygen lowers, reducing the lungs' capacity to effectively transfer oxygen from the ambient air to the blood to be carried to the tissues of the body.
    Answer (A) is incorrect. The percentage of oxygen does not change at higher altitudes, though the molecules of oxygen in ambient air get further apart, exerting less pressure per square inch. **Answer (C) is incorrect.** An incorrect balance of oxygen and carbon dioxide is primarily associated with hyperventilation.

5. If a pilot has not consumed a drink in 12 hours, and has a blood alcohol level of .04 percent, can (s)he fly?

    A. Yes, if it has been in excess of 8 hours since the pilot last consumed alcohol.

    B. No, the pilot has a blood alcohol level of .04.

    C. Yes, the FAA requires at least 12 hours and a blood alcohol level of .04.

Answer (B) is correct. (14 CFR 91.17)
    DISCUSSION: Pilots are required to have a blood alcohol level that is less than .04%, and at least 8 hours must have passed since the last alcoholic beverage was consumed.
    Answer (A) is incorrect. The FAA requires pilots to wait at least 8 hours from the time an alcoholic beverage is consumed to the time flight is attempted. In addition to the minimum of 8 hours, pilots must also have a blood alcohol level that is less than .04%. **Answer (C) is incorrect.** The FAA requires that at least 8 hours pass between the last consumption of alcohol and the beginning of a flight. Further, the blood alcohol level must be less than .04%.

6. 14 CFR 91.17 requires that blood alcohol level be less than

    A. 0.40% when piloting an aircraft.

    B. 0.08% when piloting an aircraft.

    C. 0.04% when piloting an aircraft.

Answer (C) is correct. (FAA-H-8083-25B Chap 17)
    DISCUSSION: Current regulations require that a pilot's blood alcohol level be less than 0.04% and that a minimum of 8 hours passes between consuming alcohol and piloting an aircraft.
    Answer (A) is incorrect. Pilots should have a blood alcohol level of less than 0.04%, not 0.40%. **Answer (B) is incorrect.** Pilots should have a blood alcohol level of less than 0.04%, not 0.08%.

7. According to current regulations, how many hours must elapse between consuming alcohol and piloting an aircraft?

    A. 4 hours.

    B. 8 hours.

    C. 16 hours.

Answer (B) is correct. (FAA-H-8083-25B Chap 17)
    DISCUSSION: According to 14 CFR 91.17, a minimum of 8 hours must pass between consuming alcohol and flying an aircraft.
    Answer (A) is incorrect. Regulations require that a minimum of 8 hours, not 4 hours, must pass between consuming alcohol and flying an aircraft. **Answer (C) is incorrect.** While considerable amounts of alcohol may remain in the body for over 16 hours, and it is good to be cautious about flying too soon after drinking, the regulations state that a minimum of 8 hours must elapse between consuming alcohol and flying.

8. Which of the following statements concerning the combination of alcohol and altitude is true?

    A. Judgment and decision-making abilities will only be affected at altitudes greater than 2,000 ft. MSL.

    B. Altitude multiplies the effects of alcohol.

    C. Increases in altitude do not change how alcohol affects individuals.

Answer (B) is correct. (FAA-H-8083-25B Chap 17)
    DISCUSSION: Altitude multiplies the effects of alcohol on the brain; at higher altitudes, alcohol from two drinks may have the same effect as three or four drinks at lower altitudes.
    Answer (A) is incorrect. An increase in altitude, no matter how small, can multiply the effects of alcohol on the body. **Answer (C) is incorrect.** Increasing altitude multiplies the effects alcohol will have on the body.

9. Hypoxia is the result of which of these conditions?

    A. Excessive oxygen in the bloodstream.

    B. Insufficient oxygen reaching the brain.

    C. Excessive carbon dioxide in the bloodstream.

Answer (B) is correct. (AIM Para 8-1-2)
    DISCUSSION: Hypoxia is a state of oxygen deficiency in the bloodstream sufficient to impair function of the brain and other organs.
    Answer (A) is incorrect. The problem is insufficient oxygen, not excessive oxygen. **Answer (C) is incorrect.** It is a nonsense answer. Insufficient, not excessive, carbon dioxide in the bloodstream is the result of hyperventilation, not hypoxia.

10. To rid itself of the alcohol contained in one mixed drink, the human body requires about

    A. 1 hour.

    B. 2 hours.

    C. 3 hours.

Answer (C) is correct. (FAA-H-8083-25B Chap 17)
    DISCUSSION: The body requires about 3 hours to rid itself of all the alcohol contained in one mixed drink, one beer, or one glass of wine.
    Answer (A) is incorrect. The body requires 3 hours, not 1 hour, to rid itself of all the alcohol contained in one mixed drink, one beer, or one glass of wine. **Answer (B) is incorrect.** The body requires 3 hours, not 2 hours, to rid itself of all the alcohol contained in one mixed drink, one beer, or one glass of wine.

11. Which is true regarding the presence of alcohol within the human body?

    A. A small amount of alcohol increases vision acuity.

    B. An increase in altitude decreases the adverse effect of alcohol.

    C. Judgment and decision-making abilities can be adversely affected by even small amounts of alcohol.

Answer (C) is correct. (AIM Para 8-1-1)
    DISCUSSION: As little as 1 ounce of liquor, 12 ounces of beer, or 4 ounces (one glass) of wine can impair flying skills, with the alcohol consumed in these drinks being detectable in the breath and blood for at least 3 hr.
    Answer (A) is incorrect. Any amount of alcohol decreases, not increases, virtually all mental and physical activities.
    Answer (B) is incorrect. Increases in altitude increase, not decrease, the adverse effects of alcohol.

12. To rid itself of all the alcohol contained in one beer, the human body requires about

    A. 1 hour.

    B. 4 hours.

    C. 3 hours.

Answer (C) is correct. (FAA-H-8083-25B Chap 17)
    DISCUSSION: The body requires about 3 hours to rid itself of all the alcohol contained in one mixed drink, one beer, or one glass of wine.
    Answer (A) is incorrect. The body requires 3 hours, not 1 hour, to rid itself of all the alcohol contained in one mixed drink, one beer, or one glass of wine. **Answer (B) is incorrect.** The body requires 3 hours, not 4 hours, to rid itself of all the alcohol contained in one mixed drink, one beer, or one glass of wine.

13. With a blood alcohol level below .04 percent, a pilot cannot fly sooner than

    A. 4 hours after drinking alcohol.

    B. 12 hours after drinking alcohol.

    C. 8 hours after drinking alcohol.

Answer (C) is correct. (FAA-H-8083-25B Chap 17)
    DISCUSSION: According to 14 CFR 91.17, a minimum of 8 hours must pass between consuming alcohol and flying an aircraft.
    Answer (A) is incorrect. A pilot who has consumed alcohol must wait more than 4 hours before flying. **Answer (B) is incorrect.** While considerable amounts of alcohol may remain in the body for over 12 hours and it is good to be cautious about flying too soon after drinking, the regulations state that a minimum of 8 hours must elapse between consuming alcohol and flying.

14. You attended a party last night and you consumed several glasses of wine. You are planning to fly your aircraft home and have been careful to make sure 8 hours have passed since your last alcoholic drink. You can make the flight now only if you are not under the influence of alcohol and your blood alcohol level is

    A. below .04%.

    B. below .08%.

    C. 0.0%.

Answer (A) is correct. (14 CFR 91.17)
    DISCUSSION: 14 CFR Part 91 requires that blood alcohol level be less than .04% and that a minimum of 8 hr. passes between drinking alcohol and piloting an aircraft. A pilot with a blood alcohol level of .04% or greater after 8 hr. cannot fly until his or her blood alcohol level falls below that amount. Even though the blood alcohol level may be well below .04%, a pilot cannot fly sooner than the minimum of 8 hr. after drinking alcohol.
    Answer (B) is incorrect. The legal limit for motor vehicle operation in many states is 0.08%. However, to operate an aircraft, a pilot's blood alcohol level must be below .04% and a minimum of 8 hr. must have passed since consuming the last drink. **Answer (C) is incorrect.** The legal limit to operate an aircraft is .04%. With a blood alcohol level of 0.0%, a pilot would be legally able to fly as long as it has been more than the minimum of 8 hr. since his or her last alcoholic beverage.

15. Which of the following could increase susceptibility to hypoxia?

    A. Breathing 100% oxygen at too low of an altitude.

    B. Rapidly descending from a high altitude.

    C. Flying after donating blood.

Answer (C) is correct. (FAA-H-8083-25B Chap 17)
    DISCUSSION: Anemic hypoxia can be caused by a loss of blood, such as after a blood donation. Blood volume can require several weeks to return to normal following a donation. Although the effects of the blood loss are minimal at ground level, there are risks when flying during this time.
    Answer (A) is incorrect. Hypoxia occurs due to a lack of oxygen, so breathing 100% oxygen would not increase susceptibility to hypoxia. **Answer (B) is incorrect.** Descending to a lower altitude increases the amount of breathable oxygen, so this would not increase susceptibility to hypoxia.

16. While experiencing a hangover, a pilot

   A. will have impaired motor and mental responses.
   B. is no longer under the influence of alcohol.
   C. may experience discomfort, but no impairment.

Answer (A) is correct. (FAA-H-8083-25B Chap 17)
   DISCUSSION: While experiencing a hangover, a pilot is still under the influence of alcohol. Although a pilot may think (s)he is functioning normally, motor and mental response impairment is still present.
   Answer (B) is incorrect. Considerable amounts of alcohol can remain in the body for over 16 hours, and the effects and symptoms of a hangover are because of the influence of alcohol. **Answer (C) is incorrect.** Although a pilot may think (s)he is functioning normally, motor and mental response impairment is still present.

17. A pilot making a blood donation in order to help a sick associate should be aware that for several weeks

   A. sufficient oxygen may not reach the cells in the body.
   B. fewer oxygen molecules will be available to the respiratory membranes.
   C. the ability of the body tissues to effectively use oxygen is decreased.

Answer (A) is correct. (FAA-H-8083-25B Chap 17)
   DISCUSSION: Blood donations can cause anemic hypoxia because not enough blood is available to carry a sufficient amount of oxygen to the cells.
   Answer (B) is incorrect. The amount of oxygen available to the body does not change; however, there may not be enough blood to carry the oxygen to the cells. **Answer (C) is incorrect.** The body tissues have not lost the ability to use oxygen; however, the amount of blood available to deliver the oxygen has decreased.

6.2 Hyperventilation

18. Which is a common symptom of hyperventilation?

   A. Drowsiness.
   B. Decreased breathing rate.
   C. Euphoria - sense of well-being.

Answer (A) is correct. (AIM Para 8-1-3)
   DISCUSSION: Hyperventilation is an abnormal increase in breathing, which can occur subconsciously when a stressful situation is encountered. It can cause lightheadedness, drowsiness, suffocation, tingling in the extremities, and coolness.
   Answer (B) is incorrect. Hyperventilation usually occurs from an increased, not a decreased, breathing rate. **Answer (C) is incorrect.** Euphoria is a potential symptom of hypoxia, not hyperventilation.

19. As hyperventilation progresses a pilot can experience

   A. decreased breathing rate and depth.
   B. heightened awareness and feeling of well-being.
   C. symptoms of suffocation and drowsiness.

Answer (C) is correct. (AIM Para 8-1-3)
   DISCUSSION: Hyperventilation is an abnormal increase in breathing, which can occur subconsciously when a stressful situation is encountered. It can cause lightheadedness, drowsiness, suffocation, tingling in the extremities, and coolness.
   Answer (A) is incorrect. Hyperventilation is an increase, not a decrease, of the breathing rate and depth. **Answer (B) is incorrect.** Heightened awareness and euphoria are potential symptoms of hypoxia, not hyperventilation.

20. To overcome the symptoms of hyperventilation, a pilot should

   A. swallow or yawn.
   B. slow the breathing rate.
   C. increase the breathing rate.

Answer (B) is correct. (AIM Para 8-1-3)
   DISCUSSION: A pilot should be able to overcome the symptoms of hyperventilation by slowing the breathing rate or breathing into a bag.
   Answer (A) is incorrect. Swallowing or yawning helps to equalize ear pressures, not overcome hyperventilation. **Answer (C) is incorrect.** Increasing the breathing rate aggravates hyperventilation.

21. Which would most likely result in hyperventilation?

   A. Insufficient oxygen.
   B. Excessive carbon monoxide.
   C. Insufficient carbon dioxide.

Answer (C) is correct. (AIM Para 8-1-3)
   DISCUSSION: Hyperventilation occurs when an excessive amount of carbon dioxide is passed out of the body and too much oxygen is retained.
   Answer (A) is incorrect. It describes hypoxia. **Answer (B) is incorrect.** It describes carbon monoxide poisoning.

22. Which is a common symptom of hyperventilation?

A. Tingling sensations.

B. Visual acuity.

C. Decreased breathing rate.

Answer (A) is correct. (AIM Para 8-1-3)
DISCUSSION: Hyperventilation results from an abnormal increase in the volume of air breathed in and out of the lungs. It can occur subconsciously when a stressful situation is encountered. The result is an excessive amount of carbon dioxide removed from the body. The symptoms are lightheadedness, suffocation, drowsiness, tingling of the extremities, and coolness.
Answer (B) is incorrect. Hyperventilation distorts one's abilities; it does not improve them. **Answer (C) is incorrect.** Decreasing the breathing rate is one way to overcome hyperventilation. It is not a symptom of it.

6.3 Spatial Disorientation

23. Which of the following flight conditions would indicate a pilot is experiencing spatial disorientation?

A. Steep turn.

B. Graveyard spiral.

C. Turns around a point.

Answer (B) is correct. (FAA-H-8083-25B Chap 17)
DISCUSSION: A graveyard spiral is an example of a pilot being adversely affected by spatial disorientation.
Answer (A) is incorrect. Steep turns are common maneuvers performed during training and do not indicate that a pilot is experiencing spatial disorientation. **Answer (C) is incorrect.** Turns around a point are maneuvers performed during training and do not indicate that a pilot is experiencing spatial disorientation.

24. A state of temporary confusion resulting from misleading information being sent to the brain by various sensory organs is defined as

A. spatial disorientation.

B. hyperventilation.

C. hypoxia.

Answer (A) is correct. (AIM Para 8-1-5)
DISCUSSION: A state of temporary confusion resulting from misleading information being sent to the brain by various sensory organs is defined as vertigo (spatial disorientation). Put simply, the pilot cannot determine his or her relationship to the earth's horizon.
Answer (B) is incorrect. Hyperventilation causes excessive oxygen and/or a decrease in carbon dioxide in the bloodstream. **Answer (C) is incorrect.** Hypoxia occurs when there is insufficient oxygen in the bloodstream.

25. How may a pilot overcome spatial disorientation?

A. By relying on his flight instruments.

B. By decreasing the amount of time spent looking inside.

C. By relying on all outside visual references.

Answer (A) is correct. (FAA-H-8083-25B Chap 17)
DISCUSSION: Ways to overcome the effects of spatial disorientation include relying on the airplane instruments, avoiding sudden head movements, and ensuring that outside visual references are fixed points on the surface.
Answer (B) is incorrect. Decreasing the amount of time spent looking inside is not a remedy for overcoming spatial disorientation. **Answer (C) is incorrect.** Not all visual references can be relied on, as some may be moving. A pilot must ensure that any outside visual references are fixed points on the surface.

26. You are most likely to experience somatogravic illusion during

A. a rapid descent.

B. deceleration upon landing.

C. rapid acceleration on takeoff.

Answer (C) is correct. (FAA-H-8083-25B)
DISCUSSION: A rapid acceleration, such as one experienced during takeoff, stimulates the otolith organs (in the inner ear) in the same way as tilting the head backwards. This action may create what is known as the somatogravic illusion of being in a nose-up attitude, especially in conditions with poor visual references.
Answer (A) is incorrect. A rapid acceleration, not a rapid descent, stimulates the otolith organs in the same way as tilting the head backwards, which is a common experience of somatogravic illusion. **Answer (B) is incorrect.** During landing, a rapid deceleration may cause somatogravic illusion with the opposite effect of a rapid acceleration. However, a normal deceleration upon landing should not cause a somatogravic illusion.

27. To cope with spatial disorientation, pilots should rely on

    A. body sensations and outside visual references.

    B. adequate food, rest, and night adaptation.

    C. proficient use of the aircraft instruments.

Answer (C) is correct. (FAA-H-8083-25B Chap 17)

DISCUSSION: The most important way to cope with spatial disorientation is to become proficient in the use of flight instruments and rely on them.

Answer (A) is incorrect. Body sensations should be disregarded, not relied on, to cope with spatial disorientation. Outside visual references may be used to prevent spatial disorientation but only if they are reliable, fixed points on the earth's surface. **Answer (B) is incorrect.** Adequate food, rest, and night adaptions may help you be less susceptible to spatial disorientation but should not be relied on to cope with it.

28. A pilot who needs to overcome the effects of spatial disorientation should

    A. breathe rapidly.

    B. ignore the instruments and rely on body sensations.

    C. place a greater emphasis on the flight instruments.

Answer (C) is correct. (FAA-H-8083-25B Chap 17)

DISCUSSION: A pilot can overcome the effects of spatial disorientation by placing a greater emphasis on the flight instruments. Doing this will help the pilot ignore the kinesthetic sensations encountered during spatial disorientation.

Answer (A) is incorrect. Increasing the rate of respiration will not help the pilot overcome spatial disorientation and can subsequently lead to hyperventilation. **Answer (B) is incorrect.** Relying on the sensations of the body will further increase the effects of spatial disorientation, not decrease the symptoms.

6.4 Pilot Vision

29. To scan properly for traffic, a pilot should

    A. slowly sweep the field of vision from one side to the other at intervals.

    B. concentrate on any peripheral movement detected.

    C. use a series of short, regularly spaced eye movements that bring successive areas of the sky into the central visual field.

Answer (C) is correct. (AIM Para 8-1-6)

DISCUSSION: The most effective way to scan for other aircraft during the day is to use a series of short, regularly spaced eye movements that bring successive areas of the sky into your central vision. Each movement should not exceed 10°, and each area should be observed for at least 1 sec. to facilitate detection.

Answer (A) is incorrect. You must concentrate on different segments systematically. **Answer (B) is incorrect.** Peripheral movement will not be detected easily, especially under adverse conditions such as haze.

30. Which technique should a pilot use to scan for traffic to the right and left during straight-and-level flight?

    A. Systematically focus on different segments of the sky for short intervals.

    B. Concentrate on relative movement detected in the peripheral vision area.

    C. Continuous sweeping of the windshield from right to left.

Answer (A) is correct. (AIM Para 8-1-6)

DISCUSSION: Due to the fact that eyes can focus only on a narrow viewing area, effective scanning is accomplished with a series of short, regularly spaced eye movements that bring successive areas of the sky into the central vision field.

Answer (B) is incorrect. It concerns scanning for traffic at night. **Answer (C) is incorrect.** A pilot must continually scan successive, small portions of the sky. The eyes can focus only on a narrow viewing area and require at least 1 sec. to detect a faraway object.

31. What effect does haze have on the ability to see traffic or terrain features during flight?

    A. Haze causes the eyes to focus at infinity.

    B. The eyes tend to overwork in haze and do not detect relative movement easily.

    C. All traffic or terrain features appear to be farther away than their actual distance.

Answer (C) is correct. (FAA-H-8083-25B Chap 17)

DISCUSSION: Atmospheric haze can create the illusion of being at a greater distance and height from traffic or terrain than you actually are. The pilot who does not recognize this illusion will fly a lower approach.

Answer (A) is incorrect. In haze, the eyes focus at a comfortable distance, which may be only 10 to 30 ft. outside of the flight deck. **Answer (B) is incorrect.** In haze, the eyes relax and tend to stare outside without focusing or looking for common visual cues.

32. Haze creates which of the following atmospheric illusions?

A. Being at a greater distance from the runway.

B. Being at a closer distance from the runway.

C. Haze creates no atmospheric illusions.

Answer (A) is correct. (AIM Para 8-1-5)
  DISCUSSION: Rain on a windscreen can create the illusion of greater height from the runway, and haze can create the illusion of greater distance from the runway; landing errors from these illusions can be overcome by knowledge and anticipation of the illusions.
  Answer (B) is incorrect. Haze creates the illusion of being farther from, not closer to, the runway. **Answer (C) is incorrect.** Haze creates the illusion of being at a greater distance from the runway.

33. The illusion associated with landing on a narrower than usual runway may result in the pilot flying a

A. lower approach with the risk of striking objects along the approach path or landing short.

B. slower approach with the risk of reducing airspeed below VSO or landing hard.

C. higher approach with the risk of leveling out high and landing hard or overshooting the runway.

Answer (A) is correct. (FAA-H-8083-25B Chap 17)
  DISCUSSION: A narrower-than-usual runway can create an illusion that the aircraft is at a higher altitude than it actually is, which could result in striking objects along the flight path or landing short.
  Answer (B) is incorrect. Runway width has no effect on the perceived speed in an approach to landing. **Answer (C) is incorrect.** A wider-, not narrower-, than-usual runway can create the illusion that the aircraft is lower than actual altitude, creating the risk of the pilot leveling out the aircraft high and landing hard or overshooting the runway.

6.5 Aeronautical Decision Making (ADM)

34. Aeronautical Decision Making (ADM) is a

A. systematic approach to the mental process used by pilots to consistently determine the best course of action for a given set of circumstances.

B. decision making process which relies on good judgment to reduce risks associated with each flight.

C. mental process of analyzing all information in a particular situation and making a timely decision on what action to take.

Answer (A) is correct. (AC 60-22, FAA-H-8083-25B Chap 2 and Glossary)
  DISCUSSION: ADM is a systematic approach to the mental process used by pilots to consistently determine the best course of action in response to a given set of circumstances.
  Answer (B) is incorrect. Risk management, not ADM, is the part of the decision-making process that relies on situational awareness, problem recognition, and good judgment to reduce risks associated with each flight. **Answer (C) is incorrect.** Judgment, not ADM, is the mental process of recognizing and analyzing all pertinent information in a particular situation, rationally evaluating alternative actions in response to it, and making a timely decision on which action to take.

35. Risk management, as part of the aeronautical decision making (ADM) process, relies on which features to reduce the risks associated with each flight?

A. Application of stress management and risk element procedures.

B. The mental process of analyzing all information in a particular situation and making a timely decision on what action to take.

C. Situational awareness, problem recognition, and good judgment.

Answer (C) is correct. (AC 60-22, FAA-H-8083-25B Chap 2 and Glossary)
  DISCUSSION: Risk management is that part of the ADM process that relies on situational awareness, problem recognition, and good judgment to reduce risks associated with each flight.
  Answer (A) is incorrect. Risk management relies on situational awareness, problem recognition, and good judgment, not the application of stress management and risk-element procedures, to reduce the risks associated with each flight. **Answer (B) is incorrect.** Judgment, not risk management, is the mental process of analyzing all information in a particular situation and making a timely decision on what action to take.

36. Examples of classic behavioral traps that experienced pilots may fall into are: trying to

- A. assume additional responsibilities and assert PIC authority.
- B. promote situational awareness and then necessary changes in behavior.
- C. complete a flight as planned, please passengers, meet schedules, and demonstrate the "right stuff."

Answer (C) is correct. (AC 60-22)
   DISCUSSION: There are a number of classic behavioral traps into which pilots have been known to fall. Pilots, particularly those with considerable experience, as a rule always try to complete a flight as planned, please passengers, meet schedules, and generally demonstrate that they have the "right stuff."
   Answer (A) is incorrect. Classical behavioral traps include trying to complete a flight as planned, please passengers, meet schedules, and demonstrate the "right stuff," not trying to assume additional responsibilities and assert PIC authority.
   Answer (B) is incorrect. Classical behavioral traps include trying to complete a flight as planned, please passengers, meet schedules, and demonstrate the "right stuff," not trying to promote situational awareness and then necessary changes in behavior.

37. Most pilots have fallen prey to dangerous tendencies or behavior problems at some time. Some of these dangerous tendencies or behavior patterns which must be identified and eliminated include

- A. Deficiencies in instrument skills and knowledge of aircraft systems or limitations.
- B. Performance deficiencies from human factors such as fatigue, illness, or emotional problems.
- C. Peer pressure, get-there-itis, loss of positional or situational awareness, and operating without adequate fuel reserves.

Answer (C) is correct. (AC 60-22)
   DISCUSSION: Peer pressure, get-there-itis, loss of positional or situational awareness, operating without an adequate fuel reserve, and others are dangerous tendencies or behavior patterns that must be identified and eliminated.
   Answer (A) is incorrect. Deficiencies in skills and/or knowledge may be overcome by conventional training and do not represent dangerous tendencies or behavior problems.
   Answer (B) is incorrect. Performance deficiencies caused by fatigue may be overcome by rest, and those caused by illness or emotional problems may be overcome by medical intervention. These deficiencies are physiological; they do not result from dangerous tendencies or behavior patterns.

38. The basic drive for a pilot to demonstrate the "right stuff" can have an adverse effect on safety, by

- A. a total disregard for any alternative course of action.
- B. generating tendencies that lead to practices that are dangerous, often illegal, and may lead to a mishap.
- C. allowing events, or the situation, to control his or her actions.

Answer (B) is correct. (AC 60-22)
   DISCUSSION: The basic drive to demonstrate the "right stuff" can have an adverse effect on safety and can impose an unrealistic assessment of piloting skills under stressful conditions. These tendencies ultimately may lead to practices that are dangerous and often illegal and may result in a mishap.
   Answer (A) is incorrect. "Get-there-itis," not a basic drive to demonstrate the "right stuff," has an adverse effect on safety when a pilot totally disregards any alternative course of action.
   Answer (C) is incorrect. Getting behind the aircraft, not a basic drive to demonstrate the "right stuff," has an adverse effect on safety by allowing events or the situation to control the pilot's actions.

39. The Aeronautical Decision Making (ADM) process identifies the steps involved in good decision making. One of these steps includes a pilot

- A. making a rational evaluation of the required actions.
- B. developing the "right stuff" attitude.
- C. identifying personal attitudes hazardous to safe flight.

Answer (C) is correct. (AC 60-22)
   DISCUSSION: The ADM process addresses all aspects of decision making on the flight deck and identifies the steps involved in good decision making. One step in good decision making is to identify personal attitudes hazardous to safe flight.
   Answer (A) is incorrect. Making a rational evaluation of the required actions is a part of judgment, not a step in good decision making. **Answer (B) is incorrect.** A step in the ADM process is to identify, not develop, a behavioral trap.

40. An early part of the Aeronautical Decision Making (ADM) process involves

A. taking a self-assessment hazardous attitude inventory test.

B. understanding the drive to have the "right stuff."

C. obtaining proper flight instruction and experience during training.

Answer (A) is correct. (AC 60-22)
   DISCUSSION: An early part of the ADM process includes identifying personal attitudes hazardous to safe flight by taking a self-assessment hazardous attitude inventory test.
   Answer (B) is incorrect. Taking a self-assessment hazardous attitude inventory test, not just understanding the drive to have the "right stuff," is an early part of the ADM process. **Answer (C) is incorrect.** Obtaining proper flight instruction and experience during training is critical in the development of a safe pilot but is not a part of the ADM process itself.

41. What are some of the hazardous attitudes dealt with in Aeronautical Decision Making (ADM)?

A. Antiauthority (don't tell me), impulsivity (do something quickly without thinking), macho (I can do it).

B. Risk management, stress management, and risk elements.

C. Poor decision making, situational awareness, and judgment.

Answer (A) is correct. (AC 60-22)
   DISCUSSION: ADM addresses five hazardous attitudes: antiauthority ("Don't tell me"), impulsivity ("Do something quickly without thinking"), invulnerability ("It won't happen to me"), macho ("I can do it"), and resignation ("What's the use?").
   Answer (B) is incorrect. Risk management, stress management, and risk elements are all part of the ADM process, not hazardous attitudes dealt with in ADM. **Answer (C) is incorrect.** Situational awareness and judgment are part of the mental process in ADM to prevent or stop poor judgment, not hazardous attitudes in ADM.

42. The passengers for a charter flight have arrived almost an hour late for a flight that requires a reservation. Which of the following alternatives best illustrates the ANTIAUTHORITY reaction?

A. Those reservation rules do not apply to this flight.

B. If the pilot hurries, he or she may still make it on time.

C. The pilot can't help it that the passengers are late.

Answer (A) is correct. (AC 60-22)
   DISCUSSION: By demonstrating the attitude that rules do not apply to his or her flight, the pilot is illustrating the antiauthority hazardous attitude.
   Answer (B) is incorrect. If the pilot chooses the alternative to hurry in the belief that (s)he may make it on time, the pilot is illustrating the impulsivity reaction, not the antiauthority reaction. **Answer (C) is incorrect.** If the pilot feels that (s)he cannot help that the passengers are late, (s)he is illustrating the resignation reaction, not the antiauthority reaction.

43. The pilot and passengers are anxious to get to their destination for a business presentation. Level IV thunderstorms are reported to be in a line across their intended route of flight. Which of the following alternatives best illustrates the IMPULSIVITY reaction?

A. They want to hurry and get going, before things get worse.

B. A thunderstorm won't stop them.

C. They can't change the weather, so they might as well go.

Answer (A) is correct. (AC 60-22)
   DISCUSSION: The pilot and passengers are anxious to get to their destination for a business presentation, but level 4 thunderstorms are reported to be in a line across their intended route of flight. An impulsivity hazardous attitude ("Act now; there is no time") would be to "hurry and get going" before things get worse.
   Answer (B) is incorrect. A thought of "a thunderstorm will not stop them" is an invulnerability, not impulsivity, hazardous attitude. **Answer (C) is incorrect.** A thought of "they cannot change the weather, so they might as well go" is a resignation, not impulsivity, hazardous attitude.

44. While conducting an operational check of the cabin pressurization system, the pilot discovers that the rate control feature is inoperative. He knows that he can manually control the cabin pressure, so he elects to disregard the discrepancy. Which of the following alternatives best illustrates the INVULNERABILITY reaction?

A. What is the worst that could happen?

B. He can handle a little problem like this.

C. It's too late to fix it now.

Answer (A) is correct. (AC 60-22)
   DISCUSSION: A pilot discovers that the rate control feature is inoperative on the cabin pressurization system, but he elects to disregard the discrepancy since he knows he can manually control the pressurization. An invulnerability ("Nothing bad will happen") reaction would be, "What is the worst that could happen?"
   Answer (B) is incorrect. "He can handle a little problem like this" is a macho reaction, not an invulnerability reaction. **Answer (C) is incorrect.** "It is too late to fix it now" is an impulsivity reaction, not an invulnerability reaction.

45. While on an IFR flight, a pilot emerges from a cloud to find himself within 300 feet of a helicopter. Which of the following alternatives best illustrates the "MACHO" reaction?

   A. He is not too concerned; everything will be alright.

   B. He flies a little closer, just to show him.

   C. He quickly turns away and dives, to avoid collision.

Answer (B) is correct. (AC 60-22)
   DISCUSSION: While on an IFR flight, a pilot emerges from a cloud to find himself within 300 ft. of a helicopter. A hazardous macho reaction would be to fly a little closer, just to "show" the other pilot. Macho hazardous thoughts include "I will show you."
   Answer (A) is incorrect. A reaction of "not too concerned; everything will be all right" is one of invulnerability, not macho.
   Answer (C) is incorrect. A reaction of quickly turning away and diving to avoid a collision is an impulsivity reaction, not a macho reaction.

46. What is the first step in neutralizing a hazardous attitude in the ADM process?

   A. Dealing with improper judgment.

   B. Recognition of hazardous thoughts.

   C. Recognition of invulnerability in the situation.

Answer (B) is correct. (AC 60-22)
   DISCUSSION: The first step in neutralizing hazardous attitudes is recognizing hazardous thoughts. When a pilot recognizes a hazardous thought, (s)he then should correct it by stating the corresponding antidote.
   Answer (A) is incorrect. Recognizing hazardous thoughts, not dealing with improper judgment, is the first step in neutralizing hazardous attitudes. **Answer (C) is incorrect.** Recognizing hazardous thoughts, not the invulnerability in the situation, is the first step in neutralizing hazardous attitudes.

47. A pilot and friends are going to fly to an out-of-town football game. When the passengers arrive, the pilot determines that they will be over the maximum gross weight for takeoff with the existing fuel load. Which of the following alternatives best illustrates the RESIGNATION reaction?

   A. Well, nobody told him about the extra weight.

   B. Weight and balance is a formality forced on pilots by the FAA.

   C. He can't wait around to de-fuel, they have to get there on time.

Answer (A) is correct. (AC 60-22)
   DISCUSSION: A pilot and his friends are going on a flight, but when the passengers arrive, the pilot determines the loaded airplane will be over maximum gross weight for takeoff with the existing fuel load. A resignation reaction by the pilot would be that nobody told him about the extra weight. When the responsibility is assumed to be someone else's, a pilot is in the hazardous thinking pattern of resignation.
   Answer (B) is incorrect. Considering weight and balance to be a formality forced on pilots by the FAA (ignoring the rules) is a hazardous attitude of antiauthority, not resignation. **Answer (C) is incorrect.** The pilot who cannot wait around to de-fuel because of a need to get somewhere on time illustrates the impulsivity ("I must act now; there is no time"), not the resignation, hazardous attitude.

48. Hazardous attitudes which contribute to poor pilot judgment can be effectively counteracted by

   A. early recognition of hazardous thoughts.

   B. taking meaningful steps to be more assertive with attitudes.

   C. redirecting that hazardous attitude so that appropriate action can be taken.

Answer (C) is correct. (AC 60-22)
   DISCUSSION: Hazardous attitudes that contribute to poor pilot judgment can be effectively counteracted by redirecting those hazardous attitudes so that appropriate action can be taken.
   Answer (A) is incorrect. While early recognition of hazardous thoughts is important as an initial step in dealing with hazardous attitudes, they can be effectively counteracted only by redirecting them so that appropriate action can be taken. **Answer (B) is incorrect.** Being more assertive with attitudes, if those attitudes are hazardous, would be counterproductive to safety, while redirecting the hazardous attitudes will allow appropriate action to be taken in dealing with them.

49. What should a pilot do when recognizing a thought as hazardous?

   A. Avoid developing this hazardous thought.

   B. Develop this hazardous thought and follow through with modified action.

   C. Label that thought as hazardous, then correct that thought by stating the corresponding learned antidote.

Answer (C) is correct. (AC 60-22)
   DISCUSSION: When a pilot recognizes a hazardous thought, the pilot should label it as hazardous and then correct it by stating the corresponding learned antidote.
   Answer (A) is incorrect. Once a hazardous thought is recognized, it is too late to avoid developing the thought. The pilot should label the thought as hazardous and then correct it by stating the corresponding learned antidote. **Answer (B) is incorrect.** Once a hazardous thought is recognized, it should not be developed. Instead, the pilot should label the thought as hazardous and then correct it by stating the corresponding learned antidote.

50. When a pilot recognizes a hazardous thought, he or she then should correct it by stating the corresponding antidote. Which of the following is the antidote for antiauthority?

    A. Not so fast. Think first.

    B. It could happen to me.

    C. Follow the rules. They are usually right.

Answer (C) is correct. (AC 60-22)
    DISCUSSION: When you recognize a hazardous thought, you should then correct it by stating the corresponding antidote. The antidote for an antiauthority ("Do not tell me") attitude is "Follow the rules. They are usually right."
    Answer (A) is incorrect. "Not so fast. Think first" is the antidote for the impulsivity, not the antiauthority, attitude.
    Answer (B) is incorrect. "It could happen to me" is the antidote for the invulnerability ("It will not happen to me"), not the antiauthority, attitude.

51. When a pilot recognizes a hazardous thought, he or she then should correct it by stating the corresponding antidote. Which of the following is the antidote for MACHO?

    A. Follow the rules. They are usually right.

    B. Not so fast. Think first.

    C. Taking chances is foolish.

Answer (C) is correct. (AC 60-22)
    DISCUSSION: The antidote for the macho hazardous attitude is: "Taking chances is foolish."
    Answer (A) is incorrect. "Taking chances is foolish" is the antidote for macho, not "Follow the rules. They are usually right," which is the antidote for antiauthority. **Answer (B) is incorrect.** "Taking chances is foolish" is the antidote for macho, rather than "Not so fast. Think first," which is the antidote for impulsivity.

52. What does good flight deck stress management begin with?

    A. Knowing what causes stress.

    B. Eliminating life and flight deck stress issues.

    C. Good life stress management.

Answer (C) is correct. (AC 60-22)
    DISCUSSION: Good flight deck stress management begins with good life stress management, since you will bring the stress in your life into the flight deck with you.
    Answer (A) is incorrect. Knowing what causes stress is required to reduce stress associated with crisis management in the air, but it is not the beginning of flight deck stress management. **Answer (B) is incorrect.** Eliminating life and flight deck stress issues is impossible. In fact, stress is a necessary part of life that increases motivation and heightens your response to meet a challenge.

53. To help manage flight deck stress, pilots must

    A. be aware of life stress situations that are similar to those in flying.

    B. condition themselves to relax and think rationally when stress appears.

    C. avoid situations that will degrade their abilities to handle flight deck responsibilities.

Answer (B) is correct. (AC 60-22)
    DISCUSSION: To help manage flight deck stress, pilots must condition themselves to relax and think rationally when stress occurs.
    Answer (A) is incorrect. Pilots must condition themselves to relax and think rationally when stress occurs since many of the stress coping techniques practiced for life stress management are not usually practical in flight. **Answer (C) is incorrect.** Pilots must condition themselves to relax and think rationally when unavoidable situations occur that could increase stress and degrade their abilities.

54. The Decide Model is comprised of a 6-step process to provide a pilot a logical way of approaching Aeronautical Decision Making. These steps are:

    A. Detect, estimate, choose, identify, do, and evaluate.

    B. Determine, evaluate, choose, identify, do, and eliminate.

    C. Determine, eliminate, choose, identify, detect, and evaluate.

Answer (A) is correct. (AC 60-22)
    DISCUSSION: The Decide Model, comprised of a six-step process, is intended to provide you with a logical way of approaching decision making. The six steps (in order) are detect, estimate, choose, identify, do, and evaluate.
    Answer (B) is incorrect. Detect, not determine, and estimate, not eliminate, are steps in the Decide Model. **Answer (C) is incorrect.** Do, not determine, and estimate, not eliminate, are steps in the Decide Model.

55. Which of the following is the first step of the DECIDE Model for effective risk management and Aeronautical Decision Making (ADM)?

A. Detect.

B. Identify.

C. Evaluate.

Answer (A) is correct. (AC 60-22)

DISCUSSION: The DECIDE Model, comprised of a six-step process, is intended to provide you with a logical way of approaching decision making. The six steps (in order) are detect, estimate, choose, identify, do, and evaluate.

Answer (B) is incorrect. Identify is the fourth step, not the first step, in the DECIDE Model. **Answer (C) is incorrect.** Evaluate is the final step, not the first step, in the DECIDE Model.

56. Which of the following is the final step of the Decide Model for effective risk management and Aeronautical Decision Making?

A. Estimate.

B. Evaluate.

C. Eliminate.

Answer (B) is correct. (AC 60-22)

DISCUSSION: The Decide Model, comprised of a six-step process, is intended to provide you with a logical way of approaching decision making. The six steps (in order) are detect, estimate, choose, identify, do, and evaluate.

Answer (A) is incorrect. Estimate is the second step, not the final step, in the Decide Model. **Answer (C) is incorrect.** Eliminate is not a step in the Decide Model.

57. Why is it important for pilots to obtain adequate rest and sleep?

A. Fatigue may set in and be recognized only after serious errors are made.

B. Flying while fatigued can result in a blood alcohol concentration of 0.04%.

C. Fatigue increases a pilot's tendency to rush and produces "get-there-itis."

Answer (A) is correct. (FAA-H-8083-25B Chap 17)

DISCUSSION: Fatigue can be treacherous because it may not be apparent until serious errors are made. Fatigue can be prevented by adequate rest and sleep as well as regular exercise and proper nutrition.

Answer (B) is incorrect. Fatigue impairs a pilot's judgment and decision-making abilities, but it does not raise blood alcohol concentration. **Answer (C) is incorrect.** Not all pilots react to fatigue in the same way. While some pilots may rush, others will slow down. Many pilots will not even notice a change in their performance or recognize they are fatigued.

58. The most important key to risk management is

A. understanding pilot predisposition.

B. management of external pressures.

C. the sense of security provided by experience.

Answer (B) is correct. (FAA-H-8083-25B Chap 2)

DISCUSSION: Management of external pressures is the single most important key to risk management because it is the one risk factor category that can cause a pilot to ignore all the other risk factors. External pressures put time-related pressure on the pilot and figure into a majority of accidents.

Answer (A) is incorrect. Predisposition is an attitude or tendency to act in a certain way. Although understanding this can alleviate risk, it is not the most important factor in good risk management. **Answer (C) is incorrect.** A sense of security does not necessarily mean that risks have been properly managed, and it may lead to complacency, thereby compounding the existing risks.

59. One purpose of crew resource management (CRM) is to give crews tools to

A. recognize and mitigate hazards.

B. maintain currency with regulations.

C. reduce the need for outside resources.

Answer (A) is correct. (FAA-H-8083-25B Chap 2)

DISCUSSION: CRM is focused on supporting ADM to proactively recognize safety-related hazards and mitigate the associated risks.

Answer (B) is incorrect. Maintaining currency with regulations is the responsibility of each PIC. **Answer (C) is incorrect.** The purpose of CRM is to manage all resources, both onboard and from outside sources.

STUDY UNIT SEVEN

AVIATION WEATHER

(7 pages of outline)

This study unit contains outlines of major concepts tested, sample test questions and answers regarding aviation weather, and an explanation of each answer. The table of contents above lists each subunit within this study unit, the number of questions pertaining to that particular subunit, and the pages on which the outlines and questions begin, respectively.

Recall that the **sole purpose** of this book is to expedite your passing of the FAA pilot knowledge test for the commercial pilot certificate. Accordingly, all extraneous material (i.e., topics or regulations not directly tested on the FAA pilot knowledge test) is omitted, even though much more knowledge is necessary to become a proficient commercial pilot. This additional material is presented in *Pilot Handbook* and *Commercial Pilot Flight Maneuvers and Practical Test Prep*, available from Gleim Publications, Inc. Order online at www.GleimAviation.com.

7.1 CAUSES OF WEATHER

1. Every physical process of weather is accompanied by, or is a result of, heat exchange.

2. Moisture is added to a parcel of air by evaporation and sublimation.

3. Wind is caused by pressure differences with wind flowing from high-pressure areas to low-pressure areas.

    a. When the isobars are close together, the pressure gradient force is greater, which results in a stronger wind.

4. The Coriolis force deflects wind to the right in the Northern Hemisphere.

    a. The Coriolis force tends to counterbalance the horizontal pressure gradient, causing wind to flow parallel to the isobars.

5. A cold front occlusion occurs when the air ahead of the warm front is warmer than the air behind the overtaking cold front.

6. After passage of a cold front, there will typically be a clearing of the sky with gusty, turbulent winds and a cooling of the temperature.

7.2 HIGH/LOW PRESSURE AREAS

1. A high-pressure area or ridge is an area of descending air.

    a. The general circulation of air in a high-pressure area in the Northern Hemisphere is outward, downward, and clockwise.

2. A low-pressure area or trough is an area of rising air.

    a. The circulation of air (wind system) in a low-pressure area in the Northern Hemisphere is cyclonic, i.e., counterclockwise.

    b. Thus, when flying into such a low-pressure area, the wind direction and velocity will be from the left and increasing.

    c. A low-pressure area is generally an area of unfavorable weather conditions.

3. In the Northern Hemisphere, when planning a flight from west to east, favorable winds would be encountered along the northern side of a high-pressure system or the southern side of a low-pressure system.

    a. On the return flight, the most favorable winds would be along the southern side of the same high-pressure system or the northern side of a low-pressure system.

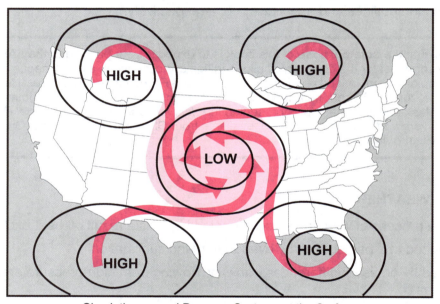

Circulation around Pressure Systems at the Surface

4. The Coriolis force prevents wind from flowing directly from high-pressure areas to low-pressure areas and produces the associated circulations.

7.3 JET STREAM

1. In the middle latitudes during the winter months, the jet stream shifts south and the wind speed increases.

    a. It is normally weaker and farther north in the summer.

2. Clear air turbulence (CAT) is typically found in an upper trough on the polar side of the jet stream.

3. The jet stream and associated CAT can sometimes be visually identified by long streaks of cirrus clouds.

4. Strong wind shears can be expected on the low-pressure side of a jet stream core where the wind speed at the core is greater than 110 kt.

5. A curving jet stream means there are abrupt weather system changes, which lend themselves to more violent turbulence.

6. The tropopause is the layer of air above the troposphere and is characterized by an abrupt change in the temperature lapse rate.

7.4 TEMPERATURE

1. Standard temperature is 15°C (59°F) at sea level; the standard lapse rate is 2°C per 1,000 ft.

    a. Thus, the standard temperature at any altitude is 15°C minus (2 times the altitude in thousands of feet).

    b. EXAMPLE: Standard temperature at 20,000 ft. is 15°C – (2 × 20) = –25°C.

    c. Normally, temperature decreases as altitude increases. A temperature inversion occurs when temperature increases as altitude increases.

2. Standard sea level pressure is 29.92 in. Hg or 1013.2 mb.

3. The temperature/dew point spread decreases as relative humidity increases.

7.5 CLOUDS

1. When air is being forced to ascend, the stability of air before lifting occurs determines the structure or type of clouds that will form.

   a. This means the stability of an air mass can usually be determined by the cloud types and the type of precipitation.

2. When a cold air mass moves over a warm surface, the result is unstable air.

   a. Unstable conditions, moist air, and a lifting action provide cumuliform clouds, good visibility, showery rain, and possible clear icing in clouds.

   b. Towering cumulus clouds indicate convective turbulence.

3. The altitude of cumuliform cloud bases can be estimated using surface temperature/dew point spread.

   a. Unsaturated air in a convective current cools at about 3.0°C per 1,000 ft., and dew point decreases about 0.5°C per 1,000 ft.

   b. Thus, temperature and dew point converge at about 2.5°C per 1,000 ft.

   c. Cloud bases are at the altitude where the temperature and dew point are the same.

4. Standing lenticular altocumulus clouds are a good indication of very strong turbulence.

5. Virga describes streamers of precipitation trailing beneath clouds but evaporating before reaching the ground.

   a. The process of evaporation cools the air around virga and can create strong downdrafts.

   b. In some cases, virga can indicate the presence of a microburst.

7.6 FOG

1. Evaporation or precipitation-induced fog arises from drops of warm rain or drizzle falling through cool air.

   a. This kind of fog is produced by frontal activity.

   b. Precipitation-induced fog is an in-flight hazard most commonly associated with warm fronts.

2. Advection fog can form when an air mass moves inland from the coastline during winter.

   a. It is most common along coastal areas.

   b. Wind stronger than 15 kt. dissipates or lifts the fog into low stratus clouds.

   c. It is usually more persistent than radiation fog and can appear suddenly during day or night.

3. Radiation fog is the result of a surface-based temperature inversion that occurs on clear, cool nights with calm or light wind.

   a. It is restricted to land areas.

   b. Temperature and radiation variations over land with a clear sky typically lead to the minimum temperature occurring just after sunrise when the incoming solar radiation is not yet strong enough to offset the terrestrial radiation from the Earth.

4. Steam fog occurs when cold air moves over relatively warm water or wet ground.

5. While flying at night, penetrating a fog layer can create the illusion of pitching up. Often, if the pilot does not recognize this illusion, (s)he will steepen the approach excessively, leading to increased speed at a steeper approach angle.

7.7 STABILITY

1. The stability of the atmosphere is determined by the ambient lapse rate, which is the decrease in temperature with altitude.

2. Warming from below decreases the stability of an air mass.

   a. Cooling from below increases the stability of an air mass.

3. The formation of either predominantly stratiform or cumuliform clouds is dependent upon the stability of the air being lifted.

   a. If clouds form as a result of stable, moist air ascending a mountain slope, the clouds will be stratus type.

4. The lifted index is computed as if a parcel of air near the surface were lifted to the 500-mb level (18,000 ft. MSL).

5. Convective circulation is caused by unequal heating of air by the Earth's surface.

   a. An example is sea and land breezes created by land absorbing and radiating heat faster than water.

   b. Cool air sinks because it is denser than warm air. The sinking cool air displaces the warmer, less dense air, which then rises.

Characteristics of Stable and Unstable Air

Condition	Stable	Unstable
Temperature decreases as altitude increases	Little or none	More than normal so air rises as soon as lifting action occurs
Temperature of air	Cool	Warm
Moisture content	Dry	Humid
Clouds	Stratiform Flat, layered	Cumuliform Billowy, cumulus
Turbulence	Relatively little	Turbulent, strong updrafts
Visibility	Poor	Good
Precipitation	Steady	Showery, intermittent

7.8 THUNDERSTORMS AND ICING

1. Extreme turbulence in a thunderstorm is indicated by very frequent lightning and roll clouds on the leading edge of cumulonimbus clouds.

    a. A lifting action and unstable, moist air are necessary for the formation of cumulonimbus clouds.

2. The life of a thunderstorm can be divided into three stages:

    a. The cumulus stage is associated with continuous updraft.
    b. The mature stage is indicated by the start of rain at the Earth's surface.
    c. The dissipating stage is characterized predominantly by downdrafts.

3. Outside thunderstorm clouds, shear turbulence can be encountered 20 NM laterally from severe storms.

    a. Do not attempt to fly under the anvil of a thunderstorm because there is still potential for severe and extreme clear air turbulence.

4. A squall line is a non-frontal, narrow band of active thunderstorms.

    a. It often contains severe steady-state thunderstorms and presents the single most intense weather hazard to aircraft.

    b. It is also associated with destructive winds, heavy hail, and tornadoes.

5. Airborne weather avoidance radar is designed to identify areas of precipitation, especially heavy precipitation, which may signify an active thunderstorm or severe weather.

    a. Instrument weather conditions can be caused by clouds that are not indicated on radar screens.

    b. Intense radar echoes should be avoided by at least 20 NM.

        1) Thus, 40 NM should exist between intense echoes before you attempt to fly between them.

6. Hail, an in-flight hazard, is likely to be associated with cumulonimbus clouds.

    a. Hailstones may be encountered in clear air several miles from a thunderstorm.

    b. Pilots should anticipate possible hail with any thunderstorm, especially beneath the anvil of a large cumulonimbus.

7. When a warm front (or a cold front) is about to pass, any rain freezes as it falls from the warmer air into air having a temperature of 32°F or less.

    a. As the freezing rain continues to fall, it turns into ice pellets.
    b. Thus, ice pellets indicate freezing rain at a higher altitude.
    c. Extreme vigilance should be exercised when flying in or around freezing conditions, especially with autopilot engaged.

        1) The autopilot will hold vertical speed on climbs or altitude in cruise regardless of whether the deicing equipment is functioning. This may cause the autopilot to allow a stall.

7.9 TURBULENCE

1. Light turbulence momentarily causes slight, erratic changes in altitude and/or attitude.

2. Moderate turbulence causes changes in altitude and/or attitude, but aircraft control remains positive.

    a. Moderate turbulence should be expected where vertical wind shear exceeds 5 kt. per 1,000 ft.

3. Clear air turbulence (CAT) is a higher-level phenomenon, i.e., above 15,000 ft. AGL, not associated with cumuliform cloudiness.

4. When wind flows over ridges or mountain ranges, it flows up the windward side and down the leeward side.

    a. A pilot who approaches mountainous terrain from the leeward side may be forced into the side of the mountain by the downward-flowing air.

    b. Wave formation should be expected with stable air at mountaintop altitude and winds of at least 20 kt. across the mountaintop.

        1) The most dangerous feature of mountain waves is the turbulent areas in and below rotor clouds.

5. Convective currents are most active on warm summer afternoons when winds are light.

7.10 WIND SHEAR

1. Wind shear is a change in wind direction and/or speed within a very short distance in the atmosphere.

    a. It can be present at any level and can exist in both a horizontal and vertical direction.

2. Hazardous wind shear is commonly encountered during periods of strong temperature inversion and near thunderstorms.

    a. Low-level wind shear may occur when there is a low-level temperature inversion with strong winds above the inversion.

3. During an approach, possible wind shear is indicated by changes in the power and vertical velocity required to remain on the proper glide path.

    a. A sudden decrease in headwind results in a loss of indicated airspeed equal to the decrease in wind velocity.

4. While approaching for landing when either possible wind shear or convective turbulence is indicated, you should increase approach airspeed slightly above normal to avoid stalling.

QUESTIONS AND ANSWER EXPLANATIONS: All of the commercial pilot knowledge test questions chosen by the FAA for release as well as additional questions selected by Gleim relating to the material in the previous outlines are provided on the following pages. These questions have been organized into the same subunits as the outlines. To the immediate right of each question are the correct answer and answer explanations. You should cover these answers and answer explanations while responding to the questions. Refer to the general discussion in the Introduction on how to take the FAA knowledge test.

Remember that the questions from the FAA knowledge test bank have been reordered by topic and organized into a meaningful sequence. Also, the first line of the answer explanation gives the citation of the authoritative source for the answer.

QUESTIONS

7.1 Causes of Weather

1. Every physical process of weather is accompanied by or is the result of

A.   a heat exchange.

B.   the movement of air.

C.   a pressure differential.

Answer (A) is correct. (AC 00-6B Chap 2)
   DISCUSSION: Every physical process of weather is accompanied by, or is the result of, a heat exchange. A heat differential (difference between the temperatures of two air masses) causes a differential in pressure, which in turn causes movement of air. Heat exchanges occur constantly, e.g., melting, cooling, evaporation, condensation, updrafts, downdrafts, wind, etc.
   Answer (B) is incorrect. Movement of air is caused by heat exchanges. **Answer (C) is incorrect.** Pressure differentials are caused by heat exchanges.

2. Moisture is added to a parcel of air by

A.   sublimation and condensation.

B.   evaporation and condensation.

C.   evaporation and sublimation.

Answer (C) is correct. (FAA-H-8083-25B Chap 12)
   DISCUSSION: Moisture is added to a parcel of air when liquid water or ice are changed into water vapor. Evaporation is the change from liquid water to water vapor. Sublimation is the change from ice directly to water vapor, without the intervening liquid stage.
   Answer (A) is incorrect. Condensation is the changing of water vapor into liquid water, which removes (not adds) moisture from the air. **Answer (B) is incorrect.** Condensation is the changing of water vapor into liquid water, which removes (not adds) moisture from the air.

3. Why does the wind have a tendency to flow parallel to the isobars above the friction level?

A.   Coriolis force tends to counterbalance the horizontal pressure gradient.

B.   Coriolis force acts perpendicular to a line connecting the highs and lows.

C.   Friction of the air with the Earth deflects the air perpendicular to the pressure gradient.

Answer (A) is correct. (AC 00-6B Chap 7)
   DISCUSSION: Normally, wind flows from areas of high pressure to areas of low pressure. Wind is deflected by the Coriolis force, however. This force, which is the result of the Earth's rotation, deflects wind to the right in the Northern Hemisphere, counterbalancing the horizontal pressure gradient. Its effects are lessened by friction with the Earth's surface at altitudes closer to the surface.
   Answer (B) is incorrect. The Coriolis force acts at a right angle to wind direction in direct proportion to wind speed. Also, the Coriolis force varies with latitude from zero at the equator to maximum at the poles. **Answer (C) is incorrect.** Surface friction tends to diminish the Coriolis force and permits the wind to follow the pressure gradient force.

4. In the Northern Hemisphere, the wind is deflected to the

A.   right by Coriolis force.

B.   right by surface friction.

C.   left by Coriolis force.

Answer (A) is correct. (AC 00-6B Chap 7)
   DISCUSSION: The Coriolis force, caused by the Earth's rotation, deflects air movements to the right in the Northern Hemisphere and to the left in the Southern Hemisphere. The Coriolis force is at a right angle to wind direction and is directly proportional to wind speed.
   Answer (B) is incorrect. Surface friction slows wind speed, which lessens the deflection to the right caused by the Coriolis force. **Answer (C) is incorrect.** Wind is deflected to the left by the Coriolis force in the Southern (not Northern) Hemisphere.

5. With regard to windflow patterns shown on surface analysis charts; when the isobars are

    A. close together, the pressure gradient force is slight and wind velocities are weaker.

    B. not close together, the pressure gradient force is greater and wind velocities are stronger.

    C. close together, the pressure gradient force is greater and wind velocities are stronger.

Answer (C) is correct. (FAA-H-8083-25B Chap 12)
    DISCUSSION: Pressure differences create a force, the pressure gradient force, which drives the wind from higher pressure to lower pressure. This force is perpendicular to isobars, or pressure contours. The closer the spacing of isobars, the stronger the pressure gradient force and the stronger the wind.
    Answer (A) is incorrect. When the isobars are close together, the pressure gradient force and wind are stronger (not weaker). **Answer (B) is incorrect.** When the isobars are not close together, the pressure gradient force and wind are weaker (not stronger).

6. What causes wind?

    A. The Earth's rotation.

    B. Air mass modification.

    C. Pressure differences.

Answer (C) is correct. (AC 00-6B Chap 2)
    DISCUSSION: Wind is caused by pressure differences with wind flowing from high-pressure areas to low-pressure areas. These pressure differences arise from the different heating of the Earth's surface.
    Answer (A) is incorrect. The Earth's rotation results in the Coriolis force, which deflects wind but does not cause wind. It deflects it to the right in the Northern Hemisphere. **Answer (B) is incorrect.** Air mass modification refers to air masses taking on the properties of the underlying region(s) after they leave their source region.

7. Which is true regarding a cold front occlusion? The air ahead of the warm front

    A. is colder than the air behind the overtaking cold front.

    B. is warmer than the air behind the overtaking cold front.

    C. has the same temperature as the air behind the overtaking cold front.

Answer (B) is correct. (FAA-H-8083-25B Chap 12)
    DISCUSSION: An occluded front, or occlusion, occurs when a cold front overtakes a warm front. A cold front occlusion occurs when the cool air ahead of the warm front is warmer than the cold air behind the overtaking cold front, lifting the warm front aloft.
    Answer (A) is incorrect. When the cool air ahead of the warm front is colder than that behind the cold front, a warm front (not cold front) occlusion occurs. **Answer (C) is incorrect.** When the cool air ahead of the warm front has the same temperature as that behind the cold front, a temperature inversion (not a cold front occlusion) is likely to occur.

8. You have delayed your flight to allow a fast moving cold front to clear your destination airport before your arrival. What type of flying conditions would you expect after the front has passed?

    A. A fast moving squall line with high winds and thunderstorms.

    B. Clear skies with gusty, turbulent winds and cooler temperatures.

    C. Low clouds, reduced visibility and showery, misty conditions.

Answer (B) is correct. (AC 00-6B Chap 10)
    DISCUSSION: The conditions that may be expected upon passage of a cold front are the clearing of precipitation and cumulus clouds; gusty, turbulent winds; and a temperature decrease.
    Answer (A) is incorrect. Fast-moving squall lines tend to form along or ahead of a cold front, often producing strong winds, large hail, frequent lightning, and heavy rainfall. **Answer (C) is incorrect.** Low clouds; reduced visibility; and showery, misty conditions are typically associated with a low-level temperature inversion layer.

9. On Surface Analysis Charts, widely spaced isobars indicate a

    A. weak pressure gradient.

    B. strong pressure gradient.

    C. relatively turbulent wind.

Answer (A) is correct. (FAA-H-8083-25B Chap 12)
    DISCUSSION: Weak pressure gradients are represented by isobars that are spaced far apart and are indicative of light winds.
    Answer (B) is incorrect. Strong pressure gradients are represented by isobars that are spaced close together and are indicative of strong winds. **Answer (C) is incorrect.** The Surface Analysis Charts do not give direct information about turbulent winds.

7.2   High/Low Pressure Areas

10. While flying cross-country in the Northern Hemisphere, you experience a continuous left crosswind which is associated with a major wind system. This indicates that you

   A. are flying toward an area of generally unfavorable weather conditions.

   B. have flown from an area of unfavorable weather conditions.

   C. cannot determine weather conditions without knowing pressure changes.

Answer (A) is correct. *(FAA-H-8083-25B Chap 12)*
DISCUSSION: Due to the counterclockwise circulation around a low-pressure area in the Northern Hemisphere, a continuous left crosswind indicates that you are flying into such an area. Low-pressure areas are areas of rising air that are conducive to cloudiness and precipitation (generally unfavorable weather conditions).
    Answer (B) is incorrect. When flying away from unfavorable weather, you are generally flying out of a low-pressure area, which means you should have a right, not left, crosswind. **Answer (C) is incorrect.** The wind can give you a general indication of pressure changes and thus weather.

11. Which is true with respect to a high- or low-pressure system?

   A. A high-pressure area or ridge is an area of rising air.

   B. A low-pressure area or trough is an area of descending air.

   C. A high-pressure area or ridge is an area of descending air.

Answer (C) is correct. *(AC 00-6B Chap 11)*
DISCUSSION: High-pressure air descends because it is heavier than low-pressure air. Ridge refers to an elongated area of high pressure.
    Answer (A) is incorrect. High-pressure air descends, not rises. **Answer (B) is incorrect.** Low-pressure air rises, not descends.

12. Which is true regarding high- or low-pressure systems?

   A. A high-pressure area or ridge is an area of rising air.

   B. A low-pressure area or trough is an area of rising air.

   C. Both high- and low-pressure areas are characterized by descending air.

Answer (B) is correct. *(AC 00-6B Chap 4)*
DISCUSSION: Low-pressure air rises because it weighs less than high-pressure air. Trough refers to an elongated area of low pressure.
    Answer (A) is incorrect. High-pressure air descends, not rises. **Answer (C) is incorrect.** High-pressure air descends, and low-pressure air rises, not descends.

13. When flying into a low-pressure area in the Northern Hemisphere, the wind direction and velocity will be from the

   A. left and decreasing.

   B. left and increasing.

   C. right and decreasing.

Answer (B) is correct. *(FAA-H-8083-25B Chap 12)*
DISCUSSION: When flying into a low-pressure area, the wind is flowing counterclockwise and thus will be from the left. Also, winds tend to be greater in low-pressure systems than in high-pressure systems, so the velocity will increase as you fly into the area.
    Answer (A) is incorrect. The wind is usually increasing, not decreasing, as you fly into a low-pressure area. **Answer (C) is incorrect.** The wind will be from the left, not right, and the wind is usually increasing, not decreasing, as you fly into a low-pressure area.

14. What prevents air from flowing directly from high-pressure areas to low-pressure areas?

   A. Coriolis force.

   B. Surface friction.

   C. Pressure gradient force.

Answer (A) is correct. *(AC 00-6B Chap 7)*
DISCUSSION: The Coriolis force, caused by the Earth's rotation, deflects air movements to the right in the Northern Hemisphere and to the left in the Southern Hemisphere. The Coriolis force is at a right angle to wind direction and is directly proportional to wind speed. Thus, air is deflected to the right as it flows from high-pressure areas to low-pressure areas.
    Answer (B) is incorrect. Surface friction encourages air movement directly from highs to lows by decreasing wind speed, which decreases the Coriolis force effect. **Answer (C) is incorrect.** The pressure gradient force causes the initial movement from high-pressure areas to low-pressure areas.

15. The general circulation of air associated with a high-pressure area in the Northern Hemisphere is

    A. outward, downward, and clockwise.

    B. outward, upward, and clockwise.

    C. inward, downward, and clockwise.

Answer (A) is correct. (FAA-H-8083-25B Chap 12)
    DISCUSSION: Air flows outward from a high-pressure area, causing a descending column of air within the high. As the air moves outward, it is deflected to the right by the Coriolis force, resulting in a clockwise rotation.
    Answer (B) is incorrect. Air flows downward (not upward) in a high-pressure area. **Answer (C) is incorrect.** Air flows outward (not inward) from a high-pressure area.

16. The wind system associated with a low-pressure area in the Northern Hemisphere is

    A. an anticyclone and is caused by descending cold air.

    B. a cyclone and is caused by Coriolis force.

    C. an anticyclone and is caused by Coriolis force.

Answer (B) is correct. (FAA-H-8083-25B Chap 12)
    DISCUSSION: Air flowing into a low-pressure area is deflected to the right in the Northern Hemisphere, resulting in a counterclockwise (or cyclonic) circulation.
    Answer (A) is incorrect. An anticyclone and descending air describes a high- (not low-) pressure area. **Answer (C) is incorrect.** An anticyclone caused by the Coriolis force describes a high- (not low-) pressure area.

17. There is a high pressure system that is located south of your planned route in the Northern Hemisphere on a west to east cross-country flight. To take advantage of favorable winds, you would plan your route

    A. on the north side of the high pressure area.

    B. on the south side of the high pressure area.

    C. through the middle of the high pressure area.

Answer (A) is correct. (FAA-H-8083-25B Chap 12)
    DISCUSSION: In the Northern Hemisphere, the flow of air from an area of high to low pressure is deflected to the right and produces a clockwise circulation around an area of high pressure. This is known as anticyclonic circulation. When planning a flight from west to east, favorable winds would be encountered along the northern side of a high-pressure system.
    Answer (B) is incorrect. On a flight from west to east, the most favorable winds would be along the northern side of the high-pressure system. **Answer (C) is incorrect.** In the Northern Hemisphere, the flow of air from an area of high to low pressure is deflected to the right and produces a clockwise circulation around an area of high pressure. This is known as anticyclonic circulation. When planning a flight from west to east, favorable winds would be encountered along the northern side of a high-pressure system or the southern side of a low-pressure system.

7.3 Jet Stream

18. During the winter months in the middle latitudes, the jet stream shifts toward the

    A. north and speed decreases.

    B. south and speed increases.

    C. north and speed increases.

Answer (B) is correct. (AC 00-6B Chap 8)
    DISCUSSION: The jet stream is a narrow band of strong winds meandering through the atmosphere at an altitude near the tropopause. In the mid-latitudes, the wind speed in the jet stream is considerably stronger in winter than in summer. Also, the jet stream shifts farther south in winter than in summer.
    Answer (A) is incorrect. The jet stream shifts south (not north) and speed increases (not decreases) in the winter months. **Answer (C) is incorrect.** The jet stream shifts south (not north) in the winter months.

19. The strength and location of the jet stream is normally

    A. weaker and farther north in the summer.

    B. stronger and farther north in the winter.

    C. stronger and farther north in the summer.

Answer (A) is correct. (AC 00-6B Chap 8)
    DISCUSSION: The jet stream is a narrow band of strong winds meandering through the atmosphere at an altitude near the tropopause. In the mid-latitudes, the wind speed in the jet stream is considerably stronger in winter than in summer. Also, the jet stream shifts farther south in winter than in summer.
    Answer (B) is incorrect. The jet stream is normally farther south (not north) in the winter. **Answer (C) is incorrect.** The jet stream is normally weaker in the summer.

20. A common location of clear air turbulence is

A. in an upper trough on the polar side of a jet stream.

B. near a ridge aloft on the equatorial side of a high-pressure flow.

C. south of an east/west oriented high-pressure ridge in its dissipating stage.

Answer (A) is correct. (AC 00-30C)
DISCUSSION: The typical location of clear air turbulence is an upper trough on the cold (polar) side of the jet stream.
Answer (B) is incorrect. Most clear air turbulence is on the northern or polar (not equatorial) side of contrasting air masses.
Answer (C) is incorrect. Most clear air turbulence is on the northern or polar (not southern) side of contrasting air masses.

21. A strong wind shear can be expected

A. in the jetstream front above a core having a speed of 60 to 90 knots.

B. if the 5°C isotherms are spaced between 7° to 10° of latitude.

C. on the low-pressure side of a jetstream core where the speed at the core is stronger than 110 knots.

Answer (C) is correct. (AC 00-30C)
DISCUSSION: When the speed of the jet stream is in excess of 110 knots, strong wind shears can be expected on the lower-pressure side.
Answer (A) is incorrect. Wind speeds of less than 100 knots are not dramatic in the jet stream. Also, the turbulence is usually to the sides or beneath the core.
Answer (B) is incorrect. This answer choice does not indicate abrupt temperature or wind changes (which cause wind shear).

22. The jet stream and associated clear air turbulence can sometimes be visually identified in flight by

A. dust or haze at flight level.

B. long streaks of cirrus clouds.

C. a constant outside air temperature.

Answer (B) is correct. (AC 00-6B Chap 21)
DISCUSSION: Streamlined, windswept cirrus clouds always indicate very strong upper winds.
Answer (A) is incorrect. The presence of dust or haze means there is not much wind or air movement to dissipate the particles. **Answer (C) is incorrect.** Clear air turbulence is caused by mixing cold and warm air at different pressure levels.

23. Which type of jetstream can be expected to cause the greater turbulence?

A. A straight jetstream associated with a low-pressure trough.

B. A curving jetstream associated with a deep low-pressure trough.

C. A jetstream occurring during the summer at the lower latitudes.

Answer (B) is correct. (AC 00-30C)
DISCUSSION: A curving jet stream indicates abrupt weather system changes, which lend themselves to more violent turbulence. In general, the more pronounced the difference in weather systems, the greater the potential for very strong turbulence.
Answer (A) is incorrect. A straight jet stream normally produces less turbulence than a curving jet stream. **Answer (C) is incorrect.** The jet stream is weaker in the summer, when it usually does not get to the lower latitudes.

24. Which feature is associated with the tropopause?

A. Constant height above the Earth.

B. Abrupt change in temperature lapse rate.

C. Absolute upper limit of cloud formation.

Answer (B) is correct. (AC 00-6B Chap 1)
DISCUSSION: The tropopause is the transition layer of atmosphere between the troposphere and the stratosphere. Height of the tropopause varies from about 65,000 ft. over the equator to 20,000 ft. or lower over the poles. A characteristic of the tropopause is an abrupt change in the temperature lapse rate, i.e., the rate at which temperature decreases with height.
Answer (A) is incorrect. The tropopause is considerably closer to the Earth's surface at the poles than at the equator.
Answer (C) is incorrect. Clouds may form above the tropopause.

7.4　Temperature

25. What is the standard temperature at 10,000 feet?

    A.　–5°C.

    B.　–15°C.

    C.　+5°C.

Answer (A) is correct. *(FAA-H-8083-25B Chap 4)*
    DISCUSSION: Standard temperature is 15°C at sea level, and the standard lapse rate is 2°C per 1,000 feet. Thus, at 10,000 feet, the standard temperature would be 20°C colder than at sea level, or –5°C (15°C – 20°C).
    Answer (B) is incorrect. The standard temperature at 15,000 feet (not 10,000 feet) is –15°C. **Answer (C) is incorrect.** The standard temperature at 5,000 feet (not 10,000 feet) is +5°C.

26. What are the standard temperature and pressure values for sea level?

    A.　15°C and 29.92" Hg.

    B.　59°F and 1013.2" Hg.

    C.　15°C and 29.92 Mb.

Answer (A) is correct. *(FAA-H-8083-25B Chap 4)*
    DISCUSSION: Standard temperature at sea level is defined as 15°C, or 59°F. Standard sea-level pressure is 29.92 in. Hg, or 1013.2 mb.
    Answer (B) is incorrect. Standard sea-level pressure is 1013.2 mb (not in. Hg). **Answer (C) is incorrect.** Standard sea-level pressure is 29.92 in. Hg (not mb).

27. Which is true regarding actual air temperature and dew point temperature spread? The temperature spread

    A.　decreases as the relative humidity decreases.

    B.　decreases as the relative humidity increases.

    C.　increases as the relative humidity increases.

Answer (B) is correct. *(FAA-H-8083-25B Chap 12)*
    DISCUSSION: Dew point refers to the temperature to which air must be cooled to become saturated by the water vapor already present in the air. Thus, as the relative humidity increases, the dew point-temperature spread decreases. As relative humidity increases to 100%, the dew point approaches the temperature and the spread approaches zero.
    Answer (A) is incorrect. As relative humidity decreases, the temperature/dew point spread increases (not decreases). **Answer (C) is incorrect.** The temperature/dew point spread decreases (not increases) as relative humidity increases.

28. What is the standard temperature at 20,000 feet?

    A.　–15°C.

    B.　–20°C.

    C.　–25°C.

Answer (C) is correct. *(FAA-H-8083-25B Chap 4)*
    DISCUSSION: Standard temperature is 15°C at sea level and the standard lapse rate is 2°C per 1,000 feet. Thus, at 20,000 feet, the standard temperature would be 40°C colder than at sea level, or –25°C (15°C – 40°C).
    Answer (A) is incorrect. The standard temperature at 15,000 feet (not 20,000 feet) is –15°C. **Answer (B) is incorrect.** The standard temperature at 17,500 feet (not 20,000 feet) is –20°C.

29. What is the standard temperature at 6,500 feet?

    A.　15°C.

    B.　2°C.

    C.　38°F.

Answer (B) is correct. *(FAA-H-8083-25B Chap 4)*
    DISCUSSION: Standard temperature is 15°C at sea level, and the standard lapse rate is 2°C per 1,000 feet. Thus, at 6,500 feet, the standard temperature would be 13°C colder than at sea level, or 2°C (15°C – 13°C).
    Answer (A) is incorrect. The standard temperature at sea level is 15°C. **Answer (C) is incorrect.** At 6,000 feet, the temperature would be approximately 3.4°C or 38.1°F.

30. An increase in temperature with an altitude increase

    A.　is indication of an inversion.

    B.　denotes the beginning of the stratosphere.

    C.　means a cold front passage.

Answer (A) is correct. *(FAA-H-8083-25B Chap 12)*
    DISCUSSION: Normally, as air rises and expands in the atmosphere, the temperature decreases. However, when the temperature of the air increases with altitude, this indicates that a temperature inversion exists.
    Answer (B) is incorrect. Although the temperature does begin to increase in the stratosphere, only specialized aircraft are likely to be able to operate high enough to see this change. **Answer (C) is incorrect.** A cold front passage does not always cause the temperature to increase with altitude. If it did, this would be an indication of an inversion.

7.5 Clouds

31. Which cloud types would indicate convective turbulence?

    A. Cirrus clouds.

    B. Nimbostratus clouds.

    C. Towering cumulus clouds.

Answer (C) is correct. (AC 00-6B Chap 17)
    DISCUSSION: Towering cumulus clouds signify a relatively deep layer of unstable air, thus indicating very strong convective turbulence.
    Answer (A) is incorrect. Cirrus clouds are high, thin, feathery ice crystal clouds in patches and narrow bands that are not generated by any convective activity. **Answer (B) is incorrect.** Nimbostratus are gray or dark, massive clouds, usually producing continuous rain or ice pellets. They form in stable air and do not produce convective activity or turbulence.

32. What is the approximate base of the cumulus clouds if the temperature at 2,000 feet MSL is 10°C and the dew point is 1°C?

    A. 3,000 feet MSL.

    B. 4,000 feet MSL.

    C. 6,000 feet MSL.

Answer (C) is correct. (FAA-H-8083-25B Chap 12)
    DISCUSSION: The height of cumuliform cloud bases can be estimated using the surface temperature/dew point spread. Unsaturated air in a convective current cools at about 3°C per 1,000 feet, and dew point decreases about 0.5°C per 1,000 feet. Thus, temperature and dew point converge at about 2.5°C per 1,000 feet. Since the temperature/dew point spread was 9°C (10 − 1), temperature and dew point will converge at 3,600 feet AGL (9 ÷ 2.5 = 3.6 or 3,600). The base of the cumulus clouds is approximately 5,600 feet MSL (3,600 + 2,000).
    Answer (A) is incorrect. This is the approximate base of the cumulus clouds if the dew point of 1°C, not the temperature/dew point spread of 9°C, is divided by 2.5. **Answer (B) is incorrect.** The base of the cumulus clouds is approximately 4,000 feet AGL, not 4,000 feet MSL.

33. What determines the structure or type of clouds which will form as a result of air being forced to ascend?

    A. The method by which the air is lifted.

    B. The stability of the air before lifting occurs.

    C. The relative humidity of the air after lifting occurs.

Answer (B) is correct. (AC 00-6B Chap 12)
    DISCUSSION: The structure of cloud types that form as a result of air being forced to ascend is determined by the stability of the air before lifting occurs. The difference between the existing lapse rate (the actual decrease in temperature with altitude) and the adiabatic rate of cooling in upward-moving air (cooling of air as a result of expansion as it ascends) determines the stability of the air. If the upward-moving air remains warmer than the surrounding air, the air is accelerated upward as a convective current. The air is considered unstable, and these conditions provide for the vertical development of cumulus clouds. If, on the other hand, the upward-moving air becomes colder than the surrounding air, it sinks. The air is considered stable, and stratiform clouds will form.
    Answer (A) is incorrect. The stability of the air (not the lifting method) determines the type of clouds that will form. **Answer (C) is incorrect.** The relative humidity of the air determines the amount (not type) of clouds that will form.

34. Which are characteristics of a cold air mass moving over a warm surface?

    A. Cumuliform clouds, turbulence, and poor visibility.

    B. Cumuliform clouds, turbulence, and good visibility.

    C. Stratiform clouds, smooth air, and poor visibility.

Answer (B) is correct. (FAA-H-8083-25B Chap 12)
    DISCUSSION: When a cold air mass moves over a warm surface, the warm air near the surface rises and creates an unstable condition. These convective currents give rise to cumuliform clouds, turbulence, and good visibility.
    Answer (A) is incorrect. Unstable air lifts and blows haze away, resulting in good (not poor) visibility. **Answer (C) is incorrect.** Unstable conditions produce cumuliform (not stratiform) clouds.

35. Which combination of weather-producing variables would likely result in cumuliform-type clouds, good visibility, and showery rain?

- A. Stable, moist air and orographic lifting.
- B. Unstable, moist air and orographic lifting.
- C. Unstable, moist air and no lifting mechanism.

Answer (B) is correct. *(FAA-H-8083-25B Chap 12)*
DISCUSSION: Unstable, moist air accompanied by lifting usually results in showery rain, good visibility, and cumuliform clouds. Orographic lifting is caused by mountain forces, mountain winds, etc.
Answer (A) is incorrect. If air is stable, stratiform rather than cumuliform type clouds will form, and the rain will be steady (not showery). **Answer (C) is incorrect.** Cumuliform clouds and showery rain cannot exist without a lifting mechanism.

36. Virga is best described as

- A. streamers of precipitation trailing beneath clouds which evaporate before reaching the ground.
- B. wall cloud torrents trailing beneath cumulonimbus clouds which dissipate before reaching the ground.
- C. turbulent areas beneath cumulonimbus clouds.

Answer (A) is correct. *(AC 00-6B Chap 13)*
DISCUSSION: Virga is streamers of precipitation, either water or ice particles, falling from a cloud in wisps or streaks and evaporating before reaching the ground.
Answer (B) is incorrect. Virga is generally thin and wispy (not a torrential wall). **Answer (C) is incorrect.** Virga is precipitation (not turbulence).

37. The presence of standing lenticular altocumulus clouds is a good indication of

- A. lenticular ice formation in calm air.
- B. very strong turbulence.
- C. heavy icing conditions.

Answer (B) is correct. *(AC 00-6B Chap 17)*
DISCUSSION: When stable air crosses a mountain barrier, turbulence usually results. Air flowing up the windward side is relatively smooth. Windflow across the barrier is laminar; i.e., it tends to flow in layers. The barrier may set up waves in these layers, much as waves develop on a disturbed water surface. Wave crests extend well above the highest mountain tops. Under each wave crest is a rotary circulation in which turbulence can be quite violent. Updrafts and downdrafts in the waves can also create very violent turbulence.
Answer (A) is incorrect. Standing lenticular clouds indicate turbulence (not calm air). **Answer (C) is incorrect.** Standing lenticular clouds indicate turbulence (not icing conditions).

38. As you approach an airport to land, you observe a convective cloud over the airport with virga below it. This could indicate

- A. smooth air.
- B. heavy rain showers.
- C. the presence of a microburst.

Answer (C) is correct. *(FAA-H-8083-25B Chap 12)*
DISCUSSION: Rain that falls through the atmosphere but evaporates prior to striking the ground is known as virga. The process of evaporation cools the air around the virga and can create strong downdrafts and in some cases microbursts.
Answer (A) is incorrect. Virga are often associated with strong downdrafts due to the cooling effect of evaporation. Therefore, the air around virga would be very turbulent, not smooth. **Answer (B) is incorrect.** Virga occur when precipitation is not able to penetrate a layer of dry air and evaporates before it reaches the surface. Thus, heavy rain showers would not be indicated by virga.

39. Cumulus clouds often indicate

- A. possible turbulence.
- B. a temperature inversion.
- C. a dry adiabatic lapse rate.

Answer (A) is correct. *(AC 00-6B)*
DISCUSSION: Cumulus clouds are formed in a convective updraft, build upward, and are associated with turbulence.
Answer (B) is incorrect. A temperature inversion prevents updrafts from forming, which is needed for the formation of cumulus clouds. **Answer (C) is incorrect.** The dry adiabatic lapse rate is a measurement of air with no moisture available to form clouds.

40. Clouds with extensive vertical development over mountainous terrain are a sign of

A. a dry adiabatic lapse rate.

B. a stable air mass.

C. an unstable air mass.

Answer (C) is correct. (AC 00-6B)
DISCUSSION: Winds across mountains cause mountain waves that are associated with severe turbulence, strong vertical currents, and icing. The extent of the turbulence is relative to the height of the ground, speed of the wind, and instability of the atmosphere. With adequate moisture, lenticular clouds will form at the top of each wave.
Answer (A) is incorrect. The dry adiabatic lapse rate is a measurement of air with no moisture available to form clouds.
Answer (B) is incorrect. The vertical development of the clouds indicates the presence of multiple waves with adequate upward motion and moisture to cause cloud formation.

41. The stability of an air mass can usually be determined by

A. the height of the tropopause.

B. measuring the dry adiabatic lapse rate.

C. cloud types and the type of precipitation.

Answer (C) is correct. (FAA-H-8083-25B Chap 12)
DISCUSSION: Atmospheric stability influences weather by affecting the vertical motion of air. Stable air suppresses vertical motion, but unstable air enhances it. Clouds formed in stable air will be shallow and layered, e.g., stratus clouds. Clouds formed in unstable air will have more height and be of the cumulus or cumulonimbus type. Precipitation from stratus clouds tends to be over large areas and lasts for long periods. Precipitation from cumulus clouds tends to be more intense and lasts for short periods.
Answer (A) is incorrect. The tropopause is a thin boundary area between the troposphere and the stratosphere. The height of the tropopause varies widely due to the location above the earth and the time of the year and is not necessarily indicative of air mass stability. Answer (B) is incorrect. Stability is determined by the change in the ambient lapse rate, not the dry lapse rate.

7.6 Fog

42. In what ways do advection fog, radiation fog, and steam fog differ in their formation or location?

A. Radiation fog is restricted to land areas; advection fog is most common along coastal areas; steam fog forms over a water surface.

B. Advection fog deepens as windspeed increases up to 20 knots; steam fog requires calm or very light wind; radiation fog forms when the ground or water cools the air by radiation.

C. Steam fog forms from moist air moving over a colder surface; advection fog requires cold air over a warmer surface; radiation fog is produced by radiational cooling of the ground.

Answer (A) is correct. (AC 00-6B Chap 16)
DISCUSSION: Radiation fog is restricted to land because water surfaces cool little from nighttime radiation. Advection fog forms when moist air moves over colder ground or water. It is most common along coastal areas. Steam fog occurs when cold air moves over relatively warm water or wet ground.
Answer (B) is incorrect. Advection fog breaks up (not deepens) when wind speed increases to 15 knots or more; steam fog requires wind to move cold air over warm, moist surfaces; and radiation fog does not form over water. Answer (C) is incorrect. Steam fog occurs when cold air moves over warm, moist surfaces, and advection fog is caused by warm air moving over a cool surface.

43. Fog produced by frontal activity is a result of saturation due to

A. nocturnal cooling.

B. adiabatic cooling.

C. evaporation of precipitation.

Answer (C) is correct. (AC 00-6B Chap 16)
DISCUSSION: Fog produced by frontal activity is known as precipitation-induced fog. It arises from drops of warm rain or drizzle falling through cool air. The evaporation from the precipitation saturates the cool air and forms fog.
Answer (A) is incorrect. Nocturnal cooling forms radiation (not precipitation-induced) fog. Answer (B) is incorrect. Adiabatic cooling forms upslope (not precipitation-induced) fog.

44. Which in-flight hazard is most commonly associated with warm fronts?

    A. Advection fog.

    B. Radiation fog.

    C. Precipitation-induced fog.

Answer (C) is correct. (AC 00-6B Chap 16)
    DISCUSSION: Precipitation-induced fog arises from drops of warm rain or drizzle evaporating as it falls through cool air. This evaporation saturates the cool air and forms fog. This kind of fog can become quite dense and continue for an extended period of time. It is most commonly associated with warm fronts.
    Answer (A) is incorrect. Advection fog results from the movement of warm, humid air over a cold water surface. **Answer (B) is incorrect.** Radiation fog results from terrestrial cooling of the Earth's surface on calm, clear nights.

45. A situation most conducive to the formation of advection fog is

    A. a light breeze moving colder air over a water surface.

    B. an air mass moving inland from the coastline during the winter.

    C. a warm, moist air mass settling over a cool surface under no-wind conditions.

Answer (B) is correct. (AC 00-6B Chap 16)
    DISCUSSION: Advection fog forms when moist air moves over colder ground or water. This type of fog is common when comparatively warm, moist oceanic air moves inland from the coastline during winter.
    Answer (A) is incorrect. A light breeze moving colder air over a warmer water surface describes steam fog. **Answer (C) is incorrect.** A warm, moist air mass settling over a cool surface under no-wind conditions describes radiation fog.

46. Advection fog has drifted over a coastal airport during the day. What may tend to dissipate or lift this fog into low stratus clouds?

    A. Nighttime cooling.

    B. Surface radiation.

    C. Wind 15 knots or stronger.

Answer (C) is correct. (AC 00-6B Chap 16)
    DISCUSSION: Advection fog deepens as wind speed increases up to 15 knots. Wind much stronger than 15 knots will lift the fog into a layer of low stratus or stratocumulus.
    Answer (A) is incorrect. Nighttime cooling forms radiation fog (not low stratus clouds). **Answer (B) is incorrect.** Surface radiation forms radiation fog (not low stratus clouds).

47. What lifts advection fog into low stratus clouds?

    A. Nighttime cooling.

    B. Dryness of the underlying land mass.

    C. Surface winds of approximately 15 knots or stronger.

Answer (C) is correct. (AC 00-6B Chap 16)
    DISCUSSION: Advection fog deepens as wind speed increases up to 15 knots. Wind much stronger than 15 knots lifts the fog into a layer of low stratus or stratocumulus.
    Answer (A) is incorrect. Nighttime cooling forms radiation fog (not low stratus clouds). **Answer (B) is incorrect.** Dryness of the underlying land mass forms radiation fog (not low stratus clouds).

48. Which conditions are favorable for the formation of a surface based temperature inversion?

    A. Clear, cool nights with calm or light wind.

    B. Area of unstable air rapidly transferring heat from the surface.

    C. Broad areas of cumulus clouds with smooth, level bases at the same altitude.

Answer (A) is correct. (AC 00-6B Chap 2)
    DISCUSSION: A temperature inversion occurs when warm air exists over cooler air. When ground heat radiates out on clear nights, the cool ground surface cools still air at the surface to a temperature below the air above it.
    Answer (B) is incorrect. The air near the surface must be stable both horizontally and vertically to permit the cool ground to cool the air near the surface. **Answer (C) is incorrect.** Cumulus clouds are well above the surface.

49. With respect to advection fog, which statement is true?

    A. It is slow to develop and dissipates quite rapidly.

    B. It forms almost exclusively at night or near daybreak.

    C. It can appear suddenly during day or night, and it is more persistent than radiation fog.

Answer (C) is correct. (AC 00-6B Chap 16)
    DISCUSSION: Advection fog is usually more extensive and much more persistent than radiation fog. Advection fog can move in rapidly regardless of the time of day or night.
    Answer (A) is incorrect. Advection fog can move in rapidly regardless of the time of day or night and is persistent. **Answer (B) is incorrect.** Radiation, not advection, fog forms almost exclusively at night or near daybreak.

50. Temperature and radiation variations over land with a clear sky typically lead to

A. minimum temperature occurring after sunrise.

B. outgoing terrestrial radiation peaking at noon.

C. temperature reaching a maximum closer to noon than to sunset.

Answer (A) is correct. (AC 00-6B)
 DISCUSSION: At night, heating is absent, but terrestrial radiation continues cooling the earth's surface. Cooling continues until shortly after sunrise, when incoming solar radiation once again exceeds outgoing terrestrial radiation. Minimum surface air temperature usually occurs shortly after sunrise.
 Answer (B) is incorrect. Outgoing radiation peaks during the nighttime when no isolation occurs. **Answer (C) is incorrect.** Peak isolation occurs around noon, but maximum surface air temperature occurs during mid-afternoon.

51. Penetrating fog while flying an approach at night, you might experience the illusion of

A. pitching up.

B. flying at a lower altitude.

C. constant turning.

Answer (A) is correct. (AIM Para 8-1-5)
 DISCUSSION: Refractory effects can cause the perception of a nose high attitude.
 Answer (B) is incorrect. This results from the illusion of being farther away from the runway; thus, the pilot responds by flying a lower approach. **Answer (C) is incorrect.** This illusion is primarily perceived during and after motion disturbances leading to spatial disorientation.

7.7 Stability

52. What are the characteristics of stable air?

A. Good visibility; steady precipitation; stratus clouds.

B. Poor visibility; steady precipitation; stratus clouds.

C. Poor visibility; intermittent precipitation; cumulus clouds.

Answer (B) is correct. (FAA-H-8083-25B Chap 12)
 DISCUSSION: Stable air is still or moving horizontally but without vertical movement. As a result, the pollutants in the air are not swept away and visibility is poor. Also, stable air forms layer-like clouds since the air is moving in layers. Relatedly, precipitation spreads over a wide area and is relatively steady and the air is smooth.
 Answer (A) is incorrect. The visibility is poor (not good) in stable air. **Answer (C) is incorrect.** The precipitation is steady (not intermittent) and the clouds are stratiform (not cumulus) in stable air.

53. Which would decrease the stability of an air mass?

A. Warming from below.

B. Cooling from below.

C. Decrease in water vapor.

Answer (A) is correct. (FAA-H-8083-25B Chap 12)
 DISCUSSION: When air is warmed from below, it tends to rise, resulting in instability; i.e., vertical movement occurs.
 Answer (B) is incorrect. Cooling from below keeps the air from rising, resulting in increased (not decreased) stability. **Answer (C) is incorrect.** A decrease in water vapor lowers the dew point of the air, which does not affect the stability.

54. What is a characteristic of stable air?

A. Stratiform clouds.

B. Fair weather cumulus clouds.

C. Temperature decreases rapidly with altitude.

Answer (A) is correct. (FAA-H-8083-25B Chap 12)
 DISCUSSION: Stable air is still or moving horizontally but without vertical movement. As a result, the pollutants in the air are not swept away and visibility is poor. Also, stable air forms layer-like clouds since the air is moving in layers. Relatedly, precipitation spreads over a wide area and is relatively steady and the air is smooth.
 Answer (B) is incorrect. Cumulus clouds are a characteristic of unstable (not stable) air. **Answer (C) is incorrect.** A rapid temperature decrease with altitude (high lapse rate) is a characteristic of unstable (not stable) air.

55. Which would increase the stability of an air mass?

A. Warming from below.

B. Cooling from below.

C. Decrease in water vapor.

Answer (B) is correct. (FAA-H-8083-25B Chap 12)
 DISCUSSION: When air is cooled from below, it does not rise, resulting in stability, i.e., no vertical movement.
 Answer (A) is incorrect. Warming from below causes the air to rise, resulting in decreased (not increased) stability. **Answer (C) is incorrect.** A decrease in water vapor lowers the dew point of the air, which does not affect stability.

56. Which is a characteristic of stable air?

    A. Cumuliform clouds.

    B. Excellent visibility.

    C. Restricted visibility.

Answer (C) is correct. (FAA-H-8083-25B Chap 12)
    DISCUSSION: Stable air is still or moving horizontally but without vertical movement. As a result, the pollutants in the air are not swept away and visibility is poor. Also, stable air forms layer-like clouds since the air is moving in layers. Relatedly, precipitation spreads over a wide area and is relatively steady and the air is smooth.
    Answer (A) is incorrect. Cumuliform clouds are a characteristic of unstable (not stable) air. **Answer (B) is incorrect.** Excellent visibility is a characteristic of unstable (not stable) air.

57. Which is a characteristic typical of a stable air mass?

    A. Cumuliform clouds.

    B. Showery precipitation.

    C. Continuous precipitation.

Answer (C) is correct. (FAA-H-8083-25B Chap 12)
    DISCUSSION: Stable air is still or moving horizontally but without vertical movement. As a result, the pollutants in the air are not swept away and visibility is poor. Also, stable air forms layer-like clouds since the air is moving in layers. Relatedly, precipitation spreads over a wide area and is relatively steady, and the air is smooth.
    Answer (A) is incorrect. Cumuliform clouds are a characteristic of unstable (not stable) air. **Answer (B) is incorrect.** Showery precipitation is a characteristic of unstable (not stable) air.

58. What type of weather can one expect from moist, unstable air, and very warm surface temperature?

    A. Fog and low stratus clouds.

    B. Continuous heavy precipitation.

    C. Strong updrafts and cumulonimbus clouds.

Answer (C) is correct. (FAA-H-8083-25B Chap 12)
    DISCUSSION: Unstable air is air that is being heated from below, producing updrafts. As a result, pollutants in the air are swept away and visibility is good. Also, unstable air forms cumulus clouds because the air is moving vertically. Relatedly, precipitation is showery and turbulence may be present.
    Answer (A) is incorrect. Fog and stratus clouds are characteristics of stable (not unstable) air. **Answer (B) is incorrect.** Continuous precipitation is a characteristic of stable (not unstable) air.

59. A moist, unstable air mass is characterized by

    A. poor visibility and smooth air.

    B. cumuliform clouds and showery precipitation.

    C. stratiform clouds and continuous precipitation.

Answer (B) is correct. (FAA-H-8083-25B Chap 12)
    DISCUSSION: Unstable air is air that is being heated from below, producing updrafts. As a result, pollutants in the air are swept away and visibility is good. Also, unstable air forms cumulus clouds because the air is moving vertically. Relatedly, precipitation is showery and turbulence may be present.
    Answer (A) is incorrect. Poor visibility and smooth air are characteristics of stable (not unstable) air. **Answer (C) is incorrect.** Stratiform clouds and continuous precipitation are characteristics of stable (not unstable) air.

60. If clouds form as a result of very stable, moist air being forced to ascend a mountain slope, the clouds will be

    A. cirrus type with no vertical development or turbulence.

    B. cumulus type with considerable vertical development and turbulence.

    C. stratus type with little vertical development and little or no turbulence.

Answer (C) is correct. (FAA-H-8083-25B Chap 12)
    DISCUSSION: Moist, stable air flowing upslope produces stratified clouds as it cools. Stable air resists upward movement.
    Answer (A) is incorrect. Cirrus are high clouds, usually consisting of ice crystals. **Answer (B) is incorrect.** There would be vertical development only if the air were unstable. Also, there is little or no turbulence in stable air.

61. The formation of either predominantly stratiform or predominantly cumuliform clouds is dependent upon the

    A. source of lift.

    B. stability of the air being lifted.

    C. temperature of the air being lifted.

Answer (B) is correct. (FAA-H-8083-25B Chap 12)
    DISCUSSION: The structure of cloud types that form as a result of air being forced to ascend is determined by the stability of the air before lifting occurs. Stability refers to the relationship of the lapse rate to the adiabatic cooling rate. If the temperature that decreases with altitude (lapse rate) is warmer than the adiabatic cooling rate (cooling of air as a result of expansion as it ascends), the air that is lifted will continue to rise, which provides for the vertical development of cumulus clouds. That is, unstable conditions exist. If, on the other hand, the lapse rate is less than (cooler than) the adiabatic rate, the air that is lifted will be as cool as or cooler than the air around it, will not lift further, and stratiform clouds will form; i.e., stable conditions exist.
    Answer (A) is incorrect. The stability of the air (not the source of lift) determines the type of clouds that will form. **Answer (C) is incorrect.** The temperature of the air (along with the dew point) determines the altitude (not type) of cloud formation.

62. When an air mass is stable, which of these conditions is most likely to exist?

    A. Numerous towering cumulus and cumulonimbus clouds.

    B. Moderate to severe turbulence at the lower levels.

    C. Smoke, dust, haze, etc., concentrated at the lower levels with resulting poor visibility.

Answer (C) is correct. (FAA-H-8083-25B Chap 12)
    DISCUSSION: Stable air is still or moving horizontally but without vertical movement. As a result, the pollutants in the air are not swept away and visibility is poor. Also, stable air forms layer-like clouds because the air is moving in layers. Relatedly, precipitation spreads over a wide area and is relatively steady, and the air is smooth.
    Answer (A) is incorrect. Towering cumulus and cumulonimbus clouds are characteristics of unstable (not stable) air. **Answer (B) is incorrect.** Turbulence is a characteristic of unstable (not stable) air.

63. Which is true regarding the development of convective circulation?

    A. Cool air must sink to force the warm air upward.

    B. Warm air is less dense and rises on its own accord.

    C. Warmer air covers a larger surface area than the cool air; therefore, the warmer air is less dense and rises.

Answer (A) is correct. (AC 00-6B Chap 11)
    DISCUSSION: When two surfaces are heated unequally, they heat the overlying air unevenly. The warmer air expands and becomes lighter or less dense than the cool air. The more dense, cool air is drawn to the ground by its greater gravitational force, lifting or forcing the warm air upward much as oil is forced to the top of water when the two are mixed.
    Answer (B) is incorrect. Cool air sinking forces the warm air up (without the cool air, the warm air would be stationary). **Answer (C) is incorrect.** Convective circulation is based on unequal heating of the Earth's surface, not the relative size of surface.

64. When conditionally unstable air with high-moisture content and very warm surface temperature is forecast, one can expect what type of weather?

    A. Strong updrafts and stratonimbus clouds.

    B. Restricted visibility near the surface over a large area.

    C. Strong updrafts and cumulonimbus clouds.

Answer (C) is correct. (AC 00-6B Chap 19)
    DISCUSSION: Unstable air is air that is being heated from below, producing updrafts. As a result, pollutants in the air are swept away and visibility is good. Also, unstable air forms cumulus clouds because the air is moving vertically. Relatedly, precipitation is showery and turbulence may be present.
    Answer (A) is incorrect. Stratonimbus clouds are a characteristic of stable (not unstable) air. **Answer (B) is incorrect.** Restricted visibility is a characteristic of stable (not unstable) air.

65. Convective circulation patterns associated with sea breezes are caused by

    A. water absorbing and radiating heat faster than the land.

    B. land absorbing and radiating heat faster than the water.

    C. cool and less dense air moving inland from over the water, causing it to rise.

Answer (B) is correct. (AC 00-6B Chap 9)
    DISCUSSION: Sea breezes are caused by cool and denser air moving inland off of the water. Once over the warmer land, the air heats up and rises. Currents push the hot air over the water where it cools and descends, starting the cycle over again. The temperature differential between land and water is caused by land absorbing and radiating heat faster than water.
    Answer (A) is incorrect. Water absorbs and radiates heat slower (not faster) than land. **Answer (C) is incorrect.** The cool air moving inland is more (not less) dense, and it rises after it is warmed, not while it is cool.

66. The difference found by subtracting the temperature of a parcel of air theoretically lifted from the surface to 500 millibars and the existing temperature at 500 millibars is called the

    A. lifted index.

    B. negative index.

    C. positive index.

Answer (A) is correct. (AC 00-45H Chap 12)
    DISCUSSION: The lifted index is computed as if a parcel of air near the surface were lifted to 500 millibars (18,000 ft. MSL). As the air is lifted, it cools by expansion. The temperature the parcel would have at 500 millibars is then subtracted from the environmental 500-millibar temperature. The difference is the lifted index, which may be positive, zero, or negative. Thus, the lifted index indicates stability at 500 millibars (18,000 ft. MSL).
    Answer (B) is incorrect. A negative index means that a parcel of air, if lifted, would be warmer than existing air at 500 mb, and thus the air is unstable. **Answer (C) is incorrect.** A positive index means that a parcel of air, if lifted, would be colder than existing air at 500 mb, and thus the air is stable.

67. From which measurement of the atmosphere can stability be determined?

    A. Atmospheric pressure.

    B. The ambient lapse rate.

    C. The dry adiabatic lapse rate.

Answer (B) is correct. (AC 00-6B Chap 12)
    DISCUSSION: The stability of the atmosphere is determined by vertical movements of air. Warm air rises when the air above is cooler. The lapse rate, which is the decrease of temperature with altitude, is therefore a measure of stability.
    Answer (A) is incorrect. While atmospheric pressure may have some effect on temperature changes and air movements, it is the actual lapse rate that determines the stability of the atmosphere. **Answer (C) is incorrect.** The dry adiabatic lapse rate is a constant rate.

68. The conditions necessary for the formation of stratiform clouds are a lifting action and

    A. unstable, dry air.

    B. stable, moist air.

    C. unstable, moist air.

Answer (B) is correct. (FAA-H-8083-25B Chap 12)
    DISCUSSION: Stable, moist air and adiabatic cooling, e.g., upslope flow or lifting over colder air, are needed to form stratiform clouds.
    Answer (A) is incorrect. Stable (not unstable), moist (not dry) air is required. **Answer (C) is incorrect.** Stable (not unstable) air is required.

69. What are the characteristics of an unstable atmosphere?

    A. A cool, dry air mass.

    B. A warm, humid air mass.

    C. Descending air in the northern hemisphere.

Answer (B) is correct. (FAA-H-8083-25B Chap 12)
    DISCUSSION: The stability of the atmosphere depends on its ability to resist vertical motion. As air temperature and air moisture increase, the density of the air decreases, causing it to rise. This creates an unstable atmosphere in which small, vertical air movements tend to become larger, resulting in turbulent airflow and convective activity.
    Answer (A) is incorrect. When air is cool, it resists rising, resulting in stability. **Answer (C) is incorrect.** The characteristics of a stable atmosphere do not change whether you are in the northern or southern hemisphere.

7.8 Thunderstorms and Icing

70. What visible signs indicate extreme turbulence in thunderstorms?

    A. Base of the clouds near the surface, heavy rain, and hail.

    B. Low ceiling and visibility, hail, and precipitation static.

    C. Cumulonimbus clouds, very frequent lightning, and roll clouds.

Answer (C) is correct. (FAA-H-8083-25B Chap 12)
DISCUSSION: Cumulonimbus clouds are thunderstorms by definition. Their intensity can be gauged by the presence of roll clouds on the lower leading edge of the storm, which mark the eddies in the shear. Roll clouds are prevalent with cold frontal or squall line thunderstorms and signify an extremely turbulent zone. Also, the more frequent the lightning, the more severe the storm.
Answer (A) is incorrect. Cloud bases and precipitation are not, in themselves, definite indicators of extreme turbulence. **Answer (B) is incorrect.** Low ceilings, hail, and precipitation static are not, in themselves, definite indicators of extreme turbulence.

71. What feature is normally associated with the cumulus stage of a thunderstorm?

    A. Roll cloud.

    B. Continuous updraft.

    C. Beginning of rain at the surface.

Answer (B) is correct. (AC 00-6B Chap 19)
DISCUSSION: The cumulus stage of a thunderstorm has continuous updrafts that build the cloud up. The water droplets are carried up until they become too heavy. Once they begin falling and creating downdrafts, the storm changes from the cumulus to the mature stage.
Answer (A) is incorrect. The roll cloud is the cloud near the ground, which is formed by the downrushing cold air pushing out from below the thunderstorm, usually in the mature stage. **Answer (C) is incorrect.** The beginning of rain at the surface indicates the start of the mature stage, which follows the cumulus stage.

72. The most severe weather conditions, such as destructive winds, heavy hail, and tornadoes, are generally associated with

    A. slow-moving warm fronts which slope above the tropopause.

    B. squall lines.

    C. fast-moving occluded fronts.

Answer (B) is correct. (FAA-H-8083-25B Chap 12)
DISCUSSION: A squall line is a non-frontal, narrow band of thunderstorms that often develops ahead of a cold front. It often contains severe steady-state thunderstorms and presents the single most intense weather hazard to aircraft.
Answer (A) is incorrect. Warm fronts generally do not produce severe weather. **Answer (C) is incorrect.** Although occluded fronts have some associated instability, the weather they produce is not nearly as severe as a squall line.

73. The conditions necessary for the formation of cumulonimbus clouds are a lifting action and

    A. unstable, dry air.

    B. stable, moist air.

    C. unstable, moist air.

Answer (C) is correct. (AC 00-6B Chap 19)
DISCUSSION: Unstable, moist air and a lifting action, i.e., convective activity, are needed to form cumulonimbus clouds.
Answer (A) is incorrect. Moist (not dry) air is required. **Answer (B) is incorrect.** Unstable (not stable) air is required.

74. Of the following, which is accurate regarding turbulence associated with thunderstorms?

    A. Outside the clouds, shear turbulence can be encountered 50 miles laterally from a severe storm.

    B. Shear turbulence is encountered only inside cumulonimbus clouds or within a 5-mile radius of them.

    C. Outside the cloud, shear turbulence can be encountered 20 miles laterally from a severe storm.

Answer (C) is correct. (FAA-H-8083-25B Chap 12)
DISCUSSION: Hazardous turbulence is present in and around all thunderstorms. Outside the cloud, shear turbulence has been encountered several thousand feet above and 20 NM laterally from a severe storm. The roll cloud signifies an extremely turbulent zone.
Answer (A) is incorrect. Shear turbulence can be encountered to 20 NM (not 50 NM) laterally from a severe storm. **Answer (B) is incorrect.** Shear turbulence can be encountered above and 20 NM (not 5 NM) laterally (not just inside) severe thunderstorms.

75. Which statement is true concerning squall lines?

A. They form slowly, but move rapidly.

B. They are associated with frontal systems only.

C. They offer the most intense weather hazards to aircraft.

Answer (C) is correct. (FAA-H-8083-25B Chap 12)
DISCUSSION: A squall line is a non-frontal narrow band of active thunderstorms. It often contains severe steady-state thunderstorms and presents the single most intense weather hazard to aircraft.
Answer (A) is incorrect. Squall lines usually form rapidly, generally reaching maximum intensity during the late afternoon and the first few hours of darkness. **Answer (B) is incorrect.** Squall lines may develop ahead of a cold front in moist and unstable air or in unstable air far removed from a front.

76. Which statement is true regarding squall lines?

A. They are always associated with cold fronts.

B. They are slow in forming, but rapid in movement.

C. They are nonfrontal and often contain severe, steady-state thunderstorms.

Answer (C) is correct. (FAA-H-8083-25B Chap 12)
DISCUSSION: A squall line is a non-frontal, narrow band of active thunderstorms that frequently develops ahead of a cold front. It can, however, occur in any area of moist, unstable air. It often contains severe steady-state thunderstorms and presents the single most intense weather hazard to aircraft.
Answer (A) is incorrect. While squall lines usually precede cold fronts, they can form in any area of unstable air. **Answer (B) is incorrect.** Squall lines usually form rapidly.

77. Select the true statement pertaining to the life cycle of a thunderstorm.

A. Updrafts continue to develop throughout the dissipating stage of a thunderstorm.

B. The beginning of rain at the Earth's surface indicates the mature stage of the thunderstorm.

C. The beginning of rain at the Earth's surface indicates the dissipating stage of the thunderstorm.

Answer (B) is correct. (AC 00-6B Chap 19)
DISCUSSION: Thunderstorms have three stages in their life cycle: cumulus, mature, and dissipating. The beginning of rain at the Earth's surface indicates the mature stage, which is characterized by numerous updrafts and downdrafts.
Answer (A) is incorrect. Updrafts do not continue during the dissipating stage of the thunderstorm; only downdrafts are present. **Answer (C) is incorrect.** The beginning of rain at the Earth's surface is the beginning of the mature (not dissipating) stage.

78. Which weather phenomenon signals the beginning of the mature stage of a thunderstorm?

A. The start of rain.

B. The appearance of an anvil top.

C. Growth rate of cloud is maximum.

Answer (A) is correct. (AC 00-6B Chap 19)
DISCUSSION: Thunderstorms have three stages in their life cycle: cumulus, mature, and dissipating. The beginning of rain at the Earth's surface indicates the mature stage, which is characterized by numerous updrafts and downdrafts.
Answer (B) is incorrect. The anvil top generally appears during (not necessarily at the beginning of) the mature stage. **Answer (C) is incorrect.** Maximum cloud growth rate occurs further into the mature stage of a thunderstorm (not at the beginning).

79. During the life cycle of a thunderstorm, which stage is characterized predominately by downdrafts?

A. Mature.

B. Developing.

C. Dissipating.

Answer (C) is correct. (AC 00-6B Chap 19)
DISCUSSION: Thunderstorms have three stages in their life cycle: cumulus, mature, and dissipating. In the dissipating stage, the storm is characterized by downdrafts as the storm rains itself out.
Answer (A) is incorrect. The mature stage has both updrafts and downdrafts, which creates tremendous wind shears. **Answer (B) is incorrect.** Cumulus is the developing stage when there are primarily updrafts.

80. What minimum distance should exist between intense radar echoes before any attempt is made to fly between these thunderstorms?

A. 20 miles.

B. 30 miles.

C. 40 miles.

Answer (C) is correct. (AC 00-24C)
DISCUSSION: Wind shear turbulence and hail have been encountered as far as 20 NM laterally from a severe thunderstorm. Thus, a minimum distance of 40 NM should exist between intense radar echoes before any attempt is made to fly between them.
Answer (A) is incorrect. Shear turbulence may be encountered 20 NM (not 10 NM) laterally from intense echoes. **Answer (B) is incorrect.** Shear turbulence may be encountered 20 NM (not 15 NM) laterally from intense echoes.

81. Which is true regarding the use of airborne weather-avoidance radar for the recognition of certain weather conditions?

A. The radar scope provides no assurance of avoiding instrument weather conditions.

B. The avoidance of hail is assured when flying between and just clear of the most intense echoes.

C. The clear area between intense echoes indicates that visual sighting of storms can be maintained when flying between the echoes.

Answer (A) is correct. (AC 00-24C)
    DISCUSSION: Airborne weather avoidance radar is designed to identify areas of precipitation, especially heavy precipitation, which may signify an active thunderstorm. Instrument weather conditions are restricted visibility due to clouds or fog which are not indicated on radar screens.
    Answer (B) is incorrect. Hail is often thrown from the tops of thunderstorms for several miles away from the cloud itself. **Answer (C) is incorrect.** Clouds without precipitation may exist between the intense echoes.

82. Which situation would most likely result in freezing precipitation? Rain falling from air which has a temperature of

A. 32°F or less into air having a temperature of more than 32°F.

B. 0°C or less into air having a temperature of 0°C or more.

C. more than 32°F into air having a temperature of 32°F or less.

Answer (C) is correct. (AC 00-6B Chap 14)
    DISCUSSION: A condition favorable for rapid accumulation of clear icing is freezing rain. Rain forms at temperatures warmer than freezing, then falls through air at temperatures below freezing and becomes supercooled. The supercooled drops freeze on impact with an aircraft surface.
    Answer (A) is incorrect. The rain must begin in temperatures of 32°F or warmer and fall through a layer of below-freezing temperatures. **Answer (B) is incorrect.** The rain must begin in temperatures of 0°C or warmer and fall through a layer of below-freezing temperatures.

83. What course of action should the pilot take if encountering freezing rain?

A. Climb because the temperature is warmer at a higher altitude.

B. Descend because the temperature is warmer at a lower altitude.

C. No change is necessary if all anti-ice/deice equipment is working.

Answer (A) is correct. (AC 00-6B Chap 14)
    DISCUSSION: The first course of action is to leave the area of visible moisture. In this case, the pilot should climb to an altitude where the temperature is above freezing.
    Answer (B) is incorrect. Once freezing rain has been encountered, by nature, the rain forms aloft at temperatures warmer than freezing, then falls through air at temperatures below freezing and becomes supercooled. A climb is the preferred course of action. **Answer (C) is incorrect.** Flight in freezing rain should be avoided when possible because ice may accumulate in a manner that mitigates the anti-ice equipment and may accrete at a rate much faster than the deicing equipment can compensate for in flight.

84. Hail is most likely to be associated with

A. cumulus clouds.

B. cumulonimbus clouds.

C. stratocumulus clouds.

Answer (B) is correct. (AC 00-6B Chap 13)
    DISCUSSION: Hail competes with turbulence as the greatest thunderstorm hazard to aircraft. Hail has been observed in clear air several miles from the parent thunderstorm. You should anticipate possible hail with any thunderstorm, especially beneath the anvil of a large cumulonimbus cloud.
    Answer (A) is incorrect. Hail is usually associated with cumulonimbus (not cumulus) clouds. **Answer (C) is incorrect.** Hail is usually associated with cumulonimbus (not stratocumulus) clouds.

85. If airborne radar is indicating an extremely intense thunderstorm echo, this thunderstorm should be avoided by a distance of at least

A. 20 miles.

B. 10 miles.

C. 5 miles.

Answer (A) is correct. (AC 00-24C)
    DISCUSSION: Wind shear turbulence has been encountered as far as 20 NM laterally from a severe thunderstorm.
    Answer (B) is incorrect. The danger of shear turbulence exists 20 NM (not 10 NM) laterally from a severe storm. **Answer (C) is incorrect.** The danger of shear turbulence exists 20 NM (not 5 NM) laterally from a severe storm.

86. Ice pellets encountered during flight normally are evidence that

   A. a warm front has passed.

   B. a warm front is about to pass.

   C. there are thunderstorms in the area.

Answer (B) is correct. (AC 00-6B Chap 18)
   DISCUSSION: Ice pellets form as a result of rain freezing at a higher altitude. This indicates that there is a layer of warm air above in which it is raining and the rain freezes as it falls through the colder air. Thus, either a warm front or a cold front is about to pass.
   Answer (A) is incorrect. The layer of warm air above cold air necessary for the formation of ice pellets occurs when a warm front is about to pass (not after it has passed). **Answer (C) is incorrect.** Ice pellets are a result of rain freezing at a higher altitude (not necessarily from a thunderstorm).

87. The greatest threats to an aircraft operating in the vicinity of thunderstorms are:

   A. thunder and heavy rain.

   B. hail and turbulence.

   C. precipitation static and low visibility.

Answer (B) is correct. (AC 00-24C)
   DISCUSSION: Hail competes with turbulence as the greatest thunderstorm hazard to aircraft. Hail has been observed in clear air several miles from the parent thunderstorm. You should anticipate possible hail with any thunderstorm, especially beneath the anvil of a large cumulonimbus cloud.
   Answer (A) is incorrect. Hail, along with turbulence, presents one of the greatest hazards to aircraft in thunderstorms; hail damages the leading edges and windshields of aircraft. **Answer (C) is incorrect.** Precipitation static may cause communications or navigational aids to fail, but precipitation static and low visibility are not considered as hazardous to aircraft as hail and turbulence. Precipitation static can be active in any rain or cloud conditions an aircraft flies in, not just thunderstorms.

88. Which statement is true concerning the hazards of hail?

   A. Hail damage in horizontal flight is minimal due to the vertical movement of hail in the clouds.

   B. Rain at the surface is a reliable indication of no hail aloft.

   C. Hailstones may be encountered in clear air several miles from a thunderstorm.

Answer (C) is correct. (AC 00-24C)
   DISCUSSION: Hail competes with turbulence as the greatest thunderstorm hazard to aircraft. Hail has been observed in clear air several miles from the parent thunderstorm. You should anticipate possible hail with any thunderstorm, especially beneath the anvil of a large cumulonimbus cloud.
   Answer (A) is incorrect. Hail, along with turbulence, presents one of the greatest hazards to aircraft in thunderstorms; hail damages the leading edges and windshields of aircraft. **Answer (B) is incorrect.** Rain at the surface does not mean the absence of hail aloft; i.e., hail vs. rain is a function of temperature.

89. Ice pellets encountered during flight are normally evidence that

   A. a cold front has passed.

   B. there are thunderstorms in the area.

   C. freezing rain exists at higher altitude.

Answer (C) is correct. (FAA-H-8083-25B Chap 12)
   DISCUSSION: Rain falling through subfreezing cold air may become supercooled, freezing on impact as freezing rain, or it may freeze during its descent, falling as ice pellets. Ice pellets always indicate freezing rain at higher altitude.
   Answer (A) is incorrect. Ice pellets may indicate that either a warm front is about to pass or a cold front has passed, not only that a cold front has passed. **Answer (B) is incorrect.** Ice pellets always indicate freezing rain at higher altitudes (not necessarily that a thunderstorm is in the area).

90. What is indicated if ice pellets are encountered at 8,000 feet?

   A. Freezing rain at higher altitude.

   B. You are approaching an area of thunderstorms.

   C. You will encounter hail if you continue your flight.

Answer (A) is correct. (FAA-H-8083-25B Chap 12)
   DISCUSSION: Ice pellets form as a result of rain freezing at a higher altitude. There is a layer of warm air above in which it is raining, and the rain freezes as it falls through the colder air. Thus, either a warm front is about to pass or a cold front has passed.
   Answer (B) is incorrect. Freezing rain can be encountered even where there are no thunderstorms. **Answer (C) is incorrect.** Ice pellets are a form of hail.

91. Thunderstorms identified as severe or giving an intense radar echo should be avoided by what distance?

    A. 5 miles.

    B. At least 25 miles.

    C. At least 20 miles.

Answer (C) is correct. (AC 00-24C)
    DISCUSSION: Wind shear turbulence has been encountered as far as 20 NM laterally from a severe thunderstorm.
    Answer (A) is incorrect. The danger of shear turbulence exists 20 NM (not 5 NM) laterally from a severe storm.
    Answer (B) is incorrect. The danger of shear turbulence exists 20 NM (not 25 NM) laterally from a severe storm.

92. On initial climbout after takeoff and with the autopilot engaged, you encounter icing conditions. In this situation you can expect

    A. ice to accumulate on the underside of the wings due to the higher AOA.

    B. the autopilot to hold the vertical speed, if the anti-icing boots are working.

    C. the increased airflow under the wings to prevent the accumulation of ice.

Answer (A) is correct. (AC 91-74B)
    DISCUSSION: Airplanes are vulnerable to ice accumulation during the initial climbout in icing conditions because lower speeds often translate into a higher angle of attack (AOA). This exposes the underside of the airplane and its wings to the icing conditions and allows ice to accumulate further aft than it would in cruise flight.
    Answer (B) is incorrect. The autopilot will hold the vertical speed whether the anti-icing boots are working or not. Therefore, extreme vigilance should be exercised while climbing with the autopilot engaged. Climbing in vertical speed (VS) mode in icing conditions is highly discouraged. **Answer (C) is incorrect.** Lower speeds and a higher AOA will expose the underside of the airplane and its wings to the icing conditions and allow the accumulation of ice, not prevent the accumulation of ice.

93. You are avoiding a thunderstorm that is in your flightpath. You are over 20 miles from the cell however, you are under the anvil of the cell. Is this a hazard?

    A. No, you are at a safe distance from the cell.

    B. Yes, hail can be discharged from the anvil.

    C. Yes, this is still in the area of dissipation.

Answer (B) is correct. (AC 00-24C, AIM Para 7-1-26)
    DISCUSSION: Pilots should anticipate possible hail with any thunderstorm, especially beneath the anvil of a large cumulonimbus.
    Answer (A) is incorrect. Even if your flightpath is over 20 mi. from the cell, there is still potential to encounter hazards such as extreme clear air turbulence and hail when under the anvil. **Answer (C) is incorrect.** When underneath the anvil, the hazards you are most likely to encounter are clear air turbulence and hail.

94. Airborne weather radar is installed to help the crew

    A. penetrate weather between storm cells.

    B. avoid severe weather.

    C. avoid storm turbulence and hail.

Answer (B) is correct. (FAA-H-8083-25B Chap 13)
    DISCUSSION: Airborne radar is equipment carried by aircraft to locate and avoid severe weather.
    Answer (A) is incorrect. Radar should not be used to penetrate storm cells. Instead, it should be used to locate and avoid dangerous weather. **Answer (C) is incorrect.** Radar shows the location and intensity of precipitation, but it does not directly detect turbulence.

7.9 Turbulence

95. A pilot reporting turbulence that momentarily causes slight, erratic changes in altitude and/or attitude should report it as

A. light chop.

B. light turbulence.

C. moderate turbulence.

Answer (B) is correct. (AIM Chap 7)
DISCUSSION: Light turbulence momentarily causes slight, erratic changes in altitude and/or attitude.
Answer (A) is incorrect. Light chop is rapid, somewhat rhythmic bumpiness. **Answer (C) is incorrect.** Moderate turbulence causes changes in altitude and/or attitude, and variations in indicated airspeed.

96. When turbulence causes changes in altitude and/or attitude, but aircraft control remains positive, that should be reported as

A. light.

B. severe.

C. moderate.

Answer (C) is correct. (AIM Chap 7)
DISCUSSION: Moderate turbulence is similar to light turbulence but of greater intensity. Changes in altitude and/or attitude occur, but the aircraft remains in positive control at all times.
Answer (A) is incorrect. Light turbulence momentarily causes slight, erratic changes in altitude and/or attitude.
Answer (B) is incorrect. Severe turbulence causes large, abrupt changes in altitude and/or attitude and the aircraft may be momentarily out of control.

97. Turbulence that is encountered above 15,000 feet AGL not associated with cumuliform cloudiness, including thunderstorms, should be reported as

A. severe turbulence.

B. clear air turbulence.

C. convective turbulence.

Answer (B) is correct. (AC 00-30C)
DISCUSSION: CAT (clear air turbulence) is turbulence encountered in air where no clouds (or only occasional cirrus clouds) are present. The name is properly applied to high-level turbulence associated with wind shear, i.e., above 15,000 feet AGL.
Answer (A) is incorrect. Severe is a degree of turbulence not related to altitude. CAT may be light, moderate, or severe.
Answer (C) is incorrect. Convective turbulence refers to cumulus clouds and the lifting action related to turbulence.

98. The minimum vertical wind shear value critical for probable moderate or greater turbulence is

A. 4 knots per 1,000 feet.

B. 5 knots per 1,000 feet.

C. 8 knots per 1,000 feet.

Answer (B) is correct. (AC 00-30C)
DISCUSSION: Moderate or greater turbulence should be expected where vertical wind shears exceed 5 knots per 1,000 feet.
Answer (A) is incorrect. Moderate or greater turbulence should be expected where vertical wind shears exceed 5 knots (not 4 knots) per 1,000 feet. **Answer (C) is incorrect.** Moderate or greater turbulence should be expected where vertical wind shears exceed 5 knots (not 8 knots) per 1,000 feet.

99. One of the most dangerous features of mountain waves is the turbulent areas in and

A. below rotor clouds.

B. above rotor clouds.

C. below lenticular clouds.

Answer (A) is correct. (AC 00-57)
DISCUSSION: When stable air flows across a mountain range, large waves occur downwind from the mountains. Underneath each wave crest is a rotary circulation called a rotor. Turbulence is most frequent and most severe in and below the rotor clouds.
Answer (B) is incorrect. The turbulent areas of a mountain wave are in and below (not above) the rotor clouds. **Answer (C) is incorrect.** The most turbulent areas of a mountain wave are in and below the rotor (not lenticular) clouds.

100. The conditions most favorable to wave formation over mountainous areas are a layer of

A. stable air at mountaintop altitude and a wind of at least 20 knots blowing across the ridge.

B. unstable air at mountaintop altitude and a wind of at least 20 knots blowing across the ridge.

C. moist, unstable air at mountaintop altitude and a wind of less than 5 knots blowing across the ridge.

Answer (A) is correct. (AC 00-57)

DISCUSSION: A mountain wave requires a layer of stable air at mountaintop altitude and a wind of at least 20 knots blowing across the ridge.

Answer (B) is incorrect. The air at the mountaintop must be stable (not unstable). Unstable air tends to deter wave formation. **Answer (C) is incorrect.** The air at the mountaintop must be stable (not unstable). Unstable air tends to deter wave formation. Also, a wind of at least 20 knots (not 5 knots) must be blowing across the ridge.

101. When flying low over hilly terrain, ridges, or mountain ranges, the greatest potential danger from turbulent air currents will usually be encountered on the

A. leeward side when flying with a tailwind.

B. leeward side when flying into the wind.

C. windward side when flying into the wind.

Answer (B) is correct. (AC 00-6B)

DISCUSSION: When wind flows over ridges or mountain ranges, it flows up the windward side and down the leeward side. Thus, a pilot who approaches mountainous terrain from the leeward side may be forced into the side of the mountain by the downward-flowing air.

Answer (A) is incorrect. You are flying away from the mountain when you fly with the wind. **Answer (C) is incorrect.** You are flying in air rising up the mountain on the windward side.

102. Convective currents are most active on warm summer afternoons when winds are

A. light.

B. moderate.

C. strong.

Answer (A) is correct. (AC 00-6B)

DISCUSSION: Convective currents are localized vertical air movements, both ascending and descending. They are most active on warm summer afternoons when winds are light. Heated air at the surface creates a shallow, unstable layer, and the warm air is forced upward. Convection increases in strength and to greater heights as surface heating increases.

Answer (B) is incorrect. Moderate wind disrupts the vertical movement of convective currents. **Answer (C) is incorrect.** Strong wind disrupts the vertical movement of convective currents.

7.10 Wind Shear

103. During departure, under conditions of suspected low-level wind shear, a sudden decrease in headwind will cause

A. a loss in airspeed equal to the decrease in wind velocity.

B. a gain in airspeed equal to the decrease in wind velocity.

C. no change in airspeed, but groundspeed will decrease.

Answer (A) is correct. (FAA-H-8083-25B Chap 12)
DISCUSSION: In such low-airspeed operations, wind shears causing a sudden decrease in headwind are critical. A sudden decrease in headwind will decrease airspeed equal to the decrease in the wind velocity.
Answer (B) is incorrect. There is a loss (not gain) in airspeed. **Answer (C) is incorrect.** Initially, there is a loss of airspeed followed by an increase (not decrease) of groundspeed.

104. During an approach, the most important and most easily recognized means of being alerted to possible wind shear is monitoring the

A. amount of trim required to relieve control pressures.

B. heading changes necessary to remain on the runway centerline.

C. power and vertical velocity required to remain on the proper glidepath.

Answer (C) is correct. (AC 00-54)
DISCUSSION: If substantial power and vertical speed adjustments are required to remain on the proper glide path during an approach, wind shear factors exist.
Answer (A) is incorrect. Trim adjustments are a function of power settings, airspeeds, and flap-gear configurations. **Answer (B) is incorrect.** Heading changes necessary to remain on the runway centerline are related to crosswind direction rather than headwind/tailwind wind shears.

105. The Low Level Wind Shear Alert System (LLWAS) provides wind data and software process to detect the presence of a

A. rotating column of air extending from a cumulonimbus cloud.

B. change in wind direction and/or speed within a very short distance above the airport.

C. downward motion of the air associated with continuous winds blowing with an easterly component due to the rotation of the Earth.

Answer (B) is correct. (AIM Para 7-1-24)
DISCUSSION: The LLWAS provides wind data and software processes to detect the presence of hazardous wind shear and microbursts in the vicinity of the airport. Wind sensors mounted on poles as high as 150 ft., are located 2,000 to 3,500 ft. from the runway centerline.
Wind shear is defined as a change in wind speed and/or direction in a short distance and can exist in either, or both, the horizontal or vertical direction.
Answer (A) is incorrect. A rotating column of air extending from a cumulonimbus cloud describes a funnel cloud or tornado, which is a phenomenon that the LLWAS cannot detect. **Answer (C) is incorrect.** The downward motion of air associated with continuous winds blowing with an easterly component due to the rotation of the Earth is describing a general circulation pattern of air in the north polar region, not something a LLWAS is designed to detect.

106. What is an important characteristic of wind shear?

A. It is present at only lower levels and exists in a horizontal direction.

B. It is present at any level and exists in only a vertical direction.

C. It can be present at any level and can exist in both a horizontal and vertical direction.

Answer (C) is correct. (FAA-H-8083-25B Chap 12)
DISCUSSION: Wind shear occurs because of changes in wind direction and wind velocity, both horizontal and vertical. It may be present at any flight level.
Answer (A) is incorrect. Wind shear occurs at all altitudes and can be both vertical and horizontal. **Answer (B) is incorrect.** Wind shear occurs at all altitudes and can be both vertical and horizontal.

107. Low-level wind shear may occur when

  A. surface winds are light and variable.
  B. there is a low-level temperature inversion with strong winds above the inversion.
  C. surface winds are above 15 knots and there is no change in wind direction and windspeed with height.

Answer (B) is correct. (AC 00-6B)
  DISCUSSION: A low-level temperature inversion forms on a clear night with calm or light surface winds. When the wind just above the inversion is relatively strong, a wind shear zone develops between the calm and the stronger winds above.
  Answer (A) is incorrect. Light surface winds alone would not cause wind shear. **Answer (C) is incorrect.** By definition, wind shear refers to abrupt changes in wind speed and/or direction.

108. Hazardous wind shear is commonly encountered

  A. near warm or stationary frontal activity.
  B. when the wind velocity is stronger than 35 knots.
  C. in areas of temperature inversion and near thunderstorms.

Answer (C) is correct. (FAA-H-8083-25B Chap 12)
  DISCUSSION: Hazardous wind shear is found near thunderstorms and also near strong temperature inversions.
  Answer (A) is incorrect. Although frontal activity implies a change in wind, i.e., wind shear, the most hazardous wind shear is found specifically near inversions and thunderstorms. **Answer (B) is incorrect.** A strong wind does not by itself result in wind shear; it occurs only if there are strong winds in another direction.

109. If a temperature inversion is encountered immediately after takeoff or during an approach to a landing, a potential hazard exists due to

  A. wind shear.
  B. strong surface winds.
  C. strong convective currents.

Answer (A) is correct. (AC 00-6B Chap 17)
  DISCUSSION: A wind shear develops in a zone between cold, calm air covered by warm air with a strong wind. This often occurs during a temperature inversion.
  Answer (B) is incorrect. Strong surface winds by themselves do not create the potential hazard that wind shear does. **Answer (C) is incorrect.** Temperature inversion precludes (not generates) strong convective currents.

110. GIVEN:

Winds at 3,000 feet AGL	30 kts
Surface winds	Calm

While on approach for landing, under clear skies with convective turbulence a few hours after sunrise, one should

  A. increase approach airspeed slightly above normal to avoid stalling.
  B. keep the approach airspeed at or slightly below normal to compensate for floating.
  C. not alter the approach airspeed, these conditions are nearly ideal.

Answer (A) is correct. (AC 00-54)
  DISCUSSION: When landing in calm wind under clear skies within a few hours after sunrise, you should be prepared for a temperature inversion near the ground. Wind shear can be expected if the winds at 2,000 to 4,000 ft. are 25 kt. or more (30 kt. at 3,000 ft. in this question). Additionally, the convective turbulence on approach can cause abrupt changes in airspeed and may result in a stall at a low altitude. The corrective action for both of these conditions is to increase approach airspeed slightly above normal to avoid stalling.
  Answer (B) is incorrect. The danger in this situation is low-level wind shear and convective turbulence, both of which may cause an abrupt loss of airspeed during the approach. Thus, you should slightly increase, not maintain or reduce, airspeed above the normal approach speed. **Answer (C) is incorrect.** Low-level wind shear and convective turbulence are not ideal landing conditions. Thus, you should increase approach airspeed slightly above normal to avoid stalling.

STUDY UNIT EIGHT

AVIATION WEATHER SERVICES

(9 pages of outline)

This study unit contains outlines of major concepts tested, sample test questions and answers regarding aviation weather services, and an explanation of each answer. The table of contents above lists each subunit within this study unit, the number of questions pertaining to that particular subunit, and the pages on which the outlines and questions begin, respectively.

Recall that the **sole purpose** of this book is to expedite your passing of the FAA pilot knowledge test for the commercial pilot certificate. Accordingly, all extraneous material (i.e., topics or regulations not directly tested on the FAA pilot knowledge test) is omitted, even though much more knowledge is necessary to become a proficient commercial pilot. This additional material is presented in *Pilot Handbook* and *Commercial Pilot Flight Maneuvers and Practical Test Prep*, available from Gleim Publications, Inc. Order online at www.GleimAviation.com.

8.1 SOURCES OF WEATHER INFORMATION

1. Current en route and destination flight information for an IFR flight should be obtained from a flight service station (FSS) or an FAA-approved online source such as www.1800wxbrief.com.

    a. Weather report forecasts that are not routinely available at the FSS can best be obtained by contacting an NWS weather forecast office (WFO).

2. Contact Flight Service by using the name of the FSS facility in your area, your airplane identification, and the name of the nearest VOR on 122.2 MHz.

3. Weather advisory broadcasts, including AWWs, convective SIGMETs, and SIGMETs, are provided by ARTCCs on all frequencies, except emergency, when any part of the area described is within 150 mi. of the airspace under their jurisdiction.

8.2 AVIATION ROUTINE WEATHER REPORT (METAR)

1. Aviation routine weather reports (METARs) are actual weather observations at the time indicated on the report. There are two types of reports:

    a. METAR is an hourly routine observation (scheduled).
    b. SPECI is a special METAR observation (unscheduled).

2. The following elements appear after the type of report:

    a. The four-letter ICAO station identifier
    b. Date and time of report
    c. Modifier (if required)
    d. Wind
    e. Visibility
    f. Runway visual range
    g. Weather phenomena

        1) **RA** means rain.
        2) **BR** means mist.

h. Sky conditions

    1) Cloud bases are reported with three digits in hundreds of feet AGL.

        a) EXAMPLE: **OVC005** means overcast cloud layer at 500 ft. AGL.

    2) To determine the thickness of a cloud layer, first add the field elevation to the reported cloud base to determine the height of the cloud base in feet MSL and then subtract this from the reported cloud layer top.

i. Temperature/dewpoint

j. Altimeter

k. Remarks (RMK)

    1) **RAB12** means rain began at 12 min. past the hour.

        a) If the time of the observation was at 1854 UTC, the rain began at 1812 UTC.

    2) **WSHFT 30 FROPA** means wind shift, 30 min. past the hour, due to frontal passage.

3. EXAMPLE: METAR KAUS 301651Z 12008KT 4SM -RA HZ BKN010 BKN023 OVC160 21/17 A3005 RMK RAB25

a. METAR is a routine weather observation.

b. KAUS is Austin, TX.

c. 301651Z is the date (30th day) and time (1651 UTC) of the observation.

d. 12008KT means the wind is from 120° true at 8 kt.

e. 4SM means the visibility is 4 statute miles.

f. –RA HZ means light rain and haze.

g. BKN010 BKN023 OVC160 means ceiling 1,000 ft. broken, 2,300 ft. broken, 16,000 ft. overcast.

h. 21/17 means the temperature is 21°C and the dewpoint is 17°C.

i. A3005 means the altimeter setting is 30.05 in. Hg.

j. RMK RAB25 means remarks, rain began at 25 min. past the hour.

4. To determine the bases of convective-type cumulus clouds in thousands of feet, divide the temperature/dewpoint spread by 2.5.

8.3 AIRCRAFT OBSERVATIONS AND REPORTS

1. No observation is more timely or needed than the one that comes directly from the flight deck.

2. Pilot weather reports (PIREPs) are transmitted in the format illustrated on the next page.

    a. They are reported as either routine (UA) or special (UUA).

    b. All heights are given as MSL. To determine AGL, subtract the field height from the given height.

    c. Turbulence is reported as

        1) Light = LGT
        2) Moderate = MDT
        3) Severe = SVR

    d. Icing is reported as

        1) Clear = CLR
        2) Rime = RIME

    e. Cloud layers are reported with heights for bases, tops, and layer type if available. "No entry" means that information was not given.

        1) EXAMPLE: SK BKN024-TOP032/BKN-OVC042 decoded means a broken layer 2,400 ft. MSL to 3,200 ft. MSL. A second layer is broken to overcast starting at 4,200 ft. MSL.

    f. Wind direction and velocity are given as a five- or six-digit code (e.g., /WV 27045 means 270° at 45 kt.).

    g. Air temperature is expressed in degrees Celsius (°C).

    h. To best determine observed weather conditions between weather reporting stations, the pilot should refer to pilot reports.

3. Aircraft reports (AIREPs) are another type of aircraft observation. Automated AIREPs are common over the United States and reported by the pilot or generated automatically, with reports delivered to a ground station.

    a. They are reported as either routine (ARP) or special (ARS).

UUA/UA	Type of report:
	URGENT (UUA) - Any PIREP that contains any of the following weather phenomena: tornadoes, funnel clouds, or waterspouts; severe or extreme turbulence, including clear air turbulence (CAT); severe icing; hail; low-level wind shear (LLWS) (pilot reports air speed fluctuations of 10 knots or more within 2,000 feet of the surface); any other weather phenomena reported that are considered by the controller to be hazardous, or potentially hazardous, to flight operations. ROUTINE (UA) - Any PIREP that contains weather phenomena not listed above, including low-level wind shear reports with air speed fluctuations of less than 10 knots.
/OV	Location: Use VHF NAVAID(s) or an airport using the three- or four-letter location identifier. Position can be over a site, at some location relative to a site, or along a route. Ex: /OV KABC; /OV KABC090025; /OV KABC045020-DEF; /OV KABC-KDEF
/TM	Time: Four digits in UTC. Ex: /TM 0915
/FL	Altitude/Flight level: Three digits for hundreds of feet with no space between FL and altitude. If not known, use UNKN. Ex: /FL095; /FL310; /FLUNKN
/TP	Aircraft type: Four digits maximum; if not known, use UNKN. Ex: /TP L329; /TP B737; /TP UNKN
/SK	Sky cover: Describes cloud amount, height of cloud bases, and height of cloud tops. If unknown, use UNKN. Ex: /SK SCT040-TOP080; /SK BKNUNKN-TOP075; /SK BKN-OVC050-TOPUNKN; /SK OVCUNKN-TOP085
/WX	Flight visibility and weather: Flight visibility (FV) reported first and use standard METAR weather symbols. Intensity (– for light, no qualifier for moderate, and + for heavy) shall be coded for all precipitation types except ice crystals and hail. Ex: /WX FV05SM -RA; /WX FV01 SN BR; /WX RA
/TA	Temperature (Celsius): If below zero, prefix with an "M." Temperature should also be reported if icing is reported. Ex: /TA 15; /TA M06
/WV	Wind: Direction from which the wind is blowing, coded in tens of degrees using three digits. Directions of less than 100 degrees shall be preceded by a zero. The wind speed shall be entered as a two- or three-digit group immediately following the direction, coded in whole knots using the hundreds, tens, and units digits. Ex: /WV 27045KT; /WV 280110KT
/TB	Turbulence: Use standard contractions for intensity and type (CAT or CHOP when appropriate). Include altitude only if different from FL. Ex: /TB EXTRM; /TB OCNL LGT-MDT BLO 090; /TB MOD-SEV CHOP 080-110
/IC	Icing: Describe using standard intensity and type contractions. Include altitude only if different from FL. Ex: /IC LGT-MDT RIME; /IC SEV CLR 028-045
/RM	Remarks: Use free form to clarify the report, putting hazardous elements first. Ex: /RM LLWS –15 KT SFC-030 DURGC RY 22 JFK

8.4 SURFACE ANALYSIS CHART

1. The Surface Analysis Chart, often referred to as a surface weather map, is the basic observed weather chart.

    a. It provides a ready means of locating observed frontal positions and pressure centers.

    b. The Surface Analysis Chart displays weather information, such as

        1) Surface wind direction and speed
        2) Temperature
        3) Dewpoint
        4) Position of fronts
        5) Areas of high or low pressure
        6) Obstructions to vision

    c. It does not show cloud heights and coverage.

2. Solid lines depicting the pressure pattern are called isobars. They denote lines of equal pressure.

    a. Isobars are placed at 4-mb intervals.

    b. When the pressure gradient is weak, dashed isobars are sometimes inserted at 2-mb intervals to more clearly define the pressure pattern.

    c. Close spacing of isobars indicates a strong pressure gradient.

8.5 TERMINAL AERODROME FORECAST (TAF)

1. A terminal aerodrome forecast (TAF) is a concise statement of the expected meteorological conditions at an airport during a specified period.

    a. TAFs are issued four times daily and are usually valid for a 24-hr. period (or 30 hr. at certain high-impact airports).

2. The elements of a TAF are the following:

    a. Type of report

        1) TAF is a routine forecast.
        2) TAF AMD is an amended forecast.
        3) TAF COR is a corrected TAF.
        4) TAF RTD is a delayed TAF.

    b. ICAO station identifier

    c. Date and time the forecast is actually prepared

    d. Valid period of the forecast

    e. Forecast meteorological conditions -- the body of the forecast, which includes

        1) Wind

            a) **VRB** means a variable wind direction.

        2) Visibility

            a) **P6SM** means the forecast visibility is greater than 6 SM.

        3) Weather

        4) Sky condition

            a) **SKC** means no clouds or less than 1/8 cloud coverage, i.e., sky clear.

8.6 AIRMETs AND SIGMETs

1. Convective SIGMETs, SIGMETs, AIRMETs, and center weather advisories (CWAs), are forecasts to advise pilots of development of potentially hazardous weather.

   a. A SIGMET provides notice of potentially hazardous en route phenomena affecting an area of at least 3,000 sq. mi., such as severe turbulence, severe icing, widespread sandstorms or dust storms, volcanic ash, etc.

   b. AIRMETs and CWAs are issued for the possibility of moderate icing, moderate turbulence, sustained surface winds of 30 kt. or more, and extensive mountain obscuration.

2. SIGMET advisories are issued as a warning of weather phenomena that are potentially hazardous to all aircraft.

3. Convective SIGMETs contain both an observation and a forecast or just a forecast for

   a. Tornadoes
   b. Lines of thunderstorms
   c. Embedded thunderstorms
   d. Thunderstorm areas greater than 3,000 sq. mi. with an area coverage of 40% or more
   e. Hail greater than or equal to 3/4 in. in diameter

4. A squall is a sudden increase in wind speed of at least 16 kt. to a sustained speed of 22 kt. or more and lasting for at least 1 min.

8.7 LOW-LEVEL AND HIGH-LEVEL PROGNOSTIC CHARTS

1. Low-Level Significant Weather Prognostic Charts depict conditions expected to exist 12 and 24 hr. in the future.

   a. The upper limit of the Low-Level Significant Weather Prognostic Chart is 24,000 ft. MSL.

2. High-Level Significant Weather Prognostic Charts are also published.

   a. They forecast significant weather between 25,000 ft. MSL and 63,000 ft. MSL.

   b. A jet stream axis with a wind speed of more than 80 kt. is identified by a bold green line.

      1) An arrowhead is used to indicate wind direction.

      2) Wind change bars positioned along a jet stream axis identify 20-kt. wind speed changes.

   c. Small scalloped lines are used in High-Level Significant Weather Prognostic Charts to indicate cumulonimbus clouds.

      1) The presence of these clouds automatically implies moderate or greater turbulence and icing.

8.8 SURFACE PROG CHARTS

1.   Surface prog charts are forecasts for surface conditions. They include

     a.   Current surface analysis issued every 3 hr.
     b.   12- and 24-hr. forecasts issued four times a day
     c.   36-, 48-, and 60-hr. forecasts issued twice a day
     d.   Medium-range forecasts issued once a day from 3 to 7 days

2.   Surface prog charts are valid for the contiguous United States.

3.   Areas of precipitation expected at the valid time of the forecast are shaded in colors depending on the type and likelihood of precipitation.

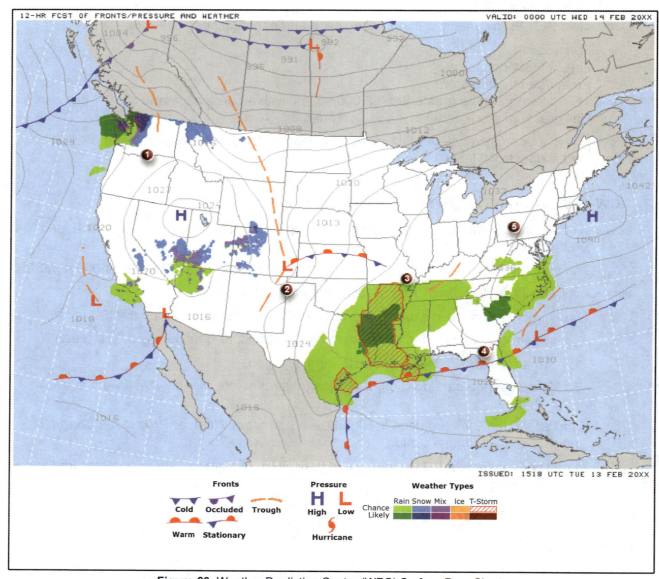

Figure 69. Weather Prediction Center (WPC) Surface Prog Chart.

8.9 OTHER WEATHER SERVICES

1. The freezing level panel found on the Lifted Index Chart is an analysis of observed freezing level data from upper air observations.

2. In the Winds Aloft Forecast, the winds are given in true direction and in knots.

3. Constant pressure charts provide information about the observed temperature, wind, and temperature/dewpoint spread at a specified altitude.

   a. Areas of strong winds (70 to 110 kt.) are denoted by hatching.

4. Flight Information Services-Broadcast (FIS-B) is a ground-based broadcast system provided through ADS-B via the 978 MHz data link that can display in-flight weather data.

   a. FIS-B information is intended for advisory use in assisting long- and near-term planning and decision making.

      1) The system lacks the updating capability necessary for tactical aerial maneuvering around localized weather phenomena.

   b. Many products are available through FIS-B, including AIRMETs, SIGMETs, convective SIGMETs, NEXRAD, D-NOTAMs, FDC-NOTAMs, METARs, TAFs, Winds Aloft, PIREPs, and Special Use Airspace status updates.

      1) Pilots should be aware that the NEXRAD uplink may be up to 20 min. old upon receipt and should not be used for navigation through severe weather.

QUESTIONS AND ANSWER EXPLANATIONS: All of the commercial pilot knowledge test questions chosen by the FAA for release as well as additional questions selected by Gleim relating to the material in the previous outlines are provided on the following pages. These questions have been organized into the same subunits as the outlines. To the immediate right of each question are the correct answer and answer explanations. You should cover these answers and answer explanations while responding to the questions. Refer to the general discussion in the Introduction on how to take the FAA knowledge test.

Remember that the questions from the FAA knowledge test bank have been reordered by topic and organized into a meaningful sequence. Also, the first line of the answer explanation gives the citation of the authoritative source for the answer.

QUESTIONS

8.1 Sources of Weather Information

1. Weather Advisory Broadcasts, including Severe Weather Forecast Alerts (AWWs), Convective SIGMETs, and SIGMETs, are provided by

   A. ARTCCs on all frequencies, except emergency, when any part of the area described is within 150 miles of the airspace under their jurisdiction.

   B. FSSs on 122.2 MHz and adjacent VORs, when any part of the area described is within 200 miles of the airspace under their jurisdiction.

   C. selected VOR navigational aids.

Answer (A) is correct. (AIM Para 7-1-8)
    DISCUSSION: ARTCCs broadcast an AWW, convective SIGMET, SIGMET, or center weather advisory (CWA) alert once on all frequencies, except emergency, when any part of the area described is within 150 mi. of the airspace under their jurisdiction.
    Answer (B) is incorrect. Weather advisory broadcasts are provided by ARTCCs on all frequencies (except emergency), not by FSSs on 122.2 MHz and adjacent VORs, when any part of the area described is within 150 mi., not 200 mi., of the airspace under their jurisdiction. **Answer (C) is incorrect.** Weather Advisory Broadcasts are provided by ARTCCs, not over VORs.

2. During preflight preparation, weather report forecasts which are not routinely available at the local service outlet (FSS) can best be obtained by means of contacting

   A. weather forecast office (WFO).

   B. air route traffic control center.

   C. pilot's automatic telephone answering service.

Answer (A) is correct. (AC 00-45H Chap 1)
    DISCUSSION: Weather report forecasts that are not routinely available at an FSS can be obtained by contacting a WFO.
    Answer (B) is incorrect. ARTCC is concerned with air traffic control, not weather briefings. **Answer (C) is incorrect.** PATWAS contains the weather products available at an FSS.

3. The most current en route and destination weather information for an instrument flight should be obtained from the

   A. FSS.

   B. ATIS broadcast.

   C. Notices to Airmen (class II).

Answer (A) is correct. (AC 00-45H Chap 1)
    DISCUSSION: FSSs are the primary source for obtaining en route and destination weather information.
    Answer (B) is incorrect. The ATIS broadcast includes information pertaining only to landing and departing operations at one airport and is thus not sufficient for en route information. **Answer (C) is incorrect.** Notices to Airmen (class II) do not contain weather information.

8.2 Aviation Routine Weather Report (METAR)

4. Refer to the excerpt from the following METAR report:

KTUS.....08004KT 4SM HZ .....26/04 A2995 RMK RAE36

At approximately what altitude AGL should bases of convective-type cumuliform clouds be expected?

   A. 4,400 feet.

   B. 8,800 feet.

   C. 17,600 feet.

Answer (B) is correct. (FAA-H-8083-25B Chap 12)
    DISCUSSION: To determine the approximate height of the cloud bases, you need the temperature and dewpoint. In the METAR report, the temperature is 26°C and the dewpoint is 4°C (26/04).
    In a convective current, temperature and dewpoint converge at a rate of 2.5°C per 1,000 ft.
    We can estimate the cumuliform cloud base in thousands of feet by dividing the temperature/dewpoint spread by 2.5. Given a temperature/dewpoint spread of 22°C (26° − 4°), the base of the convective-type cumuliform clouds is approximately 8,800 ft. AGL (22 ÷ 2.5).
    Answer (A) is incorrect. This is the approximate height of the base of cumuliform clouds if the temperature/dewpoint spread is 11°C, not 22°C. **Answer (C) is incorrect.** This is the approximate height of the base of cumuliform clouds if the temperature/dewpoint spread is 44°C, not 22°C.

5. What is the thickness of the cloud layer given a field elevation of 1,500 feet MSL with tops of the overcast at 7,000 feet MSL?

METAR KHOB 151250Z 17006KT 4SM OVC010 13/11 A2998

    A. 4,500 feet.

    B. 6,500 feet.

    C. 5,500 feet.

Answer (A) is correct. (FAA-H-8083-25B Chap 13)
    DISCUSSION: To determine the thickness of the cloud layer, find the difference between the tops and the base. Find the base in MSL by adding the field elevation (1,500 ft. MSL) to the reported base (OVC010, or 1,000 ft. AGL). The overcast cloud layer tops are reported at 7,000 ft. MSL, so the thickness of the cloud layer is 4,500 ft. (7,000 ft. − 2,500 ft.).
    Answer (B) is incorrect. To determine the thickness of the cloud layer, you must first find the base in MSL by adding, not subtracting, the field elevation (1,500 ft. MSL) to the reported base (OVC010, or 1,000 ft. AGL). This is then subtracted from the tops (7,000 ft. − 2,500 ft.). **Answer (C) is incorrect.** To determine the thickness of the cloud layer, you must first find the base in MSL by adding the field elevation (1,500 ft. MSL) to the reported base (OVC010, or 1,000 ft. AGL). Then subtract this total from the tops (7,000 ft. − 2,500 ft.).

6. The remarks section of the Aviation Routine Weather Report (METAR) contains the following coded information. What does it mean?

RMK FZDZB42 WSHFT 30 FROPA

    A. Freezing drizzle with cloud bases below 4,200 feet.

    B. Freezing drizzle below 4,200 feet and wind shear.

    C. Wind shift at three zero due to frontal passage.

Answer (C) is correct. (AC 00-45H Chap 3)
    DISCUSSION: The remark is decoded as freezing drizzle that began at 42 min. past the hour (FZDZB42) and a wind shift at 30 min. past the hour due to frontal passage (WSHFT 30 FROPA).
    Answer (A) is incorrect. FZDZB42 means that freezing drizzle began at 42 min. past the hour, not that the cloud bases are below 4,200 ft. **Answer (B) is incorrect.** Freezing drizzle began at 42 min. past the hour, not below 4,200 ft., and there was a wind shift, not wind shear, reported at 30 min. past the hour due to frontal passage.

7. The station originating the following METAR observation has a field elevation of 3,500 feet MSL. If the sky cover is one continuous layer, what is the thickness of the cloud layer? (Top of overcast reported at 7,500 feet MSL.)

METAR KHOB 151250Z 17006KT 4SM OVC005 13/11 A2998

    A. 2,500 feet.

    B. 3,500 feet.

    C. 4,000 feet.

Answer (B) is correct. (FAA-H-8083-25B Chap 12)
    DISCUSSION: In the METAR report, the base of the overcast cloud layer is reported as 500 ft. AGL (OVC005) or 4,000 ft. MSL (3,500 ft. field elevation plus 500 ft. AGL). If the overcast cloud layer top is reported at 7,500 ft. MSL, the cloud layer is 3,500 ft. thick (7,500 − 4,000).
    Answer (A) is incorrect. The cloud layer would be 2,500 ft. thick if the base of the overcast cloud layer was reported at 1,500 ft. (OVC015), not 500 ft. (OVC005). **Answer (C) is incorrect.** The top of the overcast cloud layer, not the thickness of the cloud layer, is 4,000 ft. AGL.

8. The station originating the following METAR observation has a field elevation of 5,000 feet MSL. If the sky cover is one continuous layer, what is the thickness of the cloud layer? (Top of overcast reported at 8,000 feet MSL.)

METAR KHOB 151250Z 17006KT 4SM OVC005 13/11 A2998

    A. 2,500 feet.

    B. 3,500 feet.

    C. 4,000 feet.

Answer (A) is correct. (FAA-H-8083-25B Chap 12)
    DISCUSSION: In the METAR report, the base of the overcast cloud layer is reported as 500 ft. AGL (OVC005) or 5,500 ft. MSL (5,000 ft. field elevation plus 500 ft. AGL). If the overcast cloud layer top is reported at 8,000 ft. MSL, the cloud layer is 2,500 ft. thick (8,000 − 5,500).
    Answer (B) is incorrect. To arrive at the cloud layer thickness, do not add the overcast cloud layer (OVC005) height (500 ft.) to the distance between the top of the cloud layer (8,000 ft.) and the field elevation (5,000 ft.). **Answer (C) is incorrect.** The top of the overcast cloud layer, not the thickness of the cloud layer, is 4,000 ft. AGL.

9. What is meant by the Special METAR weather observation for KBOI?

SPECI KBOI 091854Z 32005KT 1 1/2SM RA BR OVC007 17/16 A2990 RMK RAB12

 A. Rain and fog obscuring two-tenths of the sky; rain began at 1912Z.

 B. Rain and mist obstructing visibility; rain began at 1812Z.

 C. Rain and overcast at 1,200 feet AGL.

Answer (B) is correct. (AC 00-45H Chap 3)
 DISCUSSION: The SPECI report for KBOI is reporting a visibility of 1 1/2 SM in rain and mist (1 1/2SM RA BR), and the remarks indicate that the rain began at 12 min. past the hour, or 1812Z (RMK RAB12). Note the time of the SPECI is 1854Z.
 Answer (A) is incorrect. The obscuration is reported as mist (BR), not fog (FG), since the visibility is between 5/8 to 6 SM. Additionally, the rain began at 12 min. past the hour, or 1812Z, not 1912Z. **Answer (C) is incorrect.** The base of the overcast layer is reported at 700 ft. AGL (OVC007), not 1,200 ft. AGL.

10. What is meant by the Special METAR weather observation for KBOI?

SPECI KBOI 091854Z 32005KT 1 1/2SM RA BR OVC007 17/16 A2990 RMK RAB12

 A. Rain and fog are creating an overcast at 700 feet AGL; rain began at 1912Z.

 B. The temperature-dew point spread is 1°C; rain began at 1812Z.

 C. Rain and overcast at 1,200 feet AGL.

Answer (B) is correct. (AC 00-45H Chap 3)
 DISCUSSION: The SPECI report for KBOI is reporting a visibility of 1 1/2 SM in rain and mist (1 1/2SM RA BR), and the remarks indicate that the rain began at 12 min. past the hour, or 1812Z (RMK RAB12). Also, the report states temperature is 17°C and dew point is 16°C, which implies a temperature-dew point spread of 1°C. Note the time of the SPECI is 1854Z.
 Answer (A) is incorrect. The obscuration is reported as mist (BR), not fog (FG), since the visibility is between 5/8 to 6 SM. Additionally, the rain began at 12 min. past the hour, or 1812Z, not 1912Z. **Answer (C) is incorrect.** The base of the overcast layer is reported at 700 ft. AGL (OVC007), not 1,200 ft. AGL.

8.3 Aircraft Observations and Reports

11. What is the base of the ceiling in the following pilot report?

KMOB UA /OV APE230010/TM 1515/FL085/TP BE20/SK BKN065/WX FV03SM HZ FU/TA 20/TB LGT

 A. There is not a defined ceiling in this report.

 B. There is a layer reported at 8,500 feet.

 C. There is a broken layer at 6,500 feet.

Answer (C) is correct. (FAA-H-8083-25B Chap 13, AIM Para 7-1-18)
 DISCUSSION: The PIREP is reporting a broken layer of 6,500 ft. (SK BKN065).
 Answer (A) is incorrect. The PIREP is reporting a broken layer of 6,500 ft. (SK BKN065), which constitutes a ceiling. **Answer (B) is incorrect.** The altitude of the reporting aircraft is at 8,500 ft. (FL085), not the lowest overcast layer.

12. What significant cloud coverage is reported by this pilot report?

KMOB
UA/OV 15NW MOB 1340Z/SK OVC-TOP025/ OVC045-TOP090

 A. Three (3) separate overcast layers exist with bases at 2,500, 7,500, and 9,000 feet.

 B. The top of the lower overcast is 2,500 feet; the base and top of the second overcast layer are 4,500 feet and 9,000 feet, respectively.

 C. The base of the second overcast layer is 2,500 feet; the top of the second overcast layer is 7,500 feet; the base of the third layer is 9,000 feet.

Answer (B) is correct. (AC 00-45H Chap 3)
 DISCUSSION: In a PIREP, the significant cloud coverage is located in the sky cover (/SK) element. This PIREP states the top of the lower overcast cloud layer is 2,500 ft. (OVC-TOP025), and the base and top of the second overcast cloud layer are 4,500 ft. and 9,000 ft., respectively (OVC045-TOP090).
 Answer (A) is incorrect. There are two, not three, overcast cloud layers, none of which have a base of 7,500 ft. **Answer (C) is incorrect.** The top of the first, not the base of the second, overcast layer is 2,500 ft. The base of the second layer is 4,500 ft. with tops reported at 9,000 ft. There is no layer at 7,500 ft.

13. What significant cloud coverage is reported by this pilot report?

KMOB
UA/OV 15NW MOB 1340Z/SK OVC025-TOP045/ OVC075-TOP080/OVC090

A.   Three (3) separate overcast layers exist with bases at 2,500, 7,500 and 9,000 feet.

B.   The top of the lower overcast is 2,500 feet; base and top of second overcast layer are 4,500 and 9,000 feet, respectively.

C.   The base of the second overcast layer is 2,500 feet; top of second overcast layer is 7,500 feet; base of third layer is 9,000 feet.

Answer (A) is correct. (AC 00-45H Chap 3)
   DISCUSSION: The PIREP describes three overcast layers. The first layer has a base of 2,500 feet and a top of 4,500 feet. The second layer has a base of 7,500 feet and a top of 8,000 feet. The third layer begins at 9,000 feet.
   Answer (B) is incorrect. The base of the lowest layer is 2,500 feet. The base and top of the second overcast layer are 7,500 feet and 8,000 feet, respectively. **Answer (C) is incorrect.** The base of the second layer is 7,500 feet. The top of the second overcast layer is 8,000 feet. The last portion, which states a base for the third layer at 9,000 feet, is correct.

14. To best determine observed weather conditions between weather reporting stations, the pilot should refer to

A.   pilot reports.

B.   Area Forecasts.

C.   prognostic charts.

Answer (A) is correct. (FAA-H-8083-25B Chap 13)
   DISCUSSION: Pilot Weather Reports (PIREP) are observed weather conditions usually between weather reporting stations.
   Answer (B) is incorrect. Area forecasts are forecasts, not observed weather. NOTE: This product is being discontinued by the FAA. **Answer (C) is incorrect.** Prognostic charts are forecasts, not observed weather.

15. What is indicated by the following report?

TYR UUA/OV TYR180015/TM 1757/FL310/TP
   B737/TB MOD-SEV CAT 350-390

A.   An urgent pilot report for moderate to severe clear air turbulence.

B.   A routine pilot report for overcast conditions from flight levels 350-390.

C.   A special METAR issued on the 18th day of the month at 1757Z.

Answer (A) is correct. (AC 00-45H Sect 3.2)
   DISCUSSION: The UUA found in the first section of the report indicates an "Urgent Upper Air" report. The /TB MOD-SEV CAT 350-390 in the last section of the report indicates moderate to severe clear air turbulence for flight levels 350 to 390.
   Answer (B) is incorrect. If the report were a routine report, code UA would be used in the first section instead of UUA. **Answer (C) is incorrect.** The second section of the PIREP containing 1800 is the location section. In this example, /OV TYR 180015 indicates that the location of the weather-related phenomenon is on the 180° radial of the TYR VOR at 15 NM. A METAR is an aviation routine weather report; however, METAR coding is used to describe weather and visibility phenomena in the PIREP.

8.4   Surface Analysis Chart

16. The Surface Analysis Chart depicts

A.   frontal locations and expected movement, pressure centers, cloud coverage, and obstructions to vision at the time of chart transmission.

B.   actual frontal positions, pressure patterns, temperature, dewpoint, wind, weather, and obstructions to vision at the valid time of the chart.

C.   actual pressure distribution, frontal systems, cloud heights and coverage, temperature, dewpoint, and wind at the time shown on the chart.

Answer (B) is correct. (FAA-H-8083-25B Chap 13)
   DISCUSSION: The Surface Analysis Chart depicts actual frontal positions, pressure patterns, temperature, dewpoint, wind, weather, and obstructions to vision at the valid time of the chart.
   Answer (A) is incorrect. The Surface Analysis Chart reports actual surface weather as it exists at the time of observation, i.e., no forecasts. **Answer (C) is incorrect.** Surface Analysis Charts do not indicate cloud heights.

17. On a Surface Analysis Chart, the solid lines that depict sea level pressure patterns are called

A. isobars.

B. isogons.

C. millibars.

Answer (A) is correct. (AC 00-45H Chap 4)
DISCUSSION: Isobars are solid lines on the Surface Analysis Chart depicting the sea level pressure pattern. They are usually spaced at 4-mb intervals and connect points of equal or constant pressure.
Answer (B) is incorrect. Isogons are lines of magnetic variation found on navigational charts. **Answer (C) is incorrect.** Millibars are units of pressure, not lines that depict pressure patterns.

18. Dashed lines on a Surface Analysis Chart, if depicted, indicate that the pressure gradient is

A. weak.

B. strong.

C. unstable.

Answer (A) is correct. (AC 00-45H Chap 4)
DISCUSSION: When the pressure gradient is weak, dashed isobars are sometimes inserted at 2-mb intervals on the Surface Analysis Chart to more clearly define the pressure pattern.
Answer (B) is incorrect. Strong pressure gradients are depicted by closely spaced solid isobars at 4-mb intervals, not by dashed isobars at 2-mb intervals. **Answer (C) is incorrect.** Stability has to do with temperature lapse rates, not pressure levels.

19. Which chart provides a ready means of locating observed frontal positions and pressure centers?

A. Surface Analysis Chart.

B. Constant Pressure Analysis Chart.

C. Weather Depiction Chart.

Answer (A) is correct. (FAA-H-8083-25B Chap 13)
DISCUSSION: A Surface Analysis Chart provides a ready means of locating pressure systems and fronts. It also gives an overview of winds, temperatures, and dewpoint temperatures at chart time.
Answer (B) is incorrect. Constant Pressure Analysis Charts provide information on observed moisture content, temperatures, and winds aloft. **Answer (C) is incorrect.** A Weather Depiction Chart shows frontal location, cloud coverage and height, VFR-MVFR-IFR, etc., but not pressure centers. NOTE: This product is being discontinued by the FAA.

20. On a Surface Analysis Chart, close spacing of the isobars indicates

A. weak pressure gradient.

B. strong pressure gradient.

C. strong temperature gradient.

Answer (B) is correct. (FAA-H-8083-25B Chap 12)
DISCUSSION: On a Surface Analysis Chart, close spacing of the isobars indicates a strong pressure gradient. Each line represents a 4-mb change. If the lines are close together, the pressure is changing more rapidly over a given area.
Answer (A) is incorrect. The isobars will be widely, not closely, spaced when there is a weak pressure gradient. **Answer (C) is incorrect.** Isotherms, not isobars, indicate changing temperatures.

21. The distance measured in millibars separating isobars on surface analysis charts is typically

A. 2 mb.

B. 4 mb.

C. 6 mb.

Answer (B) is correct. (AC 00-45H Chap 4.1)
DISCUSSION: An isobar connects areas of similar barometric pressure. On a surface analysis chart, isobars are used to depict the sea-level pressure pattern; they are depicted with a series of solid black lines surrounding the defined pressure area. The interval between isobars is typically 4 mb, based on a standard pressure gradient.
Answer (A) is incorrect. A 2 mb distance between isobars indicates a greater rate of pressure change over a distance. **Answer (C) is incorrect.** A 6 mb distance between isobars indicates a more gradual pressure change over a distance.

22. The locations of fronts and pressure systems as of chart time are best determined by referring to a

A. constant pressure analysis chart.

B. CIP/FIP chart.

C. surface analysis chart.

Answer (C) is correct. (AC 00-45H Chap 4.1)
DISCUSSION: In addition to high and low pressure centers, a surface analysis chart depicts barometric pressures relative to sea level in MSL.
Answer (A) is incorrect. Constant pressure charts can be used to determine the observed temperature, wind, and temperature/dewpoint spread at specified flight levels. **Answer (B) is incorrect.** The current icing potential (CIP) and forecast icing potential (FIP) plots aid flight planning and situational awareness through graphical depiction of current and forecast icing conditions across an area or along a route of flight.

8.5 Terminal Aerodrome Forecast (TAF)

23. What does the contraction VRB in the Terminal Aerodrome Forecast (TAF) mean?

- A. Wind speed is variable throughout the period.
- B. Cloud base is variable.
- C. Wind direction is variable.

Answer (C) is correct. (AC 00-45H Chap 5)
   DISCUSSION: A variable wind direction forecast is noted by the contraction VRB where the three-digit wind direction usually appears.
   Answer (A) is incorrect. The contraction VRB indicates that the wind direction, not wind speed, is variable. **Answer (B) is incorrect.** The contraction VRB indicates that the wind direction, not cloud base, is variable.

24. Which statement pertaining to the following Terminal Aerodrome Forecast (TAF) is true?

TAF
KMEM 091135Z 0915 15005KT 5SM HZ BKN060
FM1600 VRB04KT P6SM SKC

- A. Wind in the valid period implies surface winds are forecast to be greater than 5 KTS.
- B. Wind direction is from 160° at 4 KTS and reported visibility is 6 statute miles.
- C. SKC in the valid period indicates no significant weather and sky clear.

Answer (C) is correct. (AC 00-45H Chap 5)
   DISCUSSION: The TAF indicates that from 1600Z the wind is forecast variable at 4 kt., visibility greater than 6 SM, no significant weather (implied since the weather element is omitted), and sky clear.
   Answer (A) is incorrect. Prior to 1600 UTC, the forecast wind is 150° at 5 kt., not greater than 5 kt. **Answer (B) is incorrect.** The wind direction is forecast to be variable, not 160°, and visibility is forecast to be greater than 6 SM (P6SM), not 6 SM (6SM).

25. The visibility entry in a Terminal Aerodrome Forecast (TAF) of P6SM implies that the prevailing visibility is expected to be greater than

- A. 6 nautical miles.
- B. 6 statute miles.
- C. 6 kilometers.

Answer (B) is correct. (AC 00-45H Chap 5)
   DISCUSSION: The visibility entry in a TAF of P6SM implies that the prevailing visibility is expected to be more than 6 statute miles (SM).
   Answer (A) is incorrect. The units of measure is statute miles (SM), not nautical miles (NM). **Answer (C) is incorrect.** The unit of measure is statute miles (SM), not kilometers.

26. In the following METAR/TAF for HOU, what is the ceiling and visibility forecast on the 7th day of the month at 0600Z?

KHOU 061734Z 0618/0718 16014G22KT P6SM
   VCSH BKN018 BKN035
FM070100 17010KT P6SM BKN015 OVC025
FM070500 17008KT 4SM BR SCT008 OVC012
FM071000 18005KT 3SM BR OVC007
FM071500 23008KT 5SM BR VCSH SCT008
   OVC015

- A. Visibility 6 miles with a broken ceiling at 15,000 feet MSL.
- B. 4 nautical miles of visibility and an overcast ceiling at 700 feet MSL.
- C. 4 statute miles visibility and an overcast ceiling at 1,200 feet AGL.

Answer (C) is correct. (AC 00-45H Chap 5)
   DISCUSSION: According to the TAF, there will be 4 statute miles visibility (4SM) and an overcast ceiling at 1,200 ft. AGL (OVC012) during the time period beginning on the 7th day of the month at 0500Z (FM070500) until the 7th day of the month at 1000Z (FM071000). The 7th day of the month at 0600Z is included within this period.
   Answer (A) is incorrect. The ceiling and visibility for the 7th day of the month at 0600Z is included within the forecast beginning on the 7th day of the month at 0500Z (FM070500). **Answer (B) is incorrect.** Prevailing visibility in the United States is in statute miles. The overcast layer is forecast to begin after 1000Z on the 7th day of the month (FM071000). The ceiling and visibility for the 7th day of the month at 0600Z is included within the forecast beginning on the 7th day of the month at 0500Z (FM070500).

27. Terminal Aerodrome Forecasts (TAF) are issued how many times a day and cover what period of time?

- A. Four times daily and are usually valid for a 24-hour period.
- B. Six times daily and are usually valid for a 24-hour period including a 4-hour categorical outlook.
- C. Six times daily and are valid for 12 hours including a 6-hour categorical outlook.

Answer (A) is correct. (AC 00-45H Chap 5)
   DISCUSSION: TAFs are issued four times daily and are usually valid for a 24-hr. period.
   Answer (B) is incorrect. TAFs are issued four, not six, times daily, and TAFs do not have a categorical outlook. **Answer (C) is incorrect.** TAFs are valid for a 24-hr., not 12-hr., period, and TAFs do not have a categorical outlook.

8.6   AIRMETs and SIGMETs

28. What single reference contains information regarding a volcanic eruption, that is occurring or expected to occur?

    A. In-Flight Weather Advisories.

    B. Terminal Area Forecasts (TAF).

    C. Weather Depiction Chart.

Answer (A) is correct. *(AIM Para 7-1-5)*
    DISCUSSION: A SIGMET, which is a type of in-flight weather advisory, will contain information regarding a volcanic eruption that is occurring or expected to occur.
    Answer (B) is incorrect. A SIGMET, not a TAF, is the single reference containing information regarding a volcanic eruption that is occurring or expected to occur. **Answer (C) is incorrect.** A Weather Depiction Chart is prepared from METAR reports and does not provide information regarding a volcanic eruption. NOTE: This product is being discontinued by the FAA.

29. In-Flight Aviation Weather Advisories include what type of information?

    A. Forecasts for potentially hazardous flying conditions for en route aircraft.

    B. State and geographic areas with reported ceilings and visibilities below VFR minimums.

    C. IFR conditions, turbulence, and icing within a valid period for the listed states.

Answer (A) is correct. *(AIM Para 7-1-5)*
    DISCUSSION: In-flight aviation weather advisories serve to notify en route pilots of the possibility of encountering hazardous flying conditions that may not have been forecast at the time of the preflight briefing. Whether or not the condition described is potentially hazardous to a particular flight is for the pilot to evaluate on the basis of experience and the operational limits of the aircraft.
    Answer (B) is incorrect. In-flight aviation weather advisories are forecasts, not reported or observed conditions. **Answer (C) is incorrect.** In-flight aviation weather advisories have a defined maximum forecast period and do not necessarily cover the entire time that IFR weather conditions, turbulence, and icing may be experienced.

30. What type of In-Flight Weather Advisories provides an en route pilot with information regarding the possibility of moderate icing, moderate turbulence, winds of 30 knots or more at the surface and extensive mountain obscurement?

    A. Convective SIGMETs and SIGMETs.

    B. Severe Weather Forecast Alerts (AWWs) and SIGMETs.

    C. AIRMETs and Center Weather Advisories (CWAs).

Answer (C) is correct. *(AIM Para 7-1-5)*
    DISCUSSION: AIRMETs are issued for the possibility of moderate icing, moderate turbulence, sustained winds of 30 kt. or more at the surface, widespread area of ceilings less than 1,000 ft. and/or visibility less than 3 SM, and extensive mountain obscurement. A CWA may be issued to supplement an AIRMET or to inform pilots when existing conditions meet AIRMET criteria but an AIRMET has not been issued.
    Answer (A) is incorrect. Convective SIGMETs concern only thunderstorms and related phenomena and imply the associated occurrence of turbulence and icing. A SIGMET is issued for severe, not moderate, icing and severe to extreme, not moderate, turbulence. **Answer (B) is incorrect.** An AWW defines an area of possible severe thunderstorms or tornado activity. A SIGMET is issued for severe, not moderate, icing and severe to extreme, not moderate, turbulence.

31. SIGMETs are issued as a warning of weather conditions which are hazardous

    A. to all aircraft.

    B. particularly to heavy aircraft.

    C. particularly to light airplanes.

Answer (A) is correct. *(AIM Para 7-1-5)*
    DISCUSSION: SIGMETs (significant meteorological information) advise of weather potentially hazardous to all aircraft other than convective activity (which is reported in a convective SIGMET). SIGMETs cover severe icing; severe or extreme turbulence; or duststorms, sandstorms, or volcanic ash lowering visibility to less than 3 SM.
    Answer (B) is incorrect. SIGMETs pertain to all, not just heavy, aircraft. **Answer (C) is incorrect.** SIGMETs pertain to all, not just light, aircraft.

32. What wind conditions would you anticipate when squalls are reported at your destination?

    A. Rapid variations in windspeed of 15 knots or more between peaks and lulls.

    B. Peak gusts of at least 35 knots combined with a change in wind direction of 30° or more.

    C. Sudden increases in windspeed of at least 16 knots to a sustained speed of 22 knots or more for at least 1 minute.

Answer (C) is correct. *(FAA-H-8083-25B Chap 12)*
    DISCUSSION: A squall is a sudden increase in wind speed of at least 16 kt. to a sustained speed of 22 kt. or more and lasting for at least 1 minute.
    Answer (A) is incorrect. Rapid variations in wind speed describe gusts (not squalls). **Answer (B) is incorrect.** Abrupt changes in both direction and speed describe wind shear (not squalls).

33. Which correctly describes the purpose of convective SIGMETs (WST)?

   A. They consist of an hourly observation of tornadoes, significant thunderstorm activity, and large hailstone activity.

   B. They contain both an observation and a forecast of all thunderstorm and hailstone activity. The forecast is valid for 1 hour only.

   C. They consist of either an observation and a forecast or just a forecast for tornadoes, significant thunderstorm activity, or hail greater than or equal to 3/4 inch in diameter.

Answer (C) is correct. *(AIM Para 7-1-5)*
   DISCUSSION: Convective SIGMETs are issued for severe thunderstorms resulting in surface winds greater than 50 kt., hail at the surface, hail of 3/4 in. diameter, tornadoes, embedded thunderstorms, lines of thunderstorms, and very severe thunderstorms.
   Answer (A) is incorrect. A WST is an unscheduled, not a scheduled, forecast. **Answer (B) is incorrect.** WSTs are issued only for severe thunderstorms and hail 3/4 in. or larger. Also, WSTs can be for periods up to 2 hr., not 1 hr.

8.7 Low-Level and High-Level Prognostic Charts

34. Which weather chart depicts conditions forecast to exist at a specific time in the future?

   A. Freezing Level Chart.

   B. Weather Depiction Chart.

   C. 12-hour Significant Weather Prognostic Chart.

Answer (C) is correct. *(AC 00-45H Chap 5)*
   DISCUSSION: U.S. Low-Level Significant Weather Prognostic Charts are issued four times daily. They contain 12- and 24-hr. forecasts indicating forecast weather at 00Z, 06Z, 12Z, and 18Z.
   Answer (A) is incorrect. There is no Freezing Level Weather Chart, per se. **Answer (B) is incorrect.** Weather Depiction Charts report current observed, not forecast, weather. NOTE: This product is being discontinued by the FAA.

35. What weather phenomenon is implied within an area enclosed by small scalloped lines on a U.S. High-Level Significant Weather Prognostic Chart?

   A. Cirriform clouds, light to moderate turbulence, and icing.

   B. Cumulonimbus clouds, icing, and moderate or greater turbulence.

   C. Cumuliform or standing lenticular clouds, moderate to severe turbulence, and icing.

Answer (B) is correct. *(AC 00-45H Chap 5)*
   DISCUSSION: Small scalloped lines are used on High-Level Significant Weather Prognostic Charts to indicate expected cumulonimbus clouds. This automatically implies moderate or greater turbulence and icing (which are not depicted separately).
   Answer (A) is incorrect. Cumulonimbus, not cirriform, clouds are indicated by small scalloped lines. **Answer (C) is incorrect.** Standing lenticular clouds would be indicated as clear air turbulence by heavy dashed lines encircling the forecast area.

36. What is the upper limit of the Low Level Significant Weather Prognostic Chart?

   A. 30,000 feet.

   B. 24,000 feet.

   C. 18,000 feet.

Answer (B) is correct. *(AC 00-45H Chap 5)*
   DISCUSSION: The upper limit of the Low-Level Significant Weather Prognostic Chart is 24,000 ft. MSL. The lower limit is the surface.
   Answer (A) is incorrect. The upper limit of the Low-Level Significant Weather Prognostic Chart is 24,000 ft. MSL, not 30,000 ft. MSL. **Answer (C) is incorrect.** The upper limit of the Low-Level Significant Weather Prognostic Chart is 24,000 ft. MSL (not 18,000 ft. MSL).

37. The U.S. High-Level Significant Weather Prognostic Chart forecasts significant weather for what airspace?

   A. 18,000 feet to 45,000 feet.

   B. 25,000 feet to 45,000 feet.

   C. 25,000 feet to 63,000 feet.

Answer (C) is correct. *(AC 00-45H Chap 5)*
   DISCUSSION: High-Level Significant Weather Prognostic Charts forecast significant weather for the altitudes from 25,000 ft. MSL to 63,000 ft. MSL.
   Answer (A) is incorrect. The base is 25,000 ft. MSL, not 18,000 ft. MSL, and the ceiling is 63,000 ft. MSL, not 45,000 ft. MSL. **Answer (B) is incorrect.** The ceiling is 63,000 ft. MSL, not 45,000 ft. MSL.

38. What is indicated by a bold green line on a High-Level Significant Weather Chart?

A. Embedded thunderstorms.

B. Moderate to severe turbulence.

C. Jet stream axis.

Answer (C) is correct. (AC 00-45H)
DISCUSSION: A jet stream axis with a wind speed of more than 80 kt. is identified by a bold green line. An arrowhead is used to indicate wind direction. Wind change bars positioned along a jet stream axis identify 20-kt. wind speed changes.
Answer (A) is incorrect. Embedded thunderstorms are located within areas of red scalloped lines. **Answer (B) is incorrect.** Turbulence is indicated by yellow dashed lines.

39. (Refer to Figure 71 on page 301.) What conditions should you expect when landing at an airport in area 3?

A. Moderate turbulence.

B. Marginal VFR conditions.

C. Instrument meteorological conditions.

Answer (C) is correct. (AC 00-45H)
DISCUSSION: The red line surrounding area 3 indicates instrument meteorological conditions, which occur when the ceiling is less than 1,000 ft. and/or visibility is less than 3 mi.
Answer (A) is incorrect. Dashed yellow lines indicating turbulence are not present in area 3. **Answer (B) is incorrect.** IFR, not MVFR, conditions are indicated by the red line surrounding area 3.

40. (Refer to Figure 71 on page 301.) At what altitude is the freezing level over area 5 on the 12-hr. significant weather prognostic chart?

A. 8,000 ft.

B. 4,000 ft.

C. At the surface.

Answer (C) is correct. (AC 00-45H)
DISCUSSION: The freezing level forecast for the first 12-hr. period is shown on the left panel. The freezing level is indicated by a dashed line and labeled in hundreds of feet MSL, or by a jagged line without a label if the freezing level is at the surface. Area 5 is north of the jagged line, indicating the freezing level begins at the surface.
Answer (A) is incorrect. The 8,000-ft. freezing level is indicated on the 12-hr. significant weather prognostic chart south of area 5 by the dashed teal line labeled 080. **Answer (B) is incorrect.** The 4,000-ft. freezing level is indicated on the 12-hr. significant weather prognostic chart south of area 5 by the dashed teal line labeled 040.

41. (Refer to Figure 71 on page 301.) How are significant weather prognostic charts best used by a pilot?

A. For determining areas to avoid (freezing levels and turbulence).

B. For overall planning at all altitudes.

C. For analyzing current frontal activity and cloud coverage.

Answer (A) is correct. (AC 00-45H)
DISCUSSION: Significant weather prognostic charts forecast conditions that exist 12 and 24 hr. in the future. They include two types of forecasts: low-level significant weather, such as IFR and marginal VFR areas, and moderate or greater turbulence areas and freezing levels.
Answer (B) is incorrect. A complete set of weather forecasts for overall planning includes terminal forecasts, graphical forecasts for aviation, etc. **Answer (C) is incorrect.** The weather depiction chart shows analysis of frontal activities, cloud coverage, ceilings, etc. NOTE: This product is being discontinued by the FAA.

42. (Refer to Figure 71 on page 301.) The U.S. Low-Level Significant Weather Prognostic Chart depicts weather conditions

A. that are forecast to exist at a specific time shown on the chart.

B. as they existed at the time the chart was prepared.

C. that are forecast to exist 6 hr. after the chart was prepared.

Answer (A) is correct. (AC 00-45H)
DISCUSSION: A low-level prognostic chart contains two panels; the one on the left is for 12 hr. after the time of issuance, and the one on the right is for 24 hr. after issuance.
Answer (B) is incorrect. Prognostic charts forecast conditions; they do not report observed conditions (as does a weather depiction chart). **Answer (C) is incorrect.** The low-level prognostic chart forecasts conditions 12 and 24 hr., not 6 hr., after the time of issuance.

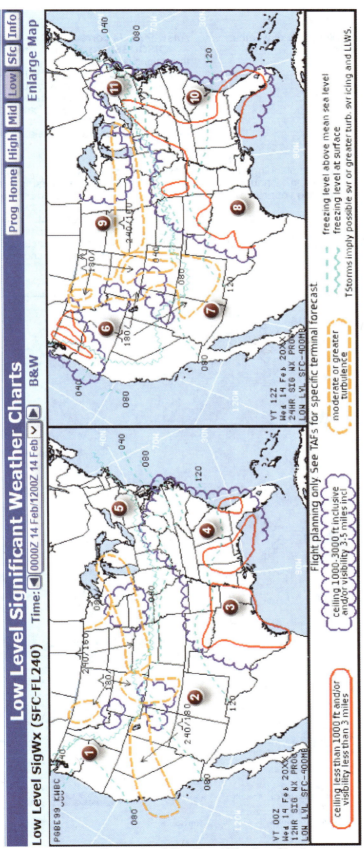

Figure 71. Low-level Significant Weather Chart.

8.8 Surface Prog Charts

43. (Refer to Figure 69 below.) What type of weather is likely to occur in area 3 at 0000Z?

A. Rain.

B. Thunderstorms.

C. Mix.

Answer (A) is correct. (AC 00-45H)
   DISCUSSION: The dark green shading in area 3 indicates that rain is likely to occur.
   Answer (B) is incorrect. The red diagonal lines in area 3 indicate that there is a chance of thunderstorms, not that thunderstorms are likely. **Answer (C) is incorrect.** There is no purple shading in area 3 indicating mixed precipitation. "Mixed" can refer to precipitation where a combination of rain and snow, rain and sleet, or snow and sleet is forecast.

44. (Refer to Figure 69 below.) You are planning to depart on a flight from area 2 to area 4 in 12 hours. What weather is forecast to occur along your route?

A. Rain and thunderstorms.

B. Thunderstorms with mixed precipitation.

C. Moderate turbulence.

Answer (A) is correct. (AC 00-45H)
   DISCUSSION: Thunderstorms and rain are forecast to exist along your route as indicated by the green shading and red diagonal lines.
   Answer (B) is incorrect. Thunderstorms and rain, not mixed precipitation, are forecast to exist. **Answer (C) is incorrect.** Turbulence forecasts are not included in this chart. Only surface conditions are shown.

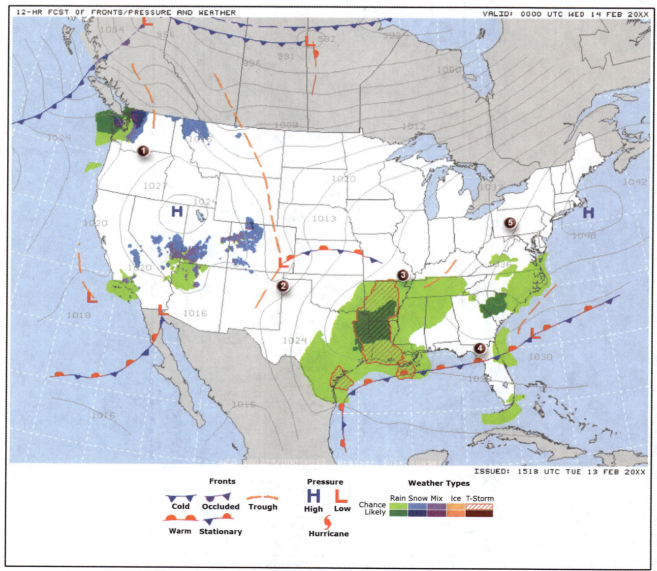

Figure 69. Weather Prediction Center (WPC) Surface Prog Chart.

45. (Refer to Figure 70 below.) At what time will the forecast conditions occur?

  A. 0000 UTC FRI.

  B. 0000 UTC TUE.

  C. 1845 UTC TUE.

Answer (A) is correct. (AC 00-45H)
    DISCUSSION: The valid time of the forecast, 0000 UTC on Friday, is listed in the top right corner of the chart.
    Answer (B) is incorrect. The valid time of the forecast is 0000 UTC on Friday, not Tuesday. **Answer (C) is incorrect.** The forecast was issued at 1845 UTC on Tuesday but is not valid until 0000 UTC on Friday.

46. (Refer to Figure 70 below.) What type of front is passing through area 1?

  A. Cold.

  B. Occluded.

  C. Stationary.

Answer (C) is correct. (AC 00-45H)
    DISCUSSION: The alternating red semicircles and blue triangles in area 1 represent a stationary front, which is a front between warm and cold air masses that is moving very slowly or not at all.
    Answer (A) is incorrect. A cold front is represented by a blue line with triangles pointing in the direction of movement. A stationary front is represented by alternating red semicircles and blue triangles. **Answer (B) is incorrect.** An occluded front is represented by a purple line with both triangles and semicircles, not alternating red semicircles and blue triangles.

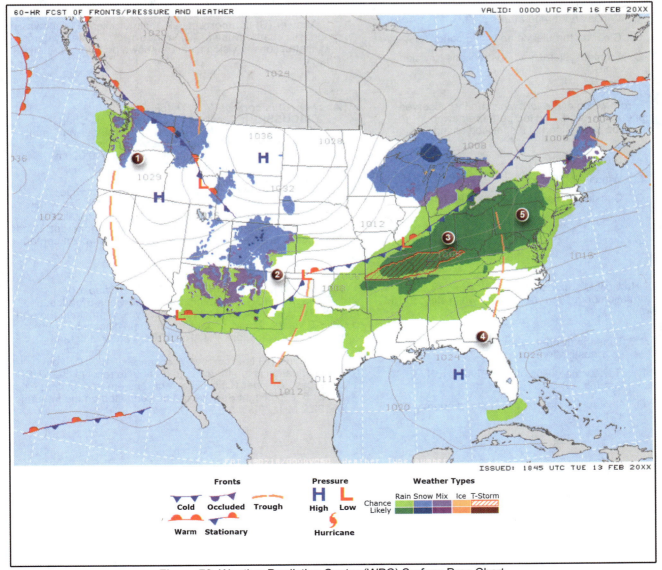

Figure 70. Weather Prediction Center (WPC) Surface Prog Chart.

8.9   Other Weather Services

47. What values are used for Winds Aloft Forecasts?

A. True direction and MPH.

B. True direction and knots.

C. Magnetic direction and knots.

Answer (B) is correct. (AC 00-45H Chap 5)
DISCUSSION: In the Winds Aloft Forecast, the temperature is in degrees Celsius, and the winds are the true direction and in knots.
Answer (A) is incorrect. The wind measurement is in knots, not MPH. **Answer (C) is incorrect.** The wind direction is true, not magnetic.

48. Hatching on a Constant Pressure Analysis Chart indicates

A. hurricane eye.

B. windspeed 70 knots to 110 knots.

C. windspeed 110 knots to 150 knots.

Answer (B) is correct. (AC 00-45H Chap 5)
DISCUSSION: On Constant Pressure Analysis Charts, areas of strong winds are indicated by hatching, or shading, which indicates winds of 70 to 110 kt.
Answer (A) is incorrect. Hurricane eyes have very low winds. **Answer (C) is incorrect.** Wind speeds between 110 and 150 kt. are shown by a clear area within a hatched area.

49. What flight planning information can a pilot derive from Constant Pressure Analysis Charts?

A. Winds and temperatures aloft.

B. Clear air turbulence and icing conditions.

C. Frontal systems and obstructions to vision aloft.

Answer (A) is correct. (AC 00-45H Chap 5)
DISCUSSION: Constant Pressure Analysis Charts provide information about the observed upper-air temperature, wind, and temperature/dewpoint spread along your proposed route.
Answer (B) is incorrect. Clear air turbulence is shown on prognostic charts. **Answer (C) is incorrect.** Frontal systems and obstructions to vision aloft are shown on Surface Analysis Charts.

50. From which of the following can the observed temperature, wind, and temperature/dewpoint spread be determined at a specified altitude?

A. Stability Charts.

B. Winds Aloft Forecasts.

C. Constant Pressure Analysis Charts.

Answer (C) is correct. (AC 00-45H Chap 5)
DISCUSSION: Constant Pressure Analysis Charts provide information about observed temperature, wind, and temperature/dewpoint spread at specified pressure altitudes. The altitudes are 850 mb (5,000 ft.), 700 mb (10,000 ft.), 500 mb (18,000 ft.), 300 mb (30,000 ft.), and 200 mb (approximately 39,000 ft.).
Answer (A) is incorrect. Stability Charts provide information about stability, freezing level, precipitable water, and average relative humidity, but they do not contain the temperature/dewpoint spread. **Answer (B) is incorrect.** Winds Aloft Forecasts do not give the temperature/dewpoint spread aloft.

51. How could you receive in-flight weather information about your destination while still 150 NM away?

A. Tune the frequency and listen to the ATIS for your destination.

B. Review the destination METAR and TAF through FIS-B.

C. Contact Flight Service on the frequency 121.5.

Answer (B) is correct. (FAA-H-8083-25B Chap 13)
DISCUSSION: Flight Information Services-Broadcast (FIS-B) is a ground-based broadcast system provided through ADS-B via the 978 MHz data link that can display in-flight weather data such as METARs, TAFs, Winds Aloft, and PIREPs.
Answer (A) is incorrect. A distance of 150 NM from the destination is too far away to be able to receive the ATIS broadcast. **Answer (C) is incorrect.** The emergency frequency is 121.5 MHz. Flight Service can be contacted on the frequency of 122.2 MHz.

STUDY UNIT NINE

NAVIGATION: CHARTS, PUBLICATIONS, FLIGHT COMPUTERS

(40 pages of outline)

This study unit contains outlines of major concepts tested; sample test questions and answers regarding navigation charts, publications, and flight computers; and an explanation of each answer. The table of contents above lists each subunit within this study unit, the number of questions pertaining to that particular subunit, and the pages on which the outlines and questions begin, respectively.

Recall that the **sole purpose** of this book is to expedite your passing of the FAA pilot knowledge test for the commercial pilot certificate. Accordingly, all extraneous material (i.e., topics or regulations not directly tested on the FAA pilot knowledge test) is omitted, even though much more knowledge is necessary to become a proficient commercial pilot. This additional material is presented in *Pilot Handbook* and *Commercial Pilot Flight Maneuvers and Practical Test Prep*, available from Gleim Publications, Inc. Order online at www.GleimAviation.com.

9.1 SECTIONAL CHARTS

1. Blue airport symbols indicate airports with at least a part-time control tower.

   a. Magenta airport symbols indicate airports without a control tower.

2. True course measurements on a sectional chart should be made along a meridian (line of longitude) near the midpoint of the course because the angles formed by lines of longitude and the course line vary from point to point.

   a. Lines of longitude are not parallel because they go from pole to pole.

3. Each rectangular area bounded by lines of latitude and longitude contains a pair of numbers in large, bold print to indicate the height of the maximum elevation of terrain or obstructions within that area of latitude and longitude. This is called the **maximum elevation figure (MEF)**.

   a. The larger number to the left indicates thousands of feet.
   b. The smaller number to the right indicates hundreds of feet.

4.   Obstructions on sectional charts are marked as shown below:

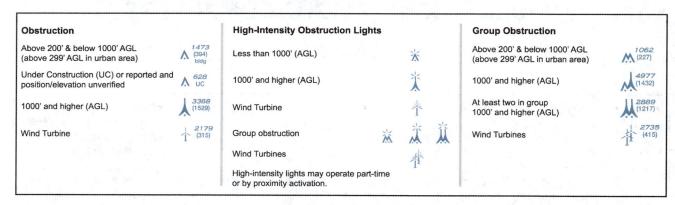

a.   The elevation of the terrain at the base of the obstruction is the bold figure of feet in MSL minus the figure in parentheses (feet AGL).

    1)   Use this computation to compute terrain elevation.

    2)   Airport elevation is also given in the airport identifier for each airport.

5.   Airport identifiers include the following information:

a.   The name of the airport.

b.   The elevation of the airport, followed by the length of the longest hard-surfaced runway. An L between the altitude and length indicates lighting.

    1)   EXAMPLE: "1008 L 70" means an airport elevation of 1,008 ft. MSL, lighting sunset to sunrise, and a length of 7,000 ft. for the longest hard-surfaced runway.

    2)   If the L has an asterisk beside it (*L), it means pilot-controlled lighting or lighting limitations exist. Refer to the Chart Supplement.

c.   Private, or **"(Pvt),"** indicating a nonpublic-use airport having emergency or landmark value.

d.   The star that follows the Control Tower (CT) frequency indicates that the control tower has limited hours of operation.

    1)   The tower frequencies table on the edge of the sectional chart lists the specific times the tower is operational.

6.   The following information illustrates how airspace is depicted on sectional charts.

   a.   Class A Airspace

      1)   Class A airspace begins at 18,000 ft. MSL, extends up to approximately 60,000 ft. MSL, and includes the airspace overlying the contiguous United States and Alaska.

      2)   Class A airspace is not depicted on sectional charts.

   b.   Class B Airspace

      1)   The lateral limits of Class B airspace are depicted by heavy blue lines on a sectional or terminal area chart.

         a)   The vertical limits of each section of Class B airspace are shown in hundreds of feet MSL.

      2)   The 30-NM veil, within which an altitude reporting transponder (Mode C) is required regardless of aircraft altitude, is depicted by a thin magenta circle.

      3)   Class B airspace is shown on the sectional chart (below left) and on the diagram (below right).

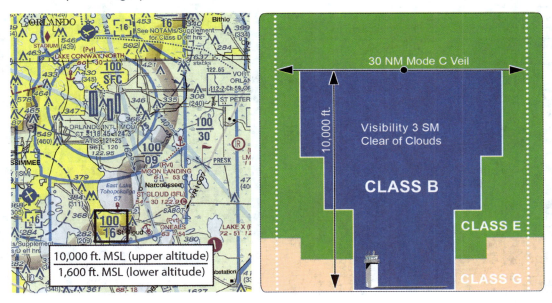

10,000 ft. MSL (upper altitude)
1,600 ft. MSL (lower altitude)

c.   Class C Airspace

1)   The lateral limits of Class C airspace are depicted by solid magenta lines on sectional and some terminal area charts.

   a)   The vertical limits of each circle are shown in hundreds of feet MSL.

   b)   The inner surface area extends from the surface upward to the indicated altitude (usually 4,000 ft. above the airport elevation) and outward 5 NM from the primary airport.

   c)   The shelf area extends from the indicated altitude (usually 1,200 ft. above the airport elevation) to the same upper altitude limit as the surface area.

2)   Class C airspace is shown on the sectional chart (below left) and on the diagram (below right).

   a)   In the example, the vertical limits of Class C airspace extend

      i)   From the surface (SFC) to 4,000 ft. MSL (40) in the surface area and
      ii)   From 1,200 ft. MSL (12) to 4,000 ft. MSL in the shelf area.

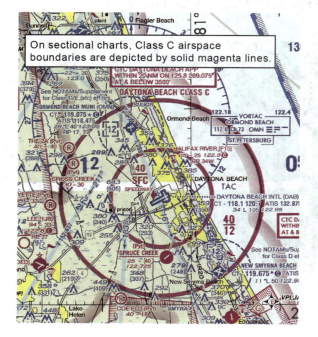
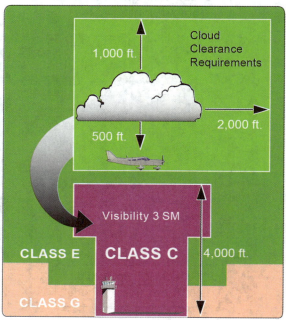

d.   Class D Airspace

   1)   The lateral limits of Class D airspace are depicted by dashed blue lines on a
        sectional or terminal area chart.

        a)   The ceiling (usually 2,500 ft. above the airport elevation) is shown within the
             circle in hundreds of feet MSL.

   2)   Class D airspace is shown on the sectional chart (below left) and on the diagram
        (below right).

        a)   The ceiling of Class D airspace in the examples is 2,700 ft. MSL.

        b)   If depicted, a dashed magenta line (see the upper right of the Class D airspace
             in the example below) illustrates an area of Class E airspace extending
             upward from the surface.

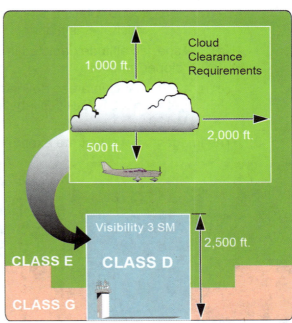

e.   Class E Airspace

1)   Class E airspace is any controlled airspace that is not Class A, B, C, or D airspace.

2)   The lower limits of Class E airspace are specified by markings on terminal and sectional charts. Class E airspace begins at

a)   The surface in areas marked by segmented (dashed) magenta lines.

b)   700 ft. AGL inside of areas marked by shaded magenta lines.

c)   1,200 ft. AGL outside of areas marked by shaded blue lines.

i)   Shaded blue lines do not appear on most sectional charts.

ii)   If shaded blue lines are not present, then Class E airspace begins at 1,200 ft. AGL, unless this airspace is otherwise designated.

iii)   Inside of an area marked by shaded blue lines, or if not defined, the floor of Class E airspace begins at 14,500 ft. MSL or 1,200 ft. AGL, whichever is higher.

d)   A specific altitude depicted in En Route Domestic Areas denoted by blue "zipper" marks.

e)   1,200 ft. AGL in areas defined as Federal Airways, indicated by blue lines between VOR facilities labeled with the letter "V" followed by numbers, e.g., V-120.

3)   The images below illustrate examples of Class E airspace depictions.

4)   Class E airspace extends up to, but does not include, 18,000 ft. MSL.

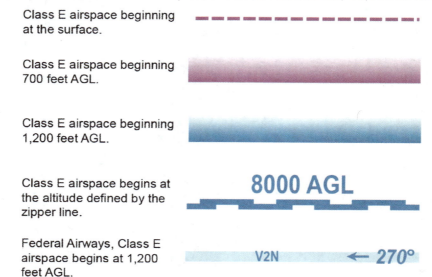

Class E airspace beginning at the surface.

Class E airspace beginning 700 feet AGL.

Class E airspace beginning 1,200 feet AGL.

Class E airspace begins at the altitude defined by the zipper line.

8000 AGL

Federal Airways, Class E airspace begins at 1,200 feet AGL.

V2N ← 270°

f.   Class G Airspace

   1)   Class G airspace is not depicted on sectional charts. It is implied to exist everywhere controlled airspace does not exist.

   2)   Class G airspace extends upward from the surface to the floor of overlying controlled airspace.

   3)   A Class G airport is any airport where Class B, C, D, or E airspace does not extend to the surface.

g.   Special Use Airspace

   1)   Prohibited areas are areas where the flight of aircraft is prohibited. These areas are established for security or other reasons associated with national welfare.

      a)   Prohibited areas are depicted by blue hashed lines labeled with a "P" followed by a number (e.g., P-40).

   2)   Restricted areas are areas where unusual, often invisible, hazards to aircraft exist. While not wholly prohibited, the flight of aircraft within these areas is subject to restrictions.

      a)   Restricted areas are depicted by blue hashed lines labeled with an "R" followed by a number (e.g., R-4009).

   3)   Warning areas are depicted by blue hashed lines labeled with a "W" followed by a number (e.g., W-103).

   4)   Military operations areas (MOAs) consist of airspace established to separate certain military training activities from IFR traffic.

      a)   MOAs are depicted by magenta hashed lines.

      b)   Pilots operating under VFR should exercise extreme caution while flying within an MOA when military activity is being conducted.

      c)   Pilots should contact any FSS within 100 mi. of the area to obtain accurate, real-time information concerning the MOA hours of operation.

         i)   Prior to entering an active MOA, pilots should contact the controlling agency for traffic advisories.

   5)   An alert area is airspace within which there is a high volume of pilot training or an unusual type of aerial activity. Pilots should be particularly alert when flying in these areas.

      a)   Alert areas are depicted on sectional charts by magenta hashed lines and labeled with an "A" followed by a number (e.g., A-293).

   6)   National security areas (NSAs) consist of airspace of defined vertical and lateral dimensions established at locations where there is a requirement for increased security and safety of ground facilities.

   7)   Controlled firing areas (CFAs) contain activities that, if not conducted in a controlled environment, could be hazardous to nonparticipating aircraft.

h.   Other Use Airspace

   1)   Military training routes are depicted on sectional charts by a thin gray line.

7. Isogonic lines are shown on most aeronautical charts as broken magenta lines, which connect points of equal magnetic variation with each line curving the length of the earth from north to south.

    a. The agonic line is the line connecting points at which there is no variation between true north and magnetic north, i.e., the 0° line.

    b. If an aircraft is heading east, the isogonic lines variation increase in increments of 5°, e.g., +5°, +10°, +15°, etc., for each line except the last line in the most eastern part of the United States, which is +24.

    c. If the aircraft is flying west, the isogonic lines decrease by 5° per isogonic line, into negative numbers to the west of the agonic line, e.g., −5°, −10°, −15°, etc., except the last line in the most western part of the United States, which is −24.

    d. Over time, the isogonic and agonic lines shift due to the movement of the magnetic north pole. However, the degree of change may vary due to unusual geological conditions affecting magnetic forces in localized areas.

9.2 CHART SUPPLEMENTS

1. Chart Supplements are published by FAA Approved Print Providers every 56 days for each of the seven geographical districts of the U.S.

    a. Chart Supplements provide information on available services, runways, special conditions at the airport, communications, navigational aids, etc.

2. The airport name is the first item listed, followed by the alternate name, if any, and then the location identifier.

3. The airport location is expressed as the distance and direction of the airport from the center of the associated city in NM.

    a. EXAMPLE: 4 NW means 4 NM northwest of the city.

4. Right-turn traffic is indicated by "Rgt tfc" following a runway number.

5. The hours of operation of a part-time control tower are found after the tower frequency in the "Communications" section.

    a. Hours of operation are expressed in Coordinated Universal Time (UTC) and are shown as "Z" time.

        1) To convert UTC to local time, use the time conversion factor shown on the first line, e.g., UTC −6(−5DT). Daylight saving time (DT) is in effect from the second Sunday in March to the first Sunday in November.

    b. When a control tower is not in operation, the CTAF frequency should be used for traffic advisories.

6. Initial communication should be with Approach Control if available where you are landing. The frequency is listed following "APP/DEP CON."

    a. It may be different for approaches from different headings.
    b. It may be operational only for certain hours of the day.

7. In Class C airspace, VFR aircraft are provided the following radar services:

    a. Sequencing to the primary Class C airport
    b. Approved separation between IFR and VFR aircraft
    c. Basic radar services, including safety alerts, limited vectoring, and traffic advisories

8. The "Airport Remarks" section contains information on pilot-controlled lighting, such as the types of lights, on which runways, and at what frequency.

    a. LDIN means lead-in lighting system, which is a type of approach light.

9. Runway gradient is not shown in the runway data if it is less than 0.3%.

10. The "Radio Aids to Navigation" section lists all the facilities by name for an airport for which the FAA has approved an Instrument Approach Procedure.

    a. The last item listed for VOR, VORTAC, or VOR/DME is the elevation and magnetic variation at the site of the facility.

        1) EXAMPLE: 560/08E means an elevation of 560 ft. MSL and a magnetic variation of 08°E at the site.

11. The Chart Supplement also contains information concerning parachute jumping sites.

12. Information regarding airport surface hot spots can be found in the Chart Supplement.

13. All of the applicable FAA legends from Appendix 1 of *Airman Knowledge Testing Supplement for Commercial Pilot* are reproduced on the following pages. The legends not included (Legends 11 and 12) pertain to military topics, helicopters, gyroplanes, and/or gliders. Gleim does not believe you will be tested on these legends on your Commercial Pilot Knowledge Test.

As you practice answering questions, keep in mind that you will need to refer to Appendix 1 of the testing supplement to find these legends on test day.

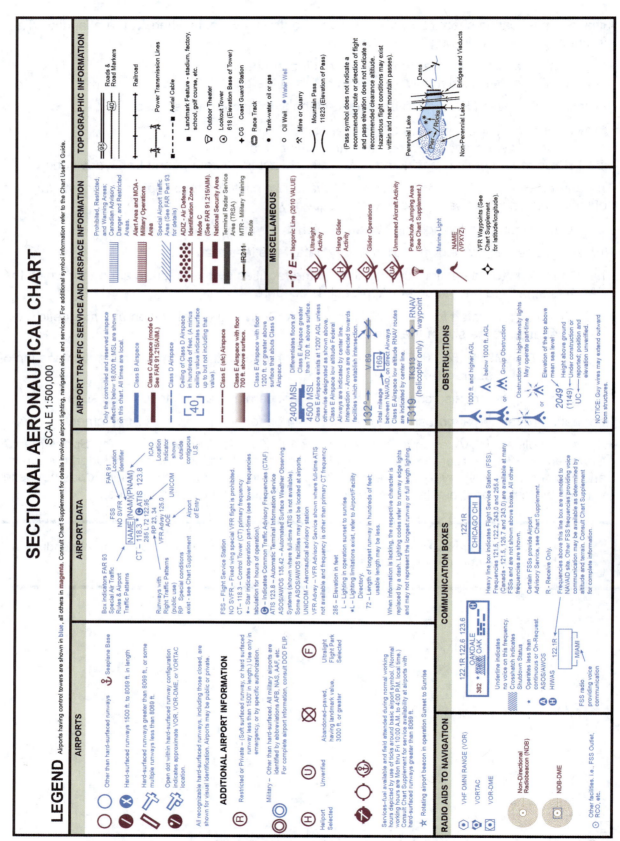

Legend 1. Sectional Aeronautical Chart.

12 **AIRPORT/FACILITY DIRECTORY LEGEND**

SAMPLE

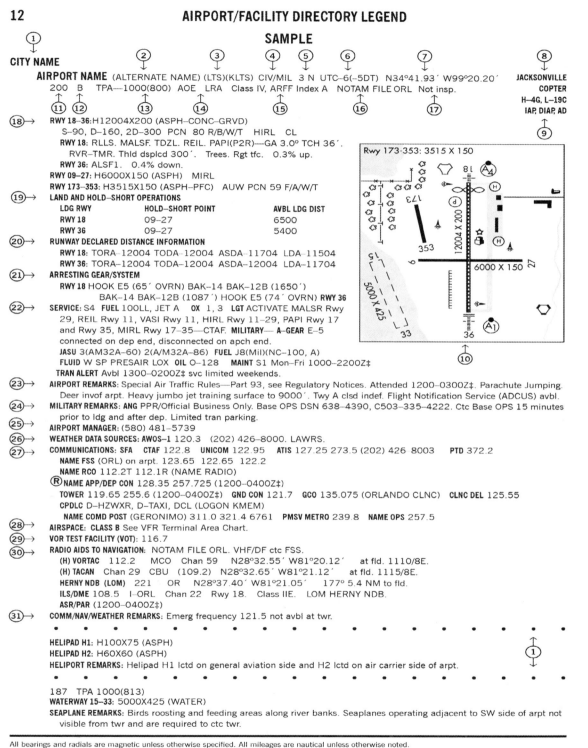

① CITY NAME

② ③ ④ ⑤ ⑥ ⑦ ⑧
AIRPORT NAME (ALTERNATE NAME) (LTS)(KLTS) CIV/MIL 3 N UTC−6(−5DT) N34°41.93′ W99°20.20′ JACKSONVILLE
200 B TPA—1000(800) AOE LRA Class IV, ARFF Index A NOTAM FILE ORL Not insp. COPTER
⑪ ⑫ ⑬ ⑭ ⑮ ⑯ ⑰ H−4G, L−19C
IAP, DIAP, AD
⑨

⑱→ RWY 18−36: H12004X200 (ASPH−CONC−GRVD)
S−90, D−160, 2D−300 PCN 80 R/B/W/T HIRL CL
RWY 18: RLLS. MALSF. TDZL. REIL. PAPI(P2R)—GA 3.0° TCH 36′.
RVR−TMR. Thld dsplcd 300′. Trees. Rgt tfc. 0.3% up.
RWY 36: ALSF1. 0.4% down.
RWY 09−27: H6000X150 (ASPH) MIRL
RWY 173−353: H3515X150 (ASPH−PFC) AUW PCN 59 F/A/W/T

⑲→ LAND AND HOLD−SHORT OPERATIONS
LDG RWY	HOLD−SHORT POINT	AVBL LDG DIST
RWY 18	09−27	6500
RWY 36	09−27	5400

⑳→ RUNWAY DECLARED DISTANCE INFORMATION
RWY 18: TORA−12004 TODA−12004 ASDA−11704 LDA−11504
RWY 36: TORA−12004 TODA−12004 ASDA−12004 LDA−11704

㉑→ ARRESTING GEAR/SYSTEM
RWY 18 HOOK E5 (65′ OVRN) BAK−14 BAK−12B (1650′)
BAK−14 BAK−12B (1087′) HOOK E5 (74′ OVRN) RWY 36

㉒→ SERVICE: S4 FUEL 100LL, JET A OX 1, 3 LGT ACTIVATE MALSR Rwy
29, REIL Rwy 11, VASI Rwy 11, HIRL Rwy 11−29, PAPI Rwy 17
and Rwy 35, MIRL Rwy 17−35—CTAF. MILITARY— A−GEAR E−5
connected on dep end, disconnected on apch end.
JASU 3(AM32A−60) 2(A/M32A−86) FUEL J8(Mil)(NC−100, A)
FLUID W SP PRESAIR LOX OIL O−128 MAINT S1 Mon−Fri 1000−2200Z‡
TRAN ALERT Avbl 1300−0200Z‡ svc limited weekends.

㉓→ AIRPORT REMARKS: Special Air Traffic Rules—Part 93, see Regulatory Notices. Attended 1200−0300Z‡. Parachute Jumping.
Deer invof arpt. Heavy jumbo jet training surface to 9000′. Twy A clsd indef. Flight Notification Service (ADCUS) avbl.

㉔→ MILITARY REMARKS: ANG PPR/Official Business Only. Base OPS DSN 638−4390, C503−335−4222. Ctc Base OPS 15 minutes
prior to ldg and after dep. Limited tran parking.

㉕→ AIRPORT MANAGER: (580) 481−5739

㉖→ WEATHER DATA SOURCES: AWOS−1 120.3 (202) 426−8000. LAWRS.

㉗→ COMMUNICATIONS: SFA CTAF 122.8 UNICOM 122.95 ATIS 127.25 273.5 (202) 426 8003 PTD 372.2
NAME FSS (ORL) on arpt. 123.65 122.65 122.2
NAME RCO 112.2T 112.1R (NAME RADIO)
Ⓡ NAME APP/DEP CON 128.35 257.725 (1200−0400Z‡)
TOWER 119.65 255.6 (1200−0400Z‡) GND CON 121.7 GCO 135.075 (ORLANDO CLNC) CLNC DEL 125.55
CPDLC D−HZWXR, D−TAXI, DCL (LOGON KMEM)
NAME COMD POST (GERONIMO) 311.0 321.4 6761 PMSV METRO 239.8 NAME OPS 257.5

㉘→ AIRSPACE: CLASS B See VFR Terminal Area Chart.

㉙→ VOR TEST FACILITY (VOT): 116.7

㉚→ RADIO AIDS TO NAVIGATION: NOTAM FILE ORL. VHF/DF ctc FSS.
(H) VORTAC 112.2 MCO Chan 59 N28°32.55′ W81°20.12′ at fld. 1110/8E.
(H) TACAN Chan 29 CBU (109.2) N28°32.65′ W81°21.12′ at fld. 1115/8E.
HERNY NDB (LOM) 221 OR N28°37.40′ W81°21.05′ 177° 5.4 NM to fld.
ILS/DME 108.5 I−ORL Chan 22 Rwy 18. Class IIE. LOM HERNY NDB.
ASR/PAR (1200−0400Z‡)

㉛→ COMM/NAV/WEATHER REMARKS: Emerg frequency 121.5 not avbl at twr.

• • • • • • • • • • • • •

HELIPAD H1: H100X75 (ASPH)
HELIPAD H2: H60X60 (ASPH)
HELIPORT REMARKS: Helipad H1 lctd on general aviation side and H2 lctd on air carrier side of arpt. ①

• • • • • • • • • • • • •

187 TPA 1000(813)
WATERWAY 15−33: 5000X425 (WATER)
SEAPLANE REMARKS: Birds roosting and feeding areas along river banks. Seaplanes operating adjacent to SW side of arpt not
visible from twr and are required to ctc twr.

All bearings and radials are magnetic unless otherwise specified. All mileages are nautical unless otherwise noted.
All times are Coordinated Universal Time (UTC) except as noted. All elevations are in feet above/below Mean Sea Level (MSL) unless otherwise noted.
The horizontal reference datum of this publication is North American Datum of 1983 (NAD83), which for charting purposes is considered equivalent to World
Geodetic System 1984 (WGS 84).

SC, 1 FEB 20XX to 29 MAR 20XX

Legend 2. Chart Supplement.

AIRPORT/FACILITY DIRECTORY LEGEND   13

18032

⑩ SKETCH LEGEND

RUNWAYS/LANDING AREAS

Hard Surfaced . . . .

Metal Surface . . . .

Sod, Gravel, etc. . . . .

Light Plane, ...
Ski Landing Area or Water

Under Construction . . . . .

Closed Rwy . . . .

Closed Pavement . . . .

Helicopter Landings Area . . . . ⒣

Displaced Threshold . . . .

Taxiway, Apron and Stopways . .

MISCELLANEOUS BASE AND CULTURAL FEATURES

Buildings . . . .

Power Lines . . . .

Fence . . . .

Towers . . . .

Wind Turbine. . . . .

Tanks . . . .

Oil Well . . . .

Smoke Stack . . . .

Obstruction   5812

Controlling Obstruction . . . .   +5812

Trees . . . .

Populated Places . . . .

Cuts and Fills . . . . . .   Cut   Fill

Cliffs and Depressions . .

Ditch . . . .

Hill . . . .

RADIO AIDS TO NAVIGATION

VORTAC . . . ⬡   VOR . . . . ⬡

VOR/DME . . ⬡   NDB . . . . ⊙

TACAN . . . . ⬠   NDB/DME . . . . ⊡

DME . . . . ▢

MISCELLANEOUS AERONAUTICAL FEATURES

Airport Beacon . . . .   ☆ ✪

Wind Cone . . . .

Landing Tee . . . .

Tetrahedron . . . .

Control Tower . . . .   or TWR

When control tower and rotating beacon
are co-located beacon symbol will be
used and further identified as TWR.

APPROACH LIGHTING SYSTEMS

A dot "•" portrayed with approach lighting
letter identifier indicates sequenced flashing
lights (F) installed with the approach lighting
system e.g. Ⓐ₁ Negative symbology, e.g., Ⓐ₁
Ⓥ indicates Pilot Controlled Lighting (PCL).

Runway Centerline Lighting . . . . .

Ⓐ Approach Lighting System ALSF-2 . .

Ⓐ₁ Approach Lighting System ALSF-1 . .

Ⓐ₂ Short Approach Lighting System
    SALS/SALSF . . . .

Ⓐ₃ Simplified Short Approach Lighting
    System (SSALR) with RAIL . . . . .

Ⓐ₄ Medium Intensity Approach Lighting System
    (MALS and MALSF)/(SSALS
    and SSALF) . . . .

Ⓐ₅ Medium Intensity Approach Lighting
    System (MALSR) and RAIL . . . .

Ⓧ Omnidirectional Approach
    Lighting System (ODALS) . . . .

Ⓓ Navy Parallel Row and Cross Bar . . .

Ⓕ Air Force Overrun . . . .

Ⓥ Visual Approach Slope Indicator with
    Standard Threshold Clearance provided

Ⓥ₂ Pulsating Visual Approach Slope Indicator
    (PVASI)

Ⓥ₃ Visual Approach Slope Indicator with a
    threshold crossing height to accomodate
    long bodied or jumbo aircraft

Ⓥ₄ Tri-color Visual Approach Slope Indicator
    (TRCV)

Ⓥ₅ Approach Path Alignment Panel (APAP)

Ⓟ Precision Approach Path Indicator (PAPI)

Legend 3. Chart Supplement.

14   AIRPORT/FACILITY DIRECTORY LEGEND
LEGEND

This directory is a listing of data on record with the FAA on public–use airports, military airports and selected private–use airports specifically requested by the Department of Defense (DoD) for which a DoD Instrument Approach Procedure has been published in the U.S. Terminal Procedures Publication. Additionally this listing contains data for associated terminal control facilities, air route traffic control centers, and radio aids to navigation within the conterminous United States, Puerto Rico and the Virgin Islands. Civil airports and joint Civil/Military airports which are open to the public are listed alphabetically by state, associated city and airport name and cross–referenced by airport name. Military airports and private–use (limited civil access) joint Military/Civil airports are listed alphabetically by state and official airport name and cross–referenced by associated city name. Navaids, flight service stations and remote communication outlets that are associated with an airport, but with a different name, are listed alphabetically under their own name, as well as under the airport with which they are associated.

The listing of an airport as open to the public in this directory merely indicates the airport operator's willingness to accommodate transient aircraft, and does not represent that the airport conforms with any Federal or local standards, or that it has been approved for use on the part of the general public. Military airports, private–use airports, and private–use (limited civil access) joint Military/Civil airports are open to civil pilots only in an emergency or with prior permission. See Special Notice Section, Civil Use of Military Fields.

The information on obstructions is taken from reports submitted to the FAA. Obstruction data has not been verified in all cases. Pilots are cautioned that objects not indicated in this tabulation (or on the airports sketches and/or charts) may exist which can create a hazard to flight operation. Detailed specifics concerning services and facilities tabulated within this directory are contained in the Aeronautical Information Manual, Basic Flight Information and ATC Procedures.

The legend items that follow explain in detail the contents of this Directory and are keyed to the circled numbers on the sample on the preceding pages.

① CITY/AIRPORT NAME
Civil and joint Civil/Military airports which are open to the public are listed alphabetically by state and associated city. Where the city name is different from the airport name the city name will appear on the line above the airport name. Airports with the same associated city name will be listed alphabetically by airport name and will be separated by a dashed rule line. A solid rule line will separate all others. FAA approved helipads and seaplane landing areas associated with a land airport will be separated by a dotted line. Military airports and private–use (limited civil access) joint Military/Civil airports are listed alphabetically by state and official airport name.

② ALTERNATE NAME
Alternate names, if any, will be shown in parentheses.

③ LOCATION IDENTIFIER
The location identifier is a three or four character FAA code followed by a four–character ICAO code, when assigned, to airports. If two different military codes are assigned, both codes will be shown with the primary operating agency's code listed first. These identifiers are used by ATC in lieu of the airport name in flight plans, flight strips and other written records and computer operations. Zeros will appear with a slash to differentiate them from the letter "O".

④ OPERATING AGENCY
Airports within this directory are classified into two categories, Military/Federal Government and Civil airports open to the general public, plus selected private–use airports. The operating agency is shown for military, private–use and joint use airports. The operating agency is shown by an abbreviation as listed below. When an organization is a tenant, the abbreviation is enclosed in parenthesis. No classification indicates the airport is open to the general public with no military tenant.

A	US Army	MC	Marine Corps
AFRC	Air Force Reserve Command	MIL/CIV	Joint Use Military/Civil Limited Civil Access
AF	US Air Force	N	Navy
ANG	Air National Guard	NAF	Naval Air Facility
AR	US Army Reserve	NAS	Naval Air Station
ARNG	US Army National Guard	NASA	National Air and Space Administration
CG	US Coast Guard	P	US Civil Airport Wherein Permit Covers Use by Transient Military Aircraft
CIV/MIL	Joint Use Civil/Military Open to the Public		
DND	Department of National Defense Canada	PVT	Private Use Only (Closed to the Public)

⑤ AIRPORT LOCATION
Airport location is expressed as distance and direction from the center of the associated city in nautical miles and cardinal points, e.g., 4 NE.

⑥ TIME CONVERSION
Hours of operation of all facilities are expressed in Coordinated Universal Time (UTC) and shown as "Z" time. The directory indicates the number of hours to be subtracted from UTC to obtain local standard time and local daylight saving time UTC–5(–4DT). The symbol ‡ indicates that during periods of Daylight Saving Time (DST) effective hours will be one hour earlier than shown. In those areas where daylight saving time is not observed the (–4DT) and ‡ will not be shown. Daylight saving time is in effect from 0200 local time the second Sunday in March to 0200 local time the first Sunday in November. Canada and all U.S. Conterminous States observe daylight saving time except Arizona and Puerto Rico, and the Virgin Islands. If the state observes daylight saving time and the operating times are other than daylight saving times, the operating hours will include the dates, times and no ‡ symbol will be shown, i.e., April 15–Aug 31 0630–1700Z, Sep 1–Apr 14 0600–1700Z.

Legend 4. Chart Supplement.

AIRPORT/FACILITY DIRECTORY LEGEND   15

⑦ **GEOGRAPHIC POSITION OF AIRPORT—AIRPORT REFERENCE POINT (ARP)**

Positions are shown as hemisphere, degrees, minutes and hundredths of a minute and represent the approximate geometric center of all usable runway surfaces.

⑧ **CHARTS**

Charts refer to the Sectional Chart and Low and High Altitude Enroute Chart and panel on which the airport or facility is depicted. Helicopter Chart depictions will be indicated as COPTER. IFR Gulf of Mexico West and IFR Gulf of Mexico Central will be referenced as GOMW and GOMC.

⑨ **INSTRUMENT APPROACH PROCEDURES, AIRPORT DIAGRAMS**

IAP indicates an airport for which a prescribed (Public Use) FAA Instrument Approach Procedure has been published. DIAP indicates an airport for which a prescribed DoD Instrument Approach Procedure has been published in the U.S. Terminal Procedures. See the Special Notice Section of this directory, Civil Use of Military Fields and the Aeronautical Information Manual 5-4-5 Instrument Approach Procedure Charts for additional information. AD indicates an airport for which an airport diagram has been published. Airport diagrams are located in the back of each Chart Supplement volume alphabetically by associated city and airport name.

⑩ **AIRPORT SKETCH**

The airport sketch, when provided, depicts the airport and related topographical information as seen from the air and should be used in conjunction with the text. It is intended as a guide for pilots in VFR conditions. Symbology that is not self-explanatory will be reflected in the sketch legend. The airport sketch will be oriented with True North at the top. Airport sketches will be added incrementally.

⑪ **ELEVATION**

The highest point of an airport's usable runways measured in feet from mean sea level. When elevation is sea level it will be indicated as "00". When elevation is below sea level a minus "–" sign will precede the figure.

⑫ **ROTATING LIGHT BEACON**

B indicates rotating beacon is available. Rotating beacons operate sunset to sunrise unless otherwise indicated in the AIRPORT REMARKS or MILITARY REMARKS segment of the airport entry.

⑬ **TRAFFIC PATTERN ALTITUDE**

Traffic Pattern Altitude (TPA)—The first figure shown is TPA above mean sea level. The second figure in parentheses is TPA above airport elevation. Multiple TPA shall be shown as "TPA—See Remarks" and detailed information shall be shown in the Airport or Military Remarks Section. Traffic pattern data for USAF bases, USN facilities, and U.S. Army airports (including those on which ACC or U.S. Army is a tenant) that deviate from standard pattern altitudes shall be shown in Military Remarks.

⑭ **AIRPORT OF ENTRY, LANDING RIGHTS, AND CUSTOMS USER FEE AIRPORTS**

U.S. CUSTOMS USER FEE AIRPORT—Private Aircraft operators are frequently required to pay the costs associated with customs processing.

AOE—Airport of Entry. A customs Airport of Entry where permission from U.S. Customs is not required to land. However, at least one hour advance notice of arrival is required.

LRA—Landing Rights Airport. Application for permission to land must be submitted in advance to U.S. Customs. At least one hour advance notice of arrival is required.

NOTE: Advance notice of arrival at both an AOE and LRA airport may be included in the flight plan when filed in Canada or Mexico. Where Flight Notification Service (ADCUS) is available the airport remark will indicate this service. This notice will also be treated as an application for permission to land in the case of an LRA. Although advance notice of arrival may be relayed to Customs through Mexico, Canada, and U.S. Communications facilities by flight plan, the aircraft operator is solely responsible for ensuring that Customs receives the notification. (See Customs, Immigration and Naturalization, Public Health and Agriculture Department requirements in the International Flight Information Manual for further details.)

U.S. CUSTOMS AIR AND SEA PORTS, INSPECTORS AND AGENTS

Northeast Sector (New England and Atlantic States—ME to MD)	407-975-1740
Southeast Sector (Atlantic States—DC, WV, VA to FL)	407-975-1780
Central Sector (Interior of the US, including Gulf states—MS, AL, LA)	407-975-1760
Southwest East Sector (OK and eastern TX)	407-975-1840
Southwest West Sector (Western TX, NM and AZ)	407-975-1820
Pacific Sector (WA, OR, CA, HI and AK)	407-975-1800

⑮ **CERTIFICATED AIRPORT (14 CFR PART 139)**

Airports serving Department of Transportation certified carriers and certified under 14 CFR part 139 are indicated by the Class and the ARFF Index; e.g. Class I, ARFF Index A, which relates to the availability of crash, fire, rescue equipment. Class I airports can have an ARFF Index A through E, depending on the aircraft length and scheduled departures. Class II, III, and IV will always carry an Index A.

AIRPORT CLASSIFICATIONS

Type of Air Carrier Operation	Class I	Class II	Class III	Class IV
Scheduled Air Carrier Aircraft with 31 or more passenger seats	X			
Unscheduled Air Carrier Aircraft with 31 or more passengers seats	X	X		X
Scheduled Air Carrier Aircraft with 10 to 30 passenger seats	X	X	X	

SC, 1 FEB 20XX to 29 MAR 20XX

Legend 5. Chart Supplement.

16   AIRPORT/FACILITY DIRECTORY LEGEND

INDICES AND AIRCRAFT RESCUE AND FIRE FIGHTING EQUIPMENT REQUIREMENTS

Airport Index	Required No. Vehicles	Aircraft Length	Scheduled Departures	Agent + Water for Foam
A	1	<90´	≥1	500#DC OR HALON 1211 or 450#DC + 100 gal H$_2$O
B	1 or 2	>90´, <126´ ———— ———— ≥126´, <159´	>5 ———— <5	Index A + 1500 gal H$_2$O
C	2 or 3	≥126´, <159´ ———— ———— ≥159´, <200´	>5 ———— <5	Index A + 3000 gal H$_2$O
D	3	≥159´, <200´ ———— ———— >200´	>5 ———— <5	Index A + 4000 gal H$_2$O
E	3	≥200´	≥5	Index A + 6000 gal H$_2$O

> Greater Than; < Less Than; ≥ Equal or Greater Than; ≤ Equal or Less Than;   H$_2$O—Water; DC–Dry Chemical.

NOTE: The listing of ARFF index does not necessarily assure coverage for non-air carrier operations or at other than prescribed times for air carrier. ARFF Index Ltd.—indicates ARFF coverage may or may not be available, for information contact airport manager prior to flight.

(16) NOTAM SERVICE

All public use landing areas are provided NOTAM service. A NOTAM FILE identifier is shown for individual landing areas, e.g., "NOTAM FILE BNA". See the AIM, Basic Flight Information and ATC Procedures for a detailed description of NOTAMs. Current NOTAMs are available from flight service stations at 1–800–WX–BRIEF (992–7433) or online through the FAA PilotWeb at https://pilotweb.nas.faa.gov. Military NOTAMs are available using the Defense Internet NOTAM Service (DINS) at https://www.notams.faa.gov. Pilots flying to or from airports not available through the FAA PilotWeb or DINS can obtain assistance from Flight Service.

(17) FAA INSPECTION

All airports not inspected by FAA will be identified by the note: Not insp. This indicates that the airport information has been provided by the owner or operator of the field.

(18) RUNWAY DATA

Runway information is shown on two lines. That information common to the entire runway is shown on the first line while information concerning the runway ends is shown on the second or following line. Runway direction, surface, length, width, weight bearing capacity, lighting, and slope, when available are shown for each runway. Multiple runways are shown with the longest runway first. Direction, length, width, and lighting are shown for sea–lanes. The full dimensions of helipads are shown, e.g., 50X150. Runway data that requires clarification will be placed in the remarks section.

RUNWAY DESIGNATION

Runways are normally numbered in relation to their magnetic orientation rounded off to the nearest 10 degrees. Parallel runways can be designated L (left)/R (right)/C (center). Runways may be designated as Ultralight or assault strips. Assault strips are shown by magnetic bearing.

RUNWAY DIMENSIONS

Runway length and width are shown in feet. Length shown is runway end to end including displaced thresholds, but excluding those areas designed as overruns.

RUNWAY SURFACE AND SURFACE TREATMENT

Runway lengths prefixed by the letter "H" indicate that the runways are hard surfaced (concrete, asphalt, or part asphalt-concrete). If the runway length is not prefixed, the surface is sod, clay, etc. The runway surface composition is indicated in parentheses after runway length as follows:

(AFSC)—Aggregate friction seal coat
(AM2)—Temporary metal planks coated with nonskid material
(ASPH)—Asphalt
(CONC)—Concrete
(DIRT)—Dirt
(GRVD)—Grooved

(GRVL)—Gravel, or cinders
(MATS)—Pierced steel planking, landing mats, membranes
(PEM)—Part concrete, part asphalt
(PFC)—Porous friction courses
(PSP)—Pierced steel plank
(RFSC)—Rubberized friction seal coat

(SAND)—Sand
(TURF)—Turf
(TRTD)—Treated
(WC)—Wire combed

SC, 1 FEB 20XX to 29 MAR 20XX

Legend 6. Chart Supplement.

AIRPORT/FACILITY DIRECTORY LEGEND   17

RUNWAY WEIGHT BEARING CAPACITY

Runway strength data shown in this publication is derived from available information and is a realistic estimate of capability at an average level of activity. It is not intended as a maximum allowable weight or as an operating limitation. Many airport pavements are capable of supporting limited operations with gross weights in excess of the published figures. Permissible operating weights, insofar as runway strengths are concerned, are a matter of agreement between the owner and user. When desiring to operate into any airport at weights in excess of those published in the publication, users should contact the airport management for permission. Runway strength figures are shown in thousand of pounds, with the last three figures being omitted. Add 000 to figure following S, D, 2S, 2T, AUW, SWL, etc., for gross weight capacity. A blank space following the letter designator is used to indicate the runway can sustain aircraft with this type landing gear, although definite runway weight bearing capacity figures are not available, e.g., S, D. Applicable codes for typical gear configurations with S=Single, D=Dual, T=Triple and Q=Quadruple:

CURRENT	NEW	NEW DESCRIPTION
S	S	Single wheel type landing gear (DC3), (C47), (F15), etc.
D	D	Dual wheel type landing gear (BE1900), (B737), (A319), etc.
T	D	Dual wheel type landing gear (P3, C9).
ST	2S	Two single wheels in tandem type landing gear (C130).
TRT	2T	Two triple wheels in tandem type landing gear (C17), etc.
DT	2D	Two dual wheels in tandem type landing gear (B707), etc.
TT	2D	Two dual wheels in tandem type landing gear (B757, KC135).
SBTT	2D/D1	Two dual wheels in tandem/dual wheel body gear type landing gear (KC10).
None	2D/2D1	Two dual wheels in tandem/two dual wheels in tandem body gear type landing gear (A340–600).
DDT	2D/2D2	Two dual wheels in tandem/two dual wheels in double tandem body gear type landing gear (B747, E4).
TTT	3D	Three dual wheels in tandem type landing gear (B777), etc.
TT	D2	Dual wheel gear two struts per side main gear type landing gear (B52).
TDT	C5	Complex dual wheel and quadruple wheel combination landing gear (C5).

AUW—All up weight. Maximum weight bearing capacity for any aircraft irrespective of landing gear configuration.

SWL—Single Wheel Loading. (This includes information submitted in terms of Equivalent Single Wheel Loading (ESWL) and Single Isolated Wheel Loading).

PSI—Pounds per square inch. PSI is the actual figure expressing maximum pounds per square inch runway will support, e.g., (SWL 000/PSI 535).

Omission of weight bearing capacity indicates information unknown.

The ACN/PCN System is the ICAO standard method of reporting pavement strength for pavements with bearing strengths greater than 12,500 pounds. The Pavement Classification Number (PCN) is established by an engineering assessment of the runway. The PCN is for use in conjunction with an Aircraft Classification Number (ACN). Consult the Aircraft Flight Manual, Flight Information Handbook, or other appropriate source for ACN tables or charts. Currently, ACN data may not be available for all aircraft. If an ACN table or chart is available, the ACN can be calculated by taking into account the aircraft weight, the pavement type, and the subgrade category. For runways that have been evaluated under the ACN/PCN system, the PCN will be shown as a five–part code (e.g. PCN 80 R/B/W/T). Details of the coded format are as follows:

NOTE: Prior permission from the airport controlling authority is required when the ACN of the aircraft exceeds the published PCN or aircraft tire pressure exceeds the published limits.

(1) The PCN NUMBER—The reported PCN indicates that an aircraft with an ACN equal or less than the reported PCN can operate on the pavement subject to any limitation on the tire pressure.

(2) The type of pavement:
R — Rigid
F — Flexible

(3) The pavement subgrade category:
A — High
B — Medium
C — Low
D — Ultra-low

(4) The maximum tire pressure authorized for the pavement:
W — Unlimited, no pressure limit
X — High, limited to 254 psi (1.75 MPa)
Y — Medium, limited to 181 psi (1.25MPa)
Z — Low, limited to 73 psi (0.50 MPa)

(5) Pavement evaluation method:
T — Technical evaluation
U — By experience of aircraft using the pavement

RUNWAY LIGHTING

Lights are in operation sunset to sunrise. Lighting available by prior arrangement only or operating part of the night and/or pilot controlled lighting with specific operating hours are indicated under airport or military remarks. At USN/USMC facilities lights are available only during airport hours of operation. Since obstructions are usually lighted, obstruction lighting is not included in this code. Unlighted obstructions on or surrounding an airport will be noted in airport or military remarks. Runway lights nonstandard (NSTD) are systems for which the light fixtures are not FAA approved L–800 series: color, intensity, or spacing does not meet FAA standards. Nonstandard runway lights, VASI, or any other system not listed below will be shown in airport remarks or military

SC, 1 FEB 20XX to 29 MAR 20XX

Legend 7. Chart Supplement.

18   AIRPORT/FACILITY DIRECTORY LEGEND

service. Temporary, emergency or limited runway edge lighting such as flares, smudge pots, lanterns or portable runway lights will also be shown in airport remarks or military service. Types of lighting are shown with the runway or runway end they serve.

NSTD—Light system fails to meet FAA standards.
LIRL—Low Intensity Runway Lights.
MIRL—Medium Intensity Runway Lights.
HIRL—High Intensity Runway Lights.
RAIL—Runway Alignment Indicator Lights.
REIL Runway End Identifier Lights.
CL—Centerline Lights.
TDZL—Touchdown Zone Lights.
ODALS—Omni Directional Approach Lighting System.
AF OVRN—Air Force Overrun 1000´ Standard
       Approach Lighting System.
MALS—Medium Intensity Approach Lighting System.
MALSF Medium Intensity Approach Lighting System with
       Sequenced Flashing Lights.
MALSR—Medium Intensity Approach Lighting System with
       Runway Alignment Indicator Lights.
RLLS—Runway Lead–in Light System

SALS—Short Approach Lighting System.
SALSF—Short Approach Lighting System with Sequenced
       Flashing Lights.
SSALS—Simplified Short Approach Lighting System.
SSALF—Simplified Short Approach Lighting System with
       Sequenced Flashing Lights.
SSALR—Simplified Short Approach Lighting System with
       Runway Alignment Indicator Lights.
ALSAF—High Intensity Approach Lighting System with
       Sequenced Flashing Lights.
ALSF1—High Intensity Approach Lighting System with Sequenced
       Flashing Lights, Category I, Configuration.
ALSF2—High Intensity Approach Lighting System with Sequenced
       Flashing Lights, Category II, Configuration.
SF—Sequenced Flashing Lights.
OLS—Optical Landing System.
WAVE–OFF.

NOTE: Civil ALSF2 may be operated as SSALR during favorable weather conditions. When runway edge lights are positioned more than 10 feet from the edge of the usable runway surface a remark will be added in the "Remarks" portion of the airport entry. This is applicable to Air Force, Air National Guard and Air Force Reserve Bases, and those joint use airfields on which they are tenants.

VISUAL GLIDESLOPE INDICATORS

APAP—A system of panels, which may or may not be lighted, used for alignment of approach path.
    PNIL   APAP on left side of runway   PNIR   APAP on right side of runway

PAPI—Precision Approach Path Indicator
    P2L   2–identical light units placed on left side of runway   P4L   4–identical light units placed on left side of runway
    P2R   2–identical light units placed on right side of runway   P4R   4–identical light units placed on right side of runway

PVASI—Pulsating/steady burning visual approach slope indicator, normally a single light unit projecting two colors.
    PSIL   PVASI on left side of runway   PSIR   PVASI on right side of runway

SAVASI—Simplified Abbreviated Visual Approach Slope Indicator
    S2L   2–box SAVASI on left side of runway   S2R   2–box SAVASI on right side of runway

TRCV—Tri–color visual approach slope indicator, normally a single light unit projecting three colors.
    TRIL   TRCV on left side of runway   TRIR   TRCV on right side of runway

VASI—Visual Approach Slope Indicator
    V2L   2–box VASI on left side of runway   V6L   6–box VASI on left side of runway
    V2R   2–box VASI on right side of runway   V6R   6–box VASI on right side of runway
    V4L   4–box VASI on left side of runway   V12   12–box VASI on both sides of runway
    V4R   4–box VASI on right side of runway   V16   16–box VASI on both sides of runway

NOTE: Approach slope angle and threshold crossing height will be shown when available; i.e., –GA 3.5° TCH 37´.

PILOT CONTROL OF AIRPORT LIGHTING

Key Mike	Function
7 times within 5 seconds	Highest intensity available
5 times within 5 seconds	Medium or lower intensity (Lower REIL or REIL–Off)
3 times within 5 seconds	Lowest intensity available (Lower REIL or REIL–Off)

Available systems will be indicated in the Service section, e.g., **LGT** ACTIVATE HIRL Rwy 07 25, MALSR Rwy 07, and VASI Rwy 07 122.8.

Where the airport is not served by an instrument approach procedure and/or has an independent type system of different specification installed by the airport sponsor, descriptions of the type lights, method of control, and operating frequency will be explained in clear text. See AIM, "Basic Flight Information and ATC Procedures," for detailed description of pilot control of airport lighting.

RUNWAY SLOPE

When available, runway slope data will be provided. Runway slope will be shown only when it is 0.3 percent or greater. On runways less than 8000 feet, the direction of the slope up will be indicated, e.g., 0.3% up NW. On runways 8000 feet or greater, the slope will be shown (up or down) on the runway end line, e.g., RWY 13: 0.3% up., RWY 31: Pole. Rgt tfc. 0.4% down.

Legend 8. Chart Supplement.

AIRPORT/FACILITY DIRECTORY LEGEND   19

RUNWAY END DATA

Information pertaining to the runway approach end such as approach lights, touchdown zone lights, runway end identification lights, visual glideslope indicators, displaced thresholds, controlling obstruction, and right hand traffic pattern, will be shown on the specific runway end. "Rgt tfc"—Right traffic indicates right turns should be made on landing and takeoff for specified runway end. Runway Visual Range shall be shown as "RVR" appended with "T" for touchdown, "M" for midpoint, and "R" for rollout; e.g., RVR-TMR.

⑲ LAND AND HOLD–SHORT OPERATIONS (LAHSO)

LAHSO is an acronym for "Land and Hold–Short Operations" These operations include landing and holding short of an intersection runway, an intersecting taxiway, or other predetermined points on the runway other than a runway or taxiway. Measured distance represents the available landing distance on the landing runway, in feet.

Specific questions regarding these distances should be referred to the air traffic manager of the facility concerned. The Aeronautical Information Manual contains specific details on hold–short operations and markings.

⑳ RUNWAY DECLARED DISTANCE INFORMATION

TORA—Take–off Run Available. The length of runway declared available and suitable for the ground run of an aeroplane take–off.
TODA—Take–off Distance Available. The length of the take–off run available plus the length of the clearway, if provided.
ASDA—Accelerate–Stop Distance Available. The length of the take–off run available plus the length of the stopway, if provided.
LDA—Landing Distance Available. The length of runway which is declared available and suitable for the ground run of an aeroplane landing.

㉑ ARRESTING GEAR/SYSTEMS

Arresting gear is shown as it is located on the runway. The a–gear distance from the end of the appropriate runway (or into the overrun) is indicated in parentheses. A–Gear which has a bi–direction capability and can be utilized for emergency approach end engagement is indicated by a (B). Up to 15 minutes advance notice may be required for rigging A–Gear for approach and engagement. Airport listing may show availability of other than US Systems. This information is provided for emergency requirements only. Refer to current aircraft operating manuals for specific engagement weight and speed criteria based on aircraft structural restrictions and arresting system limitations.

Following is a list of current systems referenced in this publication identified by both Air Force and Navy terminology:

BI–DIRECTIONAL CABLE (B)

TYPE	DESCRIPTION
BAK–9	Rotary friction brake.
BAK–12A	Standard BAK–12 with 950 foot run out, 1–inch cable and 40,000 pound weight setting. Rotary friction brake.
BAK–12B	Extended BAK–12 with 1200 foot run, 1¼ inch Cable and 50,000 pounds weight setting. Rotary friction brake.
E28	Rotary Hydraulic (Water Brake).
M21	Rotary Hydraulic (Water Brake) Mobile.

The following device is used in conjunction with some aircraft arresting systems:

BAK–14	A device that raises a hook cable out of a slot in the runway surface and is remotely positioned for engagement by the tower on request. (In addition to personnel reaction time, the system requires up to five seconds to fully raise the cable.)
H	A device that raises a hook cable out of a slot in the runway surface and is remotely positioned for engagement by the tower on request. (In addition to personnel reaction time, the system requires up to one and one–half seconds to fully raise the cable.)

UNI–DIRECTIONAL CABLE

TYPE	DESCRIPTION
MB60	Textile brake—an emergency one–time use, modular braking system employing the tearing of specially woven textile straps to absorb the kinetic energy.
E5/E5–1/E5–3	Chain Type. At USN/USMC stations E–5 A–GEAR systems are rated, e.g., E–5 RATING–13R–1100 HW (DRY), 31L/R–1200 STD (WET). This rating is a function of the A–GEAR chain weight and length and is used to determine the maximum aircraft engaging speed. A dry rating applies to a stabilized surface (dry or wet) while a wet rating takes into account the amount (if any) of wet overrun that is not capable of withstanding the aircraft weight. These ratings are published under Service/Military/A-Gear in the entry.

FOREIGN CABLE

TYPE	DESCRIPTION	US EQUIVALENT
44B–3H	Rotary Hydraulic (Water Brake)	
CHAG	Chain	E–5

UNI–DIRECTIONAL BARRIER

TYPE	DESCRIPTION
MA–1A	Web barrier between stanchions attached to a chain energy absorber.
BAK–15	Web barrier between stanchions attached to an energy absorber (water squeezer, rotary friction, chain). Designed for wing engagement.

NOTE: Landing short of the runway threshold on a runway with a BAK–15 in the underrun is a significant hazard. The barrier in the down position still protrudes several inches above the underrun. Aircraft contact with the barrier short of the runway threshold can cause damage to the barrier and substantial damage to the aircraft.

OTHER

TYPE	DESCRIPTION
EMAS	Engineered Material Arresting System, located beyond the departure end of the runway, consisting of high energy absorbing materials which will crush under the weight of an aircraft.

SC, 1 FEB 20XX to 29 MAR 20XX

Legend 9. Chart Supplement.

20   AIRPORT/FACILITY DIRECTORY LEGEND

22 **SERVICE**

SERVICING—CIVIL

S1:   Minor airframe repairs.
S2:   Minor airframe and minor powerplant repairs.
S3:   Major airframe and minor powerplant repairs.
S4:   Major airframe and major powerplant repairs.

S5:   Major airframe repairs.
S6:   Minor airframe and major powerplant repairs.
S7:   Major powerplant repairs.
S8:   Minor powerplant repairs.

FUEL

CODE	FUEL
80	Grade 80 gasoline (Red)
100	Grade 100 gasoline (Green)
100LL	100LL gasoline (low lead) (Blue)
115	Grade 115 gasoline (115/145 military specification) (Purple)
A	Jet A, Kerosene, without FS–II*, FP** minus 40° C.
A+	Jet A, Kerosene, with FS–II*, FP** minus 40°C.
A++	Jet A, Kerosene, with FS–II*, CI/LI#, SDA##, FP** minus 40°C.
A++100	Jet A, Kerosene, with FS–II*, CI/LI#, SDA##, FP** minus 40°C, with +100 fuel additive that improves thermal stability characteristics of kerosene jet fuels.
A1	Jet A–1, Kerosene, without FS–II*, FP** minus 47°C.
A1+	Jet A–1, Kerosene with FS–II*, FP** minus 47° C.

CODE	FUEL
B	Jet B, Wide-cut, turbine fuel without FS–II*, FP** minus 50° C.
B+	Jet B, Wide-cut, turbine fuel with FS–II*, FP** minus 50° C
J4 (JP4)	(JP–4 military specification) FP** minus 58° C.
J5 (JP5)	(JP–5 military specification) Kerosene with FS–II, FP** minus 46°C.
J8 (JP8)	(JP–8 military specification) Jet A–1, Kerosene with FS–II*, CI/LI#, SDA##, FP** minus 47°C.
J8+100	(JP–8 military specification) Jet A–1, Kerosene with FS–II*, CI/LI#, SDA##, FP** minus 47°C, with +100 fuel additive that improves thermal stability characteristics of kerosene jet fuels.
J	(Jet Fuel Type Unknown)
MOGAS	Automobile gasoline which is to be used as aircraft fuel.
UL91	Unleaded Grade 91 gasoline
UL94	Unleaded Grade 94 gasoline

*(Fuel System Icing Inhibitor)   **(Freeze Point)   # (Corrosion Inhibitors/Lubricity Improvers)   ## (Static Dissipator Additive)

NOTE: Certain automobile gasoline may be used in specific aircraft engines if a FAA supplemental type certificate has been obtained. Automobile gasoline, which is to be used in aircraft engines, will be identified as "MOGAS", however, the grade/type and other octane rating will not be published.

Data shown on fuel availability represents the most recent information the publisher has been able to acquire. Because of a variety of factors, the fuel listed may not always be obtainable by transient civil pilots. Confirmation of availability of fuel should be made directly with fuel suppliers at locations where refueling is planned.

OXYGEN—CIVIL

OX 1   High Pressure
OX 2   Low Pressure

OX 3   High Pressure—Replacement Bottles
OX 4   Low Pressure—Replacement Bottles

SERVICE—MILITARY

Specific military services available at the airport are listed under this general heading. Remarks applicable to any military service are shown in the individual service listing.

JET AIRCRAFT STARTING UNITS (JASU)—MILITARY

The numeral preceding the type of unit indicates the number of units available. The absence of the numeral indicates ten or more units available. If the number of units is unknown, the number one will be shown. Absence of JASU designation indicates non–availability.
The following is a list of current JASU systems referenced in this publication:

USAF JASU (For variations in technical data, refer to T.O. 35–1–7.)
ELECTRICAL STARTING UNITS:

A/M32A–86	AC: 115/200v, 3 phase, 90 kva, 0.8 pf, 4 wire
	DC: 28v, 1500 amp, 72 kw (with TR pack)
MC–1A	AC: 115/208v, 400 cycle, 3 phase, 37.5 kva, 0.8 pf, 108 amp, 4 wire
	DC: 28v, 500 amp, 14 kw
MD–3	AC: 115/208v, 400 cycle, 3 phase, 60 kva, 0.75 pf, 4 wire
	DC: 28v, 1500 amp, 45 kw, split bus
MD–3A	AC: 115/208v, 400 cycle, 3 phase, 60 kva, 0.75 pf, 4 wire
	DC: 28v, 1500 amp, 45 kw, split bus
MD–3M	AC: 115/208v, 400 cycle, 3 phase, 60 kva, 0.75 pf, 4 wire
	DC: 28v, 500 amp, 15 kw
MD–4	AC: 120/208v, 400 cycle, 3 phase, 62.5 kva, 0.8 pf, 175 amp, "WYE" neutral ground, 4 wire, 120v, 400 cycle, 3 phase, 62.5 kva, 0.8 pf, 303 amp, "DELTA" 3 wire, 120v, 400 cycle, 1 phase, 62.5 kva, 0.8 pf, 520 amp, 2 wire

SC, 1 FEB 20XX to 29 MAR 20XX

Legend 10. Chart Supplement.

AIRPORT/FACILITY DIRECTORY LEGEND   23

㉓ AIRPORT REMARKS

The Attendance Schedule is the months, days and hours the airport is actually attended. Airport attendance does not mean watchman duties or telephone accessibility, but rather an attendant or operator on duty to provide at least minimum services (e.g., repairs, fuel, transportation).

Airport Remarks have been grouped in order of applicability. Airport remarks are limited to those items of information that are determined essential for operational use, i.e., conditions of a permanent or indefinite nature and conditions that will remain in effect for more than 30 days concerning aeronautical facilities, services, maintenance available, procedures or hazards, knowledge of which is essential for safe and efficient operation of aircraft. Information concerning permanent closing of a runway or taxiway will not be shown. A note "See Special Notices" shall be applied within this remarks section when a special notice applicable to the entry is contained in the Special Notices section of this publication.

Parachute Jumping indicates parachute jumping areas associated with the airport. See Parachute Jumping Area section of this publication for additional Information.

Landing Fee indicates landing charges for private or non–revenue producing aircraft. In addition, fees may be charged for planes that remain over a couple of hours and buy no services, or at major airline terminals for all aircraft.

Note: Unless otherwise stated, remarks including runway ends refer to the runway's approach end.

㉔ MILITARY REMARKS

Joint Civil/Military airports contain both Airport Remarks and Military Remarks. Military Remarks published for these airports are applicable only to the military. Military and joint Military/Civil airports contain only Military Remarks. Remarks contained in this section may not be applicable to civil users. When both sets of remarks exist, the first set is applicable to the primary operator of the airport. Remarks applicable to a tenant on the airport are shown preceded by the tenant organization, i.e., (A) (AF) (N) (ANG), etc. Military airports operate 24 hours unless otherwise specified. Airport operating hours are listed first (airport operating hours will only be listed if they are different than the airport attended hours or if the attended hours are unavailable) followed by pertinent remarks in order of applicability. Remarks will include information on restrictions, hazards, traffic pattern, noise abatement, customs/agriculture/immigration, and miscellaneous information applicable to the Military.

Type of restrictions:

CLOSED: When designated closed, the airport is restricted from use by all aircraft unless stated otherwise. Any closure applying to specific type of aircraft or operation will be so stated. USN/USMC/USAF airports are considered closed during non–operating hours. Closed airports may be utilized during an emergency provided there is a safe landing area.

OFFICIAL BUSINESS ONLY: The airfield is closed to all transient military aircraft for obtaining routine services such as fueling, passenger drop off or pickup, practice approaches, parking, etc. The airfield may be used by aircrews and aircraft if official government business (including civilian) must be conducted on or near the airfield and prior permission is received from the airfield manager.

AF OFFICIAL BUSINESS ONLY OR NAVY OFFICIAL BUSINESS ONLY: Indicates that the restriction applies only to service indicated.

PRIOR PERMISSION REQUIRED (PPR): Airport is closed to transient aircraft unless approval for operation is obtained from the appropriate commander through Chief, Airfield Management or Airfield Operations Officer. Official Business or PPR does not preclude the use of US Military airports as an alternate for IFR flights. If a non–US military airport is used as a weather alternate and requires a PPR, the PPR must be requested and confirmed before the flight departs. The purpose of PPR is to control volume and flow of traffic rather than to prohibit it. Prior permission is required for all aircraft requiring transient alert service outside the published transient alert duty hours. All aircraft carrying hazardous materials must obtain prior permission as outlined in AFJI 11–204, AR 95–27, OPNAVINST 3710.7.

Note: OFFICIAL BUSINESS ONLY AND PPR restrictions are not applicable to Special Air Mission (SAM) or Special Air Resource (SPAR) aircraft providing person or persons on aboard are designated Code 6 or higher as explained in AFJMAN 11–213, AR 95–11, OPNAVINST 3722–8J. Official Business Only or PPR do not preclude the use of the airport as an alternate for IFR flights.

㉕ AIRPORT MANAGER

The phone number of the airport manager.

㉖ WEATHER DATA SOURCES

Weather data sources will be listed alphabetically followed by their assigned frequencies and/or telephone number and hours of operation.

ASOS—Automated Surface Observing System. Reports the same as an AWOS–3 plus precipitation identification and intensity, and freezing rain occurrence;

  AWOS—Automated Weather Observing System

  AWOS–A—reports altimeter setting (all other information is advisory only).

  AWOS–AV—reports altimeter and visibility.

  AWOS–1—reports altimeter setting, wind data and usually temperature, dew point and density altitude.

  AWOS–2—reports the same as AWOS–1 plus visibility.

  AWOS–3—reports the same as AWOS–1 plus visibility and cloud/ceiling data.

  AWOS–3P reports the same as the AWOS–3 system, plus a precipitation identification sensor.

  AWOS–3PT reports the same as the AWOS–3 system, plus precipitation identification sensor and a thunderstorm/lightning reporting capability.

Legend 13. Chart Supplement.

24   AIRPORT/FACILITY DIRECTORY LEGEND

AWOS–3T reports the same as AWOS–3 system and includes a thunderstorm/lightning reporting capability.

See AIM, Basic Flight Information and ATC Procedures for detailed description of Weather Data Sources.

AWOS–4—reports same as AWOS–3 system, plus precipitation occurrence, type and accumulation, freezing rain, thunderstorm and runway surface sensors.

HIWAS—See RADIO AIDS TO NAVIGATION

LAWRS—Limited Aviation Weather Reporting Station where observers report cloud height, weather, obstructions to vision, temperature and dewpoint (in most cases), surface wind, altimeter and pertinent remarks.

LLWAS—indicates a Low Level Wind Shear Alert System consisting of a center field and several field perimeter anemometers.

SAWRS—identifies airports that have a Supplemental Aviation Weather Reporting Station available to pilots for current weather information.

SWSL—Supplemental Weather Service Location providing current local weather information via radio and telephone.

TDWR—indicates airports that have Terminal Doppler Weather Radar.

WSP—indicates airports that have Weather System Processor.

When the automated weather source is broadcast over an associated airport NAVAID frequency (see NAVAID line), it shall be indicated by a bold ASOS, AWOS, or HIWAS followed by the frequency, identifier and phone number, if available.

㉗ COMMUNICATIONS

Airport terminal control facilities and radio communications associated with the airport shall be shown. When the call sign is not the same as the airport name the call sign will be shown. Frequencies shall normally be shown in descending order with the primary frequency listed first. Frequencies will be listed, together with sectorization indicated by outbound radials, and hours of operation. Communications will be listed in sequence as follows:

Single Frequency Approach (SFA), Common Traffic Advisory Frequency (CTAF), Aeronautical Advisory Stations (UNICOM) or (AUNICOM), and Automatic Terminal Information Service (ATIS) along with their frequency is shown, where available, on the line following the heading "COMMUNICATIONS." When the CTAF and UNICOM frequencies are the same, the frequency will be shown as CTAF/UNICOM 122.8.

The FSS telephone nationwide is toll free 1–800–WX–BRIEF (1–800–992–7433). When the FSS is located on the field it will be indicated as "on arpt". Frequencies available at the FSS will follow in descending order. Remote Communications Outlet (RCO) providing service to the airport followed by the frequency and FSS RADIO name will be shown when available. FSS's provide information on airport conditions, radio aids and other facilities, and process flight plans. Airport Advisory Service (AAS) is provided on the CTAF by FSS's for select non–tower airports or airports where the tower is not in operation.

(See AIM, Para 4–1–9 Traffic Advisory Practices at Airports Without Operating Control Towers or AC 90–42C.)

Aviation weather briefing service is provided by FSS specialists. Flight and weather briefing services are also available by calling the telephone numbers listed.

Remote Communications Outlet (RCO)—An unmanned air/ground communications facility that is remotely controlled and provides UHF or VHF communications capability to extend the service range of an FSS.

Civil Communications Frequencies–Civil communications frequencies used in the FSS air/ground system are operated on 122.0, 122.2, 123.6; emergency 121.5; plus receive–only on 122.1.

    a.   122.0 is assigned as the Enroute Flight Advisory Service frequency at selected FSS RADIO outlets.

    b.   122.2 is assigned as a common enroute frequency.

    c.   123.6 is assigned as the airport advisory frequency at select non–tower locations. At airports with a tower, FSS may provide airport advisories on the tower frequency when tower is closed.

    d.   122.1 is the primary receive–only frequency at VOR's.

    e.   Some FSS's are assigned 50 kHz frequencies in the 122–126 MHz band (eg. 122.45). Pilots using the FSS A/G system should refer to this directory or appropriate charts to determine frequencies available at the FSS or remoted facility through which they wish to communicate.

Emergency frequency 121.5 and 243.0 are available at all Flight Service Stations, most Towers, Approach Control and RADAR facilities.

Frequencies published followed by the letter "T" or "R", indicate that the facility will only transmit or receive respectively on that frequency. All radio aids to navigation (NAVAID) frequencies are transmit only. In cases where communications frequencies are annotated with (R) or (E), (R) indicates Radar Capability and (E) indicates Emergency Frequency.

TERMINAL SERVICES

SFA—Single Frequency Approach.

CTAF—A program designed to get all vehicles and aircraft at airports without an operating control tower on a common frequency.

ATIS—A continuous broadcast of recorded non–control information in selected terminal areas.

D–ATIS—Digital ATIS provides ATIS information in text form outside the standard reception range of conventional ATIS via landline & data link communications and voice message within range of existing transmitters.

AUNICOM—Automated UNICOM is a computerized, command response system that provides automated weather, radio check capability and airport advisory information selected from an automated menu by microphone clicks.

UNICOM—A non–government air/ground radio communications facility which may provide airport information.

PTD—Pilot to Dispatcher.

APP CON—Approach Control. The symbol ℞ indicates radar approach control.

TOWER—Control tower.

GCA—Ground Control Approach System.

GND CON—Ground Control.

SC, 1 FEB 20XX to 29 MAR 20XX

Legend 14. Chart Supplement.

AIRPORT/FACILITY DIRECTORY LEGEND   25

GCO—Ground Communication Outlet—An unstaffed, remotely controlled, ground/ground communications facility. Pilots at uncontrolled airports may contact ATC and FSS via VHF to a telephone connection to obtain an instrument clearance or close a VFR or IFR flight plan. They may also get an updated weather briefing prior to takeoff. Pilots will use four "key clicks" on the VHF radio to contact the appropriate ATC facility or six "key clicks" to contact the FSS. The GCO system is intended to be used only on the ground.

DEP CON—Departure Control. The symbol ⓡ indicates radar departure control.

CLNC DEL—Clearance Delivery.

CPDLC—Controller Pilot Data Link Communication. FANS ATC data communication capability from the aircraft to the ATC Data Link system.

PRE TAXI CLNC—Pre taxi clearance.

VFR ADVSY SVC—VFR Advisory Service. Service provided by Non–Radar Approach Control.
    Advisory Service for VFR aircraft (upon a workload basis) ctc APP CON.

COMD POST—Command Post followed by the operator call sign in parenthesis.

PMSV—Pilot–to–Metro Service call sign, frequency and hours of operation, when full service is other than continuous. PMSV installations at which weather observation service is available shall be indicated, following the frequency and/or hours of operation as "Wx obsn svc 1900–0000Z‡" or "other times" may be used when no specific time is given. PMSV facilities manned by forecasters are considered "Full Service". PMSV facilities manned by weather observers are listed as "Limited Service".

OPS—Operations followed by the operator call sign in parenthesis.

CON

RANGE

FLT FLW—Flight Following

MEDIVAC

NOTE: Communication frequencies followed by the letter "X" indicate frequency available on request.

㉘ AIRSPACE

Information concerning Class B, C, and part–time D and E surface area airspace shall be published with effective times, if available.

CLASS B—Radar Sequencing and Separation Service for all aircraft in CLASS B airspace.

CLASS C—Separation between IFR and VFR aircraft and sequencing of VFR arrivals to the primary airport.

TRSA—Radar Sequencing and Separation Service for participating VFR Aircraft within a Terminal Radar Service Area.

Class C, D, and E airspace described in this publication is that airspace usually consisting of a 5 NM radius core surface area that begins at the surface and extends upward to an altitude above the airport elevation (charted in MSL for Class C and Class D). Class E surface airspace normally extends from the surface up to but not including the overlying controlled airspace.

When part–time Class C or Class D airspace defaults to Class E, the core surface area becomes Class E. This will be formatted as:
AIRSPACE: CLASS C svc "times" ctc **APP CON** other times CLASS E:
or
AIRSPACE: CLASS D svc "times" other times CLASS E.

When a part–time Class C, Class D or Class E surface area defaults to Class G, the core surface area becomes Class G up to, but not including, the overlying controlled airspace. Normally, the overlying controlled airspace is Class E airspace beginning at either 700′ or 1200′ AGL and may be determined by consulting the relevant VFR Sectional or Terminal Area Charts. This will be formatted as:
AIRSPACE: CLASS C svc "times" ctc **APP CON** other times CLASS G, with CLASS E 700′ (or 1200′) AGL & abv:
or
AIRSPACE: CLASS D svc "times" other times CLASS G with CLASS E 700′ (or 1200′) AGL & abv:
or
AIRSPACE: CLASS E svc "times" other times CLASS G with CLASS E 700′ (or 1200′) AGL & abv.

NOTE: AIRSPACE SVC "TIMES" INCLUDE ALL ASSOCIATED ARRIVAL EXTENSIONS. Surface area arrival extensions for instrument approach procedures become part of the primary core surface area. These extensions may be either Class D or Class E airspace and are effective concurrent with the times of the primary core surface area. For example, when a part–time Class C, Class D or Class E surface area defaults to Class G, the associated arrival extensions will default to Class G at the same time. When a part–time Class C or Class D surface area defaults to Class E, the arrival extensions will remain in effect as Class E airspace.

NOTE: CLASS E AIRSPACE EXTENDING UPWARD FROM 700 FEET OR MORE ABOVE THE SURFACE, DESIGNATED IN CONJUNCTION WITH AN AIRPORT WITH AN APPROVED INSTRUMENT PROCEDURE.
Class E 700′ AGL (shown as magenta vignette on sectional charts) and 1200′ AGL (blue vignette) areas are designated when necessary to provide controlled airspace for transitioning to/from the terminal and enroute environments. Unless otherwise specified, these 700′/1200′ AGL Class E airspace areas remain in effect continuously, regardless of airport operating hours or surface area status. These transition areas should not be confused with surface areas or arrival extensions.

(See Chapter 3, AIRSPACE, in the Aeronautical Information Manual for further details)

SC, 1 FEB 20XX to 29 MAR 20XX

Legend 15. Chart Supplement.

26   **AIRPORT/FACILITY DIRECTORY LEGEND**

㉙ **VOR TEST FACILITY (VOT)**

The VOT transmits a signal which provided users a convenient means to determine the operational status and accuracy of an aircraft VOR receiver while on the ground. Ground based VOTs and the associated frequency shall be shown when available. VOTs are also shown with identifier, frequency and referenced remarks in the VOR Receiver Check section in the back of this publication.

㉚ **RADIO AIDS TO NAVIGATION**

The Airport/Facility Directory section of the Chart Supplement lists, by facility name, all Radio Aids to Navigation that appear on FAA, Aeronautical Information Services Visual or IFR Aeronautical Charts and those upon which the FAA has approved an Instrument Approach Procedure, with exception of selected TACANs. All VOR, VORTAC, TACAN and ILS equipment in the National Airspace System has an automatic monitoring and shutdown feature in the event of malfunction. Unmonitored, as used in this publication, for any navigational aid, means that monitoring personnel cannot observe the malfunction or shutdown signal. The NAVAID NOTAM file identifier will be shown as "NOTAM FILE IAD" and will be listed on the Radio Aids to Navigation line. When two or more NAVAIDS are listed and the NOTAM file identifier is different from that shown on the Radio Aids to Navigation line, it will be shown with the NAVAID listing. NOTAM file identifiers for ILSs and its components (e.g., NDB (LOM)) are the same as the associated airports and are not repeated. Automated Surface Observing System (ASOS), Automated Weather Observing System (AWOS), and Hazardous Inflight Weather Advisory Service (HIWAS) will be shown when this service is broadcast over selected NAVAIDs.

NAVAID information is tabulated as indicated in the following sample:

         TACAN/DME Channel   Geographical Position   Site Elevation   Magnetic Variation

NAME (L) ABVORTAC 117.55 ABE Chan 122(Y) N40°43.60' W75°27.30'   180° 4.1 NM to fld.   1110/8E   **AWOS. HIWAS.**

  Class   Frequency   Identifier   Bearing and distance   Automated   Hazardous
                                       facility to center of airport   Weather   Inflight
                                                       Observing   Weather
                                                      System   Service

      VOR unusable 020°–060° byd 26 NM blo 3,500'

    Restriction within the normal altitude/range of the navigational aid
    (See primary alphabetical listing for restrictions on VORTAC and VOR/DME).

Note: Those DME channel numbers with a (Y) suffix require TACAN to be placed in the "Y" mode to receive distance information.

HIWAS—Hazardous Inflight Weather Advisory Service is a continuous broadcast of inflight weather advisories including summarized SIGMETs, convective SIGMETs, AIRMETs and urgent PIREPs. HIWAS is presently broadcast over selected VOR's throughout the U.S.

ASR/PAR—Indicates that Surveillance (ASR) or Precision (PAR) radar instrument approach minimums are published in the U.S. Terminal Procedures. Only part-time hours of operation will be shown.

Legend 16. Chart Supplement.

9.3   IFR EN ROUTE LOW ALTITUDE CHARTS

Figure 55 on page 365 and Figure 55A on page 367 are IFR En Route Low Altitude Charts. As a commercial pilot, the FAA expects you to know how to read, interpret, and use the charts.

The following pages are reference guides to help familiarize you with these charts.

1. This symbol indicates the changeover point giving mileage between NAVAIDs.

    a. Typically used with VORs or VORTACs

2. Any of these symbols indicate there is a Minimum Crossing Altitude (MCA) or Minimum Turning Altitude (MTA).

3. This symbol indicates the ARTCC remote sites with discrete VHF and UHF frequencies.

    a. If you need to determine the ATC frequency for an area on the chart, this box will provide the name of the ATC facility (e.g., Atlanta Center) and frequency.

4. These symbols indicate Minimum Obstruction Clearance Altitude (MOCA).

＊ 0000 ＊ 0000
        ＊ 0000

5. These symbols indicate Minimum En Route Altitude (MEA).

    a. A "G" afterwards indicates the MEA for flights on a GNSS or RNAV flight plan.

0000 0000

AIRSPACE INFORMATION

AIRSPACE INFORMATION

MINIMUM ENROUTE ALTITUDE (MEA)

*All Altitudes Are MSL
Unless Otherwise Noted*

LOW ALTITUDE

RNAV/GPS MEA

3500
3000G
V4

3500
A0

Directional MEA

5500
3500
V4

5500
3500
A0

HIGH ALTITUDE

MEA-31000
J4

Shown along Routes when other than 18,000'

MINIMUM ENROUTE ALTITUDE (MEA) GAP

LOW/HIGH ALTITUDE

V4   MEA GAP

MEA is established when there is a gap in navigation signal coverage

MAXIMUM AUTHORIZED ALTITUDE (MAA)

*All Altitudes Are MSL
Unless Otherwise Noted*

LOW ALTITUDE

MAA-15500
V4

MAA-15500
A0

HIGH ALTITUDE

MAA-41000
J4

Shown along Routes when other than 45,000'

MINIMUM OBSTRUCTION CLEARANCE ALTITUDE (MOCA)

*All Altitudes Are MSL
Unless Otherwise Noted*

LOW ALTITUDE

5500
*3500
V4

MOCA

5500
*3500
A0

7000G
*6300
T266
112

CHANGEOVER POINT

LOW/ HIGH ALTITUDE

00
00

VOR Changeover Point giving mileage to NAVAIDs (Not shown at midpoint locations)

ALTITUDE CHANGE

LOW/ HIGH ALTITUDE

MEA, MOCA and / or MAA change at other than NAVAIDs

MINIMUM CROSSING ALTITUDE (MCA)

LOW/ HIGH ALTITUDE

X

X

X

SARAH
V6 4000 SW

DANEL
V6 4000 SW

T244
HANAH   7400 SE

MINIMUM RECEPTION ALTITUDE (MRA)

LOW/HIGH ALTITUDE

R

R

PAIGE
MRA 4500

MIKEL
MRA 4500

HOLDING PATTERNS

*RNAV Holding Pattern
Magnetic Reference Bearing
is determined by the isogonic
value at the waypoint or fix.*

LOW/HIGH ALTITUDE

NAMEE
N00°00.00'
W00°00.00'

NAMEE
N00°00.00'
W00°00.00'

V4

Holding reporting points have coordinate values shown

Left Turn

Right Turn

IAS   Holding Pattern with max. restricted airspeed 210K applies to altitudes above 6000' to and including 14000' 175K applies to all altitudes

IAS: Indicated Airspeed

Magnetic Reference Bearing

NAMEE

Waypoint

245

RNAV Holding

AIR DEFENSE IDENTIFICATION ZONE (ADIZ)

LOW/ HIGH ALTITUDE

CONTIGUOUS U.S. ADIZ

ALASKA ADIZ

CANADA ADIZ

Adjoining ADIZ

AIR ROUTE TRAFFIC CONTROL CENTER (ARTCC)

LOW/ HIGH ALTITUDE

NEW YORK

WASHINGTON

WASHINGTON
Hagerstown
134.15 385.4

ARTCC Remoted Sites with discrete VHF and UHF frequencies

AIR TRAFFIC SERVICE IDENTIFICATION DATA

LOW/ HIGH ALTITUDE

CTA/FIR
MIAMI OCEANIC
KZMA
FL 180
GND
NY RADIO
129.9

Type of Area Traffic Service

Ceiling
Floor
Call Sign
Frequency

ALTIMETER SETTING CHANGE

LOW ALTITUDE

QNH
ALTIMETER
QNE

FLIGHT INFORMATION REGIONS (FIR)

LOW/ HIGH ALTITUDE

MONTREAL FIR CZUL

MONTREAL FIR CZUL

TORONTO FIR CZYZ

Adjoining FIR

CONTROL AREAS (CTA)

LOW/ HIGH ALTITUDE

MIAMI OCEANIC CTA/FIR KZMA

NEW YORK OCEANIC CTA/FIR KZNY

MIAMI OCEANIC CTA/FIR KZMA

Adjoining CTA

RADIO AIDS TO NAVIGATION

122.65

WICHITA
<u>113.8</u> ICT 85 ≋·–·

N37°44.70′ W97°35.03′

FSS associated with a NAVAID

123.6   122.65

EL DORADO ELD

Name and identifier of FSS
not associated with NAVAID

Shadow NAVAID Boxes indicate Flight Service
Station (FSS) locations. Frequencies 122.2, 255.4
and emergency 121.5 and 243.0 are available
at many FSSs and are not shown. All other
frequencies are shown above the box.

Certain FSSs provide Local Airport Advisory
(LAA) on 123.6.

Frequencies transmit and receive except those followed
by R or T: R - Receive only   T - Transmit only

In Canada, shadow boxes indicate FSSs with standard
group frequencies of 121.5, 126.7 and 243.0.

JONESBORO 122.55

Remote Communications Outlet (RCO)
FSS name and remoted frequency are shown

122.6

PINE BLUFF
<u>116.0</u> PBF 107 ≣≡≣

N34°14.81′ W91°55.57′

Controlling
FSS Name ⟶ **JONESBORO**

Thin Line NAVAID Boxes without frequencies
and controlling FSS name indicate no FSS
frequencies available. Frequencies positioned
above thin line boxes are remoted to the
NAVAID sites. Other frequencies at the
controlling FSS named are available, however,
altitude and terrain may determine their
reception.

Morse Code is not shown in NAVAID
boxes on High Altitude Charts.

⊙ Flight Service Station (FSS), Remote
Communications Outlet (RCO) or
Automated Weather Observing
Station (AWOS/ASOS) not associated
with a charted NAVAID or airport.

NAME ASOS 000.0   Stand Alone
ASOS/AWOS

AIRSPACE INFORMATION

LOW ALTITUDE AIRWAYS

LOW/HIGH ALTITUDE

VHF / UHF Data is depicted in Black
LF / MF Data is depicted in Brown
RNAV Route data is depicted in Blue

V 4 — VOR Airway/ Victor Route

A0 — LF/MF Airway

- **A0** - Uncontrolled LF/MF Airway

A0 **A0** — Oceanic Route

A0 A0 — ATS Route

T000 — RNAV Route GNSS required

TK000 — RNAV Helicopter Route GNSS required

HIGH ALTITUDE ROUTES

HIGH ALTITUDE

Waypoint / NAMEE / 154 → MEA - 23000G ← 334 / **Q7** / 300 / Magnetic Reference Bearing RNAV Route

MEA-27000 MEA-23000G
Q34
256
Joint Jet/RNAV Route

SINGLE DIRECTION ROUTES

LOW/ HIGH ALTITUDE

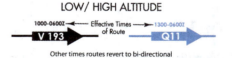

1000-0600Z ← Effective Times of Route → 1300-0600Z
V 193   **Q11**

Other times routes revert to bi-directional

HIGH ALTITUDE

R000 ▶ AIR TRAFFIC SERVICE (ATS) ROUTE

DIRECTION OF FLIGHT INDICATOR

LOW ALTITUDE - CANADA
◀ EVEN

SUBSTITUTE ROUTE

LOW/ HIGH ALTITUDE
–○–○–○–○–

All relative and supporting
data shown in brown

See NOTAMs or
appropriate publication
for specific information

Below and on the following page are the legend excerpts from IFR En Route Low Altitude Charts.

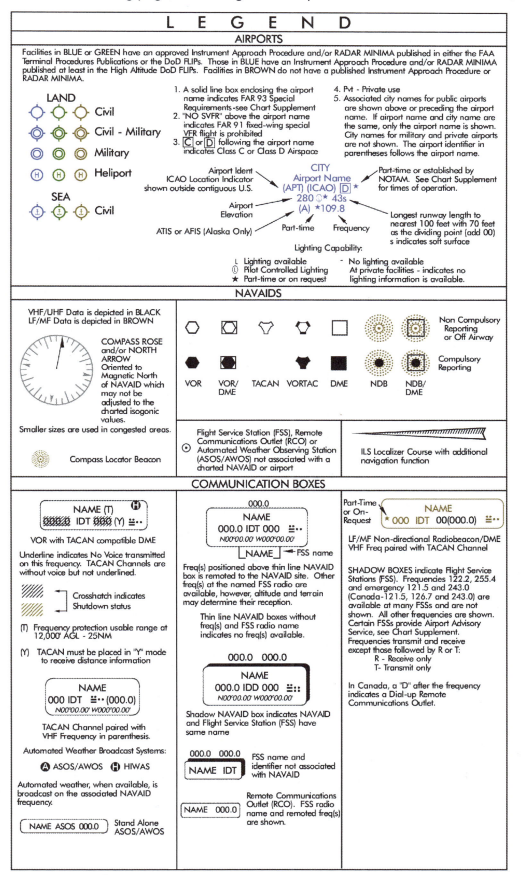

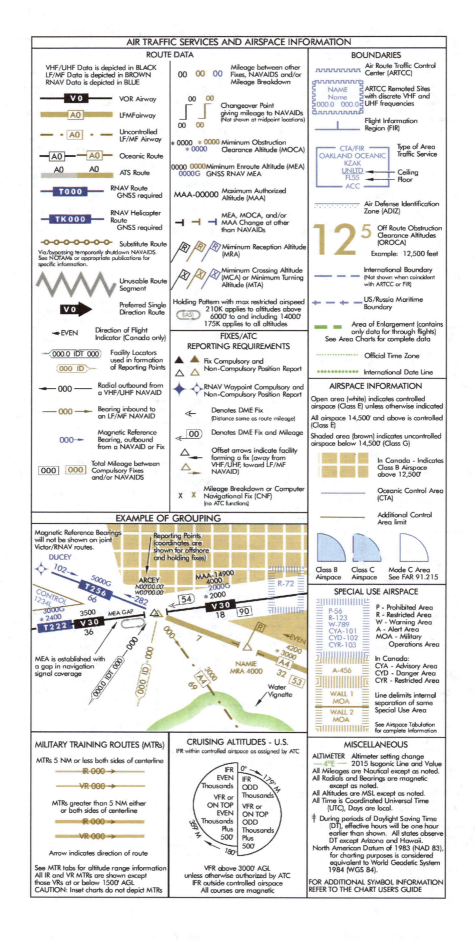

9.4 INSTRUMENT APPROACH CHARTS

1.   The questions in this subunit are wide ranging. They are best prepared for by studying the abridged approach chart legends on pages 331 and 332. You will not have the legends available for reference on the knowledge test so you need to remember the information. Remember that approach charts consist of several parts:

   a.   Top and bottom margin identification
   b.   Planview
   c.   Profile view
   d.   Minimums section
   e.   Airport diagram

2.   Runway Visual Range (RVR)

   a.   RVR is an instrumentally derived value that represents the horizontal distance the pilot can see down the runway from the approach end.

      1)   It is based on the measurement of a transmissometer near the touchdown point of the instrument runway and is reported in hundreds of feet.

   b.   If RVR is inoperative and cannot be reported, convert the RVR minimum to ground visibility, and use that as the visibility minimum for takeoffs and landings.

   c.   The normal ILS visibility minimum is 1/2 SM, which is 2400 RVR.

3.   General Approach Information

   a.   Initial approach fixes (IAF) identify the beginning of an initial approach segment of an instrument approach procedure and are identified by the letters IAF on the planview of approach charts.

   b.   Aircraft approach categories are listed as A, B, C, D, and E based upon 1.3 times the stall speed of the aircraft in the landing configuration at maximum certified gross landing weight (1.3. V_{SO}).

   c.   The symbol "T" in a point-down black triangle indicates that takeoff minimums are not standard and/or departure minimums are published and you should consult alternative takeoff procedures.

      1)   The symbol "A" in a point-up black triangle indicates that nonstandard minimums exist to list the airport as an IFR alternate.

         a)   Standard alternate minimums are 800-2 for a nonprecision approach and 600-2 for a precision approach.

   d.   An airport may not be qualified for alternate use if the NAVAIDs used for the final approach are unmonitored.

   e.   The absence of the procedure turn barb on the planview on an approach chart indicates that a procedure turn is not authorized for that approach.

      1)   The term NoPT means that there is no procedure turn.

   f.   A course reversal (procedure turn) is not required (or authorized) when radar vectors are being provided.

g.   Minimum safe-sector altitudes are depicted on approach charts. These provide at least 1,000 ft. of obstacle clearance within a 25-NM radius of the navigation facility upon which the procedure is predicated but do not necessarily ensure acceptable navigational signal coverage.

h.   Published landing minimums apply when you are making an instrument approach to an airport.

i.   If you adhere to the minimum altitudes depicted on the IAP, you can be assured of terrain and obstacle clearance.

j.   When being radar-vectored to an instrument approach, you should comply with the last assigned altitude until the airplane is established on a segment of a published route or IAP and you have been cleared for the approach, after which you should continue descents to the listed minimum altitudes.

k.   When simultaneous approaches are in progress, each pilot will be advised to monitor the tower frequency to receive advisories and instructions.

l.   When straight-in minimums are not published, you can make a straight-in landing if the active runway is in sight, there is sufficient time to make a normal landing, and you have been cleared to land.

m.   If you are doing an approach in a category B airplane but maintaining a speed faster than the maximum specified for that category, you should use category C minimums.

n.   When an instrument approach procedure involves a procedure turn, the maximum allowable indicated airspeed is 200 kt.

o.   On instrument approach segments, the minimum altitudes are indicated on the planview and profile view, which you are expected to be able to interpret and specify on the FAA instrument rating knowledge test.

p.   When holding patterns exist in lieu of outbound procedure turns, the length of the outbound leg may be indicated as a distance rather than time. This information is given in both the planview and the profile view of the approach chart.

q.   On procedure turns, there may be a distance limitation from a NAVAID, and procedural turns should be made entirely on the side of the inbound radial or bearing to which the procedural turn arrow points.

    1)   If a teardrop turn is depicted, only a teardrop course reversal can be executed.

r.   The airport diagram at the top of the IAP chart contains the following important elevation figures in MSL:

    1)   Airport elevation (ELEV)
    2)   Touchdown elevation (TDZE)
    3)   Threshold elevation (THRE)

s.   If you are not able to identify a NAVAID marking a descent to a lower altitude on a nonprecision approach, you cannot descend to the next lower altitude.

t.   The MAP of a precision approach is arrival at the DH on the glide slope.

u.   The appropriate approach and tower frequencies are indicated at the top of the planview.

v.   Some nonprecision approaches will allow descents to lower altitudes at specified DME distances.

    1)   The advantage of DME can be determined by comparing the two MDA values.

w.   Restrictions to circle-to-land procedures are found below the minimums section of the IAP chart.

x.   The height above touchdown (HAT) is the height of the MDA or DH above the touchdown zone. It is the smaller numbers that appear after the MDA or DH.

    1)   The numbers in parentheses are military minimums.

y.   The minimums section of the approach chart provides the MDA or DH and the visibility (expressed as RVR or SM).

z.   The final approach fix (FAF) for a precision approach is identified on the approach chart by a lightning bolt (✈).

    1)   The intercept altitude is indicated next to the symbol.

aa. On a nonprecision approach, the distance from the FAF to the MAP is indicated below the airport diagram.

ab. If a runway has a displaced threshold, the distance available for landing will be shown by a notation in the airport diagram. For example, "Rwy 21 ldg 5957'" signifies that 5,957 ft. of the total length of runway 21 are available for landing.

ac. A category C aircraft must use category C minimums, even if using category B approach speed.

4.   **RNAV LDA and SDF Approaches**

a.   On RNAV approaches, the MAP is identified when the TO/FROM indicator changes, which indicates station passage at the MAP waypoint.

    1)   On some RNAV approach charts, the distance from the MAP to another more prominent waypoint located along the extended final approach course may be shown in the profile and plan views.

b.   RNAV waypoints, when used for an instrument approach, contain boxes in which the latitude and longitude are listed on the first line and the VOR direction and distance are listed on the second line.

c.   RNAV approaches require an approved RNAV receiver; no other navigation equipment is specifically required.

d.   LDA (localizer-type directional aid) is as useful and accurate as a localizer (3° to 6° course width).

    1)   The LDA is very similar to an instrument landing system (ILS), but it usually does not have a glide slope (i.e., it has only a localizer) and is **not** aligned with the runway.

e.   LDA is as useful and accurate as an ILS localizer but is not part of a complete ILS.

    1)   The LDA is not aligned with the runway.

f.   SDF (simplified directional facility) has a course width of either 6° or 12°.

    1)   SDF approaches may or may not be aligned with a runway (and their courses are wider). SDF does not have a glide slope.

5.   Side-Step Approaches

   a.   A side-step approach is an instrument approach to one runway until you can see a parallel runway and "side step" to land on the parallel runway.

   b.   A side-step approach is used when a pilot (1) executes an approach procedure serving one of two or more parallel runways that are separated by 1,200 ft. or less and then (2) diverts to the other parallel runway using a straight-in approach.

   c.   Execute a side-step procedure as soon as possible after the runway environment is in sight.

6.   Localizer and ILS Approaches

   a.   ILS components include

      1)   Localizer
      2)   Glide slope
      3)   Outer marker
      4)   Middle marker
      5)   Approach lights

   b.   If more than one component is unusable, each minimum is raised to the highest minimum required by any single component that is inoperative.

   c.   A compass locator or precision approach radar (PAR) may be substituted for an inoperative OM.

   d.   When installed with the ILS and specified in the approach procedure, DME may be used in lieu of the OM.

   e.   When the glide slope fails, the ILS reverts to a nonprecision localizer (LOC) approach.

      1)   The LOC MDA and visibility minimums will be used.

   f.   If you are on the glide slope when the ILS fails and a VASI is in sight, you should continue the approach using the VASI and report the malfunction to ATC.

   g.   A second VOR receiver may be needed when doing a localizer approach with a final step-down fix to be identified by a VOR radial.

   h.   When making an LOC approach to the primary airport of the Class B airspace, the aircraft must be equipped with

      1)   Two-way radio communication
      2)   Mode C transponder
      3)   VOR

   i.   If there is penetration of the obstacle identification surfaces (OIS), the published visibility for the ILS approach can be no lower than 3/4 SM.

   j.   The ILS missed approach should be executed upon arrival at the DH on the glide slope if the visual reference requirements are not met.

   k.   The normal decision height for a Category I ILS is 200 ft. AGL.

      1)   This is the height of the glide slope centerline at the middle marker.

7. VOR Approaches

   a. The minimum navigation equipment required for a VOR/DME approach is one VOR receiver and DME.

   b. For conventional navigation systems, the MSA is normally based on the primary omnidirectional facility on which the IAP is predicated.

      1) MSAs are expressed in feet above mean sea level and normally have a 25-NM radius; however, this radius may be expanded to 30 NM if necessary to encompass the airport landing surfaces.

8. Missed Approaches

   a. When executing a missed approach prior to the missed approach point (MAP), continue the approach to the MAP at or above the minimum descent altitude (MDA) or decision height (DH) before executing any turns.

   b. If you lose visual reference in a circle to land from an instrument approach, you should make a climbing turn toward your landing runway to become established on the missed approach course.

9. Category II and III ILS Approaches

   a. These approaches often have "SA" before them, for example, "SA Category I ILS." The SA means Special Authorization because the airline or operator must get approval from the FAA before being able to conduct the approach.

   b. These approaches also require Special Aircrew and Aircraft Certification Required meaning that the crew and aircraft need special certification from the FAA before the particular approach minimums may be used.

      1) The authorization must include specific OPSPEC (operation specifications) or a letter of approval and use of Autoland or HUD (heads up display) to touch down.

   c. In the IFR Landing Minima section of CAT II approaches, the approach plate states, "RA XXX/YY" followed by the DH and the DA.

      1) EXAMPLE: "RA 111/12 100 DA 5470." The radar altimeter should be set to 111 ft., and the RVR minimum is 1,200 ft. The DH is 100 ft., and the DA is 5,470 ft.

   d. In the IFR Landing Minima section of CAT III approaches, the section will state the RVR requirement or state that it is "NA" or not applicable.

      1) Category IIIa is a type of precision instrument approach and landing with no DH or a DH below 100 ft., and controlling runway visual range not less than 700 ft.

      2) Category IIIb is a type of precision instrument approach and landing with no DH or a DH below 50 ft., and controlling runway visual range less than 700 ft., but not less than 150 ft.

      3) Category IIIc is a type of precision instrument approach and landing with no DH and no runway visual range limitation.

10. Review the information on the following pages, which consists of excerpts from the Chart Supplement (General Information and Legend).

ABBREVIATIONS

AAUP	Attention All Users Page	HAA	Height above Airport
ADF	Automatic Direction Finder	HAL	Height above Landing
ADIZ	Air Defense Identification Zone	HAT	Height above Touchdown
AFIS	Automatic Flight Information Service	HATh	Height Above Threshold
		HGS	Head-up Guidance System
ALS	Approach Light System	HIRL	High Intensity Runway Lights
ALSF	Approach Light System with Sequenced Flashing Lights	HUD	Head-up Display
		IAF	Initial Approach Fix
AP	Autopilot System	ICAO	International Civil Aviation Organization
APCH	Approach		
APP CON	Approach Control	IF	Intermediate Fix
ARR	Arrival	IM	Inner Marker
ASOS	Automated Surface Observing System	INOP	Inoperative
		INT	Intersection
ASR/PAR	Published Radar Minimums at this Airport	K	Knots
		KIAS	Knots Indicated Airspeed
ASSC	Airport Surface Surveillance Systems	LAAS	Local Area Augmentation System
ATIS	Automatic Terminal Information Service	LDA	Localizer Type Directional Aid
		Ldg	Landing
AUNICOM	Automated UNICOM	LIRL	Low Intensity Runway Lights
AWOS	Automated Weather Observing System	LNAV	Lateral Navigation
		LOC	Localizer
AZ	Azimuth	LP	Localizer Performance
BC	Back Course	LPV	Localizer Performance with Vertical Guidance
BND	Bound		
C	Circling	LR	Lead Radial. Provides at least 2 NM (Copter 1 NM) of lead to assist in turning onto the intermediate/final course.
CAT	Category		
CCW	Counter Clockwise		
CDI	Course Deviation Indicator		
Chan	Channel		
CIFP	Coded Instrument Flight Procedures	MAA	Maximum Authorized Altitude
		MALS	Medium Intensity Approach Light System
CIR	Circling		
CLNC DEL	Clearance Delivery	MALSR	Medium Intensity Approach Light System with RAIL
CNF	Computer Navigation Fix		
CTAF	Common Traffic Advisory Frequency	MAP	Missed Approach Point
		MDA	Minimum Descent Altitude
CW	Clockwise	MIRL	Medium Intensity Runway Lights
DA	Decision Altitude	MM	Middle Marker
DER	Departure End of Runway	MRA	Minimum Reception Altitude
DH	Decision Height	N/A	Not Applicable
DME	Distance Measuring Equipment	NA	Not Authorized
DTHR	Displaced Threshold	NDB	Non-directional Radio Beacon
DVA	Diverse Vector Area	NFD	National Flight Database
ELEV	Elevation	NM	Nautical Mile
EMAS	Engineered Material Arresting System	NoPT	No Procedure Turn Required (Procedure Turn shall not be executed without ATC clearance)
FAF	Final Approach Fix		
FD	Flight Director System		
FM	Fan Marker	ODALS	Omnidirectional Approach Light System
FMS	Flight Management System		
GBAS	Ground Based Augmentation System	ODP	Obstacle Departure Procedure
		OM	Outer Marker
GCO	Ground Communications Outlet	PRM	Precision Runway Monitor
GLS	Ground Based Augmentation System Landing System		
GP	Glidepath		
GPI	Ground Point of Interception		
GPS	Global Positioning System		
GS	Glide Slope		

ABBREVIATIONS

R.............................	Radial	TAA.............................	Terminal Arrival Area
RA.............................	Radio Altimeter setting height	TAC.............................	TACAN
RAIL.............................	Runway Alignment Indicator Lights	TCH.............................	Threshold Crossing Height (height in feet Above Ground level) Touchdown Zone
RCLS.............................	Runway Centerline Light System	TDZE.............................	Touchdown Zone Elevation
REIL.............................	Runway End Identifier Lights	TDZ/CL.............................	Touchdown Zone and Runway Centerline Lighting
RF.............................	Radius-to-Fix	TDZL.............................	Touchdown Zone Lights
RLLS.............................	Runway Lead-in Light System	THR.............................	Threshold
RNAV.............................	Area Navigation	THRE.............................	Threshold Elevation
RNP.............................	Required Navigation Performance	TODA.............................	Takeoff Distance Available
RPI.............................	Runway Point of Intercept(ion)	TORA.............................	Takeoff Run Available
RRL.............................	Runway Remaining Lights	TR.............................	Track
Rwy.............................	Runway	VASI.............................	Visual Approach Slope Indicator
RVR.............................	Runway Visual Range	VCOA.............................	Visual Climb Over Airport
S.............................	Straight-in	VDP.............................	Visual Descent Point
SALS.............................	Short Approach Light System	VGSI.............................	Visual Glide Slope Indicator
SSALR.............................	Simplified Short Approach Light System with RAIL	VNAV.............................	Vertical Navigation
SDF.............................	Simplified Directional Facility	WAAS.............................	Wide Area Augmentation System
SM.............................	Statute Mile	WP/WPT.............................	Waypoint (RNAV)
SOIA.............................	Simultaneous Offset Instrument Approach		

TERMS/LANDING MINIMA DATA

IFR LANDING MINIMA

The United States Standard for Terminal Instrument Procedures (TERPS) is the approved criteria for formulating instrument approach procedures. Landing minima are established for six aircraft approach categories (ABCDE and COPTER). In the absence of COPTER MINIMA, helicopters may use the CAT A minimums of other procedures.

LANDING MINIMA FORMAT

In this example airport elevation is 1179, and runway touchdown zone elevation is 1152.

Straight-in ILS to Runway 27

Visibility (RVR 100's of feet)

DA

Aircraft Approach Category
HAT/HATh

CATEGORY	A	B	C	D
S-ILS 27	1352/24		200 (200-½)	
S-LOC 27	1440/24	288	(300-½)	1440/50 288 (300-1)
CIRCLING	1540-1 361 (400-1)	1640-1 461 (500-1)	1640-1½ 461 (500-1½)	1740-2 561 (600-2)

Straight-in with Glide Slope Inoperative or not used to Runway 27

MDA   HAA   Visibility in Statute Miles

All **weather** minimums in parentheses not applicable to Civil Pilots.

Military Pilots refer to appropriate regulations.

Comparable Values of RVR and Visibility

The following table shall be used for converting RVR to ground or flight visibility. For converting RVR values that fall between listed values, use the next higher RVR value; do not interpolate. For example, when converting 1800 RVR, use 2400 RVR with the resultant visibility of ½ mile.

RVR (feet)	Visibility (statute miles)	RVR (feet)	Visibility (statute miles)
1600	¼	4500	⅞
2400	½	5000	1
3200	⅝	6000	1¼
4000	¾		

INSTRUMENT APPROACH PROCEDURES (CHARTS)

PLANVIEW SYMBOLS

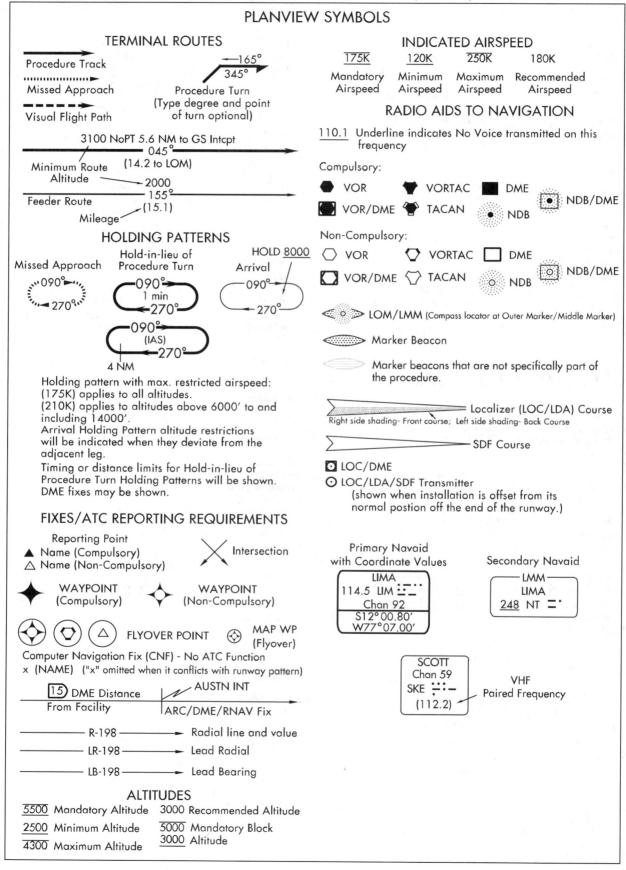

TERMINAL ROUTES

Procedure Track

Missed Approach

Visual Flight Path

165°
345°
Procedure Turn
(Type degree and point
of turn optional)

3100 NoPT 5.6 NM to GS Intcpt
045°
(14.2 to LOM)
Minimum Route Altitude
2000
155°
Feeder Route
(15.1)
Mileage

INDICATED AIRSPEED

175K	120K	250K	180K
Mandatory Airspeed	Minimum Airspeed	Maximum Airspeed	Recommended Airspeed

RADIO AIDS TO NAVIGATION

110.1 Underline indicates No Voice transmitted on this frequency

Compulsory:

VOR   VORTAC   DME   NDB/DME

VOR/DME   TACAN   NDB

Non-Compulsory:

VOR   VORTAC   DME   NDB/DME

VOR/DME   TACAN   NDB

LOM/LMM (Compass locator at Outer Marker/Middle Marker)

Marker Beacon

Marker beacons that are not specifically part of the procedure.

Localizer (LOC/LDA) Course
Right side shading- Front course; Left side shading- Back Course

SDF Course

LOC/DME

LOC/LDA/SDF Transmitter
(shown when installation is offset from its normal postion off the end of the runway.)

HOLDING PATTERNS

Missed Approach
090°
270°

Hold-in-lieu of Procedure Turn
090°
1 min
270°

090°
(IAS)
270°
4 NM

HOLD 8000
Arrival
090°
270°

Holding pattern with max. restricted airspeed:
(175K) applies to all altitudes.
(210K) applies to altitudes above 6000' to and including 14000'.
Arrival Holding Pattern altitude restrictions will be indicated when they deviate from the adjacent leg.
Timing or distance limits for Hold-in-lieu of Procedure Turn Holding Patterns will be shown. DME fixes may be shown.

FIXES/ATC REPORTING REQUIREMENTS

Reporting Point
▲ Name (Compulsory)
△ Name (Non-Compulsory)

✕ Intersection

◆ WAYPOINT (Compulsory)

◇ WAYPOINT (Non-Compulsory)

FLYOVER POINT

MAP WP (Flyover)

Computer Navigation Fix (CNF) - No ATC Function
x (NAME) ("x" omitted when it conflicts with runway pattern)

15 DME Distance From Facility

AUSTN INT
ARC/DME/RNAV Fix

———— R-198 ————▶ Radial line and value
———— LR-198 ————▶ Lead Radial
———— LB-198 ————▶ Lead Bearing

Primary Navaid with Coordinate Values

| LIMA |
| 114.5 LIM |
| Chan 92 |
| S12° 00.80' |
| W77° 07.00' |

Secondary Navaid

| LMM |
| LIMA |
| 248 NT |

SCOTT
Chan 59
SKE
(112.2)

VHF Paired Frequency

ALTITUDES

5500 Mandatory Altitude   3000 Recommended Altitude
2500 Minimum Altitude   5000 Mandatory Block
4300 Maximum Altitude   3000 Altitude

INSTRUMENT APPROACH PROCEDURES (CHARTS)

PLANVIEW SYMBOLS

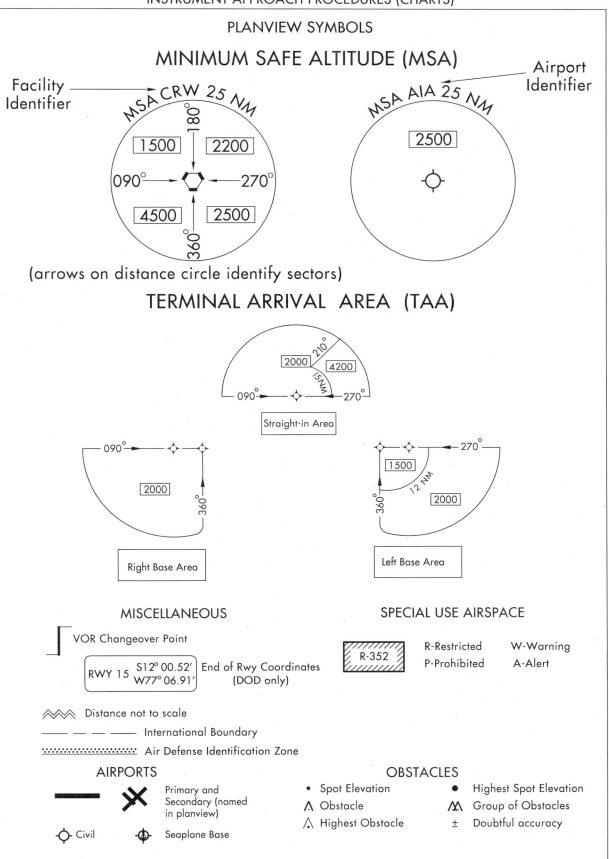

INSTRUMENT APPROACH PROCEDURES (CHARTS)

PROFILE VIEW

Three different methods are used to depict either electronic or vertical guidance: "GS", "GP", or "VDA".

1. "GS" indicates that an Instrument Landing System (ILS) electronic glide slope (a ground antenna) provides vertical guidance. The profile section of ILS procedures depict a GS angle and TCH in the following format: $\frac{\text{GS } 3.00°}{\text{TCH } 55}$.

2. "GP" on GLS and RNAV procedures indicates that either electronic vertical guidance (via Wide Area Augmentation System - WAAS or Ground Based Augmentation System - GBAS) or barometric vertical guidance is provided. GLS and RNAV procedures with a published decision altitude (DA/H) depict a GP angle and TCH in the following format: $\frac{\text{GP } 3.00°}{\text{TCH } 50}$.

3. An advisory vertical descent angle (VDA) is provided on non-vertically guided conventional procedures and RNAV procedures with only a minimum descent altitude (MDA) to assist in preventing controlled flight into terrain. On Civil (FAA) procedures, this information is placed above or below the procedure track following the fix it is based on. Absence of a VDA or a note that the VDA is not authorized indicates that the prescribed obstacle clearance surface is not clear and the VDA must not be used below MDA. VDA is depicted in the following format: $\frac{\measuredangle \, 3.00°}{\text{TCH } 55}$.

ILS or LOC APPROACH

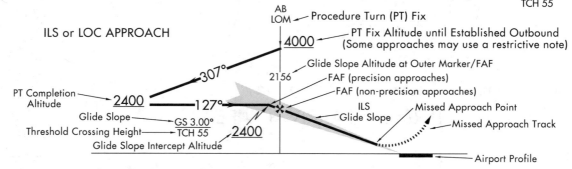

RNAV and GLS PROCEDURES WITH VERTICAL GUIDANCE

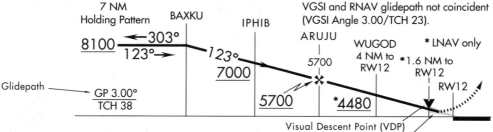

NON-VERTICALLY GUIDED CONVENTIONAL PROCEDURES AND RNAV PROCEDURES WITH MDA ONLY

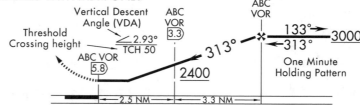

DESCENT FROM HOLDING PATTERN

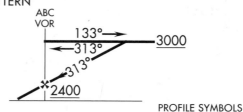

ALTITUDES		PROFILE SYMBOLS	
__5500__ Mandatory Altitude	3000 Recommended Altitude	Glide Slope/Glidepath Intercept Altitude and final approach fix for vertically guided approach procedures.	▬ ▬ ▶ Visual Flight Path
__2500__ Minimum Altitude	$\frac{\text{5000}}{\underline{\text{3000}}}$ Mandatory Block Altitude	2400	Note: Facilities and waypoints are depicted as a solid vertical line while fixes and intersections are depicted as a dashed vertical line.
$\overline{\text{4300}}$ Maximum Altitude		▼ Visual Descent Point (VDP)	

9.5 FUEL CONSUMPTION

1. To determine the time en route, divide the number of miles by your groundspeed.

2. To determine the fuel consumed, multiply the time en route by the fuel consumed per hour.

3. EXAMPLE: If an airplane uses 10.5 GPH and has a TAS (or groundspeed) of 145 kt., you may be asked to estimate the fuel burn on a 460 NM trip.

   a. First, determine the time en route by dividing the distance of 460 NM by 145 kt. to arrive at 3.17 hr.

   b. Second, multiply the time of 3.17 hr. by 10.5 GPH to arrive at 33 gal.

9.6 WIND DIRECTION AND SPEED

1. To estimate your wind given true heading and a true course, simply use the wind side of your flight computer backwards.

   a. Place the groundspeed under the grommet (the hole in the center) with the true course under the true index.

   b. Then on the true airspeed arc, place a pencil mark reflecting the right or left wind correction angle you are holding.

   c. Rotate the inner scale so the pencil mark is on the centerline and read the wind direction under the true index.

   d. The distance up from the grommet is the wind speed.

2. To determine the total course correction needed to converge on (fly direct to) your destination, use the following steps:

   a. Since 1° off course equals 1 NM per 60 NM from the station, the following formula applies:

   $$\frac{\text{NM off}}{\text{NM flown}} \times 60 = \text{Degrees off course from departure point}$$

      1) Turning back this number of degrees will parallel the original course.

   b. To fly direct to your destination, calculate the number of degrees off course.

   $$\frac{\text{NM off}}{\text{NM remaining}} \times 60 = \text{Degrees off course to destination}$$

      1) Turning this number of degrees farther will take you direct to your destination.

   c. EXAMPLE: You are 140 NM from your departure point and have determined that you are 11 NM off course. If 71 NM remain to be flown, the approximate total correction to be made to converge on the destination is 14°, as computed below.

   $$\frac{11\ \text{NM}}{140\ \text{NM}} \times 60 = 4.7°$$

   $$\frac{11\ \text{NM}}{71\ \text{NM}} \times 60 = \underline{9.3°}$$
   $$\underline{\underline{14.0°}}$$

9.7   TIME, COMPASS HEADING, ETC., ON CLIMBS AND EN ROUTE

1.   You may be asked to determine the minutes, compass heading, distance, and fuel consumed during a climb or en route.

2.   The first step is to determine the number of minutes to climb.

    a.   Divide the amount of climb required by the rate of climb.

        1)   EXAMPLE: If you must climb 5,000 ft. at 500 fpm, the climb takes 10 min. (5,000 ÷ 500).

3.   If there are several alternative answers with the correct number of minutes, you may be able to determine the correct answer based upon the amount of fuel burned.

    a.   Convert the time required to climb into hours by dividing by 60.

    b.   Then multiply by the rate of fuel consumption to determine the amount of fuel used.

4.   Finally, if you must determine the compass heading, begin by converting the true course to true heading by adjusting for wind effect using the wind side of your flight computer.

    a.   Align the wind direction on the inner scale under the true index (top of the computer) on the outer scale.

    b.   Measure up the vertical line the amount of wind speed in kt., and put a pencil mark on the plastic.

    c.   Rotate the inner scale so the true course is under the true index.

    d.   Slide the grid so that your pencil dot is superimposed over the true airspeed. The location of the grommet will indicate the groundspeed.

    e.   The pencil mark will indicate the wind correction angle (if to the left, it is a negative wind correction, and if to the right, a positive wind correction).

    f.   True heading is found by adjusting the true course for the wind correction.

    g.   Magnetic heading is found by adjusting the true heading for magnetic variation.

        1)   Subtract easterly variation ("east is least").
        2)   Add westerly variation ("west is best").

    h.   Convert magnetic heading to compass heading by adjusting for the compass deviation, which is given in these questions as + or −.

9.8   TIME, COMPASS HEADING, ETC., ON DESCENTS

1.   These questions are calculated the same as for climbs (Subunit 9.7), except you are descending.

2.   Note that the questions require you to arrive at some elevation AGL above the airport, not the airport elevation.

    a.   Add the airport elevation to the altitude AGL required; then subtract that amount from the cruising altitude.

QUESTIONS

9.1 Sectional Charts

1. Which is true concerning the blue and magenta colors used to depict airports on Sectional Aeronautical Charts?

A. Airports with control towers underlying Class A, B, and C airspace are shown in blue; Class D and E airspace are magenta.

B. Airports with control towers underlying Class C, D, and E airspace are shown in magenta.

C. Airports with control towers underlying Class B, C, D, and E airspace are shown in blue.

Answer (C) is correct. (ACUG)
DISCUSSION: On sectional charts, airports with control towers underlying Class B, C, D, E, or G airspace are shown in blue. Airports with no control towers are shown in magenta.
Answer (A) is incorrect. There are no airports in Class A airspace. Airports with control towers are shown in blue, all others in magenta. **Answer (B) is incorrect.** Airports with control towers are shown in blue, not magenta.

2. True course measurements on a Sectional Aeronautical Chart should be made at a meridian near the midpoint of the course because the

A. values of isogonic lines change from point to point.

B. angles formed by isogonic lines and lines of latitude vary from point to point.

C. angles formed by lines of longitude and the course line vary from point to point.

Answer (C) is correct. (FAA-H-8083-25B Chap 15)
DISCUSSION: Because meridians (lines of longitude) converge toward the poles, the angles formed by meridians and the course line may vary from point to point. Thus, course measurement should be taken at a meridian near the midpoint of the course rather than at the departure point.
Answer (A) is incorrect. Isogonic lines are used to calculate magnetic (not true) course. **Answer (B) is incorrect.** Isogonic lines are used to calculate magnetic (not true) course.

3. What must a pilot do or be aware of when transitioning an Alert Area?

A. All pilots must contact the controlling agency to ensure aircraft separation.

B. Non-participating aircraft may transit the area as long as they operate in accordance with their waiver.

C. Be aware that the area may contain unusual aeronautical activity or high volume of pilot training.

Answer (C) is correct. (AIM Para 3-4-6, FAA-H-8083-25B)
DISCUSSION: Alert areas are depicted on aeronautical charts with an "A" followed by a number (e.g., A-211) to inform non-participating pilots of areas that may contain a high volume of pilot training or an unusual type of aerial activity. Pilots should exercise caution in alert areas. Pilots of participating aircraft and pilots transiting the area are equally responsible for collision avoidance.
Answer (A) is incorrect. It is not necessary to contact any agency when transiting an alert area. However, it is imperative that pilots exercise caution within an alert area. Pilots of participating aircraft and pilots transiting the area are equally responsible for collision avoidance. **Answer (B) is incorrect.** Non-participating aircraft do not need a waiver to fly through an alert area.

4. When a dashed blue circle surrounds an airport on a sectional aeronautical chart, it will depict the boundary of

A. Special VFR airspace.

B. Class B airspace.

C. Class D airspace.

Answer (C) is correct. (AIM Para 3-2-5)
DISCUSSION: On a sectional aeronautical chart, the boundary of Class D airspace is depicted by a dashed (segmented) blue circle around an airport.
Answer (A) is incorrect. There is no airspace designated as special VFR. **Answer (B) is incorrect.** On a sectional chart, a solid, not dashed, blue circle that surrounds an airport depicts the boundary of Class B airspace.

5. (Refer to Figure 52 on page 347.) (Refer to point 1.) The floor of the Class E airspace above Georgetown Airport (Q61) is at

A. the surface.

B. 3,823 feet MSL.

C. 700 feet AGL.

Answer (B) is correct. (ACUG)
DISCUSSION: Georgetown Airport is located within 4 NM of the blue shaded area representing a federal airway, which means the floor of Class E airspace is at 1,200 ft. AGL. The airport elevation is given in the first line of the airport data as 2,623 ft. MSL. Thus, the floor of Class E airspace above Georgetown Airport is 3,823 ft. MSL (2,623 + 1,200).
Answer (A) is incorrect. Class E airspace would begin at the surface only if the airport were surrounded by a magenta segmented circle. Answer (C) is incorrect. The floor of Class E airspace would begin at 700 ft. AGL if Georgetown Airport were inside, not outside, the magenta-shaded areas.

6. (Refer to Figure 52 on page 347.) (Refer to point 2.) The highest obstruction with high intensity lighting within 10 NM of Sacramento International Airport (SMF) is how high above ground?

A. 533 feet.

B. 559 feet.

C. 512 feet.

Answer (C) is correct. (ACUG)
DISCUSSION: Obstructions with high-intensity lights are depicted by lightning bolt symbols around the top of the obstruction symbol. The only symbol having high-intensity lights within 10 NM of SMF is located approximately 3 NM southeast of the airport. The height above ground of this obstruction is the number in parentheses, which is 512 ft. AGL.
Answer (A) is incorrect. This is the height of the obstruction above sea level, not the ground. Answer (B) is incorrect. This is the height above ground of the group of obstructions located approximately 8 NM southeast of the airport. While these obstructions are the highest above ground, they do not have high-intensity lighting.

7. (Refer to Figure 52 on page 347.) (Refer to Area 2.) When departing the RIO LINDA (L36) Airport to the northwest at an altitude of 1,000 feet AGL, you

A. must make contact with MC CLELLAN (MCC) control tower as soon as practical after takeoff.

B. are not required to contact any ATC facilities if you do not enter the Class C Airspace.

C. must make contact with the SACRAMENTO INTL (SMF) control tower immediately after takeoff.

Answer (B) is correct. (FAA-H-8083-25B, ACUG)
DISCUSSION: At 1,000 ft. AGL, the planned flight to the northwest would not require any contact with ATC facilities as long as Class C airspace is avoided immediately to the west.
Answer (A) is incorrect. McClellan Airport is a Class E airport and does not have a control tower, as indicated by the magenta airport symbol. Answer (C) is incorrect. As long as Class C airspace is avoided, there is no requirement to contact the Sacramento Intl tower.

8. (Refer to Figure 52 on page 347.) (Refer to Area 6.) What is the purpose of the star that follows the CT-120.65 in the information box for the Sacramento Mather (MHR) Airport?

A. That the control tower has limited hours of operation.

B. The airport has maintenance facilities.

C. There is a rotating beacon on the field.

Answer (A) is correct. (Sectional Chart legend)
DISCUSSION: The star that follows the Control Tower (CT) frequency indicates that the control tower has limited hours of operation. The tower frequencies table on the edge of the sectional chart lists the specific times the tower is operational.
Answer (B) is incorrect. Ticks around the airport symbol indicate that the airport has fuel available, but there is no symbol to indicate that the airport has maintenance facilities. Answer (C) is incorrect. The star on top of the airport symbol, not the star that follows the Control Tower (CT) frequency, indicates that there is a rotating beacon on the field.

9. (Refer to Figure 52 on page 347.) (Refer to point 4.) The terrain at the obstruction approximately 8 NM east southeast of the Lincoln Airport is approximately how much higher than the airport elevation?

A. 418 feet.

B. 827 feet.

C. 1,245 feet.

Answer (B) is correct. (ACUG)
DISCUSSION: The obstruction approximately 8 NM east-southeast of the Lincoln Airport (point 4) is marked as having an elevation of 1,245 ft. MSL, and a height of 297 ft. AGL. Thus, the terrain elevation at that point is 948 ft. MSL (1,245 − 297). The Lincoln Airport elevation is shown to be 121 ft. MSL, which is 827 ft. (948 − 121) lower than the terrain elevation at the obstruction.
Answer (A) is incorrect. The terrain at the obstruction is 827 ft., not 418 ft., higher than the Lincoln Airport elevation. Answer (C) is incorrect. This is the MSL height of the obstruction.

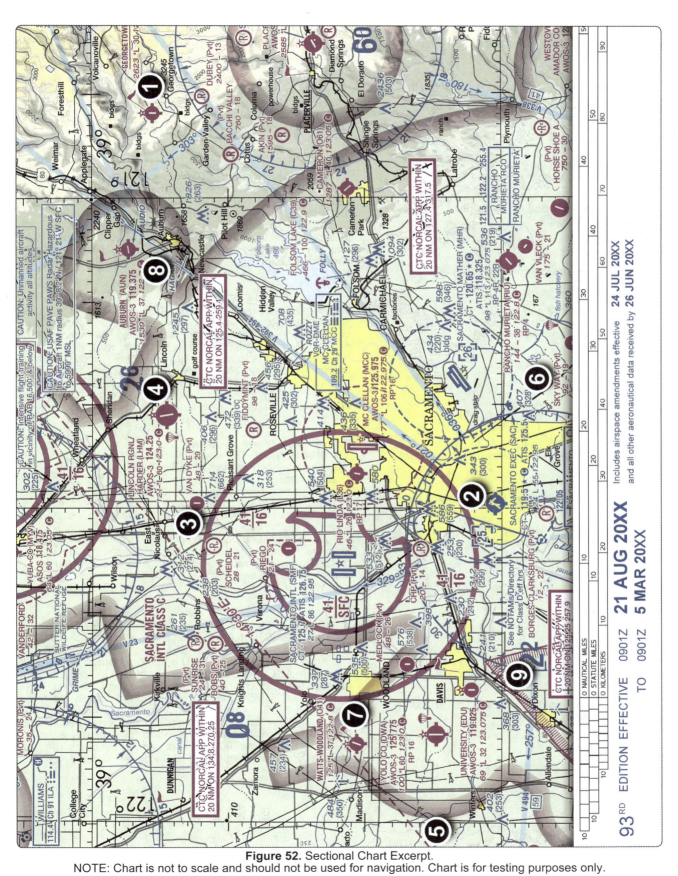

Figure 52. Sectional Chart Excerpt.
NOTE: Chart is not to scale and should not be used for navigation. Chart is for testing purposes only.

10. (Refer to Figure 52 on page 349.) (Refer to point 5.) The floor of the Class E airspace over University Airport (area 5) is

A. the surface.

B. 700 feet AGL.

C. 1,200 feet AGL.

Answer (B) is correct. (ACUG)
   DISCUSSION: University Airport (east of point 5) is located within the magenta shading, which means the floor of Class E airspace is at 700 ft. AGL.
   Answer (A) is incorrect. Class E airspace would begin at the surface only if the airport were surrounded by a magenta segmented circle. **Answer (C) is incorrect.** Class E airspace would begin at 1,200 ft. only if the airport were surrounded by a shaded blue line.

11. (Refer to Figure 52 on page 349.) (Refer to point 2.) Borges-Clarksburg Airport is

A. an airport restricted to use by private and recreational pilots.

B. a restricted military stage field within restricted airspace.

C. a nonpublic use airport.

Answer (C) is correct. (ACUG)
   DISCUSSION: Borges-Clarksburg Airport (south of 2) is a private, i.e., nonpublic-use, airport as indicated by the term "(Pvt)" after the airport name. Private airports that are shown on the sectional charts have an emergency or landmark value.
   Answer (A) is incorrect. The airport symbol with the letter "R" in the center means it is a nonpublic-use airport, not that only private and recreational pilots may use the airport. **Answer (B) is incorrect.** Military airfields are labeled as AFB, NAS, AAF, NAAS, NAF, MCAS, or DND.

12. (Refer to Figure 52 on page 349.) (Refer to area 6.) How long is the longest runway at Sacramento Mather airport (MHR)?

A. 9,800 ft.

B. 11,300 ft.

C. 7,500 ft.

Answer (B) is correct. (ACUG)
   DISCUSSION: The length of the longest runway is noted in the airport information on the second line. The number "113" means that the length of the longest runway is 11,300 ft.
   Answer (A) is incorrect. The number "98" in the airport information does not show runway length but indicates that the field elevation is 98 ft. MSL. **Answer (C) is incorrect.** The number "075" is the last three digits of the tower frequency and does not indicate the runway length.

13. (Refer to Figure 52 on page 349.) (Refer to point 7.) The floor of Class E airspace over the town of Woodland is

A. 700 feet AGL over part of the town and no floor over the remainder.

B. 1,200 feet AGL over part of the town and no floor over the remainder.

C. both 700 feet and 1,200 feet AGL.

Answer (C) is correct. (ACUG)
   DISCUSSION: The town of Woodland (just east of point 7) has magenta shading over part of it. To the inside of the shading, Class E airspace begins at 700 ft. AGL. Where the outer edge of the magenta area ends, Class E airspace begins at 1,200 ft. AGL. One can assume the town of Woodland is to the inside of a shaded blue line not depicted on the chart excerpt.
   Answer (A) is incorrect. No floor would imply Class E airspace begins at the surface. Class E airspace at the surface is depicted with a dashed magenta line. **Answer (B) is incorrect.** The area to the inside of the magenta shading indicates the floor of Class E airspace is at 700 ft. AGL.

14. (Refer to Figure 52 on page 349.) (Refer to Area 8.) The traffic pattern altitude at the Auburn (AUN) airport is 1,000 feet AGL. May you practice landings under VFR when the AWOS is reporting a ground visibility of 2 miles?

A. Yes, you will be operating in a combination of Class E and G airspace.

B. No, the reported ground visibility must be at least 3 miles.

C. No, the Class E airspace extends to the airport surface.

Answer (B) is correct. (14 CFR 91.119, 14 CFR 91.155)
   DISCUSSION: In Class E airspace below 10,000 ft. MSL, the minimum reported visibility for VFR operations is 3 SM.
   Answer (A) is incorrect. The traffic pattern altitude at AUN is 1,000 ft. AGL, and Class E airspace begins at 700 ft. AGL, as indicated by the magenta shading. In Class E airspace below 10,000 ft. MSL, the minimum reported visibility for VFR operations is 3 SM. Practicing landings in these conditions would only be legal if the entire traffic pattern remained in Class G airspace. **Answer (C) is incorrect.** The area around Auburn (AUN) below 700 ft. AGL is Class G airspace. The floor of Class E airspace begins at 700 ft. above Auburn.

15. (Refer to Figure 52 below.) (Refer to point 8.) The floor of the Class E airspace over the town of Auburn is

A. 1,200 feet MSL.

B. 700 feet AGL.

C. 1,200 feet AGL.

Answer (B) is correct. *(ACUG)*
DISCUSSION: The town of Auburn (southeast of point 8) is located inside the magenta-shaded area, which means the floor of Class E airspace is 700 ft. AGL.

Answer (A) is incorrect. The floor of Class E airspace over the town of Auburn is 700 ft. AGL, not 1,200 ft. MSL. The town of Auburn is within the magenta shading. **Answer (C) is incorrect.** The floor of Class E airspace inside the magenta-shaded area is 700 ft. AGL, not 1,200 ft. AGL.

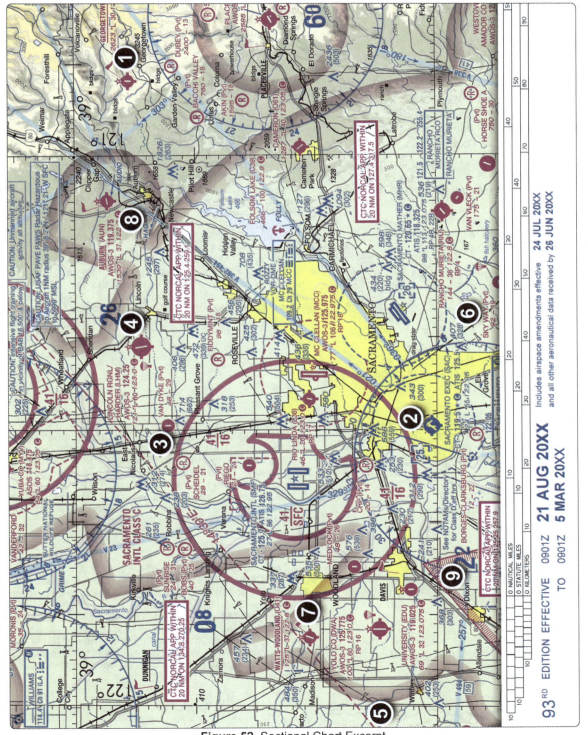

Figure 52. Sectional Chart Excerpt.
NOTE: Chart is not to scale and should not be used for navigation. Chart is for testing purposes only.

16. (Refer to Figure 53 on page 351.) You are planning a VFR west bound flight departing the FRESNO CHANDLER EXECUTIVE (FCH) airport and you will be passing through the active Lemoore C and A MOAs. What action should you take?

    A. Exercise extreme caution while in the boundaries of the MOA.

    B. Avoid the MOA, VFR, and IFR flights are prohibited during day light hours.

    C. Contact the aircraft operating in the MOA on the Guard frequency of 121.5.

Answer (A) is correct. *(AIM Para 3-4-5, FAA-H-8083-25B)*
    DISCUSSION: Pilots operating under VFR should exercise extreme caution while flying within an MOA when military activity is being conducted. Pilots should contact any FSS within 100 mi. of the area to obtain accurate, real-time information concerning the MOA hours of operation. Prior to entering an active MOA, pilots should contact the controlling agency for traffic advisories.
    Answer (B) is incorrect. Flight within MOAs is not prohibited, but pilots should contact any FSS within 100 mi. of the area to obtain accurate, real-time information concerning the MOA hours of operation. Prior to entering an active MOA, pilots should contact the controlling agency for traffic advisories. **Answer (C) is incorrect.** Pilots should contact any FSS within 100 mi. of the area to obtain accurate, real-time information concerning the MOA hours of operation. Prior to entering an active MOA, pilots should contact the controlling agency for traffic advisories.

17. (Refer to Figure 53 on page 351.)

GIVEN:

Location	Madera Airport (MAE)
Altitude	1,000 ft. AGL
Position	7 NM north of Madera (MAE)
Time	3 p.m. local
Flight visibility	1 SM

You are VFR approaching Madera Airport for a landing from the north. You

    A. are in violation of the Federal Aviation Regulations; you need 3 miles of visibility under VFR.

    B. are required to descend to below 700 feet AGL to remain clear of Class E airspace and may continue for landing.

    C. may descend to 800 feet AGL (Pattern Altitude) after entering Class E airspace and continue to the airport.

Answer (B) is correct. *(ACUG)*
    DISCUSSION: If you are 7 NM north of Madera Airport (middle of Fig. 53), you are outside of the magenta shaded area, which means the floor of Class E airspace is at 1,200 ft. AGL. Since you are flying at 1,000 ft. AGL (i.e., Class G airspace) during daylight hours, the minimum flight visibility required for VFR flight is 1 SM. At the edge of the magenta shading the floor of Class E is at 700 ft. AGL. Thus, to maintain VFR you must remain in Class G airspace and descend below 700 ft. AGL to remain clear of Class E airspace, and you may continue for landing.
    Answer (A) is incorrect. You are currently in Class G airspace at 1,000 ft. AGL during daylight hours, and thus you need only 1 SM, not 3 SM, visibility. **Answer (C) is incorrect.** In order to remain VFR, you must descend below 700 ft. AGL, not the pattern altitude of 800 ft. AGL, to remain clear of Class E airspace.

18. (Refer to Figure 53 on page 351.) (Refer to Area 4.) You plan to depart on a day VFR flight from the Firebaugh (F34) airport. What is the floor of controlled airspace above this airport?

    A. 1,200 feet above the airport.

    B. 700 feet above the airport.

    C. 1,500 feet above the airport.

Answer (B) is correct. *(14 CFR 91.155)*
    DISCUSSION: The floor of Class E airspace over the Firebaugh (F34) Airport is 700 ft. AGL, which is indicated by its location within the magenta shading.
    Answer (A) is incorrect. F34 is surrounded by magenta shading, indicating a Class E floor of 700 ft. AGL, not 1,200 ft. AGL. **Answer (C) is incorrect.** The floor of Class E airspace over the Firebaugh (F34) Airport is 700 ft. AGL, which is indicated by its location within the magenta shading.

19. (Refer to Figure 53 on page 351.) (Refer to Area 2.) What is indicated by the star next to the "L" in the airport information box for the MADERA (MAE) airport north of area 2?

    A. Special VFR is prohibited.

    B. There is a rotating beacon at the field.

    C. Lighting limitations exist.

Answer (C) is correct. *(ACUG)*
    DISCUSSION: The "*L" in the airport information box for Madera Airport indicates that lighting limitations exist and to refer to the Chart Supplement.
    Answer (A) is incorrect. The "*L" in the airport information box for Madera Airport indicates that lighting limitations exist and to refer to the Chart Supplement. **Answer (B) is incorrect.** The star above the airport symbol indicates the existence of a rotating or flashing airport beacon operating from sunset to sunrise.

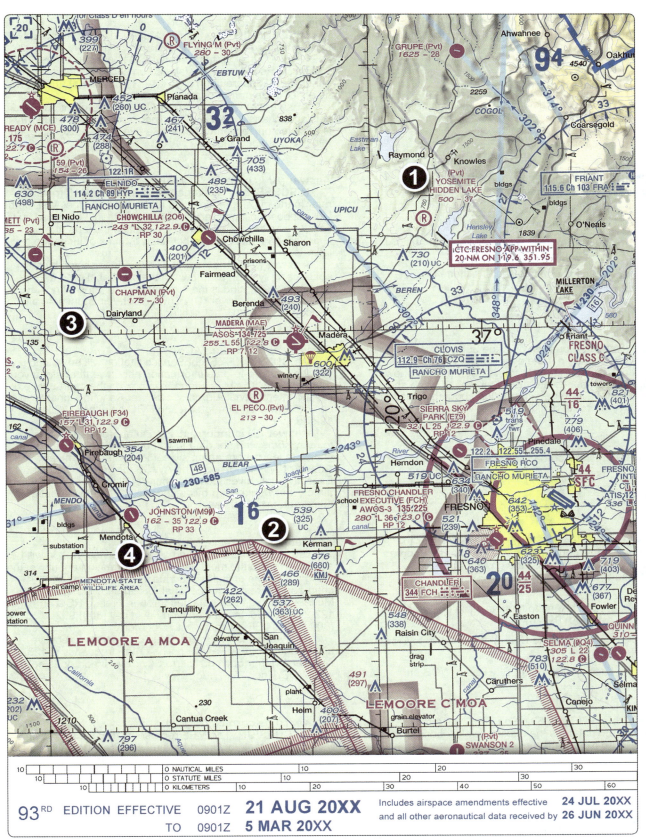

Figure 53. Sectional Chart Excerpt.
NOTE: Chart is not to scale and should not be used for navigation. Chart is for testing purposes only.

20. (Refer to Figure 53 on page 353.) (Refer to point 1.) This thin black shaded line is most likely

    A. an arrival route.

    B. a military training route.

    C. a state boundary line.

Answer (B) is correct. (ACUG)
    DISCUSSION: The thin black shaded line is most likely a military training route (MTR). Generally, MTRs are established below 10,000 ft. MSL for operations at speeds in excess of 250 kt. MTRs are normally labeled on sectional charts with either IR (IFR operations) or VR (VFR operations) and followed by either three or four number characters.
    Answer (A) is incorrect. Arrival routes are not depicted on sectional charts. **Answer (C) is incorrect.** A state boundary line is depicted on sectional charts by a thin black broken line, not a thin black shaded line.

21. (Refer to Figure 53 on page 353.) (Refer to point 2.) The 16 indicates

    A. an antenna top at 1,600 feet AGL.

    B. the maximum elevation figure for that quadrangle.

    C. the minimum safe sector altitude for that quadrangle.

Answer (B) is correct. (ACUG)
    DISCUSSION: The large bold 1 and smaller 6 (point 2) refer to the maximum elevation figure (MEF) in feet MSL of the highest obstruction or terrain in the quadrangle bounded by tick lines of longitude and latitude. On sectional charts, the MEF is provided in each square bounded by lines of longitude and latitude.
    Answer (A) is incorrect. An antenna is shown by an obstruction symbol (as shown to the southeast of 2) and the height above ground is the number in parentheses, not large, bold numbers. **Answer (C) is incorrect.** Minimum safe altitudes are depicted on IAP, not sectional, charts.

22. (Refer to Figure 53 on page 353.) (Refer to area 2.) While en route over Fresno Chandler Executive airport (FCH), your airborne radar shows unforecast thunderstorms 20 mi. ahead. Who should you contact for more information about the weather along your route of flight?

    A. Flight Service Station (FSS) on 122.55.

    B. Fresno Approach on 119.6.

    C. Fresno Chandler Executive AWOS on 135.225.

Answer (A) is correct. (ACUG)
    DISCUSSION: A Flight Service Station will be able to give you the most up-to-date information about weather along your route of flight. The blue information box on the chart above Fresno International Airport shows that Rancho Murieta radio can be contacted through Fresno RCO on either 122.2 or 122.55.
    Answer (B) is incorrect. Fresno approach may be able to relay some weather data to you but would not be the best choice to learn more about a weather system 20 mi. away. **Answer (C) is incorrect.** The AWOS for Fresno Chandler Executive only gives local weather data in the vicinity of the airport and would not provide specific information about a thunderstorm 20 mi. away.

23. (Refer to Figure 53 on page 353.) (Refer to area 2.) How could you receive a weather update while in your aircraft on the ground at Fresno Chandler Executive airport (FCH)?

    A. Contact Rancho Murieta radio on 122.55 or call (800) 992-7433.

    B. Contact Fresno Chandler Executive tower on 123.0.

    C. Listen to the Sierra Sky Park AWOS on 122.9.

Answer (A) is correct. (ACUG)
    DISCUSSION: Contacting a Flight Service Station will be able to give you the most up-to-date information about weather along your route of flight. The blue information box on the chart above Fresno International Airport shows that Rancho Murieta radio can be contacted through Fresno RCO on either 122.2 or 122.55. In addition, you could call (800) 992-7433 (800-WX-BRIEF) to speak with a briefer.
    Answer (B) is incorrect. Fresno Chandler Executive airport does not have a tower. The CTAF frequency is 123.0. **Answer (C) is incorrect.** Sierra Sky Park airport does not have an AWOS. The CTAF frequency is 122.9.

24. (Refer to Figure 53 on page 353.) (Refer to area 2.) What does the maximum elevation figure (MEF) 16 represent?

    A. The highest elevation within this quadrant, including terrain and other vertical obstacles, is 1,600 ft. MSL.

    B. The highest elevation within this quadrant, including terrain and other vertical obstacles, is 1,600 ft. AGL.

    C. The minimum safe altitude in this quadrant is 1,600 ft. MSL.

Answer (A) is correct. (ACUG)
    DISCUSSION: The MEF represents the highest elevation within a quadrant, including terrain and other vertical obstacles (towers, trees, buildings, etc.). A quadrant on sectional charts is the area bounded by ticked lines dividing each 30 min. of latitude and each 30 min. of longitude. MEF figures are rounded up to the nearest 100-ft. MSL value, and the last two digits of the number are not shown.
    Answer (B) is incorrect. The MEF is an MSL value, not AGL. **Answer (C) is incorrect.** The MEF shows the height of the tallest known obstacle in a quadrant, not the minimum safe altitude.

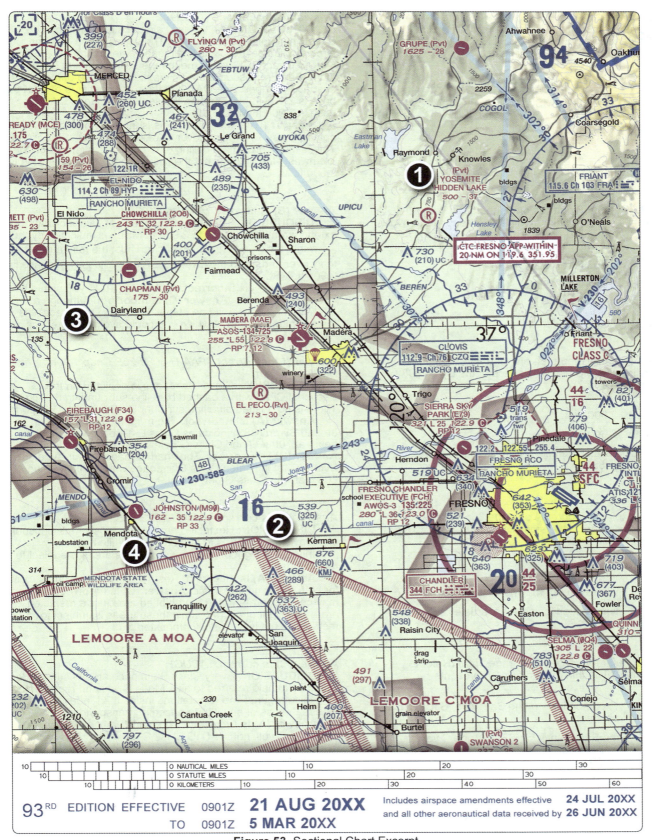

Figure 53. Sectional Chart Excerpt.
NOTE: Chart is not to scale and should not be used for navigation. Chart is for testing purposes only.

25. (Refer to Figure 54 on page 355.) (Refer to point 6.) The Class C airspace at Metropolitan Oakland International (OAK) which extends from the surface upward has a ceiling of

A. both 2,100 feet and 3,000 feet MSL.

B. 10,000 feet MSL.

C. 2,100 feet AGL.

Answer (A) is correct. (ACUG)
   DISCUSSION: The Class C airspace at OAK (point 6) is shown in solid magenta lines. The surface area over the airport indicates the Class C airspace extends from the surface (SFC) upward to T, which means the ceiling ends at the base of the San Francisco Class B airspace. The base of the Class B airspace changes over OAK. On the northwest side of OAK the base is 2,100 ft. MSL and on the southeast side of OAK the base is 3,000 ft. MSL.
   Answer (B) is incorrect. This is the ceiling of the Class B, not the Class C, airspace over OAK. Answer (C) is incorrect. This is the approximate ceiling of the Class C airspace on the northwest side of OAK, but the ceiling on the southeast side is 3,000 ft. MSL.

26. (Refer to Figure 54 on page 355.) (Refer to point 1.) What minimum altitude is required to avoid the Livermore Airport (LVK) Class D airspace?

A. 2,503 feet MSL.

B. 2,901 feet MSL.

C. 3,297 feet MSL.

Answer (B) is correct. (AIM Para 3-2-5)
   DISCUSSION: The Class D airspace at Livermore Airport extends from the surface to 2,900 ft. MSL, as indicated by the 29 within the blue segmented circle. Thus, the minimum altitude to fly over and avoid the Livermore Airport Class D airspace is 2,901 ft. MSL.
   Answer (A) is incorrect. At 2,503 ft. MSL, you would be in Class D airspace. Answer (C) is incorrect. Although at 3,297 ft. MSL you would be above the Class D airspace, it is not the minimum altitude at which you could avoid the airspace.

27. (Refer to Figure 54 on page 355.) What is the ceiling of the Class D Airspace of the Byron (C83) airport (Area 2)?

A. 2,900 feet.

B. 7,600 feet.

C. Class D Airspace does not exist at Byron (C83).

Answer (C) is correct. (FAA-H-8083-25B Chap 14 and Sectional Chart)
   DISCUSSION: Class D airspace is depicted on the Sectional Chart with a dashed blue line surrounding the airport. There is no dashed blue line surrounding Byron (C83) Airport.
   Answer (A) is incorrect. The magenta shaded circle around Byron (C83) indicates Class E airspace with the floor being at 700 feet and Class G below that, not 2,900 feet. Answer (B) is incorrect. The shaded magenta surrounding Byron (C83) indicates Class E airspace with the floor being at 700 feet with Class G below that, not 7,600 feet.

28. (Refer to Figure 54 on page 355.) (Refer to Area 3.) What is the significance of R-2531? This is a restricted area

A. for IFR aircraft.

B. where aircraft may never operate.

C. where often invisible hazards exist.

Answer (C) is correct. (FAA-H-8083-25B Chap 15)
   DISCUSSION: Restricted areas are areas where unusual, often invisible, hazards to aircraft exist. While not wholly prohibited, the flight of aircraft within these areas is subject to restrictions.
   Answer (A) is incorrect. Restrictions in these areas exist for both VFR and IFR traffic. Answer (B) is incorrect. Aircraft may never operate within a prohibited area, not a restricted area. The flight of aircraft within these areas is subject to restrictions but is not wholly prohibited.

29. (Refer to Figure 54 on page 355.) (Refer to point 4.) The thin magenta line represents

A. the outer limits of the San Jose (SJC) Class C airspace.

B. the San Francisco (SFO) Mode C veil, which requires a mode C transponder from 1,200 feet AGL up to 10,000 feet MSL.

C. the San Francisco Mode C veil, which requires the use of an appropriate transponder.

Answer (C) is correct. (ACUG)
   DISCUSSION: Every Class B airspace area is surrounded by a 30 NM halo referred to as a Mode C veil and represented by a thin magenta line. Operations inside the Mode C veil require the use of an altitude-encoding transponder.
   Answer (A) is incorrect. The magenta line represents the Mode C veil, not the SJC Class C boundary. Answer (B) is incorrect. The requirement for an altitude-encoding transponder within the Mode C veil begins at the surface, not 1,200 feet AGL.

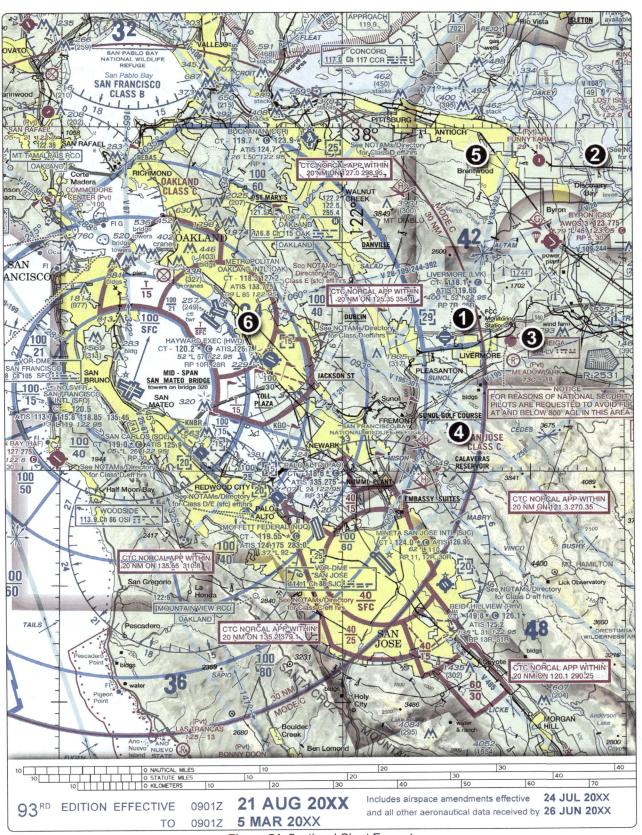

Figure 54. Sectional Chart Excerpt.
NOTE: Chart is not to scale and should not be used for navigation. Chart is for testing purposes only.

30. Which statement is true about isogonic lines?

A. Isogonic lines are lines of equal variation.

B. Isogonic lines do not vary for different headings of the same aircraft.

C. Varies over time as the Agonic line shifts.

Answer (A) is correct. (FAA-H-8083-25B Chap 8)
    DISCUSSION: Isogonic lines are shown on most aeronautical charts as broken magenta lines, which connect points of equal magnetic variation. The 0° line is known as the agonic line. The agonic is the line connecting points at which there is no variation between true north and magnetic north.
    Answer (B) is incorrect. If an aircraft is heading east, the isogonic lines increase in increments of 5°, e.g., +5°, +10°, +15°, etc., except the last line in the most eastern part of the United States, which is +24. If the aircraft is flying west, the isogonic lines decrease in increments of 5°, into negative numbers to the west of the agonic line, e.g., –5°, –10°, –15° etc., except the last line in the most western part of the United States, which is –24. **Answer (C) is incorrect.** Over time, the isogonic and agonic lines shift due to the movement of the magnetic north pole. However, the degree of change may vary due to unusual geological conditions affecting magnetic forces in localized areas.

31. Alert Areas are special use airspace depicted within magenta lines on sectional charts in which

A. there is a high volume of pilot training activities or an unusual type of aerial activity, neither of which is hazardous to aircraft.

B. the flight of aircraft is prohibited.

C. the flight of aircraft, while not prohibited, is subject to restriction.

Answer (A) is correct. (ACUG)
    DISCUSSION: Alert areas are depicted on charts to inform non-participating pilots of areas that may contain a high volume of pilot training or an unusual type of aerial activity, neither of which is hazardous to aircraft.
    Answer (B) is incorrect. A prohibited area, not an alert area, is airspace within which the flight of aircraft is prohibited. **Answer (C) is incorrect.** A restricted area, not an alert area, is airspace within which the flight of aircraft, while not prohibited, is subject to restriction.

32. What action should a pilot take when operating under VFR in a Military Operations Area (MOA)?

A. Obtain a clearance from the controlling agency prior to entering the MOA.

B. Operate only on the airways that transverse the MOA.

C. Exercise extreme caution when military activity is being conducted.

Answer (C) is correct. (AIM Para 3-4-5)
    DISCUSSION: Military operations areas consist of airspace established for separating military training activities from IFR traffic. VFR traffic should exercise extreme caution when flying within an MOA. Information regarding MOA activity can be obtained from flight service stations (FSSs) within 100 mi. of the MOA.
    Answer (A) is incorrect. A clearance is not required to enter an MOA. **Answer (B) is incorrect.** VFR flights may fly anywhere in the MOA.

9.2 Chart Supplements

33. (Refer to Figure 68 on page 357.) Where is Air Park Dallas located with relation to the city?

A. North, approximately 9 miles.

B. Northeast, approximately 16 miles.

C. North, approximately 33 miles.

Answer (B) is correct. (Chart Supplement)
    DISCUSSION: Fig. 68 contains the Chart Supplement excerpt for Air Park Dallas. On the first line, the third item listed, 16 NE, means that Air Park Dallas is located approximately 16 NM northeast of the associated city.
    Answer (A) is incorrect. North, approximately 9 mi., is the approximate distance from ADS Airport to the associated city, not Air Park Dallas. **Answer (C) is incorrect.** The airport is approximately 16 NM northeast, not 33 NM north, of the associated city.

34. (Refer to Figure 68 on page 357.) Refer to Air Park Dallas (N33°01.41' W96°50.22'). Is fuel ever available at Air Park Dallas?

A. Yes, whenever the airport is attended by airport personnel.

B. No, since there is no "star" symbol near the airport on the chart, there is no fuel available at this airport.

C. Yes, fuel services can be arranged by calling the listed phone number prior to arrival.

Answer (C) is correct. (Chart Supplement)
    DISCUSSION: Look at Fig. 68, the Chart Supplement excerpt for Air Park Dallas, located at the given coordinates. Locate the "Airport Remarks." You will see on the first line that fuel is available by calling the listed phone number prior to arrival (arr).
    Answer (A) is incorrect. The airport is unattended, and there are no regular fuel services available. **Answer (B) is incorrect.** The star symbol on a Chart Supplement diagram represents the airport beacon, not fuel services.

TEXAS   265

DALLAS

ADDISON (ADS)(KADS)   9 N   UTC–6(–5DT)   N32°58.11´ W96°50.19´

645   B   TPA—See Remarks   LRA   NOTAM FILE ADS

RWY 15–33: H7203X100 (ASPH–GRVD)   S–60, D–120   HIRL

  RWY 15: MALSR. PAPI(P4R)—GA 3.0° TCH 60´. Thld dsplcd 979´.
Tree.

  RWY 33: REIL. PAPI(P4L)—GA 3.0° TCH 60´. Thld dsplcd 772´. Bldg.

RUNWAY DECLARED DISTANCE INFORMATION

  RWY 15: TORA–7203   TODA–7203   ASDA–7203   LDA–6224

  RWY 33: TORA–7203   TODA–7203   ASDA–7203   LDA–6431

ARRESTING GEAR/SYSTEM

  RWY 15: EMAS

SERVICE: S4   FUEL 100LL, JET A   OX 2, 3   LGT ACTIVATE HIRL Rwy
15–33 and MALSR Rwy 15—CTAF.

AIRPORT REMARKS: Attended continuously. Birds on and invof arpt. No
touch and go ldgs without arpt mgr apvl. Numerous 200´ bldgs within
1 mile east, and south of arpt, transmission twrs and water tanks west
of arpt. Noise sensitive areas surround arpt. Pilots req to use NBAA std
noise procedures. TPA—1601 (956) for light acft, 2001 (1356) for
large acft. Be alert, rwy holding position markings lctd at the west
edge of Twy A. Flight Notification Service (ADCUS) available.

AIRPORT MANAGER: 972-392-4850

WEATHER DATA SOURCES: AWOS–3 (972) 386–4855 LAWRS.

COMMUNICATIONS: CTAF 126.0   ATIS 133.4 972–628–2439

UNICOM 122.95

®REGIONAL APP/DEP CON 124.3

  TOWER 126.0 (1200–0400Z‡)   GND CON 121.6   CLNC DEL 119.55

AIRSPACE: CLASS D svc 1200–0400Z‡, other times CLASS G.

RADIO AIDS TO NAVIGATION: NOTAM FILE FTW.

  MAVERICK (H) VORW/DME 113.1   TTT   Chan 78   N32°52.15´ W97°02.43´   054° 11.9 NM to fld. 540/6E.
All acft arriving DFW are requested to turn DME off until departure due to traffic overload of Maverick DME
DME unusable:
    180°–190°

  ILS/DME 110.1   I–ADS   Chan 38   Rwy 15.   Class IT.   Unmonitored when ATCT closed. DME also serves Rwy 33.

  ILS/DME 110.1   I–TBQ   Chan 38   Rwy 33.   Class IB.   Localizer unmonitored when ATCT closed. DME also serves
Rwy 15.

DALLAS–FT WORTH
COPTER
H–6H, L–17C, A
IAP, AD

AIR PARK–DALLAS (F69)   16 NE   UTC–6(–5DT)   N33°01.41´ W96°50.22´

695   TPA—1890(1195)   NOTAM FILE FTW

RWY 16–34: H3080X30 (ASPH)   LIRL(NSTD)

  RWY 16: Thld dsplcd 300´. Pole.

  RWY 34: Tree. Rgt tfc.

SERVICE: S4   FUEL 100LL   LGT ACTIVATE LIRL Rwy 16–34—CTAF. Rwy 16–34 NSTD LIRL; 2780´ of rwy lgtd. Thld and
dsplcd thld not lighted.

AIRPORT REMARKS: Uattended. For fuel call 972-248-4265 prior to arr. Rwy 16–34 pavement cracking, loose stones on rwy.
Rwy 34 NSTD cntrln marking incorrect size and spacing.   Rwy numbers 25´ tall, markings faded.   Rwy number 34 not
located at rwy end.

AIRPORT MANAGER: 972-248-4265

COMMUNICATIONS: CTAF 122.9

RADIO AIDS TO NAVIGATION: NOTAM FILE FTW.

  MAVERICK (H) VORW/DME 113.1   TTT   Chan 78   N32°52.15´ W97°02.43´   042° 13.8 NM to fld. 540/6E.
All acft arriving DFW are requested to turn DME off until departure due to traffic overload of Maverick DME
DME unusable:
    180°–190°

COMM/NAV/WEATHER REMARKS: For Clnc Del ctc Regional Apch at 972–615–2799.

DALLAS–FT WORTH
COPTER
L–17C, A

Figure 68. Chart Supplement.

35. You are preflight planning in the morning before an afternoon flight. Where would you find information regarding an "Airport surface hot spot?"

    A. Call the Automated Flight Service Station.

    B. In the Chart Supplements U.S.

    C. In the NOTAM's during your preflight briefing.

Answer (B) is correct. (FAA-H-8083-25B Chap 14)
    DISCUSSION: An "airport surface hot spot" is a runway safety related problem area or intersection on an airport. Information regarding airport surface hot spots can be found in the Chart Supplements U.S.
    Answer (A) is incorrect. Information regarding airport surface hot spots can be found in the Chart Supplements U.S. **Answer (C) is incorrect.** Information regarding airport surface hot spots can be found in the Chart Supplements U.S.

36. (Refer to Figure 66 on page 359.) Traffic patterns in effect at Wiley Post are

    A. to the right on Runways 35R, 35L, and 31; to the left on Runways 17L, 17R, and 13.

    B. to the left on Runways 35R, 35L, and 31; to the right on Runways 17L, 17R, and 13.

    C. to the right on Runways 17L-35R.

Answer (B) is correct. (Chart Supplement)
    DISCUSSION: Fig. 66 contains the Chart Supplement excerpt for Wiley Post. For this question, you need to locate the runway end data elements, i.e., Rwy 17L-35R, Rwy 17R-35L, and Rwy 13-31. Traffic patterns are to the left unless right traffic is noted by the contraction "Rgt tfc." The only runways with right traffic are Rwy 17L, 17R, and 13.
    Answer (A) is incorrect. Traffic patterns are to the left, not right, for Rwy 35R, 35L, and 31. Traffic patterns are to the right, not left, for Rwy 17L, 17R, and 13. **Answer (C) is incorrect.** The traffic pattern for Rwy 35R is to the left, not right.

37. (Refer to Figure 66 on page 359.) What is the recommended communications procedure for landing at Wiley Post during the hours when the tower is not in operation?

    A. Monitor airport traffic and announce your position and intentions on 126.9 MHz.

    B. Contact UNICOM on 122.95 MHz for traffic advisories.

    C. Monitor ATIS for airport conditions; then announce your position on 122.95 MHz.

Answer (A) is correct. (Chart Supplement)
    DISCUSSION: When the Wiley Post tower is closed, you should monitor airport traffic and announce your position and intentions on the CTAF. Fig. 66 contains the Chart Supplement excerpt for Wiley Post. Locate the section titled "Communications" and note that on that same line the CTAF frequency is 126.9.
    Answer (B) is incorrect. When the tower is not in operation, you should monitor other traffic and announce your position and intentions on the specified CTAF. At Wiley Post, the CTAF is the tower frequency of 126.9, not the UNICOM frequency of 122.95. **Answer (C) is incorrect.** When the tower is not in operation, you should monitor other traffic and announce your position and intentions on the specified CTAF. At Wiley Post, the CTAF is the tower frequency of 126.9, not the UNICOM frequency of 122.95.

200   **OKLAHOMA**

WILEY POST (PWA)(KPWA)   7 NW   UTC–6(–5DT)   N35°32.05´ W97°38.82´   DALLAS–FT WORTH
   1300   B   TPA—See Remarks   NOTAM FILE PWA   H–6H, L–15D
   RWY 17L–35R: H7199X150 (CONC)   S–35, D–50, 2D–90   HIRL   IAP, AD
     RWY 17L: MALSR. PAPI(P4L)—GA 3.0° TCH 54´. Rgt tfc.
     RWY 35R: MALSR. PAPI(P4L)—GA 3.0° TCH 54´. Thld dsplcd 355´.
     Trees.
   RWY 17R–35L: H5002X75 (ASPH–CONC)   S–26, D–45   MIRL
     RWY 17R: REIL. PAPI(P4L)—GA 3.0° TCH 43´. Tree. Rgt tfc.
     RWY 35L: REIL. PAPI(P4L)—GA 3.0° TCH 42´.
   RWY 13–31: H4214X100 (CONC)   S–35, D–50, 2D–90   MIRL
     0.6% up SE
     RWY 13: Rgt tfc. 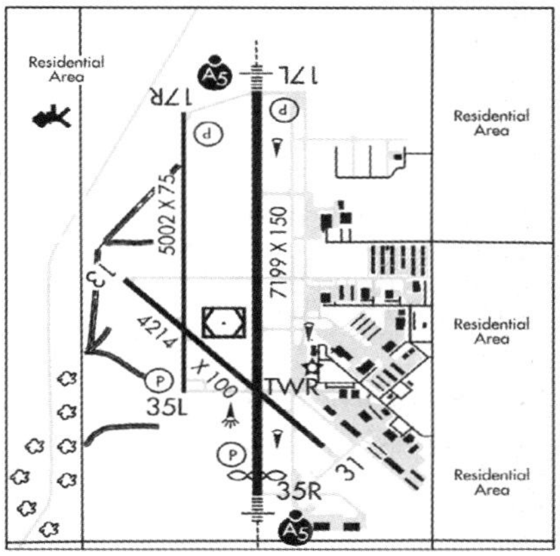
   RUNWAY DECLARED DISTANCE INFORMATION

	TORA	TODA	ASDA	LDA
RWY 13:	4214	4214	4214	4214
RWY 17L:	7199	7199	6844	6844
RWY 17R:	5002	5002	5002	5002
RWY 31:	4214	4214	4214	4214
RWY 35L:	5001	5001	5001	5001
RWY 35R:	7198	7198	7198	6844

   SERVICE: S4   **FUEL** 100LL, JET A   **OX** 1, 2, 3, 4   **LGT** Dusk–Dawn. When
     twr clsd ACTIVATE HIRL Rwy 17L–35R and MALSR Rwy 17L and Rwy
     35R—CTAF.
   AIRPORT REMARKS: Attended continuously. 100LL fuel avbl 24 hrs self serve with credit card. Surface conditions reported
     Mon–Fri 1400–2300Z‡. Rwy 13–31 CLOSED 0400–1300Z‡. Rwy 13–31 CLOSED to tkof and Rwy 31 CLOSED to acft
     over 12,500 lbs gross weight. Flocks of birds on and invof arpt all quadrants. Noise abatement procedure: Acft in excess
     of 12,500 pounds departing Rwy 17L–35R climb at a maximum rate consistent with safety to an altitude of 1500´ AGL
     then reduce power setting and climb rate to 3000´ AGL or 2 NM from arpt depending on air traffic control and safety
     conditions. TPA for Rwy 17R/35L 1900(600) 2300(1000) all other rwys. Rwy 13–31 unlighted 0400–1300Z‡. Touch
     & go or stop & go ldgs not authorized Rwy 13–31.
   AIRPORT MANAGER: 405-316-4061
   WEATHER DATA SOURCES: ASOS (405) 798–2013
   COMMUNICATIONS: CTAF 126.9 **ATIS** 128.725 **UNICOM** 122.95
     RCO 122.65 (MC ALESTER RADIO)
   Ⓡ **OKE CITY APP/DEP CON** 124.6 (171°–360°) 120.45 (081°–170°) 124.2 (001°–080°)
     TOWER 126.9   (1300–0400Z‡) **GND CON** 121.7
   AIRSPACE: CLASS D svc 1300–0400Z‡ other times CLASS E.
   RADIO AIDS TO NAVIGATION: NOTAM FILE PWA.
     (T) VORW/DME 113.4   PWA   Chan 81   N35°31.98´ W97°38.83´   at fld. 1271/8E.
     ILS 110.15   I–PWA   Rwy 17L.   Unmonitored when ATCT clsd. DME also serves Rwy 35R.
     ILS/DME 110.15   I–TFM   Chan 38(Y)   Rwy 35R.   Class IT.   DME also serves Rwy 17L.

Figure 66. Chart Supplement.

38. To avoid landing at the wrong airport or runway, pilots should

    A. consult the *Aeronautical Information Manual*.

    B. consult airport diagrams and Chart Supplements.

    C. contact the airport UNICOM frequency for runway advisory.

Answer (B) is correct. (FAA-H-8083-25B Chap 14)
    DISCUSSION: Chart Supplements are published every 56 days and include the most accurate information about an airport, including runways and lighting.
    Answer (A) is incorrect. The *Aeronautical Information Manual* does not include airport-specific information regarding runways and is used as a recommendation. **Answer (C) is incorrect.** Although recommended runway information can be received on the UNICOM frequency, not all airports have active UNICOMs and it is better practice to use the Chart Supplements, which include more detailed information such as LAHSO operations.

39. (Refer to Figure 67 on page 361.) When approaching Lubbock Preston Smith Airport from the west at noon for the purpose of landing, initial communications should be with

    A. Lubbock Approach Control on 119.2 MHz.

    B. Fort Worth Center on 128.75 MHz.

    C. Lubbock Tower on 120.5 MHz.

Answer (A) is correct. (Chart Supplement)
    DISCUSSION: Fig. 67 contains the Chart Supplement excerpt for Lubbock Preston Smith Airport. Locate the section titled "Airspace" and note that Lubbock Preston Smith Airport is located in Class C airspace. You should contact approach control (app con) before entering. Move up two lines to "APP/DEP CON" and note that aircraft should initially contact Lubbock Approach Control on 119.2 MHz.
    Answer (B) is incorrect. The frequencies shown in the communications section for App/Dep Con do not include 128.75 MHz. **Answer (C) is incorrect.** When approaching Lubbock Preston Smith Airport, your initial contact should be with approach control, not the tower.

40. (Refer to Figure 67 on page 361.) Which type of radar service is provided to VFR aircraft at Lubbock Preston Smith Airport?

    A. Sequencing to the primary Class C airport and standard separation.

    B. Sequencing to the primary Class C airport and limited vectoring so that radar targets do not touch, or 1,000 ft. vertical separation.

    C. Sequencing to the primary Class C airport, traffic advisories, limited vectoring, and safety alerts.

Answer (C) is correct. (AIM Para 4-1-17, Chart Supplement)
    DISCUSSION: Fig. 67 contains the Chart Supplement excerpt for Lubbock Preston Smith Airport. Locate the section titled "Airspace" to determine that Lubbock Preston Smith Airport is located in Class C airspace. Once communications and radar contact are established, VFR aircraft are provided the following services:

1. Sequencing to the primary airport
2. Approved separation between IFR and VFR aircraft
3. Basic radar services, i.e., safety alerts, limited vectoring, and traffic advisories

    Answer (A) is incorrect. In addition to sequencing to the primary Class C airport and standard separation, Class C radar service also includes basic radar services, i.e., traffic advisories and safety alerts. **Answer (B) is incorrect.** One radar service provided to VFR aircraft in Class C airspace provides for traffic advisories and limited vectoring so that radar targets do not touch, or 500 ft., not 1,000 ft., of vertical separation.

TEXAS

337

LUBBOCK

LUBBOCK EXECUTIVE AIRPARK (F82)   5 S   UTC–6(–5DT)   N33°29.14´ W101°48.76´
DALLAS–FT WORTH
L–6H

3200   B   TPA—4200(1000)   NOTAM FILE FTW
RWY 17–35: H3500X70 (ASPH)   S–13   HIRL
RWY 07–25: 1500X110 (TURF)
  RWY 07: P–line.
SERVICE: S4   FUEL 100LL, JET A
AIRPORT REMARKS: Attended 1400–0000Z‡. After hrs 806–789–6437, 806–589–8143. Fuel avbl 24 hrs with major credit card. Rwy 17 road located at thld. Farm equipment ops AER 17, Rwy 25 and Rwy 35.
AIRPORT MANAGER: 806–789–6437
COMMUNICATIONS: CTAF/UNICOM 122.8
RADIO AIDS TO NAVIGATION: NOTAM FILE LBB.
  (L) VORTACW 109.2   LBB   Chan 29   N33°42.30´ W101°54.84´   148° 14.1 NM to fld. 3310/11E.   HIWAS.
  VOR portion unusable:
    140°–190° byd 20 NM blo 5,100´

- -

LUBBOCK PRESTON SMITH INTL (LBB)(KLBB)   4 N   UTC–6(–5DT)   N33°39.82´ W101°49.23´
DALLAS–FT WORTH
H–6G, L–6H
IAP, AD

3282   B   LRA   Class I, ARFF Index C   NOTAM FILE LBB
RWY 17R–35L: H11500X150 (CONC–GRVD)   S–100, D–170, 2S–175, 2D–350 PCN 65 R/B/W/T   HIRL
  RWY 17R: MALSR. PAPI(P4R)—GA 3.0° TCH 69´. RVR–T Rgt tfc. 0.4% down.
  RWY 35L: ODALS. VASI(V4L)—GA 3.0° TCH 54´. RVR–R 0.3% up.
RWY 08–26: H8003X150 (CONC–GRVD)   S–100, D–170, 2S–175, 2D–350 PCN 71 R/B/W/T   HIRL
  RWY 08: REIL. PAPI(P4L)—GA 3.0° TCH 50´. RVR–R Rgt tfc.
  RWY 26: MALSR. PAPI(P4L)—GA 3.0° TCH 50´. RVR–T
RWY 17L–35R: H2891X74 (ASPH)   S–12.5
  RWY 35R: Road. Rgt tfc.

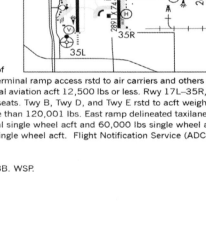

RUNWAY DECLARED DISTANCE INFORMATION
RWY 08: TORA–8003   TODA–8003   ASDA–8003   LDA–8003
RWY 17L: TORA–2891   TODA–2891   ASDA–2891   LDA–2891
RWY 17R: TORA–11500 TODA–11500   ASDA–11500   LDA–11500
RWY 26: TORA–8003   TODA–8003   ASDA–8003   LDA–8003
RWY 35L: TORA–11500 TODA–11500   ASDA–11500   LDA–11500
RWY 35R: TORA–2891   TODA–2891   ASDA–2891   LDA–2891
SERVICE: S4   FUEL 100LL, JET A, A1+   OX 1, 2, 3, 4
AIRPORT REMARKS: Attended continuously. Numerous birds on and invof arpt. PAEW adjacent Rwy 08–26 and Rwy 17R–35L. Passenger terminal ramp access rstd to air carriers and others with prior permission call 806–775–2044. Rwy 17L–35R rstd to general aviation acft 12,500 lbs or less. Rwy 17L–35R, Twy B, Twy D, and Twy E not avbl for air carrier acft with over 9 psgr seats. Twy B, Twy D, and Twy E rstd to acft weighing less than 50,000 lbs. Twy L between Twy F and Twy J clsd to more than 120,001 lbs. East ramp delineated taxilane and apron area rstd to 120,000 lbs dual tandem acft, 89,000 lbs dual single wheel acft and 60,000 lbs single wheel acft. All other east ramp pavements rstd to acft less than 12,500 lbs single wheel acft.   Flight Notification Service (ADCUS) available.
AIRPORT MANAGER: 806–775–3126
WEATHER DATA SOURCES: ASOS 125.3 (806) 766–6432. HIWAS 109.2 LBB. WSP.
COMMUNICATIONS: ATIS 125.3 UNICOM 122.95
  RCO 122.55 (FORT WORTH RADIO)
Ⓡ APP/DEP CON 119.2 119.9
  TOWER 120.5 GND CON 121.9 CLNC DEL 125.8
AIRSPACE: CLASS C svc ctc APP CON
RADIO AIDS TO NAVIGATION: NOTAM FILE LBB.
  (L) VORTACW 109.2   LBB   Chan 29   N33°42.30´ W101°54.84´   107° 5.3 NM to fld. 3310/11E.   HIWAS.
  VOR portion unusable:
    140°–190° byd 20 NM blo 5,100´
  LUBBI NDB (LOMW) 272   LD   N33°39.76´ W101°43.39´   265° 4.9 NM to fld. 3198/6E.
  POLLO NDB (LOM) 219   LB   N33°44.26´ W101°49.76´   168° 4.5 NM to fld.
  ILS/DME 111.7   I–LBB   Chan 54   Rwy 17R.   Class IA.   LOM POLLO NDB.
  ILS 111.9   I–LDT   Rwy 26.   Class IA.   LOM LUBBI NDB.

Figure 67. Chart Supplement.

41. (Refer to Legend 14 below.) What is the acronym for a computerized command response system that provides automated weather, radio check capability, and airport advisory information selected from an automated menu by microphone clicks?

A. GCA.

B. AUNICOM.

C. UNICOM.

Answer (B) is correct. *(Chart Supplement)*
   DISCUSSION: The AUNICOM provides automated weather, radio check capability, and airport advisory information selected from an automated menu by microphone clicks.
   Answer (A) is incorrect. A GCA is a Ground Control Approach system. **Answer (C) is incorrect.** A UNICOM is a nongovernment air/ground radio communications facility that may or may not provide airport information.

---

24   AIRPORT/FACILITY DIRECTORY LEGEND

AWOS–3T reports the same as AWOS–3 system and includes a thunderstorm/lightning reporting capability.
   See AIM, Basic Flight Information and ATC Procedures for detailed description of Weather Data Sources.
AWOS–4—reports same as AWOS–3 system, plus precipitation occurrence, type and accumulation, freezing rain, thunderstorm and runway surface sensors.
HIWAS—See RADIO AIDS TO NAVIGATION
LAWRS—Limited Aviation Weather Reporting Station where observers report cloud height, weather, obstructions to vision, temperature and dewpoint (in most cases), surface wind, altimeter and pertinent remarks.
LLWAS—indicates a Low Level Wind Shear Alert System consisting of a center field and several field perimeter anemometers.
SAWRS—identifies airports that have a Supplemental Aviation Weather Reporting Station available to pilots for current weather information.
SWSL—Supplemental Weather Service Location providing current local weather information via radio and telephone.
TDWR—indicates airports that have Terminal Doppler Weather Radar.
WSP—indicates airports that have Weather System Processor.
   When the automated weather source is broadcast over an associated airport NAVAID frequency (see NAVAID line), it shall be indicated by a bold ASOS, AWOS, or HIWAS followed by the frequency, identifier and phone number, if available.

㉗ **COMMUNICATIONS**
Airport terminal control facilities and radio communications associated with the airport shall be shown. When the call sign is not the same as the airport name the call sign will be shown. Frequencies shall normally be shown in descending order with the primary frequency listed first. Frequencies will be listed, together with sectorization indicated by outbound radials, and hours of operation. Communications will be listed in sequence as follows:
Single Frequency Approach (SFA), Common Traffic Advisory Frequency (CTAF), Aeronautical Advisory Stations (UNICOM) or (AUNICOM), and Automatic Terminal Information Service (ATIS) along with their frequency is shown, where available, on the line following the heading "COMMUNICATIONS." When the CTAF and UNICOM frequencies are the same, the frequency will be shown as CTAF/UNICOM 122.8.
The FSS telephone nationwide is toll free 1–800–WX–BRIEF (1–800–992–7433). When the FSS is located on the field it will be indicated as "on arpt". Frequencies available at the FSS will follow in descending order. Remote Communications Outlet (RCO) providing service to the airport followed by the frequency and FSS RADIO name will be shown when available. FSS's provide information on airport conditions, radio aids and other facilities, and process flight plans. Airport Advisory Service (AAS) is provided on the CTAF by FSS's for select non–tower airports or airports where the tower is not in operation.
(See AIM, Para 4–1–9 Traffic Advisory Practices at Airports Without Operating Control Towers or AC 90–42C.)
Aviation weather briefing service is provided by FSS specialists. Flight and weather briefing services are also available by calling the telephone numbers listed.
Remote Communications Outlet (RCO)—An unmanned air/ground communications facility that is remotely controlled and provides UHF or VHF communications capability to extend the service range of an FSS.
Civil Communications Frequencies–Civil communications frequencies used in the FSS air/ground system are operated on 122.0, 122.2, 123.6; emergency 121.5; plus receive–only on 122.1.
   a.   122.0 is assigned as the Enroute Flight Advisory Service frequency at selected FSS RADIO outlets.
   b.   122.2 is assigned as a common enroute frequency.
   c.   123.6 is assigned as the airport advisory frequency at select non–tower locations. At airports with a tower, FSS may provide airport advisories on the tower frequency when tower is closed.
   d.   122.1 is the primary receive–only frequency at VOR's.
   e.   Some FSS's are assigned 50 kHz frequencies in the 122–126 MHz band (eg. 122.45). Pilots using the FSS A/G system should refer to this directory or appropriate charts to determine frequencies available at the FSS or remoted facility through which they wish to communicate.
Emergency frequency 121.5 and 243.0 are available at all Flight Service Stations, most Towers, Approach Control and RADAR facilities.
Frequencies published followed by the letter "T" or "R", indicate that the facility will only transmit or receive respectively on that frequency. All radio aids to navigation (NAVAID) frequencies are transmit only. In cases where communications frequencies are annotated with (R) or (E), (R) indicates Radar Capability and (E) indicates Emergency Frequency.

TERMINAL SERVICES
SFA—Single Frequency Approach.
CTAF—A program designed to get all vehicles and aircraft at airports without an operating control tower on a common frequency.
ATIS—A continuous broadcast of recorded non–control information in selected terminal areas.
D–ATIS—Digital ATIS provides ATIS information in text form outside the standard reception range of conventional ATIS via landline & data link communications and voice message within range of existing transmitters.
AUNICOM—Automated UNICOM is a computerized, command response system that provides automated weather, radio check capability and airport advisory information selected from an automated menu by microphone clicks.
UNICOM—A non–government air/ground radio communications facility which may provide airport information.
PTD—Pilot to Dispatcher.
APP CON—Approach Control. The symbol ® indicates radar approach control.
TOWER—Control tower.
GCA—Ground Control Approach System.
GND CON—Ground Control.

SC, 1 FEB 20XX to 29 MAR 20XX

Legend 14. Chart Supplement.

42. (Refer to Legend 15 below.) What depicts a Class E airspace that begins at 700 ft. AGL?

A. A dashed blue circle around an airport.

B. A solid magenta circle around an airport.

C. A magenta vignette that goes around an airport.

Answer (C) is correct. (AIM Para 3-2-6)
   DISCUSSION: Class E airspace floor begins at 700 ft. AGL. It is depicted by a magenta vignette circle or area around an airport.
   Answer (A) is incorrect. A dashed blue circle around an airport depicts Class D airspace. **Answer (B) is incorrect.** A solid magenta circle going around an airport depicts Class C airspace.

AIRPORT/FACILITY DIRECTORY LEGEND   25

GCO—Ground Communication Outlet—An unstaffed, remotely controlled, ground/ground communications facility. Pilots at uncontrolled airports may contact ATC and FSS via VHF to a telephone connection to obtain an instrument clearance or close a VFR or IFR flight plan. They may also get an updated weather briefing prior to takeoff. Pilots will use four "key clicks" on the VHF radio to contact the appropriate ATC facility or six "key clicks" to contact the FSS. The GCO system is intended to be used only on the ground.

DEP CON—Departure Control. The symbol Ⓡ indicates radar departure control.

CLNC DEL—Clearance Delivery.

CPDLC—Controller Pilot Data Link Communication. FANS ATC data communication capability from the aircraft to the ATC Data Link system.

PRE TAXI CLNC—Pre taxi clearance.

VFR ADVSY SVC—VFR Advisory Service. Service provided by Non–Radar Approach Control.
   Advisory Service for VFR aircraft (upon a workload basis) ctc APP CON.

COMD POST—Command Post followed by the operator call sign in parenthesis.

PMSV—Pilot–to–Metro Service call sign, frequency and hours of operation, when full service is other than continuous. PMSV installations where weather observation service is available shall be indicated, following the frequency and/or hours of operation as "Wx obsn svc 1900–0000Z‡" or "other times" may be used when no specific time is given. PMSV facilities manned by forecasters are considered "Full Service". PMSV facilities manned by weather observers are listed as "Limited Service".

OPS—Operations followed by the operator call sign in parenthesis.

CON

RANGE

FLT FLW—Flight Following

MEDIVAC

NOTE: Communication frequencies followed by the letter "X" indicate frequency available on request.

㉘ AIRSPACE

Information concerning Class B, C, and part–time D and E surface area airspace shall be published with effective times, if available.

CLASS B—Radar Sequencing and Separation Service for all aircraft in CLASS B airspace.

CLASS C—Separation between IFR and VFR aircraft and sequencing of VFR arrivals to the primary airport.

TRSA—Radar Sequencing and Separation Service for participating VFR Aircraft within a Terminal Radar Service Area.

Class C, D, and E airspace described in this publication is that airspace usually consisting of a 5 NM radius core surface area that begins at the surface and extends upward to an altitude above the airport elevation (charted in MSL for Class C and Class D). Class E surface airspace normally extends from the surface up to but not including the overlying controlled airspace.

When part–time Class C or Class D airspace defaults to Class E, the core surface area becomes Class E. This will be formatted as:
AIRSPACE: CLASS C svc "times" ctc **APP CON** other times CLASS E:
or
AIRSPACE: CLASS D svc "times" other times CLASS E.

When a part–time Class C, Class D or Class E surface area defaults to Class G, the core surface area becomes Class G up to, but not including, the overlying controlled airspace. Normally, the overlying controlled airspace is Class E airspace beginning at either 700´ or 1200´ AGL and may be determined by consulting the relevant VFR Sectional or Terminal Area Charts. This will be formatted as:
AIRSPACE: CLASS C svc "times" ctc **APP CON** other times CLASS G, with CLASS E 700´ (or 1200´) AGL & abv:
or
AIRSPACE: CLASS D svc "times" other times CLASS G with CLASS E 700´ (or 1200´) AGL & abv:
or
AIRSPACE: CLASS E svc "times" other times CLASS G with CLASS E 700´ (or 1200´) AGL & abv.

NOTE: AIRSPACE SVC "TIMES" INCLUDE ALL ASSOCIATED ARRIVAL EXTENSIONS. Surface area arrival extensions for instrument approach procedures become part of the primary core surface area. These extensions may be either Class D or Class E airspace and are effective concurrent with the times of the primary core surface area. For example, when a part–time Class C, Class D or Class E surface area defaults to Class G, the associated arrival extensions will default to Class G at the same time. When a part–time Class C or Class D surface area defaults to Class E, the arrival extensions will remain in effect as Class E airspace.

NOTE: CLASS E AIRSPACE EXTENDING UPWARD FROM 700 FEET OR MORE ABOVE THE SURFACE, DESIGNATED IN CONJUNCTION WITH AN AIRPORT WITH AN APPROVED INSTRUMENT PROCEDURE.
Class E 700´ AGL (shown as magenta vignette on sectional charts) and 1200´ AGL (blue vignette) areas are designated when necessary to provide controlled airspace for transitioning to/from the terminal and enroute environments. Unless otherwise specified, these 700´/1200´ AGL Class E airspace areas remain in effect continuously, regardless of airport operating hours or surface area status. These transition areas should not be confused with surface areas or arrival extensions.

(See Chapter 3, AIRSPACE, in the Aeronautical Information Manual for further details)

SC, 1 FEB 20XX to 29 MAR 20XX

Legend 15. Chart Supplement.

9.3   IFR En Route Low Altitude Charts

43. (Refer to Figure 55 on page 365.) En route on V112 from BTG VORTAC to CARBY intersection, the minimum altitude crossing GYMME intersection is

    A. 6,400 feet.

    B. 6,500 feet.

    C. 7,000 feet.

Answer (C) is correct. (14 CFR 91.177)
    DISCUSSION: When no minimum crossing altitude (MCA) is specified, e.g., at GYMME intersection, the intersection may be crossed at or above the preceding MEA. Since the MEA along V112 eastbound is 7,000 ft., GYMME may be crossed no lower than 7,000 ft.
    Answer (A) is incorrect. This is the MOCA, not the MEA, along V112. **Answer (B) is incorrect.** This is the MEA west of GYMME when westbound, not eastbound.

44. (Refer to Figure 55 on page 365.) When en route on V448 from YKM VORTAC to BTG VORTAC, what minimum navigation equipment is required to identify LEARN intersection?

    A. One VOR receiver.

    B. One VOR receiver and DME.

    C. Two VOR receivers.

Answer (A) is correct. (FAA-H-8083-15B Chap 10)
    DISCUSSION: To identify LEARN INT., only one VOR receiver is required. It is important to establish yourself on V448 and maintain heading while you orient yourself to LTJ VORTAC R-285. Your position checks and tuning will need to be done quickly and accurately.
    Answer (B) is incorrect. Since LEARN INT. can be determined by cross radials, only one VOR receiver is required; a DME is not. **Answer (C) is incorrect.** Only one VOR receiver, not two, is required to identify LEARN INT.

45. (Refer to Figure 55 on page 365.) En route on V468 from BTG VORTAC to ADOJA, the minimum altitude at TROTS intersection is

    A. 7,200 feet.

    B. 10,000 feet.

    C. 11,500 feet.

Answer (C) is correct. (14 CFR 91.177)
    DISCUSSION: TROTS intersection (45 NM northeast of BTG VORTAC on V468 in Fig. 55) shows a minimum crossing altitude (MCA) of 11,500 ft. when northeastbound on V468.
    Answer (A) is incorrect. This is the MOCA along V468, not the MCA at TROTS. **Answer (B) is incorrect.** This is the MEA before TROTS, not the MCA at TROTS.

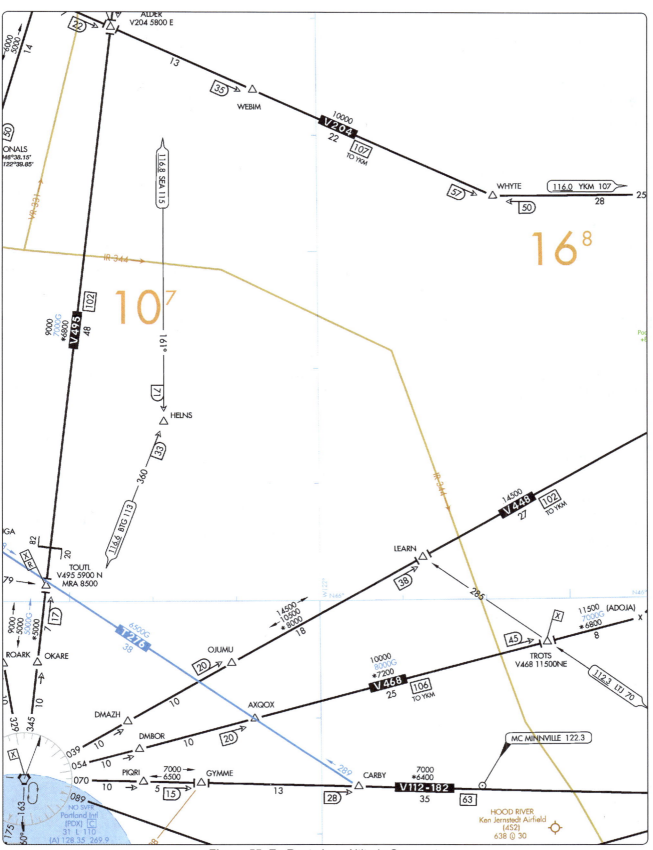

Figure 55. En Route Low Altitude Segment.

46. (Refer to Figure 55A on page 367.) While passing near the KLICKITAT VOR, southbound on V497, contact is lost with Seattle Center. You should attempt to reestablish contact with Seattle Center on

    A. 119.65 MHz.

    B. 112.3 MHz.

    C. 122.65 MHz.

Answer (A) is correct. (ACUG)
    DISCUSSION: To the southeast of the KLICKITAT VOR is a box with serrated edges. This box shows the frequency for Seattle Center in the KLICKITAT VOR area as 119.65.
    Answer (B) is incorrect. A frequency of 112.3 is the frequency for the KLICKITAT VOR, not Seattle Center. Additionally, 112.3 is underlined, indicating that the VOR has no voice capability (i.e., that there would be nothing to receive on 112.3). **Answer (C) is incorrect.** This is the frequency you would use to contact Seattle Flight Service when in the vicinity of the KLICKITAT VOR, not Seattle Center.

47. (Refer to Figure 55A on page 367.) En route on V448 from FEBUS to ANGOO, the minimum altitude crossing YKM is

    A. 5,000 feet.

    B. 8,500 feet.

    C. 9,500 feet.

Answer (C) is correct. (14 CFR 91.177)
    DISCUSSION: The YKM VORTAC has a flag with an x. If you look below the Yakima VORTAC box, you will see text indicating that the MCA for V448 is 9,500 feet in the southwest direction.
    Answer (A) is incorrect. The directional MEA is 5,000 feet when traveling northeast bound between HITCH intersection and YKM VORTAC, not the MCA when traveling from FEBUS to ANGOO on V448. **Answer (B) is incorrect.** As you travel on V468 from east to west from YKM, the MEA is 8,500 feet.

48. (Refer to Figure 55A on page 367.) What is the MOCA between HITCH and TROTS intersections on V468?

    A. 6,800 feet MSL.

    B. 7,000 feet MSL.

    C. 8,500 feet MSL.

Answer (A) is correct. (14 CFR 91.177)
    DISCUSSION: The MOCA (minimum obstruction clearance altitude) appears with an asterisk under the MEA on V468. It is 6,800 ft. MSL.
    Answer (B) is incorrect. This is the MEA if you have GPS or WAAS equipment and you filed your IFR plan as such. **Answer (C) is incorrect.** This is the MEA, not MOCA, between HITCH and SWANY intersections.

49. (Refer to Figure 55A on page 367.) At what point should a VOR changeover be made from FEBUS intersection to YKM VORTAC southbound on V448?

    A. 15 NM north of YKM.

    B. 31 NM north of YKM.

    C. 45 NM north of YKM.

Answer (A) is correct. (AIM Para 5-3-6)
    DISCUSSION: The VOR changeover point is depicted on V448, southwest of FEBUS intersection, and depicts the mileage between the VORTAC stations. It shows the COP as being 15 NM northeast of YKM VORTAC.
    Answer (B) is incorrect. The distance between FEBUS intersection and YKM is 31 NM. **Answer (C) is incorrect.** The COP is 45 NM southwest of Moses Lake VORTAC, not Yakima VORTAC.

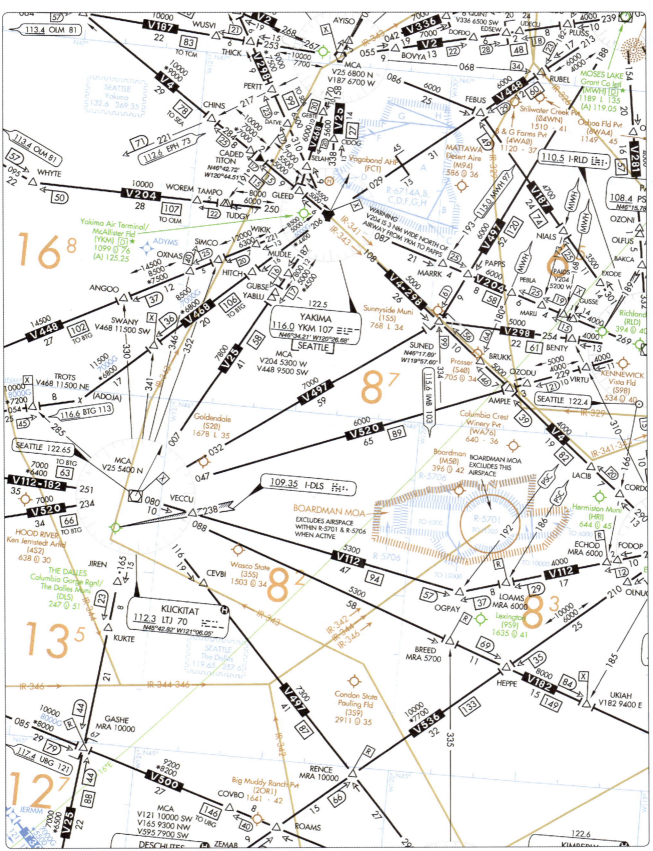

Figure 55A. En Route Low Altitude Segment.

9.4 Instrument Approach Charts

50. (Refer to Figure 30 on page 369.) What minimum navigation equipment is required to complete the VOR/DME-A procedure?

    A. One VOR receiver.

    B. One VOR receiver and DME.

    C. Two VOR receivers and DME.

Answer (B) is correct. (FAA-H-8083-15B Chap 10)
    DISCUSSION: The minimum navigation equipment required for a VOR/DME approach is one VOR receiver and DME.
    Answer (A) is incorrect. The minimum equipment required for a VOR/DME approach includes DME. **Answer (C) is incorrect.** The approach requires one VOR receiver, not two.

51. (Refer to Figure 30 on page 369.) The minimum safe altitude (MSA) for the VOR/DME or GPS-A at 7D3 is geographically centered on what position?

    A. DEANI intersection.

    B. WHITE CLOUD VOR/DME.

    C. MAJUB intersection.

Answer (B) is correct. (AIM Para 5-4-5)
    DISCUSSION: Minimum safe altitudes provide obstacle clearance within 25 NM of the specified navigational facility. In Fig. 30, the MSA circle specifies WHITE CLOUD VOR/DME.
    Answer (A) is incorrect. DEANI intersection is the point of descent to the final approach fix. **Answer (C) is incorrect.** An MSA will normally be based on a navigation facility or a waypoint (GPS or RNAV approach), not the airport.

52. (Refer to Figure 30 on page 369.) When approaching the VOR/DME-A, the symbol [2800] in the MSA circle represents a minimum safe sector altitude within 25 NM of

    A. DEANI intersection.

    B. White Cloud VOR/DME.

    C. Baldwin Municipal Airport.

Answer (B) is correct. (AIM Para 5-4-5)
    DISCUSSION: For conventional navigation systems, the MSA is normally based on the primary omnidirectional facility on which the IAP is predicated. The MSA depiction in Fig. 30 contains the facility identifier of White Cloud VOR/DME. MSAs are expressed in feet above mean sea level and normally have a 25 NM radius; however, this radius may be expanded to 30 NM if necessary to encompass the airport landing surfaces.
    Answer (A) is incorrect. DEANI intersection is the point of descent to the final approach fix, not the point of reference for the MSA. **Answer (C) is incorrect.** White Cloud VOR/DME is the designated point of reference for the MSA, not Baldwin Municipal Airport.

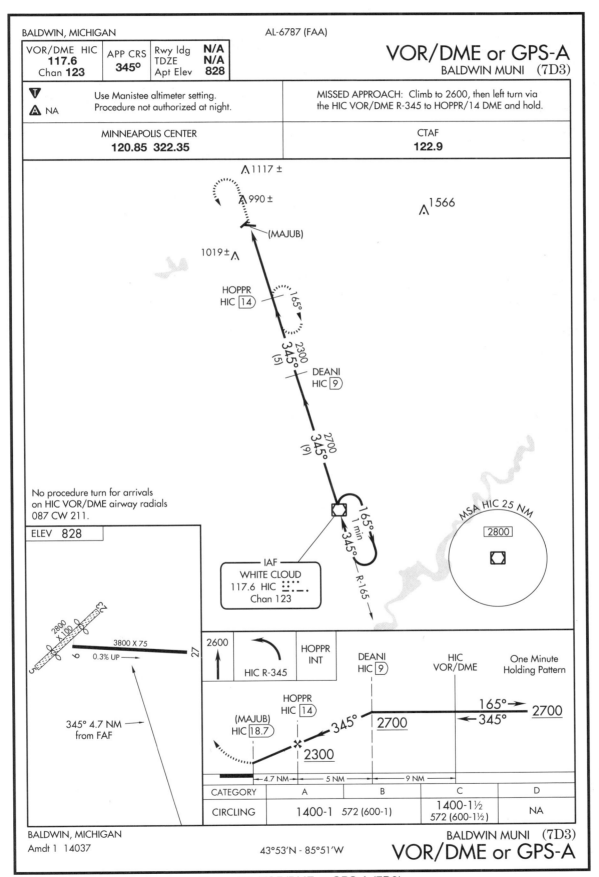

Figure 30. VOR/DME or GPS-A (7D3).

53. (Refer to Figure 28 on page 371.) When conducting a missed approach from the LOC RWY 31 approach at KDSM, what is the Minimum Safe Altitude (MSA) while maneuvering?

    A. 1,600 feet.

    B. 2,800 feet.

    C. 4,000 feet.

Answer (B) is correct. (AIM Para 5-4-5)
    DISCUSSION: The approach plate indicates that 2,800 feet MSL is the MSA in the sector in which maneuvering for the missed approach occurs. Minimum safe altitudes are published for emergency use on IAP. MSAs provide 1,000 feet of clearance over all obstacles but do not necessarily assure acceptable navigation signal coverage. The MSA depiction on the plan view of an approach chart contains the identifier of the center point of the MSA, the applicable radius of the MSA, a depiction of the sector(s), and the minimum altitudes above MSL which provide obstacle clearance.
    Answer (A) is incorrect. The initial altitude to climb to in the missed approach procedure is 1,600 feet. **Answer (C) is incorrect.** The MSA from the DSM 330 through 060 degree radials is 4,000 feet. Additionally, 4,000 feet is the emergency safe altitude from 25 NM to 100 NM from DSM. When conducting the missed approach procedure hold, the inbound turn commences at 22 NM DME, which would keep the outermost turning radius within the 25 NM MSA protected area.

54. (Refer to Figure 28 on page 371.) During the ILS RWY 31 procedure at DSM, the minimum altitude for glide slope interception is

    A. 2,365 feet MSL.

    B. 2,400 feet MSL.

    C. 3,000 feet MSL.

Answer (B) is correct. (AIM P/C Glossary)
    DISCUSSION: The minimum glide slope interception altitude for an ILS is the FAF (marked by a lightning bolt). In Fig. 28, the FAF is 2,400 ft. MSL.
    Answer (A) is incorrect. This is the glide slope altitude over the LOM. **Answer (C) is incorrect.** This is the MSA when south of the LOM.

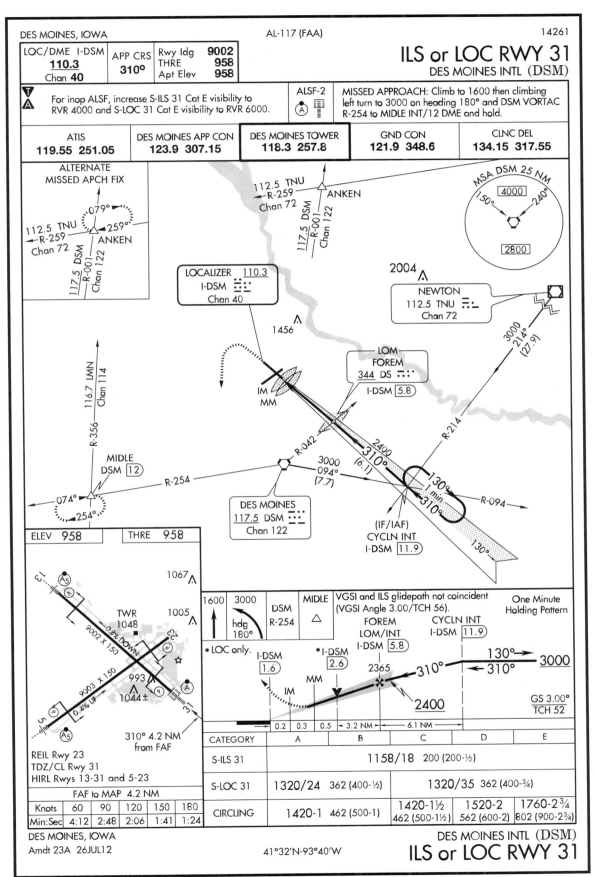

Figure 28. ILS or LOC RWY 31 (DSM).

55. (Refer to Figure 27 on page 373.) Refer to the DEN ILS RWY 35R procedure. The FAF intercept altitude is

    A. 6,120 feet MSL.

    B. 5,570 feet MSL.

    C. 7,000 feet MSL.

Answer (C) is correct. (FAA-H-8083-16B Chap 4)
    DISCUSSION: The glide slope intercept altitude at the FAF (lightning bolt) is 7,000 feet MSL.
    Answer (A) is incorrect. The minimum altitude for the nonprecision approach is 6,120 feet MSL. **Answer (B) is incorrect.** The DH is 5,570 feet MSL.

56. (Refer to Figure 27 on page 373.) Which reported ground visibility at DEN is the lowest that a flight crew could use for this approach?

    A. 1/4 mile.

    B. 1/2 mile.

    C. RVR 10.

Answer (B) is correct. (14 CFR 91.175)
    DISCUSSION: The conversion from 1/2 mi. visibility to RVR is 2400, and 1/4 mi. is 1600 RVR. The approach requires at least 1800 RVR. Therefore, of the choices provided, the lowest reported ground visibility acceptable for the approach is 1/2 mi.
    Answer (A) is incorrect. The conversion from 1/4 mi. visibility to RVR is 1600. This approach requires a minimum of 1800 RVR. Therefore, a 1/4 mi. visibility is not an acceptable ground visibility to use this approach. **Answer (C) is incorrect.** The RVR needs to be equal to or greater than 1800 (RVR 18).

57. (Refer to Figure 27 on page 373.) The symbol on the plan view of the ILS RWY 35R procedure at DEN represents a minimum safe sector altitude within 25 NM of

    A. Denver VOR/DME.

    B. GLL VORTAC.

    C. Denver International Airport.

Answer (A) is correct. (AIM Para 5-4-5)
    DISCUSSION: Minimum safe altitudes provide obstacle clearance within 25 NM of the specified navigational facility. In Fig. 27, the MSA circle specifies DEN VOR/DME.
    Answer (B) is incorrect. An MSA for the ILS RWY 35R at DEN is based on Denver VOR/DME, not the GLL VORTAC. **Answer (C) is incorrect.** An MSA will always be based on a navigation facility or a waypoint (GPS or RNAV approach), not an airport.

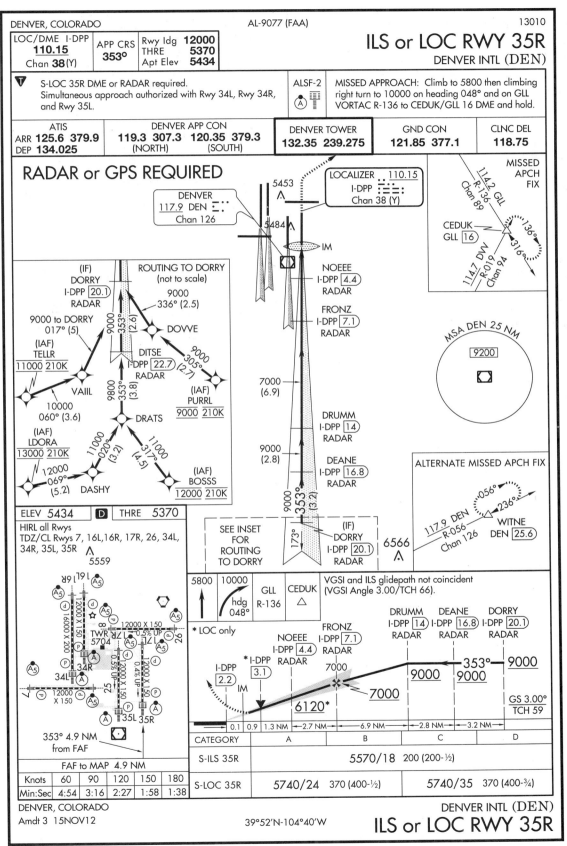

Figure 27. ILS or LOC RWY 35R (DEN).

58. (Refer to Figure 26 on page 375.) The final approach fix for the precision approach is located at

- A. RIIVR intersection.
- B. Glide slope intercept (lightning bolt).
- C. JETSA intersection.

Answer (B) is correct. (FAA-H-8083-16A Chap 4)
   DISCUSSION: On a precision approach, the final approach fix is the glide slope intercept point at the published altitude. It is identified on an IAP chart by a lightning bolt.
   Answer (A) is incorrect. RIIVR intersection is an IAF, not the FAF. **Answer (C) is incorrect.** JETSA intersection is the FAF for the LOC 24R, not the ILS 24R, approach.

59. (Refer to Figure 26 on page 375.) During the ILS RWY 24R procedure at LAX, what altitude minimum applies if the glide slope becomes inoperative?

- A. 580 feet.
- B. 460 feet.
- C. 320 feet.

Answer (B) is correct. (AIM Para 1-1-9)
   DISCUSSION: If the glide slope fails during an ILS approach, the approach can be continued as a nonprecision localizer approach. The MDA for the LOC RWY 24R is 460 ft.
   Answer (A) is incorrect. This is the sidestep, not straight-in, MDA for Categories A, B, and C. **Answer (C) is incorrect.** This is the DH for the ILS, not the MDA for the localizer.

60. (Refer to Figure 26 on page 375.) The final approach fix for the ILS RWY 24R is located at

- A. MERCE intersection.
- B. Glide Slope Intercept (lightning bolt).
- C. JETSA intersection.

Answer (B) is correct. (FAA-H-8083-16A Chap 4)
   DISCUSSION: The final approach fix for an ILS approach is indicated on an instrument approach procedure by a lightning bolt symbol. This is also the point of glide slope intercept.
   Answer (A) is incorrect. The MERCE intersection is an intermediate fix (indicated by the "IF" notation), not the final approach fix. **Answer (C) is incorrect.** The Maltese cross symbol indicates that JETSA is the final approach fix for the nonprecision localizer approach, not for the precision ILS approach.

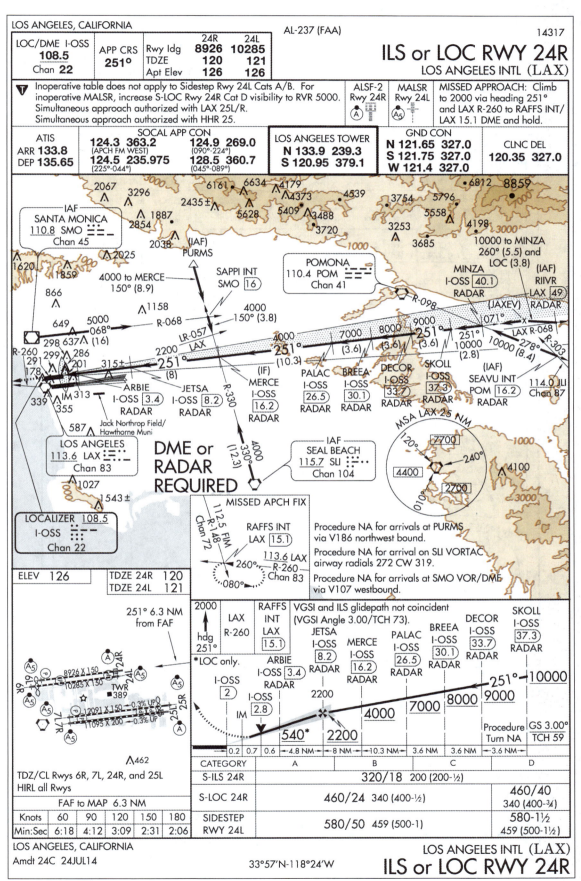

Figure 26. ILS or LOC RWY 24R (LAX).

61. (Refer to Figure 29 below.) The missed approach point of the ATL S-LOC 8L procedure is located how far from SCHEL intersection?

A. 5.7 NM.

B. 4.7 NM.

C. 5.8 NM.

Answer (C) is correct. (AIM Para 5-4-5)
DISCUSSION: In Fig. 29, the profile view indicates that SCHEL intersection is the FAF for the S-LOC 8L approach, as indicated by the Maltese cross. At the lower right corner of the IAP chart, it indicates that from the FAF (i.e., SCHEL INT) to the MAP is 5.8 NM for the S-LOC 8L approach.

Answer (A) is incorrect. This is the distance from the FAF to the IM, not the MAP. **Answer (B) is incorrect.** This is the distance from the FAF to the visual descent point (VDP), not the MAP.

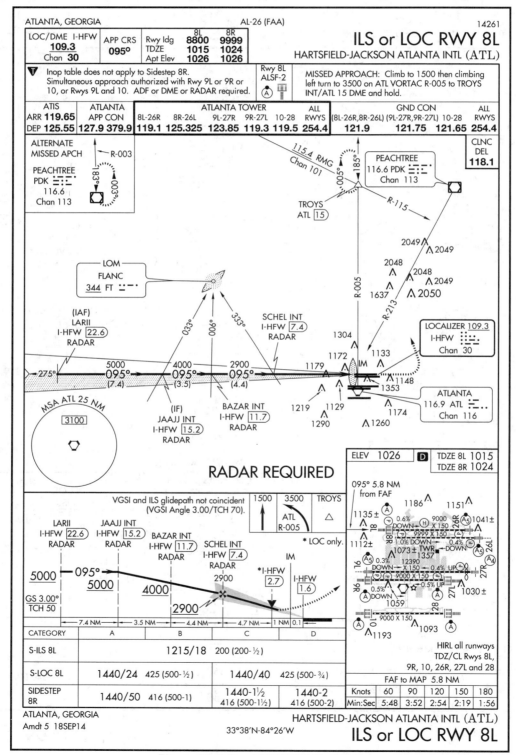

Figure 29. ILS or LOC RWY 8L (ATL).

9.5 Fuel Consumption

62. If an airplane is consuming 95 pounds of fuel per hour at a cruising altitude of 6,500 feet and the groundspeed is 173 knots, how much fuel is required to travel 450 NM?

    A. 248 pounds.

    B. 265 pounds.

    C. 284 pounds.

Answer (A) is correct. (FAA-H-8083-25B Chap 11)
    DISCUSSION: At a groundspeed of 173 kt., it will take 2.60 hr. to go 450 NM (450 NM ÷ 173 NM/hr.). At 95 lb./hr., it will take approximately 248 lb. (2.60 × 95) of fuel.
    Answer (B) is incorrect. This is required to travel 483 NM, not 450 NM. **Answer (C) is incorrect.** This is required to travel 517 NM, not 450 NM.

63. If fuel consumption is 80 pounds per hour and groundspeed is 180 knots, how much fuel is required for an airplane to travel 477 NM?

    A. 205 pounds.

    B. 212 pounds.

    C. 460 pounds.

Answer (B) is correct. (FAA-H-8083-25B Chap 11)
    DISCUSSION: At a groundspeed of 180 kt., it will take 2.65 hr. to go 477 NM (477 NM ÷ 180 NM/hr.). At 80 lb./hr., it will take approximately 212 lb. (2.65 × 80) of fuel.
    Answer (A) is incorrect. This is required to travel 461 NM, not 477 NM. **Answer (C) is incorrect.** This is required to travel 1,035 NM, not 477 NM.

64. If fuel consumption is 80 pounds per hour and groundspeed is 180 knots, how much fuel is required for an airplane to travel 460 NM?

    A. 205 pounds.

    B. 212 pounds.

    C. 460 pounds.

Answer (A) is correct. (FAA-H-8083-25B Chap 11)
    DISCUSSION: At a groundspeed of 180 kt., it will take 2.56 hr. to go 460 NM (460 NM ÷ 180 NM/hr.). At 80 lb./hr., it will take approximately 205 lb. (2.56 hr. × 80 lb./hr.) of fuel.
    Answer (B) is incorrect. This is required to travel 477 NM, not 460 NM. **Answer (C) is incorrect.** This is required to travel 1,035 NM, not 460 NM.

65. If an airplane is consuming 12.5 gallons of fuel per hour at a cruising altitude of 8,500 feet and the groundspeed is 145 knots, how much fuel is required to travel 435 NM?

    A. 27 gallons.

    B. 34 gallons.

    C. 38 gallons.

Answer (C) is correct. (FAA-H-8083-25B Chap 11)
    DISCUSSION: At a groundspeed of 145 kt., it will take 3.0 hr. to go 435 NM (435 NM ÷ 145 NM/hr.). At 12.5 GPH, it will take approximately 38 gal. (3 × 12.5) of fuel.
    Answer (A) is incorrect. This amount is required to travel 313 NM, not 435 NM. **Answer (B) is incorrect.** This amount is required to travel 394 NM, not 435 NM.

66. If an airplane is consuming 9.5 gallons of fuel per hour at a cruising altitude of 6,000 feet and the groundspeed is 135 knots, how much fuel is required to travel 490 NM?

    A. 27 gallons.

    B. 30 gallons.

    C. 35 gallons.

Answer (C) is correct. (FAA-H-8083-25B Chap 11)
    DISCUSSION: At a groundspeed of 135 kt., it will take 3.63 hr. to go 490 NM (490 NM ÷ 135 NM/hr.). At 9.5 GPH, it will take approximately 35 gal. (3.63 × 9.5) of fuel.
    Answer (A) is incorrect. This amount is required to travel 384 NM, not 490 NM. **Answer (B) is incorrect.** This amount is required to travel 426 NM, not 490 NM.

67. If an aircraft is consuming 9.7 gallons of fuel per hour at a cruising altitude of 6,000 feet and the groundspeed is 115 knots, how much fuel is required to travel 350 NM?

    A. 36 gallons.

    B. 30 gallons.

    C. 41 gallons.

Answer (B) is correct. (FAA-H-8083-25B Chap 11)
    DISCUSSION: At a groundspeed of 115 kt., it will take 3.04 hr. to go 350 NM (350 NM ÷ 115 NM/hr.). At 9.7 GPH, it will take approximately 30 gal. (3.04 hr. × 9.7 GPH) of fuel.
    Answer (A) is incorrect. This amount is required to travel 426 NM, not 350 NM. **Answer (C) is incorrect.** This amount is required to travel 490 NM, not 350 NM.

68. If an aircraft is consuming 9.3 gallons of fuel per hour at a cruising altitude of 6,000 feet and the groundspeed is 135 knots, how much fuel is required to travel 390 NM?

A. 27 gallons.

B. 30 gallons.

C. 35 gallons.

Answer (A) is correct. (FAA-H-8083-25B Chap 11)
 DISCUSSION: At a groundspeed of 135 kt., it will take 2.89 hr. to go 390 NM (390 NM ÷ 135 NM/hr.). At 9.3 GPH, it will take approximately 27 gal. (2.89 hr. × 9.3 GPH) of fuel.
 Answer (B) is incorrect. This amount is required to travel 435 NM, not 390 NM. **Answer (C) is incorrect.** This amount is required to travel 510 NM, not 390 NM.

69. If an aircraft is consuming 9.5 gallons of fuel per hour at a cruising altitude of 6,000 feet and the groundspeed is 135 knots, how much fuel is required to travel 380 NM?

A. 27 gallons.

B. 30 gallons.

C. 35 gallons.

Answer (A) is correct. (FAA-H-8083-25B Chap 11)
 DISCUSSION: At a groundspeed of 135 knots, it will take 2.81 hr. to go 380 NM (380 NM ÷ 135 NM/hr.). At 9.5 GPH, it will take approximately 27 gal. (2.81 hr. × 9.5 GPH) of fuel.
 Answer (B) is incorrect. This amount is required to travel 427 NM, not 380 NM. **Answer (C) is incorrect.** This amount is required to travel 497 NM, not 380 NM.

70. If an aircraft is consuming 9.5 gallons of fuel per hour at a cruising altitude of 6,000 feet and the groundspeed is 135 knots, how much fuel is required to travel 420 NM?

A. 27 gallons.

B. 30 gallons.

C. 35 gallons.

Answer (B) is correct. (FAA-H-8083-25B Chap 11)
 DISCUSSION: At a groundspeed of 135 knots, it will take 3.11 hr. to go 420 NM (420 NM ÷ 135 NM/hr.). At 9.5 GPH, it will take approximately 30 gal. (3.11 hr. × 9.5 gal./hr.) of fuel.
 Answer (A) is incorrect. This amount is required to travel 384 NM, not 420 NM. **Answer (C) is incorrect.** This amount is required to travel 497 NM, not 420 NM.

71. If an airplane is consuming 14.8 gallons of fuel per hour at a cruising altitude of 7,500 feet and the groundspeed is 167 knots, how much fuel is required to travel 560 NM?

A. 50 gallons.

B. 53 gallons.

C. 57 gallons.

Answer (A) is correct. (FAA-H-8083-25B Chap 11)
 DISCUSSION: At a groundspeed of 167 kt., it will take 3.35 hr. to go 560 NM (560 NM ÷ 167 NM/hr.). At 14.8 GPH, it will take approximately 50 gal. (3.35 × 14.8) of fuel.
 Answer (B) is incorrect. This amount is required to travel 598 NM, not 560 NM. **Answer (C) is incorrect.** This amount is required to travel 643 NM, not 560 NM.

72. If fuel consumption is 14.7 gallons per hour and groundspeed is 157 knots, how much fuel is required for an airplane to travel 612 NM?

A. 58 gallons.

B. 60 gallons.

C. 64 gallons.

Answer (A) is correct. (FAA-H-8083-25B Chap 11)
 DISCUSSION: At a groundspeed of 157 kt., it will take 3.90 hr. to go 612 NM (612 NM ÷ 157 NM/hr.). At 14.7 GPH, it will take approximately 58 gal. (3.90 × 14.7) of fuel.
 Answer (B) is incorrect. This amount is required to travel 641 NM, not 612 NM. **Answer (C) is incorrect.** This amount is required to travel 684 NM, not 612 NM.

9.6 Wind Direction and Speed

73. GIVEN:

True course	105°
True heading	085°
True airspeed	95 kts
Groundspeed	87 kts

Determine the wind direction and speed.

    A. 020° and 32 knots.

    B. 030° and 38 knots.

    C. 200° and 32 knots.

Answer (A) is correct. (E6B)
    DISCUSSION: To estimate your wind, given a true heading and a true course, simply use the wind side of your flight computer backwards. First, place your groundspeed of 87 kt. under the grommet with your true course of 105° under the true index. Since your true heading is 085°, you are holding a 20° left wind correction angle. Next, place a pencil mark on the 95-kt. true airspeed arc, 20° left of the centerline. Finally, rotate the wheel until the pencil mark is on the centerline, and read a wind of 020° (under the true index) at 32 kt. (up from your grommet).
    Answer (B) is incorrect. A wind from 030° at 38 kt. would result in less wind correction and a slower groundspeed.
    Answer (C) is incorrect. A wind from 200° at 32 kt. would result in a higher, not lower, groundspeed than airspeed.

74. GIVEN:

True course	345°
True heading	355°
True airspeed	85 kts
Groundspeed	95 kts

Determine the wind direction and speed.

    A. 095° and 19 knots.

    B. 113° and 19 knots.

    C. 238° and 18 knots.

Answer (B) is correct. (E6B)
    DISCUSSION: To estimate your wind, given a true heading and a true course, use the wind side of your flight computer backwards. First, place your groundspeed of 95 kt. under the grommet with your true course of 345° under the true index. Since your true heading is 355°, you are holding a 10° right wind correction angle. Next, place a pencil mark on the 85-kt. true airspeed arc, 10° right of centerline. Finally, rotate the wheel until the pencil mark is on the centerline, and read a wind of 113° (under the true index) at 19 kt. (up from the grommet).
    Answer (A) is incorrect. A wind from 095° at 19 kt. would result in more wind correction angle and a slower groundspeed.
    Answer (C) is incorrect. A wind from 238° at 18 kt. would require a left, not right, wind correction angle.

75. GIVEN:

Distance off course	9 mi
Distance flown	95 mi
Distance to fly	125 mi

To converge at the destination, the total correction angle would be

    A. 4°.

    B. 6°.

    C. 10°.

Answer (C) is correct. (FAA-H-8083-25B Chap 11)
    DISCUSSION: To determine the total correction angle to converge on your destination, use the following steps:

1. Since 1° off course equals 1 NM per 60 NM from the station, the following formula applies:

$$\frac{\text{NM off}}{\text{NM flown}} \times 60 = \text{Deg. off course from departure point}$$

$$\frac{9 \text{ NM}}{95 \text{ NM}} \times 60 = 5.68°$$

Turning back this number of degrees will parallel the original course.

2. To converge on your destination, calculate the number of degrees off it.

$$\frac{\text{NM off}}{\text{NM remaining}} \times 60 = \text{Deg. off course to destination}$$

$$\frac{9 \text{ NM}}{125 \text{ NM}} \times 60 = 4.32°$$

3. Turning this number of degrees farther will take you to your destination. Thus, the total correction angle is approximately 10° (5.68 + 4.32).

    Answer (A) is incorrect. Turning 4° would converge you on your destination if you were already paralleling the original course. **Answer (B) is incorrect.** Six degrees is the amount of correction required to parallel the original course.

76. You have flown 52 miles, are 6 miles off course, and have 118 miles yet to fly. To converge on your destination, the total correction angle would be

A. 3°.

B. 6°.

C. 10°.

Answer (C) is correct. (FAA-H-8083-25B Chap 11)
DISCUSSION: To determine the total correction angle to converge on your destination use the following steps:

1. Since 1° off course equals 1 NM per 60 NM from the station, the following formula applies:

$$\frac{\text{NM off}}{\text{NM flown}} \times 60 = \text{Deg. off course from departure point}$$

$$\frac{6\ \text{NM}}{52\ \text{NM}} \times 60 = 6.92°$$

Turning back this number of degrees will parallel the original course.

2. To converge on your destination, calculate the number of degrees off it.

$$\frac{\text{NM off}}{\text{NM remaining}} \times 60 = \text{Deg. off course to destination}$$

$$\frac{6\ \text{NM}}{118\ \text{NM}} \times 60 = 3.05°$$

3. Turning this number of degrees farther will take you to your destination. Thus, the total correction angle is approximately 10° (6.92 + 3.05).

Answer (A) is incorrect. Turning 3° would converge you on your destination if you were already paralleling the original course. **Answer (B) is incorrect.** Six degrees is the amount of correction required to parallel the original course.

9.7   Time, Compass Heading, Etc., on Climbs and En Route

77. An airplane departs an airport under the following conditions:

Airport elevation	1000 ft
Cruise altitude	9,500 ft
Rate of climb	500 ft/min
Average true airspeed	135 kts
True course	215°
Average wind velocity	290° at 20 kts
Variation	3° W
Deviation	−2°
Average fuel consumption	13 gal/hr

Determine the approximate time, compass heading, distance, and fuel consumed during the climb.

    A. 14 minutes, 234°, 26 NM, 3.9 gallons.

    B. 17 minutes, 224°, 36 NM, 3.7 gallons.

    C. 17 minutes, 242°, 31 NM, 3.5 gallons.

Answer (B) is correct. (E6B)
    DISCUSSION: The requirement is the time, compass heading, distance, and fuel consumed during the climb. The airport elevation is 1,000 ft. and the climb is to 9,500 ft., which is a climb of 8,500 ft. At 500 fpm, this requires 17 min. In 17 min., the fuel burned would be 3.7 gal. [(17 ÷ 60) × 13].
    To determine the compass heading, first determine the true heading using the wind side of your flight computer. Then adjust the true heading to magnetic heading, and then to compass heading.
    To determine the distance, multiply the time by the groundspeed also found on the wind side of the computer.
    Answer (A) is incorrect. The time required to climb is 17 min., not 14 min. **Answer (C) is incorrect.** The fuel used during 17 min. of climb is 3.7 gal., not 3.5 gal.

78. An airplane departs an airport under the following conditions:

Airport elevation	1,500 ft
Cruise altitude	9,500 ft
Rate of climb	500 ft/min
Average true airspeed	160 kts
True course	145°
Average wind velocity	080° at 15 kts
Variation	5° E
Deviation	−3°
Average fuel consumption	14 gal/hr

Determine the approximate time, compass heading, distance, and fuel consumed during the climb.

    A. 14 minutes, 128°, 35 NM, 3.2 gallons.

    B. 16 minutes, 132°, 41 NM, 3.7 gallons.

    C. 16 minutes, 128°, 32 NM, 3.8 gallons.

Answer (B) is correct. (E6B)
    DISCUSSION: The requirement is the time, compass heading, distance, and fuel consumed during the climb. The airport elevation is 1,500 ft. and the climb is to 9,500 ft., which is a climb of 8,000 ft. At 500 fpm, this requires 16 min., which narrows the answer choices down to two. In 16 min. at 14 gal./hr., just over one-fourth of 14 gal. would be burned, which is approximately 3.7 gal. To determine the compass heading, first determine the true heading using the wind side of your flight computer. Then adjust the true heading to magnetic heading, and then to compass heading. To determine the distance, multiply the time by the groundspeed also found on the wind side of the computer.
    Answer (A) is incorrect. The time required to climb is 16 min., not 14 min. **Answer (C) is incorrect.** The fuel used during 16 min. of climb is 3.7 gal., not 3.8 gal.

79. GIVEN:

Wind	175° at 20 kts
Distance	135 NM
True course	075°
True airspeed	80 kts
Fuel consumption	105 lb/hr

Determine the time en route and fuel consumption.

    A. 1 hour 28 minutes and 73.2 pounds.

    B. 1 hour 38 minutes and 158 pounds.

    C. 1 hour 40 minutes and 175 pounds.

Answer (C) is correct. (E6B)
    DISCUSSION: Using the wind side of your flight computer, follow these steps:

1. Place the wind direction under the true index (175°).
2. Mark the wind velocity up from the grommet (+20 kt.).
3. Place the true course under the true index (75°).
4. Slide the wind velocity mark to the (80-kt.) TAS line, and the groundspeed is under the grommet which is 81 kt.

Using the computer side, determine the time it takes to travel 135 NM by placing the index under 81 kt. and locating 135 NM on the outer scale. Under it is the time of 1 hr. 40 min. Next, place the index under 105 lb./hr. and locate 1 hr. 40 min. on the inner scale, and determine the fuel consumption on the outer scale to be 175 lb.
    Answer (A) is incorrect. To travel 135 NM in 1 hr. and 28 min. would require a groundspeed of 92 kt., not 81 kt. **Answer (B) is incorrect.** In 1 hr. and 38 min. at 105 lb./hr., the fuel consumption would be 171 lb., not 158 lb.

9.8 Time, Compass Heading, Etc., on Descents

80. An airplane descends to an airport under the following conditions:

Cruising altitude	6,500 ft
Airport elevation	700 ft
Descends to	800 ft AGL
Rate of descent	500 ft/min
Average true airspeed	110 kts
True course	335°
Average wind velocity	060° at 15 kts
Variation	3°W
Deviation	+2°
Average fuel consumption	8.5 gal/hr

Determine the approximate time, compass heading, distance, and fuel consumed during the descent.

   A. 10 minutes, 348°, 18 NM, 1.4 gallons.

   B. 10 minutes, 355°, 17 NM, 2.4 gallons.

   C. 12 minutes, 346°, 18 NM, 1.6 gallons.

Answer (A) is correct. (E6B)
DISCUSSION: A descent is to be made from 6,500 ft. to 1,500 ft. MSL (airport elevation of 700 ft. + 800 ft. AGL), which is a 5,000-ft. descent. At 500 fpm, it would take 10 min. Thus, the correct answer must either be 10 minutes, 348°, 18 NM, 1.4 gallons or 10 minutes, 355°, 17 NM, 2.4 gallons. At 8.5 gal./hr., 1.4 gal. would be burned in 10 min. (10/60 × 8.5). Thus, 10 minutes, 348°, 18 NM, 1.4 gallons is correct.
    Compute the compass heading by using the wind side of your flight computer. Convert true course to true heading based upon the wind effect. Then convert the true heading to magnetic heading by adjusting for the magnetic variation. The compass heading is determined by adjusting the magnetic heading for the compass deviation.
    Answer (B) is incorrect. At 8.5 gal./hr., 1.4 gal., not 2.4 gal., would be used in 10 min. **Answer (C) is incorrect.** It would take approximately 12 min. to descend from 6,500 ft. MSL to the surface of the airport, not the level altitude of 1,500 ft. MSL (800 ft. AGL).

81. An airplane descends to an airport under the following conditions:

Cruising altitude	7,500 ft
Airport elevation	1,300 ft
Descends to	800 ft AGL
Rate of descent	300 ft/min
Average true airspeed	120 kts
True course	165°
Average wind velocity	240° at 20 kts
Variation	4°E
Deviation	−2°
Average fuel consumption	9.6 gal/hr

Determine the approximate time, compass heading, distance, and fuel consumed during the descent.

   A. 16 minutes, 168°, 30 NM, 2.9 gallons.

   B. 18 minutes, 164°, 34 NM, 3.2 gallons.

   C. 18 minutes, 168°, 34 NM, 2.9 gallons.

Answer (C) is correct. (E6B)
DISCUSSION: A descent is to be made from 7,500 ft. to 2,100 ft. MSL (airport elevation of 1,300 ft. + 800 ft. AGL), which is a 5,400-ft. descent. At 300 fpm, it would take 18 min. Thus, the correct answer must either be 18 minutes, 164°, 34 NM, 3.2 gallons or 18 minutes, 168°, 34 NM, 2.9 gallons. Based on fuel consumption of 9.6 gal./hr., the fuel consumption would be 2.9 gal. (18/60 × 9.6), which makes the answer 18 minutes, 168°, 34 NM, 2.9 gallons correct.
    Compute the compass heading by using the wind side of your flight computer. Convert true course to true heading based upon the wind effect. Then convert the true heading to magnetic heading by adjusting for the magnetic variation. The compass heading is determined by adjusting the magnetic heading for the compass deviation.
    Answer (A) is incorrect. The time to descend is 18 min., not 16 min. **Answer (B) is incorrect.** At 9.6 gal./hr., 2.9 gal., not 3.2 gal., would be used in 18 min.

82. An airplane descends to an airport under the following conditions:

Cruising altitude	10,500 ft
Airport elevation	1,700 ft
Descends to	1,000 ft AGL
Rate of descent	600 ft/min
Average true airspeed	135 kts
True course	263°
Average wind velocity	330° at 30 kts
Variation	7°E
Deviation	+3°
Average fuel consumption	11.5 gal/hr

Determine the approximate time, compass heading, distance, and fuel consumed during the descent.

   A. 9 minutes, 274°, 26 NM, 2.8 gallons.

   B. 13 minutes, 274°, 28 NM, 2.5 gallons.

   C. 13 minutes, 271°, 26 NM, 2.5 gallons.

Answer (C) is correct. (E6B)
DISCUSSION: A descent is to be made from 10,500 ft. to 2,700 ft. MSL (airport elevation of 1,700 ft. + 1,000 ft. AGL), which is a 7,800-ft. descent. At 600 fpm, it would take 13 min. Thus, the correct answer must either be 13 minutes, 274°, 28 NM, 2.5 gallons or 13 minutes, 271°, 26 NM, 2.5 gallons and you must compute the compass heading.
    Place the wind direction of 330° under the true index. With a pencil, mark the wind velocity of 30 kt. above the grommet. Then turn the inner scale so that the true course of 263° is under the true index. Next, slide the wind scale such that the pencil mark is on the true airspeed of 135 kt., and note that the groundspeed is 121 kt. Also note that a 12 right correction is required. Thus, the true heading will be 275° (263° + 12°). To convert to magnetic, subtract the 7 easterly variation to get 268° (275° − 7°). Then add the compass deviation of 3° to determine the compass heading of 271° (268° + 3°). Thus, 13 minutes, 271°, 26 NM, 2.5 gallons is correct.
    Answer (A) is incorrect. The time to descend is 13 min., not 9 min. **Answer (B) is incorrect.** The compass heading is 271°, not 274°.

STUDY UNIT TEN

NAVIGATION SYSTEMS

(3 pages of outline)

This study unit contains outlines of major concepts tested, sample test questions and answers regarding navigation systems, and an explanation of each answer. The table of contents above lists each subunit within this study unit, the number of questions pertaining to that particular subunit, and the pages on which the outlines and questions begin, respectively.

Recall that the **sole purpose** of this book is to expedite your passing of the FAA pilot knowledge test for the commercial pilot certificate. Accordingly, all extraneous material (i.e., topics or regulations not directly tested on the FAA pilot knowledge test) is omitted, even though much more knowledge is necessary to become a proficient commercial pilot. This additional material is presented in *Pilot Handbook* and *Commercial Pilot Flight Maneuvers and Practical Test Prep*, available from Gleim Publications, Inc. Order online at www.GleimAviation.com.

10.1 VOR USE AND RECEIVER CHECKS

1. When checking the course sensitivity of a VOR receiver, the OBS should be rotated 10° to 12° to move the CDI from the center to the last dot.

    a. One-fifth deflection represents 2° off course, or 2 NM at 60 NM from the VOR station.

2. When using a VOT to make a VOR receiver check, the CDI should be centered and the OBS should indicate that the aircraft is on the 360° radial.

    a. To use a designated checkpoint on an airport surface, set the OBS on the designated radial.

        1) The CDI must center within ±4° of that radial with a FROM indication.

    b. When the CDI is centered during an airborne check, the OBS and the TO/FROM indicator should read within ±6° of the selected radial.

3. To track outbound on a VOR radial, set the OBS to the desired radial, and make heading corrections toward the CDI.

    a. To track inbound on a VOR radial, set the OBS to the reciprocal of the desired radial, and make heading corrections toward the CDI.

    b. Flying a heading that is reciprocal to the bearing selected on the OBS would result in reverse sensing of the VOR receiver.

4. For IFR operations off established airways, VORs that are no more than 80 NM apart should be listed in the "route of flight" portion of an IFR flight plan.

5. VOR/DME-based RNAV units need both VOR and DME signals to operate.

    a. If the NAVAID selected is a VOR without DME, RNAV mode will not function.

6. The Very High Frequency Omnidirectional Range Minimum Operational Network (VOR MON) provides a conventional navigation backup service in the event of a loss of global positioning system (GPS) signal.

10.2 HORIZONTAL SITUATION INDICATOR (HSI)

1. The horizontal situation indicator (HSI) is a combination of a heading indicator and a VOR/ILS indicator, as illustrated and described below.

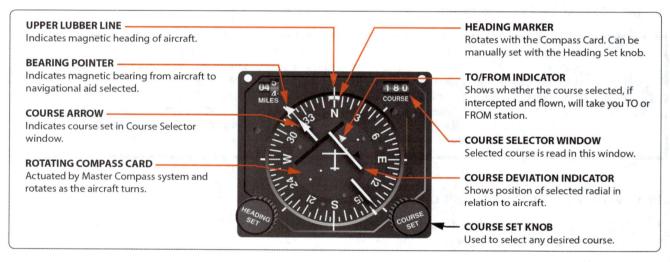

UPPER LUBBER LINE
Indicates magnetic heading of aircraft.

BEARING POINTER
Indicates magnetic bearing from aircraft to navigational aid selected.

COURSE ARROW
Indicates course set in Course Selector window.

ROTATING COMPASS CARD
Actuated by Master Compass system and rotates as the aircraft turns.

HEADING MARKER
Rotates with the Compass Card. Can be manually set with the Heading Set knob.

TO/FROM INDICATOR
Shows whether the course selected, if intercepted and flown, will take you TO or FROM station.

COURSE SELECTOR WINDOW
Selected course is read in this window.

COURSE DEVIATION INDICATOR
Shows position of selected radial in relation to aircraft.

COURSE SET KNOB
Used to select any desired course.

    a. Upper lubber line shows the current heading.

    b. Bearing pointer can be used to quickly determine the bearing to the station, and the tail of the bearing pointer indicates what radial the aircraft is currently on.

    c. Course arrow indicates desired course used for navigation.

    d. Rotating compass card rotates so that the heading is shown under the index at the top of the instrument.

    e. Heading marker is used to mark a desired heading and is set with the heading set knob.

    f. TO/FROM indicator shows whether the aircraft is flying toward or away from the station.

    g. Course selector window displays the selected course in a numerical format.

    h. Course deviation indicator indicates the direction the aircraft would have to turn to intercept the desired radial if on the approximate heading of the course selection.

    i. Course set knob is used to adjust the course arrow.

10.3 GLOBAL POSITIONING SYSTEM (GPS)

1.   To effectively navigate by means of GPS, pilots should

     a.   Determine the GPS unit is approved for their planned flight

     b.   Determine the status of the databases

          1)   The current status of navigational databases, weather databases, NOTAMs, and signal availability should be ensured prior to takeoff.

     c.   Understand how to make and cancel all appropriate entries

          1)   Stressful situations, heavy workloads, and turbulence make data entry errors real problems, and pilots should know how to recover basic aircraft controls quickly.

     d.   Program and review the planned route

          1)   Because each GPS layout can vary widely in type and function (knobs, switches, etc.), programming of the units should be verified for accuracy.

          2)   Name changes or spelling mistakes contribute to errors in flying appropriate routes.

     e.   Ensure the track flown is approved by ATC

     f.   Consider that when using a hand-held GPS for VFR navigation, position accuracy may degrade without notification

2.   One of the primary benefits of GPS navigation is that it permits aircraft to fly optimum routes and altitudes.

     a.   The "Direct To," or **D→** , key is a primary function key on most GPS units. A user hits the button and, using a series of knobs or switches, programs the intended waypoint or airport using the proper identifier. This feature shows the quickest way to fly to any given point, which is usually in a straight line.

     b.   The "nearest" button, abbreviated on most units as NRST, will show the closest airports in relation to the aircraft's current location.

          1)   The "nearest" function is very beneficial in emergency situations. A pilot simply presses this button to see the name, location, and direction to the nearest airport for landing.

          2)   Information such as navigation and communication frequencies, runway numbers and lengths, and other pertinent data is also provided.

3.   Due to the use of and reliance on GPS systems for navigation, it is easy for pilots to lose proficiency in performing manual calculations on courses, times, distances, headings, etc.

     a.   Emergency situations (e.g., electrical failures) make it important to maintain proficiency in these calculations.

10.4 PILOTAGE AND DEAD RECKONING

1.   Pilotage is navigation by reference to landmarks or checkpoints.

     a.   It is a method of navigation that can be used on any course that has adequate checkpoints, but it is more commonly used in conjunction with dead reckoning and VFR radio navigation.

2.   Dead reckoning is navigation solely by means of computations based on time, airspeed, distance, and direction.

     a.   It can be used when ground references are not visible, such as flights over water, but is usually used in conjunction with pilotage for cross-country flying.

QUESTIONS AND ANSWER EXPLANATIONS: All of the commercial pilot knowledge test questions chosen by the FAA for release as well as additional questions selected by Gleim relating to the material in the previous outlines are provided on the following pages. These questions have been organized into the same subunits as the outlines. To the immediate right of each question are the correct answer and answer explanations. You should cover these answers and answer explanations while responding to the questions. Refer to the general discussion in the Introduction on how to take the FAA knowledge test.

Remember that the questions from the FAA knowledge test bank have been reordered by topic and organized into a meaningful sequence. Also, the first line of the answer explanation gives the citation of the authoritative source for the answer.

QUESTIONS

10.1 VOR Use and Receiver Checks

1. When checking the course sensitivity of a VOR receiver, how many degrees should the OBS be rotated to move the CDI from the center to the last dot on either side?

   A. 5° to 10°.

   B. 10° to 12°.

   C. 18° to 20°.

Answer (B) is correct. (FAA-H-8083-15B Chap 9)
   DISCUSSION: Course sensitivity may be checked on a VOR by noting the number of degrees of change in the course selected as you rotate the OBS to move the CDI from center to the last dot on either side. This should be between 10° and 12°.
   Answer (A) is incorrect. Normal VOR sensitivity is 10° to 12°, not 5° to 10°. **Answer (C) is incorrect.** Normal VOR sensitivity is 10° to 12°, not 18° to 20°.

2. When using VOT to make a VOR receiver check, the CDI should be centered and the OBS should indicate that the aircraft is on the

   A. 090 radial.

   B. 180 radial.

   C. 360 radial.

Answer (C) is correct. (AIM Para 1-1-4)
   DISCUSSION: To use a VOT, tune in the published VOT frequency on your VOR receiver. With the course deviation indicator (CDI) centered, the omnibearing selector (OBS) should read 0° with the TO-FROM indicator showing FROM or the OBS should read 180° with the TO-FROM indicator showing TO. This indicates you are on the 360° radial.
   Answer (A) is incorrect. A VOT sends out a 360°, not 090°, radial in all directions. **Answer (B) is incorrect.** A VOT sends out a 360°, not 180°, radial in all directions.

3. How should the pilot make a VOR receiver check when the aircraft is located on the designated checkpoint on the airport surface?

   A. Set the OBS on 180° plus or minus 4°; the CDI should center with a FROM indication.

   B. Set the OBS on the designated radial. The CDI must center within plus or minus 4° of that radial with a FROM indication.

   C. With the aircraft headed directly toward the VOR and the OBS set to 000°, the CDI should center within plus or minus 4° of that radial with a TO indication.

Answer (B) is correct. (AIM Para 1-1-4)
   DISCUSSION: On ground checkpoints, you must have the aircraft on the location of the checkpoint and have the designated radial set on the OBS. The CDI must center within ±4° of the designated radial.
   Answer (A) is incorrect. It relates to VOT receiver checks, but on a VOT, with the OBS on 180°, there should be a TO, not a FROM, indication. **Answer (C) is incorrect.** It relates to VOT receiver checks, but VOTs, or any other VOR receiver check, do not require the airplane to be pointed in a particular direction.

4. Which situation would result in reverse sensing of a VOR receiver?

   A. Flying a heading that is reciprocal to the bearing selected on the OBS.

   B. Setting the OBS to a bearing that is 90° from the bearing on which the aircraft is located.

   C. Failing to change the OBS from the selected inbound course to the outbound course after passing the station.

Answer (A) is correct. (FAA-H-8083-15B Chap 9)
   DISCUSSION: By flying a heading that is a reciprocal of the course set in the OBS, you will have two situations: You will be flying to the station with a FROM indication, or you will fly from the station with a TO indication. Either will result in reverse sensing.
   Answer (B) is incorrect. This situation will result in the TO/FROM flag indicating the "cone of confusion." **Answer (C) is incorrect.** Although this situation may put you off course, it would not cause reverse sensing.

5. An aircraft 60 miles from a VOR station has a CDI indication of one-fifth deflection, this represents a course centerline deviation of approximately

  A. 6 miles.

  B. 2 miles.

  C. 1 mile.

Answer (B) is correct. *(FAA-H-8083-15B Chap 9)*
  DISCUSSION: Assuming a receiver with normal course sensitivity and full-scale deflection at 5 dots, aircraft displacement from course is approximately 200 ft. per dot per NM. Because one-fifth deflection equals 1 dot, the aircraft is 12,000 ft. or 2 NM off course (200 ft./NM × 60 NM = 12,000 ft.).
  Answer (A) is incorrect. Six NM off course would be indicated by a three-fifth, not one-fifth, CDI deflection.
  Answer (C) is incorrect. One NM off course would be indicated by a one-fifth CDI deflection if the aircraft were 30 NM, not 60 NM, from the station.

6. When the CDI needle is centered during an airborne VOR check, the omnibearing selector and the TO/FROM indicator should read

  A. within 4° of the selected radial.

  B. within 6° of the selected radial.

  C. 0° TO, only if you are due south of the VOR.

Answer (B) is correct. *(AIM Para 1-1-4)*
  DISCUSSION: For an airborne VOR receiver check, the maximum permissible bearing error of a VOR is ±6°.
  Answer (A) is incorrect. The airborne check tolerance is 6°, not 4°. **Answer (C) is incorrect.** The airborne check is performed over points designated by the FAA or over specific landmarks, not only due south of the VOR.

7. To track outbound on the 180 radial of a VOR station, the recommended procedure is to set the OBS to

  A. 360° and make heading corrections toward the CDI needle.

  B. 180° and make heading corrections away from the CDI needle.

  C. 180° and make heading corrections toward the CDI needle.

Answer (C) is correct. *(FAA-H-8083-15B Chap 9)*
  DISCUSSION: The recommended procedure is to set 180° on the OBS (your outbound course). This will give you a FROM indication while flying away from the station. This is normal sensing and you correct towards the needle.
  Answer (A) is incorrect. This procedure would give you reverse sensing. Thus, corrections are made away from, not toward, the needle. **Answer (B) is incorrect.** This procedure would take you away from your course (it is the way you navigate when using reverse sensing, e.g., on the back course of a localizer approach).

8. To track inbound on the 215 radial of a VOR station, the recommended procedure is to set the OBS to

  A. 215° and make heading corrections toward the CDI needle.

  B. 215° and make heading corrections away from the CDI needle.

  C. 035° and make heading corrections toward the CDI needle.

Answer (C) is correct. *(FAA-H-8083-15B Chap 9)*
  DISCUSSION: Because radials emanate outward from the VOR, tracking inbound on R-215 means you are flying the reciprocal course of 035°. Thus, you should set 035° on the OBS, and make heading corrections toward the needle.
  Answer (A) is incorrect. This procedure would result in reverse sensing by the CDI. **Answer (B) is incorrect.** This procedure would result in reverse sensing by the CDI.

9. Why does the FAA maintain a VOR Minimum Operational Network (MON)?

  A. To provide VOR navigation service in the Western Mountainous USA below GPS signal coverage.

  B. To maintain the en route Victor airway structure on overwater routes in the Gulf of Mexico.

  C. To support navigation of non-DME/DME equipped RNAV aircraft in the event of GPS outage.

Answer (C) is correct. *(FAA-H-8083-3B Chap 3)*
  DISCUSSION: The FAA maintains VORs geographically situated in the contiguous United States (CONUS) necessary to provide coverage at and above 5,000 ft. AGL, supporting approaches to MON airports and meeting other criteria to provide a conventional navigation backup service in the event of a loss of GPS signal.
  Answer (A) is incorrect. The VOR MON is designed to enable aircraft that have lost GPS service to revert to conventional navigation procedures. **Answer (B) is incorrect.** VOR MON allows continued navigation through an outage area using VOR station-to-station navigation to proceed to a MON airport where an instrument landing system (ILS), localizer (LOC), or VOR approach procedure can be flown without the necessity of GPS, DME, automatic direction finder (ADF), or surveillance.

10. For IFR operations off established airways, ROUTE OF FLIGHT portion of an IFR flight plan should list VOR navigational aids which are no more than

   A. 80 miles apart.

   B. 70 miles apart.

   C. 40 miles apart.

Answer (A) is correct. (AIM Para 5-1-8)
   DISCUSSION: The *Aeronautical Information Manual* indicates that, in order to facilitate the use of VOR signals, the distance between VORs defining a direct route of flight in controlled airspace off established airways below 18,000 ft. MSL should not exceed 80 NM.
   Answer (B) is incorrect. The recommended maximum distance between VOR navigational aids is 80 NM, not 70 NM.
   Answer (C) is incorrect. The recommended maximum distance between VOR navigational aids is 80 NM, not 40 NM.

11. When navigating using only VOR/DME based RNAV, selection of a VOR NAVAID that does not have DME service will

   A. result in loss of RNAV capability.

   B. have no effect on navigation capability.

   C. not impact navigation provided enough GPS is operating.

Answer (A) is correct. (FAA-H-8083-25B Chap 16)
   DISCUSSION: VOR/DME-based RNAV units need both VOR and DME signals to operate. If the NAVAID selected is a VOR without DME, RNAV mode will not function.
   Answer (B) is incorrect. VOR/DME-based RNAV units need both VOR and DME signals to operate. If the NAVAID selected is a VOR without DME, RNAV mode will not function.
   Answer (C) is incorrect. GPS is not needed when navigating using only VOR/DME-based RNAV.

10.2 Horizontal Situation Indicator (HSI)

12. (Refer to Figure 17 on page 389.) Which illustration indicates that the airplane will intercept the 060 radial at a 75° angle outbound, if the present heading is maintained?

   A. 4

   B. 5

   C. 6

Answer (B) is correct. (FAA-H-8083-15B Chap 9)
   DISCUSSION: The present magnetic heading of the airplane in illustration 5 is 345°, so you will cross R-060 at a 75° angle. The TO indication indicates you are east of the 330° – 150° radials. The right deflection on the 240° OBS selection means you are south of the 060° radial.
   Answer (A) is incorrect. Illustration 4 shows the airplane intercepting R-060 at a 15° angle (255° – 240°). **Answer (C) is incorrect.** Illustration 6 shows the airplane intercepting R-060 at a 60° angle (300° – 240°).

13. (Refer to Figure 17 on page 389.) Which statement is true regarding illustration 2, if the present heading is maintained? The aircraft will

   A. cross the 180 radial at a 45° angle outbound.

   B. intercept the 225 radial at a 45° angle.

   C. intercept the 360 radial at a 45° angle inbound.

Answer (A) is correct. (FAA-H-8083-15B Chap 9)
   DISCUSSION: Illustration 2 indicates that the airplane is heading approximately 227°. The bearing pointer indicates that a heading of 235° will take you to the station; thus, you are on the 055 radial (i.e., east-northeast of the station heading southwest). If you maintain the present heading, the station will remain to the right of the aircraft, and you will cross the 180 radial at approximately a 45° angle outbound (227 – 180 = 47).
   Answer (B) is incorrect. You would intercept the 180 radial, not the 225 radial, at a 45° angle outbound.
   Answer (C) is incorrect. The bearing point is currently to the right of the airplane's heading; thus, the station would remain to the right. The airplane would fly south, not north, of the station and would cross the 180, not the 360, radial at a 45° angle outbound, not inbound.

14. (Refer to Figure 17 on page 389.) Which illustration indicates you will comply with ATC instructions if the current heading is maintained and ATC instructs you to intercept the 360° radial north of the station?

   A. 1

   B. 2

   C. 3

Answer (C) is correct. (FAA-H-8083-15B Chap 9)
   DISCUSSION: Illustration 3 indicates that the aircraft is northeast of the station. The bearing pointer indicates the station is towards the south; thus, if the present heading is maintained, the aircraft will intercept the 360° radial while still north of the station.
   Answer (A) is incorrect. Illustration 1 indicates that the aircraft is currently northeast of the station on a heading of 030°. Therefore, if the present heading is maintained, the aircraft will fly further away from the 360° radial, not towards it. **Answer (B) is incorrect.** Illustration 2 indicates that the aircraft is northeast of the station. The bearing pointer indicates that the station is to the right of your present heading. In order to intercept the 360° radial, a turn to the right is required. If the current heading is maintained, the aircraft will eventually intercept the 180° radial south of the station, not the 360° radial north of the station as ATC instructed.

15. (Refer to Figure 17 below.) Which HSI indicates you will comply with ATC instructions if the current heading is maintained and ATC instructs you to intercept the 240° radial southwest of the station?

   A. 4

   B. 5

   C. 6

Answer (A) is correct. *(FAA-H-8083-15B Chap 9)*
    DISCUSSION: Illustration 4 indicates that the aircraft is currently east of the station on a southwesterly heading of 255°. If this heading is maintained, you will eventually intercept the 240° radial southwest of the station.
    Answer (B) is incorrect. Illustration 5 indicates that the aircraft is east of the station on a northwesterly heading of 345°. If this heading is maintained, the aircraft will never intercept the 240° radial. **Answer (C) is incorrect.** Illustration 6 indicates that the aircraft is east of the station on a northwesterly heading of 300°. If this heading is maintained, the aircraft will never intercept the 240° radial.

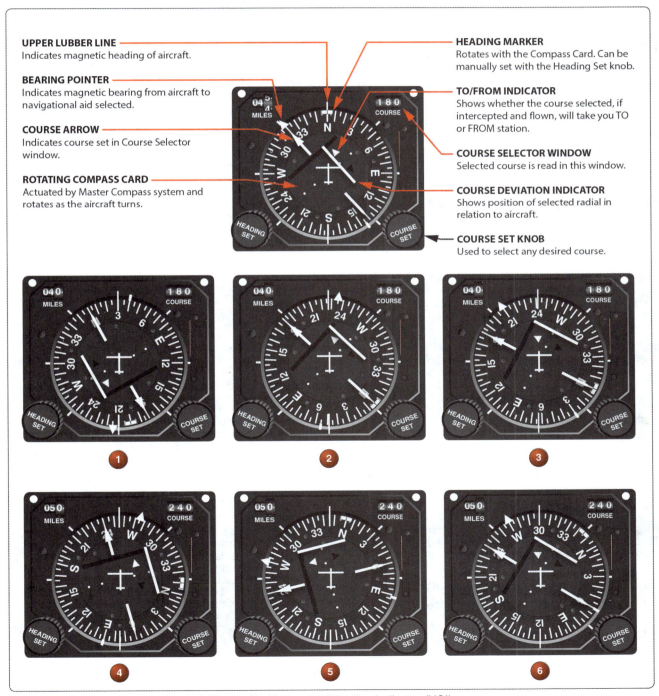

Figure 17. Horizontal Situation Indicator (HSI).

16. (Refer to Figure 17 on page 391.) Which illustration indicates that the airplane will intercept the 060 radial at a 60° angle inbound, if the present heading is maintained?

   A. 6

   B. 4

   C. 5

Answer (A) is correct. (FAA-H-8083-15B Chap 9)
   DISCUSSION: Illustration 6 indicates that the airplane is east of the station on a heading of 300°. The course selector is set to 240 and a TO indication. On a heading of 300°, the airplane will intercept the 060 radial inbound, which is 240° TO the station, at a 60° angle (300 – 240 = 60).
   Answer (B) is incorrect. In illustration 4, the airplane is east of the station heading 255°. The airplane will intercept the 240 radial, not the 060 radial, at a 15° angle outbound. **Answer (C) is incorrect.** In illustration 5, the airplane is east of the station heading 345°. The airplane will intercept the 060 radial at a 105° angle inbound (345 – 240 = 105), not a 60° angle inbound.

17. (Refer to Figure 17 on page 391.) Which illustration indicates that the airplane should be turned 150° left to intercept the 360 radial at a 60° angle inbound?

   A. 1

   B. 2

   C. 3

Answer (A) is correct. (FAA-H-8083-15B Chap 9)
   DISCUSSION: By turning the airplane as indicated in illustration 1 (150° left), your heading will be 240°. This would be a 60° interception to the 360° radial.
   The TO indication on a 180° OBS means you are north. The right deflection on the 180° OBS means you are east of the 360° radial. A 240° MH will intercept the 360° radial at a 60° angle.
   Answer (B) is incorrect. Airplane 2 is inbound from the northeast. If you turn 150° left from 227°, your new heading will be 077°. You will fly away from the 360° radial. **Answer (C) is incorrect.** Airplane 3 is inbound from the northeast. If you make a 150° left turn from 244°, your new heading will be 094°. You will fly east, away from the 360° radial.

18. (Refer to Figure 17 on page 391.) Which is true regarding illustration 4, if the present heading is maintained? The airplane will

   A. cross the 060 radial at a 15° angle.

   B. intercept the 240 radial at a 30° angle.

   C. cross the 180 radial at a 75° angle.

Answer (C) is correct. (FAA-H-8083-15B Chap 9)
   DISCUSSION: Illustration 4 indicates that the airplane is heading 255°. The bearing pointer indicates that a heading of 275° will take you to the station; thus, you are on the 095 radial (i.e., east of the station heading southwest). If you maintain the present heading, you will cross the R-180 at a 75° angle (255 – 180 = 75).
   Answer (A) is incorrect. You will cross the 240 radial, not the 060 radial, at a 15° angle. **Answer (B) is incorrect.** You will cross the 240 radial at a 15°, not 30°, angle.

19. (Refer to Figure 17 on page 391.) Which illustration indicates that the airplane is crossing the 030 radial?

   A. 1

   B. 3

   C. 6

Answer (B) is correct. (FAA-H-8083-15B Chap 9)
   DISCUSSION: The bearing pointer can be used to quickly determine the bearing to the station, and the tail of the bearing pointer indicates which radial the aircraft is currently on. In illustration 3, the bearing pointer shows the bearing to the station is 210°. Check the reciprocal to see that the aircraft is crossing the 030 radial.
   Answer (A) is incorrect. In illustration 1, the aircraft's heading is 030°, but the bearing pointer indicates that the aircraft is currently crossing the 040 radial, not the 030 radial. **Answer (C) is incorrect.** In illustration 6, the bearing pointer indicates that the aircraft is currently crossing the 090 radial, not the 030 radial.

20. (Refer to Figure 17 on page 391.) (Refer to illustration 1.) If the aircraft turns to the heading indicated by the heading marker, it will

   A. intercept the 180° radial after station passage.

   B. intercept the 180° radial prior to station passage.

   C. not intercept the 180° radial.

Answer (A) is correct. (FAA-H-8083-15B Chap 9)
   DISCUSSION: Station passage is indicated when the aircraft crosses the radial 90° from the selected radial. Since the 180° radial is selected, station passage will occur when the aircraft crosses the 090° radial. The bearing pointer on illustration 1 shows that the aircraft is currently on the 040° radial (using the tail of the bearing pointer) northeast of the station. If the aircraft is turned to 200° as indicated by the heading marker, the aircraft would intercept the 180° radial after station passage.
   Answer (B) is incorrect. The aircraft would intercept the 180° radial after, not prior to, station passage. **Answer (C) is incorrect.** The bearing pointer in illustration 1 indicates that the aircraft is currently on the 040° radial northeast of the station. If the aircraft is turned to 200° as indicated by the heading marker, the aircraft would intercept the 180° radial after station passage.

21. (Refer to Figure 17 below.) (Refer to illustration 2.) If the aircraft turns to the heading indicated by the heading marker, it will

A. intercept the 360° radial after station passage.

B. intercept the 360° radial prior to station passage.

C. not intercept the 360° radial.

Answer (C) is correct. (FAA-H-8083-15B Chap 9)
DISCUSSION: The 360° radial is west of the aircraft. If the aircraft turns to a heading of 360°, it will fly parallel to, but not intercept, the radial.
Answer (A) is incorrect. On a heading of 360°, the aircraft will not intercept the 360° radial. **Answer (B) is incorrect.** On a heading of 360°, the aircraft will not intercept the 360° radial.

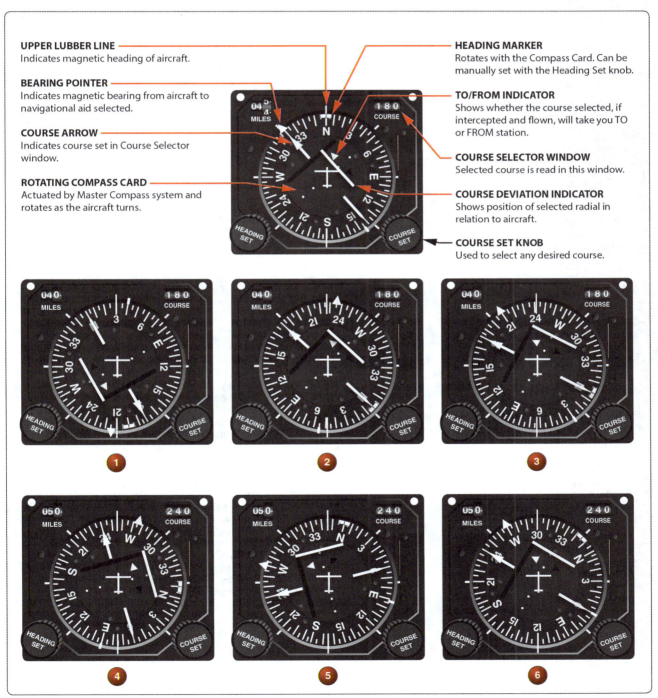

Figure 17. Horizontal Situation Indicator (HSI).

10.3 Global Positioning System (GPS)

22. Effective navigation by means of GPS includes

    A. determining the current status of all databases.

    B. ensuring that ATC approves your planned route.

    C. relying solely on the GPS for course information.

Answer (A) is correct. (FAA-H-8083-6 Chap 3)
    DISCUSSION: A pilot must determine the status of all appropriate databases. If a database is not current, the pilot must use an alternate means of navigation as a primary form.
    Answer (B) is incorrect. Pilots may be, and frequently are, given changes to their requested planned route by ATC. A pilot must ensure that the route flown is approved by ATC whether it is his or her requested plan or not. **Answer (C) is incorrect.** All systems have the possibility of failing at some point, and it would not be effective to rely solely on a GPS unit for navigation. It is wise to have another means (paper charts, approach plates, etc.) from which to navigate.

23. Why should pilots understand how to cancel entries made on a GPS?

    A. Because GPS units frequently provide wrong or false information.

    B. Because heavy workloads and turbulence can increase data entry errors.

    C. Because published route names commonly change.

Answer (B) is correct. (FAA-H-8083-6 Chap 3)
    DISCUSSION: Stressful situations, heavy workloads, and turbulence make data entry errors real problems, and pilots should know how to recover basic aircraft controls quickly.
    Answer (A) is incorrect. GPS units provide a high degree of accuracy and are unreliable very infrequently. **Answer (C) is incorrect.** It is not common for names of published routes to change.

24. Reliance on GPS units

    A. can cause pilots to lose proficiency in performing manual calculations of time, distance, and heading.

    B. will increase a pilot's skill in navigating by visual reference.

    C. does not decrease pilot workload.

Answer (A) is correct. (FAA-H-8083-6 Chap 3)
    DISCUSSION: Due to the reliance on GPS systems for navigation, it is easy for pilots to lose proficiency in performing manual calculations on courses, times, distances, headings, etc.
    Answer (B) is incorrect. Reliance on GPS units for navigation does not increase skill in navigating by outside references. **Answer (C) is incorrect.** Navigation by GPS does decrease pilot workload.

25. The primary purpose of the direct-to button is to

    A. provide waypoints to a given runway.

    B. give routing to the nearest airport.

    C. show the quickest way to fly to any given point.

Answer (C) is correct. (FAA-H-8083-6 Chap 3)
    DISCUSSION: The "direct-to" feature shows the quickest way to fly to any given point, whether an airport or waypoint.
    Answer (A) is incorrect. A pilot would not use the "direct-to" function to see all the waypoints to a given airport. The "flight plan" feature should be used to see this information. **Answer (B) is incorrect.** The "nearest," or NRST, button provides information about the closest airport at any given time.

26. Which button/feature provides information on the closest airport at any given time?

    A. Direct-to.

    B. Nearest.

    C. Flight plan.

Answer (B) is correct. (FAA-H-8083-6 Chap 3)
    DISCUSSION: The "nearest," or NRST, button will provide information including frequencies, direction, and distance to the closest airport. It is especially beneficial in emergency situations because very few keystrokes are needed to gather information.
    Answer (A) is incorrect. The "direct-to" button shows the quickest way to fly to any given point, whether an airport or waypoint, but does not necessarily provide airport information. **Answer (C) is incorrect.** The "flight plan" button shows all waypoints to a given airport. A pilot has to program all this information manually.

27. What is a consideration when using a hand-held GPS for VFR navigation?

A. Position accuracy may degrade without notification.

B. RAIM capability will be maintained for entire flight.

C. Waypoints will still be accurate even if database is not current.

Answer (A) is correct. (FAA-H-8083-25B Chap 16)
DISCUSSION: While a hand-held GPS receiver can provide excellent navigation capability to VFR pilots, position accuracy may degrade without notification.
Answer (B) is incorrect. When using a hand-held GPS for VFR navigation, loss of navigation signal may occur, possibly with no RAIM warning to the pilot. **Answer (C) is incorrect.** Waypoints may not be accurate if the database is not current.

10.4 Pilotage and Dead Reckoning

28. What procedure could a pilot use to navigate under VFR from one point to another when ground references are not visible?

A. Dead reckoning.

B. Pilotage.

C. VFR is not allowed in these circumstances.

Answer (A) is correct. (FAA-H-8083-25B Chap 16)
DISCUSSION: Dead reckoning is navigation solely by means of computations based on time, airspeed, distance, and direction. If ground references are not visible, such as when flying over water, dead reckoning can be used to navigate.
Answer (B) is incorrect. Pilotage is navigation by reference to landmarks or checkpoints and cannot be used if ground references are not visible. **Answer (C) is incorrect.** Pilots may still operate under VFR in some cases when ground references are not visible, such as when flying over water.

394

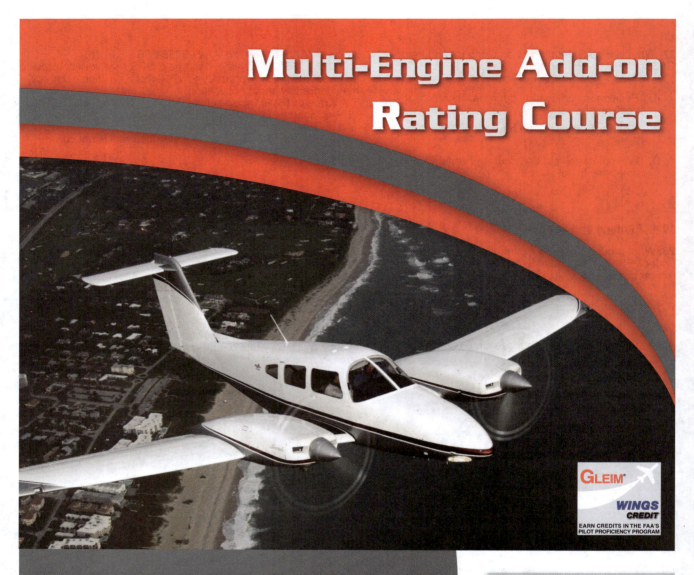

STUDY UNIT ELEVEN

FLIGHT OPERATIONS

(3 pages of outline)

This study unit contains outlines of major concepts tested, sample test questions and answers regarding flight operations, and an explanation of each answer. The table of contents above lists each subunit within this study unit, the number of questions pertaining to that particular subunit, and the pages on which the outlines and questions begin, respectively.

Recall that the **sole purpose** of this book is to expedite your passing of the FAA pilot knowledge test for the commercial pilot certificate. Accordingly, all extraneous material (i.e., topics or regulations not directly tested on the FAA pilot knowledge test) is omitted, even though much more knowledge is necessary to become a proficient commercial pilot. This additional material is presented in *Pilot Handbook* and *Commercial Pilot Flight Maneuvers and Practical Test Prep*, available from Gleim Publications, Inc. Order online at www.GleimAviation.com.

11.1 FLIGHT FUNDAMENTALS

1. The four flight fundamentals involved in maneuvering an airplane are

    a. Straight-and-level flight

    b. Turns

    c. Climbs

    d. Descents

11.2 TAXIING

1. When taxiing in a strong quartering tailwind, the aileron control should be opposite the direction from which the wind is blowing.

    a. This keeps the aileron down on the side from which the wind is blowing.

2. On crosswind takeoffs,

    a. The rudder is used to maintain directional control,

    b. The aileron pressure should be into the wind to keep the upwind wing down, and

    c. There should be a higher-than-normal liftoff speed so the airplane does not skip sideways during liftoff.

11.3 LANDINGS

1.   During gusty wind conditions, a power-on approach and power-on landing should be conducted.

2.   On crosswind landings, at the moment of touchdown, the direction of motion of the airplane and its longitudinal axis should be parallel to the runway, i.e., not skipping sideways, which would impose side loads on the landing gear.

3.   When turbulence is encountered during the approach to a landing, you should increase the airspeed slightly above normal approach speed to attain more positive control.

4.   If landing downwind or with a tailwind, expect the likelihood of overshooting the intended landing spot and a faster groundspeed at touchdown.

5.   When conducting a go-around, the pilot must be aware that the airplane is trimmed for a power-off condition, and application of takeoff power will cause the nose to rise rapidly.

11.4 EMERGENCIES

1.   The vital and most immediate concern in the event of complete power failure after becoming airborne on takeoff is maintaining a safe, i.e., best glide, airspeed to avoid stalls/spins.

2.   When diverting to an alternate airport in an emergency, time is usually of the essence. Accordingly, you should divert to the new course as soon as possible. Rule of thumb computations, estimates, and any other shortcuts are appropriate.

11.5 ANTI-COLLISION LIGHT SYSTEM

1.   Pilots are required to have the aircraft's anti-collision lighting system operating during all operations, night and day, unless the pilot in command determines that it should be turned off for safety reasons.

11.6 COLD WEATHER OPERATION

1.   The cabin area as well as the engine should be preheated for cold weather operation.

2.   In cold weather, crankcase breather lines should be inspected to determine whether they are clogged with ice from crankcase vapors that have condensed and frozen.

3.   When taking off from a slushy runway, you can minimize the freezing of landing gear mechanisms by waiting to retract the landing gear immediately to allow it to air dry.

11.7 TURBULENCE

1. In severe turbulence, set power for the design maneuvering airspeed (V_A) and maintain a level flight attitude.

    a.   Accept changes in airspeed and altitude.

2. Flight at or below V_A means the airplane will stall before excessive loads can be imposed on the wings.

3. When entering an area where significant clear air turbulence (CAT) has been reported, reduce the airspeed to that recommended for rough air at the first indication of turbulence.

11.8 NIGHT FLYING OPERATIONS

1. For night flying operations, the best night vision is achieved when the rods in the eyes become adjusted to the darkness in approximately 30 min.

2. When planning a night cross-country flight, you should check the availability and status of en route and destination airport lighting systems.

3. Light beacons producing red flashes indicate obstructions or areas considered hazardous to aerial navigation.

4. When flying VFR at night, the first indication of flying into restricted visibility conditions is the gradual disappearance of lights on the ground.

5. When planning for an emergency landing at night, two of the primary considerations should include

    a.   Planning the emergency approach and landing to an unlighted portion of an area
    b.   Selecting a landing close to public access, if possible

QUESTIONS AND ANSWER EXPLANATIONS: All of the commercial pilot knowledge test questions chosen by the FAA for release as well as additional questions selected by Gleim relating to the material in the previous outlines are provided on the following pages. These questions have been organized into the same subunits as the outlines. To the immediate right of each question are the correct answer and answer explanations. You should cover these answers and answer explanations while responding to the questions. Refer to the general discussion in the Introduction on how to take the FAA knowledge test.

Remember that the questions from the FAA knowledge test bank have been reordered by topic and organized into a meaningful sequence. Also, the first line of the answer explanation gives the citation of the authoritative source for the answer.

QUESTIONS

11.1 Flight Fundamentals

1. Name the four fundamentals involved in maneuvering an aircraft.

   A.   Power, pitch, bank, and trim.

   B.   Thrust, lift, turns, and glides.

   C.   Straight-and-level flight, turns, climbs, and descents.

Answer (C) is correct. (FAA-H-8083-3B Chap 3)
   DISCUSSION: Maneuvering the airplane is generally divided into four flight fundamentals: straight-and-level flight, turns, climbs, and descents. All controlled flight consists of either one or a combination of more than one of these basic maneuvers.
   Answer (A) is incorrect. Power, pitch, bank, and trim are the components of aircraft control by which the four fundamental maneuvers are performed. **Answer (B) is incorrect.** Thrust and lift are two of the forces that act on an airplane, and glides are a type of descent.

11.2 Taxiing

2. While taxiing a light, high-wing airplane during strong quartering tailwinds, the aileron control should be positioned

   A.   neutral at all times.

   B.   toward the direction from which the wind is blowing.

   C.   opposite the direction from which the wind is blowing.

Answer (C) is correct. (FAA-H-8083-3B Chap 2)
   DISCUSSION: When taxiing with a quartering tailwind, the aileron control should be positioned opposite the direction from which the wind is blowing so that the aileron is down on the side from which the wind is blowing. This will prevent the wind from lifting the wing or getting under it and blowing the airplane over.
   Answer (A) is incorrect. The ailerons can assist in keeping the wind from blowing the airplane over in strong crosswinds. **Answer (B) is incorrect.** Pilots should position the aileron control toward the direction from which the wind is blowing when taxiing with a quartering headwind, not tailwind.

3. With regard to the technique required for a crosswind correction on takeoff, a pilot should use

   A.   aileron pressure into the wind and initiate the lift-off at a normal airspeed in both tailwheel- and nosewheel-type airplanes.

   B.   right rudder pressure, aileron pressure into the wind, and higher than normal lift-off airspeed in both tricycle- and conventional-gear airplanes.

   C.   rudder as required to maintain directional control, aileron pressure into the wind, and higher than normal lift-off airspeed in both conventional- and nosewheel-type airplanes.

Answer (C) is correct. (FAA-H-8083-3B Chap 5)
   DISCUSSION: For crosswind takeoffs, the aileron control must be held into the crosswind, which raises the aileron on the upwind wing to impose a downward force on the wing to counteract the lifting force of the crosswind and prevents that wing from rising. The rudder is used to maintain directional control. Finally, a higher than normal lift-off airspeed is appropriate in both conventional and nosewheel-type airplanes to keep the airplane from skipping sideways during a possible slow transition from the directional control down the runway to crabbing into the wind once airborne.
   Answer (A) is incorrect. The lift-off speed should be increased slightly and rudder pressure should be applied as necessary to maintain directional control. **Answer (B) is incorrect.** The amount of rudder pressure required to maintain directional control of the airplane should be applied, not necessarily only right rudder pressure.

4. When taxiing during strong quartering tailwinds, which aileron positions should be used?

A. Neutral.

B. Aileron up on the side from which the wind is blowing.

C. Aileron down on the side from which the wind is blowing.

Answer (C) is correct. (FAA-H-8083-3B Chap 2)
DISCUSSION: When taxiing with a quartering tailwind, the aileron control should be positioned opposite the direction from which the wind is blowing so that the aileron is down on the side from which the wind is blowing. This will prevent the wind from lifting the wing or getting under it and blowing the airplane over.
Answer (A) is incorrect. The ailerons can assist in keeping the wind from blowing the airplane over in strong crosswinds. **Answer (B) is incorrect.** Pilots should position the aileron up on the side from which the wind is blowing in a quartering headwind, not tailwind.

11.3 Landings

5. Which type of approach and landing is recommended during gusty wind conditions?

A. A power-on approach and power-on landing.

B. A power-off approach and power-on landing.

C. A power-on approach and power-off landing.

Answer (A) is correct. (FAA-H-8083-3B Chap 8)
DISCUSSION: Power-on approaches at airspeeds slightly above normal should be used for landing in gusty or turbulent wind conditions. To maintain good control in a gusty crosswind, the use of partial wing flaps may be necessary. The touchdown will be at a higher airspeed to ensure more positive control. An adequate amount of power should be used to maintain the proper airspeed throughout the approach, and the throttle should be retarded to idling position only after the main wheels contact the landing surface.
Answer (B) is incorrect. A power-on, not power-off, approach should be used during gusty conditions. **Answer (C) is incorrect.** A power-on, not power-off, landing should be used during gusty conditions.

6. When turbulence is encountered during the approach to a landing, what action is recommended and for what primary reason?

A. Increase the airspeed slightly above normal approach speed to attain more positive control.

B. Decrease the airspeed slightly below normal approach speed to avoid overstressing the airplane.

C. Increase the airspeed slightly above normal approach speed to penetrate the turbulence as quickly as possible.

Answer (A) is correct. (FAA-H-8083-3B Chap 8)
DISCUSSION: Power-on approaches at airspeeds slightly above normal should be used for landing in gusty or turbulent wind conditions. To maintain good control in a gusty crosswind, the use of partial wing flaps may be necessary. The touchdown will be at a higher airspeed to ensure more positive control. An adequate amount of power should be used to maintain the proper airspeed throughout the approach, and the throttle should be retarded to idling position only after the main wheels contact the landing surface.
Answer (B) is incorrect. Because normal approach speed is generally well below V_A, a slightly higher approach speed will improve control effectiveness without overstressing the airplane. **Answer (C) is incorrect.** The increased approach speed is for improved control effectiveness. In general, turbulence should be penetrated slowly, not as quickly as possible.

7. A proper crosswind landing on a runway requires that, at the moment of touchdown, the

A. direction of motion of the airplane and its lateral axis be perpendicular to the runway.

B. direction of motion of the airplane and its longitudinal axis be parallel to the runway.

C. downwind wing be lowered sufficiently to eliminate the tendency for the airplane to drift.

Answer (B) is correct. (FAA-H-8083-3B Chap 8)
DISCUSSION: At the moment of touchdown, the upwind wing must be held down and opposite rudder applied so that the direction of motion of the airplane and its longitudinal axis are both parallel to the runway. Failure to accomplish this results in severe sideloads being imposed on the landing gear and imparts ground looping tendencies.
Answer (A) is incorrect. The direction of motion of the airplane must be parallel, not perpendicular, to the runway. **Answer (C) is incorrect.** Pilots should lower the upwind wing, not the downwind wing, to eliminate drift.

8. When conducting a go-around, the pilot must be aware that

  A. radio communications are key to alerting other aircraft in the pattern that a go-around maneuver is being conducted.

  B. the airplane is trimmed for a power-off condition, and application of takeoff power will cause the nose to rise rapidly.

  C. flaps should be raised as quickly as possible to reduce drag and increase airspeed for a successful go-around.

Answer (B) is correct. (FAA-H-8083-3B)
  DISCUSSION: Because the airplane is trimmed for the approach (a low-power and low-airspeed condition), application of maximum allowable power requires considerable control pressure to maintain a climb pitch attitude. The addition of power tends to raise the airplane's nose suddenly and make it veer to the left. Forward elevator pressure must be anticipated and applied to hold the nose in a safe climb attitude. Right rudder pressure must be increased to counteract torque and P-factor and keep the nose straight.
  Answer (A) is incorrect. The most important factor in conducting a go-around safely is maintaining control of the aircraft. Radio communications should not be made until the aircraft is established in a stable climb at a safe distance from the ground. **Answer (C) is incorrect.** A sudden and complete retraction of the flaps could cause a loss of lift, resulting in the airplane settling into the ground. Flaps should be retracted intermittently in small increments to allow time for the airplane to accelerate progressively as they are being raised.

9. What should be expected when making a downwind landing? The likelihood of

  A. undershooting the intended landing spot and a faster airspeed at touchdown.

  B. overshooting the intended landing spot and a faster groundspeed at touchdown.

  C. undershooting the intended landing spot and a faster groundspeed at touchdown.

Answer (B) is correct. (FAA-H-8083-25B, AC 91-79A)
  DISCUSSION: The effect of a downwind landing is an increased groundspeed, which can increase the likelihood of overshooting the intended landing spot.
  Answer (A) is incorrect. When making a downwind landing, an aircraft will likely overshoot, rather than undershoot, the intended landing spot. In addition, the indicated airspeed will be the same, but the groundspeed will be increased. **Answer (C) is incorrect.** When making a downwind landing, an aircraft will likely overshoot, rather than undershoot, the intended landing spot due to increased groundspeed.

11.4 Emergencies

10. A pilot's most immediate and vital concern in the event of complete engine failure after becoming airborne on takeoff is

  A. maintaining a safe airspeed.

  B. landing directly into the wind.

  C. turning back to the takeoff field.

Answer (A) is correct. (FAA-H-8083-3B Chap 8)
  DISCUSSION: The most immediate concern in the event of complete engine failure while airborne in all phases of flight is establishing and maintaining a safe (i.e., best glide) airspeed. This is especially true when an engine failure occurs after becoming airborne on takeoff since the airplane is in a nose-up attitude and a relatively slow airspeed, which may be near the stall speed.
  Answer (B) is incorrect. Landing into the wind may not always be the best choice, given available landing areas and obstructions. **Answer (C) is incorrect.** Turning back to the takeoff field will not be possible until sufficient altitude has been gained.

11. When diverting to an alternate airport because of an emergency, pilots should

  A. rely upon radio as the primary method of navigation.

  B. climb to a higher altitude because it will be easier to identify checkpoints.

  C. apply rule-of-thumb computations, estimates, and other appropriate shortcuts to divert to the new course as soon as possible.

Answer (C) is correct. (FAA-H-8083-25B Chap 16)
  DISCUSSION: When diverting to an alternate airport because of an emergency, time is usually of the essence. Accordingly, pilots should divert to the new course as soon as possible. Rule of thumb computations, estimates, and any other shortcuts are appropriate.
  Answer (A) is incorrect. Any appropriate means of navigation is satisfactory. **Answer (B) is incorrect.** Climbs may consume valuable time and/or fuel.

12. If you experience an engine failure in a single-engine aircraft after takeoff, you should

A. establish the proper glide attitude.

B. turn into the wind.

C. adjust the pitch to maintain V_Y.

Answer (A) is correct. (FAA-H-8083-3B)
DISCUSSION: If an actual engine failure occurs immediately after takeoff and before a safe maneuvering altitude is attained, a proper glide attitude should be immediately established and a field should be selected directly ahead or slightly to either side of the takeoff path.
Answer (B) is incorrect. Most takeoffs are already made into the wind. In the event of a tailwind departure, turning into the wind would result in the loss of considerable altitude during the turn and should not be attempted. **Answer (C) is incorrect.** The proper glide speed, not V_Y, should be established.

11.5 Anti-Collision Light System

13. Pilots are required to have the anti-collision light system operating

A. during all types of operations, both day and night.

B. anytime the pilot is on the flight deck.

C. anytime an engine is in operation.

Answer (A) is correct. (AIM Para 4-3-23)
DISCUSSION: Aircraft equipped with an anti-collision lighting system are required to have that system operating during all types of operations, both day and night, except when the pilot in command determines that it should be turned off for safety reasons.
Answer (B) is incorrect. The anti-collision light system need not be operated if the pilot is on the flight deck of an aircraft that is not performing an operation (e.g., the system does not have to be on while the pilot preflights the flight deck). **Answer (C) is incorrect.** The anti-collision light system is required to be operational during all types of operations, day and night, not just when an engine is in operation (e.g., a motor-glider equipped with anti-collision lights must use them during power-off soaring as well as during powered flight).

11.6 Cold Weather Operation

14. If necessary to take off from a slushy runway, the freezing of landing gear mechanisms can be minimized by

A. recycling the gear.

B. delaying gear retraction.

C. increasing the airspeed to V_{LE} before retraction.

Answer (B) is correct. (FAA-H-8083-25B Chap 5)
DISCUSSION: Delaying the landing gear retraction will ensure that any ice in the process of forming will be broken off and blown away before it completely freezes.
Answer (A) is incorrect. Recycling the landing gear several times after takeoff will impede the climbout and should only be done if an abnormal indication is present when attempting to extend the gear. **Answer (C) is incorrect.** The landing gear should always be retracted well below V_{LE}.

15. Which is true regarding preheating an aircraft during cold weather operations?

A. The cabin area as well as the engine should be preheated.

B. The cabin area should not be preheated with portable heaters.

C. Hot air should be blown directly at the engine through the air intakes.

Answer (A) is correct. (AC 91-13C)
DISCUSSION: Low temperatures may cause a change in the viscosity of engine oils, batteries to lose a high percentage of their effectiveness, and instruments to stick. Thus, preheating of the engine as well as the cabin area is desirable during cold weather operations.
Answer (B) is incorrect. The flight deck area can be preheated with portable heaters if they are available and appropriate. **Answer (C) is incorrect.** The engine should be heated by blowing warm air on the entire engine surface, not through the air intake areas.

16. During preflight in cold weather, crankcase breather lines should receive special attention because they are susceptible to being clogged by

   A.   congealed oil from the crankcase.

   B.   moisture from the outside air which has frozen.

   C.   ice from crankcase vapors that have condensed and subsequently frozen.

Answer (C) is correct. (FAA-P-8740-24)
   DISCUSSION: Frozen crankcase breather lines prevent oil from circulating adequately in the engine and may even result in broken oil lines or oil being pumped out of the crankcase. Accordingly, pilots must always visually inspect to make sure that the crankcase breather lines are free of ice. The ice may have formed as a result of the crankcase vapors freezing in the lines after the engine has been turned off.
   Answer (A) is incorrect. Oil in the crankcase virtually never gets into the breather lines but rather remains in the bottom of the crankcase. Answer (B) is incorrect. Very cold outside air has a low moisture content.

17. When departing from a runway that is covered with snow or slush, what could a pilot do to prevent damage to the landing gear due to the conditions?

   A.   Do not retract the landing gear immediately to allow the gear to air-dry.

   B.   Immediately retract the landing gear so it can be heated in the gear wells.

   C.   Fly at a speed above the green arc of the airspeed indicator to remove the snow and slush.

Answer (A) is correct. (FAA-H-8083-25B)
   DISCUSSION: If departing from an airstrip with wet snow or slush on the takeoff surface, the gear should not be retracted immediately so that any wet snow or slush can be air-dried.
   Answer (B) is incorrect. If departing from an airstrip with wet snow or slush on the takeoff surface, the gear should not be retracted immediately so that any wet snow or slush can be air-dried. Answer (C) is incorrect. The top of the green arc is V_{NO}, which is the maximum structural cruising speed. Operations above V_{NO} move into the yellow arc and should only be flown at those speeds in smooth air. In addition, V_{LE} would be exceeded if operating above V_{LO}. If departing from an airstrip with wet snow or slush on the takeoff surface, the gear should not be retracted immediately, but there is no need to accelerate to remove any wet snow or slush or to allow it to be air-dried.

11.7 Turbulence

18. If severe turbulence is encountered during flight, the pilot should reduce the airspeed to

   A.   minimum control speed.

   B.   design-maneuvering speed.

   C.   maximum structural cruising speed.

Answer (B) is correct. (FAA-H-8083-25B Chap 8)
   DISCUSSION: Flight at or below design maneuvering speed (V_A) means the airplane will stall before excess loads can be imposed on the wings and cause structural damage.
   Answer (A) is incorrect. Minimum control speed is just above stall speed. In turbulence, the changing airspeeds would result in the airplane stalling and/or significant control problems. Answer (C) is incorrect. The maximum structural cruising speed (V_{NO}) is considerably above V_A.

19. Which is the best technique for minimizing the wing-load factor when flying in severe turbulence?

   A.   Change power settings, as necessary, to maintain constant airspeed.

   B.   Control airspeed with power, maintain wings level, and accept variations of altitude.

   C.   Set power and trim to obtain an airspeed at or below maneuvering speed, maintain wings level, and accept variations of airspeed and altitude.

Answer (C) is correct. (AC 00-6B Chap 11)
   DISCUSSION: In severe turbulence, pilots should set power and trim to obtain an airspeed at or below maneuvering speed (V_A), maintain a level pitch and bank attitude, and accept variations of airspeed and altitude.
   Answer (A) is incorrect. Maintaining a constant airspeed in severe turbulence is impossible. Answer (B) is incorrect. Maintaining a constant airspeed in severe turbulence is impossible.

20. A pilot is entering an area where significant clear air turbulence has been reported. Which action is appropriate upon encountering the first ripple?

   A.   Maintain altitude and airspeed.

   B.   Adjust airspeed to that recommended for rough air.

   C.   Enter a shallow climb or descent at maneuvering speed.

Answer (B) is correct. (FAA-H-8083-25B Chap 8)
   DISCUSSION: When entering an area where significant air turbulence has been reported, pilots should adjust their airspeed to that recommended for rough air (V_A) at the first indication of turbulence.
   Answer (A) is incorrect. Pilots should reduce their airspeed to V_A. Answer (C) is incorrect. Pilots do not need to adjust altitude; just slow to V_A.

11.8   Night Flying Operations

21. For night flying operations, the best night vision is achieved when the

    A. pupils of the eyes have become dilated in approximately 10 minutes.

    B. rods in the eyes have become adjusted to the darkness in approximately 30 minutes.

    C. cones in the eyes have become adjusted to the darkness in approximately 5 minutes.

Answer (B) is correct. *(FAA-H-8083-3B Chap 10)*
    DISCUSSION: In the eye's adaptation to darkness process, the pupils of the eyes first enlarge (dilate) to receive as much of the available light as possible. After about 5 to 10 min., the cones become adjusted and the eyes become 100 times more sensitive to the light than they were before the process began. The best night vision is achieved when the rods in the eyes have become adjusted to the darkness, which takes about 30 min. At this time, the eyes are about 100,000 times more sensitive to light than they were in a lighted area.
    Answer (A) is incorrect. The eyes dilate (enlarge) at the beginning of the eye's adaptation to darkness. Additionally, the cones become adjusted after 10 min., but the best night vision is achieved when the rods become adjusted in approximately 30 min. **Answer (C) is incorrect.** The best night vision is achieved when the rods, not cones, in the eyes become adjusted to the darkness in approximately 30 min., not 5 min.

22. When planning a night cross-country flight, a pilot should check for

    A. availability and status of en route and destination airport lighting systems.

    B. red en route course lights.

    C. location of rotating light beacons.

Answer (A) is correct. *(FAA-H-8083-3B Chap 10)*
    DISCUSSION: When planning a night cross-country flight, pilots should check the availability and status of lighting systems at en route and destination airports. Information about their availability can be found on aeronautical charts and in the Chart Supplement. The status of each facility can be determined by reviewing pertinent NOTAMs.
    Answer (B) is incorrect. Red lights indicate obstructions or areas considered hazardous to aircraft. There are no red en route course lights. **Answer (C) is incorrect.** Although knowing the location of rotating light beacons will assist pilots during night navigation, it is more important that they know the availability and status of en route and destination airport lighting systems. These lighting systems include runway lights, taxiway lights, and rotating beacons.

23. When planning a night cross-country flight, a pilot should check for the availability and status of

    A. all VORs to be used en route.

    B. airport rotating light beacons.

    C. destination airport lighting systems.

Answer (C) is correct. *(FAA-H-8083-3B Chap 10)*
    DISCUSSION: When planning a night cross-country flight, pilots should check the availability and status of lighting systems at the destination airport. These lighting systems include runway lights, taxiway lights, and rotating beacons. Information about their availability can be found on aeronautical charts and in the Chart Supplement. The status of each facility can be determined by reviewing pertinent Notices to Airmen (NOTAMs).
    Answer (A) is incorrect. Although knowing the availability and status of VORs to be used en route will assist pilots in night navigation, it is more important that they know the availability and status of lighting systems at the destination airport. **Answer (B) is incorrect.** Although knowing the availability and status of rotating light beacons at airports along the route will assist pilots in night navigation, it is more important that they know the availability and status of the entire lighting system, not just the rotating beacon, at the destination airport.

24. Light beacons producing red flashes indicate

    A. end of runway warning at departure end.

    B. a pilot should remain clear of an airport traffic pattern and continue circling.

    C. obstructions or areas considered hazardous to aerial navigation.

Answer (C) is correct. *(FAA-H-8083-3B Chap 10)*
    DISCUSSION: Light beacons producing red flashes indicate obstructions or areas considered hazardous to aerial navigation.
    Answer (A) is incorrect. End of runway lights are steady, not flashing, red lights. **Answer (B) is incorrect.** In the case of ATC light signals to an airplane in flight, a steady red, not a flashing red, light signal means to give way to other aircraft and continue circling.

25. When operating VFR at night, what is the first indication of flying into restricted visibility conditions?

A. Ground lights begin to take on an appearance of being surrounded by a halo or glow.

B. A gradual disappearance of lights on the ground.

C. Flight deck lights begin to take on an appearance of a halo or glow around them.

Answer (B) is correct. (FAA-H-8083-3B Chap 10)
DISCUSSION: When operating VFR at night, the first indication of flying into restricted visibility conditions is the gradual disappearance of lights on the ground.
Answer (A) is incorrect. Ground fog, not flying into restricted visibility, is indicated when ground lights begin to take on an appearance of being surrounded by a halo or glow. Caution should be used in attempting further flight in that same direction. **Answer (C) is incorrect.** Ground fog, not flying into restricted visibility, is indicated when ground lights, not flight deck lights, begin to take on an appearance of a halo or glow around them.

26. After experiencing a powerplant failure at night, one of the primary considerations should include

A. turning off all electrical switches to save battery power for landing.

B. planning the emergency approach and landing to an unlighted portion of an area.

C. maneuvering to, and landing on a lighted highway or road.

Answer (B) is correct. (FAA-H-8083-3B Chap 10)
DISCUSSION: After experiencing an engine failure at night, one of the primary considerations should include planning the emergency approach and landing to an unlighted portion of an area. This is to avoid the possibility of landing in an area where the airplane could hurt people on the ground and/or avoid buildings on the ground during landing.
Answer (A) is incorrect. Turning off all electrical switches to save battery power for the landing is a procedure to use for an alternator failure, not an engine failure, at night. **Answer (C) is incorrect.** After experiencing an engine failure at night, one of the primary considerations should include turning away from, not maneuvering toward, a lighted highway or road. Highways or roads are hazardous to the pilot and people on the ground.

27. When planning for an emergency landing at night, one of the primary considerations should include

A. turning off all electrical switches to save battery power for the landing.

B. selecting a landing area close to public access, if possible.

C. landing without flaps to ensure a nose-high landing attitude at touchdown.

Answer (B) is correct. (FAA-H-8083-3B Chap 10)
DISCUSSION: When planning for an emergency landing at night, one of the primary considerations should include selecting an emergency landing area close to public access, if possible. This may facilitate rescue or help, if needed.
Answer (A) is incorrect. Turning off all electrical switches to save battery power for landing is a procedure to use for an alternator failure, not an engine failure, at night. **Answer (C) is incorrect.** When planning for an emergency landing at night, the pilot should plan to land in the normal landing configuration. The flaps should be extended to ensure to land at the slowest possible speed in a nose-high attitude at touchdown.

APPENDIX A
COMMERCIAL PILOT PRACTICE TEST

The following 100 questions have been randomly selected from the airplane-related questions in our commercial pilot test bank. You will be referred to figures (charts, tables, etc.) throughout this book. Be careful not to consult the answers or answer explanations when you look for and at the figures. Topical coverage in this practice test is similar to that of the FAA commercial pilot knowledge test. Use the correct answer listing on page 414 to grade your practice test.

1. (Refer to Figure 17 on page 389.) Which illustration indicates that the airplane will intercept the 060 radial at a 75° angle outbound, if the present heading is maintained?

A — 4
B — 5
C — 6

2. (Refer to Figure 17 on page 389.) Which illustration indicates that the airplane will intercept the 060 radial at a 60° angle inbound, if the present heading is maintained?

A — 6
B — 4
C — 5

3. (Refer to Figure 9 on page 209.) Using a normal climb, how much fuel would be used from engine start to 10,000 feet pressure altitude?

Aircraft weight	3,500 lb
Airport pressure altitude	4,000 ft
Temperature	21°C

A — 23 pounds.
B — 31 pounds.
C — 35 pounds.

4. An airplane departs an airport under the following conditions:

Airport elevation	1000 ft
Cruise altitude	9,500 ft
Rate of climb	500 ft/min
Average true airspeed	135 kts
True course	215°
Average wind velocity	290° at 20 kts
Variation	3° W
Deviation	–2°
Average fuel consumption	13 gal/hr

Determine the approximate time, compass heading, distance, and fuel consumed during the climb.

A — 14 minutes, 234°, 26 NM, 3.9 gallons.
B — 17 minutes, 224°, 36 NM, 3.7 gallons.
C — 17 minutes, 242°, 31 NM, 3.5 gallons.

5. An airplane descends to an airport under the following conditions:

Cruising altitude	6,500 ft
Airport elevation	700 ft
Descends to	800 ft AGL
Rate of descent	500 ft/min
Average true airspeed	110 kts
True course	335°
Average wind velocity	060° at 15 kts
Variation	3°W
Deviation	+2°
Average fuel consumption	8.5 gal/hr

Determine the approximate time, compass heading, distance, and fuel consumed during the descent.

A — 10 minutes, 348°, 18 NM, 1.4 gallons.
B — 10 minutes, 355°, 17 NM, 2.4 gallons.
C — 12 minutes, 346°, 18 NM, 1.6 gallons.

6. (Refer to Figure 35 on page 225.)

GIVEN:

Temperature	80°F
Pressure altitude	4,000 ft
Weight	2,800 lb
Headwind	24 kts

What is the total landing distance over a 50-foot obstacle?

A — 1,125 feet.
B — 1,250 feet.
C — 1,325 feet.

7. (Refer to Figure 14 on page 205.)

GIVEN:

Aircraft weight	3,700 lb
Airport pressure altitude	4,000 ft
Temperature at 4,000 ft	21°C

Using a normal climb under the given conditions, how much fuel would be used from engine start to a pressure altitude of 12,000 feet?

A — 30 pounds.
B — 37 pounds.
C — 46 pounds.

8. (Refer to Figure 12 on page 217.)

GIVEN:

Pressure altitude	18,000 ft
Temperature	−1°C
Power	2,200 RPM – 20" MP
Best fuel economy usable fuel	344 lb

What is the approximate flight time available under the given conditions? (Allow for VFR day fuel reserve.)

A — 4 hours 50 minutes.
B — 5 hours 20 minutes.
C — 5 hours 59 minutes.

9. (Refer to Figure 8 on page 221.)

GIVEN:

Fuel quantity	47 gal
Power-cruise (lean)	55 percent

Approximately how much flight time would be available with a night VFR fuel reserve remaining?

A — 3 hours 8 minutes.
B — 3 hours 22 minutes.
C — 3 hours 43 minutes.

10. If an airplane is consuming 14.8 gallons of fuel per hour at a cruising altitude of 7,500 feet and the groundspeed is 167 knots, how much fuel is required to travel 560 NM?

A — 50 gallons.
B — 53 gallons.
C — 57 gallons.

11. You have flown 52 miles, are 6 miles off course, and have 118 miles yet to fly. To converge on your destination, the total correction angle would be

A — 3°.
B — 6°.
C — 10°.

12. (Refer to Figure 31 on page 223.) Rwy 30 is being used for landing. Which surface wind would exceed the airplane's crosswind capability of 0.2 V_{S0}, if V_{S0} is 60 knots?

A — 260° at 20 knots.
B — 275° at 25 knots.
C — 315° at 35 knots.

13. (Refer to Figure 11 on page 215.) If the cruise altitude is 7,500 feet, using 64 percent power at 2,500 RPM, what would be the range with 48 gallons of usable fuel?

A — 635 miles.
B — 645 miles.
C — 810 miles.

14. The CG of an aircraft may be determined by

A — dividing total arms by total moments.
B — dividing total moments by total weight.
C — multiplying total weight by total moments.

15. GIVEN:

	WEIGHT	ARM	MOMENT
Empty weight	957	29.07	?
Pilot (fwd seat)	140	−45.30	?
Passenger (aft seat)	170	+1.60	?
Ballast	15	−45.30	?
TOTALS	?	?	?

The CG is located at station

A — −6.43.
B — +16.43.
C — +27.38.

16. Aeronautical Decision Making (ADM) is a

A — systematic approach to the mental process used by pilots to consistently determine the best course of action for a given set of circumstances.
B — decision making process which relies on good judgment to reduce risks associated with each flight.
C — mental process of analyzing all information in a particular situation and making a timely decision on what action to take.

17. (Refer to Figure 54 on page 355.) (Refer to point 1.) What minimum altitude is required to avoid the Livermore Airport (LVK) Class D airspace?

A — 2,503 feet MSL.
B — 2,901 feet MSL.
C — 3,297 feet MSL.

18. (Refer to Figure 3 on page 40.) If an airplane glides at an angle of attack of 10°, how much altitude will it lose in 1 mile?

A — 240 feet.
B — 480 feet.
C — 960 feet.

19. The remarks section of the Aviation Routine Weather Report (METAR) contains the following coded information. What does it mean?

RMK FZDZB42 WSHFT 30 FROPA

A — Freezing drizzle with cloud bases below 4,200 feet.
B — Freezing drizzle below 4,200 feet and wind shear.
C — Wind shift at three zero due to frontal passage.

20. (Refer to Figure 53 on page 353.) (Refer to point 1.) This thin black shaded line is most likely

A — an arrival route.
B — a military training route.
C — a state boundary line.

21. (Refer to Figure 32 on page 199.)

GIVEN:

Temperature	100°F
Pressure altitude	4,000 ft
Weight	3,200 lb
Wind	Calm

What is the ground roll required for takeoff over a 50-foot obstacle?

A — 1,180 feet.
B — 1,350 feet.
C — 1,850 feet.

22. (Refer to Figure 38 on page 231.)

GIVEN:

Empty weight (oil is included)	1,271 lb
Empty weight moment (in-lb/1,000)	102.04
Pilot and copilot	400 lb
Rear seat passenger	140 lb
Cargo	100 lb
Fuel	37 gal

Is the airplane loaded within limits?

A — Yes, the weight and CG is within limits.
B — No, the weight exceeds the maximum allowable.
C — No, the weight is acceptable, but the CG is aft of the aft limit.

23. The angle of attack of a wing directly controls the

A — angle of incidence of the wing.
B — amount of airflow above and below the wing.
C — distribution of pressures acting on the wing.

24. Which is true concerning the blue and magenta colors used to depict airports on Sectional Aeronautical Charts?

A — Airports with control towers underlying Class A, B, and C airspace are shown in blue; Class D and E airspace are magenta.
B — Airports with control towers underlying Class C, D, and E airspace are shown in magenta.
C — Airports with control towers underlying Class B, C, D, and E airspace are shown in blue.

25. True course measurements on a Sectional Aeronautical Chart should be made at a meridian near the midpoint of the course because the

A — values of isogonic lines change from point to point.
B — angles formed by isogonic lines and lines of latitude vary from point to point.
C — angles formed by lines of longitude and the course line vary from point to point.

26. Detonation may occur at high-power settings when

A — the fuel mixture ignites instantaneously instead of burning progressively and evenly.
B — an excessively rich fuel mixture causes an explosive gain in power.
C — the fuel mixture is ignited too early by hot carbon deposits in the cylinder.

27. An airplane is loaded to a gross weight of 4,800 pounds, with three pieces of luggage in the rear baggage compartment. The CG is located 98 inches aft of datum, which is 1 inch aft of limits. If luggage which weighs 90 pounds is moved from the rear baggage compartment (145 inches aft of datum) to the front compartment (45 inches aft of datum), what is the new CG?

A — 96.13 inches aft of datum.
B — 95.50 inches aft of datum.
C — 99.87 inches aft of datum.

28. Which is true regarding the forces acting on an aircraft in a steady-state descent? The sum of all

A — upward forces is less than the sum of all downward forces.
B — rearward forces is greater than the sum of all forward forces.
C — forward forces is equal to the sum of all rearward forces.

29. If the same angle of attack is maintained in ground effect as when out of ground effect, lift will

A — increase, and induced drag will decrease.
B — decrease, and parasite drag will increase.
C — increase, and induced drag will increase.

30. During preflight in cold weather, crankcase breather lines should receive special attention because they are susceptible to being clogged by

A — congealed oil from the crankcase.
B — moisture from the outside air which has frozen.
C — ice from crankcase vapors that have condensed and subsequently frozen.

31. What is the minimum flight visibility and proximity to cloud requirements for VFR flight, at 6,500 feet MSL, in Class C, D, and E airspace?

A — 1 mile visibility; clear of clouds.
B — 3 miles visibility; 1,000 feet above and 500 feet below.
C — 5 miles visibility; 1,000 feet above and 1,000 feet below.

32. Which is a characteristic typical of a stable air mass?

A — Cumuliform clouds.
B — Showery precipitation.
C — Continuous precipitation.

33. Applying carburetor heat will

A — not affect the mixture.
B — lean the fuel/air mixture.
C — enrich the fuel/air mixture.

34. Which cloud types would indicate convective turbulence?

A — Cirrus clouds.
B — Nimbostratus clouds.
C — Towering cumulus clouds.

35. How can you determine if another aircraft is on a collision course with your aircraft?

A — The nose of each aircraft is pointed at the same point in space.
B — The other aircraft will always appear to get larger and closer at a rapid rate.
C — There will be no apparent relative motion between your aircraft and the other aircraft.

36. When in the vicinity of a VOR which is being used for navigation on VFR flight, it is important to

A — make 90° left and right turns to scan for other traffic.
B — exercise sustained vigilance to avoid aircraft that may be converging on the VOR from other directions.
C — pass the VOR on the right side of the radial to allow room for aircraft flying in the opposite direction on the same radial.

37. The general circulation of air associated with a high-pressure area in the Northern Hemisphere is

A — outward, downward, and clockwise.
B — outward, upward, and clockwise.
C — inward, downward, and clockwise.

38. A pilot's most immediate and vital concern in the event of complete engine failure after becoming airborne on takeoff is

A — maintaining a safe airspeed.
B — landing directly into the wind.
C — turning back to the takeoff field.

39. Which statement is true about magnetic deviation of a compass? Deviation

A — varies over time as the agonic line shifts.
B — varies for different headings of the same aircraft.
C — is the same for all aircraft in the same locality.

40. Name the four fundamentals involved in maneuvering an aircraft.

A — Power, pitch, bank, and trim.
B — Thrust, lift, turns, and glides.
C — Straight-and-level flight, turns, climbs, and descents.

41. Fog produced by frontal activity is a result of saturation due to

A — nocturnal cooling.
B — adiabatic cooling.
C — evaporation of precipitation.

42. Lift on a wing is most properly defined as the

A — force acting perpendicular to the relative wind.
B — differential pressure acting perpendicular to the chord of the wing.
C — reduced pressure resulting from a laminar flow over the upper camber of an airfoil, which acts perpendicular to the mean camber.

43. In theory, if the airspeed of an airplane is doubled while in level flight, parasite drag will become

A — twice as great.
B — half as great.
C — four times greater.

44. In small airplanes, normal recovery from spins may become difficult if the

A — CG is too far rearward, and rotation is around the longitudinal axis.
B — CG is too far rearward, and rotation is around the CG.
C — spin is entered before the stall is fully developed.

45. If an airplane is loaded to the rear of its CG range, it will tend to be unstable about its

A — vertical axis.
B — lateral axis.
C — longitudinal axis.

46. Fuel/air ratio is the ratio between the

A — volume of fuel and volume of air entering the cylinder.
B — weight of fuel and weight of air entering the cylinder.
C — weight of fuel and weight of air entering the carburetor.

47. Which statement is true concerning the hazards of hail?

A — Hail damage in horizontal flight is minimal due to the vertical movement of hail in the clouds.
B — Rain at the surface is a reliable indication of no hail aloft.
C — Hailstones may be encountered in clear air several miles from a thunderstorm.

48. Turbulence that is encountered above 15,000 feet AGL not associated with cumuliform cloudiness, including thunderstorms, should be reported as

A — severe turbulence.
B — clear air turbulence.
C — convective turbulence.

49. When checking the course sensitivity of a VOR receiver, how many degrees should the OBS be rotated to move the CDI from the center to the last dot on either side?

A — 5° to 10°.
B — 10° to 12°.
C — 18° to 20°.

50. From which of the following can the observed temperature, wind, and temperature/dewpoint spread be determined at a specified altitude?

A — Stability Charts.
B — Winds Aloft Forecasts.
C — Constant Pressure Analysis Charts.

51. What values are used for Winds Aloft Forecasts?

A — True direction and MPH.
B — True direction and knots.
C — Magnetic direction and knots.

52. Which weather chart depicts conditions forecast to exist at a specific time in the future?

A — Freezing Level Chart.
B — Weather Depiction Chart.
C — 12-hour Significant Weather Prognostic Chart.

53. The Surface Analysis Chart depicts

A — frontal locations and expected movement, pressure centers, cloud coverage, and obstructions to vision at the time of chart transmission.
B — actual frontal positions, pressure patterns, temperature, dewpoint, wind, weather, and obstructions to vision at the valid time of the chart.
C — actual pressure distribution, frontal systems, cloud heights and coverage, temperature, dewpoint, and wind at the time shown on the chart.

54. Which conditions are favorable for the formation of a surface based temperature inversion?

A — Clear, cool nights with calm or light wind.
B — Area of unstable air rapidly transferring heat from the surface.
C — Broad areas of cumulus clouds with smooth, level bases at the same altitude.

55. Which type of jetstream can be expected to cause the greater turbulence?

A — A straight jetstream associated with a low-pressure trough.
B — A curving jetstream associated with a deep low-pressure trough.
C — A jetstream occurring during the summer at the lower latitudes.

56. (Refer to Figure 5 on page 60.) The vertical line from point D to point G is represented on the airspeed indicator by the maximum speed limit of the

A — green arc.
B — yellow arc.
C — white arc.

57. Baggage weighing 90 pounds is placed in a normal category airplane's baggage compartment which is placarded at 100 pounds. If this airplane is subjected to a positive load factor of 3.5 Gs, the total load of the baggage would be

A — 315 pounds and would be excessive.
B — 315 pounds and would not be excessive.
C — 350 pounds and would not be excessive.

58. To track inbound on the 215 radial of a VOR station, the recommended procedure is to set the OBS to

A — 215° and make heading corrections toward the CDI needle.
B — 215° and make heading corrections away from the CDI needle.
C — 035° and make heading corrections toward the CDI needle.

59. Which is not a type of hypoxia?

A — Histotoxic.

B — Hypoxic.

C — Hypertoxic.

60. Which is a common symptom of hyperventilation?

A — Drowsiness.

B — Decreased breathing rate.

C — Euphoria - sense of well-being.

61. As hyperventilation progresses a pilot can experience

A — decreased breathing rate and depth.

B — heightened awareness and feeling of well-being.

C — symptoms of suffocation and drowsiness.

62. A state of temporary confusion resulting from misleading information being sent to the brain by various sensory organs is defined as

A — spatial disorientation.

B — hyperventilation.

C — hypoxia.

63. What will occur if no leaning is made with the mixture control as the flight altitude increases?

A — The volume of air entering the carburetor decreases and the amount of fuel decreases.

B — The density of air entering the carburetor decreases and the amount of fuel increases.

C — The density of air entering the carburetor decreases and the amount of fuel remains constant.

64. For internal cooling, reciprocating aircraft engines are especially dependent on

A — a properly functioning cowl flap augmenter.

B — the circulation of lubricating oil.

C — the proper freon/compressor output ratio.

65. While maintaining a constant angle of bank and altitude in a coordinated turn, an increase in airspeed will

A — decrease the rate of turn resulting in a decreased load factor.

B — decrease the rate of turn resulting in no change in load factor.

C — increase the rate of turn resulting in no change in load factor.

66. A fixed-pitch propeller is designed for best efficiency only at a given combination of

A — altitude and RPM.

B — airspeed and RPM.

C — airspeed and altitude.

67. Which of the following are considered aircraft class ratings?

A — Transport, normal, utility, and acrobatic.

B — Airplane, rotorcraft, glider, and lighter-than-air.

C — Single-engine land, multiengine land, single-engine sea, and multiengine sea.

68. No person may operate a large civil aircraft of U.S.-registry which is subject to a lease, unless the lessee has mailed a copy of the lease to the FAA Aircraft Registration Branch, Oklahoma City, OK, within how many hours of its execution?

A — 24

B — 48

C — 72

69. Who is primarily responsible for maintaining an aircraft in an airworthy condition?

A — The lead mechanic responsible for that aircraft.

B — Pilot in command or operator.

C — Owner or operator of the aircraft.

70. For an airport without an approved instrument approach procedure to be listed as an alternate airport on an IFR flight plan, the forecasted weather conditions at the time of arrival must have at least a

A — ceiling of 2,000 feet and visibility 3 SM.

B — ceiling and visibility that allows for a descent, approach, and landing under basic VFR.

C — ceiling of 1,000 feet and visibility 3 NM.

71. Pilots who change their permanent mailing address and fail to notify the FAA Airmen Certification Branch of this change, are entitled to exercise the privileges of their pilot certificate for a period of

A — 30 days.

B — 60 days.

C — 90 days.

72. In the contiguous U.S., excluding the airspace at and below 2,500 feet AGL, an operable coded transponder equipped with Mode C capability is required in all airspace above

A — 10,000 feet MSL.

B — 12,500 feet MSL.

C — 14,500 feet MSL.

73. If weather conditions are such that it is required to designate an alternate airport on your IFR flight plan, you should plan to carry enough fuel to arrive at the first airport of intended landing, fly from that airport to the alternate airport, and fly thereafter for

A — 30 minutes at slow cruising speed.
B — 45 minutes at normal cruising speed.
C — 1 hour at normal cruising speed.

74. Airplane A is overtaking airplane B. Which airplane has the right-of-way?

A — Airplane A; the pilot should alter course to the right to pass.
B — Airplane B; the pilot should expect to be passed on the right.
C — Airplane B; the pilot should expect to be passed on the left.

75. NTSB Part 830 requires an immediate notification as a result of which incident?

A — Engine failure for any reason during flight.
B — Damage to the landing gear as a result of a hard landing.
C — Any required flight crewmember being unable to perform flight duties because of illness.

76. Approved flotation gear, readily available to each occupant, is required on each airplane if it is being flown for hire over water,

A — in amphibious aircraft beyond 50 NM from shore.
B — beyond power-off gliding distance from shore.
C — more than 50 statute miles from shore.

77. A new maintenance record being used for an aircraft engine rebuilt by the manufacturer must include previous

A — operating hours of the engine.
B — annual inspections performed on the engine.
C — changes as required by Airworthiness Directives.

78. No person may operate an aircraft in simulated instrument flight conditions unless the

A — other control seat is occupied by at least an appropriately rated commercial pilot.
B — pilot has filed an IFR flight plan and received an IFR clearance.
C — other control seat is occupied by a safety pilot, who holds at least a private pilot certificate and is appropriately rated.

79. A person with a Commercial Pilot certificate may act as pilot in command of an aircraft for compensation or hire, if that person

A — is qualified in accordance with 14 CFR Part 61 and with the applicable parts that apply to the operation.
B — is qualified in accordance with 14 CFR Part 61 and has passed a pilot competency check given by an authorized check pilot.
C — holds appropriate category, class ratings, and meets the recent flight experience requirements of 14 CFR Part 61.

80. To act as pilot in command of an airplane that is equipped with retractable landing gear, flaps, and controllable pitch propeller, a person is required to

A — hold a multiengine airplane class rating.
B — make at least six takeoffs and landings in such an airplane within the preceding 6 months.
C — receive and log ground and flight training in such an airplane, and obtain a logbook endorsement certifying proficiency.

81. To act as pilot in command of a tailwheel airplane, without prior experience, a pilot must

A — log ground and flight training from an authorized instructor.
B — pass a competency check and receive an endorsement from an authorized instructor.
C — receive and log flight training from an authorized instructor.

82. If an ATC transponder installed in an aircraft has not been tested, inspected, and found to comply with regulations within a specified period, what is the limitation on its use?

A — Its use is not permitted.
B — It may be used when in Class G airspace.
C — It may be used for VFR flight only.

83. Which is the correct symbol for the stalling speed or the minimum steady flight speed in a specified configuration?

A — V_s.
B — V_{s1}.
C — V_{s0}.

84. When weather information indicates that abnormally high barometric pressure exists, or will be above ___ inches of mercury, flight operations will not be authorized contrary to the requirements published in NOTAMs.

A — 31.00
B — 32.00
C — 30.50

85. One of the main functions of flaps during the approach and landing is to

A — decrease the angle of descent without increasing the airspeed.
B — provide the same amount of lift at a slower airspeed.
C — decrease lift, thus enabling a steeper-than-normal approach to be made.

86. The stalling speed of an airplane is most affected by

A — changes in air density.
B — variations in flight altitude.
C — variations in airplane loading.

87. (Refer to Figure 52 on page 347.) (Refer to point 8.) The floor of the Class E airspace over the town of Auburn is

A — 1,200 feet MSL.
B — 700 feet AGL.
C — 1,200 feet AGL.

88. With regard to the technique required for a crosswind correction on takeoff, a pilot should use

A — aileron pressure into the wind and initiate the lift-off at a normal airspeed in both tailwheel- and nosewheel-type airplanes.
B — right rudder pressure, aileron pressure into the wind, and higher than normal lift-off airspeed in both tricycle- and conventional-gear airplanes.
C — rudder as required to maintain directional control, aileron pressure into the wind, and higher than normal lift-off airspeed in both conventional- and nosewheel-type airplanes.

89. Which is true regarding the development of convective circulation?

A — Cool air must sink to force the warm air upward.
B — Warm air is less dense and rises on its own accord.
C — Warmer air covers a larger surface area than the cool air; therefore, the warmer air is less dense and rises.

90. What feature is normally associated with the cumulus stage of a thunderstorm?

A — Roll cloud.
B — Continuous updraft.
C — Beginning of rain at the surface.

91. Select the true statement pertaining to the life cycle of a thunderstorm.

A — Updrafts continue to develop throughout the dissipating stage of a thunderstorm.
B — The beginning of rain at the Earth's surface indicates the mature stage of the thunderstorm.
C — The beginning of rain at the Earth's surface indicates the dissipating stage of the thunderstorm.

92. If severe turbulence is encountered during flight, the pilot should reduce the airspeed to

A — minimum control speed.
B — design-maneuvering speed.
C — maximum structural cruising speed.

93. (Refer to Figure 51 on page 95.) The pilot generally calls ground control after landing when the aircraft is completely clear of the runway. This is when the aircraft

A — passes symbol D.
B — is on the dashed-line side of symbol G.
C — is past the solid-line side of symbol G.

94. An aircraft 60 miles from a VOR station has a CDI indication of one-fifth deflection, this represents a course centerline deviation of approximately

A — 6 miles.
B — 2 miles.
C — 1 mile.

95. Which data must be recorded in the aircraft logbook or other record by a pilot making a VOR operational check for IFR operations?

A — VOR name or identification, place of operational check, amount of bearing error, and date of check.
B — Date of check, place of operational check, bearing error, and signature.
C — VOR name or identification, amount of bearing error, date of check, and signature.

96. Which procedure should you follow to avoid wake turbulence if a large jet crosses your course from left to right approximately 1 mile ahead and at your altitude?

A — Make sure you are slightly above the path of the jet.
B — Slow your airspeed to V_A and maintain altitude and course.
C — Make sure you are slightly below the path of the jet and perpendicular to the course.

97. Which is true regarding a cold front occlusion? The air ahead of the warm front

A — is colder than the air behind the overtaking cold front.
B — is warmer than the air behind the overtaking cold front.
C — has the same temperature as the air behind the overtaking cold front.

98. Weather Advisory Broadcasts, including Severe Weather Forecast Alerts (AWWs), Convective SIGMETs, and SIGMETs, are provided by

A — ARTCCs on all frequencies, except emergency, when any part of the area described is within 150 miles of the airspace under their jurisdiction.
B — FSSs on 122.2 MHz and adjacent VORs, when any part of the area described is within 200 miles of the airspace under their jurisdiction.
C — selected VOR navigational aids.

99. During an approach, the most important and most easily recognized means of being alerted to possible wind shear is monitoring the

A — amount of trim required to relieve control pressures.
B — heading changes necessary to remain on the runway centerline.
C — power and vertical velocity required to remain on the proper glidepath.

100. GIVEN:

Pressure altitude	5,000 ft
True air temperature	+30°C

From the conditions given, the approximate density altitude is

A — 7,800 feet.
B — 7,200 feet.
C — 9,000 feet.

PRACTICE TEST LIST OF ANSWERS

The listing below gives the correct answers for your FAA commercial pilot practice knowledge test and the page number in this book on which you will find each question with the complete Gleim answer explanation.

Q. #	Answer	Page	Q. #	Answer	Page	Q. #	Answer	Page	Q. #	Answer	Page
1.	B	388	26.	A	65	51.	B	304	76.	B	160
2.	A	390	27.	A	233	52.	C	299	77.	C	169
3.	C	208	28.	C	36	53.	B	295	78.	C	150
4.	B	381	29.	A	43	54.	A	269	79.	A	144
5.	A	382	30.	C	402	55.	B	264	80.	C	138
6.	B	225	31.	B	92	56.	A	61	81.	C	139
7.	C	204	32.	C	271	57.	B	48	82.	A	168
8.	C	216	33.	C	64	58.	C	387	83.	B	132
9.	B	220	34.	C	266	59.	C	241	84.	A	154
10.	A	378	35.	C	104	60.	A	244	85.	B	30
11.	C	380	36.	B	104	61.	C	244	86.	C	35
12.	A	222	37.	A	263	62.	A	245	87.	B	349
13.	C	214	38.	A	400	63.	C	63	88.	C	398
14.	B	226	39.	B	59	64.	B	67	89.	A	272
15.	B	227	40.	C	398	65.	B	46	90.	B	274
16.	A	247	41.	C	268	66.	B	68	91.	B	275
17.	B	354	42.	A	39	67.	C	136	92.	B	402
18.	B	40	43.	C	37	68.	A	147	93.	C	94
19.	C	293	44.	B	35	69.	C	166	94.	B	387
20.	B	352	45.	B	44	70.	B	156	95.	B	157
21.	B	198	46.	B	63	71.	A	142	96.	A	105
22.	A	230	47.	C	277	72.	A	163	97.	B	261
23.	C	30	48.	B	279	73.	B	155	98.	A	292
24.	C	345	49.	B	386	74.	B	151	99.	C	281
25.	C	345	50.	C	304	75.	C	171	100.	A	196

APPENDIX B
INTERPOLATION

The following is a tutorial based on information that has appeared in the FAA's *Pilot's Handbook of Aeronautical Knowledge*. Interpolation may be required in several questions found in this book.

A. To interpolate means to compute intermediate values between a series of given values.

    1.   In many instances when performance is critical, an accurate determination of the performance values is the only acceptable means to enhance safe flight.

    2.   Guessing to determine these values should be avoided.

B. Interpolation is simple to perform if the method is understood. The following are examples of how to interpolate, or accurately determine the intermediate values, between a series of given values.

C. The numbers in column A range from 10 to 30, and the numbers in column B range from 50 to 100. Determine the intermediate numerical value in column B that would correspond with an intermediate value of 20 placed in column A.

A	B
10	50
20	X = Unknown
30	100

    1.   It can be visualized that 20 is halfway between 10 and 30; therefore, the corresponding value of the unknown number in column B would be halfway between 50 and 100, or 75.

D. Many interpolation problems are more difficult to visualize than the preceding example; therefore, a systematic method must be used to determine the required intermediate value. The following describes one method that can be used.

    1.   The numbers in column A range from 10 to 30 with intermediate values of 15, 20, and 25. Determine the intermediate numerical value in column B that would correspond with 15 in column A.

A	B
10	50
15	
20	
25	
30	100

    2.   First, in column A, determine the relationship of 15 to the range between 10 and 30 as follows:

$$\frac{15 - 10}{30 - 10} = \frac{5}{20} \text{ or } 1/4$$

        a.   It should be noted that 15 is 1/4 of the range between 10 and 30.

3.   Now determine 1/4 of the range of column B between 50 and 100 as follows:

$$100 - 50 = 50$$
$$1/4 \text{ of } 50 = 12.5$$

a.   The answer 12.5 represents the number of units, but to arrive at the correct value, 12.5 must be added to the lower number in column B as follows:

$$50 + 12.5 = 62.5$$

4.   The interpolation has been completed and 62.5 is the actual value which is 1/4 of the range of column B.

E.   Another method of interpolation is shown below:

1.   Using the same numbers as in the previous example, a proportion problem based on the relationship of the number can be set up.

Proportion: $\dfrac{5}{20} = \dfrac{X}{50}$

$$20X = 250$$
$$X = 12.5$$

a.   The answer, 12.5, must be added to 50 to arrive at the actual value of 62.5.

F.   The following example illustrates the use of interpolation applied to a problem dealing with one aspect of airplane performance:

Temperature (°F)	Takeoff Distance (ft.)
70	1,173
80	1,356

1.   If a distance of 1,173 feet is required for takeoff when the temperature is 70°F and 1,356 feet is required at 80°F, what distance is required when the temperature is 75°F? The solution to the problem can be determined as follows:

$$\frac{5}{10} = \frac{X}{183}$$
$$10X = 915$$
$$X = 91.5$$

a.   The answer, 91.5, must be added to 1,173 to arrive at the actual value of 1,264.5 ft.

CROSS-REFERENCES TO
THE FAA ACS CODES

Airman Knowledge Test Reports list the Airman Certification Standards (ACS) code of each question answered incorrectly. The total number of questions missed may differ from the number of ACS codes shown on the report if more than one question is missed for a certain code. We have created an online cross-reference of all the questions from our commercial pilot knowledge test bank to their ACS codes to help you determine which Gleim subunits to focus on.

> To view the online listing of questions and ACS codes, visit www.GleimAviation.com/ACSXRefs.
>
> To determine what topic each code pertains to, the ACS may be viewed at www.faa.gov/training_testing/testing/acs.

The codes are derived from the Commercial Pilot ACS, which consists of Areas of Operation arranged in a logical sequence, beginning with Preflight Preparation and ending with Postflight Procedures. Each Area of Operation includes appropriate tasks, and each task begins with an objective that states what the applicant should know, consider, and/or do. The ACS then lists the aeronautical knowledge, risk management, and skill elements relevant to each task, along with the conditions and standards for acceptable performance. Each task element is assigned a unique code, such as CA.I.A.K1, which can be broken down as follows:

CA = Applicable ACS (Commercial Pilot – Airplane)
I = Area of Operation (Preflight Preparation)
A = Task (Pilot Qualifications)
K1 = Task Element Knowledge 1 (Certification requirements, recent flight experience, and recordkeeping)

In the online cross-reference, we present our study unit/question number and our answer to the right of each code. For example, a cross-reference to 4-1 represents our Study Unit 4, question 1. Multiple questions may be associated with a single ACS code. Applicants should discuss their test results with a CFI and study the entire task element of identified weakness instead of merely studying a specific question.

The FAA will periodically revise the existing codes and add new ones. As Gleim learns about any changes, we will update our materials.

AUTHORS' RECOMMENDATIONS

Gleim cooperates with and supports all aspects of the flight training industry, particularly organizations that focus on aviation recruitment and flight training. Below are some of the top organizations for anyone interested in aviation.

EXPERIMENTAL AIRCRAFT ASSOCIATION: YOUNG EAGLES PROGRAM

The Experimental Aircraft Association's (EAA) Young Eagles Program has provided free introductory flights to over 1 million young people ages 8 to 17. This program helps young people understand the important role aviation plays in our daily lives and provides insight into how an airplane flies, what it takes to become a pilot, and the high standards flying demands in terms of safety and quality.

NOTE: The Gleim Learn to Fly booklet (available for free at www.GleimAviation.com/learn-to-fly) is used as "ground school" training for Young Eagles programs. For more information about the Young Eagles Program, visit www.youngeagles.org or call 1-800-564-6322.

AIRCRAFT OWNERS AND PILOTS ASSOCIATION

The Aircraft Owners and Pilots Association (AOPA) hosts an informational web page on getting started in aviation for those still dreaming about flying, those who are ready to begin, and those who are already making the journey. Interested individuals can order a FREE subscription to Flight Training Magazine, which explains how amazing it is to be a pilot. Other resources are available, such as a flight school finder, a guide on what to expect throughout training, an explanation of pilot certification options, a FREE flight training newsletter, and much more. To learn more, visit www.aopa.org.

CIVIL AIR PATROL: CADET ORIENTATION FLIGHT PROGRAM

The Civil Air Patrol (CAP) Cadet Orientation Flight Program is designed to introduce CAP cadets to flying. The program is voluntary and primarily motivational, and it is designed to stimulate cadets' interest in and knowledge of aviation.

Each orientation flight is approximately 1 hour, follows a prescribed syllabus, and is usually in the local area of the airport. Except for takeoff, landing, and a few other portions of the flight, cadets are encouraged to handle the controls. For information about the CAP cadet program nearest you, visit www.gocivilairpatrol.com.

WOMEN IN AVIATION INTERNATIONAL

Women in Aviation International (WAI) is a nonprofit organization dedicated to the encouragement and advancement of women in all aviation career fields and interests. Its diverse membership includes astronauts, corporate pilots, maintenance technicians, air traffic controllers, business owners, educators and learners, journalists, flight attendants, air show performers, airport managers, and many others.

WAI provides year-round resources to assist women in aviation and encourage young women to consider aviation as a career and offers educational outreach programs to educators, aviation industry members, and young people nationally and internationally. WAI also hosts an annual Girls in Aviation Day for girls ages 8 to 17. Learn more at www.wai.org.

NINETY-NINES

The Ninety-Nines (99s) is an international organization of women pilots with thousands of members from over 40 countries. Its goal is to promote advancement of aviation through education, scholarships, and mutual support. The 99s have co-sponsored over 75% of FAA pilot safety programs in the U.S. and annually sponsor hundreds of educational programs, such as aerospace workshops for teachers, airport tours for school children, fear-of-flying clinics for airline passengers, and flight instructor revalidation seminars. Learn more at www.ninety-nines.org.

INSTRUCTOR CERTIFICATION FORM
COMMERCIAL PILOT KNOWLEDGE TEST

Name: _____

I certify that I have reviewed the above individual's preparation for the FAA Commercial Pilot —
Airplane knowledge test [covering the topics specified in 14 CFR 61.125(b)(1) through (16)] using the
Commercial Pilot FAA Knowledge Test Prep book, software, and/or online course by Irvin N. Gleim
and Garrett W. Gleim and find him/her competent to pass the pilot knowledge test.

_____ _____ _____ _____ _____
Signed   Date   Name   CFI or CGI   Expiration Date
                                                                 Number   N/A if CGI

GLEIM®

Aviation

ABBREVIATIONS AND ACRONYMS IN
COMMERCIAL PILOT FAA KNOWLEDGE TEST PREP

14 CFR	Title 14 of the Code of Federal Regulations
AAF	Army Airfield
AC	Advisory Circular
AC 00-6B	*Aviation Weather*
AC 00-45H	*Aviation Weather Services*
ACS	Airman Certification Standards
ACUG	Aeronautical Chart Users' Guide
AFB	Air Force Base
AGL	above ground level
AIM	*Aeronautical Information Manual*
AIREP	aircraft report
AIRMET	Airman's Meteorological Information
AME	aviation medical examiner
ATC	Air Traffic Control
BHP	brake horsepower
CAT	clear air turbulence
CDI	course deviation indicator
CFA	controlled firing area
CFI	Certificated Flight Instructor
CG	center of gravity
DA	decision altitude
DH	decision height
E6B	flight computer
EAS	equivalent airspeed
EFB	electronic flight bag
EFD	electronic flight display
ELT	emergency locator transmitter
ETE	estimated time en route
FAA	Federal Aviation Administration
FAA-H-8083-1B	*Weight and Balance Handbook*
FAA-H-8083-3B	*Airplane Flying Handbook*
FAA-H-8083-6	*Advanced Avionics Handbook*
FAA-H-8083-15B	*Instrument Flying Handbook*
FAA-H-8083-16B	*Instrument Procedures Handbook*
FAA-H-8083-25B	*Pilot's Handbook of Aeronautical Knowledge*
FAA-H-8083-32A	*Aviation Maintenance Technician Handbook–Powerplant*
FAA-P-8740-24	*Winter Flying Tips*
FBO	Fixed-Base Operator
FIS-B	Flight Information Services-Broadcast
FL	flight level
FSS	Flight Service Station
GPH	gallons per hour
Hg	mercury
HSI	horizontal situation indicator
IAP	instrument approach procedure
IFR	instrument flight rules
ILS	instrument landing system
IR	instrument route
ISA	international standard atmosphere
LDA	localizer directional aid
L/D	lift/drag
L/D_{MAX}	maximum lift-to-drag ratio
LIFR	low IFR
MAP	missed approach point
Mb	millibar
MDA	minimum descent altitude
MEF	maximum elevation figure
MEL	minimum equipment list
METAR	aviation routine weather report
MFD	multi-function display
MH	magnetic heading
MMEL	master minimum equipment list
MOA	Military Operations Area

MSA	minimum safe altitude
MSL	mean sea level
MTR	Military Training Routes
MVFR	marginal VFR
NAS	National Airspace System
NM	nautical mile
NOTAM	notice to airmen
NSA	national security area
NTSB	National Transportation Safety Board
OAT	outside air temperature
OBS	omnibearing selector
PFD	primary flight display
PIC	pilot in command
PIREP	Pilot Weather Report
PPH	pounds per hour
RAIM	Receiver Autonomous Integrity Monitoring
RNAV	area navigation
RNP	required navigation performance
SFC	surface
SIC	second in command
SIGMET	Significant Meteorological Information
SL	sea level
SM	statute mile
SRM	single-pilot resource management
ST	standard temperature
STAR	standard terminal arrival
SUA	special use airspace
SVFR	Special VFR
TAF	terminal aerodrome forecast
TAS	true airspeed
TIS-B	Traffic Information Services-Broadcast
UTC	Coordinated Universal Time
V_1	maximum speed in the takeoff at which the pilot must take the first action to stop the airplane within the accelerate-stop distance
V_2	takeoff safety speed
V_A	maneuvering speed
V_{EF}	speed of assumed critical engine failure (takeoff)
V_F	design flap speed
V_{FE}	maximum flap extended speed
VFR	visual flight rules
V_G	speed for best glide
VHF	very high frequency
V_{LE}	maximum landing gear extended speed
V_{MC}	minimum control speed with the critical engine inoperative
V_{MO}/M_{MO}	maximum operating limit speed
V_{NE}	never-exceed speed
V_{NO}	maximum structural cruising speed
VOR	VHF omnidirectional range
VOR MON	VOR Minimum Operational Network
VORTAC	Collocated VOR and TACAN
VOT	VOR test facility
VR	visual route
V_S	stalling speed or the minimum steady flight speed at which the airplane is controllable
V_{S0}	stalling speed or the minimum steady flight speed in the landing configuration
V_{S1}	stalling speed or the minimum steady flight speed obtained in a specific configuration
V_X	speed for best angle of climb
V_Y	speed for best rate of climb
Z	Zulu or UTC time

INDEX OF LEGENDS AND FIGURES

INDEX